PONTIFF

PONTIFF

GORDON THOMAS
AND
MAX MORGAN-WITTS

GRANADA
London Toronto Sydney New York

Granada Publishing Limited
Frogmore, St Albans, Herts AL2 2NF
and
36 Golden Square, London WIR 4AH
515 Madison Avenue, New York, NY 10022, USA
117 York Street, Sydney, NSW 2000, Australia
60 International Boulevard, Rexdale, Ontario R9W 6J2, Canada
61 Beach Road, Auckland, New Zealand

Published by Granada Publishing 1983

Copyright © Gordon Thomas and Max Morgan-Witts Productions Limited 1983

British Library Cataloguing in Publication Data

Thomas, Gordon
Pontiff.
1. Papacy—History—20th century
I. Title   II. Morgan-Witts, Max
262'.13'09047   BX1390

ISBN 0–246–11879–2

Phototypeset by
Wyvern Typesetting Ltd, Bristol
Printed in Great Britain by
Mackays of Chatham Ltd

Granada ®
Granada Publishing ®

Contents

Authors' Note vii

Some of the People Prominent in the Story ix

THE STORY SO FAR 1

THE JACKAL 5

PART ONE
THE LAST DAYS 17

PART TWO
THE WILL OF GOD 121

PART THREE
CONSPIRACY 305

THE POPE AND THE JACKAL 443

THE STORY THEREAFTER 461

Note on Sources 469

Textual Notes 471

Abbreviated Bibliography 489

Index 491

v

Authors' Note

This is the true story of three very public figures, a trio of popes ruling during the most critical time in the recent history of the Roman Catholic Church. It is also often an account of their very private lives; much of this may surprise and astonish. To obtain the truth required the co-operation of, and an understanding with, those who were, and still are, close to the persons and events portrayed. Our collaborators – for that is what they were, and we acknowledge our debt to them; indeed, without their unstinted frankness there would be no story – were prompted by all sorts of reasons to help. Some felt it really was time to look honestly and realistically behind the mystery and secrecy which is more than a way of life in the Vatican. Others recognized the importance of examining in detail the process and decision-making which creates popes; they were the ones who felt the only way to begin to understand that system was to see how popes actually live as human beings: what motivates them, who tries to influence them, how they respond to pressures, threats and much else. Our helpers ranged from cardinals to the personal staff of these popes. They provided detailed information which they had never before made available. Much of it was intimate data which showed that the men who attain the most powerful spiritual office on earth are human to a degree seldom suspected. This then is their story – Paul VI, John Paul I and John Paul II.

Some of the Persons Prominent in the Story

THE POPES

Paul VI (Giovanni Montini). Elderly and isolated. Knows death is near and fears it may come violently at the hands of the terrorists he sees all around.

John Paul I (Albino Luciani). Did not want to be pope but was thrust upon the throne of St Peter to replace Paul. Is immediately confronted with the divided factions of the Curia – the Church's civil service. Pinocchio and a mysterious herbal elixir help to sustain him. In a month he does more than anyone thought possible – and many in the Curia think undesirable. Then on the thirty-third day of his pontificate he dies – the circumstances of his death paving the way for all that was to follow.

John Paul II (Karol Wojtyla). Charismatic, pragmatic – and always very Polish. Assumes power at the climax of a struggle in that most secret of places – Conclave, the process which elects popes. He returns the papacy to the very centre of the world's political stage, bringing it into open confrontation with its old enemy, Communism. The result is traumatic.

THE ENEMIES

Agca, Mehmet Ali. Teenage Turkish fanatic, steeped in fundamentalist Muslim politics, violently anti-Christian. Recruited for the express purpose of assassinating John Paul II. Trained in Libya and the Lebanon by a renegade CIA agent.

Andropov, Yuri. Present position: President of the Soviet Union; formerly Head of the KGB.

Tore, Teslin. Agca's KGB controller in the Balkans.

Folini, Maurizio. KGB paymaster and another of Agca's controllers.

And sundry other terrorists.

THE PAPAL ENTOURAGE

Father John Magee. Private secretary to all three popes. Knows their secrets, the very private foibles of very public figures. Protective, tough and very Irish.

Father Pasquale Macchi. Paul VI's senior secretary. Feared, if not always respected; his critics said he was pope-in-residence, the bossy assistant who manipulated the old pontiff.

Cardinal Jean Villot. Secretary of State. Chain-smoking and long-suffering, he collected enemies even his few influential friends could not fend off. In the end, over the death of John Paul I, he made a fateful mistake — one which opened the door to the KGB.

Cardinal Agostino Casaroli. Replaced Villot. Known as the Vatican's Kissinger because of his special role in developing *Ostpolitik*, the Vatican's attempt to reach an 'understanding' with the Soviet bloc.

Cardinal Franz Koenig. Archbishop of Vienna. Intellectual giant, the Church's expert on religions and how to handle the threat of Communism. An old friend of John Paul II, he mounted an astonishing campaign to have him elected.

Cardinal John Cody. Archbishop of Chicago. The most controversial figure in the American Church. Money and questions of morality beset him.

Bishop Paul Marcinkus. Vatican banker extraordinary. Financial scandal swirls around his towering figure. He dismisses it all and says God knows the truth.

Michele Sindona. Financier friend of Paul VI. Currently serving a long-term sentence in an up-state New York penitentiary, the end result of swindling that almost bankrupted the Vatican.

Cardinal Sebastiano Baggio. Papal troubleshooter. The energetic prefect of the Congregation of Bishops whose most spectacular failure was to unseat Cody.

Cardinal Giovanni Benelli. Powerful prelate who thought his moment had come when John Paul I became pope.

Cardinal Pericle Felici. Prefect of the Supreme Tribunal of the Apostolic Signatura, the papal appelate court. Knows everybody in the Church who matters. Even his friends fear him.

Father Lambert Greenan. English-language editor of the Vatican newspaper, *L'Osservatore Romano*. Witty, waspish and wise.

Father Sean MacCarthy. Radio Vatican commentator. He could not quite believe it when he learned colleagues had bugged Conclave.

Archbishop Gaetano Alibrandi. Papal Nuncio to Ireland. A diplomat with unusual links to people and places that diplomats normally avoid.

Father Andrew Greeley. The Church's Critic-in-Residence.

And sundry other members of the Sacred College of Cardinals, the Curia and the Church.

THE STORY
SO FAR

1

From the time Jesus said to Simon, 'You are Peter, and on this rock I will build my Church', there have been popes. Some were holier than others; many found the office a high-risk occupation. Each of the first eighteen popes was a victim of violence, either crucified, strangled, poisoned, beheaded or smothered to death. Some found no peace even in the grave. Formosus (891–6) was disinterred nine months after burial, his rotting corpse robed in pontifical vestments and placed on a chair to face trial before a religious court presided over by his successor. The corpse of John XIV (983–4) was skinned and hauled through the streets of Rome. Other popes have been imprisoned, exiled and deposed. Some were confronted with rival claimants, faced intense secular interference, heresies, mass defections and schisms.

Yet few institutions in the whole of history have displayed a greater capacity for survival. Roman Catholics often believe this longevity to be striking theological testimony to the divinity of the papacy; much is made of the power of the Holy Spirit for ensuring that the highest office of the Universal Church continues the ministry given by Christ to Peter. The papacy, called by Toynbee the greatest of all Western institutions, exerts a fascination for everybody. Believers find it a comforting symbol of Catholic identity. The rest are mesmerized by its complexities and contradictions.

Popes have civilized barbarians yet encouraged the Inquisition. They condemned torture yet approved it against heretics. Popes, the apostles of peace, have waged war. A few – John XII (955–64) and Alexander VI (1492–1503) – led shocking lives. The papacy, the epitome of unity, has itself been a significant barrier to church unity.

It remains so in 1978, when Paul VI, the two hundred and sixty-first pope to hold the office, is still on the Throne of St Peter. It is the fifteenth year of his pontificate and 740 million baptized Catholics, whatever else they feel about him, agree he is firmly rooted in the 1900-year-old papal tradition. He is as insistently imperious, magnificently monarchic and absolutely absolute as any pope before him. He is also old and waiting to die, preferably in bed.

But in this year of violence, of urban terrorism and religious fanatics and senseless brutal killing wherever he looks, not even Paul VI knows with certainty whether his death will be peaceful.

The worry helps to keep him awake at night.

THE
JACKAL

Now hatred is by far
The lasting pleasure

Byron

2

The creeping grey where night ends and another day begins, 4.30 by the clock, the moment his mother still calls the first dawn, awakens him.

For a moment Mehmet Ali Agca lies motionless. Only his eyes move, small, red-rimmed, watchful eyes, set deep in a long face. He also has cropped hair, bushy eyebrows and a thin nose which flares under his steady breathing. He is nineteen years and five months old on this July morning in 1978. But those eyes make him look at least a decade older. They are the eyes of an insomniac, scanning a room which is all too familiar to him. He was born in it and has experienced all his worthwhile memories so far within the confines of its plain whitewashed walls. Here he cried himself to sleep after his first street fight. Later he experienced his first sexual fantasy on this bed he has slept in since a boy. And here, too, beneath the small window in the wall, he regularly pleads with Allah to make him famous. Agca is still waiting. In the meantime his mind is filled with other thoughts, ugly and dangerous ideas which excite and frighten him.

His eyes continue to scan. The walls are covered with posters. Many bear the photograph of the same man, Colonel Arpaslan Turkes, leader of Turkey's paramilitary Idealists. Modelled on Hitler's SS and equipped with a variety of World War II weapons, the Idealists, better known as the Grey Wolves, are becoming as formidable as some of the more well-known terrorist groups in Europe. Turkish law forbids the display of such posters under penalty of imprisonment. But Agca does not care about the risk. He has been a Grey Wolf for two years. So far he has killed nobody. Yet he is willing to do so, and to die, for Turkes.

Agca finds nothing unusual in such fanaticism. He was born and raised with it. There are countless thousands of other Turks like him, all caught up in the Anarchy, the generic term for the appalling violence which sweeps Turkey, Islam's last free society, a democracy of forty-five million persons in a Moslem world of six hundred million; only the Catholic Church can claim more souls. The Anarchy, for all its tentacles which feed off the interstices of Turkish life, is concerned with one ultimate goal: the end of the present system of authentic elections and multiple parties. Violence, insane and numbing and continuous, has been chosen as the means to do this. Entire cities are now closed citadels controlled by either the Right or Left. During the first six months of this year there have been six hundred murders; there is an average of twenty armed bank robberies a day. Nobody knows who is behind the Anarchy; most likely, no single hand any longer controls it, no one voice issues threats, demands, communiqués, chooses the victims. The Anarchy makes no special effort to gouge out the heart of the Turkish state – as the Red Brigades concurrently do in Italy. In Turkey, army officers, judges, politicians and policemen are not specifically singled out; the killing is far more indiscriminate. Nor is it a straight clash between Right and Left. There are as many as forty-five Marxist revolutionary groups in Turkey fighting each other. The Right is dominated by the hard profile of Turkes and his Grey Wolves, who howl when their Leader addresses them. Agca regularly practises the chilling animal sound in his bedroom.

The only furniture in the room, apart from his iron bedstead, is a rickety old table and chair. A strip of carpet is on the bare concrete floor that is icy cold in winter but pleasantly cool in the hot summers. On top of the strip lies a smaller and grander rug. It is hand-woven with an intricate pattern of gold and red threads. It belonged to Agca's grandfather; when he died it was passed on, a family tradition, to his eldest grandson. It is Agca's prayer mat, one of his two most prized possessions.

Above his head is a shelf. It contains a row of books: an English primer, well thumbed, its pages repeatedly folded at the corners to mark important passages; the others are paperbacks, thrillers for the most part, including a reprint of *The Day of the Jackal*. Agca has read it at least ten times, fascinated by the details of how to assassinate a public figure. Beside the books is an old cigar box. It contains his second treasured keepsake, an old Mauser pistol, oiled, wrapped in rags. There are several bullets in the box.

Staring around the room, the dull heaviness he feels is more pronounced. Fear? Expectation? The residue of the malaise which had once again gripped him? He does not know. He is only aware of the tightening in his chest, the queasy feeling in his stomach. But at least he no longer shows any surface anger, no clenching and unclenching of his hands or the sudden curling of his lips to expose discoloured teeth. His mother has shown him how to control such indications of inner torment, just as she taught him, in the shrill voice people call intimidating but which he finds comforting, that at first dawn he must scramble from bed and recite one of the five *sourates*, the daily prayers of the Koran.

Agca's nervous energy is evident as he gets up, clad in the vest and underpants in which he always sleeps. Standing, he is an unprepossessing figure; hands and feet seem out of proportion to his puny body with its concave chest, protruding shoulder blades and thin arms and legs. He looks painfully undernourished. Besides insomnia, Agca suffers from anorexia nervosa, a severe psychological illness more usually found in teenage girls, and crippling bouts of depression. Not even his mother can fully understand his suffering.

Just as she had first shown him years earlier, he now spreads his prayer rug, prostrates himself three times, each time touching his forehead to the ground, murmuring the name of Allah, Master of the World, the All-Meaningful and All-Compassionate, the Supreme Sovereign of the Last Judgement.

Then he begins quietly to recite his long list of hatreds.

The eldest son of the widow Muzzeyene will need a long time to get through his list.

The light is still too diffuse to identify the bleakness of this room. There are four others similarly austere in the house. The largest is his mother's bedroom with its double bed no one has shared since the day her husband died eleven years before; two smaller bedrooms, one for Fatma, Agca's seventeen-year-old sister, the other for Adnan, his fifteen-year-old brother. There is also the family room, where they eat, squatting on the floor around a pot-bellied wood-burning stove and, at nights, watch television on an old black and white set.

Muzzeyene has painted the living room walls a sickly green from a tin of paint she found on a local refuse dump she regularly scours. The ceiling is dirty from the stove. There is an outside toilet and water from a pump. For this hovel Muzzeyene pays an absentee landlord the equivalent of one US dollar a week. When he learned the amount, Agca felt it was extortionate. From then on all landlords, absentee or otherwise, were put on his hate list.

The list is extraordinary in its diversity and implication. It includes: all the long-dead Russian Tsars and their imperial dreams; NATO, whose bases are scattered throughout Turkey; Sheik Yamani, for refusing to use Arab oil to destroy the West. On a more personal level Agca hates hamburgers, ketchup, Levis, *I Love Lucy*, *Time* and *Newsweek* – anything connected with the most powerful nation in the world, its way of life, values and customs, the very well-springs of its existence. He needs a full five minutes to remind himself of everything he hates about America.

He especially hates those Americans who buy the staple of village life, and not just the staple of his village, but of hundreds of other villages scattered from end to endless end of Turkey: the poppy. For a thousand years – Agca dates it from the time Sultan Arpaslan defeated the Byzantine emperor at the Battle of Malazgrit and ancient Anatolia became Turkish – the poppy has been tilled, its oil used for cooking, its leaves in salad, its seeds in bread, its pods fed to cattle, its stalks in building. Only its gum remained untouched by villagers. The Americans have found a special use for it, converting the gum into a morphine base which in turn is refined into heroin.

Officially, this no longer happens. On 30 June 1971, the United States government and the Turkish regime signed an agreement banning all opium poppy growing in Turkey. The last legal crop was harvested in 1972. America paid $35 million to Turkey to compensate the poppy growers while they sought replacement crops. President Nixon hailed the agreement as a significant step towards stemming the heroin crisis in the United States. The farmers took the money but went on growing the poppy.

Agca knows what heroin can do. Fresh in his mind is the incident in Istanbul. A drug courier had been caught cheating by his employers. The man was held down and forcibly injected with high-grade pure heroin. The process was repeated every day for a week. By then he was an incurable addict. To complete his punishment his employers arranged that he would receive no further heroin. In another week the demented courier jumped into the Bosphorus, drowning in its pollution. Agca finds the episode exhilarating in its violence and deeply satisfying – the way the courier was finally driven to kill himself.

Months afterwards the details have lost nothing in his repeated retelling of the story. What he does not add – preferring instead to keep it for this time at dawn when he rekindles all his other hatreds – is his burning resentment for those unknown American drug bosses on the other side of the world. Indirectly, they employ him; he occasionally drives a truck on the heroin trail. He gets only a fistful of Turkish lire for each trip. But it is not that which fuels his anger. It is directly related to his discovery of the vast profits made by the Americans. A poppy farmer might get $15 for a pound of gum. On the streets of New York, refined and processed, the price was $200,000 a pound. All profiteers are now on Agca's list.

So, too, are employers, dating from that day his father was killed in a road accident on a Tuesday and his employer had refused to pay the last full week of salary.

When he thinks of his father nowadays, he can only clearly remember his hands, calloused, broad-fingered and practical; violent, too, suddenly lashing out, sending his mother reeling and the cheap crockery shattering over the floor. Agca remembered how he had smiled at his father's funeral; his mother looked at him and they both understood. Only in deference to her had Agca kept his father off his list.

His death had altered the family's position. Already poor they plunged still further down the village social scale. All three children, from an early age, were expected to find work. By the time he was ten, Agca sold water by the cup to travellers at a bus stop near his home. It was about this time his eating problems began. He deliberately missed meals, or ate no more than he had to when at table. His mother did not seem unduly concerned. Perhaps because she was so busy with other problems – finding the rent money, clothes for the children, scouring the refuse tip for a scrap of window curtain or a usable cooking pot – she did not seriously consider her son's eating habits. Nor did she immediately recognize the psychological changes in him, that he was growing into a young man rather different from his companions. Often he would fall into silent, inactive periods, retreating to his room. When she did think about such behaviour, like him, she had no idea of the complex process causing it. Part was associated with the guilt he felt at not loving his father. Yet that same guilt stopped him from speaking about the feeling, let alone seeking help. Instead, all the hostility he had felt towards his father he turned on himself during these periods of depression. Eventually he had come to believe he could only expunge this feeling by hatred. He once mentioned this to his mother, and from then on she encouraged him to hate. And so his list was created.

The light was strengthening now. He could hear the sounds of his mother and sister preparing breakfast, and beyond the windows the first stirrings of life in the community somebody had cruelly called Yesiltepe, Green Hill.

Only the largest-scale maps of Turkey pinpoint Yesiltepe, 465 miles due east of Ankara. It huddles on the road along which the Crusaders trudged to and from Jerusalem. Every thirty years or so the buildings begin to crumble into dust, their dung bricks turning to powder under the fierce heat of summer and the biting cold which sweeps the Turkish steppes from October to April. Yesiltepe has clung for six hundred years to the stony ground that extends to the mountains which ring the community. Eleven hundred people in 1978 live here: suspicious, insular men in dark suits and flannel shirts, and women who clutch their veils as they drive the cattle through the unpaved streets and work the fields. There are a good number of children; even the very young ones smoke and hawk and spit. The small mosque has a tall, tapering minaret. Many of the houses do not have electricity or running water. The restrictive Moslem code keeps all women outside the tea-houses where the men spend their days talking and playing cards.

In this remote corner of the earth, Agca learned the facts of his life. He was an unusually small child, but gifted: he could read and write at the age of five. Yesiltepe school has no accelerated programme for advanced children. Instead Agca was 'skipped' ahead by his teachers. At eight he was in the fourth grade, sharing lessons with twelve-year-olds. At first he liked to show off his abilities, but after he had been beaten several times by his classmates he learned to disguise his brilliance. Nevertheless, by the age of fourteen he had learned all the school could offer. He stayed another year, coming and going as he pleased. Almost naturally, because of his impoverished background, he drifted into one of the gangs in the nearby town of Malatya. He found himself running errands for the local crime bosses. He was good. He was recommended to the bigger bosses running the local sector of the heroin trail; when they wanted an extra driver they used him. On a trip to Istanbul he casually made contact with the Grey Wolves; he liked what he heard of their plans to overthrow established government. He joined the group. At the same time he made arrangements to continue his studies at the University of Ankara; young though he was, his grades guaranteed him a place. He spent an uneventful year there. Then the onset of one of his depression cycles cut short his studies. He returned to Yesiltepe and discovered the Grey Wolves had a cell in Malatya. He attended their meetings but found little in common with his fellow revolutionaries. He drifted back onto the heroin trail. The money he made from smuggling he gave to his mother. She did not ask where it came from. It was another of their understandings.

In the past five years Agca has owned five hand guns. So far his only victim has been a neighbour's cockerel whose head he blew off for target practice. His mother had to pay double the market price for the bird; from that moment on the neighbour had been marked down as another profiteer.

Puberty hardened Agca, but his melancholia gave him a curious charm which made him welcome enough in one of Malatya's brothels. Apart from these visits he avoided all contact with the opposite sex. Yet throughout his blossoming process part of him stood off to one side, cold and watchful. It was the part which recognized the ignorance of his teachers, the part which made him constantly replay little vignettes where he had been made to suffer. It was that part which said he must seek revenge.

As a young man he now functions well enough. He is a respected and feared figure among his contemporaries. His affiliation with the Grey Wolves is sufficient to make even the most threatening of Yesiltepe's bullies steer clear of him; Colonel Turkes has shown he can wreak terrible retribution on anybody who dares touch his men.

To Yesiltepe's elders Agca is a strange person. He does not gamble and cannot bear personal competition. Nor does he ever let his feelings get out of control, at least publicly. Though he understands limited aggression objectively, he cannot take part in it. He makes no distinction between friendly competition and total combat to the death. That is why he finds all organized sport boring. The only time he shows real passion is when he is alone, when he is reciting his hate list. It's a year now since he began collecting it, a desperate, confusing catalogue no outsider can quantify or explain. It is his only outlet, the one thing which allows him to burn off some of the inner furies. His mental state is dangerously balanced, yet some primeval instinct protects him, ensuring nobody, not even his mother, realizes what is happening to him.

A doctor would undoubtedly recognize the symptoms as alarming: the withdrawal from food, the frequent escape from normal daily contact, the sudden inner anger that precedes the dull pain. A psychiatrist would assuredly probe Agca's self-reproach, his perfection-ist behaviour – the books on his shelf are lined up in careful symmetry, his clothes are laid out in the same way on the floor by his boots – small clues, but indications of how far his obsessional ideas are expiatory, an attempt to overcome, by a kind of mental magic, deeper distress. And if the psychiatrist was an analyst he might probe Agca about his correct and prudish manners to discover it hid a rather perverse sexuality. He might learn of Agca's compulsion to step over cracks in the ground, to touch wood for luck, to keep a single tune running through his head for days. And all this might, in the end, lead to Agca telling him about his hate list.

But there is no doctor in Yesiltepe and the nearest psychiatrist is in Ankara.

Agca continues with his task, moving steadily through the list, knowing he has time, realizing today will probably pass like any other now that he is again ready to leave the self-imposed isolation of this room. He will spend most of it in the town's tea-room, sipping *cay*, aromatic tea, and catching up on the latest talk.

Nowadays there is much to discuss. Yesiltepe is caught up in the latest sectarian slaughter sweeping Turkey. There have been five deaths in the community, polarizing further the extreme right- and left-wing elements in Yesiltepe. Throughout Turkey hundreds are dead and thousands injured. The victims are clubbed, shot in the stomach, set on fire with petrol, hacked to pieces with machetes. There have been waves of arrests. In one prison alone, a morning's drive from Yesiltepe, 807 defendants will shortly face a collective trial in the jail yard. Rumour says the guilty ones will be shot in batches of fifty.

Many are Agca's friends, fellow Grey Wolves; most are younger than he is. Killers under eighteen are much in demand among the various factions because Turkish law precludes the death penalty below that age.

Agca also knows most certainly that he, too, would now be under arrest but for the depression which has kept him in this bedroom for almost two months, bowed down, withdrawn, refusing anything but the minimum of food. After a time, he had slowly climbed out of his apathy, returning gradually to his present aggressive state.

He is coming to the end of his list. Slowly, in the guttural peasant patois of Malatya province which made city people underestimate him, he reminds himself he hates the Queen of England because she symbolizes the worst kind of imperialism; South Africa because of its apartheid and links with Israel.

Finally only his religious hatreds are left. He keeps them for the end because they are the most virulent, consuming him like a cancer, burrowing into his mind, even capable at times of making him weep. Then, real tears fall down his cheeks, the crying of an unforgiving fanatic who hates all religions save his own. He sees them as threatening, plotting and determined to overthrow the faith to which he subscribes. He has been able to reduce them to one instantly recognizable ideograph. It is that of an old man, dressed in white with a skull cap who lives in a huge palace far beyond the mountains. He rules like a caliph, issuing decrees and orders many millions must obey. And when he dies another old man takes his place, ruling in the same inflexible manner.

When Agca eventually comes to the end of his hate list, he reserves himself one final pleasure: to make a wish of who, given the chance, he would like to destroy.

There is nowadays no doubt in his mind. He would like to kill the old man.

All Agca knows about him and the vast kingdom he rules is contained in a school exercise book which he keeps beneath the cigar box holding his Mauser.

This morning, as he does every other, part of the obsessive ritual which rules his life, Agca rises from his squatting position and reaches for the exercise book. Sitting on his bed he turns the pages. The notes are fragmentary, scribbled in his spidery long-hand and difficult to decipher.

The message they contain is both revealing and disturbing. Agca believes the old man is in the vanguard of a calculated campaign to erode the very foundations of Islam. He is doing so by carefully encouraging the introduction of modern life into countries which are the last bastion of the Moslem religion. He is doing so under the guise of progress, pretending to be improving conditions when all the time he is cunningly eroding the essential purity of Islam, making it face compromises which will weaken, and ultimately destroy it or, at the very least, transform it into a political ideology which could actually rob it of its deep religious power. Islam, if the old man had his way, would be cast on the religious rubbish heap, little more than an ethnic or cultural irrelevance. Finally it would wither and die, another victim of the extraordinary plotting the old man, his predecessors and all those they represent, are capable of. So Agca believes.

Stuck in the exercise book are also faded newspaper and magazine photographs, and stories detailing the old man's travels around the world: to India, to America, to Pakistan, to so many countries, spreading his hateful message, the way his predecessors have done for 1900 years. Surrounded by pomp and glory, rejoicing in even more titles than Allah himself has, the old man is known, variously, as Servant of the Servants of God, Patriarch of the West, Vicar of Christ on Earth, Bishop of Rome, Sovereign of the State of Vatican City, Supreme Pontiff, His Holiness Pope Paul VI.

Ideally Agca would like to kill Paul. But if, as Agca has written in his exercise book, 'the biological solution, death, intervenes', then he is equally determined to kill his successor.

Agca has come to realize that almost certainly he will not be able to achieve this on his own. It will require a great deal of careful planning, money and back-up. In Agca's mind there are only two possible places from which this support can come, Russia or Libya. He has read that the rulers of these countries hate and fear the pope as much as he does. Agca is positive one of them will help him.[1]

PART ONE

THE LAST
DAYS

He went unterrified
Into the gulf of death
— Shelley

3

For months there has been something missing in St Peter's Square. From midnight it is closed to traffic and its fountains switched off until the wooden shutters on two corner windows on the top floor of the Apostolic Palace open the next morning. Romans say the time of their opening is a good guide to the current health and temper of the man in the bedroom behind the shutters. If they open before the first rays of the sun pass above the limpid Tiber to light the cross on top of the Basilica, Paul will have spent another restless night. If the shutters remain closed until the sun illuminates the vaulted dome of the greatest church in Christendom, then the pope has spent a relatively peaceful one – perhaps with the help of the two vials kept at his bedside. One holds a supply of Mogadon sleeping tablets; the other contains capsules whose contents are a mixture known only to the pope's doctor, the omniscient Mario Fontana. They are to ease his patient's arthritis. Just as they speculate about the shutters, so people do about the medicine.

It is by such means that the mood of the papacy is assessed in this, the fifteenth year of the pontificate of Giovanni Battista Montini, elected in 1963 to be the spiritual leader of the largest church in the world and the bearer of awesome titles, offices and power which, in theory, can reach out from this bedroom in a fifteenth-century Vatican palace and directly affect the lives of 740 million baptized Roman Catholics. In reality, he reigns over a restless church which increasingly pays little more than lip service to his teachings. Many Catholics flaunt his now-famous encyclical, *Humanae Vitae – On Human Life* – by continuing to practise birth control; women want to be priests, priests wish to marry, bishops desire to be regional popes, theologians claim a teaching authority even more absolute than the powers vested in the body of the tired and frail old man in the brass bed which faces the closed shutters.

The Vatican's Secretary of State, Cardinal Jean Villot, had arranged for the traffic to be halted and the fountains silenced to help Paul sleep.[1] But even Villot felt unable to hush the ringing of the six massive bells of St Peter's; for three hundred years they have peeled their joy for a new saint and tolled their sorrow at the death of a pope. In this, the eightieth year of his life, and preoccupied now with the physical act of dying – Paul wonders what he would feel, how it would come upon him, would it be quick, would he be conscious to the very end – the pope could ponder that his four predecessors had lain in this same bedroom waiting for death. He had mused recently, and mentioned it to those of his personal staff who are not excluded by the carapace he has created between himself and the world of ordinary feelings, whether those other popes experienced the feeling he increasingly has: that it will be a blessed relief finally to lay down the heavy burden of his office.

Nobody will ever know what his first thought is on awakening this particular July morning in 1978. Unlike Pius XII, who kept a diary filled with such private details, and John XXIII, who delighted in telling everybody his inner feelings at the dawn of each day, Paul neither writes down nor speaks about such intimate matters.

Nor, indeed, would anybody know the precise moment he has awoken, or even whether he has slept at all. Years ago he ordered that nobody must come knocking on his bedroom door and wish him good morning. He would emerge when he felt like it. Barring the gravest of crises – in this era it includes a sudden nuclear attack by the Soviet Union or the assassination of an important head of state, like the American President or the Queen of England – almost no one is permitted to enter his bedroom until he says so.

It is a surprisingly small room, square, with a high ceiling. The bed dominates it. Paul brought it with him from Milan where he was archbishop before the Conclave of 1963 elected him pope by a runaway majority. They say – those cynical Romans – the Holy Spirit worked overtime to achieve that result. The bedding is a pastel shade, matching the linen cloth covering on the walls. There is a fine mahogany chest of drawers supporting a bevelled mirror and a small desk with an old-fashioned black telephone which rarely rings. Paul does not favour the instrument as a means of communication; he likes to look into a person's eyes when he or she speaks. There is an Afghan rug on the polished wooden floor. The window drapes are pastel. On the wall above the bed is a painting of Jesus's agony on the Cross; it, too, came from Milan, a gift from the priests of the City to commemorate his election. Beside the bed is a table. As well as the vials, there is an old Bible his father gave him the day he made his first Holy Communion on 6 June 1907; seventy-one years later the Bible has been lovingly preserved in a heavy leather cover. Near the table is a prie-dieu where Paul kneels and says his private prayers. Above it a wooden crucifix has been fixed to the wall. Close by, reducing the impact of the Cross, is a fine picture of the Virgin. Crucifix and portrait are also gifts he accepted on the long and lonely journey which brought him to this room.

But there is none of the bric-à-brac a person who has travelled so widely might be expected to have on view: no signed portraits of other heads of state, no photographs to show he has journeyed to places no other pope has ever been. The bedroom is tastefully anonymous. It is as if here, where he now spends a quarter of his daily life, Paul does not wish to be cluttered with his past.

There is one exception, an object that is not a gift, which the pope is almost childishly obsessive about. Wherever he travels it goes with him, carefully packed into his baggage by the senior of his two personal secretaries, Don Pasquale Macchi. This morning it stands in its accustomed place between the Bible and the vials. It is a cheap alarm clock with a lacquered brass frame and Roman numerals on its plain white face. It has two stubby brass legs. Every night Paul winds the clock. Every morning, at precisely 6.30, the alarm gives its tinny summons. He lets it ring for a few seconds and then presses the button on top of the bell, as if concerned not to awaken anybody in the vicinity of the bedroom. It is a ritual he has followed for fifty-five years, from that day in May 1923, when he was made *addetto*, second secretary, to the nunciature in Warsaw. Every night for the seven months he spent there he set the alarm for 6.30; in those days he slept deeply and the alarm would often shrill its course before he was fully awake. He would rise and do an hour's work before breakfast. This habit of an early start stuck.

Nowadays, he frequently beats the clock, awakening from at best a fitful sleep an hour or more before the alarm rings. Then – he has confided to Macchi – he watches the minutes tick by. Sometimes he silently recites a favourite passage from Shakespeare's *Troilus and Cressida*, the one about 'The end crowns all,/And that old common arbitrator, Time/Will one day end it.'

Paul's thin body, clad in a white nightshirt, barely disturbs the bedding. His feet are encased in bedsocks because of his poor circulation. Medically, Fontana does not approve of the socks, but the wise old physician – Fontana is seventy and belongs to a different school from the brisk young men of medicine today – recognizes the psychological importance the socks have for the pope.

Physically, Paul has been ill for years. A delicate child, he grew into a far from robust man. In middle age troublesome bladder and kidney disorders surfaced. In the end his prostate was surgically removed. But in spite of Fontana's secret capsules, the arthritis in the pope's right knee remains so painful he often finds it difficult to walk. He has also become prone to bronchitis and influenza. Fontana had already treated an attack in the spring of 1978 with antibiotics; the side-effects of the drugs left Paul's resistance even lower. Now, in July, another bout seems to be developing. The doctor fears the heat and humidity of a Roman summer will further debilitate his patient. He has urged the pope to go to Castel Gandolfo. Paul demurs: he would go to the papal palace, the retreat of popes for centuries in the Alban hills outside Rome, on the same day as every other year. His physician could do no more than visit Paul daily, listen to his chest, and silently count the time before the pope would leave Rome.

Paul now has only one more night to spend in this room high above St Peter's Square.

In bed, like anyone else, he appears at his most vulnerable. His skin is taut on the skull, his hair wispy grey, without vigour. The veins stand out on the back of his long, thin hands, the fingers tapering to nails which need paring. Yet, in the depths of his winter of age, there is still something left which the years have not dimmed: his eyes. Miraculously, they have retained their brilliant blue colour, their luminosity and, above all, their look of piercing yet somehow gentle enquiry. They seem at variance with a face which is lined and haggard and etched deeply with personal pain.

Shortly after he has silenced the alarm, Paul presses one of three buttons on a buzzer system. It is the signal to those waiting beyond the bedroom that he is officially awake.

*

Sister Giacomina has been waiting for the sound of the buzzer in the comfortable bed-sitting room she occupies close to the pope's room. The two other buttons link Paul with Macchi's apartment on the third floor of the Apostolic Palace, and with Franco Ghezzi, the pope's valet-chauffeur, who is married and lives in an apartment in the rear of the vast rambling building which has 10,065 suites, salons, rooms, reception areas, audience chambers, halls, passageways and cellars; these are linked by 997 flights of stairs and three elevators, one of which is reserved exclusively for Paul and his personal staff. The elevator door is near Giacomina's room, a strategic position which allows her to monitor and, when occasion demands, head off unwanted visitors.

She is one of five nuns who take care of the papal household, washing and cooking and cheerfully complaining about the electric carpet sweeper when its cable becomes entangled in their habits as they vacuum the eighteen rooms of the apartment.

Giacomina is in charge of this domestic retinue. She has served in that capacity for more years than anybody cares to remember. Church regulations stipulate that women who work and live in the households of priests and prelates must be of 'canonical age', assumed to mean beyond the age of physical attraction.

Giacomina has filled the requirement for many years. But despite her evident age there is a resilience about her which even the most overbearing of cardinals finds daunting. She knows her position is secure so long as Paul is alive; nobody is allowed to forget that she is more than a mere housekeeper. She combines the management of the papal household with her role as the pope's personal nurse. She is trained in the techniques of mouth-to-mouth resuscitation and how to administer painkilling and life support injections. She knows where Fontana is any moment of the day or night, and she will not hesitate to call him at the first sign her beloved Paul displays of distress. People say she is more formidable than even the legendary Sister Pasqualina who looked after Pius XII. It was Pasqualina who ended the unwritten rule that the papal household was to be run exclusively by men. But whereas there was endless gossip over the influence Pasqualina had on Pius, there is no doubt about the effect Giacomina has on Paul. With a few well-chosen words she can make light of even the gloomiest of starts to his day.

She knocks once on the pope's bedroom door and waits. When she is bidden to, she enters and greets the pope with words which seldom vary: 'Holy Father, it is going to be a wonderful day'.

Then she walks to the window and opens the shutters.

*

Two hundred feet below, in St Peter's Square, a City of Rome policeman who has been waiting for this moment speaks into his two-way radio to tell colleagues on the far side of Bernini's colonnade – a complex of 284 columns and 88 pilasters surmounted by 162 statues each twelve feet high – what has happened. They begin to remove the crash barriers which diverted traffic around the square during the night. Shortly afterwards the fountains in the great piazza, 215 yards at its greatest breadth, begin to spout water.

*

Alone now, Paul gets slowly out of bed and gingerly stands up to test the degree of pain in his right knee; he has been told to do this by Fontana. The pope eases his 130 pounds on to his right leg. The pain is no worse, or better, than it has been for months. Walking slowly, the way Fontana suggested, Paul reaches the bathroom.

It is as featureless as any bathroom in any luxury hotel; it might have been designed by Hilton or one of the world's other innkeepers. There are pastel-tiled walls and a matching suite in lime green. The bath is fitted with a shower attachment and a non-slip bottom. The pope washes, and shaves with an electric razor: its make is a secret because the Vatican fears the manufacturer might advertise that Paul uses their model.

While he is in the bathroom Ghezzi enters the bedroom – the only employee allowed to do so without knocking – and lays out Paul's clothes for the day: a white linen cassock, caped across the shoulders, white cotton underpants and vest, white stockings and shoes and a white skull cap. The garments bear no label. They do not need one; there probably isn't a priest in Rome who would not recognize the distinctive cut of a vestment tailored by the House of Gammarelli, papal tailors and outfitters for almost 200 years. From a tiny workshop in the centre of the city they have dressed popes for mourning and for rejoicing; in the rag trade they are probably the most exclusive establishment in the world. During the past fifteen years, Gammarelli's cutters and seamstresses have made over a score of cassocks, stoles, rochets, mozzettas and skull caps for Paul. But, like any old man, he has developed a fondness for certain clothes: apart from ceremonial occasions he chooses the comfort of a few old favourite cassocks.

Having laid out the garments, Ghezzi leaves.

Paul prefers to dress in private. He does so slowly; the arthritic stiffness in his fingers makes it difficult to close the buttons on his cassock. Finally, he drapes a solid gold cross around his neck; it hangs on his chest on a 24-carat gold chain. A journalist recently wrote the cross and chain could be worth $100,000.

His next move is another of those private little rituals which have always filled his life. He lowers himself on to the prie-dieu and prays. Then he rises to his feet and walks to the windows. Standing well in the shadow of the drapes – he has a genuine concern that some photographer might be lurking outside with a telephoto lens and snap him off-guard – Paul looks out over the vast expanse of St Peter's Square, and beyond. It is understandably a view of which he has never tired.

At this early hour it is at its best. Below him, stretching into the distance, are a hundred and more hooded domes glinting in the sun between the spires, towers, monuments, palaces and parks. There are streets that run long and straight, others which are curved and short, broad or narrow. Even up here he can hear the unique sound of Rome, an echoing hum created as a result of the city being built on hardened volcanic ash, the *tufo*.

To his immediate right, about 1,200 feet from his bedroom window, is the mass of Michelangelo's dome on top of the Basilica of St Peter's.

Long ago, when Paul first entered Vatican service, he had memorized the proportions of the Basilica. He found the facts useful when later, a fully fledged diplomat, he spent time making polite smalltalk at official functions. Nowadays, when he looks at the Basilica, his thoughts may be on the day he will be buried in a vault deep beneath the ground which supports the edifice. Nevertheless, old though he is, and forgetful too, the pope can, if asked, still recite the dimensions of this masterpiece: the interior 611 feet long, 435 feet high, with 77 supporting columns, 44 altars, 395 statues, and a bronze ball on top of the dome large enough to contain sixteen persons comfortably. Nor can he easily forget that, even when the Roman Empire declined and Peter became the Great Fisherman, it still needed 1,000 years for his successors – each of them wearing the Fisherman's Ring which, because of his arthritis, Paul no longer wears – to create this Basilica as the focal point of a new empire, Christianity. Though his memory is failing, he will surely not have forgotten that hardly had the last stone been put into place before the Christian world was torn apart by hatred and dissensions.

In the distance he can see the American College on the Janiculum Hill. If he does not look long in that direction it is understandable. The Church in America is a source of endless problems for him. It is still young and he is old; he does not know, he has told his confidants, how best he can handle the serious challenges from the other side of the Atlantic. But they cannot be ignored.

And over there, to the right of his window, is the roof of the Sistine Chapel – ordinary enough on the outside, affording no clue to the splendour beneath – where, all those years ago, he was elected by his fellow cardinals as the ideal man to govern the church, reduce the hate, eliminate the animosity, heal the divisions. Some say he has failed to do any of these things. Others ask how it could have been otherwise.

And below, in the still empty piazza of St Peter's, is another painful reminder. Early though it is, the square is sprinkled with armed policemen; they have carbines, and radios to call for reinforcements. Their presence is grim evidence of the threat Paul now faces.

Out there in Rome are the persons who killed one of his closest friends, Aldo Moro, the Christian Democratic leader. Moro's life was political conciliation. On the day he was kidnapped, in March 1978, Moro took the historic step of bringing the Communists into the Parliamentary alliance to support a Christian Democratic government. For Paul, Moro's kidnapping personalizes the whole question of urban terrorism. He repeatedly appealed to Moro's captors to free him, writing a final entreaty in his own neat hand, a few poignant lines imploring the 'men of the Red Brigades' on his knees to show mercy.

Their response was predictable. Moro was murdered with a circle of bullets around his heart which left him twenty minutes to drown in his own blood.

Paul, some say, has never forgiven the killers. Certainly, what they have done still haunts him as he turns away from the window and shuffles slowly towards the bedroom door ready to begin another long day.

*

In the corridor outside the bedroom two priests, their severe black soutanes relieved only by the white of stiff Roman collars, stand and make smalltalk. They respect each other but do not always agree on policies to be pursued. At this hour of the day, by tacit agreement, they confine themselves to non-controversial subjects: the weather and the holiday from which the younger of the pair has just returned.

The older man is Macchi, Paul's personal private secretary for twenty-three years. His companion is Father John Magee, an Irishman who has served in a similar capacity for three years.

Macchi retains the cultivated hand-flourishes of the seminary professor he once was. But over the years an almost permanent scowl has settled on his darkly handsome face. His once thick thatch of black hair has thinned and greyed. And even here within the papal apartment Macchi is restless. His eyes flicker constantly from the pope's bedroom door back to the corridor. The slightest sound – voices from somewhere else in the apartment, a door opening – tenses him. He has been like this from the day a psychopath tried to kill Paul in the Philippines. Only Macchi's fast reflexes and physical courage in wresting the dagger from a madman dressed as a priest saved the pope from assassination. Macchi, perhaps more than anyone else on the pope's staff, knows of the very real new threats to the pontiff's life. The Red Brigades would like to kill Paul. And the West German government has just secretly informed Secretary of State Villot that a unit of the Red Army Fraction, a spin-off from the German Baader-Meinhof gang, is in Rome attempting to carry out a plan to kidnap Paul and fly him to Libya. There he would be held hostage, with the Libyan leader's connivance, against the release of all convicted terrorists in Israeli jails. Confirmation of this plan came to the Vatican from the MOSSAD, the Israeli Intelligence Service. Even now, MOSSAD agents are in Rome trying to locate the Red Army unit. One result of this threat is that plans for Paul to travel by car, as he usually does, to Castel Gandolfo, are cancelled. Instead he will fly by helicopter. Macchi has ordered the Vatican Press Office to announce that the reason for the switch is to avoid creating the traffic congestion which inevitably arises whenever the pope drives through the city. Nobody really believes the excuse. Macchi does not care: public relations are not his forte. He is singular, ruthless, impatient, sometimes rude and always totally dedicated to Paul. His enemies, and he has many, say he is a one-man papal praetorian guard and presidential secret service detail rolled into one. He is the pope's ears, and often his voice. Only Giacomina stands up to him. Some of their clashes have been memorable.

Magee has never been known to exchange a cross word with anybody in the Vatican during the time he has worked there. He is a muscular, well-proportioned man, built like a good hurling player. He has an open face and keen, searching eyes. But it is his voice, the soft lilt of Newry, County Down, where he was born forty-one years ago, which other members of the papal entourage find so attractive. The nuns listen appreciatively to Magee's fluent Italian; they like his unfailing courtesy and humility, his fund of Irish stories and jokes. Magee is probably one of the most popular men in the Vatican. At times he finds this embarrassing. He is still feeling his way; he does not wish to put noses out of joint, particularly the long, sensitive nose of Macchi.

Generally these past three years have gone swimmingly for Magee, mainly because he has ruefully confirmed the validity of many things Macchi explained. He has discovered that cardinals *do* lie, sometimes habitually, often for no reason except they feel the truth can be used as a trade-off, a commodity to bargain with for personal advantage. And cardinals *do* try to manipulate him, though now Magee more easily recognizes the signs of an impending con: the frank and open unblinking look, the smile just that much too accommodating, the casual too-relaxed style of speaking; he knows all the little tricks and has learned that the way to survive is not to become personally involved in the machinations of those who attempt to use him as a stepping stone to the pope. With these people he maintains a polite, low-key and neutral manner and responds to their wheedling by following one inflexible rule: if a case has merit he will place it before Paul, otherwise nobody can circumnavigate Magee. He has found that his job requires infinite patience, a finicky attention to detail, tenacity and the sheer physical strength to work for absurdly long periods. Magee and Macchi regularly put in a hundred working hours a week, almost all of them under pressure. Both men welcome the month a year vacation which frees them from the considerable burden of their office.

Magee has in fact just returned from a holiday in America, flying home through Ireland where he visited St Patrick's Mission Society – the order to which he belongs – in the Wicklow Hills. His fellow missionaries at Kiltegan greeted him with pride. Magee is the first member of the order in living memory to serve on the pope's personal staff. Indeed, his whole career has been striking proof of the rapid promotion possible in the Church. Ordained in 1962, Magee was sent to Nigeria as a missionary. Four years later a Vatican talent-spotter heard about this young priest in the bush. Magee was brought to Rome. For nine years he worked for the prestigious Propagation of the Faith movement. Then Paul personally picked him to be his English-language secretary.

Magee is saddened to see the deterioration in the pope's physical condition since he has been away from the Vatican. Paul has visibly aged. Magee knows well the signs of impending death; he has seen it many times among the tribesmen of Nigeria. He doubts very much whether the pope will live to see his next birthday, this coming September. Almost certainly he will not be alive at Christmas. Even now, as he comes out of his bedroom towards the waiting secretaries, Magee cannot help but think the pope walks like a man who has accepted his fate.

First Macchi, then Magee, wish him a good morning, addressing Paul as *Santissimo Padre*, Holy Father. They fall in on either side of him, matching their pace to the pope's slow, shambling gait.

In the rarefied atmosphere of clerical Rome, the two priests wield immense power. All sorts of people court their favour. The pope consults them on every serious matter. Both are brilliant aides to His Holiness, partly because neither has any compunction about being a thorn in the side of the more senior prelates in the Vatican. In contrast to the ever-calm Magee, Macchi is highly strung. Yet one of his many tasks is to stop the pope worrying about minor details. Magee, among other things, is Paul's conduit to the world's youth. He also keeps a careful eye on the pope's private charity. Its funds come from many sources. Bishops making their annual reports to the pope will generally present him with a cash gift; the size depends on the wealth of the diocese. American bishops usually give cheques for $2,000; Cardinal Cody of Chicago, who rules over one of the richest dioceses in the Catholic world, habitually hands over $10,000.

Cody's tangled finances – indeed his entire behaviour – have come seriously to trouble Paul. There are well-founded accusations: that the cardinal is a racist, is in conflict with many of the Chicago clergy, is unpopular with many of the laity and displays some extraordinary political and military views. There are also disturbing reports about Cody's vindictiveness, his obsession with secrecy, his refusal to make annual spiritual retreats. The worst charge of all – the one the Vatican is most shocked about – is that the cardinal has misused Church funds.

But now, moving along beside the shuffling Paul, is not the time for Macchi or Magee to mention such grave matters. Instead, a confidential, detailed report will be prepared, confined only to the facts which can be proved. It will make no recommendations. That is not the report's function. But both secretaries can have no doubt what will happen. When Paul reads the report he will almost certainly do what he has threatened to do for some time: despatch on the first scheduled flight to Chicago the Vatican's trouble-shooter, the tough-minded Sebastiano Baggio, prefect of the Congregation of Bishops and the one man with the skill to convey Paul's 'request' that Cody should give up his office.

The three men reach double doors half-way down the corridor. Paul leads them into his private chapel. Its walls are of white marble, cool to the touch, their hardness softened by diffused light coming through glass mosaics of religious scenes. These are the Stations of the Cross which Paul specially installed at the onset of his pontificate. The three men quickly genuflect towards the wooden cross above the altar. Then, with some difficulty, for the arthritis has affected his hip, Paul bends to kiss the altar and begins Mass with the traditional words: 'Oh Lord, I raise to you my prayer . . . '

*

In St Peter's Square police are setting up barriers which will allow them some control over the crowds expected for the pope's weekly public audience later in the morning. For a very long time Wednesday has been the day of the general audience, when the pope receives people 'without rank or name' from the whole world. Since 1971 he has greeted them in the auditorium designed for the purpose by the architect Pier Luigi Nervi. The building stands partially outside the Vatican State boundary, and Rome police fear that somebody – a terrorist, a fanatic, a madman – could enter the hall and attack the pope. All reasonable steps are now taken to minimize the risk. The drably dressed Civil Guards, under the direction of the Central Security Office of the Vatican, are equipped with metal detectors and carefully scrutinize everybody who goes into the hall. There are also armed policemen at strategic points around the building. Their weapons are concealed, in deference to an order from Cardinal Villot, but each Civil Guard is trained in the Rome police armoury to hit a moving target at thirty paces. The city police on duty in St Peter's Square, even though it is also Vatican State property, have no compunction about displaying their guns. They believe keeping a high profile is one way to reduce the risks.

*

Paul is back in his bedroom, fortified by the ninety minutes he has spent in the chapel going through the Matins, Lauds and Prime of his daily office. Once more he kneels on his prie-dieu to commune directly with God. The hum from the *tufo* is louder, reinforced by a miscellany of noise from the square below as the tourist coaches arrive in ever greater frequency. Shortly before nine o'clock, Paul rises from his knees to attend to his frugal earthly needs. He leaves the bedroom and walks the few feet to the dining room where there is a carved walnut table, seating for ten persons, two sideboards and a serving table. A crucifix hangs on the wall. One sideboard holds decanters of liqueurs. The other supports a carved statue of Jesus. There is a twenty-one-inch television set in the corner. Before it was installed the maker promised never to reveal his was the set the pope preferred.

The table is laid with fruit, homemade bread, cheese and butter, all brought in fresh every day. At Paul's place at the head of the table there is a cut-crystal water glass, a plate, cup and saucer. Beside the glass is one of Dr Fontana's little capsules, placed there by Giacomina.

There are two other place settings, for Macchi and Magee. Apart from Sundays – when Giacomina and some of the other nuns sit at table, their turn carefully rotated by Giacomina – the pope almost invariably dines only with his secretaries.

They are already seated when he enters and takes his place. For a moment he bows his head in silent prayer, raising it as Giacomina enters the room to serve coffee and bring the pope a selection from the local and international morning newspapers available in Rome. They include *Le Monde*, *Figaro*, the *International Herald-Tribune* and the *Rome Daily-American*. Italian publications include Communist ones.

Giacomina stands watchfully until Paul swallows his capsule. Satisfied, she leaves; throughout the day she will regularly make sure he takes his medicine.

The pope begins to read, going first to the editorial page of each newspaper and then moving through the other sections. As he finishes a paper he passes it to Macchi who, after scanning it, hands it to Magee. There is little conversation. Each is absorbed with the news. It is another of Paul's small rituals, this systematic scrutiny of the print media every morning. Though he will not concede it to anyone else, he has told his table companions that the mounting attacks on his pontificate both sadden and hurt him. He can date them from that summer day in 1968 when he published his long-expected encyclical on birth control. It had been a catalyst. Everyone in the Church afterwards judged him by that pronouncement. Everything he said before, or since, was seen in the light of *Humanae Vitae*. The most strident attacks, perhaps not surprisingly, had come from America. He no longer reads them, though he is aware they are still circulated within the Vatican. He does not understand nor wish to know of such disloyalty, just as he cannot understand the process which has made the media feel free to criticize the papacy openly. The son of a newspaperman, Paul now wonders what journalism has come to. He finds it difficult to accept the finite judgements which are beginning to appear; people are already starting to write and speak as though his long pontificate were over. It is a curious feeling, he has more than once told Macchi and Magee, to read of himself in the past tense. Yet that is what is happening. And journalists now regularly trawl through his long life, searching for portents which can explain his actions. They have even gone back to his beginnings, to the village of Concesio in the foothills of the Italian Alps, to see what can be dredged up.

But if the clues were there, they have long gone. Concesio is no longer a small farming village; it has become a suburb of the industrial city of Brescia. The Montini family are now shadowy figures. People remember them only vaguely. Paul's father, Giorgio, was a middle-class landowner and newspaper editor. His mother, Giuditta, was a fragile, shy woman, devoutly religious, very like her son. Both parents raised him in a strong Christian rhythm. Early on his thoughts turned to the priesthood. But the prudence, caution and doubts which would haunt him throughout later life had already taken root. Did he have a vocation? Was he physically strong enough to become a priest? A good constitution was essential and he was plagued with delicate health. Did he have the temperament? The stamina and the zeal? Was God guiding him in the right direction? Those doubts had been resolved but others took their place – doubts which had left him awkward about himself and his mission.

If he was critical of others, he was even more so of himself. John XXIII had called him, when Paul was Archbishop of Milan, 'Our Hamlet cardinal'. In a way it was true; he did believe suffering was a precondition for overcoming doubt and, with God's grace, reaching a higher certainty and an agreement with those who opposed the cause of good, especially Communists and terrorists. Yet some of those passing judgement on him took little of this into account. They saw him only as the pope who gave moral support to guerrillas in Spain and left-wing parties in Latin America; as the pontiff who allowed himself and his office to be exploited by the Communist government of North Vietnam in order to help make their 1968 Tet offensive a reality; as the Holy Father who looked benignly on Castro's Cuba, and allowed Marxist bishops and priests and nuns to say Mass in the Church in America, the Third World and Asia; as Paul, who never said a word in protest publicly about the suppression of the Church in Hungary,

Romania and Czechoslovakia. They judged him, he would sometimes sigh across the breakfast table to Macchi and Magee, without full knowledge of the facts.

He reads on, moving steadily from one column to the next, the way he devours official documents. Much of the newspapers' contents he finds trivializing, not at all like the serious, sobering writing his father had produced.On an inside page of an Italian newspaper is another summation of his pontificate. This one is no more banal or vindictive than any of the others. He scans it quickly and responds as he so often does to such attacks. He tosses aside the paper and shrugs his shoulders.

Macchi, who has been waiting for such a moment, begins to run through with Paul his list of appointments for the day.

*

In St Peter's Square, the atmosphere is Roman carnival. Long lines of visitors wend their way towards the Arch of the Bells, one of the entrances to Vatican City. Beyond the gates is the Nervi Audience Hall. Souvenir sellers batten on the lines offering an astonishing selection of junk: fake papal coins, tin medallions, plastic crucifixes, rosaries, emblems, stamps and postcards of the Virgin, Jesus, the Crucifixion and Paul. There are few buyers for the pope's portrait. It is an old one, taken perhaps five years ago. The colouring is unreal; Paul seems to have been wearing make-up or fallen victim to a re-brush artist. From time to time the police move in and pull a person from the lines. These are pickpockets. On a good morning a score can be arrested. They go quietly to one of the police vans parked beneath the Bernini colonnade. There is no sign of any other trouble. But the police commander in charge of the square moves busily among his men, who deploy and redeploy themselves in no apparent order around the tourists.

*

Fully briefed on his appointments, Paul waits in his private study adjoining his bedroom. His official office is two floors below. But he prefers to spend the first segment of his busy, compartmentalized day in this perfectly square room with its floor-to-ceiling shelves filled with books which reflect the breadth of his reading. The sciences are well represented, as are the classics. One shelf is given over to the works of major modern novelists: Graham Greene and Saul Bellow each have space on this shelf; Norman Mailer has a place with his *The Naked and the Dead*, a book Paul regards as an important contribution to the more serious anti-war literature of Bertrand Russell and other pacifist writers whose works are also neatly arranged on the shelves. There are rows of books on theology and religious subjects of all kinds. The writings of the French philosopher Jacques Maritain are in evidence. On a side table is the Italian edition of Maritain's *Integral Humanism*. Paul, when he was a cardinal, eagerly wrote a preface to the translation. The words, in a sense, sum up his view of the papacy and the Church. He argues it is best to be 'a witness by service, and do not think that any other initiative is possible, practical or called for'. He is sympathetic, not surprisingly, to integral humanism's springboard that all men and women are naturally good, and will readily respond to good and reject evil, when shown the difference. He sees it as the role of the Church to make every effort to identify that difference rather than only to make attempts to Catholicize politics, science, education and literature or any other aspect of life. The call to be a 'witness by service' is what the Church must answer before all others. Only then will it keep its rightful place in a world which increasingly excludes any form of Christianity, let alone recognizes the central authority of the pope as the Vicar of Jesus. In Paul's view the papacy and the Church must find a new and more compatible way to attract believers; there is a need to free both the papacy and the Church from their isolation, to recognize past differences and correct them as part of a dedicated new drive to make the twin institutions more palatable to the world.

The words were written before Paul returned to Rome after nine years in Milan. He came south on a train carrying the sort of hangers-on most cardinals acquire. His 'Milan Mafia' of designers, architects, financiers and clerics of all kinds stamped their authority on his papacy.

Among them was the man Paul now awaits, his doctor, Mario Fontana. The pope is resigned to these daily visits; he accepts them as yet another pinprick from the invisible thicket of thorns which he has allowed to surround him.

Fontana as always is punctual. He enters the study on the first stroke of ten o'clock, a dark-blue-suited figure with a gold fob chain across his waistcoat. Even without his black bag he could be nothing but a doctor; he exudes that special bedside manner which only very successful physicians possess. As papal doctor his official title is *archiatro*, a derivation from the Greek meaning physician to an emperor.

No pope ever had a more devoted doctor than Fontana. He has searched the world for a drug which could ease, if not cure, Paul's arthritis. He has even gone to 'fringe' medicine – the world of homoeopathic remedies often not recognized by orthodox practitioners – to find a medicament. In doing so he followed a well-established precedent: several popes had used rejuvenating treatments and elixirs to try to combat the ravages of age. Fontana eventually produced the little capsules which the pope has been swallowing for months. If there are no great signs of improvement, neither has there been a dramatic decline.

Fontana greets Paul with a deeply reverential, 'Good morning, Your Holiness', placing his bag on a small desk in the centre of the room. He does not open it at once but instead starts an innocuous conversation; one morning it is about the weather, another about the tourist season. But the talk is more than polite filling-in. Fontana uses it to judge his patient's responses. Is Paul alert? Does he respond with animation? Or is he listless, not really listening? The answers help the doctor decide what sort of night the pope has had. Paul dislikes being questioned on such matters.

The physical examination is quick. Fontana produces a stethoscope from his bag, slips the disc inside the pope's cassock and listens to his chest. It takes only a minute to complete the examination. Fontana does not say anything. Later he will tell Giacomina and Macchi that Paul still needs very careful watching. The doctor intends to travel with the pope to Castel Gandolfo.

Paul and Fontana leave the study and walk to the elevator. They ride down together to the second floor. The elevator is silent and swift, no longer the creaky water-propelled type so common in the Vatican when Paul first arrived. Yet the overall atmosphere is the same: quiet, almost serene, a mood created, he would sometimes say to a visiting dignitary, by the Holy Spirit.

Fontana continues on out to the Courtyard of San Damaso, across which must come all visitors to the papal apartments or the offices of the Secretariat of State.

The Swiss Guards kneel in salute as Paul passes them on his way to his official office, known as the 'private library'. Each Guard carries a sword or medieval pike as his only visible weapon to protect the Apostolic See. Each soldier comes from a good Swiss Catholic family to serve in the *Cohors Helvetica*, the sole surviving unit of the armed forces of the papacy. The Swiss Guards are under the direct authority of the pontiff. Paul disbanded the Noble Guard and the Palatine Guard in 1970; after years of loyal service he decided they had no useful role to perform. It is yet another decision which has brought him stinging criticism. Now the Swiss Guards – four officers, a chaplain, twenty-three non-commissioned officers, sixty halberdiers and two drummers, in their billowy Renaissance costume with the dark-blue, orange and yellow stripes – are all that remain of ceremonial protocol.

The real protection for the pope is in the hands of men such as the pair of blue-uniformed Civil Guards who stand near the door to his private study. Both are armed with revolvers concealed beneath their jackets. They regularly practise being fast on the draw. They stiffen and salute quickly as the pope passes, but do not bow in case, at that moment, an assassin chooses to strike. A year ago, such an idea would have been preposterous. Now, nobody can be certain.

*

News of any further threats of violence against the pope will almost certainly be first received, and swiftly acted upon, on the floor immediately above Paul's office. Here, on the third floor of the Apostolic Palace, is the Secretariat of State, with its staff of around one hundred, including a dozen diplomats who hold Holy See passports, and about twenty members of religious orders. This is the over-crowded, artificially lit and inadequately ventilated head office of the papal foreign service – the only one in the world which regularly calls upon the Holy Spirit for assistance when faced with a serious political problem. And since the attempt on Paul's life at Manila Airport, the Secretariat has discreetly created a reporting system which allows key members of its staff to be reached day or night by secular governments with news of any new threat to the pope. The system has already been used by the West German and Israeli governments.

Working closely with the pope, the Secretariat is largely responsible for the proper governing of the Holy See and Vatican State. Although coming under the supreme authority of the pontiff, these are separate and distinct entities. The Holy See is the central headquarters of Roman Catholicism. It regulates the religious life of every Catholic, making decisions which affect the faithful in every corner of the world. The Catholic stand on birth control, the Catholic attitude towards Protestantism, the Catholic position on Communism, Judaism, Islam, all in the end emanate from the Holy See. Here, too, all kinds of doctrinal questions, from the wording of the catechism to the validity of baptism, are settled. Every aspect of Church policy and practice is formulated on the third floor of the Apostolic Palace. For 740 million baptized Catholics, for 421,839 priests and 986,686 nuns, for 3,700 bishops, for 130 cardinals, for a Church which makes up 18.1 per cent of the estimated population of the world; for them all the decisions made in these offices are supposedly binding. It is the Holy See, not Vatican State, which has diplomatic relations with over fifty nations and maintains a diplomatic corps of some forty apostolic nuncios and delegates in various capitals or, in Africa, roving about their territory. Vatican State – a mere 108 acres, a landlocked and walled enclave within the City of Rome, 1,132 yards in length and 812 yards across – is the shell of temporal sovereignty which allows the Church to carry out its mission through the Holy See and the offices of the Secretariat of State.

For the last nine years the Secretariat has been run by Villot, the cardinal everybody likes to label. To journalists he is a xenophobic Frenchman – only Gallic newsmen write with pride that he is God's de Gaulle – pinch-nosed and purse-lipped, whose smile never quite reaches behind his steel-framed spectacles. His detractors postulate that even when he sleeps, Villot's eyes are on guard, staring unblinkingly at the ceiling. A more serious observation is that he has developed his bureaucratic capability after a lifetime of minor victories.

His office is close to a small and beautiful bathroom, designed and painted by Raphael, which is both entrancing and gently salacious. Villot's office, by contrast, is elegantly functional. There is little clutter, but an immediate impression of constant achievement: a variety of paperwork comes and goes all the time, passing in and out of the fug of Gauloises which wreathes the room during Villot's working hours. He smokes forty a day. His staff shake their heads and say his Eminence will surely die of lung cancer. Villot gives a Frenchman's shrug: he is seventy-two years old and it is too late to change the habit of a lifetime. Socially, he is a renowned *bon vivant*; his cellar is said to be the finest in a Vatican of fine wine cellars. He likes small dinner parties when he listens a great deal to some of the world's leading opinion-makers. Listening has always been his strong point in a steady climb to power: auxiliary bishop of Paris in 1954, archbishop of Lyons in 1965 and then the short, sudden leap to this office on the third floor. Here, the world's problems, as perceived in the Vatican, are sifted, analysed and pronounced upon, but not always for public consumption. Villot is a passionate advocate of the Holy See's renowned skill at low-key, often secret diplomacy. He dreads those times when the Secretariat's role in some delicate negotiation surfaces before a satisfactory conclusion. Then his daily cigarette consumption goes over the fifty mark. Villot is presently involved with the Middle East, Poland and Rhodesia. Moderate success in these areas is keeping him within his usual two packets a day.

For weeks, too, he has been aware of another matter which will likely come to a head shortly. Careful questioning of Fontana has left Villot in no doubt that Paul could die soon. When the moment comes, Villot, as Secretary of State, would become the Camerlengo, or Chamberlain, of the Universal Church, in full charge until a new pope is elected, and totally responsible for the organization of the Conclave which will elevate a cardinal to pontiff. Villot has already studied the bulky file on John XXIII's funeral and reminded himself of Paul's apostolic constitution, *On Electing a Supreme Pontiff*, his guidelines for the appointment of his successor. It is another of those documents which has created dissent. Paul has decreed all cardinals over eighty years of age are to be banned from the next Conclave. And the strict secrecy of Conclave – a tradition which stems from 1903 when it was deployed to stop the Austrian emperor, Franz Joseph I, from influencing the cardinal voters – has been considerably tightened. Cardinals must solemnly swear before God to keep their mouths shut. The Conclave area must be swept electronically for bugs. Paul, Villot has wryly remarked, is determined there will be no Vaticangate to leak details of the power plays behind the next papal election. But even Villot cannot guarantee the secrets will be kept. Not any more. Not the way some of the more ambitious cardinals have started to behave. Even now, while Paul still lives, they are jockeying and lobbying, testing the ground for support. It is all illegal and against the express wishes of the Holy Spirit. But it *is* going on. And Villot senses it could reach a point where, among other things, he will be forced to increase his consumption of cigarettes under the nervous strain of coping with some of the manoeuvrings of his fellow cardinals.

*

In the office where he now sits, Paul, two years earlier, made a decision which many still say marks one of the peaks of his pontificate. Against all the advice he received from the Roman Curia – the highly complicated and structured hierarchical body which is the Holy See's civil service – Paul looked outside Italy for many of the twenty new cardinals he appointed in 1976. Several of them – Evaristo Arns and Aloisio Lorscheider of Brazil, Bernardin Gantin of Benin, Hyacinthe Thiandoum of Senegal, Jaime Sin of the Philippines and Eduardo Pironio of Argentina – were men for whom the Curia had no special liking; they are progressives, eager for reform, prepared to challenge the Curia. In promoting them, Paul made his own curial enemies. He feels the risk was worthwhile and hopes that the newcomers, when they come to vote for his successor, will look for a candidate who will wish to continue the reforms he has introduced. But he does not underestimate the ability of those in the Curia to manipulate the situation for their own ends. He has seen them do it before; and he is still trapped in their skilful snares, this northern Italian who has never found it easy to get the Romans to welcome him. Even here, in his inner sanctum, their influence is as tangible as ever: many of the decisions he will be asked to endorse at the end of the day will have been prepared, shaped, honed and polished by the Curia. They will be presented to him as carefully argued memos, papers which have been written and rewritten to get their meaning right to the very last nuance, documents which have been patiently worked over by many clever minds.

There is no way Paul can change matters. He himself spent thirty years within the curial system. He knows too well how it works. He also realizes, despite his great achievement in appointing the cardinals he wanted, in the end he cannot beat the system. No pope ever has.

Such thoughts may well have contributed to the sense of failure people now openly detect in Paul. It has been there for a long time, perhaps from that day in 1966, just three years after he became pope, when he visited the grave of Celestine V. Celestine is remembered now only as the pope who resigned in 1294. Paul chose the visit to speak of resignation. His words, as always, were open to interpretation. But the consensus was that Paul would abdicate under certain conditions. Already he had become involved in a running battle with the Jesuits; the first shocking whispers of Cody's behaviour in Chicago had reached him; the implementation of Vatican II was causing serious difficulties; the Holy See was caught up in Vietnam. Over the years all these crises had deeply troubled him. His sense of failure grew. Even to his secretaries, the discreet and loyal Macchi and Magee, Paul now cuts a lonely and tragic figure – very much Hamlet's cardinal – as he sits and waits for his first official visitor.

More than any of the other rooms he occupies, Paul has taken pains over the décor of this spacious salon with its three windows looking down on St Peter's Square. He removed the gilt furniture John XXIII favoured; gone, too, are his predecessor's predilection for patterned rugs and the busts of dead popes. They have all been taken to one of the cavernous basement stores in the Apostolic Palace to be inventoried, covered by dust sheets and left to await the pleasure of some future pope. From the same cellars Paul ordered up fine Renaissance paintings and wooden statues of the saints and the creamy velours he favours as wall and floor coverings.

He sits at a sixteenth-century desk, crafted in the days of Paul IV. It has a hand-tooled leather writing pad, a small clock in a solid gold frame, a gold-topped roll blotter, a combination scissors and letter opener. Every item is carefully laid out; it is all so neat any visitor knows this is not Paul's real working desk. This is a showcase where he sits and receives a stream of people. Behind him is a shelf with a white telephone. No one can remember when he last used it. No incoming calls ever get this far: they end at the desks of Macchi and Magee. Beside the white telephone are carefully chosen reference books: a Latin Bible and index; a leather-bound volume of Vatican II documents; Paul's celebrated encyclical, *Ecclesiam Suam*; a dictionary of missions; a code of canon law; the latest edition of the Vatican yearbook, which has been specially bound for him in white leather. The lighting, the flower arrangements, the position of every piece of furniture combine to suggest a designer's concept of what a pope's office should look like. It is both overpowering and deadening.

Shortly after ten o'clock, as per Macchi's appointment schedule, Villot comes into the room. He visits it regularly twice a day, more often when there is a particular crisis on which Paul needs special briefing. He stands before the desk and greets the pope in Italian, spoken impeccably with no trace of a French accent. There is nothing in Villot's manner to suggest any truth in the stories written by those journalists who first lampoon his physical features and then go on to report that the Secretary feels an outsider in the Vatican, that he might even be going to tender his resignation – again.

In the media Villot has been offering his resignation for years. He is supposed to have done so after opposing Italy's referendum on divorce; after failing to persuade the United States to allow the Vatican to become more involved in finding a settlement for the Vietnam war; over his continual jousting with the Jesuits. The times he is said to have threatened to go are as legion as the crises alleged to have provoked his reaction. Many of the tales are probably baseless. But there have been occasions – particularly over Vietnam – when Villot found his efforts suddenly torpedoed by those Curia officials who are not above leaking to the press sensitive material. Almost certainly Villot then spoke to Paul about going and the pope begged him to stay.

Paul is not by nature a pleader. Any more than he relished symbolically going down on his painful knees to the Red Brigades in a futile bid to save his friend, Moro, so he has not liked repeating the process each time Villot wants to quit. But they are both old and weary men; in the end they had briefly embraced each other and Villot continued to soldier on.

Yet between them lies an issue which both have spoken about to their confidants – and perhaps their confessors – but have never fully explored with each other. It is the rise and fall and rise again of Giovanni Benelli. Even now, only two years later, the roots of the story have become obscured; those who really know all the facts keep them under careful guard, but the moral of the story is obvious. It most likely began with Paul anticipating the day when the long-suffering Villot would resign. To prepare for such an eventuality, the pope appointed Benelli as Under-Secretary of State. Benelli had learned his diplomatic ringcraft in such tricky Holy See postings as Dublin, Paris, Rio de Janeiro and Madrid. Looking much younger than his fifty-five years, with a flashing smile to match his wit, Benelli soon raised Villot's hackles. The pair were simply incompatible. Then, with a swiftness which left even hardened curialists dumbfounded, Benelli was gone – raised to the cardinalate and sent off to be archbishop of Florence, not exactly the wilderness but also not a place for a restless, ambitious prince of the Church. Villot led the coup which ousted him. He found a ready ally in the pope's trouble-shooter, Sebastiano Baggio, and a surprising one in Macchi, who had grown tired of Benelli's abrupt Tuscan manners and high-minded attitudes. The clincher came when Fr Romeo Panciroli, who runs a tight-lipped Vatican Press Office, and Bishop Paul Marcinkus, president of Vatican Bank, supported Villot. Paul had little alternative. Benelli went.

But nobody now thinks sending him to Florence has ended his ambitions. Vatican scuttlebutt openly predicts there is one certain papal candidate for the next Conclave, the cardinal in Florence. And rumour adds that if the archbishop is successful in becoming the two hundred and sixty-second successor to the Throne of St Peter the Apostle, one of his first actions will be to ensure Villot, Baggio, Macchi, Panciroli and Marcinkus end their days in some of the Church's loneliest outposts. Unless, of course, they resigned. It was the sort of scenario which could drive Villot to chain-smoking.

This morning there are yet other related issues to make Secretary of State Villot ponder his future. Baggio, having helped to see off Benelli, has begun to make his own play for the papacy. Since May, the man who is known around the Vatican as 'Viaggio Baggio', a curial-created pun meaning 'Baggio the traveller' – itself an allusion to the endless journeys he takes on behalf of Paul to dampen down some local Church crisis – has been trying to muster support. And the brief alliance between the trouble-shooter and the Secretary of State is over. Again there are any number of possible reasons: incompatibility (always a safe bet in the fiercely competitive Vatican arena); outrage by Villot that anybody should be campaigning as though the papacy was a presidential office; Baggio's view that Villot is just a tired old man who should have resigned years ago. There is as much grist as there are mills. The outcome is that nowadays the pair openly avoid each other. And everybody says the ruptured relationship is yet another sign Paul will die soon.

It is in this frame of mind that Villot begins to discuss with the pope matters of state. Better than anybody, the Secretary knows the Vatican is grinding to a halt.[2] No decision which can be put off is being taken. Everybody is waiting, biding their time and preparing their position for what must follow after Paul is laid to rest.

4

Almost at the moment Villot concludes his far-ranging presentation for Paul, which as usual incorporated a review of the latest developments in such perennial trouble-spots as Beirut, Hanoi, Warsaw and Salisbury, Rhodesia, the door to the salon opens and a prelate enters.

He has not knocked or been summoned, nor has he sought permission before walking in unannounced. He does not need to. His position and office, prefect of the Prefecture of the Pontifical Household, Casa Pontificia, gives Monsignor Jacques Martin the right to enter the papal presence at any time he chooses. Only the pope's personal valet, Ghezzi, shares this jealously guarded privilege. It allows Martin to keep a proper, and satisfying, distance between himself and the other members of the Pontifical Family. As its titular head, Martin is nowadays busier than ever. After centuries of independence, the duties of the Pontiff's Ceremonial Congregation, the offices of the Major-domo, the Chamberlain, and the Heraldic Commission have all been placed under the control of the Casa Pontificia, where Martin's responsibilities already include running the internal affairs of the pope's household in the Vatican and at Castel Gandolfo, and arranging almost all of Paul's meetings. Martin is also the elderly priest in a plain black cassock and simple gold cross who is always close to the pope in the obligatory photographs of important personages who call on Paul. Martin's suite of rooms near the Courtyard of San Damaso are filled with leather-bound albums commemorating hundreds of such occasions. They go well with the frescoed walls and ceilings, the religious scenes, the sportive-looking cherubs and satyrs, the triptych in oils, all of which also help make the prefect's apartment one of the most beautifully appointed among those who work for Paul.

Having entered, Martin stands by the door. His nose is almost the beak-shape cartoonists depict when they sketch him as the pope's fixer, the priest who ultimately decides who sees Paul; there are an average of 5,000 requests a week for a private, semi-private or small-group audience. Inevitably, most applicants are disappointed. But those who make it into the papal presence usually come to see Martin as one of the most fascinating men in the Vatican. With some truth, Paul's

administration is characterized as 'horizontal'; it is uniformly compe-
tent but short on intellectual giants. Martin is one of the exceptions,
and he knows it. Perhaps that is why behind his courtly manners there
is a sardonic wit and a glitter in his eye when he detects a worthwhile
challenge to his vast knowledge of how the Vatican works. Few offer
one. His reputation is renowned for overwhelming anybody who
doubts the astonishing range of facts he possesses.

It was he, using his knowledge of the layout of the Apostolic Palace,
who found just the right room to be converted into an infirmary for
Paul to have his prostate operation. It is he who knows all about the
holy relics on which faith is built: the bones of Magi, the skull of John
the Baptist, the hand of St Gregory, the robe of Jesus, the Virgin's cloak,
Mary Magdalene's foot, even part of the foreskin of Christ, said to be
the only known sliver of him, reposing in a ruby and emerald-studded
casket watched over by two solid silver angels in a shrine in Calcate,
north of Rome. And it is Martin, too, who can chart the steady growth
in the number of cardinals: the thirty-eight popes who reigned from
1198 to 1492 created 540; during the next three hundred years a
further thirty-seven popes named 1,275 cardinals. Some popes, such as
Celestine IV and Leo XI, appointed none. Others created them with
astonishing rapidity. But until February 1965, the maximum number
of living cardinals at any one time remained seventy, the limit fixed to
commemorate the seventy ancient scholars of Alexandria who are
traditionally thought to be the translators of the Hebrew Bible into
Greek.

Paul, the man Martin has come to fetch, raised the number to 101,
and then, in 1976, yet again, to a record 136 cardinals.

Martin always has a fresh story, fact or theory to keep his very private
dinner parties going right up to the witching hour of midnight when all
the gates of the Vatican are closed and no one can leave or enter
without a permission which is rarely granted. The Vatican is the only
state in the free world which physically seals its boundaries every night.
Martin likes the custom; it gives him a chance to get to bed at a
reasonable time after spending an hour or so going over Paul's schedule
for the following day.

Now, he remains by the door, a precise and self-effacing man with
the lightest of blue eyes, which become glacial when something, or
somebody, doesn't please him. By some extraordinary means those
eyes seem to draw Paul to his feet.

The pope rises slowly, using his desk for support, again feeling the
pain in his right knee. Followed by Villot he walks towards Martin.

The three men converse for a moment in French; Paul has a scholar's
facility to speak several languages fluently. He has even considered

learning Russian so that he may communicate more directly with Soviet leaders; Foreign Minister Gromyko has already paid him four long visits during the last ten years.

Villot makes his farewell, always a formal moment, for both pope and Secretary of State are punctilious about protocol, then Martin escorts Paul slowly towards the first of eight ante-chambers where small groups are waiting.

These are Martin's chosen ones, those he has found a place for in the carefully structured scale of audiences which begin with the large general mass audiences, move on to group audiences, then to semi-private audiences, *baciamano*, when it is permitted to kiss the pope's hand and engage him in carefully prepared conversation. Finally there are the private meetings, usually held in the salon the pope has just left; these are invariably restricted to heads of state, ambassadors, cardinals or bishops on urgent or important business.

Those waiting in the ante-chamber are *baciamano*. Each of them – all these men in dark lounge suits and women in long severe dresses – has been able to convince Martin they are worthy of this moment: they may have raised funds for their local Church, made an outright gift to a Catholic hospital, a Catholic charity, a Catholic mission; perhaps they have a close connection with a powerful bishop or cardinal. Their very presence here denotes special status.

They have been waiting patiently for an hour, shepherded into position by Martin's staff of eight priests who placed them according to a typed list. The most important are in the first room where, in theory, Paul will spend a little more time; if his schedule runs too far behind, Martin will shorten the pope's stay in the final salons. His aides have been moving among the groupings, reminding them, again, that the ritual demands the most punctilious decorum and protocol. No one must ask the pope personal questions or attempt to obtain a blessing for any object such as a pocket Bible or rosary. All should bend at the knee when the pope comes into their presence. At all times they should address him as 'Your Holiness'. They may kiss his right hand.

*

As eleven o'clock approaches there is hardly an empty space in the Nervi Hall. It is filled with twelve thousand people. So many want to see Paul before he dies – though nobody is sufficiently crass to give that as the reason when applying for a ticket to the public audience – there has been standing room only for months. The endless ranks seem lost in the vast area, causing some people to say that if the hall is supposed to represent one of the entrance halls to Heaven, then surely God needs a new architect. Others argue it is difficult to see what else Pier Nervi could have done, given his brief from Paul to build the largest audience chamber in the Western world. Nervi finally settled for four prestressed concrete walls, an undulating ceiling and a ramped floor running 2,756 feet from the entrance down to the elevated stage at the western wall. There are no frescoes, no canvas reminders of God, Heaven, Christ or Eternity to soften the vaulted ceiling supported by forty-two white, geminate arches. Set into each of the two long side walls is an oval stained-glass window. Like so much else about the building, the windows have been the object of fierce controversy. Marc Chagall was first asked to suggest designs for them. His sketches were judged too confused and earthy for a setting supposed to suggest Heavenly peace. Giovanni Hajnal's impression of the serenity of God now fill the two windows. Set high in one wall are the glass-fronted booths for television, radio and print commentators. This morning, as usual, they are crammed with journalists; the rumour persists Paul might yet announce his resignation.

Macchi and Magee have been out to check the microphone standing before the pope's throne; their amplified testing, one, two, three, four, has brought ripples of applause.

The massive theatre is dwarfed by the largest bronze sculpture on earth, the Risen Christ. Paul commissioned it in 1965 – a full year before workmen began excavating the foundation for the hall, demolishing in the process a number of buildings between the Holy Office and the Leonine Wall of the Vatican. The bronze is the creation of Pericle Fazzini, one of Jacqueline Kennedy's favourite sculptors. The choice of Fazzini was not a universal one; Romans thought Paul should have engaged a local man.

Since 30 June 1971 Paul has come, every Wednesday he is in Rome, to this gargantuan mass of engineering dynamism to speak to the people. It is here he revealed the interpretation and shaping of many of the ideas which have led to endless debate. He has used the audiences both to welcome the Test Ban treaty and to indicate that an accommodation with Communism is necessary. In this hall he has spoken about the problems of underdeveloped countries, showing a good understanding of the divisive forces currently at work in the world; about the new era of space travel; about the meaning of democracy in an age of increasing totalitarianism.

Yet over the years there has been a shift in emphasis: the sensitive and modest pronouncements of his first speeches have gradually hardened to a more protective attitude, the human relations aspect giving way to a more authoritarian stand. He was the boss showing he must boss. Never a charismatic or utopian leader like his predecessor,

John XXIII, Paul's public pronouncements became tinged with conservatism. Collegiality, the sharing of power between the pope and the episcopate, which he had looked upon with favour during the early days of his reign, now appeared to him a dangerous novelty that could usurp traditional papal prerogatives. Inevitably, this change of attitude forged him into an alliance with the conservatives of the Curia. They shrewdly encouraged Paul in his belief he must say or do nothing which would cause him to go down in history as the pope who presided over the dismantling of the Church. That, whispered those conservatives, would happen if he pursued the initiatives and freedom John had begun to introduce.

Paul was elected at a time when the Church was already seriously divided, polarized between opposing tendencies. He maintained a form of unity by refusing, at first, to push any line resolutely for fear of further weakening the institution. But by following a middle course he had come to be seen as indecisive, pessimistic and, some even said, underhand. Few realized he was engaged upon a skilful holding operation. Initially he entered this hall intending merely to restate some of the ancient truths. Gradually, instead of trying to please everybody by making concessions all around, he developed fewer qualms about favouring conservatives, both religious and political. They came to see him as their own. This had helped ease his Hamletic hesitation and provided the resolve for *Humanae Vitae*. The message of that encyclical was one he continued to convey at his weekly audiences.

Nevertheless, just when he had secured the approbation of the right, Paul had shifted again. He began to argue that the issue of Catholic–Marxist dialogue needed re-examining following the spectacular gains made by the Left in various Latin countries; this papal initiative was correctly diagnosed as stemming from fear – the fear that the new political situation would adversely affect the Church unless the Church quickly came to terms with it. The result was equally inevitable: there was a right-wing backlash which produced powerful splinter groups. The most publicized was the movement led by the reactionary traditionalist Archbishop Marcel Lefèbvre. Even to mention his name in Paul's presence is to draw a stinging rebuke. In part the reporters in the booths awaiting the pope's progress down the ramp are there to see whether Lefèbvre's disciples will stage a demonstration during the audience which will show once more the bitterness of the controversy.

The prospect of trouble, and a good story, excites the journalists. Many of them have covered the Lefèbvre saga from the day it started, 8 December 1965, the last day of the Second Vatican Council. The reporters spend their waiting time remembering events that, looking back, have an inevitability about them.

*

At some point in the history of the four-year-long Vatican Council, Lefèbvre, a French-born archbishop few had heard of, decided Vatican II was moving the Church dangerously near to a position of 'neo-Modernism and neo-Protestantism'. On the closing day of the Council he went further. Flanked by two of his priests, the archbishop told a group of newsmen he had legal grounds on which to oppose the decisions of the Council; consequently they were invalid and non-binding. Lefèbvre had gone on in an androgynous voice which would soon become as famous as Paul's, stating there was nothing in any Church document which declared that to disobey the decisions of Vatican II would bring anathema, the ultimate ecclesiastical condemnation for a breach of the true faith.

The reporters who had been there that cool December afternoon still remember how they had reached for their pencils and switched on their cassette recorders. Here was not merely a challenge; here were the makings of a running controversy. Lefèbvre might not be well known, but he *was* an archbishop and senior Churchmen didn't usually talk so outspokenly. Lefèbvre's language was uncompromising. The basis of this two-pronged attack hinged on his idea that traditional Catholic belief and dogma were being altered fundamentally in an ill-guided attempt to keep up with the changing times. What was happening, argued the archbishop, was 'a new kind of Reformation'. But unlike Luther in the sixteenth century, who had revolted against the Church of Rome and left it to carry on the fight outside, this time those behind the 'new Reformation' intended to stay in the Church and burrow away from that secure position to destroy well-established patterns.

It was heady stuff, the sort of copy which put the Church back on the front pages.

So it had begun. The headlines were followed by profiles of Lefèbvre, the son of a textile manufacturer from Tourcoing, France, who became a scholarly priest, a valued member of the Holy Spirit Missionary Order, a bishop in Senegal and later archbishop of Dakar. Until the Vatican Council it was a career not exceptional for a talented sixty-year-old who always had ambitions to make his way in the Church. Then, just as suddenly as he had emerged, Lefèbvre dropped from sight. He might have remained forgotten if, in 1969, Paul had not promulgated a new official text for celebrating Mass – the *Mass Ordinal*. It consisted of an *Introduction* and a new text for both the existing Mass and the ceremonial instructions. It was intended as a replacement for the

Tridentine order of Mass published by Pius V in 1570, which had been in use ever since.

Two Italian priests, sympathetic to the views Lefèbvre had expressed in 1965, wrote a biting criticism of the new *Ordinal* and *Introduction* as flying in the face of traditional Catholic beliefs. The priests, following Lefèbvre's example, made themselves available to the media. The tabloids reduced it to: Paul or Pius – it's Mass-make-your-own-mind-up-time. Paul asked the Sacred Congregation for the Faith – previously known as the Holy Office, and before that the Congregation for the Holy Inquisition of Heretical Error, with a history going back more than four hundred years – to examine his *Introduction*. The Congregation reported favourably. And there the story might have once again stopped.

But Lefèbvre told a journalist he had obtained permission from the Vatican to start his own institute and seminary at Econe in Switzerland. Here was another good tale and the media made the most of it. Lefèbvre helped by launching a series of attacks on the established Church in Europe and the United States. On 21 November 1974, he published a manifesto castigating the Vatican Council as a 'fake', the Pauline Mass as 'illegal', and the teachings of the bishops 'in error'. He became an international figure. He quickly opened other seminaries, produced a scathing newsletter, and wrote a book, *J'accuse le Concile*. He became a firm media favourite. Now there was no way the story would die.

Paul – trapped trying to be all things to all persons – hesitated fatally, ignoring Villot's advice to act ruthlessly, crush Lefèbvre and totally destroy his movement. Paul tried to reason with a man who was beyond persuasion. Then, too late, Paul allowed the full fury of the Vatican to fall on the archbishop. Canonical approval was withdrawn from his seminaries. The Vatican Court of Appeals refused to review this decision. By 1976 almost weekly threats, demands and orders from Rome were winging their way to Lefèbvre's mountain fastness to try to bring him to heel. He refused. Instead he took his mission to the United States, stomping the country, confirming children, preaching against the teachings of Vatican II. He returned to Switzerland in June 1976 and announced he was about to ordain twenty-six young men into the priesthood at his Econe seminary. Legally he still had the right to do so. Then Paul did something no other pope had done for 217 years. He publicly attacked a prelate of the Church. The pope felt he had no alternative. The danger was too real: Lefèbvre could not only ordain priests but also create bishops and even dioceses to compete with the established ones. He could set up his own Church. It was a nightmare.

The day before Lefèbvre was due to ordain his priests, Paul suddenly tried a more direct approach. He sent Cardinal Thiandoum as his special emissary, begging Lefèbvre to desist – in much the same way Paul later beseeched the Red Brigades to spare Moro. Lefèbvre, like the terrorists, did not respond to the plea. He ordained his priests and delivered a sermon about the 'traitors of our faith', a reference presumed to be aimed at Paul and the Vatican.

Villot tried. He sent a courier and a letter demanding Lefèbvre cease. The response was icy. The Secretary of State then suspended the archbishop from office. Lefèbvre promptly preached a sermon about the Vatican creating 'confusion through bastardization'. There was, he thundered, 'a bastard rite [the Pauline Mass], bastard sacraments, bastard priests'. He had one final defiance: 'If the pope is in error, he ceases to be pope.'

The Church closed its collective doors. Lefèbvre promptly celebrated a Latin rite Mass in a wrestling hall. Six thousand people came to join in the responses. Paul, the same day, drew seven thousand to Castel Gandolfo to hear his appeal: 'Help Us to prevent a schism in the Church. Our brother prelate has challenged the Keys placed in our hands by Christ. We will not answer the archbishop in the tone he uses with Us.'

The battle waged on, with Paul alternatively trying reason and threats, with Lefèbvre always stubbornly obstinate and maddeningly able to get his point across the front pages. Finally, when Lefèbvre eventually persuaded Paul they should meet at Castel Gandolfo – 'I want to work under your authority, but I must speak to you personally' – the media were on hand to hear the outcome of this historic confrontation.

The reporters would remember the archbishop's appearance that September day. He looked a man possessed by the all-devouring idea that he was right. An hour later he emerged from Paul's summer retreat to give a blow-by-blow account of how Paul had listened while Lefèbvre insisted on his 'rights': the right to say the Tridentine Mass; the right to ordain more priests; the right to go his own way. Paul had asked whether the archbishop intended to consecrate new bishops. The response was unequivocal: Lefèbvre would do so when he thought it was necessary. He had lectured the pope and Paul had briefly lost his temper. Then they had prayed together, reciting an Our Father, a Hail Mary and the prayer to the Holy Spirit, *Veni, Sancte Spiritus*. They made their responses in Latin. Lefèbvre believed it was a sign he was winning.

But peace was still a long way off. The more Lefèbvre denies he is anti-Vatican or 'unfaithful' to the pope, or that he has any intention of creating a 'Tridentine Vatican' or of building a basilica to rival St Peter's, or that he intends to become the latest anti-pope, a man whom the Church decides is not validly elected: the more he denies such charges, the more plausible they become to many of the journalists now waiting for Paul to arrive in the audience hall.

*

Paul waits patiently while the *sediari*, the throne bearers, in full morning dress, their starched shirt fronts whiter even than Paul's cassock, approach with the *sedia gestatoria*, the ornately sculpted chair on which Paul is borne into the audience hall.

Surrounding the throne, eyes constantly scanning the tumultuous crowd, security men lead the procession down the aisle. The noise is one continuous roar of singing, cheering, handclapping and crying. This is the time the pope's entourage most fear, when Paul is most vulnerable to attack. Somewhere among the waving hands could be one holding a weapon. Camilio Ciban, head of the security detail, keeps close to the swaying chair, ready to throw himself between the pope and an attacker. Macchi is on the other side of the *sedia gestatoria*, prepared to fulfil a similar function. Magee is in front, viewing the throng ahead for the first sign of anything untoward. Ciban also has men on either side of Paul's chair. He has told all of them to watch people's eyes; eyes are the giveaway which can provide that vital split-second's advantage.

None of the security men look at Paul. His head moves from side to side as he smiles wanly out over the crowds, occasionally leaning down towards outstretched hands. He is careful not actually to make contact for fear he is yanked from his throne; that nearly happened in India. The procession moves slowly, far more so than Ciban likes. But Paul has specifically ordered there must be no unseemly hurry. People have come from all corners of the earth for this moment and he will not disappoint them. It takes twenty minutes for the chair to reach the dais. There Macchi and Magee help Paul to the throne on the stage. Thunderous applause continues. From the dais the body of the hall seems to be a mass of exploding flashbulbs.

The chair bearers and security detail disappear through a door near the Fazzini sculpture. Now the only protection the pope has are four Swiss Guards, plumed and helmeted, halberds held rigidly before them. To Paul's left sit two rows of visiting cardinals, bishops, Macchi and Magee. The pope looks at them nodding and smiling. The applause roars on. He turns to face the crowd and slowly extends his arms as though embracing everyone. Suddenly, as if drilled to recognize the signal, the crowd becomes silent.

The pope makes the sign of the cross and then begins his weekly homily with the words he has always used: 'Dear sons and daughters . . .'

He pauses and closes his eyes. His face is drawn and haggard.

One of the journalists overlooking the scene wonders whether Paul has suffered another sudden spasm of pain. Everybody knows of his arthritis; it has become as talked about as was Kennedy's back, de Gaulle's liver and Adenauer's pancreas.

A companion shakes his head. The pope, he ventures, is probably wondering what new there is for him to say. He's said it all before, to everybody who will listen.

It's true. No pope has travelled so far to speak to so many.

*

When all the judgements are in: when his contribution to the Church has been weighed; when the truth assessed of whether timid by temperament he became brave out of virtue; whether he is right to see tradition not as the dead hand of the past weighing down on the present but as a positive concept of living reality; whether the implementation of so many of the Second Vatican Council's teachings, such a personal triumph for him, ultimately paved the way for a sharing of power while allowing the papacy to be of even greater service to the Church; whether all the liturgical changes he introduced were really only what some critics claimed, more aesthetic than pastoral; whether he too often invoked his personal authority when he should have sheltered behind his fellow bishops; whether, as in the case of *Humanae Vitae*, he was right to pronounce on complex issues of personal liberty about which the world had become so sensitive; whether his well-publicized oecumenism would have been better understood had his utterances been in the form of clear doctrinal statements instead of parables, or what he called 'gestures'; when all these and many other matters came to be judged, it is almost certain they would be seen in the context of Paul's most newsworthy achievement – that of being the first modern pilgrim pope, the man who personally brought his message from Rome and, like so many other messengers, found himself not always welcome.

Early on Paul spoke of himself as a pilgrim and of his pontificate as a pilgrimage. All those hard lessons he had learned while a papal diplomat were called into play when, in his role as the prophet of peace and justice to all men, he made journeys which stirred the imagination. He went to the source of Christian faith, the Holy Land, and embraced Patriarch Athenagorus. He went to India and prayed with the people, receiving in Bombay the most tumultuous welcome the nation has ever bestowed upon a foreign visitor. Fulfilling his description of himself as an 'apostle on the move', Paul went to Uganda where, in Kampala, he made a special effort to speak of the Anglican martyrs. As he stepped from the Alitalia plane on his arrival in Bogotá, Colombia – the first pope to use jet travel – he astonished everyone by kissing the soil of Latin America; that gesture alone ensured his visit was a massive personal triumph. In Manila he was attacked by the mad painter dressed as a priest. But it made no difference: everywhere he went he carried his message of spiritual brotherhood. It was part of Paul's dialogue with other religions.

But it was not always easy – in the Far East, in South America, in Central Africa – for the faithful to understand his attitude on birth control, divorce and other inflexible Church teachings. Nor could everyone grasp why large sums of money should be spent on soaring, open-air altars and triumphal arches for parade routes when so many of the spectators were near to starvation.

Wherever Paul travelled he gave the impression the weight of the world bore down on his narrow shoulders, threatening to crush his diminutive, white-clad figure. Yet when he spoke he had the ears of the world. Only afterwards, once he had gone, did some people pause to consider what he had said. They came to see his words as providing no more than a kindly recognition of their existence, a benign acknowledgement of their difficulties – but very few practical solutions.

He addressed the General Assembly of the United Nations, beginning with the words he knew assured him respectful attention: 'We have a message to deliver to each of you.' On that occasion his words had been simultaneously translated into thirty-five languages. He was heard by representatives of almost all the nations on earth. His hopes were compelling: relations between peoples must be regulated by reason, justice and negotiation, not by fear, force or fraud.

The sixty journalists who had flown with Paul from Rome to New York had heard it all before. Some were now listening to it again, in the Nervi Hall where Paul concludes his homily with a universal blessing.

*

Escorted by Macchi, Magee, Ciban and his security men who have silently returned, Paul leaves the throne and walks slowly down to a group of infirm people waiting in a special area to the left of the stage. There are men, women and some children; limbless, wheelchair bound, many bear the unmistakable mark of terminal illnesses.

Paul places his hand on the head of a blind boy. The child looks up sightlessly at the pope, who bends and whispers words he has used before. 'Courage, be brave.' The boy shakes his head as though he cannot be brave any longer. Paul whispers again. 'I will pray for you. Will you pray for me?' The boy frowns, not certain what to answer. Finally he says: 'How can I pray for you, Your Holiness?' And Paul answers, very softly, so that Macchi and Magee must strain to hear the words. 'You are my son. You can pray for your father.' The boy smiles, understanding.

The pope moves to an old woman. She is without arms, a huge goitre on her neck. She is burnt reddish-black from radiation treatments. The cancer, she says, is still spreading. She knows she must die soon. Will the Holy Father bless her? He quickly places his hand on her head and does so.

It takes almost thirty minutes for him to move among the sick. Clearly the occasion inspires him. His eyes are filled with genuine compassion. He finds the right words for every person. Even the nearby security men are moved.

Other security men are politely urging those in the body of the hall to leave. Barriers stop them from coming close to the pope as he concentrates on his mission to the lame. The crowd begins slowly to drift out into St Peter's Square.

Paul eventually turns, makes his way painfully up the steps and across the dais, disappearing, without once looking back, behind the bronze sculpture.

The public will not officially see him again until he appears at the special window of his summer retreat this coming Sunday to deliver another homily.

At the rear entrance to the hall, Ghezzi waits with the Mercedes to take Paul and his secretaries back to the Apostolic Palace. During the audience, Ghezzi has polished the car; he does so several times a day. It is without doubt the most cared-for car in Rome. The return journey takes two minutes. It needs only another thirty seconds for the elevator to carry Paul, Macchi and Magee up to the papal apartment.

Paul goes to his bedroom to wash his hands and pray. By the time he returns to the dining room Ghezzi is there – now wearing a white jacket with gold buttons – ready to serve luncheon to the pope and his secretaries.

During the meal they review the morning. The conversation gradually widens to well beyond the audience hall. Magee, in particular, is very good at opening up the talk, bringing the world to Paul's table now that he is too infirm to go out into the world.

The discussion is interrupted by the lunchtime news on television. Paul pushes aside his plate – in any case nowadays he eats very little – and tries to concentrate on the headlines to see whether they have any relevance to the political briefing Villot gave him.

They do. As usual the affairs of the Vatican produce a crop of speculations. There is an item from Hong Kong stating the delicate manoeuvring between Communist China and the Holy See is continuing: the Vatican may soon have to accept more government-appointed Catholic priests in China and work within those limits. There is a report from Vienna claiming Eastern Europe is where the focus of Vatican policy remains. The reporter reminds viewers that recent visits to Paul by Hungary's leader Janos Kadar and Poland's Edward Gierek were bitterly criticized, that opposition to the pope's global strategy comes not only from known right-wingers but also from those who argue that arrangements in Eastern Europe are reminiscent of the concordats made with Fascists before World War II. The story ends with an unnamed Vatican source saying full churches in Poland are clear proof Paul's strategy works. A commentator picks up the theme, arguing the pope is now so completely committed to rapprochement with Eastern Europe's Communist regimes no successor will be able to reverse the process. The main objective of his activist foreign policy, claims the commentator, is to ameliorate the plight of fifty million Catholics behind the Iron Curtain.

As the news ends Paul rises and leaves the room. Outside, Giacomina waits to escort him to the door of his bedroom. They exchange little conversation but Paul clearly benefits from the presence of this caring woman who has given her celibate self to him. She opens the bedroom door and stands aside while he shuffles in. Then she closes the door and retraces her steps.

*

At four o'clock Paul emerges from his bedroom and goes to the chapel to pray once more, saying Nones and Vespers from his breviary. He then returns to his private study and sits at his desk. He fidgets, as he is wont to do nowadays, with the portraits of his mother and father and the three small Byzantine pictures. He has taken to repositioning them from one day to the next, sometimes pushing them to the back of the desk, other times bringing them closer to him. Nobody knows why. No one asks. Paul is not the sort of person to volunteer an explanation.

Giacomina appears with a cup of espresso coffee and another capsule. This is the time of day the nun and the pope exchange domestic smalltalk. Does His Holiness have a preference for dinner? Will there be guests? She hopes for a response to the latter question other than the brief headshake it draws. Since the death of Moro, Paul has invited almost no outsider to his table. It is another sign of how deeply the crime has affected him. He sees it as a stain which is irremovable and irredeemable. His grief remains obvious. But it did nothing to soothe the feelings of Moro's family, who saw in his death a terrible object lesson for Paul and his policy of trying to reach an accommodation with Communists. Few of the family attended the elaborate memorial service where Paul publicly upbraided God for not saving his 'good, wise and innocent friend'.

Afterwards the pope retired to the Vatican to brood endlessly on the deeper meaning of the crime. It was more than just another in a long catalogue of spectacular and bloody murders. It was a calculated blow to the State and, consequently, to the Church. Almost all of those involved in the Red Brigades' activities had grown up in Italy's two most rigid orthodoxes: Communism and Catholicism; a large percentage of the terrorists were basically religious persons who came to politics and violence with the convictions of zealots.[1] For them force was a way of life. In adopting that credo they had made Italy the main arena for terrorism in Western Europe. The reason, as Paul often said, was not hard to see: sapped by social decay, Italy had become a fertile breeding ground because its economic decline had alienated workers and left thousands of well-educated young persons jobless. There was no ready solution; Moro's murder merely showed no one was immune from the guerrilla warfare being waged in the streets of every major Italian city.

Most ominous of all, in the wake of the killing, another figure had been nominated for possible assassination. Repeatedly, the question was now asked: when will there be an attempt to kidnap or kill the pope?

Paul has told his trusted staff on more than one occasion it would be dangerous to ignore the possibility. As he put it to Giacomina, 'We are no longer inviolate.'

Not even the optimistic nun has found words to comfort him.

5

It is five o'clock, the hour Villot makes his second formal appearance of the day. He enters Paul's study followed by an assistant, a priest in a soutane who carries a tray filled with papers. The priest leaves them on Paul's desk and departs. Villot remains for a few moments, drawing the pope's attention to various documents in the tray. Paul will initial some, sign others with his formal signature – Paulus PP VI. Satisfied he has overlooked nothing, Villot once more takes his formal leave.

Paul can now do what he enjoys most: carefully perusing the paperwork of his administration. There has probably never been a modern pope so capable of assimilating such a prodigious amount of information so quickly. It was one of the qualities noted when he studied at Rome's Gregorian University. The knack helped shape his destiny; after graduating, and that brief spell in Warsaw where he took his alarm clock and found the climate affected his health, he returned to Rome. Pius XI heard about this wan-faced priest who could read and evaluate at high speed for hours on end. Paul was given a tiny office in the Secretariat of State. He climbed the clerical promotion ladder in a straightforward and successful way, ending as one of two principal advisers to Pius XII. Paul had by then developed an astonishing memory; he could recall totally documents he had seen years before. This remains a tremendous asset as he now studies the contents of the tray before him.

It contains the latest proof that the Holy See long ago accepted it should deal with politics as well as religion; it has frequently achieved its ends by deliberately confusing spiritual prerogative with political ambition. Popes, the very apex of these policies, have challenged emperors, undermined kings and queens, led armies into battle and now, in the case of Paul, passed judgement on Vietnam, disarmament and the problems of the Third World.

Paul does so because he is, in part, speaking from the security of a bedrock of immense secular influence wielded in the name of religion. Perhaps more than at any time in modern history, his pontificate has made its views known on international affairs. Not only has he broken a long tradition by travelling far outside Italy to places ever further removed from the atmosphere of the Vatican in which he has been formed and nurtured, but in doing so he created a situation where the Holy See ended the narcissistic provincialism of its daily outlook and squarely faced harsh realities. Although he has done a great deal by way of innovation – while at the same time frequently repeating allusions to the heavy and rather frightening responsibilities of his office, references which often make him seem welcomingly human rather than merely holy – Paul is nevertheless not an innovator. Long years as a bureaucrat have left their mark.

The real Paul is now seen only by those very close to him. To the rest he is autocratic on a grand scale, living proof a pope is absolute and answerable to no legislature; in everything he does he is advised, not constitutionally controlled, by lawmakers. In his world there is no such thing as collective responsibility. That may be why he spends so long agonizing over a relatively small matter: the appointment of a new bishop, the moving of a nuncio from one diplomatic post to another, the wording of some minor document. Those around him say, without malice, he is only really satisfied a decision is right when it is added to his already heavily burdened conscience.

By seven o'clock, about the same time most nights, Paul is well into the paperwork from the Secretariat of State. All three of its departments have made their customary submission.

The first department deals with relations with secular powers and matters arising mainly from concordats. It functions rather like a Foreign Ministry. The second department handles correspondence with the nuncios, pro-nuncios and the legates; the latter are specially appointed to represent the pope at specific occasions, such as the dedication of a new cathedral, a religious conference or a minor state funeral. This department also receives all requests from diplomats of the fifty-one nations accredited to the Holy See, and submits names to the pontiff of potential future nuncios. The pope must approve each appointment. The third department, the one whose papers always cause Paul to hesitate longest, is responsible for compiling and transcribing the final drafts of Papal Briefs from the working language of Italian into English, French, German, Portuguese and Spanish. Paul is fluent in each and is forever concerned how words prepared for his approval will translate into those tongues. There is less problem when he writes to heads of state. He does so in Latin, the text prepared by the Secretariat of Briefs to Princes.

He has barely finished with the contents of the tray when Macchi appears with another. This contains the day's output from other curial departments which also need Paul's attention.

Cardinal Franjo Seper from Yugoslavia controls the old Sacred

Congregation of the Inquisition, established by Paul III in 1542 to combat heresy and still known as the Holy Office in spite of its name having been changed by papal order in 1965 to the Sacred Congregation for the Doctrine of the Faith. The Holy Office is the most authoritarian of the Church's institutions: the correspondence it submits to Paul about alleged misdemeanours, reports on doubtful theological books and teachings have a chilling ring about them. With his strongly legalistic viewpoint, the seventy-two-year-old Seper, say liberal Roman Catholics, is perfectly suited for the role of the now-abolished Inquisitor. He writes to the pope most days about the action he wishes Paul to approve against some major infraction of dogma.

Equally regular is correspondence from the Sacred Congregation for the Sacraments and Divine Worship. Much of its work is concerned with granting annulments for marriages which have not been consummated, and releases for priests who wish to relinquish their orders. There is also a steady flow of paperwork from the Sacred Congregation for Religion and Secular Institutes, which settles questions affecting religious orders and examines the status of new foundations. It is now actively concerned with the activities of Lefèbvre.

Paul always finds relief in the infrequent reports from the Sacred Congregation for the Causes of Saints, founded in 1588 to handle such pleasurable matters for a pope as canonization and the preservation of holy relics. He reads on, through reports from the Sacred Congregation for Bishops, and those of the Sacred Congregation for the Clergy. He then turns to the crisply clear paperwork of Cardinal Gabriel-Marie Garrone, who not only presides over the Sacred Congregation for Catholic Education but is also Chancellor of the Gregorian University – the proving ground for all those destined for high office in the Church – and Chamberlain of the College of Cardinals. The austere seventy-six-year-old Frenchman, who served with distinction in World War II, includes with his report another of his famous theological conundrums for Paul to ponder. Over the years there has developed an almost continuous intellectual running debate between the two men. Paul, as always, will take time formulating a reply; he will end it, as he does each of his letters, with the words, 'Yours in Christ'.

Much of the work near the bottom of the tray requires no more than careful reading and initialling. The Apostolic Penitentiary handles complex problems of conscience: can a priest kill to protect himself; should he, as some are doing in Latin America, bear arms? It also advises on the penalties a pope may impose for such a dire crime as a priest saying a black mass. Every year there are a number of such cases;

they frighten Paul more than anything else. He regards them as proof the Devil is alive and well and hiding inside the Church. Cardinal Giuseppe Paupini, the seventy-one-year-old Italian whom Paul placed in charge of the Apostolic Penitentiary five years ago, is the Vatican's resident expert on sorcery of all kinds. His work is adjudged so important and urgent that he will be the only cardinal allowed during the next Conclave to remain in contact with his office.

There are reports for Paul from the Supreme Tribunal of the Apostolic Signature, the tribunal responsible for preparing petitions, usually relating to pardons, for papal approval. Paul has made its main responsibility that of settling conflicts between curial departments. It is the nearest thing to an ombudsman the Vatican has.

Finally, the tray contains the latest reports from the three special Secretariats. The Secretariat for Christian Unity, presided over by one of the undisputed leaders of the Church in Western Europe, Cardinal Jan Willebrands, sixty-eight-year-old Archbishop of Utrecht, was created by John XXIII to handle some of the preparatory work for the Second Vatican Council. It made its mark as a vigorous, optimistic and liberalizing body. Paul is now not always happy with some of its recommendations.

Paul himself established the Secretariat for Non-Christians in 1964. It is now in the sure hands of Cardinal Sergio Pignedoli; at sixty-eight he is as energetic as ever. There is a salty flavour to Pignedoli's tongue, a throwback to the days he was a chaplain in the Italian navy.

The Secretariat for Non-Believers is under the presidency of Franz Koenig, Archbishop of Vienna and one of the Church's few authentic experts on *Ostpolitik*, the détente between Church and Communism. The progressively minded Koenig – unlike Willebrands he has never caused Paul concern over a recommendation as he has an almost uncanny flair for knowing how and when to offer a suggestion for the pope's ear – accepted the job on Paul's assurance he would not have to move to Rome. With engaging frankness Koenig explained he had no 'great desire to be at head office'. Besides, he could better continue to serve Vatican interests by remaining at his strategic post in Vienna, monitoring developments behind the Iron Curtain. Paul likes and respects the courteous Viennese with the mellifluous voice and unrivalled knowledge of the history of religions. Despite his age, seventy-three, Koenig remains a healthy and compelling figure; many in the Curia think they could do much worse than have him as the next pope.

*

In St Peter's Square the tourists have thinned out and the souvenir sellers gone downtown to see who else they can catch. Only the policemen remain in strength. One of them walks towards the seventy-seven-foot-high obelisk in the middle of the most visited square in the world. Another policeman stands at the foot of the obelisk which had taken ninety men and four hundred horses to position after it had been brought to Rome by the Emperor Caligula. Legend says that on 13 October AD 64, Peter was crucified upside down near the spot where the policemen now stand, 1,914 years later. The presence of the policemen continues the theme of violence which dominated this place nineteen centuries earlier. They wear flak jackets protecting their chests, crotches, backs and buttocks. They cradle machine pistols. Only a few tourists find incongruous the sight of two heavily armed men standing in the deepening shadow of an obelisk dwarfed by Michelangelo's cupola on St Peter's Church, the very symbol of peace.

*

At 8.30 pm – the time has never varied in Magee's memory – Paul joins his two secretaries for dinner. Ghezzi stands by one of the sideboards and, like the others, bows his head while Paul murmurs grace. Then the valet serves the meal: thin soup, the way Paul likes it, followed by his favourite veal casserole, vegetables and side salad. Veal alternates with chicken and, very occasionally, steak. Magee, accustomed to the hearty portions of his missionary days, has learned to accept the smaller helpings at Paul's table. But the wine is excellent. And there is plenty of mineral water. Paul uses some to swallow another capsule Giacomina has placed beside his plate.

The dinner talk, as so often recently, hinges on the problems the Church faces in the secular world. Paul is on record as saying he is well aware that he is the principal obstacle to church unity. Now, years after he made that typically anguished confession, the rifts are wider than ever. What he calls 'the forces of darkness' – a generic term for Communism, terrorism, the abortion-on-demand movement, the drive against priests remaining celibate, even the antics of Lefèbvre – are wedging themselves ever deeper into the gaps. Moral and ideological schisms have developed to such an extent they often seem unbridgeable. Everywhere he looks, Paul can see churches destroyed, religious rights curtailed, the blood of his priests and nuns flowing. This is the year the Church is celebrating the eighteenth anniversary of the convocation of the Second Vatican Council and the tenth anniversary of *Humanae Vitae*. Paul had intended the celebrations to help bond the faithful together. Yet what is happening? Dissension on all sides.

Both Macchi and Magee work hard to lift Paul's spirits. Nevertheless tonight is to be no exception. The pope doggedly moves back through half a century of events he has either been directly involved with or has observed closely from the wings. Names and incidents drift in and out of his conversation. His memory is impressive but the tone is melancholic. His listeners detect a feeling of betrayal deep inside Paul. But has he himself betrayed the promise of his background – a member of the northern Italian 'liberal wing' of the twenties, a man whose career as an archbishop suggested someone ready to act boldly and imaginatively as a pastoral leader – or has he been betrayed by the more vicious elements of the faction-ridden Curia? Macchi and Magee suspect, and they have told each other as much, elements of both played their part in taking toll of Paul. But the time has long gone when they might have dared try to lead him away from the abyss he totters towards in conversation. All they can do now is sit quietly and let him ramble on. They feel deep compassion and love for this man who has been, and tries to remain, like a father to them. The secretaries see him not at all as the cold and stern figure of the media, but as a very old and tired man who knows his life is ending, and who is inwardly troubled that when the moment comes he may still have left so much undone.

Paul's ruminations end when Macchi switches on the television set for the nightly news. They sit silent, gripped by the flickering images of strife in the world. Macchi, as he has done before, floats the idea of a programme devoted only to Good News. The senior secretary does not much care for television as such: he believes it frequently distorts by over-emphasizing items which happen to be caught on film. He instances an ambush in Vietnam, a shoot-out in some street; it's all far, far too violent for Macchi – but he also feels the day must come when the Vatican will use orbiting satellites to reinforce the faith in every corner of the earth. Magee joins in. He is enthusiastic about such global communications; he sees the possibility of unifying the church by bringing Catholics of South America and Scandinavia together through one satellite. He sees all sorts of benefits. Paul sits quietly, listening carefully, sometimes smiling indulgently at the enthusiasm of the younger men. The flow of bad news from the TV is forgotten. It is the cue for Ghezzi to switch off the set. The valet has come to marvel at the skills the secretaries display nightly in their attempt to distract the pope from the realities of the world.

When the discussion has run its course – both Macchi and Magee are skilled conversationalists and know how far to go and how much to leave for another occasion – Paul rises and returns to his study. For the next hour he will write letters to his family and old friends; he is a loyal correspondent and has been writing regularly to some people for over forty years.

His personal correspondence completed, Giacomina arrives with

Macchi – Magee has, by custom, gone to his own quarters to catch up on paperwork – and for the next hour they sit with Paul while he listens to his recordings of the classics and opera. Sometimes, when the mood takes him, he will play *Jesus Christ, Superstar*. He has a particular favourite from the show, the song Mary Magdalene sings: 'I Don't Know How to Love Him'. The musical interlude ends, the secretary and the nun leave. Paul once more returns to his desk.

From now until he chooses to go to bed he will be alone. It won't halt the speculation. Reporting the imagined and real thoughts of the pope has become a growth industry. With the Vatican officially more secret than ever over its affairs – always a sign things may not be as ordered as they should – Paul is surrounded, both from within and outside the Apostolic Palace, by those who make a living from conjecture. For a handful of lire, or perhaps a good dinner, they will answer all questions. Does Paul think at times about forgiving those who have wronged him? By any count the list of such offenders is long – and lengthening. Does he worry about the impecunity of the Vatican? The question is hardly original; Paul can still remember, so people say, his sense of shock on discovering that when Benedict XV died in 1922, the Vatican had to float a loan of $100,000 from a Rome bank to help pay for his funeral. Does Paul think that, because of what he has encouraged, the Vatican is now in a bigger financial mess than before? The conjecturalists shake their collective head. He would certainly not think about *that*. Not just before going to bed. That would be one guaranteed way to give himself nightmares.

*

In St Peter's Square the policemen play the nightly game which helps them while away the hours. They know who sleeps behind every window in the papal apartment. They bet between themselves on the exact moment the light in each bedroom will go out. The stakes are not high because it is not much of a gamble. The household keeps very regular hours. Giacomina's light is the first to be doused. Then Macchi's window becomes dark. Next the light of Magee's bedroom goes out.

It is now after midnight and the three entrances to the Vatican are locked. At the Porta Sant'Anna, the Bronze Doors, and the Arco delle Campane Swiss Guards patrol slowly, caped against the cool night air. Behind them shadowy figures from the Vatican Central Office of Vigilance plod between the various buildings. Many of these guards, rumour has it, are armed and as tough as any anti-terrorist squad. In February 1971, Paul placed security on a far more stringent and professional footing when he decreed the members of Vigilance must 'maintain awareness of the value of the promise of fidelity to the

Supreme Pontiff which implies the strict observance of the orders imparted by superiors, and the responsible and diligent execution of their tasks and special duties attached to them. The tasks of each are not limited materially only to the execution of what they have been ordered to do, but include all that alert and unceasing activity which, by discovering, anticipating and restraining every action contrary to the laws and rules, makes up the singular character of those who are concerned with vigilance and the defence of order, the safety of persons and the safeguarding of material goods.' The Vigilance guards do not bet on lights out. They are a dour and watchful lot, the real muscle behind the fancy-costumed Swiss Guards.

In the square the fountains have been turned off and the traffic diverted. But the light from Paul's study burns on. Then it is gone. A moment later his bedroom light comes on. It is a little patch of brightness against the dark sky. Then suddenly it, too, is no more.

The policemen start a new game. Is the pope asleep? Is he lying awake thinking? About what? There is no betting but the man who comes up with the unlikeliest answer will be judged the winner. The policemen have good imaginations; the game may run the duration of their shift. Tomorrow it will be different. The helicopter will come and Paul will have gone. The fountains and traffic will run continuously. And the policemen will have to invent new games to play to overcome their boredom.

*

A detachment of Swiss Guards – in their distinctive steel helmets and starched neck ruffs, the morning breeze making their Renaissance costume seem more billowy than ever – march out of their barracks opposite the pope's parish church, Santa Anna dei Palafrenieri. Built in 1573 for the papal grooms, the oval church is now almost exclusively used only by the guards and the domestic staff of the Vatican. Hardly anyone can remember when Paul last said Mass there. The area itself is the tradesmen's entrance to the Vatican. The Porta Sant'Anna, a gate set in the middle of a narrow street, is the way in for produce lorries and vans. It is a noisy spot and, because it is so busy, a magnet for tourists. This morning they stand and gape at the Swiss Guards breaking ranks and boarding a bus which will take them to Castel Gandolfo. They are Paul's advance party, the men who will help protect his summer palace. Everything about the guards seems alien in the essentially Italian environment. This has not helped their relationship with the Vigilance. There is tension between them. The Vigilance look on the Swiss Guards as little more than toy soldiers. The Swiss Guards feel the presence of the hard-nosed, drab-blue uniformed security men is unnecessary;

they believe they can do all that is required to protect the pope on Vatican soil. The guards are hardened young men, drilled and honed in the official parade-ground language of their unit, German. Each has pledged to serve for a minimum of two years, swearing his oath of personal loyalty to the pope by holding the Vatican standard in one gloved hand while raising the other aloft, two fingers and thumb outstretched to represent the Trinity. It is a highly unusual unit in which guards need only obey their colonel, one other officer and their sergeant, all of whom wear identically coloured plumes. Their other officers can be ignored; so can the Vigilance.

The bus drives out of the gate. Shortly afterwards a second, smaller detachment of guards, halberds held aloft, march from their barracks and board a couple of jeeps. The vehicles drive slowly along the Via del Belvedere, past the Vatican's printing concern and the separate printing shop of the Vatican's semi-official daily newspaper, *L'Osservatore Romano*, and its associated papers and publications. The convoy drives on beyond the Vatican generating station, its pharmacy, the self-service duty-free store, the health centre, the telephone exchange and the public offices of the Vatican Bank. In minutes the jeeps are travelling through the Vatican Gardens, wending their way close to the remains of a tower, all that stands of a wall built by Innocent III for a reason only Prefect Martin now knows.

The gardens are, for all the magnificence of their statues, fountains and grottoes, a mess. Too many effects have been sought after – there are overtones of England, France and the tropics in the landscaping – making the final result a mish-mash. Box hedges crowd palm trees, willows stand beside banana plants, rockeries of coral and evergreens are placed side by side. Everywhere there is a jumble of religious artifacts: a representation of the grotto at Lourdes where St Bernadette saw her vision of the Virgin; a plaster replica of Our Lady of Guadelupe who appeared in Mexico to an Indian peasant, the Madonna imprinting her image on his work apron. Paul has ordered that this statue, above all others, must be properly tended. It is regularly cleaned with soapy water.

The jeeps are climbing now, past a shrubbery and a flowerbed with the pope's coat of arms picked out in blooms, past the Ethiopian College, and the pseudo-palace housing Vatican Radio's director-general. The convoy stops by the heliport at the very western tip of Vatican City. The guards get out and take up their positions at the four corners of the pad, specially built to foil any terrorist attempt to kidnap Paul. Another truck arrives bringing a crew of *sampietrini*, skilled maintenance men who normally spend their days repairing and maintaining St Peter's Basilica. The *sampietrini* have a special place in

Vatican affections since that memorable day when, during the pontificate of Pius XII, they discovered a crypt under the Basilica filled with a double row of mausoleums, a high altar and the bones of a big man thought to be those of the first pope, St Peter the Apostle. Today they will merely roll out the wool carpet they have brought from a store room in the Apostolic Palace. The men work carefully to ensure the carpet will run from the exact spot Paul will alight from his car to the point where he will board the helicopter.

*

In the papal apartment Macchi and Magee have been supervising the exodus to Castel Gandolfo. Trunks and chests have been packed and sent down by elevator to San Damaso Courtyard, once the private garden, *hortus secretus*, of medieval and Renaissance popes. The area is filled with trucks and men loading not only the personal effects of Paul and his staff but boxes from the Secretariat of State and other curial departments; the summer retreat to the Alban Hills south-east of Rome does not mean even, in this almost moribund pontificate, that the administrative wheels can actually stop turning. From doors around the courtyard frockcoated officials bustle forth to urge the loading be completed. All sorts of people seem to have business in the area: the pope's Almoner is here, chatting to some of the Prelates of the Ante-chamber; here, too, are the Gentlemen of the Pope and the Attachés of the Ante-chamber. Prefect Martin, his nose more beaky than ever, appears to be everywhere, checking that each box, case, trunk and chest is loaded in some preordained order only he and his staff seem to know. Suddenly, everything fits into place. The loading is over, the trucks begin to move. Ghezzi arrives with the Mercedes and parks it as close as possible to the elevator. He stands expectantly beside the car, its nearside rear door open.

Martin is already riding up to the papal apartment. Moving a pope outside the Vatican is always a difficult task; transporting the aged and infirm Paul demands the very best from the prefect. He emerges on the fourth floor to be met by the two secretaries. Giacomina and her nuns have already departed for Castel Gandolfo; the summer palace has a caretaker staff but Giacomina wants to make the place shipshape in her way. Before leaving she ensured Paul had taken his morning capsule and that Fontana had pronounced the pope was fit enough to travel. Now there is a more than usual air of death about the apartment as Macchi and Magee wait for Paul to emerge from his bedroom.

*

Once Paul has reached the San Damaso Courtyard, still flanked by

Macchi and Magee, he pauses to talk to Martin and other members of the household who will be travelling by road to Castel Gandolfo. Villot and Archbishop Giuseppe Caprio, the Secretary of State's *sostituto*, or deputy, are also there. Later each will clearly recall two things: the real reluctance of Paul to leave and his last words before he gets into the car. Caprio bends forward to wish Paul a pleasant stay at Castel Gandolfo. For a moment the pope looks at the *sostituto*. They are old friends and have remained close. Then Paul speaks, his voice little more than a whisper. 'We will go, but we don't know whether we will return.' He pauses again before completing the sentence in the stiffly formal language he still uses in public: 'Or how we shall return.'

Caprio remains numbed by the words as Ghezzo drives off with the pope and his secretaries.

Villot now feels more certain than ever. He walks across the courtyard towards the entrance to the Secretariat of State, head bowed and hands clasped just below the solid gold cross on his silk soutane; it is a familiar position when he is thinking deeply. The Secretary of State has no doubts. Paul has just given the clearest sign yet he is expecting to die soon.

Macchi and Magee instinctively decide – though there is no way they can consult each other, seated as they are on jump seats facing the pope – they will not pursue the remark.

For his part Paul appears to be concentrating on the scene outside. The car swings round the right side of St Peter's, past a small door leading down to the tombs of almost all of his predecessors, clustered in no special order around the monument to Apostle Peter. It is here Paul's body will eventually rest. The Mercedes continues between the Vatican's mosaic factory and the rather over-powering *governatorato* building, home of the civil administration which runs Vatican City for the pope. In its basement is the *magazzino*, a veritable bargain basement where those with special permits can buy anything from the latest model automobile to cigarettes duty-free. It is a privilege jealously guarded and, on Paul's orders, one no insider is encouraged to discuss. He is concerned the concession will be misunderstood in the inflation-ridden secular world outside. Close by is the Vatican's railway station, a branch line from Rome built in the 1930s. The last pope to use it was John XXIII when he made a train pilgrimage to Loreto and Assisi. The Sistine Chapel choir lined the platform singing psalms as the train pulled out of Vatican City. Since then the station has seen no more than a weekly train taking out Vatican mosaics for various churches and bringing in the heavier commercial goods, marble for statues and replacement plant for the print works.

The Mercedes eventually reaches the helicopter pad, Ghezzi parking it precisely so he can open the rear door just where the carpet begins. His passengers alight and he drives off, heading for Castel Gandolfo. With his special Vatican registration plates he knows he has nothing to fear from any Rome traffic policeman as he speeds across the city to pick up the *autostrada* heading into the hills.

There are no ceremonies before Paul, Macchi and Magee board the aircraft. The Swiss Guards go down on one knee and remain in that position as the helicopter lifts off.[1]

Seventeen minutes later – every yard of its flight scanned by Italian air force radar at their base beside Rome Airport where a squadron of Italian fighters stands ready to scramble at the first hint of any attempt to intercept the helicopter – it touches down in the grounds of Castel Gandolfo. Since the seventeenth century, popes have come here, to the cool of the Alban Hills, to rest inside an enclave which nowadays provides the main source of income – tourism – for the 3,000 villagers who live in its shadow. There are four palaces inside the hundred acres. The Pope's Palace appears the most forbidding, a fortified bastion built for Urban VIII in the early 1600s and extended first by Alexander VII and then by Clement XIII. Compared to its immediate neighbours, the Cybo Palace and the Villa Barberini, Paul's residence lacks architectural character. It looks like a place for a beleaguered man. But his own apartment has an unrivalled view of the lake and hills where the Emperor Diocletian, persecutor of the first Christians, had a villa.

The helicopter comes to a stop between the formal French and Italian gardens and close to a magnificent cryptoporticus, a sheltered walkway decorated with frescoes. Paul, escorted by Macchi and Magee, shuffles its length, oblivious of his surroundings – the splendour of the Roman countryside, the twin domes of the Vatican Observatory brought to Castel Gandolfo by Pius XI in 1935 and still manned by some of those Jesuits Paul has never found easy to handle.

Once upon a time Paul used to visit the observatory regularly and stare through its telescope at some of the hundred billion stars spanning a thousand, and more, light years across the heavens. He would look up to the Belt of Orion and at Sirius, the Dog Star, the most glittering of them all, its blinding white light forming the bottom hole in the Belt. When the night was especially clear and his eyes were not tired, he would search for Aldebaran the Bull, and, beyond, the tiny clusters of stars known as the Pleiades. Then, traversing the telescope westwards, he would locate the twins, Castor and Pollux, so far away in space so vast, his astronomers liked to tell him, that matter was being formed at the rate of a million million million million tons a second.

Out there, too, was Andromeda, a galaxy very similar to the Milky Way. They, the dozen or more Jesuit astronomers who manned the observatory, had first intrigued him with the thought there were billions of stars in the Andromeda galaxy and then excited him with the idea one of them could be – if the laws of probability mean anything – a planet like Earth, perhaps even inhabited by people not unlike earthlings. He had listened, entranced – as he suspected they knew he would be – as they unfolded to him the secrets of the galaxies: they were teachers and knew how to arouse and hold his curiosity. His nights with them were one of his few real pleasures. But since his anger over the general behaviour of the Society of Jesus, the order of the Jesuits, he had deliberately stayed away from the observatory.

Paul had no quarrel with the astronomers. Yet his rigidity insisted they must be included as part of the general displeasure he felt towards their order. Nobody had spoken in Paul's presence for over a year now about the reasons for the deep rift between himself and the Jesuits. It was another of the taboo subjects. But everybody knew the crisis was worsening and a solution, however unpleasant, could not be put off forever.

Like Cody, the American Church, Vatican finances, the radical priests of South America, the demands of Catholic Africa and Asia – like so many problems, the question of what to do about the Jesuits lingered on.

Inside the palace he takes the lift to his apartment. The Swiss Guards are already in position. One of their special tasks is to seal this building should Paul die here.

6

Throughout July 1978, Pope Paul VI became increasingly weak. His devoted aides grew more concerned. Dr Fontana saw him twice a day; Giacomina was never far away. On good days the pontiff walked in the garden, either in the early morning or late afternoon, moving beneath a series of awnings the gardeners had erected to protect him from the sun and the prying lenses of photographers. On those occasions the pope supported himself on the arm of one of his secretaries. He spent much time praying, either in his chapel or bedroom. He ate very little; Fontana gave him vitamin injections regularly. Only the most essential of papers were brought from the Vatican for the pope to sign. On Sundays he somehow found sufficient strength to greet visitors from his window at the traditional noon Angelus. He used the occasions to attack Soviet harshness towards dissidents. He received one special visitor, Mrs Lillian Carter, mother of the American President. They spent their time together speaking about the infringement of human rights in Russia.

The pope also carefully followed the news, paying special attention to reports of terrorist outrages. The Iraqi prime minister was assassinated in London, seventeen persons were massacred in Rhodesia, a Spanish general was murdered in Madrid, a new wave of bombings engulfed Italy. In all, over 500 persons were killed or injured in atrocities around the world during July.

There was also other news to concern the pontiff. A newly formed group in the United States, called the Committee for Responsible Election of the Pope (CREP), urged that the next Conclave should be less secretive. CREP was largely the creation of a priest, Andrew Greeley. The pope let it be known he found CREP's ideal unacceptable. That did not stop Greeley pushing his case.

And the world's first test-tube baby, Louise Brown, conceived outside her mother's womb, was born in Oldham, England. The pope stated the Roman Catholic Church had not changed its stance against any form of artificial insemination. Shortly afterwards the French National Institute of Applied Sciences announced that after ten years of research the first test-tube fly had been born. The Vatican made no comment.

In the first week of August the weather turned exceptionally humid, causing a sudden flare-up in the pope's already severely painful arthritis. His doctor *ordered him to bed. On Saturday, 5 August the Vatican announced that the pope had cancelled his next Sunday blessing.*

The brief statement heightened the perception of observers both in and outside the Vatican.

7

At 6.30 on the morning of 6 August, the Feast of the Transfiguration, a group of listeners outside Paul's bedroom door at Castel Gandolfo hear a familiar sound. It is the tinny summons of his alarm clock. It shrills for a moment and is then silent. There is no other sound from the bedroom beyond the door. Macchi murmurs that the pope is still alive.

It has been an anxious night for all of those grouped in this short corridor which ends at the polished wooden door: Macchi, Magee, Fontana and especially Giacomina and her nuns who took turns standing near the door in case Paul called for help. But nothing disturbed the long hours of darkness. Since he whispered goodnight to Macchi eight hours previously, nobody has seen or heard from Paul.

The group still finds it difficult to believe how quickly the crisis developed. The previous day, in spite of agreeing to cancel his Sunday balcony appearance, Paul insisted on getting up for supper. He had sat at the table for forty-five minutes, listening to Macchi expound his passion for modern art. The discussion was interrupted by the television news. There had been another terrorist outrage, this time a PLO bomb had ripped apart the middle of a Tel Aviv market. After the news ended, both secretaries joined the pope in saying the Rosary. They then retired to Paul's private chapel and said Compline together. Soon afterwards the pope said he felt hot and that his arthritis was unusually painful. Macchi escorted him to his bedroom while Magee summoned Fontana. The doctor diagnosed Paul's fever as caused by acute cystitis, which had exacerbated his severe arthritic condition. Fontana ordered total bedrest and began a course of antibiotics. After the doctor left, Paul asked Macchi to read him part of Jean Guitton's latest book, *Mon petit catéchisme: dialogues avec un enfant*. Macchi chose the chapter on Jesus.[1] Guitton had long been one of the pope's favourite French theologians; indeed his intellectual outlook was largely formed through French thinkers such as Pascal, Congar, Bernanos and Simone Weil. Paul had said goodnight and fallen asleep. Afterwards the two secretaries and doctor met in the palace library to discuss the situation. Fontana had left them in no doubt the prognosis was grave. In a man of Paul's age and weakened physical condition it

70

was quite impossible to predict whether the drugs would work or what side-effects they might produce. All Fontana could do was observe closely his patient and ensure Paul was in no way disturbed. Nobody – and certainly no Church crisis – must be allowed to interfere with this very explicit order of Fontana's. Before parting, the three men had agreed that unless an emergency brought them together sooner, they would meet again the following morning outside Paul's room shortly before his alarm clock was due to go off.

Now, in the silence which follows its ringing, nobody in the corridor moves. Paul is still the pope: everybody in the group recalls his clear instruction that no one except Ghezzi was to enter his bedroom unless called. Fontana decides the circumstances are exceptional. He knocks quietly on the door – it is no more than the gentlest of taps – and enters alone, carrying his bag of drugs and needles. After a few moments Macchi follows.

Paul is lying very still in bed. Macchi can see at once there has been no improvement overnight. The pope's face is flushed, his eyes are red-rimmed and, if anything, more sunken. His skin seems waxy and damp. He looks a very sick man. Fontana examines him fully. The pope has a temperature of over a hundred degrees Fahrenheit, his heartbeat has become weaker and his blood pressure is up several points. Paul complains of increased pain in his right knee, the seat of the arthritis which long ago shrunk him into a prematurely old man. Fontana decides to inject the pope with a heart stimulant and to give him antibiotics intravenously. While he prepares the syringes the doctor makes cheerful conversation, trying to draw Paul out so he can form some assessment of his mental state. Fontana knows that the pope's willpower, his very desire to live, is going to be a crucial factor in the coming days. The doctor is almost certain the illness has not peaked and Paul's success in coping with that serious time will, in part, depend on how positive he is in his thinking.

The pope, in fact, is quite alert. When Macchi mentions today is the thirty-third aniversary of the atomic attack on Hiroshima and that the world will be specially praying for peace, Paul reveals he had intended to touch upon the subject of the perils of atomic weapons during his balcony appearance at noon. Next Sunday, *Santissimo Padre*, says Fontana, maybe next Sunday His Holiness will be strong enough to make an appearance.

The doctor gives the pope his injections and says he will return in a couple of hours. In the meantime His Holiness should try to drink as much as possible. Fontana is worried the pope's poor intake of fluids could affect his organs.

Fontana goes away to telephone a urologist at Rome's Gemelli

Polyclinic, one of the best medical centres in Europe. He discusses the desirability of the specialist coming to examine Paul. After reviewing the symptoms the urologist agrees to stand by. Fontana is acutely aware of the very special problems associated with calling in help from outside. Already the fact that Paul's noon appearance has been cancelled has alerted the Rome press corps. They are even now setting up camp around the papal enclave, their telephoto lenses trained on its windows ready to capture anything which moves. There is no way the urologist, or any other outside specialist, can reach the pope's bedside without first running the media gauntlet. Calling in a consultant, especially on a Sunday, would immediately suggest the pope's situation was serious; soon wire service bells would be ringing around the world, causing unease and alarm. Yet Fontana will not hesitate to do anything to help his patient. Those close to Paul say these past months the doctor's devotion has scaled new peaks. He has made hundreds of phone calls to distinguished colleagues all over the world; he has pored over the latest literature on the treatment of arthritic conditions. He has done far more than any physician could reasonably be expected to do. Magee has said that if Fontana wasn't Italian, he would surely have been an Irish country doctor. It is the highest form of praise Magee knows. Like everyone else in the papal household, the young Irishman is now desperately worried. But he has learned to hide his feelings. It was one of the first things he absorbed from Macchi. A pope's secretary, the suave Milanese had said, is like a barometer; everybody sets their sails by him.

Macchi is himself at his inscrutable best as he stands by Paul while Giacomina and one of her nuns changes the pope's sheets. Macchi then helps Paul back into bed and sits at his side, outwardly as unconcerned as his inner self will let him appear. For years now the senior secretary has been the victim of a vicious press campaign. The scandal sheets portray him upbraiding the pope when he becomes morbid or depressed, sending Paul off to bed when he stays up too late, bullying him to make decisions. And plotting. Always plotting, with Baggio, with Levi, editor of *L'Osservatore Romano*, with Panciroli in the Vatican Press Office or with Marcinkus – especially Marcinkus – at Vatican Bank.

Recently these attacks have come from a new source. Greeley, the one-time Chicago parish priest who is the moving force behind CREP, has been writing about the Church and the Vatican for a long time; he is said to be the author of eighty books, a feat explained by one critic as possibly only because their author has never had an unpublished thought in his life; and when he produced a book called *Sexual Intimacy*, another critic added that Greeley had now never had an unpublished fantasy in his life. For three years Greeley has been coming to Rome to prepare the ground for his eighty-first work, this one concerned with the making of the next pope, to be written along the lines of Theodore White's books on how recent US presidents were elected. Greeley's trips to Rome have not made the city seem more attractive to him; its plumbing and eating arrangements increasingly irk this quirky man. But he likes the present Vatican even less. He has come to the conclusion it is out of step with almost everything he holds to be true, though it is never easy to be sure what this Catholic 'in good standing' really means, or indeed just whom he talks to in the Vatican. He has decided to give pseudonyms to many of them while at the same time somewhat weakening this protection by composing detailed physical descriptions of priests with finely chiselled features and slender aristocratic hands and voices which purr with power. Certainly Greeley's attacks on Macchi are real enough: he blames him for much of what is wrong with Paul, from the way he smiles to the grand designs of his pontificate.

Greeley's Macchi seems far removed from the Macchi who sits by Paul in his spacious bedroom with its décor almost universally beige; chairs, drapes, carpet and silk bedspread are all in this neutral colour. In these surroundings the secretary is genuinely caring and attentive to Paul's slightest wish. He gently persuades the pope to sip the glucose drink Giacomina has left. Afterwards Macchi offers to read another excerpt from Jean Guitton's book.

Paul wants to know whether there is any news from Baggio. The pope finally moved against Cody in Chicago by secretly despatching his trouble-shooter with the 'request' the cardinal resign on whatever grounds he chose. There are any number of factors which decided Paul on this action. There was the confidential report prepared for him by his secretaries. There was another and far more lethal report from Monsignor Agostino Casaroli, secretary of the Council for the Public Affairs of the Church in the Secretariat of State. The sixty-three-year-old Casaroli is known in the Vatican as 'our non-Jewish Kissinger', because of his freewheeling style and frequent travels as part of his special responsibility for the more delicate aspects of the Holy See's foreign policy.

Casaroli first learned about Cody from trusted sources in Warsaw. What he heard was sufficiently alarming for him to urge that no matter how great was Cody's past contributions to the Polish Church – a guaranteed way to win the support of Chicago's large Polish community – no matter how powerful a figure he was in the American Church hierarchy, Cody should go, either willingly or by force. Casaroli believed it only a matter of time before the Church's enemies began to exploit Cody's behaviour, doing irreparable harm to the Church and the policies Casaroli was helping to further.

From Vienna, Cardinal Franz Koenig had weighed in with a report indicating that the bad news from Cody's diocese had already been gratefully picked up in Eastern Europe. From Latin America Cardinal Aloisio Lorscheider, showing considerable courage for someone who had only recently been elected to the permanent council of the Synod of Bishops, sent a note bluntly saying Cody's racist image created a poor impression in South America. And even one of Cody's North American colleagues, Archbishop Joseph Bernardin of Cincinnati, also a permanent member of the Synod, let Paul know of his concern in, and beyond, Chicago over Cody.

The precise words in all these alarm signals Paul has decided must forever remain secret. He has already told Macchi the reports should be closely guarded and, after he dies, destroyed along with his most private papers. Despite such thoroughness, the allegations against Cody are now becoming public. In part this is due to campaigning by the voice of CREP, Andrew Greeley.

The same wonderfully anonymous sources which allow Greeley to write so enticingly about Vatican affairs have helped him identify the grounds which made Paul send Baggio flying to Chicago with what amounts to a papal demand. No one in the Vatican, where he is cordially disliked, can seriously dispute that this time Greeley has got it absolutely right; there isn't a junior secretary who hasn't heard about the shenanigans of Cody, the most controversial cardinal in the Church.[2]

The first charge against Cody, in Casaroli's view, provides ample ground to act: racism. In his globe-trotting, the tough-minded monsignor has come to see racial discrimination as one of the greatest barriers to Church unity. John XXIII first recognized something had to be done about this blight, but it was Paul, through his journeys, who worked hard to implement racial equality abroad; the impact he had is one of his major achievements. Yet in Casaroli's view there is still a long way to go. During his regular accounts to Villot of his journeys into the Third World, Casaroli reports that the continued racism of America, Australia, South Africa and in some ways of Great Britain has created a gulf which leaves the Church in 'the position of trying to dance an Irish jig on a minefield sown by the Chinese'. Whenever a prelate comes to Rome it is now virtually mandatory for him to receive Casaroli's lecture against racism. There is not a senior member of the Church who does not know where the Vatican stands on the matter. Yet Cody supported the decision in Chicago to close any number of schools teaching black children in the inner city ghettos. Liberal black community leaders called Cody's intervention the worst kind of racism.

Casaroli does not believe Cody is a racist, but he thinks the cardinal should have known better than to allow the Church to be placed in a position of disrepute. And he hopes Cody will go quietly; Casaroli hates any form of public breastbeating. But he fears that is what Cody will do, for although the evidence is certainly there, not all of it is all that damning. Cody is charged with being in constant conflict with most of his clergy. This the Vatican doesn't normally worry about; it knows there are often disagreements between a strong bishop and his priests and on the whole this is seen as no bad thing: it keeps both sides on their toes. But the situation in Chicago had gone far beyond that. The Association of Chicago priests publicly condemned their cardinal for lying to them habitually. Some of the most respected prelates in the diocese sent protests to the apostolic delegation in Washington and even to the Vatican itself. When asked for an explanation by those in Rome, Cody refused to answer. Paul himself sent a handwritten note requesting he be more reasonable and co-operative. Cody's reply was typical: he had nothing to answer for. Yet apart from his priests a large segment of Chicago laity are up in arms. Hundreds of upsetting letters regularly reach Rome containing evidence of Cody's intransigence. Many contain details which suggest he may be suffering from some mental disorder. The writers document Cody's contact with extreme right-wing organizations such as the John Birch Society; they instance evidence of his obsession with secrecy and mystery; they tell of a spy network he has set up to keep track of every visiting priest who comes to Chicago; they speak of his personal spite and bouts of uncontrollable pique. The Vatican doesn't think all the accusations are true; there is always a lunatic fringe which writes to Rome about every bishop in every diocese. But these letters from Chicago often come from important and influential Catholics. They can no longer be answered by a polite *pro forma* letter.

Many of the charges, especially from the Catholic business community, accuse Cody of poor management of the diocese; the cardinal, they say, concentrates all the power in his own hands, refuses to delegate, consults nobody except a very small circle of cronies. Important decisions and appointments get shunted aside. But the real nub of the case against Cody concerns his alleged financial maladminis-tration. While treasurer of the American bishops, Cody invested several million dollars of Church funds in Penn Central only days before the railroad went bankrupt. In addition there is the accusation that sixty million dollars of parish funds are on deposit at the Chicago chancery and Cody has refused to reveal either to the diocese or the Vatican what he intends doing with the money or who gets the interest. Again, he has poured millions of dollars into a TV network which operates only in rectories and schools. Even this would not seriously deplete the finances of one of the world's most affluent archdioceses but, coupled with Cody's life style, the accusation that he uses Church funds to buy expensive presents for those few members of the Curia prepared to overlook his behaviour; the charge that he refuses to make spiritual retreats, that his rudeness, temper, at times even fury, are demonic: all these, together with the reports Paul has studied since arriving at Castel Gandolfo, had left him no alternative but to despatch Baggio to Chicago.

He has been gone now a week. Only Macchi knows what happened. In total secrecy Baggio arrived at O'Hare Airport and was driven to Cody's villa in the grounds of the seminary at Mundelein. Over dinner he laid out the evidence and Paul's 'request'. There had been a shouting match which lasted into the early hours of the morning. After breakfast Baggio left, his mission to Chicago a total failure. Macchi has been waiting for the right moment to break the news to Paul. Now is not the time. Instead he diverts the pope with the thought no news from Baggio could only be good news in the end. Paul does not question the excuse. He is too exhausted to do so.

Beyond the sick room the mood of the household is one of increasing anxiety. Everyone knows the Holy Father's condition has not improved: the domestic staff have seen a grave Fontana huddling with Prefect Martin and then Magee; the gardeners report that the reporters, television and radio technicians are constantly growing in number. Tourists are also arriving by the bus-load.

During the morning Fontana pays two further visits to Paul. The pope's condition has not altered. Fontana makes another phone call to his colleague at the Gemelli Hospital. They agree the illness should peak during the next twelve hours; if Paul can survive the day he may yet recover. Fontana's hope that this may happen quickly permeates the household. By midday the staff appear almost happy as they go about preparations for lunch.

Paul has a bowl of soup and sips the fresh lemon drink Giacomina has prepared. The nun and Fontana stand either side of his bed while he drinks. He is lucid and cheerful, thanking them and, through them, everybody else who is so solicitous for his welfare.

When Giacomina leaves the room she is nearly in tears. Macchi, waiting in the corridor for news, is alarmed and asks urgently whether *Santissimo Padre* is worse. The nun shakes her head: no, no, he is being the Holy Father they all knew – only thinking of others.

Relieved, the secretary goes to tell Martin, who in turn phones Villot in the Vatican. The Secretary of State informs those he has decided should be kept in touch with events at Castel Gandolfo. Calls go to his deputy, Caprio; the dean of the College of Cardinals, Carlo Confalonieri; the vicar-general of Rome, Cardinal Ugo Poletti, who tends to the religious needs of the city of which Paul, among his many titles, is bishop. The pope's brother, Senator Ludovico Montini, and his favourite nephew, Marco Montini, are also contacted. Villot knows almost nothing about medicine, but he knows a great deal about the effects even a minor illness can have on someone as old and infirm as Paul; the Secretary of State has seen several friends die suddenly in such situations. He asks all those he rings to remain close to their phones. He then makes one more call, to the mayor of Rome, Giulio Carlo Argan, asking him to have police motorcyclists standing by to escort at short notice to Castel Gandolfo the cars of those Villot has previously telephoned. Argan is a Communist, a shrewd and capable man who still resents the way the Vatican interceded against the Communists during the last election. He listens politely, asks few questions but understands fully what could be happening. He gives his orders to the city's chief of police. Motorcyclists are despatched to wait beside St Peter's Square and outside the homes of Paul's relatives.

*

In mid-afternoon Paul awakes from a restless sleep. Fontana, who has been watching over his patient, slips on the blood pressure cuff and checks the reading: the pressure is up, dangerously so. He checks Paul's pulse. It is erratic. Hiding his alarm as best he can, Fontana listens to the pope's heart. The beat is weak and uneven. He checks Paul's temperature. It is well over the hundred mark. The climax could be coming sooner than Fontana expected.

He gives Paul an injection to steady his heart-beat, and presses a bedside buzzer. It brings Giacomina running. Between them the nun and doctor place cooling towels around Paul's forehead and assist him to drink.

The pope's treasured bedside clock, standing beside the Bible his father gave him, helps the doctor count off the minutes as he waits for the first sign of reaction to the injection. Thirty minutes later, Paul's blood pressure has dropped almost to normal and his heart-beat, although weak, is regular. His temperature, too, has been lowered by repeated towel applications and drinks. Fontana cannot be certain, but he hopes the crisis has come and gone. He waits another thirty minutes and, at five o'clock, leaving Giacomina by the pope's bedside, he goes off to make another call to his medical colleague in Rome.

Later the question will be asked – one of many – why Fontana at this stage didn't either have Paul transferred by helicopter ambulance to the Gemelli, or request the clinic's mobile intensive-care team come to Castel Gandolfo. But Fontana feels not only that he is more than medically capable of handling the situation but there is also the protocol involved. Popes just don't go to hospital, however private or good the facilities may be. The custom dates back to the days when royal personages were treated in their homes because the care there was better than in hospital. When Fontana operated on Paul's prostate he had set up a temporary theatre in the room that Prefect Martin found. Calling in the mobile intensive-care unit was another matter – one of judgement. Using his considerable experience, weighing the medical and sociological factors involved – the headlines and clamour which would inevitably follow – Fontana decides this is not yet the stage to seek such radical outside help.

The doctor explains his thinking to Martin, Macchi and Magee. They immediately agree with Fontana. The three are still discussing the situation when the buzzer brings them running to Paul's room. Giacomina has noticed the pope's blood pressure has risen. Magee, who has not seen the pope for some hours, is shaken by his appearance: the matted hair, the flushed cheeks in contrast to his general pallor, the tremble in his hand – all signal Paul is entering another crisis. It passes as quickly as it manifests itself, leaving the pope sunk back on his pillows, Macchi holding one hand, Fontana the other, the others grouped around the bed.

Paul asks Macchi to say Mass for him at six o'clock and then requests that his brother and nephew be sent for. Martin hurries from the room, close to tears; Paul has often told him he will know when the end is near and when it is, he will want, if possible, his immediate relatives at hand.

The prefect's phone call activates the plans Villot has prepared for this moment. In minutes cars are speeding out of the Vatican and from the two Montini family residences. Each car is preceded by police motorcyclists who leave the Sunday afternoon holiday traffic in no doubt of the seriousness of their mission. Their sirens cut a path for the cars as they roar down the *autostrada* towards Castel Gandolfo.

The Cardinal Secretary of State's limousine is in the lead. Villot sits in the back beside the case which for months he has kept packed for this occasion. It contains his vestments, anointing oil and a small solid silver hammer.

Less than thirty minutes after leaving Rome, the cars sweep past the press corps and up to the Pope's Palace. The agency reporters note who have arrived and it is the Associated Press man who manages to get off the first flash: 17.55 POPE'S FAMILY JOIN SENIOR VATICAN AIDES AT PONTIFF'S BEDSIDE.

*

Outside Paul's bedroom Macchi briefly explains the position to the new arrivals. The Holy Father is considerably weakened by his two attacks, but he is conscious and most anxious to follow the Mass and take Communion with them. The service will be held in the chapel leading off the pope's bedroom. They should all go in, greet the Holy Father briefly, and then move on to the chapel.

If Villot is incensed at being treated in this cavalier way, he does not show it. Macchi is still the pope's closest confidant; he still has more effective power than even the most powerful cardinal. Villot goes in and greets Paul, formal as ever.

At six o'clock Macchi begins the celebration of Mass. Those present make their responses: Confalonieri, Poletti, Caprio and Villot fill one row of chairs. The Montinis are behind them. In another row Giacomina and her nuns kneel in prayer. Martin and Magee are closest to the open door of the chapel and, like Fontana who is beside them, the two priests regularly glance over their shoulders at the pope propped up in bed.

Paul follows the Mass avidly; during the recitation of the Creed, Magee and Martin clearly hear him twice repeat the words, *Apostolicam Ecclesiam*.

At 6.15 Fontana suddenly rises to his feet in the middle of a response and goes to Paul's bedside. Instinctively the other worshippers turn, some even half rising to follow him but Macchi's voice firmly holds them in place. The doctor checks Paul's pulse. It is wild. He places the stethoscope disc on the pope's chest. The heart beat is irregular. But it is Paul's breathing which is of most concern to the doctor: it is fast and laboured. The pope has suffered a heart attack and there is nothing his doctor can do. The effects of the attack pass and Paul lies motionless on his pillow. After some moments he nods towards the chapel and whispers he would like to receive Communion as soon as possible. Fontana conveys the request to Martin. Macchi comes to the bedside and proffers the ritualistic wafer and wine. Afterwards there is a marked change in Paul. He appears totally calm and at peace. He even manages a small wave to those in the chapel. Only Fontana is fully aware of what has happened. The heart attack was not massive but in his opinion it would be decisive. He takes Macchi aside and says the pope can have little time left.

The secretary, observing the protocol, goes to Villot, now standing uncertainly near the chapel door, and tells him the worst. The Secretary of State immediately comes to Paul's side and asks whether he would like to be anointed.

The pope nods. '*Subito, subito.*'

Villot goes to his bag and removes the anointing oil. He pours some into a small silver chalice and returns to the bedside to begin administering the Last Sacrament.

Paul clasps Villot's hand as he prays. Everyone is now grouped around his bed: Giacomina and her nuns on one side, the two Montinis and the Vatican prelates on the other. Macchi and Magee stand at the foot of the bed, watching Villot complete the anointing. The Secretary of State steps back as Paul closes his eyes. Fontana bends over him, listening to his heart. He rises and says the Holy Father is still alive. The doctor looks at Paul's bedside clock; in all the years he has known the pope, Fontana has never known it to be too fast or too slow. Its hands point to 6.30.

There is no sound except the clock's ticking and the steady clicking of the nuns' rosaries.

*

Shortly after 7.30, the pope opens his eyes. Magee is not certain but he thinks they have lost their lustre, their ability to penetrate deep into a person's soul. They now seem glazed in their sockets.

Fontana is at once by the bedside, bending down and listening to the sounds of ebbing life filling his stethoscope. Paul's breathing is harsher and shallower. But somehow, between the labouring, he manages to speak.

'We have arrived at the end. We thank . . .'

He is unable to complete the sentence before his eyes close once more.

Villot and the Montinis look towards Fontana. He checks again with his stethoscope. Paul is still alive.

The doctor, Villot, Macchi, Magee and Martin draw to one side. Fontana tells them he is now certain. There is virtually no hope. Barring a miracle the pontificate of Paul VI will be over by midnight. Martin hurries from the room.

*

In his office in the Pontifical Commission for Social Communications – the Vatican Press Office – its secretary, Fr Romeo Panciroli, is grateful to hear from Martin. The withdrawn and precise press aide has been bombarded all afternoon by the world's media. He is totally ill-equipped to deal with such an onslaught. He prefers his encounters with the media – when they must occur – to be through those

Rome-based correspondents he knows and who, in turn, know how to treat him with proper respect; not at all like the pushy, aggressive, rude and demanding voices which have almost blocked the Vatican switchboard for hours. Martin and Panciroli discuss the wording of a communiqué. They agree it should be brief. That settled, Panciroli has only to decide who shall first have the news. He consults his press directory. The Associated Press is the first name on his list. Moments later its wires carry: FLASH. AT 18.15 HOURS POPE PAUL VI SUFFERED A HEART ATTACK. HE IS SEMI-CONSCIOUS VATICAN PRESS SECRETARY PANCIROLI STATED.

It was the AP's Rome Bureau's second world scoop of the day.

*

At nine o'clock the pope once more opens his eyes. He looks around. Nobody knows whether he can see or whether it is only a reflex action.

Villot breaks the silence: '*Santissimo Padre.*'

Paul turns to him, nodding. Then he speaks. 'Pray for me . . .' He lapses back into semi-consciousness.

Fontana checks the pope's heart. Afterwards he removes the blood pressure cuff. The readings won't make any difference now. The doctor says, quite loudly, that the Holy Father's life is hanging by a thread.

At 9.30 Paul again opens his eyes. Magee fancies he can see the pope's lips starting to move. He strains forward, trying to catch the words. Villot, closer, can actually make them out without too much difficulty. Paul is reciting Our Father. The others pick up the cadence of the Lord's Prayer:

'. . . Who art in Heaven,
Hallowed be Thy Name,
Thy Kingdom come,
Thy will be . . .'

The pope's eyes close and his lips become still. The others falter through the prayer.

Fontana bends over Paul, listening for an unusually long time to his chest. He feels for the pope's pulse. The doctor straightens and looks at the others. Then he glances at Paul's alarm clock to verify the time. It is 9.40. There is a distinct tremor in his voice as he pronounces: 'It is over.'

At that precise moment the ancient alarm clock, which had rung at 6.30 that morning and which had not been rewound or reset, begins to shrill, filling the bedroom with its tinny sound.

*

Martin is the first to leave the room. The prefect goes to telephone Panciroli. The world must be told.

His departure is a signal for Villot. He is no longer just the Secretary of State: he is now also Camerlengo, the cardinal who will run the Church, with the help of the College of Cardinals, until the conclusion of the forthcoming Conclave. Villot will supervise the funeral preparations, send out the formal invitations and decide a thousand and one matters until a new pontiff is chosen. But first, before he does anything, he must attend to a hallowed ritual.

Villot walks to his case, aware all eyes in the bedroom are upon him. He removes the small silver hammer and returns to stand over the body. Using the hammer, he taps Paul lightly on the forehead and, in a strong voice nobody can remember him using before, Villot poses a question asked over the corpses of popes for centuries.

'Giovanni Battista Enrico Antonio Marie, are you dead?'

He waits a full minute for any response. He then repeats his action and question. After another minute he completes the ritual a third time. He then turns and addresses no one in particular. 'Pope Paul is truly dead.'

Villot lifts the pope's right hand. For a moment he stares at it, unbelieving. He looks at Macchi and demands to know where is the Fisherman's Ring. Villot must take possession of it; later, before the assembled cardinals, the Camerlengo will use a pair of silver shears to break the ring and Paul's seals of office. From that moment no one can use either to authenticate a false document.

Macchi does not know where the ring is.

Villot's instructions are sharply clear: the ring must be found – and quickly.

Those words signify the transfer of power from Macchi and all the others who have held it for the fifteen years, one month and fifteen days Paul occupied the Throne of St Peter.

8

During the next hours a number of events occurred essentially simultaneously and in no special order. In some cases they were the result of planning. In others they were spontaneous reactions. Some were significant, others less so. All arose directly from what had occurred. Each suggested there was nothing on earth quite like the aftermath of the death of a pope. So, almost simultaneously . . .

Vatican Press Secretary Panciroli gave the Associated Press its third clear beat on the story by again first telephoning the wire service's Rome bureau. At 9.44 pm, Italian time, the AP sent a five bell flash to all its subscribers: POPE DEAD.

Over four thousand miles away in the Chicago News Center of CBS – where the wall clocks showed the local time as 2.45 in the afternoon – a duty editor dialled Andrew Greeley at his home in Grand Beach to say he was flying a film crew across Lake Michigan for the voice of CREP to explain the pontificate of Paul. The crew arrived while Greeley was saying Mass in his garden. He stopped the service to address the camera. He was as critical as CBS may have hoped he would be. But Greeley's views never made the evening news. The tape was lost. Paul's death had not much moved Greeley – nor did the prospect of flying yet again to Rome, although this time he would spearhead the Universal Press Syndicate 'task force' covering the funeral and Conclave. Greeley would be one of two thousand news persons to reach Rome in the next seventy-two hours.

By 9.55 pm Vatican time, every position on its switchboard was manned. Each nun had a head-set clipped over her coif. Usually the Sunday night shift was as quiet as each of the three graveyards in the Vatican. But since the AP flash the world had begun to call the Holy See number – Rome 6982 – and been answered with the invariable greeting, 'Vaticano'. In the coming twenty-four hours the nuns would receive and make 27,800 calls.

Macchi was the second person to leave Paul's bedroom. The once all-powerful private secretary had begun his first task of the interregnum, the period between the death of one pope and the election of the next. He was trying to find the Fisherman's Ring. Four days passed before the discomfited Macchi located it at the back of a drawer in the desk of Paul's private study.

The secretary's departure from the bedroom was the signal for the others to leave. Giacomina and her nuns remained behind to bathe the pope's body *before it was handed over to the embalmers. The nuns reportedly wept as they worked.*

Villot drove back to the Vatican with Confalonieri, Poletti and Caprio. As Camerlengo, Villot had already accomplished a great deal since the moment of death. He had ordered Martin and Fontana back to Rome to prepare the preliminary work for the death certificate. He had phoned the Papal Master of Ceremonies, Monsignor Virgilio Noé, and various members of the Apostolic Camera, the body responsible for administering the property of the Holy See during the vacancy. Before leaving Castel Gandolfo, Villot had also symbolically taken possession of its palaces and grounds. During the journey to the Vatican the four cardinals discussed the next steps. Poletti would go on radio and television to tell the people of Rome their bishop had died. Confalonieri would inform the cardinals, the diplomatic corps and the secular governments of the fifty-one nations with whom the Holy See had diplomatic ties. Villot would formally seal the pope's private apartment, in which nobody was allowed to live during the interregnum. He would also take symbolic possession of the Vatican Palace and the Lateran Palace, formerly the official residence of the Bishop of Rome and now the administrative headquarters of Rome diocese.

Magee remained at Castel Gandolfo to help supervise the arrangements for the lying in state.

RAI, the Italian television and radio network, interrupted its programme with the news. Stations all over the Western world did the same. Radio Moscow and Peking Radio, along with most other Communist satellites, would wait a further ten hours before briefly noting the passing of the pontiff. Albanian Radio would not report it for three days.

Vatican Radio had closed its offices just off the Via della Conciliazione at eight pm. Only engineers were on duty to transmit pre-recorded programmes. None of them heard the RAI flash. Not that it would have made any difference: the station's director-general, Fr Roberto Tucci, a Jesuit and the only person with the authority, now the pope was dead, to pre-empt the schedules, was out of Rome. His team of broadcasters, Jesuits and other missionaries were either at supper or saying devotions in their religious houses throughout the city. They went to bed not knowing the pope was dead or that their station, sometimes known as 'the voice of God', was about to face its greatest challenge.

Tailor Anibaile Gammarelli heard the news on the radio. He immediately drove to his shop at 34 Santa Chiara to double-check what he already knew, that the House of Gammarelli, Sartoria Pontifica, had ample cloth for the task ahead.

Tourists started to drift into St Peter's Square. They stood waiting, they said, for some sort of announcement, expecting a Vatican official to emerge on the balcony of the Basilica and say something. When no one appeared they drifted away again.

The first tributes were full of praise. From the White House, Downing Street, the President's Palace in Paris, the Chancellor's Residence in Bonn, came the verdicts: the pope's contribution to religious harmony had been considerable; he had steered the Second Vatican Council to port; he had strengthened power-sharing in the Church by founding the Synod of Bishops and broken down so many barriers by his trips to all five continents. In Ireland they reminded themselves he had visited them twice, not as pope but as a senior member of the Secretariat of State. In India, where it was the middle of the night, newspapers dusted off obituaries already set in print. Their eulogies were generous. His papacy had been a dramatic turning point in the history of the Roman Catholic Church's relationship with other religions. It was a point of view echoed on a thousand and more editorial pages in the coming days. Later they would be carefully perused in the Vatican as a means of evaluating the Church's position in the world.

Everywhere reporters followed up the AP flash. They reached Hans Küng in Switzerland and asked the Catholic theologian for a comment on a pope who had done nothing to stop the constant harassment Küng had experienced at the hands of the Curia for daring to keep open the debate on the infallibility of the pope. Küng begged time to consider his comment. Lefèbvre also avoided immediate public judgement. But everybody knew it was only a matter of time before both made their positions known.

Religious scholars of other persuasions began to sharpen their prose to deliver verdicts. For those wishing to criticize, the material was there. The Curia was as strife-ridden as ever. The pope's oecumenical gestures had been weakened by this struggle within the Vatican. The Synod of Bishops had not lived up to its promise. Such opinions at best left a question mark. Paul was certainly not the worst pope but he was a long way from being called great.

Some of the ambassadors accredited to the Holy See did not wait for official notification. The British Envoy Extraordinary and Minister Plenipotentiary dialled the duty officer at the Foreign Office in London to break the news. The duty officer informed the Permanent Under-Secretary of State. He called the Foreign Secretary, who informed the Prime Minister, who decided, as it was the death of the head of state, to inform Buckingham Palace. A court chamberlain brought the news to the Queen at the end of dinner. She immediately asked her personal private secretary to prepare a suitable message of condolence. From the British Envoy's call from Rome to the start of drafting formal royal regret needed no longer than fifteen minutes.

Working from an alphabetical list, the staff of the Secretariat of State telephoned and cabled all over the world. The telegrams were in Italian or French. Nobody could mistake the message sent to each cardinal. THE POPE IS DEAD. COME AT ONCE. VILLOT. The phone calls were equally abrupt, little more than a voice from the Vatican reading out the text of the cable. The hard-pressed staff at the Secretariat had no time to accept condolences or enter into conversations.

At 10.20, Austrian summer time, the telephone rang at Wollzeile 2 in Vienna, the massive palace of the Cardinal Archbishop, Franz Koenig.

The State Secretariat priest double-checked the number on his list – Vienna 532561 – to make sure it was right. He was about to put down the phone and send a telegram when the call was answered . . .

9

Sunday in the archbishop's palace in Vienna's Second District provides a relief from the sounds which permeate even the inner reaches of the thick-walled building during weekday peak traffic hours. In the relative peace of the deserted business quarter of the city on the Sabbath, the palace retains certain features: architecturally it looks like a scaled-down version of the Apostolic Palace, with its courtyard from which floor after floor rises; it has the same faded outer elegance and the same inner magnificence. Yet, unlike the Apostolic Palace, this edifice makes no secret of its security systems. A heavy milled-steel gate bars the entrance. Closed-circuit television monitors anyone who approaches the building. There is a constant guard at the gate-house. The Vienna police are never far off. In a way it is all a tribute to the power and integrity of the man who has lived here through some of the most tumultuous events in post-war European history. He predicted how the Cold War would develop, he warned the Berlin Wall was on the way, he foresaw the Hungarian Uprising and the end of Dubček in Czechoslovakia. He arranged to free Cardinal Mindszenty from his enforced exile in the American Embassy in Budapest and was a guiding hand in a hundred lesser incidents. The Russians and their satellites both fear and respect Franz Koenig, the Cardinal Archbishop of Vienna. He is a man some of the Communist leaders, in their wilder moments, would like to kill, so the American CIA have told him. Koenig is a prudent man. That is why he has accepted the sort of protection more customary in a high-security prison than the residence of a religious leader.

Yet Koenig has done more than anyone, with the exception of Agostino Casaroli, to break the massive moral and ideological conflict between the Roman Church and Communism. He sees the dangers of a continuing enmity between two rock-solid monoliths. He believes that while the Vatican can never condone Communist doctrine, it is not always wise for it to be rigidly dogmatic. Koenig remembers the futility of that during the reign of Pius XII. In the course of his pontificate fifteen countries came under Communist rule. Pius's threat to excommunicate all Catholics who willingly remained in the Communist Party or supported its policies had no effect. Koenig long ago abandoned the ingenuous idea Communism would soon be overturned. Instead he argues that the objective should be to win and preserve a better position for the Church under Communism.

He has been holding these views since John XXIII's encyclical *Pacem in Terris* – *Peace on Earth* – published in 1963, which provides the intellectual justification for rapprochement. No one is more adept at walking this tightrope than Koenig. He knows every subtlety of the encyclical, where and how it distinguishes between false ideas and the historical truths based on them. He played his part in encouraging bishops' delegations from Communist countries to attend the Second Vatican Council; later he counselled on how to respond to Khrushchev's encouraging messages to John. And throughout Paul's pontificate, Koenig's advice was regularly sought. As a result, Paul sent Casaroli to Moscow to sign the Holy See's adherence to the treaty prohibiting the proliferation of atomic weapons. One unlikely effect of the signing is that the Swiss Guards are annually inspected, under the terms of the treaty, to ascertain whether they possess any secret nuclear warheads.

Again, Koenig played an important part in persuading Communist satellites to ease restrictions on religious education. And it was his nod which encouraged the Vatican to establish diplomatic relations with Yugoslavia. Many of Koenig's views were reached after a Sabbath of meditation.

He works in his study, when not attending to his own devotions or ministering to others at the regular Sunday Masses which are punctuated by the three good meals a day the archbishop still relishes in this, his seventy-third year. He looks not only ten years younger but, even without his cardinal's robes and biretta, there is no mistaking he is a prince of the Church. He exudes that rare mix of a deeply pious scholar crossed with a very shrewd politician. He is witty and expansive on matters of record, but a staunch keeper of what are known in the Vatican as 'the secrets' – all those confidences only very senior cardinals hear. He speaks German with a velvety Viennese accent and can be fluent and amusing in several other languages. He has a face made for sculpting. Even when he is silent, contemplating or listening, he has this habit of sitting with his strong hands intertwined.

Koenig has heard the telephone ringing, but has made no attempt to answer it. Instinctively he knows it brings both important and grave news. No one would otherwise call at this late hour. His thoughts immediately go back to the evening television news. There was no hint of a crisis there. Something must have happened suddenly. He feels he knows the answer even before his private secretary walks in. The man is young, but the archbishop sees that he seems to have aged. In a voice Koenig barely recognizes, the priest says the pope died forty-one minutes ago.

The archbishop nods: he had been right about the call. He has expected it, he now remembers, for months. The last time he saw Paul, Koenig knew he was looking at a doomed man. The archbishop had returned to his palace near the Danube and done something he had never done before. He packed a special suitcase for Conclave. It contains sufficient personal effects to keep him in confined comfort for a week. If Conclave were to go beyond that time he would have to send out for more razor blades – or grow a beard.

He gives his secretary an order: reserve the first available airline seat to Rome.

Koenig wants to get there as quickly as possible because he feels intuitively the run-up to Conclave will be the most decisive in the history of the modern Church. He wants to be in at the beginning so he can play to the full his very proper role as one of the great cardinal electors.

*

Shortly after 8.50 pm in Dublin – Irish summer time is one hour behind continental Europe – the telephone rings in a secluded mansion on the outskirts of the city. It is one of the operators in the telegraphic section of Ireland's not very efficient telephone service. But nobody can complain about the time this telegram has taken to reach Dublin, a swift twenty-two minutes. The operator reads the message: DEEPLY REGRET INFORM YOU HOLY FATHER PASSED AWAY. INFORM ALL RELEVANT. YOURS IN CHRIST. VILLOT-CAMERLENGO. The operator spontaneously adds his own condolences and poses the question people will soon be asking all over the world: 'What does this mean for the Church?'

'A great deal. *Sì*, a great deal.'

Even this brief response cannot disguise the Sicilian accent of the man who has spent nine eventful years in this mansion.

It is set in the vast expanse of Phoenix Park. Neighbours include the American ambassador and the President of Ireland. That, some say, is only one of the reasons for the discreet garda presence outside the house. The police are there, it is claimed, to note the unusual callers at the most unlikely hours. Yet, true or not, the man who lives here is certainly sufficiently important to warrant protection. A measure of his position is that he is now the first person in Ireland to be told Paul is dead.

There are those in the British Embassy on the other side of the city, in the Protestant northern enclaves of this troubled island, and certainly across the Irish Sea in the fastness of Whitehall, who would not grieve if this man was no longer in Ireland. They sometimes refer to him disparagingly as 'the Green Sicilian', or 'the pope's spy'. They would pay well to know the contents of the weekly diplomatic pouch he personally seals and sends on the Aer Lingus flight to Rome. As well as details about the work of the Irish Church, its various charities and cultural activities, the pouch frequently contains a shrewd assessment of the people and pressures involved in Britain's battle with the IRA. The man who lives in this mansion is often the first to know details of some new initiative directly from the IRA. In the Vatican's discreet but continuous efforts to bring a just settlement in Ulster, the Apostolic Papal Delegate to Ireland, Dean of the Diplomatic Corps, His Grace, Archbishop Dr Gaetane Alibrandi, has been a key figure. During his nine years at the nunciature he has secretly met many of the IRA leaders. He sees these contacts as part of an intelligence gathering process which can provide unique insights and information for collation in the Vatican, and eventual study by the pope. Alibrandi's reports on the North often go far beyond what the Vatican learns from its constant contacts with bishops in Ireland and elsewhere. The nuncio is almost certainly the only diplomat in Dublin to deal directly with such prime sources – the political leaders of the men who do the shooting. That is why the Special Branch likes to know who visits this secluded mansion, that is why members of Ireland's coalition rumble that the nuncio should be quietly withdrawn by the Vatican.[1]

The diminutive diplomat – Alibrandi is barely five feet in his old-fashioned lace-up shoes – sees his close connection with those he insists on calling 'guerrilla fighters', not 'gunmen' nor 'terrorists', as yet another way for him to learn of the deeper roots of the Ulster conflict. With a passion even his opponents find mesmeric, Alibrandi argues that most of the IRA act as they do because of the presence of a situation not of their making: that to reject or condemn them, without any attempt to understand them, is simply a different form of violence. To those appalled by this argument, the nuncio serenely responds that any form of killing has a blunting effect.

Alibrandi's involvement in the strife is balanced in his mind by the undisputed truism that ever since Northern Ireland was created, many of its Protestant clergymen have openly and dangerously manipulated the political life of the province to the detriment of Catholics. He is appalled by Orange Order rituals which include calling a football 'the pope' and kicking it around a field. He cannot conceive, even in the most Catholic of northern ghettos, a similar game being played with a football called 'the Queen'. Alibrandi remains convinced that by refusing to condemn such behaviour, the most extreme of Ulster's

Protestant clergymen are, willy-nilly, cast as officers in the bitter war which engages their troops; that, quite deliberately, they have allowed religion and politics to meld into a single, potent, all-pervading force; that, behind the many other motives for Ulster's peculiar anti-Catholic discrimination, lurks one dominant factor: the attitude of these clergymen and their determination to sustain the myths about, and the frenetic fear of, Catholicism.

The nuncio possesses an impressive and depressing collection of Northern Protestant bigotry – all of it abrasive, strident, uncharitable, unyielding and off-putting. It is an effective counter to slip across his dining table when the occasional non-Catholic guest raises a question about some alleged excess of the Church Alibrandi represents in a country which has a long and compliant religious relationship with Rome.

It is this which allows him to remain largely unperturbed by the hostile reaction he attracts from Dublin politicians and members of the diplomatic corps of which he is titular head. It also allows him to be a vigorous defender of the role of Vatican diplomacy in the modern world. He will remind anybody his functions are clearly defined in a document Paul issued in June 1969: 'The primary and specific purpose of the mission of a papal representative is to render ever closer and more operative the ties that bind the Apostolic See and its local Church; the ordinary function of a pontifical representative is to keep the Holy See regularly and objectively informed about the conditions of the ecclesiastical community to which he has been sent, and assert what may affect the life of the Church and the good of souls.'

This is enough for Alibrandi. He will go on meeting the IRA if it means he receives a fuller picture of what is happening in Ireland. The papal directive makes this permissible in the view of the sixty-four-year-old diplomat who holds a doctorate in canon law and is an acknowledged expert on ecclesiastical history, international law, sociology and economics. He speaks several languages, and began his career at the Secretariat of State by opening and sometimes secretly copying the most private letters of Paul. It is the memory of that misdemeanour which now fills the nuncio's mind when he puts down the phone.

The scene of a few months ago wells up in his memory. Paul is sitting on a couch in his office when the nuncio arrives to make his annual report. He motions for Alibrandi to sit beside him. They have known each other for nearly forty years and have stayed in touch all the time. Nevertheless Alibrandi detects a feeling of surprise in Paul when he says, 'Holy Father, I wish to make a special confession to you.' Paul, he remembers, said nothing. Instead his eyes had dwelled on Alibrandi, 'wonderful eyes, able to make you want to speak'. Alibrandi had begun to talk in little more than a whisper, finding it difficult to admit what he had done so long ago. 'Holy Father, do you remember that you gave me sometimes some private letters, very private letters?' Paul had answered, 'I remember, I remember.' Encouraged, Alibrandi continued, 'And nobody but the person receiving the letters was to read them?' Again, 'I remember, I remember.' Then in a surge of words, 'Holy Father, before I sealed your letters I read them.' Paul had sat there 'not angry, just interested and understanding', as the nuncio completed his confession. 'Holy Father, those were the best letters I have ever read. And the very best I always copied so I could use the thoughts later in my own letters.' Suddenly Paul leaned forward and smiled. 'I am very happy that you found my words so useful.'[2]

Glad now to be alone with his thoughts, the tiny figure of the nuncio is momentarily a tragic one as the full impact of the news dawns on him. His nut-brown face crinkles with inner pain, his hands pluck nervously at his pectoral cross. Until this moment he has never fully realized how much he will miss Paul, not just as pope but also as a friend.

Alibrandi feels especially sad Paul will never see the splendid new nunciature which is being built for the apostolic delegate. It has only one drawback so far as Alibrandi can tell, now that the need to make the chapel larger than originally envisaged has been agreed, namely that the new building, out on the busy Navan Road, will make it much more difficult for IRA men to slip in and out.

But, for the moment, the problems of moving to a new home and dealing with members of proscribed organizations will have to take second place to the demands the death of the pope places on the hard-working nuncio.

Paul's death means that in the coming days Alibrandi will be 'chained to my typewriter', executing Villot's telegraphed order to 'inform all relevant'. These will include the President of Ireland, the Minister of Foreign Affairs, the bishops and the nuncio's fellow ambassadors in Ireland. All will receive a personally typed letter. Alibrandi learned to type when acting as Paul's secretary in 1938. He feels it particularly appropriate that the skill Paul encouraged should now be used to inform 'all relevant' of his death.

*

It is teatime in Buenos Aires when the cable from the Vatican confirms what Juan Carlos Aramburu has known for hours. Each of the city's newspapers and TV stations called him for comment following the AP flash. But the sixty-six-year-old cardinal archbishop of the largest Catholic diocese in the world – he is directly responsible for nine million souls – determinedly refuses to say anything until he has Villot's cable in his hands. It is not that he wishes to be unhelpful, it is that he needs every minute to work out the deeper implications of Paul's death. The more he thinks about it, Aramburu will later admit in his pleasant singsong Spanish, the more the situation has the makings of one of those sudden explosive crises which South America itself seems so often able to produce.

Aramburu has a donnish shyness, a throwback to his days as a professor. But it masks a powerful certainty: by the end of the century the numerical power-base of the Church will have shifted from Europe to Latin America. There are about 204,100,000 baptized Catholics in South America. There are a further 79,114,000 in Central America and another 17,529,000 in the Caribbean islands. Even these figures are likely to be out of date, such is the high birth rate. At present forty per cent of the Church's strength comes from this part of the world. But by the end of the century – at the present rate of one Catholic born and baptized every ninety-three seconds in the area – Latin America will have over fifty per cent of that strength. Aramburu believes that in the coming Conclave he and his eighteen fellow cardinals from the region, coupled with the Spanish cardinals and perhaps the Portuguese, could provide a voting bloc hard to ignore. Given, that is, they can agree on a common strategy. Better than anybody Aramburu knows it is a big proviso. Yet it is one for the future. His more immediate concerns are caused by the fact that in every sense Paul's death comes at the worst possible time.

It follows hard on the heel of a calculated snub by Italy's Socialist president, Sandoro Pertini, who decided against sending a message of congratulation to Jorge Rafael Videla, former head of yet another Argentinian military junta and, since five days ago, 1 August, civilian president of the country. Pertini felt he could not offer good wishes to a man who has done more than most of Argentina's dictators to abuse human rights.

The fiercely nationalistic Argentinians, forty per cent of whom are of Italian descent, reacted strongly to the slight. Many feel they, too, have been insulted by the motherland they left to begin a new life in Buenos Aires or on the pampas. Aramburu recognizes that the South American Church is likely to be dragged into the controversy: such situations invariably lead to demands for denunciations from the pulpits. In the minds of the masses the issue is simplistically clear: Pertini, an upstart Socialist, has insulted their new president. With a fervour of new-found *patria*, some Argentinians are prepared to see the situation burst into flame; there have already been bomb scares at Alitalia offices and other Italian places of business.

Aramburu fears Paul's death could be the touch fuse. Almost certainly, reasons the cardinal, Videla will wish to attend the funeral and stay on for the installation of the next pope. Aramburu can see how it would provide the president with a badly needed shop window, one in which the general with the Clark Gable moustache would have a chance to score an important public relations coup; for a man ultimately responsible for the torture and death of thousands, the visit to Rome could be used to make the world think he was, at heart, simply another deeply caring Catholic.

The cardinal feels that if Videla goes he could spark off riots in Rome and mar the solemnities. Yet Aramburu can think of no means of stopping the president. In the three years he has been a cardinal the gifted Aramburu has not faced a tougher problem.

It is one almost as serious as the national malaise which grips Argentina. Inflation is running at 155 per cent. Wages have dropped in real terms to between forty and sixty per cent of their level before Videla seized power. Bankruptcies are at a new high. While the remnants of the old Peronist regime are totally discredited, there is no evidence Videla can get the country moving as a modern industrial nation with stable political institutions.

There are other reasons for Aramburu to look with concern on the idea of Videla going to Rome. In his absence the president might be ousted; his power base is far from secure. Those who seek to replace him could also bring about the one conflict, above all others, which Aramburu privately fears. It would be caused by the dispute over the Malvinas, those near-barren islands five hundred miles off the coast of Argentina which remain almost embarrassingly as one of the last outposts of Britain's once-great empire. Personally, Aramburu has little doubt the islands will eventually become the property of Argentina. But he has always cautioned that the only way to achieve this is by patient negotiation. He knows that whenever matters become particularly uncomfortable for a junta – when the protests become more than tolerated whispers about brutalities, about kidnappings, about anything which could precipitate yet another coup – those who currently hold the country down by military force almost inevitably trot out the question of the Malvinas. It is a guaranteed way to stifle opposition and unite public opinion.

Aramburu has been telling the Vatican for years there is the growing possibility of a military offensive by Argentina against the islands.[3] The prospect bothers the cardinal deeply. For as a prince of the Church he must condemn all violence. Equally, he suspects that if he does that in the case of the Malvinas, he would be flying in the face of what his flock wants and, perhaps, even against what he himself believes. But Aramburu is also painfully aware that dictator Videla is probably the worst possible person to go to Rome to put forward any claim to the islands which hinges on moral rights.

*

In Rome, a member of the African Missionary Order, Father Sean MacCarthy, is dressing in the open-necked white shirt and blue trousers he favours for work. MacCarthy is a broadcaster – one of the few in all Rome who does not yet know the biggest news story since the kidnapping of Aldo Moro has broken.

For the past nine years MacCarthy has hosted Vatican Radio's English-language programme to Africa; he also at times broadcasts to Europe. He is fifty-nine, a compact man with a shock of grey hair and a studio pallor. Like his friend, John Magee, MacCarthy retains his soft Irish brogue, a well-modulated voice ideal for conveying the Sacred Word on the 16/25 metre short-wave band.

Having breakfasted and driven from his mission house to Vatican Radio headquarters, MacCarthy still has no inkling of what has happened. He casually strolls onto the third floor of the broadcast centre where he has his office to find himself caught up in what passes for panic in the usually serene atmosphere of the most powerful religious station on earth: people are almost running; some are even talking a little faster than usual.

Slightly puzzled, MacCarthy goes to his desk in the English-language section and is further surprised when his telephone rings. A radio station in Los Angeles – where it is the middle of the night – is calling for a reaction to the pope's death. Instinctively the broadcaster in MacCarthy surfaces; he begins to speak off the cuff, formulating elegantly interlinked thoughts and offering the sort of careful and balanced judgements long experience has taught him to give. It is a masterly example of the delicate art of avoiding pitfalls. The California station will replay the recording regularly throughout the night, billing it as: 'The voice of the Vatican expresses its grief.'

It's the sort of hyperbole which makes MacCarthy wince. He just wishes the secular media weren't so tasteless. But in the coming days he will shudder quite often at such lapses. Those will be the moments when he is fervently glad he does not have to compete for a news-break or earn his living searching for the next sensation. As a religious, a member of a monastic order, he receives no salary, only expenses and his keep; that's the way he likes it – three good meals a day, a comfortable bed and probably the most faithful listeners a broadcaster could want.

Yet he is no stuffed shirt. He understands the requirements of his calling, the need neither to play up nor down to his audience. He is careful to provide a source for everything, and his judgements are based on the sort of meticulous research even Prefect Martin would accept.

Having quickly assimilated the basic circumstances surrounding Paul's passing, throughout the morning MacCarthy fields calls from English-language stations around the world, while at the same time preparing his own programme for airing from Studio One later in the day. He plans it to be a straight recital of the facts; how and when the pope died, who was there, what his last words were. Nearby broadcasters in thirty-four other languages are preparing their bulletins, from Tamil to Esperanto, from the dialects of the highlands of China to the patois of New Guinea, from the guttural sounds of bush Africa to the resonant growl of the Polish steppes: to almost anywhere there are Catholics ready and able to listen, Vatican Radio will bring its version of the death of the pope.

MacCarthy completes his script. Suddenly he grins. Come to think of it, he is not really going to sound much different from the secular bulletins. Yet no doubt his details will seem more authoritative because, after all, they are being beamed from the transmitters of 'the voice of God'.

*

Father Lambert Greenan, editor of the English-language edition of *L'Osservatore Romano*, as usual manages to cope with several matters at once. In one hand he holds a large gin and tonic. In the other he has a newspaper brought along for the Aer Lingus flight to Rome. At the same time, the Dominican is keeping one watchful eye on a particularly powerful cardinal who is dressed as a simple country priest sitting two rows behind him, while his other eye is on a photographer festooned with what the editor thinks must be the entire contents of a camera shop. Greenan wonders how the situation will develop. But nothing will surprise him – not after the events of the past twenty-four hours.

The tall and avuncular Irish-born Greenan – he comes from the same Newry parish as Magee and the pair are close friends, partly because of their dissimilar personalities, and partly because they are members of the Celtic fraternity who have always held key posts in the Vatican and are consequently sometimes known there as the 'Irish Mafia' – had left Rome to holiday with relations in Ireland. Upon entering Irish air space Greenan had suddenly felt compelled to say a rosary for the pope: 'I just prayed he wouldn't die while I was on holiday.' On Sunday night, home with his family, having uncorked a choice wine for dinner Greenan felt another compulsion – to catch the headlines on RTE's nine o'clock television news. He was in time to hear the newscaster announce Paul's death. Greenan spent much of the night arranging to fly back to Rome. As editor of the 'almost official' English-language weekly of the Vatican, his presence is mandatory to publish the documentation associated with the funeral and aftermath.

Greenan relishes the prospect of the unremitting pressure ahead; eighteen thousand very select readers in ninety-one countries will look to his paper to provide the plain, unvarnished truth of what has happened and what is going to happen. There won't be a line of speculation – just all the facts the Vatican deems fit to print, translated often from flowery Italian or arid Latin into perfect English by one of the sharpest and finest minds working in the service of the Holy See.

He is also waggish. Greenan once found himself seated beside Archbishop Alibrandi at one of the interminable dinners Irish prelates like to give. Smiling broadly at the swarthy-faced Sicilian, Greenan remarked in mock surprise, 'I had no idea we had Arabs in the Church's diplomatic service.' The puzzled nuncio looked uncertain, waiting for Greenan to continue. The editor carried on blithely: 'Your name. Ali Brandi. That's Arabic for sure in my book.' The two didn't exchange a further word during dinner. Greenan tabbed Alibrandi as 'a fella who couldn't see a joke'.

Behind his daffiness, Greenan is a noted theologian and philosopher of impeccable credentials. He is sixty-one years old, suffers fools badly, but has an unshakeable loyalty to a circle of friends which extends through the Vatican into the papal apartment itself. People say he knows almost as many secrets as Macchi and Magee. Greenan keeps them locked behind an ironic smile. He is a formidable man in every sense; those who abuse his trust do so at their peril.

On this Monday morning, sipping his gin and tonic – no easy feat since the plane is being buffeted by a fierce summer storm over France – Greenan wonders why Cardinal Paolo Bertoli is travelling incognito. Greenan knows the seventy-year-old loves his little mysteries; Bertoli has been Scarlet Pimpernelling so long Roman satirists say he should really wear a cloak instead of a cassock. But recently, after a distinguished career as nuncio in Turkey, Colombia, the Lebanon and France, Bertoli's star has waned. He had a fierce quarrel with Giovanni Benelli and, like Benelli, Bertoli simultaneously fell victim of Vatican hatchetry. While Benelli was despatched to be archbishop of Florence, Bertoli was pressurized to the point where he did the unthinkable – he resigned as prefect of the Sacred Congregation for the Cause of Saints. He had gone off, again, as Paul's delegate to try to bring peace between

Christians and Moslems in the Lebanon. Nobody really felt his heart was in the mission; in any event it failed. Personally, Greenan didn't think such an intervention could work in the political cesspit of the Middle East. Afterwards hardly anyone had seen Bertoli for months. Now, here he was, slimmed down, leaner than he had been for years, a glint in his eyes, having boarded the plane at Lourdes. He surely hadn't been to look at the grotto, not dressed like this, in an unadorned black soutane, as unprepossessing as any curate. But it hadn't taken the photographer long to penetrate the disguise. As the plane begins to come out of the turbulence, the cameraman starts to move into position, but hesitatingly: even the brashest of photographers knows Bertoli is explosive over having his picture taken without permission.

Still musing, Greenan is tapped on the shoulder. It is Bertoli, speaking perfect English, a gift Greenan had not known him to display before. Can he borrow the newspaper? Instinctively Greenan replies, 'Of course, Eminence.' There follows one of those brief conversations which come under the heading of the games people play.

'You know me?'

'Of course, Eminence.'

'How do you know me?'

'We meet quite often, Eminence.'

'Why do we meet?'

'I edit the English edition of L'Osservatore Romano.'

'Oh yes, there are several language editions aren't there?'

'Yes, Eminence.'

'It's terrible news, isn't it?'

'Yes, Eminence.' Greenan hands over the newspaper, the convoluted conversation at an end, and resumes pondering how his next edition should present its all-important judgement on Paul.

Since 1890 the daily edition of L'Osservatore Romano – published at three o'clock every afternoon with weekly editions in English, French, Spanish, Portuguese, German, Italian and Polish – has promulgated the nearest the Vatican has to an 'official' printed word. Like Vatican Radio and the Press Office, the group of newspapers is owned by the Holy See and answers directly on all editorial matters to a department of the Secretariat of State, the Office of Information and Documentation. The papers' funding comes from the Administration of the Patrimony of the Holy See; its administration is in the hands of a religious order, the Salesian Congregation of John Bosco.

For nine years Greenan has edited the English-language weekly on a shoestring; the entire group is in financial straits. Greenan's paper carries little advertising, has no overseas correspondents and just one editorial assistant in a cramped office in a featureless building beside the

Porta Sant'Anna. Greenan rigorously follows the editorial line of the parent daily, loyally and, when necessary, pugnaciously upholding the papacy. He provides a valuable record of nearly everything the pope says and does, including publishing the official texts of papal speeches. He also prints occasional articles of real political significance or historical interest. The editorials have a special importance, particularly the unsigned ones. They are usually 'inspired' by the pope; sometimes Paul even wrote them himself.

Now, as the plane heads for Rome, Greenan is shaping his thoughts about a man he has loved deeply and respected. He fears the secular media will once again focus on the *Humanae Vitae* encyclical and miss so much else in the pontificate. Among other things Paul revised the rite of concelebration, that moment the priests of a diocese gather around their bishop to celebrate the Eucharist with him, or when the cardinals congregate around the pope to create visible evidence of collegiality, simple but striking proof all priests and bishops share with him responsibility for the entire Church. While the five meetings of the Synod of Bishops have not been an unqualified success – they could not be since Paul's idea of 'open government' in the Church was simply too great a change to absorb in just over a decade – Greenan believes substantial progress has been achieved in the revision of canon law, doctrine, liturgy and the delicate question of mixed marriages. All this he attributes to Paul's commitment to change. And right to the end he remained the pope of oecumenism. Paul seized every opportunity to demonstrate this. Who could forget the moment when Paul once more publicly displayed his innate humility during an historic moment in the Sistine Chapel: the Pope had dropped to his knees before Metropolitan Melitone of Constantinople, on a rare visit to Rome, and kissed his feet. And Dr Michael Ramsey, then the Archbishop of Canterbury, had been embraced like a brother on his visit to the Vatican. Such gestures were inspired by Paul's greatest triumph, the bringing of Vatican II to a successful conclusion. This was the pope Greenan will wish to eulogize in print. He is still contemplating the matter when the photographer makes his approach to Bertoli.

Quick as a flash, Greenan is out of his seat and, with a murmured, 'Excuse me, Eminence', Greenan plucks the newspaper from Bertoli's astonished grasp. Greenan folds the paper to hide the large photo he suspects has galvanized the photographer into action. It is one of Benelli. Above it is the headline: THE NEXT POPE?

Bertoli smiles tightly. The last thing Bertoli would wish, Greenan suspects, is to be photographed staring at a picture of his old enemy – and undoubtedly a rival in the coming Conclave. His 'good deed for the day' done, Greenan sits back and continues planning his commemoration issue on Paul.

*

Aboard an Austrian Airways jet converging on Rome, Koenig is also considering the prospects for Conclave. He sees himself as something of a veteran, one of the eleven cardinals still living who attended the 1963 Conclave which elected Paul. Koenig has already issued his judgement on the third pope he has served; he remembers Paul as a genuinely holy man whose pontificate set the Church firmly on course towards the next century: no matter who succeeds him, much of what Paul did cannot easily be undone. There are no surprises in Koenig's verdict. Nobody expected there would be. Some, though, are already interpreting Koenig's words as an indication he will not resist any serious attempt to promote him to the papacy.

Even as the plane is completing its seventy-minute flight from Vienna, speculators have been busy trying to stand up this prospect. They point out that in the last few years Koenig has done a great deal of travelling, presuming he has done so in order that other cardinals may come to know him better; it helps to be a familiar face around Conclave. But many cardinals have been travelling lately. The speculators therefore look for another clue. Back in 1975, Sebastiano Baggio and Koenig each wrote articles in support of Opus Dei. Now that *is* interesting. Opus Dei is a right-wing semi-secret secular society founded in Spain which wields huge background power in the Church. It is not the sort of fellow traveller in whose company the liberal Koenig would normally be expected to be found; the same can be said of Baggio. Unless, of course, three years ago, both were even then laying the ground for the next papal election. For Opus Dei is a firm favourite with Cardinal Pericle Felici, the influential sixty-seven-year-old prefect of the Supreme Tribunal of the Apostolic Signatura, the person whom Paul placed in charge of settling inter-Curia disputes but whom many have come to see as the curial cardinal determined to undo many of the progressive initiatives begun by Vatican II. The bull-necked Felici, with a Roman Emperor's head and a huge, imperious nose, can sniff out the first whiff of anything faintly liberalizing.

He seems, at first glance, an unlikely person to support Koenig. But, say the experts, times are a-changing. Felici may be better off endorsing Koenig – or, less likely, Baggio, for the two men dislike each other – in the hope that when his man is elected, he will remember who helped put him there. That's how the theory goes. The supposition does not take into account Koenig's own great strength of character and his well-known individualism; it is more likely that if he became pope he would be nobody's man. Popes have a habit of turning out like that. But in the Conclave stakes which have now been declared open, few take account of such trifles. The name of the game is to float stories and watch how they develop. It's a time-honoured tradition and one the experienced Koenig recognizes.

Sipping coffee with Viennese cookies, aware that everyone on board knows the purpose of his journey, the cardinal archbishop is careful to say nothing to anybody that might indicate what he himself thinks about the future.

*

At eleven o'clock on this sweltering Monday in Rome, nineteen cardinals, the majority of whom are permanently based in the city, assemble in the Sala Bologna on the third floor of the Apostolic Palace. Several are over eighty, including Carlo Confalonieri who most people cannot believe is actually eighty-five. The Dean of the College of Cardinals doesn't look a day over seventy. He thinks it nonsense that Paul's *Romano Pontifici Eligendo* – the matrix for the next Conclave – should bar any cardinal over eighty from voting.

Confalonieri, as tradition demands, takes the chair at this, the first of the General Congregations – pre-Conclave meetings when, during the interregnum, the assembled cardinals direct the day-to-day running of the Church. On this occasion they must also decide the funeral arrangements.

It is Villot who quickly takes charge. He is one of the few curial cardinals still holding office. Paul's *Eligendo* requires most cardinals in charge of departments to resign automatically on the death of a pope so that his successor may have a free hand over whom he appoints. In the *sede vacante*, the period between popes, Villot is the official keeper of the keys of St Peter. He is now both Secretary of State and Camerlengo, the second person this century to combine the two functions. The first was Eugenio Pacelli in 1939. He became Pius XII. The coincidence is sufficient for Villot's name to be touted as a candidate by all those Vaticanologists who would dearly love to know what is happening in this salon with its frescoes and obligatory wooden crucifix on one wall.

The decisions are few. The funeral is set for Saturday, 12 August, five days hence. There would then follow *Novemdiales*, nine days of mourning. Conclave will not actually begin until Friday, 25 August, eighteen days away, the latest possible date allowed by Paul's *Eligendo*. Villot reports he has sealed all the palaces he is supposed to seal. He reminds them the next meeting will be the same time tomorrow. This one has lasted a mere ten minutes.

The starting date for Conclave decided by these nineteen cardinals and binding on each cardinal elector will produce a welter of criticism, exhortation and raise speculation to fever pitch. But not yet.

Everybody on the outside is at present more puzzled about why there are to be six full days between Paul's death and the moment he is placed in his tomb. It's not because the time is required for all the cardinals to reach Rome or for the statesmen of the world to fly in. If necessary they could almost all be here in the next forty-eight hours. Accordingly, somebody starts the story – which spreads like wildfire – that Villot has made his first mistake as Camerlengo, that he wants to spin out his moment of glory and preside over the longest papal wake anyone can remember. What else is to be expected, shrug the cynical Romans, from a foreigner – and a Frenchman at that?

It is just the right level of bitchiness to get everybody talking. There's only one thing better than a papal funeral: one with a living scapegoat to mock. The hapless Villot fits the bill perfectly.

*

Shortly before noon at Castel Gandolfo, Giacomina leads her nuns into Paul's bedroom. They stand around the bed, the only sound the clicking of their rosaries and their prayers.

Paul is covered by a sheet. The drapes are drawn. A powerful fan plays across the room. After one final look, the nuns leave. Giacomina is the last to go. Even so she wants to be away from here well before what will begin to occur in this room at 9.40 tonight – the earliest possible moment under Italian law it can happen. She prefers to remember Paul as she now sees him, a man at peace at last. This is the way Giacomina has been raised to believe a pope should look when he dies.

But Paul must soon become a subject for that very American illusion – making the dead appear approximately alive.

*

At Dublin Airport, Archbishop Alibrandi looks searchingly into the face of a fellow priest whom he is seeing off on a flight to Rome, already seriously delayed through a strike by French air traffic controllers which has plunged Europe into chaos. Yet Alibrandi's house guest for the past two weeks, Cardinal Salvatore Pappalardo, remains calm and relaxed. Surely this is another good sign, muses Alibrandi happily. But then there are so many positive things about his fellow Sicilian, the sixty-year-old archbishop of Palermo, to give substance to the scenario the nuncio sees as a distinct possibility. Indeed Pappalardo's entire career is perfect for what Alibrandi envisages. As a seasoned papal diplomat, Pappalardo knows almost all there is to know about the ways and wiles of the Secretariat of State; as former president of the Pontifical Ecclesiastical Academy in Rome, where future Holy See diplomats are trained, he has closely observed the crafty ways of the Curia. And in his pastoral work in Palermo, he continues to perform brilliantly: he fights municipal corruption, helps the poor, stays out of party politics, faces up to the Mafia, denounces anything which smacks of chicanery. Further, Pappalardo is physically strong, cultured, well-travelled and absolutely middle-of-the-road in matters of Church dogma. Behind his youthful smile is an iron will. All in all, Alibrandi believes the next time he sees his closest friend he will happily kneel and kiss the Fisherman's Ring on Pappalardo's finger.

During the last sixteen hours, between a brief sleep and planning all else he must do, Alibrandi's thoughts have constantly dwelt on this exciting idea. Now, as Pappalardo's flight is finally called, the nuncio gives him one last appraising look. There is no doubt at all: Pappalardo would appear very fine in papal vestments; he already has the face plus that special aura of authority and humility which go with the position.

Driving back from the airport across the city whose newspapers carry pages of obituaries on Paul, Alibrandi wonders how long it will be before the same newspapers may be heralding the election of his friend. Yet even the euphoric nuncio does not minimize the obstacles Pappalardo must overcome. There has not been a Sicilian pope for over a thousand years. And, like most Italians, those in the Curia might not easily accept any change in that situation; there's a degree of racism behind many Italians' thinking. But Alibrandi remains quietly confident that if anybody can alter this attitude it will be Pappalardo.

His election could only enhance the career of the nuncio. Alibrandi might reasonably expect to be made a cardinal, plucked from the turmoil of Irish politics and brought to Rome to be at the very centre of things. It is a prospect heady enough to give added dash to the nuncio's great pleasure, driving. He speeds on his way, deftly moving in and out of the traffic, almost tingling with expectation at what the future could hold.

*

Quickly settling into Rome, absorbing all those sounds and mores which, Vienna apart, make it one of the most agreeable cities Koenig knows, the cardinal archbishop begins to evaluate the situation. It is more or less what he'd expected. Some good judgements on Paul are surfacing. He is emerging not only as the most travelled pope in history – even Koenig has to pause to remember it really was twenty-three pilgrimages in all – but as the pontiff who contributed a 'remarkable corpus of thought' to his times. People are beginning to realize his pontificate was altogether broader and more complicated than that of a mere social critic and philosopher: he may yet emerge as among the most intellectually accomplished of world leaders in the past twenty-five years. Paul had the vision that all roads lead to Rome; through his diplomatic ties he was more aware of the important trends than almost any other major modern leader. In a way Paul knew too much rather than too little. He is perceived by his proponents – and Koenig is glad they are at last having their day – as the man who encouraged the world in its hopes. And now the world is being reminded of the multitude of milestones along Paul's long road. He had abolished the traditional abstinence from meat on Fridays. He nullified the notorious Index of Prohibited Books, which had included the works of Victor Hugo and Voltaire. He ensured Mass could be celebrated in as many languages as there are people to speak them. He warned that rich nations must share their wealth with impoverished ones or risk 'the judgement of God and the wrath of the poor'. Now, in death, Paul is being seen as an open-minded conservative guiding a radical reformation; not many reformers have been so hesitant, not many conservatives have wrought such far-reaching change.

It is a verdict Koenig cannot fault. He wishes, though, he could feel the same about the rumours. People, some of whom he thinks should know better, are saying factions have started to form, that groundwork more appropriate to the secular world is already starting to influence the Holy Spirit in deciding the outcome of Conclave. In other words the politicking has started. So they say.

Koenig cannot abide this sort of talk. He regards it as demeaning both the memory of Paul and the serious business of choosing his successor. Koenig also senses how things will develop: every time a pair of cardinals are spotted together it is going to be presented as the makings of a plot.

Yet, he must admit, some cardinals don't discourage speculation. In Florence, Benelli has been telling a radio audience that Villot 'had purely formal relations with the Holy Father while I saw him every day', just the sort of words to get the secular press pot bubbling. And of course there is friction: a hundred and twenty cardinals can't all be expected to like each other; of course there will be dinner parties, very private ones, where the mix of Church guests will be as carefully chosen as any intimate gathering planned by a Parisian or Washington hostess; of course the first table reservations are being made at L'Eau Vive, an agreeable French cuisine restaurant behind the Pantheon reportedly one of the places where cardinals like to 'consult' – the only sort of lobbying officially permitted under Paul's *Eligendo*. But does it all add up to an orchestrated campaign for the papacy like the contest for the US presidency? Of course not – not in Koenig's view. And he does not wish to get into the semantics of where consultation stops and wheeler-dealing begins.

If there is an answer to that, it doesn't interest Koenig. He has already decided on his opening strategy. He is going to be very careful in whose company he dines. And at all times he will keep his own counsel, listen a great deal and then, in the privacy of his own room in one of the Vatican colleges, he will prepare his next moves.

There is, though, one thought he is prepared to share with others. Having studied the list, surveyed the form, looked at the possible runners, considered their track record, assessed the odds, the cardinal archbishop, not normally a betting man, has a tip: the race is wide open.

Whether he intends it or not, that forecast is going to give rise to the very thing he abhors – further speculation.[4]

*

Late in the afternoon, seventy-four-year-old Renato Zottich packs five bottles of embalming fluid into a carton at the head office of Zega and Company, Rome's largest funeral establishment. It is not the sort of work the gregarious Egyptian-born professor of mechanics normally does; he is in charge of Zega's fleet of hearses and funeral cars. But Armando Zega himself has entrusted Zottich with this 'very special mission', carrying out instructions personally ordered by Villot. The bottles of pinkish chemicals have been imported from the Epic Corporation of America. Zottich has been warned by the Vatican that under no circumstances must the company be informed their chemical was used. Villot is concerned Epic might use the information to promote their products.

Zottich checks the typewritten cards he has prepared. They contain precise details of how the Epic preparations are to be used. He seals the cards in a company envelope with its distinctive logo – a bold 'Z' on a red background – places the envelope on top of the bottles and scotch-tapes the carton. He then checks a second package. It contains a huge hypodermic syringe capable of holding half a pint of fluid. He reseals this carton and hands both boxes to a company employee. In keeping with the extraordinary secrecy surrounding the entire operation, the man, at the Vatican's insistence, is only to be known as 'the Technician'.

The Vatican is divided on the question of embalming, as is most of Italy. Zega and Co. provide the service mainly for Americans who die in Italy and whose remains are to be shipped home. Few Italians like the idea of their loved ones undergoing the process.

Zottich was surprised and delighted when Zega was contacted by

105

Villot's office and told that Paul was to be embalmed – the decision to do so was taken because of the length of time his body would be on public display – and that the firm should provide 'all technical requirements'. Zottich feels that in gossipy Rome Zega and Co.'s role will soon be an open secret; this might encourage others to use the process at 500,000 lire a corpse. There is no question of charging the Vatican: Zottich sees 'the honour and potential' as beyond recompense.

He tells the Technician the instruction cards must be faithfully followed. The man drives to Castel Gandolfo with Zottich's words in his mind – 'no mistakes, Zega and Company depend on you'. His van is loaded with equipment which includes a range of ingenious aids to prop and keep a cadaver in place on a catafalque.

The Technician carries the accoutrements in through a side door of the Papal Palace; Fontana and his assistant, Dr Renato Buzzonetti, escort him to the pope's bedroom. They lay out the equipment and the two doctors study the instruction cards. Fontana and Buzzonetti have only limited experience of embalming procedures but these seem clear enough. Nothing more can be done before 9.40 pm: Italian law insists that even for a pope there must be a twenty-four hour interval between the moment of death and the onset of embalming to ensure a person is 'medically and legally' dead.

Only when that formality is satisfied do the two doctors and the Technician get to work. They drain all Paul's body fluids. Then they inject a succession of embalming fluids into the corpse. The chemicals harden all the organs and give the skin a firm, pinkish texture. The process takes two hours.

Close to midnight Monsignor Virgilio Noé, Papal Master of Ceremonies, enters the room. Noé carries a silver urn which he has removed from a cabinet under the Altar of the Confession, which itself stands over the tomb of St Peter in the Vatican Basilica. Noé placed the urn there on 28 June, the eve of the Feast of Saints Paul and Peter. It was one of the ceremonial high spots of his year, the papal blessing of the pallium repositing in the urn. Made from the wool of two lambs – suggesting Christ, the Lamb of God and the Good Shepherd – the pallium was fashioned by Benedictine Sisters of St Cecilia in their convent in the salubrious suburb of Trastevere just beyond the Vatican walls.

Noé now places the urn by the bedside. Then, with the help of the two doctors, he dresses Paul in full pontifical vestments. Noé goes to the door and summons a detachment of Swiss Guards. They enter carrying the catafalque. The pope's body is manoeuvred into place on the bier. The silent procession then slowly makes its way to the ground-floor Hall of the Swiss Guard. The catafalque is placed in the centre of the large salon. The Technician adjusts the rubber neck support and shoulder blocks which help hold the body in position. Noé motions everyone away while he makes the final arrangements to the vestments. Then, with infinite care, he lifts the pallium from the urn and drapes the circular two inch band of white wool around Paul's neck, arranging it over the chasuble so that the pallium's six black crosses repose above his breast, shoulders and abdomen. Noé kneels for a moment in prayer beside the bier before walking slowly from the Hall. As he does so the four-man Swiss Guard of honour takes up its position, one at each corner of the catafalque. From now until Paul is finally laid to rest, the Swiss Guards will be in constant attendance.

10

In the next four days Rome became the focus of world attention. Nearly all the cardinals had arrived by Wednesday, 9 August when, in the evening, Paul's body was conveyed by road from Castel Gandolfo to lie in state in St Peter's. Over a hundred million watched the occasion on television. The endless tributes continued to be published. Still more came as the statesmen of the world arrived to pay their last respects. The Vatican Press Office was under constant siege by thousands of journalists, many of whom complained about the poor arrangements for the media. Among them was Andrew Greeley and the team from CREP. The organization had produced a book, The Inner Elite, *which supposedly indicated the 'mind set' of the cardinals who would vote in the coming Conclave. That very experienced Vatican observer, Peter Hebblethwaite, noted that the slim volume was 'riddled with errors, misleading statements and faulty deductions'. But it had sold out by Friday, when Rosalynn Carter and Senator Edward Kennedy made a late but opportune appearance. They got almost as much air time as Paul's will, which the Vatican released in time for the evening television news. The thirteen-page document confirmed the essential goodness and simplicity of the man. It ended with Paul's request for a simple funeral and a plea for pardons from all those he had harmed.*

11

Saturday's dawn reddens the sky, warning of another fiercely hot and humid day, as Macchi enters the Vatican by the tradesmen's entrance – the Porta Sant'Anna gate. It is symbolic of his new status. The former senior secretary is now just another priest, divested of the power to make or break a man's career. The Swiss Guards still salute him, but they need no longer fear he might find some small fault with their appearance as he has done in the past.

This morning Macchi is too preoccupied to notice how burnished are the guards' boots or how clean are their hands. His mind is on the days which have gone and the task ahead. The past week has etched haggard lines into his imperious face, leaving his eyes black-rimmed from exhaustion and grief. Macchi has hardly slept since Villot ordered him to find Paul's Fisherman's Ring. When he had done so the Camerlengo brusquely ordered Macchi to deliver the ring to the Sala Bologna. There, before the assembled cardinals, Villot split the ring with silver shears and shattered Paul's seals of office with the same hammer he had used to tap the forehead of the dead pope.

That had been on Wednesday. By then Macchi was in temporary accommodation, living in one of the poky rooms the Vatican always has available around Rome. He had hardly visited it. Instead, by special permission of Villot and under the express terms of Paul's will, the secretary had worked from dawn to midnight, when the closing of the Vatican gates drove him out, alone in the papal apartment.

Paul had appointed Macchi executor of his will. The handwritten document, surmounted by the papal coat of arms, was drawn up on 30 July 1965. Macchi could clearly remember the occasion. He had sat with Paul while the pope began to write: 'Some notes for my will. In the name of the Father and of the Son of the Holy Spirit. Amen.' The long list of clauses did not read like a last testament. They were more the thoughts of a man who, in that, the third year of his pontificate, was already preoccupied with death. Paul wanted to die *un povero*, a poor man. He wished his funeral to be 'pious and simple'. He requested no monument over his grave. 'Now that the day draws to its close and everything comes to an end and I must leave this wonderful and turbulent world, I thank you, Lord.' Buried in the will is the reason Macchi has been toiling these past two days in the eerie silence of the apartment he knows so well. Paul specially ordered in a codicil that Macchi destroy all personal notes and correspondence. Macchi was surprised to discover how great is the accumulation. The papers fill a stack of boxes. Unlike Paul's official papers, which will go to the Secret Archives, these private ones must remain undisclosed forever. They do not include the batch of confidential reports on Cody. Villot has confiscated these, telling Macchi they must be handed to the next pope. The Camerlengo regards them as a time-bomb, capable not only of destroying Cody, but also of rending the Church asunder.[1]

Macchi reaches the San Damaso Courtyard where two Vigilance security men wait with the boxes loaded on a trolley. The cartons have been guarded overnight in the old Vatican jail. In silence the men follow Macchi to an elevator. It takes them to the third floor warren of the Secretariat of State. There is nobody about at this early hour, which is why Macchi has chosen this time. The Vigilance wheel the trolley to a small room. It contains a large shredding machine. Macchi begins to feed in the very intimate thoughts of Paul; they come out the other end as unintelligible strips of paper. Even then Macchi is not satisfied. He orders the Vigilance to pack the waste into plastic sacks and have it burned.

Then the secretary leaves the Apostolic Palace for the last time. Now he has only one further act to perform. He slips through a side door and enters the vast nave of St Peter's Basilica. His shoes echoing on the stone floor, Macchi moves purposefully past some of the altars, the colonnades, the statue of St Peter whose right foot gleams from constant kissing by the faithful, the huge throne in the tribune with its ancient wooden chair said to have been sat on by the Apostle, the black and gold monument to Urban VIII teeming with Barberini's bees, the Virgin and Christ, the Pietà – past centuries of work by artisans of every skill. He eventually stops before the simple bier built by the *sampietrini* in their workshops behind St Peter's; they have also constructed the triple papal coffin – the inner is made of bronze, the second of cedar and the outer coffin is of cypress, the latter to symbolize the simplicity Paul has requested.

Paul lies in a red vestment over his white garments. The pallium Noé positioned with such loving care is precisely in place. A solitary Easter candle burns with a steady flame in the still air. The four Swiss Guards stand motionless.

Apart from them there is nobody to see Macchi kneel beside the bier and pray in silent farewell. Close to tears, he rises and walks slowly out of the Basilica, his mind settled. Even if asked, he will not work for the next pope. Instead he will take up pastoral duties. It is, Macchi feels, the best tribute he can pay to the memory of the man he loved and revered more than any other.

*

Greeley has concluded that Paul's lying in state reminds him of 'the King Tut exhibit in Chicago'. When he had viewed the pope's body on Thursday, it appeared to him 'very purple and pasty and corpselike'; the passing crowds, muses Greeley, showed 'lots of curiosity, but no sign of mourning or grief'. His latest observations are added to the rag-bag of impressions Greeley has gathered since arriving in Rome. It's been a busy time: some 'quick interviews' with those tantalizingly anonymous sources of his; a culling of the Italian media: the news magazines have all been quick off the mark but Greeley thinks it poor taste the way *Gente, Epoca, Oggi* and *Panorama* placed their papal obituaries cheek-by-jowl with more normal fodder – sexual confessions, nude photographs and auto-eroticism. He has been sniffing around the cardinals and come to the conclusion that the secrecy, the ban on explicit campaigning and the protocol which forbids cardinals divulging their real differences are all going to affect their decision-making.

Greeley's mysterious sources have served him well. Yet he is not happy. In fact he admits: 'I'm afraid I'm going to pieces. I've lost my glasses, I've walked out of the hotel without my wallet, I've forgotten phone numbers, and am in mortal terror of missing appointments.' It's nerves, of course, brought on by the thought that tomorrow, Sunday, he is going to unveil publicly his personally conceived, nurtured and so far jealously guarded blinding revelation – just what kind of pope the cardinals should choose if they wish to stay in good standing with Greeley.

*

One prince of the Church already knows Greeley's intentions. Long ago Cardinal John Cody found it expedient to add the name of the one-time priest in his diocese to the list of those of whom he likes to keep track. Cody sees nothing sinister in this. Greeley is a declared foe and the cardinal thinks it would be foolish not to keep abreast of an opponent's thinking. It is the way he has always operated and it has helped to make him what he is – the most powerful religious leader Chicago has ever had. Cody has seen the likes of Greeley come and go, yet for Cody the priest remains one more prick from his crown of thorns. The cardinal is already savouring the moment he will be asked to comment on CREP's proposals. That may well be the time for Cody to launch a carefully staged counter-attack against the insidious smears and aspersions which surround him. No reference to those accusations, naturally, just a short statement indicating CREP and its cohorts are trying to trivialize the Church. That will be enough. People can always read between the lines.

In any case, nobody but Cody knows the truth behind the accusations, and he has chosen – whether on advice or personal decision even his closest associates cannot be certain – to maintain total silence in face of the mounting storm. He knows reporters say he's trying to ride it out, that he is behaving like a maddened bull at the Chicago stockyards, almost demanding to be slaughtered at the first opportunity. This does not disturb Cody. People can go on complaining about him to Rome as long as they like; the Vatican can send as many emissaries as it wishes; Cody knows, in the end, there is little anyone can do. To sack him outright would create a scandal which could rip through the American Church, perhaps even cause a few figures to fall in the Vatican. This, too, he knows. So he's going to continue playing it his way. Greeley and his ilk, Cody is convinced, will simply run out of steam. The cardinal has seen it happen before. And besides, he is a master of the waiting game.

This Saturday morning Cody rises early in his private room in the palatial Villa Stritch, perhaps the finest in a row of fine mansions on the Via della Nocetta. He has slept soundly, shows no sign of jet lag and, since getting up, has been making telephone calls to his network of friends in the Vatican. He has sources in all the right places. With each one he gossips a bit, laughs a little, listens a lot. In a surprisingly short time he has a picture of what is happening. The funeral arrangements do not concern him: he assumes Villot and his functionaries have planned them down to the last amen.

Cody is interested in Conclave. He assures a friend in the Pontificio Collegio Irlandese – the Irish College out on Via Santa Quattro and traditionally a clearing house for such scuttlebutt – that the Americans want a Pope 'in the image of Paul', but preferably a non-Italian European who is 'definitely not Curial'. Cody's Irish contact suggests Hume of Westminster as a possibility. The cardinal asks whether his English colleague can speak Italian yet. Hardly a word. Certainly not fluently. Then, pronounces Cody, Hume has no chance: the Italians would never tolerate a Bishop of Rome who cannot speak their language. Does his Irish source know of any cardinal who has been taking a crash course in Italian? No, but he'll ask around.

More calls by Cody – who sees them all as the permissible 'consultation' allowed under Paul's rules – and he learns there is mounting concern among many of the non-Italian cardinals about the long delay before Conclave has been scheduled to start. The Italians are up to their old tricks, Cody is told, wanting to do what they are best at, preparing their ground at a leisurely pace before Conclave begins. Cody can interpret this two ways. It is just the Italians being Italian. Or the Curia thinks it has a potential deadlock on whom it wants to see succeed Paul; if that is the case, those in the Curia need all the time possible to do some very hard 'consulting' before the cardinals are locked up.

Cody calls Prefect Martin – with whom when in Rome he likes to mull over Vatican history and also gain some shrewd insights into how the immediate papal family is coping – and he says he favours the view that the Curia may be alarmed. They go on to speak of Cardinal Leo Suenens's recent revolutionary suggestion, the one Vatican Radio reported with the sort of raised inflection which mirrored the shock-wave felt throughout the Holy See at the Belgian's proposal that this time no less than four popes should be elected, one to be stationed in each quarter of the globe. Coming from anybody else the thought would have caused an even bigger reaction, but people are becoming used to hearing Suenens's radical ideas. He has also suggested the pope should no longer be chosen only by cardinals who, in any case, have no justification in scripture, but by a body more representative of the entire Church. Cody considers Suenens's opinions are immaterial, especially as he has ceased to be one of the driving forces in that faction the press have come to call 'European progressives'. Its members include Koenig, Willebrands of Utrecht and Marty of Paris. Suenens is said to have lost interest in their ideals since becoming an influential member of the charismatic movement. And Koenig himself has just made it clear, though not publicly, that he thinks he is too old to allow his name to go forward as a potential future pope.

Still more calls and Cody gets another slant on how the future could go: while he was flying the Atlantic, cardinals Sin, Hume and Lorscheider were having the first of what will become regular meetings – either in the English College or Lorscheider's room in the Latin American College – to see whether a loose coalition might be formed which would combine the voting power of South and Central America, the Caribbean, Asia and Africa. It could be a very powerful bloc. But who should get its vote in the crucial first ballot? Not even Martin is prepared to go that far.

Within a few hours of arriving in Rome Cody knows more than most curial cardinals about how the land really lies. He likes the look of it. It seems there will be some good old-fashioned politicking ahead – all in the name of 'consultation', naturally.

*

At noon the doors of the Basilica close behind the last of an estimated 250,000 persons who have filed past Paul's bier. Outside in St Peter's Square, on the balustrades of Bernini's colonnade, cameras of Italian television are positioned among the baroque statues of saints. The cameramen rehearse their shots. One pans across the frieze under the drum of the Basilica where letters six feet high proclaim in Latin: 'You are Peter and on this rock I will build my Church . . . I will give you the keys of the kingdom of heaven'. Another camera focuses on the great dome of St Peter's. A third looks down on the square itself where squads of *sampietrini* are setting out over nine thousand seats for the first outdoor funeral in the history of the papacy. A group of Americans have occupied some of the seats, bringing with them a cooler of soft drinks. On the marble steps of St Peter's, velvet-covered kneelers and chairs are placed for dignitaries of the Church and the secular world. The first of nearly ten thousand city of Rome police, *carabinieri* and squads of DIGOS, the anti-terrorist force, are in position. If the expected crowds materialize, there will be one policeman for every ten mourners. Though street vendors are barred for the day from the square, souvenir shops along the Via della Conciliazione are packed; any fake artifact connected with Paul is snapped up. More Pauline junk-mementos have probably been sold during the last five days than in the previous four years of his pontificate.

Elsewhere in the city, US senator Edward Kennedy of Massachusetts places a bouquet on the spot at the street corner where Aldo Moro was kidnapped and then stands silently for two minutes. The only sound is the click and whirr of still and film cameras and the nervous shuffling of the large police detail protecting Kennedy. At the American Embassy Mrs Carter talks to a CBS correspondent about her impressions and describes how the president's mother had prayed for rain in drought-stricken Africa when she had visited Paul at Castel Gandolfo, and how the pope told her he would die very soon.

It all seems so irrelevant.

*

Walking briskly, his soutane swishing softly in rhythm with his stride, Magee enters the Vatican through the Arch of the Bells and moves on into St Peter's through a side door. It is pleasantly cool inside the transept, and the barley-sugar columns of Bernini's *baldacchino*, ninety-five feet high, soar upwards towards the sixteen windows in the dome which filter the fierce sun and give a soft, almost surreal light to the scene Magee has come to observe.

He has no official responsibility here. This is in the hands of Villot and Noé. The secretary is present because, like Macchi, Magee wishes to say

114

a personal farewell to the man who most shaped his life. Outwardly, Magee is not an emotional or sentimental person. But the death of Paul, though he had expected it, has drained him. His is a deeply felt wrench and only his faith has been able to sustain him in genuine grief. Unlike so many who hardly knew the pope, Magee does not choose publicly to share his judgement of the man; it is something too private, this feeling that the world has lost a living saint.

At a nod from Villot, the *sediari*, who carried Paul on his portable throne throughout his pontificate, now lift his body off the bier and place it in the coffin. One of them drapes an ermine-coloured blanket over his body and covers the pope's face with a purple veil. Then the lid of the coffin is positioned and held in place by sixteen solid gold screws specially made in the Vatican workshops.

Magee turns and walks slowly from the Basilica. He does not know what his future will be. He does not much care. Besides, it is much too early to think of such things.

*

The cardinal who has built his reputation by trying to think of everything, Baggio, trouble-shooter by appointment to Paul, arrives in the early afternoon by car outside the imposing portico of the Sacred Congregation for Bishops, whose prefect he has been for five years, and hurries into the building. He has been spotted, of course; there is hardly a cardinal who can now safely move in the city without being observed by one of the tipsters who feed titbits to the army of reporters. And there are any number of good reasons for them to be interested in this squat, muscular man with a wrestler's broad shoulders and hands. Baggio is sixty-five and definitely *papabile*, a candidate for the papacy. He is also perfectly cast to play the role of pope-maker. He knows well everybody who matters, the majority of his fellow cardinals and all the most important bishops of the Church: he knows what they think, what they feel about each other; he knows their fears, ambitions, wishes and often their private desires. Acquiring such secrets is all part of his work as prefect. Nobody wants to be on the wrong side of Baggio. That is why he is so respected and courted.

Until now he has not been seen by the secular world since news leaked about his secret visit to Cody. But lurking in the corner of the Square of Pius XII, The Saviour of the City, dedicated to that pope's intercession to save Rome from being seriously bombed during World War II, the informer observes that Baggio is carrying a bulky briefcase. There is nothing unusual in this as Baggio is famous for taking with him wherever he goes the most secret papers he is working on; as part of his security system he also never receives visitors in his office for fear they

115

might see a confidential document momentarily removed from the safe behind his desk.

Yet in spite of these measures there is a mole in his ministry – as there are in so many Congregations – who, for money, regularly betrays some of the secrets Baggio labours to protect. And so, by this unsavoury route, details surface about the latest contents of Baggio's briefcase.

It is more pay-dirt on Cody. There are new and potentially explosive allegations about the long relationship the Chicago cardinal has had with a sixty-eight-year-old divorcee who, since at least 1967, has been a close companion of Cody's. He even brought her to Rome when he was made cardinal. The precise nature of their relationship has produced just the sort of speculation Baggio dreads. Cody and his friend constantly claim they are cousins. But Baggio now knows, after some discreet digging in Chicago – he has relatives in nearby Oak Park – that the couple are only distantly related through the remarriage of her father to Cody's aunt. And the woman has listed Cody's residence as her summer address. Worse, Cody arranged, when he was in St Louis, for her to draw $11,500 a year from the diocese; there is no evidence she did much work for this stipend. Finally, there is the allegation that Cody is diverting church funds into her private account; it is rumoured that as much as $1 million has gone in this way.

Nobody outside the Vatican knows whether Baggio put these charges to Cody when they met in Chicago. But they do exist. Yet for the moment Baggio must keep them in limbo. Baggio is many things: aggressive, witty, charming, uncompromising, cheerful and enlightened; he knows all about the 'human aspect' of life. Even so this 'Chicago affair' may be something else. He is sure the problem will not go away. It will be carried over into the next pontificate.

And that raises a question not even the prescient Baggio can possibly answer: how will the next pontiff react? Will he weigh it all against the wider effect the removal of Cody could have on the American Church as a whole? A scandal of this nature would assuredly draw worldwide publicity; the harm to the Universal Church could be incalculable. Might the decision be taken not to pursue the matter further? Holy See scandals have been hushed up before. Is this why Baggio, when he leaves the building and is driven off to prepare for Paul's funeral, has a deeply troubled look on his face?

These questions help the rumour mills grind away the last hours before the moment they, too, must fall silent in face of the awesome ceremony in St Peter's Square.

*

Vatican Radio's MacCarthy is one of a couple of hundred broadcasters working the square. Dressed in a black suit and Roman collar, toting a tape recorder, MacCarthy is slowly moving through the crowd gathering impressions, comments and assessments. He is tired, understandably so. Few broadcasters have made such an effort to immerse themselves in the action of the past week. MacCarthy has read almost everything available on papal wakes and funerals; he has found the work of his friend, Lambert Greenan in the English-language edition of *L'Osservatore Romano* most helpful. Greenan has just published a sympathetic and authoritative account of Paul's life and times. Commentators around the square are quoting the obituary.[2]

MacCarthy is preparing a pastiche of this climactic day so listeners down through Africa to the Cape of Good Hope will have a feeling for the mood in the square. He describes the scene: 'Perhaps as many as one hundred thousand persons, many dressed in black. But this is not merely a time of mourning. It is also a time for thoughtful consideration of the hope for eternal life. There is a mood of silent dignity.'

He moves through the crowd towards the white marble steps. Once more he speaks into his microphone: 'To all of us this scene is new. There has probably never been such an immense congregation for a Christian funeral. It is another reminder of all His Holiness stood for. He had always sought to meet his flock in the square on the great religious festivals of the year. He once said, "I will make this square an altar." And so he has.'

MacCarthy has now reached the edge of the steps leading up to the doors of St Peter's, open again. Away to his right he can see Rosalynn Carter and Imelda Marcos, wife of the president of the Philippines. Edward Kennedy is close by. Near him is the former Archbishop of Canterbury, Dr Michael Ramsey, and the Patriarch of Moscow. Around them are crowned heads of Europe and statesmen of the world. Delegations from over a hundred nations are here. Others can describe their dress and try to interpret the whispers and smiles they exchange; MacCarthy is more concerned to place in perspective what is about to happen: 'His Holiness requested in his will a simple and pious funeral. That has been faithfully adhered to. There is to be no catafalque, nothing to raise his coffin to public view. Instead it will be laid on the ground. It will be bare and unadorned, except for an open Bible. All this is another reminder of His Holiness – his very real wish to reduce as far as possible the symbols of pomp and power which used to characterize the papal court.'

*

Inside the Basilica the procession forms up. The cardinals are paired off according to seniority. Near the front is the primate of Poland, Stefan

Wyszynski, and Giuseppe Siri, each of whom has been a cardinal for a quarter of a century. Close behind follow the Canadian archbishop of Montreal and the patriarch of Alexandria in Egypt. Koenig is paired with the archbishop of Dar-es-Salaam. A little further back Cardinal John Carberry, the spunky seventy-four-year-old archbishop of St Louis, is close to the august figure of John Krol, Cardinal archbishop of Philadelphia. The lofty Krol and the diminutive Carberry will make a striking physical contrast for the commentators to seize upon. Another American, Cardinal Terence Cooke of New York, is behind the solid-looking Cardinal archbishop of Cracow, Karol Wojtyla, whose halting English Cooke does not always find easy to follow. Timothy Manning, Cardinal archbishop of Los Angeles, the only one in the entire procession who speaks Gaelic – he was born in Ballingeary, Co. Cork, sixty-nine years ago – is near with the patriarch of Venice, Cardinal Albino Luciani. Luciani bridges the conversational gaps with gentle little smiles. Manning instinctively likes this Italian – which is more than he can say for some of them. Cody is paired with Felici. They appear to have nothing to say to each other. If Cody's case ever reaches the stage where it must officially be examined by the Church, Felici, in his capacity as Prefect of the Apostolic Signatura, the highest court of appeal in the Church, will have to recommend judgement for the pope's final approval. Aramburu of Buenos Aires is in front of Sin of Manila. They have come to know and like each other over the years. Aramburu cannot conceal his relief that Argentina's junta leader, Videla, decided at the last moment not to attend the funeral; he has said he may come to the inauguration of the next pope. But that is at least three weeks away. And in the stormy atmosphere of South American politics, anything can happen in the interval. Baggio and Bertoli make another pair. They are outwardly affable.

*

MacCarthy holds the microphone close to his lips to ensure his words are not drowned by the singing: 'The chair-bearers are carrying Pope Paul's coffin down the steps and lying it directly in front of the altar. One of the many new features of this Mass is that the cardinals will concelebrate it around the altar. Now they come. The last one, a tall, handsome man, is Cardinal Confalonieri. He will be the main celebrant in today's Mass. He is wearing a slightly different-coloured robe from the others. Theirs are purple. But his is a bright scarlet – the special colour of his office as Dean.'

MacCarthy has just time to say that the Mass proper is beginning when the amplified voice of Confalonieri intones the words of the *confiteor*, the prayer for God's forgiveness of sins.

During the brief pause which follows Bible readings in various languages, MacCarthy has time to explain that Confalonieri will next deliver the homily in Latin. MacCarthy lets the first flowing phrases roll before beginning faultlessly to translate them. He describes the procession which brings bread and wine to the altar for consecration while the choir sings the offertory hymn, Psalm 17. The broadcaster then lets the actual sound of this very solemn moment of the Mass speak for itself.

*

Koenig has been standing almost two hours in heavy vestments in a temperature of over eighty degrees. He is a fit man, but wonders what the heat is doing to some of the more elderly cardinals. It cannot be easy for them. Then, as the offertory procession returns to the altar, Koenig notices something he will never forget: a gentle breeze has begun to ruffle the open Bible on Paul's coffin; slowly the pages begin to turn. Koenig thinks it symbolic – almost as uncanny as the moment Paul's alarm clock rang the instant he died.

*

MacCarthy once more slips in a few sentences to link the singing of the Litany of the Saints with the closing prayers and the slow procession of the cardinals past either side of the coffin. Then Confalonieri himself describes the final stage of the funeral. In halting English he explains: 'The pope now enters for the last time the Vatican Basilica where so often he celebrated the Eucharist and addressed his word to the Church. The remains of His Holiness will be laid to rest in the tomb in the Vatican crypt. There he will remain in the gentle presence of a Madonna gracefully sculpted by Donatello to await his resurrection in glory.'

The moon is rising over the Janiculum Hill, picking out a line of cypress trees, as the choir sing the Magnificat and Paul's coffin, the pages of the Bible still slowly turning, is carried back up the steps to the tolling of the bells of St Peter's.

Moments later the doors of the Basilica are shut.

MacCarthy's microphone catches the sound. And around him the speculation is renewed: which of all the cardinals who have spent the past one hundred and fifty-nine minutes burying Paul, will next emerge on the balcony above these doors as pope?

PART TWO

THE WILL
OF GOD

*If this is the way God ordained it,
  so it must be*

— old Arabic saying

12

This, they will say, is how it was.

For six weeks Agca led a peaceful life, spending his days for the most part in the company of other men in the tea-room of Yesiltepe. They spoke about the Anarchy, the official executions, the reprisals. But nobody can remember Agca displaying any strong views on the terrorism infesting Turkey. He seemed to be a man apart.

At home he was cheerful, wrestling with Adnan and joking with Fatma that she must not eat so much if she wanted to keep her figure. He was a model elder brother. One day he had delighted his mother, Muzzeyene, by returning home with two cooking pots. He planted them proudly on the table before her, grinning, but not saying how he came by them. His mother did not ask; she wished to do nothing to disturb the tranquil domestic atmosphere which had helped to make bearable the furnace-like heat of Malatya province in the middle of summer. That night she cooked him bean curd in one of the pots. He ate a double helping, and there was some gentle joshing from Fatma and Adnan about Agca's new-found appetite. Muzzeyene could not remember being more happy. Allah, she felt, was at last listening to all those prayers she had offered up to him.

And thus it continued until this Saturday evening.

Agca is not a television viewer; too many of the programmes are imported from the America he hates, but he recognizes the pleasure some of them give to his mother and Fatma – they especially like soap operas – and so he tolerates the set in the corner of the living room. Normally, out of deference to his views, they wait until he leaves the house before turning it on and giggling over the antics of *Lucy* and *Sergeant Bilko*.

Tonight, though, Agca has decided to remain at home. Muzzeyene, sensitive to such matters, detects a familiar restlessness in her son; it is there in the way he abstractedly bites his lip and digs his fingers into the palms of his hands. She hopes it's just a passing phase and not the onset of another full-scale depression.

Thinking it might distract him, and knowing his interest in world

123

events – or so he has often told her – she switches the set on for the late evening news.

Flickering across the screen is a short clip of the funeral of Paul in Rome.

Agca's reaction startles his mother. He leaps to his feet, switches off the set with a violence which threatens to topple it from its table, and stands facing his family, screaming. They do not understand his horrifying rage. He looks and sounds like a man possessed. Suddenly, he starts to howl like an animal. It is the call of the Grey Wolves. Still howling, he runs to his room.

None of them can remember ever seeing Agca behaving like this. Both Adnan and Fatma are frightened by their brother's behaviour. After a time Muzzeyene manages to calm them. By then the howling has died away. She moves to stand outside Agca's bedroom door. Now she can hear him steadily chanting. She is relieved. Agca is going through his hate list. Though she does not know the word, Muzzeyene feels it must be therapeutic for him.

Next morning, at the customary hour of 4.30, she awakens, expecting to hear Agca reciting *sourates*, the first Koran prayer of the day. Instead, there is not a sound coming from his room.

She checks. During the night Agca has silently slipped away.

Muzzeyene is a practical woman; there is no point worrying where he has gone. He has done this before. On these occasions Muzzeyene has her own routine to follow. She enters his room to see what he has taken. The Mauser and bullets are no longer in the cigar box. This does not unduly disturb her. Her son always carries the weapon and ammunition on him when he leaves home. Muzzeyene does not like the idea, but she has come to accept he is entitled to protect himself; he lives in a violent world, she rationalizes, where it is often kill or be killed.

She checks whether anything else has been removed. Everything seems to be in order. She looks again at the shelf of books. Muzzeyene can hardly read or write, and it is a source of pride to her that Agca has more books on this shelf than are in all the other houses of Yesiltepe combined. She is careful not to touch them; she knows every book has its specially designated place in the collection. Only Agca knows why. If he were to discover she had been in his room during his absence, Muzzeyene feels it could destroy the close bond between them. She studies the spines of the books. They all seem in place. Yet she senses something is wrong. Muzzeyene counts the books, saying the numbers aloud, the way a child or semi-literate counts.

There are none missing.

Her eyes continue to search the shelf. And then, at last, she realizes.

The exercise book beneath the empty cigar box – the one filled with all those photographs and stories about the old holy man of the infidels who has just died – is no longer there.

Muzzeyene wonders why her son has taken it with him.[1]

13

She screams at Greeley that he is evil and has sexual problems. He responds that the data on sexual attitudes he has been discussing come from 'sample research', not personal experience. Inwardly he thinks having sexual problems is part of the human condition, but that this woman would surely never cause him any. She is 'wild-eyed', young, Italian, and has 'Catholic Action written all over her'. She is also one of the two hundred or so journalists attending Greeley's press conference to unveil his 'job description' of a pope. It is Greeley and CREP's big moment, and they are milking it for all its sociological worth, claiming the job description 'a contribution of significance to the Church and the cardinal electors'.

The reporters scribble furiously as Greeley advances the idea that it does not matter whether the next pope is a curial cardinal or a non-curial cardinal, whether he is Italian or not, whether he is from the First, Second or Third World, whether he is an intellectual or non-intellectual, a diplomat or a pastor, progressive or moderate, an efficient administrator or lacking in administrative experience, a 'liberation' theologian or a traditional theologian, or how he regards the political issues facing the world.

Barely pausing for breath, in full talk-show stride, well aware of the headlines he is bound to attract, Greeley continues that 'doubtless someone in the papal entourage must be an efficient administrator, someone must be a theologian, someone must be a diplomat, someone must be a pastor, someone must understand Italy, someone must be sensitive to the Third World, someone must know how the Roman Curia runs and how it can be brought under control' – a well-timed pause to see how that little broadside has gone over – and then on to the nub of his case: it is not necessary for the pope to have any of these abilities; men with such talents can be found to assist him, consequently they are not needed for the 'top position in the Catholic Church'.

Greeley has this knack of talking the language of the tabloids, of reducing some of the most complex issues of the religious world to a few pithy sentences. He delivers them. 'At the present critical time in its history, faced with the most acute crisis, perhaps, since the Reformation and dealing with a world in which both faith and community are desperately sought, the papacy requires a man of holiness, a man of hope, a man of joy; a sociologically oriented job description of the pope, in other words, must conclude that the Catholic Church needs as its leader a holy man who can smile.'

That screaming Italian reporter is not the only one at Greeley's throat. He is accused of trying to merchandise the pope, of attacking the Church, of attempting mass-media manipulation. He fights back, mentally labelling his attackers as 'pietists and paranoids'. Insults are traded. Greeley, throwing caution completely to the wind, says he is not even against a woman pope. 'A *papessa* could not make more of a mess of the Church than we men have over the last 1900 years.'

Inevitably, the attitude of American Catholics to *Humanae Vitae* is raised; it's a running sore everybody likes to pick. Greeley snaps that the fault lies with the Church: 'If an organization fails to communicate, it must assume that *it* has failed, not that the *people* have failed.' It's a good note to end on – and another headline for tomorrow. He leaves the press conference, the screams of the wild-eyed young Italian fixed in his mind, convinced she and the rest of the Italian media 'will murder us tomorrow; however, it doesn't make much difference'.

Precisely. Greeley and CREP are up and running. It's the sort of stage-managing even Cody, no slouch in such matters, must reluctantly admire. But Cody has decided this is not the time to launch a counter-campaign against Greeley's attacks. He is going to ignore them.

*

Vatican Radio and *L'Osservatore Romano* disregard the wire service reports of Greeley's press conference. Nowadays staff on each of these Vatican organs, in addition to their usual work, are going about the delicate and difficult task of deciding who should be placed on a realistic short list of *papabili*. There are, by this Wednesday, 16 August, any number of such lists on offer in Rome; one even presents the entire membership of the College of Cardinals, one hundred and thirty, ignoring the fact that fifteen have reached the age of eighty and are consequently barred from voting under Paul's *Eligendo*, three have not come to Rome owing to ill-health and one is seriously sick in the city after suffering a heart attack during Paul's funeral; it is highly unlikely any of these nineteen cardinals absent from Conclave would be chosen as pontiff. The remaining one hundred and eleven cardinal electors are now preparing for Conclave.

It is from this number that Lambert Greenan is attempting to narrow the choice to a dozen or so names. Each editor in the other language sections of *L'Osservatore Romano* is doing the same. Later the names on these confidential lists will be compared and a final master list of most-favoured possible popes drawn up. Special biographies will then be prepared on each cardinal chosen, and a portrait, either from photographer Luigi Felici's files or from the newspaper's extensive picture library, will be selected. An entire series of newspaper editions will be set in advance, each featuring a different candidate. When the name of the next pope is telephoned to *L'Osservatore Romano*, the correct plate will be locked onto the paper's presses and in minutes a special edition will be on sale in St Peter's Square. That is the theory. The success of the operation depends entirely on accurate prediction at this early stage.

There are few better on the paper's staff for this job than Father Greenan. Long ago, during the days he worked in the Secretariat of State, Greenan learned the rules of Vatican secrecy; consequently, people trust him. They tell him all sorts of things they would never mention to others. He is a receptacle for information on the strengths and weaknesses of those he is now trying to assess.

Greenan looks first at the likeliest source for a new pope – the European cardinals. Fifty-seven of them are eligible to vote. He soon discounts a number of names. Frantisek Tomasek of Czechoslovakia is not only too old at seventy-eight but would also be too daring a choice. Paul made him a cardinal *in pectore*, secretly, not publicly revealing Tomasek's appointment for an entire year for fear of disturbing the delicate *Ostpolitik* of Casaroli. The Czechs have not liked that; they would resent even more Tomasek sitting on the Throne of St Peter. Antonio Ribeiro, patriarch of Lisbon, is, at fifty, simply too young, even though his career suggests that in the 1990s, should there be a Conclave, he could be a serious candidate: he was co-president of the 1977 Synod of Bishops and his fundamental theology is impeccable. For the reason Greenan ruled out Tomasek he now rejects Alfred Bengsch, bishop of West Berlin for the past seventeen years and an implacable opponent of the Wall and Communism. Bengsch, muses Greenan, will probably end his days in the city he was born in and to which he returned after being wounded and captured by the Americans at Normandy in 1944, afterwards becoming a priest and then cardinal in 1967.

There are four other German cardinals. The most powerful, without doubt, is the forbidding archbishop of Cologne, seventy-one-year-old Joseph Hoeffner. He is tough, acerbic and conservative; he learned his theology from Pius XII – nothing wrong with that, but is it what the Church now wants? Would the Americans go with such deeply traditional thinking? Hoeffner is involved – something the Vatican never likes – in fighting Hans Küng. Küng, in Greenan's view, is wrong: he has a mandate from Rome to teach what Rome approves; that is the end of the matter. But for Hoeffner to pursue the fight publicly is something else. Greenan passes over Hoeffner to the next German.

Joseph Ratzinger, the fifty-one-year-old archbishop of Munich has a career which bears the hallmark of a churchman going places. Almost single-handed, he revitalized the German Church in the post-war years, driving himself and others with uncharacteristic Bavarian energy. He recognized that the real challenge lay with the youth: he taught dogmatic theology in Bonn, Münster, Tübingen and Regensburg. His classes were packed. It seemed only natural that Ratzinger should be a *peritus*, expert adviser, to Vatican II. But there are problems. Ratzinger is not only young but speaks Italian with a thick German accent. He is also cast in the image of Paul – scholarly, reticent, hardly a charismatic figure. Yet Greenan puts a query against the Bavarian's name; he will look again at it later after he has reflected further.

Joseph Schroffer, the seventy-five-year-old West German curial cardinal is a non-starter; apart from the age factor Schroffer has been tucked away for much of his life in the Congregation for Catholic Education; important work, certainly, but a post which doesn't offer the breadth of experience a pope ideally needs. Hermann Volk, bishop of Mainz, is seventy-four and unless Greenan is seriously mistaken, Conclave will not be looking for a caretaker pope who will simply keep the Throne of St Peter warm for a few years while some of the younger cardinals establish their worth.

The Spanish have four cardinals. A very definite possibility is the shrewd and personable archbishop of Madrid, Enrique y Tarancon. He is not only the acknowledged leader of the Spanish Church, he has done more than any other Spanish cardinal to lessen the chains which fettered the country's Catholics under Franco. More important, he is in good standing with the Curia and, during the Second Vatican Council, displayed brilliant strategy in a number of crucial debates. Enrique y Tarancon has the ability to reach both progressives and conservatives. His age, seventy-one, engaging personality, command of Italian, understanding of Latin America and the need for the European and American Churches to build bridges there – all these go towards ensuring the Spaniard is *papabile*.

Greenan discounts the next two Spanish cardinals, Bueno y Monreal of Seville and Gonzales Martín of Toledo – both are virtually unknown outside their own hierarchy – and hesitates over Jubany Arnau, archbishop of Barcelona. He teaches law at a local seminary and at sixty-five is in the right age-bracket. He has a good reputation with his priests and knows how to deliver a sermon. But in the end Arnau is also ruled out. There are so many better possibilities.

The Dutch, despite what's been written in recent months in the Italian secular press, still have, in Greenan's view, a strong contender in Jan Willebrands. It is not just that he is so widely admired and respected: the man has style. Everything Willebrands does has a natural polish about it. And he learned about the Roman Curia's methods from the legendary Cardinal Bea, the scholarly Jesuit who was private confessor to Pius XII: if Bea was alive now, he might have a real chance of being chosen pope by acclamation – that rare occasion in Conclave when one cardinal proposes a name and all others accept it at once, so avoiding any balloting. Willebrands is unlikely to achieve that, but he goes on Greenan's list.

Reluctantly he rules out Bernard Alfrink, who retired three years ago from the Utrecht archbishopric which Willebrands inherited. Alfrink is a cautious liberal; he knew how to keep a tight rein on Utrecht and has never let the Curia control him. But he is too old, a shaky seventy-eight. It is virtually the same for the last Dutchman, Cardinal Maximilian de Furstenberg. He had been an apostolic diplomat most of his working life before taking over as prefect of the Sacred Congregation for Oriental Churches; de Furstenberg directed this sensitive body brilliantly. Eventually, though, he had found the strain too much and retired. A good and worthy man, his time for high office appears to be over.

Greenan works on steadily, weighing and judging. There is still a long way to go, over one hundred cardinals to assess. He must spend many hours poring over confidential files, searching his memory, telephoning the right persons and holding the sort of cryptic conversations he is renowned for, then thinking some more – all to help him guess 'which way the Holy Spirit may be thinking'.

Even for the ebullient and very confident editor it is a testing challenge.

*

The Lancia 2000 with the Venetian registration draws no attention in Rome; there are a thousand cars like it on the streets of this city, in spite of Rome being gripped in *ferragosto*, the period when everybody who can escapes from the enervating August heat. The Lancia's driver is actually a confidential secretary, Diego Lorenzi. He is only thirty-nine but looks older from the effects of the exhausting past eleven days he has spent chauffeuring the man he is devoted to, and who sits beside him in the car, a sign of their close and informal relationship: Cardinal Albino Luciani, the sixty-five-year-old patriarch of Venice.

Daily, at all hours, Lorenzi has fetched the car from a garage and brought it to the Augustinian College near the Vatican where he and Luciani have modest rooms. He has driven the patriarch to one meeting after another. Luciani is determined to consult with every cardinal voter possible before Conclave, exploring with each his views on which way the Church should be going. This is typical of the patriarch; he is dedicated to preparatory work. He says it makes it so much easier to come to the right decision in the end.

Sometimes the meetings continue late into the night. Yet Luciani always manages to smile as he leaves, a full-scale boyish grin which lights up his face, sheds years from it and makes him look almost impish. The smile is his trademark, as recognizable as Cody's back-thumping, Pericle Felici's nervous shuffle and Hume of Westminster's languid good manners.

Only later, when Lorenzi has helped Luciani to his room and there is no one to see them, does the patriarch slump on his bed and admit the pain in his legs is at times almost unbearable. He suffers from phlebitis, a painful circulatory disease that is an off-shoot from the four minor heart attacks Luciani has had during the past fifteen years. None have been serious and his doctor in Venice has assured him he has made a complete recovery. Inevitably though, those attacks and the phlebitis have exacted their toll; as a result Luciani's overall health is not robust. And he is a worrier. This, in part, is why he is taking these soundings among his fellow cardinals: he wants to know how the Holy Spirit – the Word of God which is supposed to 'guide the spirit' of each cardinal – may be directing them.

Luciani has kept secret from the Vatican his physical condition. He feared that if Paul had heard about it, he might have suggested he gave up his duties. For a man whose life is dedicated to his ministry, such a prospect was unthinkable. His secret is safe with Lorenzi; the ties between them are as close as those of brothers. The secretary, in turn, does everything he can to ease Luciani's physical path. He insists the patriarch watches his intake of pasta and wine and that he soaks his feet twice a day in the herbal preparation Luciani's housekeeper, Sister Vincenza, has obtained. The remedy is from the Dolomites where Luciani and Vincenza were born. She swears the elixir works. The sophisticated Lorenzi is not so certain. But he will approve anything which may make his employer more comfortable.

The Lancia eases through the noonday traffic this Thursday, 17 August, and stops outside the Collegio Pio Latino on the Via Aurelia. Luciani has come here to lunch with the Latin American cardinals, many of whom he knows well: Venetians have traditionally emigrated to South America, and the migrants often have settling-in problems which require Luciani's intercession. The patriarch has brought each cardinal a gift – a signed copy of his book, *Illustrissimi*, a series of make-believe letters Luciani has written to famous authors and characters in history or fiction.

Lorenzi carries the books while Cardinal Aramburu of Buenos Aires, an old friend, leads the patriarch inside. Eighteen cardinals await in the college's main reception room, the entire South and Central American contingent. Their presence in force is a tribute to Luciani. Like him they are dressed in simple black cassocks, the only symbols of rank their scarlet skullcaps. Luciani seems to have a problem keeping his in place; it is frequently askew at an almost raffish angle. The effect, combined with his infectious grin, makes him look more than ever a cheeky schoolboy.

His secretary tactfully manoeuvres Luciani to a chair. From there the patriarch distributes the books, nodding happily at the obvious pleasure the gifts create.

Aramburu, while knowing the story well, for the benefit of his fellow cardinals asks Luciani how he came to write the letters in *Illustrissimi*. And Luciani, who has answered the question often, does so now as if for the first time. It is another of his endearing, almost child-like qualities. The reason he gives is engagingly simple, yet holds important truths for all of those present. 'When I preach in St Mark's, I may have a few hundred listeners. Half of them are tourists who do not understand Italian, and the other half are wonderful people but they are . . . well, getting on in years.' He pauses, smiling. 'Then the editor of *Messagero di San Antonio* said to me that if I wrote for him, my audience would increase a thousandfold. I was convinced.'

There are appreciative chuckles. *Illustrissimi*, Luciani says modestly, is only the result of his desire to reach a wider audience. While doing so, he has frequently used a celebrated name merely as an excuse to develop a serious moral or religious point. He reveals how his simulated letter to the English dramatist, Christopher Marlowe, who wrote *Doctor Faustus*, gave him the opportunity to talk about the Devil. His listeners nod, captivated by the technique. When he penned his letter to Goethe he was actually exploring the question of *noblesse oblige* in the present-day cinema. His essay to Chesterton was a warning that progress when confined only to materialism could lead mankind to catastrophe.

Luciani explains it is his way of bringing theology to the masses, to try and bolster their faith by relating the Gospel to people and events which everyone can grasp.

The lesson is well received. Aramburu leads the guest of honour into lunch where much of the table-talk is about having *Illustrissimi* translated into other languages.

Aramburu also thinks that 'this fine and wonderful man could be a good pope'. Such thoughts, of course, do not surface now. They are for later.

The Argentinian does not notice what Lorenzi has seen. Under the table Luciani is using one leg to massage the back of the other. It's a bad sign. It means the pace is once more beginning to affect the patriarch. The secretary is glad it will soon be over and he can drive his beloved cardinal back to the comparative quiet of Venice.[1]

*

MacCarthy's office in Vatican Radio – a large corner one on the third floor, its size and position indicating his importance in the station – has a wall map of Africa. It reminds MacCarthy, if ever he needs reminding, of the vastly disparate potential audience he broadcasts to every day. There are Boers and bushmen, jungle tribesmen and desert dwellers; often suspicious or even hostile to each other, they all trust MacCarthy to tell them the truth. For many he also provides almost their only contact with the English language. He never preaches but tries always to inform. For the past twelve days MacCarthy has been preparing his listeners for Conclave.

This Friday evening, 18 August, he is devoting part of his broadcast to describing what is a cardinal. MacCarthy carefully explains that the word came from the Latin, *cardo*, a hinge, indicating the pivotal importance cardinals have in the affairs of the Church. Although the title of cardinal goes back well over a thousand years, it was not until 1150 that the Sacred College of Cardinals – consisting of cardinal bishops, cardinal priests and cardinal deacons – came into being. Since 1179 the Sacred College has had the exclusive right to elect the pope. In 1945, Pius XII began to select his cardinals from all over the world. His successors have followed this practice. The aim of the Church is to have each Christian nation represented by a member of the College. Paul decreed that the number of cardinals entitled to vote must not exceed one hundred and twenty. He never disclosed his reason.

MacCarthy pauses, aware his unseen audience needs time to absorb what he's said. Then he continues, describing how a cardinal is created. It begins, says MacCarthy, when the pope declares the appointment during a secret consistory, a meeting with the cardinals who reside permanently in Rome. Afterwards, the promotion is generally made known at a public consistory. And it is then the pope sometimes also announces he has created one or more cardinals *in pectore*, which MacCarthy translates as 'in his breast'. He explains: 'This means their names are not publicly revealed. Such cardinals date their seniority from the moment they are nominated *in pectore*, but all their other privileges begin only on the day their names are revealed. If the pope should die before divulging their names, their promotion is void.'

Once more he pauses. he briefly wonders how many letters he will receive asking which living cardinals began *in pectore*. MacCarthy has his reply ready: so far as is known, only Tomasek of Czechoslovakia and Trinh Van Can of Vietnam were elevated this way.

He carries on, explaining that a cardinal has numerous legal and other privileges including the right to use mitre and crosier, 'to celebrate Mass pontifically and to be judged by none other but the pope'. Temporally, a cardinal ranks 'with the princes of reigning houses'. Yet cardinals possess no constitutional rights under the absolute government of the papacy and cannot even meet together without the pope's permission. A cardinal may resign, but he can only be deprived of his title for the gravest of reasons.

MacCarthy goes on to say that in the unlikely event of some nomad in Central Africa coming unexpectedly upon a cardinal, the proper form of address is 'Eminence' or 'Your Eminence'; the style 'Most Reverend Lord' is, suggests MacCarthy *sotto voce*, perhaps a little old-fashioned these days. Before the broadcast ends, he deftly slips in 'God's commercial', reminding his listeners that a person of such 'eminence' can be as humble as a parish priest, 'but I imagine he has a greater cross to bear'.

*

In common with everyone in the Pontifical Household, its prefect, Jacques Martin, is temporarily at least, out of work. He expects he will be reappointed by the next pope. But nothing is certain. In the meantime he is doing a good deal of thinking and listening.

Martin is not alone in wanting to know which way the wind is blowing. And there is, he is prepared to concede, a lot of interesting chaff flying around. He is not going to say exactly how much reliance he puts on some of it – probably very little – but he doesn't dismiss altogether what secular spectators are saying: Conclave will be marked by the presence of many great electors, the euphemism applied to those cardinals who wield the most influence.

Koenig is widely held to be one. Enrique y Tarancon is another. Baggio, Benelli, Bertoli – given they don't think they themselves are in with a chance for the Throne of St Peter – will each doubtless be influential. But none of these names is new to an old hand like Martin. He is more interested in some of the other cardinals on offer as decision-makers.

There is Aloisio Lorscheider. He is fifty-three, too young to become pope unless there is a startling reversal of what has historically been the case. Martin is not altogether surprised the name of the Brazilian archbishop is being put forward by the tabloids as 'a pope-maker', a phrase the prefect detests. Lorscheider's reputation has gone far beyond the remote corners of the world where he has his diocese. He is a superb theologian and was relator-general of the 1977 Synod of Bishops. Paul was much impressed by him – now not necessarily a help in the pre-Conclave mood shaping up. But Lorscheider could emerge as a decisive influence on his fellow Latin Americans and perhaps even the Asians.

Nor is Martin surprised to see the name of Sin of Manila being toyed with; nobody is even remotely suggesting he could become pope, yet Sin's record as a campaigner for human rights, his desire to see the Church more involved in such issues, his astute sense of political timing – all are helping make him potentially an important elector.

And there is Gantin, whose behaviour during the funeral Mass for Paul deeply impressed Martin. There can be little doubt almost every African cardinal will continue to 'consult' with Gantin. As Chairman of the Commission for Justice and Peace, he is a curial cardinal. He knows the ropes, who is pulling where – and whether that pull can be sustained.

Martin has his own favourite – naturally – but only he knows who. It is almost forty years since he came to work in the city-state. He has experienced its history and is familiar with most of the worthwhile secrets of the period. He has kept all the really good ones to himself. That's how some people survive in the Vatican – acquiring precious information but never revealing it; around the Apostolic Palace it's called 'heavenly insurance'. The saying goes that the man who knows too much will never be dispensed with; popes come and go but shrewd old retainers like Martin remain securely in their niches.

This Saturday evening, 19 August, Martin has invited Macchi to dinner, the last time they will meet before the secretary leaves Rome.

What they discuss remains their secret. The very fact they have chosen to spend this time together – when at least Martin could expect any number of other invitations to dinner for, after all, the prefect of the Casa Pontificia is an invaluable sounding-board for the possibilities being endlessly discussed – will ferment yet further speculation. Are they planning in some way to use their years of prestige under Paul to influence the choice of his successor? Are they casting themselves in the role of spiritual godfathers about to call in past favours? Are they preparing to float one of those little initiatives, watch it climb and drift over the Vatican walls and then see where it will eventually settle? All –

at least for the record – nonsense of course. But the questions are almost as interesting as the fact that they are never answered. The entire scenario fits in very well with the way it is as the first week of the interregnum closes.

14

During the next four days important questions began to be aired about the kind of pope the Church now needed. Ten Catholic theologians, including Hans Küng, issued a joint statement, Open Letter to Conclave, *which was the most determined effort to date to influence its deliberations.*

Arguing that not only was the world divided into hostile power blocs and political systems, estranged races and classes, but pointing out that Christianity was itself split into various ideologies, the Open Letter *stated that if the Catholic Church was 'truly united', it could perform a significant service by helping to diminish these tensions and differences. This could only be achieved by choosing the right sort of pope: he should be open to the world, a spiritual leader, an authentic pastor, a true fellow bishop, an oecumenical mediator, a genuine Christian, a pope who would above all overcome the conflicts and contradictions which had left even the Universal Church often hopelessly divided. In short, he ought to be a pope of reconciliation, one open to 'the signs of the times and the changing attitudes of men'. This was taken to mean looking again at* Humanae Vitae.

He should, wrote the theologians, 'encourage others rather than merely scolding and admonishing. He should not be authoritarian, but he should possess real authority in his office. What he needs is not only a formalistic, official and institutional, but also a personal, objective and charismatic authority'. This was seen as dancing on Paul's tomb.

There was a resounding call for an end to the 'outmoded curial style', for positive guidance rather than prohibition in all the decisive questions affecting life and death and good and evil, including 'those matters where human sexuality is involved'. This was interpreted as a cry for contraception for Catholics and the removal of the Church's ban on divorce.

There was a demand for real power-sharing between the papacy and the Synod of Bishops. This was seen as a second jig on the Pauline pontificate.

There was insistence that the next pope exercise his moral authority with objectivity, that he take seriously the spiritual relationship with the Jews and activate that 'which we share in common with Islam', and also make room in the Church's teachings for more than traditionalist theology. That was taken as Küng being traditionally Küng.

The blueprint sparked off other issues. There was an appeal for the next pope to commission serious research into the workings of the Curia, to analyse exactly what was going on in the central organization of the Church, to unravel the levels at which the greatest power lay. There should be studies of Church officials, 'an analysis of the social background, ideology, financial investment and social interaction of holders of authority in the Church': that is how one of the many sociologists in Rome to observe the run-up to Conclave saw the situation. He was understood to mean that such a survey might reveal whether those who ran the Church had much in common with its members.

Everything added up to a call for change, a radical and dramatic switch in direction during which the papacy was asked to take stock and, confident of its unique heritage, to make the fullest use of its spiritual power, recognize the need for proper collegial participation, become less monarchical and more pastoral, loosen the mantle of tradition for tradition's sake – while never forgetting the adage that the man who married the spirit of the time soon found himself a widower.

Not surprisingly, no immediate name sprang to mind who could fill this role of religious superstar.

Instead, an extremist fringe, two broadly-based pressure groups, and a London bookmaker emerged, reducing what Küng intended as a means of settling the very future of the Catholic Church to more malleable proportions. The reporters, running out of specifics, were grateful: there was not much sense repeating that the cardinals were still meeting secretly every morning in the Sala Bologna to rubber-stamp decisions taken by Villot to keep the Church ticking over; or to rehash the boring biographies of cardinals given out by the Vatican Press Office, which was about all it did provide; or to try to make sense of the more obtuse articles in L'Osservatore Romano which suggested that the Holy Spirit, and nothing else, was already hovering over every cardinal elector; or to attempt to interpret the sermons some of those cardinals gave in the city's churches – should they be taken at their surface banality or was there an inner meaning to be gleaned from the preaching?

Ladbrokes, the London bookmakers, tried to make it easier to spot the winner by opening a book on who would be the next pope. A Roman Catholic member of parliament complained that the Church was 'electing a successor to Jesus Christ and that is not a matter for Ladbrokes'. In reply the bookmakers claimed to have 'a lot of clergymen laying bets'. The current odds placed Pignedoli at 5–2, favourite; Baggio and Poletti, 7–2; Benelli, 4–1; Willebrands, 8–1; Pironio, 12–1; Koenig, 16–1; Hume, 25–1; Cordeiro, Lorscheider and Suenens, 33–1.

One thing was certain: the radical element was everywhere evident in Rome. An organization called Civiltà Cristiana – so far out on the religious right wing some of its members even questioned whether Lefèbvre wasn't really a liberal – was rushing around the city sticking up posters: ELECT A CATHOLIC POPE. And Lefèbvre finally declared himself, saying he would 'reject in advance a pope *who was elected by a Conclave which excluded the over-eighties'; indeed, thundered the cantankerous archbishop from his Swiss mountain eyrie, the Conclave was anyway invalid because it did not allow these older cardinals to vote. Lefèbvre deemed this part of Paul's 'deviations' which had allowed the Church to become influenced by Marxist and Masonic infiltrators. The extreme left also saw Conclave as little more than a farce. One former Benedictine monk told a press grateful for every little sensation that Conclave was actually the secret stage 'where the psycho-drama of Christian alienation is being played out'. Nobody asked what* that *meant.*

While the religious buffoons had their moments, the two main pressure groups were making their views known. The conservatives were led by Felici, who spoke darkly of 'past blunders' – which turned out to mean vacillation over birth control, the ordination of married men and, even worse, the possible ordination of women, on which a special commission had been working before Paul died. Felici argued all this had helped pave the way for an increasing number of priests to give up the ministry, for religious to become laicized; oecumenism, he pronounced in a voice some said would have frightened a covey of devils, had gone too far, while talk of trying to understand Marxism made the Church seem an ally of the revolution. Felici, perhaps recognizing he was virtually unelectable for holding such intransigent views, was promoting – the word used, of course, was 'consulting' – two candidates. One was Giuseppe Siri, archbishop of Genoa. That was not very surprising; Siri faithfully reflected his sponsor's attitudes: he saw red in more ways than one. Felici's second choice was a surprise. With Koenig now out of the running – he had let that much become public, though as Ladbrokes' book showed, it no way lengthened the odds against him – Felici had started to support Baggio as well, in case Siri stumbled at any stage before acquiring the minimum seventy-five votes needed to become pope. Where and when Baggio and Felici had made up their differences, or whether it was just a piece of pragmatic trading on the goodwill of the Holy Spirit, nobody really knew. But there it was: Felici and Paul's trouble-shooter, if not actually hand in hand, were now at least no more than a cassock apart.

Benelli was both the pope-maker and a candidate of the progressives. His supporters included Confalonieri, Koenig and a number of other European cardinals. That is, if the next pope had to be an Italian. On the other hand, if that tradition wasn't adhered to, then all sorts of possibilities opened up. Here Willebrands led the field. Out on the rails, showing no special form, was Leon Duval: the archbishop of Algiers, known as 'Archbishop Mohammed' because of his efforts to bridge the Christian–Moslem divide, was seen as a Third World longshot. Ranked with him was another outsider, Maurice Roy, archbishop of Quebec City who, in World War II, was probably the most famous chaplain in the Canadian Army; the idea still persisted that if Hume of Westminster didn't gather sufficient support, then what was being loosely labelled 'the

Anglo-Saxon camp' – a coalition of American, Canadian and French cardinals – might run Roy, especially if he showed signs of picking up Third World support. Bracketed with Duval and Roy was another possible, Stefan Wyszynski, archbishop of Warsaw since 1948: people spoke of his great courage and skill in walking the tightrope of Church–state relations in Poland, the most Catholic of Communist countries; if a caretaker pope was needed, then the seventy-seven-year-old Wyszynski could be the man. Jogging along at his heels was Karol Wojtyla, archbishop of Cracow; he was a real outsider, but Koenig had begun murmuring to fellow cardinals that Wojtyla had a lot of unsuspected qualities. Nobody really asked the Viennese to amplify; there seemed little point with Wojtyla so far down the track.

By Thursday, 24 August, the day before the cardinals would enter Conclave, in response to an Italian newspaper which published a computer forecast predicting Baggio would win, the pained voice of Vatican press spokesman Panciroli recalled the words of Cardinal Roncalli who, on the eve of the 1958 Conclave which elected him John XXIII, had said that combined prayers would ensure the next pope would be a wise and gentle man, and that he would be a holy man who spread holiness.

John's description sounded just the sort of man only the Holy Spirit could again put into office.

15

On Thursday morning Villot gets up a full hour earlier than usual in his Vatican apartment. Everything he now does is out of keeping with the routine he has maintained since becoming Secretary of State. Dressed and shaved, he stands at his bedroom window, a tall and gaunt figure staring out at a Rome still asleep; he can barely remember when last he saw a sunrise, this moment the sky lightens and is gilded before dissolving into the deep blue of another cloudless day. At this hour the *tufo* is barely audible; there is nothing in sight to disturb the tranquillity. Yet Villot is filled with inner torment; even in those really bad days during Paul's reign – when he wanted to resign over so many issues – he never felt so miserable. He chainsmokes furiously. The Frenchman has hardly ever done this before, smoking before his first coffee; at this rate he will easily exceed his two packs a day norm.

His eyes constantly return to the huddle of buildings and courtyards away to his right. He cannot see them all, but Villot knows every inch of the area. He has walked it dozens of times this past week. Each time it took him nine minutes to complete this journey around the perimeter of Conclave. Villot spent many days supervising the preparation of the place, doing everything in his power to make it as sealed off from the outside world as it was possible to be. Now, he fears, his work has been in vain.

The Secretary is deeply troubled, and has been since the telephone call late the previous night from Camilio Ciban, chief of Vatican security. Ciban had requested an appointment at this unusually early hour. He had said nothing else. He did not have to. The arrangement between them was that Ciban would only call when he was certain.

Villot's manservant notes that his master has almost filled with ash and butts one of the many ashtrays scattered around the apartment when, at six am, the appointed hour, he ushers in Ciban.

Ciban is wearing one of his expensive custom-tailored silk suits. It looks well on him. He is a compact man, greying at the temples, with worry-lines around his mouth and eyes. Some say the lines come from all the secrets his Roman memory stores. If this morning the lines are deeper than usual, it is understandable. Ciban is worried; his face appears more granite-hard and weatherbeaten than ever. He looks a man who has yet again had his belief in the worst of human nature confirmed. Ciban waits while the servant pours coffee and removes the ashtray. Only after the man has closed the door behind him does the security chief begin to explain the reason for his early-morning visit.

Secret though their meeting is, the very reason which makes it necessary also ensures that at least the broad lines of the discussion will become known.

Ciban tells Villot of the plan to bug Conclave.

It is the second time in a year the Secretary has had to grapple with the threat of illegal electronic surveillance inside the Vatican.

The previous incident had deeply shocked and frightened him. From the beginning the episode had an odour which Villot found repugnant. During the closing months of Paul's pontificate, members of the domestic staff in the Apostolic Palace had stolen a selection of the pope's treasured antique coins. Ciban traced the thieves when they tried to sell the coins in Rome. He recovered almost all of them and the Vatican *governatorato* had wanted to hand over the culprits to the Italian authorities. When the thieves appealed for clemency to Paul, he had forgiven them. The unsavoury episode would have ended there but for the intervention of Casaroli.

During his years of floating through the corridors of Communist power on delicate missions for the Vatican, the sharp-eyed diplomat had come to ponder why it was that his hosts behind the Iron Curtain seemed so often able to anticipate the finer nuances of Holy See strategy. In Budapest, in 1964, the foreknowledge of the Hungarian government had, Casaroli decided, resulted in only a limited agreement being signed which was less than satisfactory to the Holy See. Again, in the same period, when he had travelled frequently to Prague to negotiate Archbishop Baran's release from prison into exile, the diplomat was sometimes dismayed how knowledgeable the Czechs were about highly sensitive issues which should have been closely guarded Vatican secrets. It was the same when Casaroli saw Tito in Yugoslavia, when he went to Moscow, when he attended the Helsinki Conference on Security, when he visited Cuba, East Germany, Poland and Romania. Wherever he travelled within the Soviet Bloc, Casaroli increasingly had the uncomfortable feeling that those he was dealing with knew far more than they should about the inner thinking of the Holy See.

The theft of Paul's coins gave Casaroli the perfect opening to test the validity of his suspicions. He went to Villot and proposed a counter-surveillance team from the Italian secret service be called in to sweep the Vatican for electronic listening devices. Villot was against the idea. Both his diplomatic training and old-fashioned instincts combined to make him resist the thought that the Vatican may have been penetrated by modern weapons. Casaroli patiently explained that during his trips behind the Iron Curtain he was certain his quarters had been rigged with listening devices. Still Villot hesitated. To sweep the Vatican might defeat the purpose of the exercise. News of the operation was bound to get out. If nothing else, it might lead to all sorts of internal labour-relations problems; in recent years Vatican lay staff had become more militant and were even talking of taking industrial action should their demands for better working conditions and pay not be met. If word leaked to them, it might well precipitate a crisis which could see the Vatican locked in a very unholy dispute with its employees. Even worse, the slightest hint of suspicion on the part of the Holy See would undoubtedly alert the Communists to try other methods to penetrate the Vatican – if that was indeed what Casaroli was suggesting had happened. Villot still found it very hard to believe that what he perceived as one of the most secure places on earth – his Secretariat of State – could be under outside surveillance. Casaroli had persisted, and found in Ciban ready support. The security man finally convinced Villot. Ciban assured him that the Italian team had been trained by the CIA, probably the world's ranking experts on electronic sweeping.

Once Villot was convinced, the rest was easy. Two men, posing as estimators for badly needed rewiring of the electrical system in the Apostolic Palace and other buildings, spent a week inside the Vatican. (Two senior Vatican staffers recalled the day the phoney estimators checked their offices. Both men insisted they were suspicious because the estimators 'worked far harder than any Italian normally does'.) By the end of their stay they had discovered eleven separate bugs in the Secretariat of State and the *governatorato* building. The devices were of Soviet and American manufacture. There was no way of knowing how long they had been there or who placed them in position. Some of the bugs were so super-sophisticated they were capable of picking up telephone calls and conversations in far away corners of the Vatican. Villot had sat there, ashen-faced, while Ciban explained the way the gadgets worked.

Now, several months later, Ciban is back with further devastating news. He has learned of at least one plan to bug Conclave. There may be others. Though he cannot be certain, the plot he knows of seems comparatively harmless. Some of the staff at Vatican Radio propose to have placed within Conclave a relatively innocuous device so they will be the first outsiders to learn a pope has been elected. Ciban does not know who is involved or how exactly the plan will work.

Villot is appalled. The implications are truly alarming. If the stage has been reached where, however unofficially – for Ciban is sure the scheme is outside the knowledge of the station's director-general or his programme, technical and news directors – Vatican Radio personnel propose to break the stringent terms of Paul's *Eligendo*, who else may be contemplating a similar breach? Given everything Casaroli has told him, Villot is in no doubt the deliberations of Conclave would be of great interest to the enemies of the Holy See; in the confines of Conclave, where cardinals expect to talk frankly and freely about matters they may never wish mentioned outside, the possibility they will be overheard is most alarming.

Villot wonders what should be done. Should he warn the cardinals of the risk?

Ciban is emphatic: *no*. To do that could create other problems; it might even wreck Conclave. Almost certainly the majority of cardinals would feel inhibited if they knew there was a chance their private deliberations were being listened to. Some, especially the Americans, still very much caught up by Watergate, might demand the sort of electronic protection which could be self-defeating. Nor did Ciban think Villot should discuss the matter with Tucci of Vatican Radio: there was little the director-general could do except issue a stern reminder to staff of the severe penalties facing anyone involved in bugging Conclave – they include instant dismissal and excommunication from the Church with the possibility of criminal proceedings to follow in the Italian courts. That may stop a faint heart, but Ciban suspects the persons involved in the Vatican Radio caper are made of stronger stuff. They surely realize the risks, therefore they probably believe they have a plan which virtually eliminates any risk of discovery.

The measure of Villot's desperation is that he again asks Ciban what should be done.

The security chief is in no doubt. They must work within the existing procedures. He will have two experts inside the Conclave area regularly sweeping it. Even the Sistine Chapel, where the cardinals cast their secret ballots, will not escape scrutiny: when the electors are not in session, the experts will carefully check the Chapel.

Villot asks the one salient question: supposing the bugging device is so tiny, so sophisticated, so easily hidden that unless every person inside Conclave is under constant monitoring by electronic scanners – when they eat together, go to their separate rooms, see their confessors, go to the bathroom, pick up their medicine from one of the two St John of God male nurses in the enclosed area – unless all this is done, what chance is there of ever finding a bug?[1]

*

144

Walking purposefully, bull neck thrust forward, Cardinal Pericle Felici strides through a sparsely furnished room in the Vatican, his shoes echoing on the marble floor. His expensive cassock – Gammarelli charges him $600 for each hand-stitched one – contrasts starkly with the pale wooden walls. He ignores the custodian seated at the large, businesslike table, bare except for a book every visitor is supposed to sign before proceeding beyond this point. Felici hasn't signed the book in the eleven years he has been cardinal. Nobody has dared challenge him about this.

His sudden, unexpected visits make those who work in this building nervous. Many of them are quite young and casually dressed; they have introduced a Coca-Cola dispenser, and a coffee-maker which gurgles all day. They suspect, correctly, that Felici does not like these innovations. Nor are they the only changes which have been introduced since Felici first came here in the 1940s; then he was Rector of the Pontifical Seminary for Legal Studies and he frequently consulted the records of ancient judgements that are stored only here. In those days the furniture was medieval; now it is austerely modern. One entire floor is virtually filled with photocopiers, duplicating documents for every department in the Vatican. There is even an elevator. This Felici avoids: he prefers to walk everywhere in this building, which has no name-plate at its entrance, but which all who have business here know as L'Archivio Segreto Vaticano, the secret archives of the Vatican.

It may well be what Felici claims it is, the most important archive in the world. There are thirty miles of shelves filled with books, parchment and paper manuscripts of the greatest historical importance. Here are slips of paper detailing long forgotten sins, broken promises, indulgences and special exemptions from ecclesiastical law. Here are the records of Consistory – the senate of cardinals which once advised the pope on such important matters as the appointment of theologians to refute the thesis of Luther. Here are records of Conclaves from the fifteenth century on; beside the bare official tallies of votes there are marvellously detailed accounts by the Camerlengos of the day. And there is more – much, much, more: documents on the Inquisition, thirteenth-century reports about the Mongols, monographs on the papacy's exodus to Avignon. There is a vast repository of papers which run from Barbarossa to Napoleon, from Luther to Calvin. There are registers which contain nightmarish drawings of Draculas and women with the bodies of nymphs and the faces of beasts, dating from the days of Innocent III. There are no less than 4,837 other registers detailing forgotten wars, uprisings and civil disturbances.

But the Secret Archives are more than the storehouse of a dead past.

145

Here, too, are highly sensitive records of the Church's contemporary involvement. There are detailed files on Richard Nixon, Leonid Brezhnev, Harold Wilson, Giscard d'Estaing – the leaders of every nation the Holy See has deemed it necessary to deal with. Hitler and Stalin have their secret boxes; so do the lesser tyrants. Felici is one of a handful of persons allowed to examine this material.

He enters the study room. Here at least nothing has changed. The big black desks have not been replaced this century, nor have the bookracks for volumes too heavy to handle. And the straight-backed chairs look as uncomfortable now as when Felici first sat on them. In those days he was too lowly to be allowed beyond this chamber, with its great clock and carved throne where the prefect of the establishment sometimes sits watching his assistants silently fetch and carry records for people who have been granted special permission to inspect them only in this room. For certain files they need the personal consent of the pope before doing so. And only scholars of the highest repute can come here. Even they are limited in what they can see. There is a rule that nothing less than a hundred years old can be shown; many papal records are marked to remain closed for three centuries. Some of Pius XII's files on his relations with the Nazis, and details of his attempts to help the Jews, will not be available until the twenty-second century – and only then if the pope of the time agrees the documents can be inspected.

Yet Felici has business far beyond this relatively public place.

He leaves the study room and continues into the heart of the building, picking his way through corridors of shelves and past the small private chapel of the profligate Pope Borgia, where, legend says, his illegitimate daughter Lucrezia debated with the philosophers of her day the meaning of passion. Felici crosses the high-roomed cavern called the Hall of the Parchments, filled with tens of thousands of documents dealing with the rights of the papal state: many of the manuscripts are tinged purple because of a violet-coloured fungus which defies the most scientific of treatment. Beyond is another room, lined with steel bookshelves holding the registers of petitions. There are over seven thousand volumes of requests for every kind of ecclesiastical grace and favour going back five hundred years: the supplications of kings stand beside the requests of parish priests. Here are also the annulments; the details they contain are often more personal and intimate than the case files of a secular psychiatrist. Nobody, except the likes of Felici, can open these records. But they hold no interest for him, at least not today.

Felici strides past the *Miscellanea*, a room filled with fifteen enormous closets. This *fondo*, or archive, contains data on early political and religious history: reports on nuncios long before there were permanent nunciatures; accounts of observers at the Battle of Waterloo and the Charge of the Light Brigade. In one closet are records of trials for sorcery; in its own special *busta*, or file, are the letters of Joan of Arc to the Comte d'Armagnac – a correspondence that helped have her burnt as a witch. Close by are the one hundred and fifty volumes of *avvisi*, reports to the Curia by nuncios and other papal officers. They go back to the Middle Ages, capturing perfectly the mood at the great courts of Versailles, Vienna, Venice, Paris and London. In another *busta* are details of the scandalous lives led by the Nuns of Monza; in another is correspondence between the popes and Michelangelo; a third contains the parchment petitions of Copernicus, Boccaccio and Rabelais. In a separate archive, a sign of its special importance in this unparalleled collection, is a bound volume of the original, handwritten records of the trial of Galileo. Felici once spent days poring over them, trying to understand this genius who had challenged the Church.

He turns yet another corner, and there, waiting for him beside a huge safe, is the head of this vast treasure house, Cardinal Antonio Samore. Almost all his Church life has been spent in curial service; he is a witty, agreeable man with a flair for remembering more medieval *bon mots* than even Prefect Martin relishes. Four years ago Samore took over the Archives at the personal request of Paul. It was Samore himself who delivered to Paul those references to death which had so preoccupied the pope.

Samore has often met Felici by this safe, which holds in its drawers the most precious of all the ancient documents in the Secret Archives. One drawer contains four sheets of crumbling parchment bearing 305 wax seals, each with a coat of arms attesting to the authenticity of the signature of a member of the Swedish Parliament – ratification for the abdication in 1654 of their bi-sexual queen, Christina, on her conversion to Catholicism. In a separate drawer is the last letter of the Catholic Queen of Scots, Mary, written to the pope just before she was beheaded on the orders of the Protestant Queen of England, Elizabeth I. There is another letter, this from a Ming Empress, written in 1655 on a sheet of embroidered silk, requesting the pope's help to Christianize China. There is the futile petition of seventy-five lords of England begging the pope to annul the marriage between Henry VIII and Catherine of Aragon; the same drawer contains love letters from the king to Anne Boleyn. There are the famous gold seals of the Spanish kings, Philip II and Philip III, each seal weighing almost a kilo. There are the scrolls exchanged between Byzantine emperors and popes, going back to 1146, asking protection for the Crusaders and written on purple parchment in gold script. There is the dogma of the Immaculate

Conception, illustrated in delicate colours and bound in pale blue velvet. Locked in a separate steel box – which only a pope can open – is said to be the last secret of 'Our Lady of Fatima', who reportedly appeared in 1916 as a vision to three young children in the small Portuguese village of that name. Two of her prophecies – the two world wars – have already come true, say the faithful. Her third prophecy was entrusted to the Vatican with instructions it should be opened by the reigning pope in 1960. This was John XXIII; what he read – runs the story – made him 'tremble with fear and almost faint with horror'. And Paul's depressions increased, say some of his staff, after he studied the prophecy. Believers claim it gives the date for World War III, describing a holocaust in which several nations are wiped out; before that happens the reigning pope will have been assassinated.

Dire though it is, such speculation is not the reason Felici is meeting with Samore. Felici is concerned with what he might find behind a solid oak door, blackened with age and always kept locked, the key never out of the possession of the Archives' custodian.

Samore uses it now to open the door. The two men enter and Samore locks the door behind them.

They are in another corridor off which are small cell-like rooms. Each one holds some of the most sensitive contemporary documents the Vatican possesses. They invariably involve living persons, existing political situations and running scandals. It is the latter which interests Felici.

He has come to check on the truth of an extraordinary development. In the past forty-eight hours an unsigned statement has been circulated to a number of cardinals impugning the morality and honesty of a *papabile*. The document bears all the hallmarks of having been written by somebody with inside knowledge. The detail is impressive, the conclusion inescapable: to elect this particular cardinal as pope would ultimately involve the Church in unmitigated scandal.

If the accusations have substance, Felici knows the evidence will be in one of these cells. The idea a fellow cardinal could be guilty of serious chicanery he finds shocking enough. Yet equally appalling is the way the charges have surfaced. For even if the cardinal in question is exonerated – and nothing is found in any of the box files Felici begins to pursue – one thing remains disturbingly clear. A 'dirty tricks department' seems determined to intervene in Conclave.

*

Paul Marcinkus, the prelate his staff call *il gorilla* – though only when he is out of earshot – lopes into a seventeenth-century tower near Porta Sant'Anna.

A small plate on the door identifies the tower as the Istituto per le Opere Religiose (IOR), the Institute for Religious Works; it is another of those misleading Vatican titles which, in this particular case, may also be the best misnomer in the world. For the institute is far more concerned with money than religion. Since 1942 it has been the Vatican's bank, established in wartime by Pius XII to transfer funds from Fascist Italy to Catholic religious and charitable organizations throughout the world. Now, in 1978, it invests the resources of the Church almost everywhere a justifiable profit is to be made. The bank also holds some three billion US dollars in deposits for about 7,000 customers. These include nearly all the diplomats accredited to the Holy See. But the majority of its private clients are very wealthy Italians worried about Communism, terrorism and the declining lira. After proper introduction – virtually only on the personal recommendation of an existing depositor – a new customer may open an account with the IOR and then funnel his funds to the hard-currency haven of Switzerland. The Italian authorities can do nothing about this, as the IOR is the financial agency of an independent sovereign state and exports its customers' money with impunity. Further, the IOR participates in the secretive Caribbean Eurocurrency market and also works closely with some of the biggest banking houses in Europe and the United States. Few other institutions are able to claim such uncommon connections and privileges. IOR customers pay the going rate for bank charges, but each must agree before being accepted as a client to bequeath ten per cent of their holdings to the Church – either on death or the closure of an account. For nine years this extraordinary and mysterious financial entity has been in the iron grasp of Marcinkus.[2]

As he crosses the marble floor of the IOR banking hall, his eyes flick from the tasteful wall prints to the gleaming polished wooden counters where blue-uniformed ushers escort those allowed to do business here to tellers who dress as soberly as morticians. Marcinkus hardly ever acknowledges the existence of these flunkeys; indeed few people nowadays receive more than the wintriest of smiles from the towering bishop before he closes his office door on the world.

It's always like this, remember the older hands, when the grapeshot may again be about to fly. It was like this when the news broke that the IOR was investing in the casino at Monte Carlo, had bought shares in the Beretta firearms factory and owned stock in a Canadian company making oral contraceptives. Each of these incidents created its own furore. They also revealed Marcinkus at his imperious best. He had risen to every occasion, displaying a formidable fighting spirit.

That quality had been there from the beginning of his days at IOR. He may not have known much about the finer points of high finance, but he did know all about keeping secrets secret. He still does. Now though, they say – these minions Marcinkus ignored on his way to his office – he is increasingly fearful that the great solid wall of secrecy he has constructed around everything he does, and has done in the past, is beginning to crumble. There is quiet satisfaction in some of the voices which report this as fact. They dislike both Marcinkus and his methods. They believe his policies have led to the IOR being accused of widespread 'mercantile' speculation in everything from currency to high-flying stocks, of helping rich Italians evade tax and currency laws, of using the most unscrupulous channels that capitalism offers. As a result, next to Macchi, Marcinkus has for years run close second as the most unpopular person in the Vatican.

Although there is no way of telling by looking at him, his heavy-lidded eyes and perpetually clenched lips rarely varying their position in public, Marcinkus, say his well-placed allies in the Vatican – these include Tucci at Vatican Radio, Levi at *L'Osservatore Romano* and Panciroli at the Press Office – can be forgiven for believing he is the victim if not of a full-scale dirty tricks campaign, then something almost as sinister. Some even go so far as to suggest that this Lithuanian-American priest-banker with his McCarthylike fervour for anti-Communism is a prime target for the KGB's Department of Disinformation. What other explanation, they ask, can there be for the way *il crack Sindona* continues to haunt him?

What else can Marcinkus expect, retort his growing number of enemies both in and outside the Vatican, after what he has done?

Undoubtedly the answer to both of these questions continue to trouble the fifty-six-year-old bishop.

Born and raised in Cicero – the Chicago suburb which was also the birthplace of Al Capone – Marcinkus still takes pride in his mid-European ancestry, almost as much as he does in his physical toughness, the way he swings a golf club. He is at home in Wall Street and other major stock exchanges, and now knows as much about blue chip and gilt-edged investments as he does about the Creed. There is not a bank who will refuse to talk to him; there is hardly a financial institution which won't do business with him – not even in the stormy wake of *il crack Sindona*, the most reverberating scandal to illuminate the very murky world of Vatican high finance.

It broke in the closing years of Paul's pontificate, casting the gravest doubts on the way the Vatican conducts its financial affairs, strongly suggesting it had played fast and loose with the money entrusted to it – and may still be doing so. The most accusing fingers have been pointed at Marcinkus.

But now, on the eve of Conclave, Marcinkus can be certain *il crack Sindona* will carry over into the next pontificate. What happens then will almost certainly depend on who is elected. His friends, including Cody, have told him not to worry, that the worst is over. They argue that no matter who emerges as pope, there is no way he can easily get rid of his banker. To do so would be to admit what the Vatican has so far denied – that there has been some very odd goings-on in the affairs of IOR. Besides, there are all those secrets Marcinkus has locked in his head. Nobody, says Cody, could risk them coming out; the cardinal is convinced Marcinkus should feel safe.

Yet not even Cody knows whether Marcinkus really sees it like this; his very nature does not allow him to share such confidences. One thing, though, is clear: there is no one in the IOR who knows as much as Marcinkus about the bank's operations.

His choice of who would best suit him as pope is also something he keeps in his head; everybody is sure he has not written down a short list of favourites. Unless forced to, Marcinkus never writes down anything: everything is stored in his extraordinary brain which can handle a score of complex issues without any obvious effort. Marcinkus is the nearest the Vatican has to a human computer. Not even his friends say this makes him an easy man to live with.

Like Macchi, Marcinkus does not care about his unpopularity; good public relations are not high on his list of priorities. His obsession with secrecy precludes it. He has made secrecy a prime consideration in his handling of the Vatican's vast portfolio. Some say it's now worth in total ten billion US dollars, and that each year as much as ten million dollars' profit goes directly into the pope's account – number 16/16 – which the pontiff may use in any way he wishes. The figures could be even higher. During this interregnum nobody except Marcinkus really knows them.

And in spite of all that has happened – the highly embarrassing headlines and stories of financial betrayal – the way money can be utilized continues to fascinate Marcinkus. His three-room apartment in the Villa Stritch is filled with books on the subject; seriously talking about high finance is one of the few guaranteed ways to excite this tall, heavy-set man with grey, thinning hair and rasp-file voice. It has been so for years.

From the day he took over as president of the IOR in 1969, Marcinkus set out to learn everything possible about the Vatican's investments. He discovered it held two per cent of all the shares quoted on Italian stock exchanges; it was a stockholder in a dozen Italian banks, including one called the Bank of the Holy Spirit; it held blocks of stocks in insurance firms, steel corporations, mining companies, construction concerns and auto conglomerates. The Vatican had provided funding to help build Rome's Hilton and the Watergate complex in Washington. Its total worth went far beyond shareholdings. Apart from churches and other properties owned by dioceses around the world – which are independent of direct Vatican control – the value of the Vatican's real estate ran into billions of dollars; it owned scores of apartment blocks in Rome, a large portion of the city's Trastevere tourist-trap area; it had land in the hills outside Rome and properties throughout Europe, South America and the United States. It had handsomely multiplied the eighty-three million US dollars equivalent Mussolini paid in 1929 under the Lateran Treaty to compensate the Church for territory lost to Italy. In the aftermath of the Wall Street Crash of that year, the money was invested in markets which were bound to rise, though it needed World War II to produce the first fat profits for the Vatican portfolio. Marcinkus has told Cody – who, being Cody, passed on the good news to others – that from 1940, 'It's been a real gravy train.'

This, then, was the happy situation Marcinkus inherited the day he was plucked by Paul from the obscurity of the Roman Curia and put in control of more money than many of the world's private banking houses handle.

Having made his review of the Vatican's financial position, Marcinkus decided it could be improved upon. He first virtually cut himself free from the tiresome supervision of the Prefecture for the Economic Affairs of the Holy See, and then set off on a breathtaking programme of expansion, emerging in the process as the Vatican's true financial *éminence grise*. Whether in the beginning he was given the job simply on a whim of Paul's, a bonus for the way he had doted on the pope – at least in public – once running the IOR Marcinkus swiftly became the best-known Vatican figure in world banking circles. It seemed, indeed, a success story hard to equal, this saga of an unknown priest with a rat-trap mind who climbed to the very pinnacle of financial peaks without ever having to publish a balance sheet or face the hazards of a stockholders' meeting. Marcinkus liked to joke he was only answerable to the pope – and to God.

He no longer makes the jest – not since Michele Sindona came to blight his life. It has even made it harder for Marcinkus to enjoy a round at the Aquasanta – Rome's most exclusive golf club. For it was there, out on the immaculate greens, that Sindona and his aides wove spells which eventually embroiled Marcinkus and his IOR as their business partners.

Marcinkus's staff believe the repercussions of this association are again about to plague him. For they, too, realize that the danger to him

– and the continuing embarrassment to them all – is likely to be greater than ever on this eve of Conclave. During the last two weeks most of the cardinals have been fed a devastating stream of information claiming the IOR is still operating in too independent and cavalier a fashion; this, allied to growing rumours the Church may be having cash-flow problems, further calls into question the role of Marcinkus.

Even now it may not be easy for him fully to understand the tangled sequence of events which have led to open calls for his replacement, mainly as a result of his alleged part in propping up Sindona at the very time Sindona was at the height of his swindling career. Yet since the death of Paul evidence has also emerged showing that the links between the Vatican and Sindona can be traced back directly to Paul himself: that he, and no one else, was instrumental in opening the way for Sindona to enter the previously closed world of Vatican finance; that Marcinkus merely inherited the situation and, with the pope's approbation already bestowed on Sindona, Marcinkus then fatally lowered his banker's guard.

It is an intriguing theory and one that Marcinkus's friends are energetically advocating. Support for their claim comes from one of the Vatican's many *bêtes noires*, Malachi Martin, a former Jesuit professor at the Pontifical Biblical Institute in Rome and close associate of John XXIII. Martin has given up holy orders and, say his former colleagues, publishes endless criticisms of the Church and the Vatican with the benefit of his first-hand experience. His latest work, *The Final Conclave*, has come at a most opportune moment. Although largely fictional, it also contains a predictably subtle critique of Paul's mission, and his account of the ties between Paul and Sindona is being hotly debated by cardinals. The Americans are furious that Martin has made such allegations public; some of the Europeans, who are anyway closer to the events of *il crack Sindona*, point out that the Vatican, which has the resources to do so, has not yet denied Martin's claims. By now any number of knowledgeable persons in Rome are quite prepared to accept the substance of Martin's story. For that which is checkable, checks out. But even Martin does not know all the links between the old pope and the young financier. Even stronger are the ties between Sindona and the Church.

*

Michele Sindona was born in 1920 of a humble family in the Sicilian village of Patti, which sprawls across a low hill overlooking the Mediterranean. It is about fifty miles from Messina and, in the words of Mafia mobster Lucky Luciano, Patti is a good place to be – from.

Early in life Sindona became imbued with a desire to improve, and prove, himself. Unwilling to become a priest, he decided upon the other most respected profession in Sicilian society, law. He studied for the bar at Messina University, and to pay his way through law school worked during his vacations in the local tax office. Sindona displayed natural gifts for spotting evasions of all kinds. These skills brought him to the notice of the bishop of Messina. On his advice, after he qualified as a lawyer Sindona opened his own tax office in the town and began to advise the local church on how to save on its investments.

His relationship with the bishop demonstrated another of Sindona's lifelong skills, his ability to make useful friends. Sindona helped along their relationship by teaching the bishop origami, the Japanese art of paper folding. The two men spent happy evenings together creating paper boats and crowns. Between sipping the fiery local brandy, the bishop told Sindona about an authentic Italian hero, an emigrant called Amadeo Giannini who founded the Bank of America. When Sindona candidly admitted he wished to be another Giannini, the kindly bishop urged him to go to Milan. He even wrote Sindona a glowing introduction to the Church authorities in the city.

Milan in 1946 was another of Europe's post-war ruined cities. But Sindona, with the instinct which was another of his attributes, recognized that in the forthcoming economic recovery – the Italian miracle of the fifties – Milan would become once more the country's financial centre. He correctly predicted there would be a boom in the construction industry as bombed properties were rebuilt. Sindona soon became the city's leading property tax expert; he seemed to know a hundred different ways to avoid duty on all kinds of speculation and redevelopment deals. Many of his grateful clients paid him in shares. By 1952 Sindona had one of the most comprehensive private portfolios in Milan. It was but a short step from there to a seat on his first bank board. Within a year he was on the board of several banks and holding companies, and was becoming known in other financial centres around Europe. He was just thirty-two years old.

By then Paul had arrived in Milan. He brought with him all the anguish and trauma he had so recently experienced in Rome. There, in the Vatican, Paul had risen to become one of Pius XII's closest advisers. He was respectful and grateful to his mentor. In turn, Pius had encouraged him to probe where he liked and to keep nothing back. Paul, out of curiosity more than anything, began to look at the way the Vatican's financial empire was run. What he learned shocked him. Pius's own nephews were engaged in some very dubious transactions. Paul wrote a detailed report on the abuses to Pius. The reward for Paul's diligence was swift and unexpected: he was banished to Milan, sent into exile without even the cardinal's red hat which traditionally went with the appointment of archbishop of this northern city. Paul was hurt; not angry, but deeply wounded. He had done his job without fear or favour, the way he thought Pius wished him to. Instead, this — abrupt, curt, cruel dismissal from the seat of papal power. So be it: Paul accepted his fate stoically. But he also resolved if ever he returned to the Vatican he would make it his business to shake up its financial institutions: it would be a clean-out, he promised Macchi, which would be every bit as thorough as that day Jesus had thrown the money-lenders from the temple.

Perhaps anxious to know how this purge might best be accomplished, Paul invited Sindona to lunch.

It was, on the face of it, a meeting unlikely to succeed: the shy, diffident Paul and the mercurial Sicilian with the Midas touch. Yet, according to both men, Paul found from the very beginning rare common ground with his guest. He liked the way Sindona had tried to conform: his southern accent, always a handicap in Milanese society, had been carefully disguised. Sindona wore the soberest of suits and was coolly deferential. Possibly most important of all to Paul, Sindona made it clear he did not gossip: for Sindona omertà meant more than the historic code of silence protecting the closed society of Sicily; omertà for him was tantamount to an oath of personal loyalty to Paul. Such a pledge made it easier for Paul to accept Sindona's professed love of the Church and the way he spoke so sincerely about making 'God's money work for God'. The two men began to meet; Paul even allowed Sindona to interest him briefly in origami. But what cemented their relationship was the astonishing ease with which Sindona answered Paul's anxious musing about where the diocese would find the money to build a badly needed old people's home. Sindona raised the equivalent in lire of 2.4 million dollars in a matter of hours from Milanese business friends.

Gradually, though this would only emerge as hindsight, Sindona worked his way into Paul's confidence; it was a technique one of Sindona's colleagues would later brand as a 'snake charmer in the business of seduction'. During this period the unsuspecting Paul voiced his concern over the way Vatican finances were handled. Sindona was sympathetic. He wondered how he could help. Perhaps the first thing would be for Paul to effect an introduction to the 'right person' in the Vatican?

Paul obliged. Sindona travelled south to Rome to meet Prince Massimo Spada, then head of the IOR. It was a scouting mission, testing the ground. Spada, like Paul, was captivated by Sindona's good manners and quiet style. It seemed the most natural thing in the world for Spada to satisfy Sindona's casual request for an introduction to the

Banco di Roma per la Svizzera, a Swiss bank of which the Vatican owned fifty-one per cent. In return Sindona offered the Vatican, through Spada, controlling interest in a private Milan bank whose board he sat on, the Banca Privata Finanziaria (BPF); Spada accepted.

By now Sindona was advancing on all fronts. He sold a small Milan steel foundry to the American Crucible Steel Company, making a tidy two-million-dollar profit. He used the money to establish a holding company in the tax haven of Liechtenstein. He acquired control of Finabank in Geneva and took over the Banco di Messina in Sicily. He now had the basic props to support the vast criminal enterprise he was embarking upon.

It began to operate in the utmost secrecy against the background of the very public blitz Sindona launched against almost every centre of Western financial power. He first established a close working relationship with Hambros Bros of London, one of the capable lay bankers who advise the Vatican; others include J. P. Morgan and Rothschilds of Paris. Sindona soon persuaded the Continental Bank of Illinois, based in Chicago, to take a fifteen per cent stake in the BPF bank. Continental's president, David Kennedy, was another of those names Sindona flagged as most useful for the future: Kennedy became Nixon's Secretary to the Treasury. One of the two men who arranged the Continental–BPF deal was Marcinkus.

For by then a new triumvirate existed in the Vatican. Paul was pope, Marcinkus was in charge of the IOR, and Sindona was often seen in the company of the third important member, Macchi.

In those early days of the pontificate, the pope, his secretary and his banker would all sit at Paul's table after dinner, mesmerized – 'rabbits before a stoat' was how one observer portrayed them – while Sindona described the results of his latest forays. He bought his way into the American Oxford Electric Company, into the Brown pulp and paper concern and even into the canning giant, Libby's. At one time he was directly involved with no less than twenty-two companies as well as acting as consultant to dozens more. *Time* magazine called him 'the most successful Italian since Mussolini'.

Who better than Sindona for Paul to turn to for advice on the reforms he had promised himself to carry out? Pius's relatives were removed. And it was Sindona who fed Paul thoughts for his explosive papal encyclical, *Populorum Progressio*, which had stunned the Catholic Establishment by attacking 'the international imperialism of money', whereby in the end, 'the poor always remain poor and the rich become ever richer'.

Paul and the loyal Marcinkus were now in command of the largest undisclosed fortune in the Christian world: the Vatican's gold reserves in Fort Knox alone were said to be over three billion dollars. Increasingly they accepted the advice of Sindona on how that fortune should be used; and this at a time when Sindona was ruthlessly looting companies of all kinds.

In 1968 the Vatican lost a six-year battle with Italy's tax authorities. The Vatican had claimed exemption from tax on its 1962 Italian company dividends. Sindona advised Paul the time had come to relinquish the Church's troublesome involvement with Italian capitalism.

Late one night, in the spring of 1969, Paul received Sindona in his private study. Not even Macchi was permitted to be present; the secretary and Marcinkus sat in Paul's dining room sipping liqueurs and smoking cigars. For ninety minutes the pope and the tycoon discussed the best way to sell the Vatican's controlling interest in the 350-million-dollar conglomerate, Società Generale Immobiliare (SGI), Italy's biggest property and construction concern. Its president was a former governor of Vatican City and four of the Vatican's financial advisers sat on SGI's august board. Apart from owning Italian hotels, office blocks and construction companies, SGI was truly a multinational, owning the Pan-Am building on the Champs-Elysées, the Montreal Stock Exchange Building and the Watergate complex in Washington.

Paul wanted to sell the Vatican's SGI stock. For one thing he felt it was too obvious a reminder of the earthly resources he ultimately controlled; for another, following the long wrangle over tax exemption, he wished to divest the Vatican of as many of its local, Italian, interests as possible.

Sindona advised against selling SGI through the already weakened Italian Stock Exchange. Instead, the Vatican should go for the glamorous and convertible Eurodollars.

Paul agreed. Ever helpful, Sindona drew up an agreement in which he personally would be responsible for divesting the Vatican of its SGI involvement. Paul signed the document. Sindona retained one copy. The other was deposited in that corner of the Secret Archives where records of the most sensitive of papal financial transactions are kept.

With one stroke of the pen Paul had brought to fruition years of careful planning on the part of Sindona. The Sicilian became the Vatican's main financial consultant. The way was clear for him to step up his criminal activities, for who would dare challenge the pope's most trusted financial helper?

For three years Sindona, ruthlessly using the *imprimatur* of the Vatican, bought and sold, manoeuvred and manipulated, juggled and cheated his way through the financial centres of Europe. It did not take long to settle the SGI deal: the Vatican received its money and kept a nominal five per cent interest in the conglomerate. Marcinkus allowed huge amounts of money to be plunged into Sindona-backed ventures. At one stage half a billion dollars were tied up in these dazzling but dangerous exploits. By 1972 the Vatican was probably one of the biggest – if not the biggest – source of hard cash for Sindona to plunder.

Then, at a few hours' notice, Sindona told the dumb-founded Marcinkus he was moving his headquarters to New York. It should have made Marcinkus ponder; instead he appeared to accept at face value Sindona's claim that from New York he would 'make God's money work even harder for God'.

Sindona took an apartment in the Pierre Hotel and opened a sumptuous office at 450 Park Avenue. Coincidentally it was a mere block away from where Jesse Livermore conducted his machinations during the Wall Street Crash of 1929; initially Livermore had scored a triumph, but in the end, the man Sindona so wished to emulate, Amadeo Giannini, had been one of those responsible for crushing Livermore, who had eventually blown out his own brains. Unfortunately for him, Sindona did not know his American financial history.

What he did know was that his time had run out in Italy. For twenty years he had waded through labyrinthine deals and disentangled the almost impenetrable Italian company laws. But ultimately it all meant very little where it mattered most: the Milan Establishment to whom Sindona was still a pushy Sicilian; they would never let him break the hold of the Lombard bankers, the Bank of Italy, the Bastogi and Agnelli families. For them he remained just an upstart peasant – never to be admitted to the inner elite despite his much-vaunted Vatican connection.

And now he was gone, his opponents set about destroying him. The Italian police began an intensive probe into Sindona's dealings. And Marcinkus, who had entrusted so much to Sindona, began to hear the terrible clay-feet truth about the man he had almost idolized. The full extent of Sindona's looting emerged slowly. It was a tale of massive shenanigans involving fraudulent foreign-exchange trading, commodity flim-flams, regular bribery – he allegedly spent a million dollars a year fixing some of Aldo Moro's associates in the Christian Democratic Party – and the illegal exportation of hundreds of millions of Italian lire through his privately owned banks. Further, he had systematically robbed many of the companies he had taken over, leaving stockholders ruined. He had also perfected a *modus operandi* for forcing companies in which he acquired even partial control to pay excessively high interest rates, commissions and expenses to his own banks.

And he had done a great deal of this by invoking the name of the

Vatican. Even worse, it looked as though the Vatican had lost a staggering sixty billion lire through its association with Sindona.

Marcinkus had barely time to digest the implications before Sindona's great American venture collapsed. Within thirty-six months of arriving in New York he had been picked clean by Wall Street's three-card-monte traders. The Franklin National Bank he had bought as a base for his American operations foundered. From then on it was all downhill. The Italian authorities began extradition proceedings to bring Sindona back to Milan to face charges of looting $200 million from the Italian banks he controlled. The American Securities and Exchange Commission stepped in to look at US-based Sindona enterprises – and halted trading in one of them on the American Stock Exchange. With mounting horror the Vatican discovered it was involved in this operation; it was ordered to pay $320,000 in penalties. Crack after crack appeared in the carefully constructed edifice Sindona had created with the unwitting help of the pope and his chief banker.

The immediate drama, so far as the Vatican was concerned, was over. Sindona could do no more direct financial harm. But one question remained: why had it taken so long for Marcinkus to wake up to the true nature of the man he had been so closely involved with, blindly maintaining his trust in Sindona, even placing large sums of money in his banks, to the end?

The question had been asked before – with no answer.

Now it was being asked again. Both Macchi and Cody – who is one of the cardinals closely associated with the Prefecture for Economic Affairs – had, in the past, been able to stamp on demands for the proper reckoning which, such powerful voices as Villot said, was long due. They successfully resisted these demands by insisting an enquiry would ultimately have involved and embarrassed Paul.

But with the pope dead, Marcinkus knows there is no guarantee a searching in-Vatican investigation can still be headed off. Indeed all the signs suggest quite the contrary.

Even Cody is bruiting it about that the best thing which could happen, 'for everyone concerned', is for Conclave to elect a pastoral pope who would close the door on the past and let those 'who know best' tidy up financial loose ends in the way the Vatican always prefers to handle such 'problems', quietly and very much out of the public eye.

*

Greenan and his desk look like something out of *The Front Page* by this Thursday lunchtime. He has removed his Roman collar, unbuttoned his clerical shirt and rolled up his sleeves. In braces and puffing a cigar, all he needs is an eye-shade to complete the picture of an old-fashioned editor at work. His desk is littered with paper: items clipped from the Italian press, notes on telephone conversations, Vatican Press Office biographies of cardinals and other less official, but often more revealing, accounts of their lives. They are all jumbled together. Yet Greenan seems to know where everything is: time and again his hands reach out unerringly to locate a piece of paper.

It has all helped him complete his list of *papabili*. Ratzinger of Munich, the one German Greenan had hesitated over, has not made it.

Not unexpectedly, the list contains a number of Italians, the result of Greenan's careful review of the twenty-seven Italian cardinals.

Giuseppe Siri, archbishop of Genoa since 1946, is included. Greenan divines the seventy-two-year-old Siri will probably gather a goodly percentage of the conservative votes in the first ballot. But from there on is anybody's guess: a rule of thumb might be that the longer Conclave takes, the more will Siri's chances improve: he could end up as a makeshift compromise candidate accepted by all the conservatives. Should this occur, other cardinals may follow past form and bow under the pressure from that bloc.

Like every other cardinal, Siri has stoutly disclaimed he is in the running. Nobody believes him, but his protest is entered in the daily verbiage the Italian press devotes to the upcoming Conclave. At least Siri has not fallen back on the now rather overworked claim that it does not matter what anyone thinks because, in the end, the pope will be chosen by the Holy Spirit. Most of the Roman cynics see this as another example of cardinal-speak, a ruling out of the possibility of any human error producing the wrong kind of pope. Siri sees such thinking as a misuse of the Holy Spirit. At one of the *Novemdiales* Masses celebrated in St Peter's, he cleverly developed this point. Choosing as his text Matthew 14: 22–33, the story of how Peter walked on the water but began to sink when he thought more about himself than of Jesus, Siri warned his fellow cardinals they could not avoid their duties by leaving it all to the Holy Spirit: 'nor should they abandon themselves, without toil and suffering, to their first impulse or to unreasonable suggestions'. This was straight talking when measured against the convoluted sayings of some other cardinals. Siri had gone on to give an interview to an Italian newspaper which could only be viewed as a carefully timed pitch on his part for those votes not yet committed elsewhere. Siri spoke soothingly of the need to continue the work of Paul, to ensure that 'the positive and great accomplishments' of that pontificate 'be continued with courage'.

Benelli – another name on Greenan's list – has also been courting the press. His interview is about the need for collegiality within the Church and for the power of the Synod of Bishops to be increased. Paul did a noble thing in creating the Synod, but his successor must be even bolder, ensuring the Synod keeps in balance the papacy and the Church. This fascinates Greenan. For he has deduced, correctly, that in the past week or so Benelli has revised his position. No longer is he running, however discreetly, as *papabile*; instead everything he says and does is designed to promote the candidature of a fellow cardinal – Albino Luciani. This is why Benelli has spoken so strongly about collegiality, an issue he has not previously dwelt upon. Collegiality is a cause very close to the heart of the patriarch of Venice, so much so that Luciani has never overturned a decision of his priest senate. Benelli himself might appear briefly on the first ballot – two or three votes at the outside is Greenan's guess – but his real strength will be in mobilizing support for Luciani. Benelli is also preparing his ground for a triumphal return as the power behind the throne in what he now confidently believes will be the next pontificate, Luciani's. Then, while the patriarch continues his pastoral path, Benelli, if all goes as he thinks it should, can set about dealing with those who drove him from Paul's side. It could be quite a blood-bath.

Sergio Pignedoli, a firm candidate of the Italian news magazines, as well as Ladbrokes' odds-on favourite, has finally crept onto Greenan's list. It is not that the editor hesitated over the memory of the cardinal's momentous gaffe in Libya: attending a Christian–Moslem seminar in Tripoli, Pignedoli had signed his name to a resolution condemning 'Zionism as racism'; afterwards he complained bitterly that he couldn't read Arabic and that the Libyan leader had slipped in the condemnation at the very last moment. Greenan, like many others, feels the whole episode has been grossly exaggerated. This is not what made him hesitate. Conceding Pignedoli could make a showing in the beginning, he might well not have the support to go further. His presence on Greenan's list is really an indication of how wide-open is the choice of candidates.

Bertoli is there. As a strong favourite of many curial cardinals it would be unthinkable for him not to be included. In the past three weeks he has not put a well-shod foot wrong. His tribute to Paul was exemplary. His *Novemdiales* sermon covered all the right curial ground: an Italian was called for because of the special needs of the diocese of Rome and the complexities of the Italian political scene; what is wanted is both a pastoral bishop and a cardinal already resident in Rome. Bertoli wrapped it all up in delectable cardinal-speak, but the underlying message was clear. There is only one person of whom Bertoli was speaking – himself.

Ugo Poletti is on the list as a longshot. The vicar-general of Rome cannot really be expected to show beyond the first ballot. Like Benelli, he is cast in the role of pope-maker – in Poletti's case, on behalf of Bertoli. If he has calculated correctly, Poletti, too, can expect a suitable reward. There is a rumour he would like to take Villot's job as Secretary of State; others say he will get the Holy Office in a Bertoli pontificate. Poletti set the tone of his approach a week ago when he delivered a sermon devoted entirely to Paul's 'jealous love' of Rome. He told his congregation, including a large number of cardinals, that throughout his pontificate and in spite 'of the worries of his daily ministry as Universal pastor', Paul never forgot his 'special' responsibility to the diocese of Rome. Now, more than at any time in living memory, Poletti had wheezed in a voice which often seemed unable to finish a thought, Rome, with its violence, kidnappings and political murders, was a microcosm of the troubled world. Paul had often implied, suggested Poletti, that if Rome could be put right, the rest of the world would fall into step. And the only way to do this – wheeze-wheeze – was to give Rome what it needed. The congregation thought Poletti had finished. He stood there, exhaling air noisily. But then the dénouement: Rome needed a Roman pope, able to speak the language of the Romans. And if not a Roman, then certainly an Italian. Bertoli had sat and nodded as if the idea had never before occurred to him.

Finally, there is the name on his list Greenan finds in many ways most intriguing of all – Luciani's. He is present not just by virtue of Benelli's support; Luciani is included because Greenan feels the patriarch is one of the most refreshingly unusual of all the cardinal electors. On matters of church doctrine he is conventionally conservative. Yet Greenan knows that Luciani wrote to Hans Küng to congratulate him on his book, *On Being a Christian*, and sent him a copy of *Illustrissimi* which, when the news leaks out – as it is bound to – is not going to please some of the German cardinals who have been going round Rome hinting that the patriarch is their man. Again, on matters of ecclesiastical discipline, Luciani is conservative; he expects his people to go along with him on the decisions he takes. But in coming to them he is remarkably flexible and liberal in his thinking. It is the same with his attitude to what people label the theological revolution. Greenan dislikes such tags but thinks this one almost apt; since John XXIII there *has* been a lot of rethinking that not even the last years of Paul has completely stifled – and certainly not in Luciani. The patriarch feels the Church can only benefit from re-examining the writings of, for instance, the nineteenth-century liberal theologian Antonio Rosmini. All this is agreeably surprising.

But what really intrigues Greenan – and he is not alone in this reaction – has been Luciani's response to an event tailor-made to make any cardinal do some nifty hop-skip-and-jumping: it is the continuing controversy over the birth of Louise Brown, the English test-tube baby. Every churchman in Rome is being pestered by reporters for comment. Most of them refuse to say anything or else follow Paul's condemnatory line on artificial insemination. Luciani has gone his own and very different way. He has told a Rome newspaper: 'I send the most heartfelt congratulations to the English baby girl whose conception took place artificially. As far as the parents are concerned, I have no right to condemn them. If they acted with honest intention and in good faith, they could even be deserving of merit before God for what they wanted and asked the doctors to carry out.'

Now *that*, thinks Greenan, is both moving and shrewd; the more so because, having delivered his warmest good wishes, Luciani went on carefully to express his reservations in the matter. He observed that while progress is often a good thing, it is not necessarily always a good thing: after all, progress produced atomic weapons. On balance he feels he has yet to be shown reason to modify the accepted view within the Church on artificial insemination. Those who carefully study his words note that Luciani did not say *no* reasons exist for the change, nor did he discount the arguments of some moral theologians that even under the restrictions of Pius XII some sort of test-tube procreation might be acceptable. What he was doing, Luciani stressed, was merely expressing his very personal point of view in the hope it would initiate a reasoned and calm debate.

The subtleties of this are not lost on Greenan. Here is a strongly motivated cardinal not afraid to speak publicly and intelligently on a very difficult issue. He managed to do so without giving offence; no one can fail to notice his concern for the teachings of the Church or his clear belief that change is still possible. It is the judgement of a man who maintains an open mind and pastoral sensitivity within the existing framework of Catholic dogma; Luciani's pronouncement is also one of the very few genuine acts of religious statesmanship during the entire interregnum.

Greenan can only contemplate, but he thinks Luciani's statement has given the cardinal an appreciably better chance of becoming pope than the editor ever has of winning the Irish Sweep Stakes.

*

MacCarthy can sense the excitement mounting. Many of his 329 colleagues in Vatican Radio are walking that much quicker and talking that much faster on this Thursday evening. Tucci has left his director-general's office and is strolling through the station's four floors, dropping in on broadcasters and technical staff.

Tucci is proud of the way his team have handled themselves these past three weeks. Between them they have transmitted 700 broadcasts into Eastern Europe, 300 to Western Europe, 200 to Africa – of which MacCarthy's programme is one of the most popular – 130 to the Middle East, Asia and the Pacific, and almost 100 to America. It has amounted to 240 hours of broadcasts a week, 175 of them in foreign languages. This Thursday evening the thrust of the station's output continues to be concentrated on Conclave.

MacCarthy has chosen to recount the history of Conclave itself. Seated in the cramped confines of Studio One he waits for the red cue light, and begins.

'The term Conclave – derived from the Latin, *cum-clave* – was originally used to indicate an area of the house which was particularly reserved and therefore locked with a key. In the language of the Church, it is used today to indicate the closed place where the election of the pope takes place.'

With the words rolling off his tongue, pacing himself, MacCarthy goes on to explain that the first formal Conclave elected Honorius III in 1216, but that an even earlier pope, Alexander III, had, in 1179, reserved the right to elect the pontiff only to cardinals.

'In those days it was all so much easier. The College of Cardinals never exceeded thirty until the end of the thirteenth century. And they never seemed to be in much of a hurry . . .'

MacCarthy explains how the cardinals were forced to change their easy-going ways. 'In 1216 they were locked into a palace without proper food. The same happened in 1241 and again in 1243. Finally, in 1268, they were not only locked up but also walled in. When that failed to produce a speedy result, the roof of their palace was removed and the voters left exposed to the elements. They still took two years, nine months and two days to elect a pope.'

Another short pause. It has taken MacCarthy hours of patient research to break down a very long story for a few minutes of air time. Even now, as he scans his script, he is not certain he has shortened it enough. All those foreign phrases are a problem.

'To avoid in the future a repetition of such a long and harmful *sede vacante* – which as you know from a previous broadcast means the period between popes – Gregory X, in the Second Council of Lyons in 1274, promulgated the constitution *ubi periculum*, which officially instituted Conclave. The rules were rigid. Ten days after the death of a pope, the cardinals had to meet in the same palace as he had died. They must do so, and I quote "in one hall, without walls nor dividing curtains, living in common" – that's a nice way of putting it, isn't it? – without contact with the outside world, without speaking secretly with any other cardinal. The keys of the Conclave were guarded. Even in those days there was a Cardinal Camerlengo and a Marshal of the Conclave who stopped anybody entering or leaving. Food was introduced by means of revolving turntables, and great care was taken that no messages were smuggled in . . . or, for that matter, out.'

Another pause for breath; time enough for MacCarthy to glance at the studio clock. He had two minutes left – just enough time.

'If after three days the Conclave had not managed to elect a pope, then during the next five days they could only have one course for luncheon and one for supper. When those five days had passed, they were then only allowed bread, wine and water.'

He had hesitated over that: such restrictions might not appear very severe to some of his audience half starving in some remote corner of Africa. Yet, equally, they might make some of his more affluent listeners in South Africa stop and ponder. It was never easy to strike a balance between so many worlds.

MacCarthy resumes speaking. His modulated voice covers the reforms of centuries. With seconds to spare he signs off with the reminder that he will be on hand tomorrow to describe the start of what could be one of the most momentous Conclaves of all. He of course knows nothing of the plan to bug it.

16

Jaime Sin of Manila may well be the first cardinal awake in Rome on this Friday morning, 25 August. Long before dawn he is shaved and dressed in a soutane. In common with Cardinal Manning of Los Angeles, Sin will admit he feels, 'like a new boy going to a new school, just very excited'. He has packed his suitcase for Conclave; it holds clothes sufficient 'for a few days'. However he now thinks, after all he has gleaned, the proceedings may last even longer.

This is his first Conclave and Sin's main guide for what to expect is a recently published account of the previous one, which elected Paul. The detailed reconstruction of that event goes some way towards explaining Paul's stringent rules about the secrecy of future Conclaves as well as his warning against making pacts and deals; there seems to have been a number of these in the 1963 Conclave, yet the same thing is happening again.

But Sin has come to realize that everything depends on what is meant by pacts and deals; during the past three weeks the wheeling and dealing has at times been as subtle as a Chinese paradigm.

In his first few days in Rome he had been surprised by the way national jealousies flared. There is no doubt in his mind that many Italian cardinals want the papacy to continue its unbroken line of the past 455 years, and to elect an Italian. This entrenched attitude has caused its own backlash. Certain of the non-Italians expected to support an Italian candidature have indicated they are having second thoughts. That did not surprise Sin. But he is genuinely astonished by what he learned over dinner with some of the Latin American cardinals the previous night. Aramburu of Buenos Aires then delivered a well-timed bombshell, indicating he would not, after all, be voting for Luciani. The Argentinian doggedly refused to say more, but rumour has it Aramburu does not think Luciani strong enough for the job. There is even a suggestion Aramburu made some very discreet enquiries in Venice and knows the patriarch is in poor physical shape. Can this be the only reason for his switch? Is it a sign of the times – that a potential pope must have a clean bill of health before he can be considered?

Sin does not know. Yet he is aware that Koenig is now in the forefront of the move to elect a non-Italian. The Viennese – whom Sin sees as one of the few genuine elder-statesmen cardinals – is murmuring it is not going to be easy for any Italian to achieve the necessary majority of two-thirds plus one; there are so many Italians in the running that by the time they have sorted themselves out, Conclave could have reached an impasse. So why not go for another European – like Willebrands? Or, to be really daring, the cardinal from Cracow, Wojtyla. That's what Koenig is saying.

The Filipino thinks the problems go far deeper than nationalism, and are certainly nothing much to do with the way the press is labelling every cardinal a conservative or a moderate. Sin believes this far too simplistic; the shades of opinion he has detected during the 'consultations' he has enjoyed cover a far broader spectrum, which cannot be reduced to convenient expressions such as freedom versus authority. Liberal cardinals can be as authoritarian as any conservative, and all but the most reactionary of them at least pay lip service to the thought that the new pope must place more emphasis on the problems of under-developed countries.

Sin feels the real issue lies there. The next pontiff, whatever nationality he is, whatever grouping puts him into office, will have to answer two major and interlinked questions. How far should the Church pursue cordial relations with Marxist governments? How far should it seek social change and political action through its growing membership in the Third World? Asia, Africa and Latin America are major areas of expansion for the Church. But, as Sin well knows, its leaders in these regions are often under conflicting pressures from oppressive regimes and revolutionary movements. In his own Manila diocese there are priests involved in anti-government activity. The next pope must give a clear definition of how far the Church will allow clergy to be involved in open and often violent conflict. Sin is also uncomfortably aware that in the eyes of many of his flock, the papacy has not lived up to its role as a servant of the underprivileged; this has helped create secular and political obstacles to the spread of the faith.

While in Rome, Sin has learned a great deal about some of the other problems facing the Church. There is an increasing number of young drop-outs from the priesthood, especially in Europe. Many give their reason for leaving as disappointment that the Church is not maximizing its commitment to the poor, the very bastion of its mission. From the American cardinals Sin has learned of the resistance of millions of US Catholics to the traditional ban on contraception, abortion and divorce. And some of the Europeans have told him there is a renewed challenge from certain influential theologians to the doctrine of papal infallibility, indicating perhaps a weakening of Church authority over clergy and the laity.

These issues, too, Sin believes, will confront the new pope. So will the question of the Church's fading initiative for closer ties with other Christian faiths. In these past years unresolved questions of doctrine have slowed down oecumenism.

One other thing is clear to Sin. The next pope must follow Paul's most dramatic innovation – breaking the papacy's relative isolation to become the most travelled pontiff in history. And yet the youngest cardinal in Rome is not certain whether, even if the new pope deals with all this, he will satisfy both the conservative and liberal elements in the Church.

The liberals say the only way to appease them, and also halt the steady fall in Church attendance – especially in Western Europe, the traditional heartland of Roman Catholicism – is for the next pope to be more responsive to the needs of the modern world, to re-examine existing doctrine, possibly even to amend *Humanae Vitae*. Conservatives oppose anything resembling such radical reform. Time and again Sin has been quoted Paul's own message of 1974 in which he warned against the Church teaching 'an easier, experimental, rational and scientific conception of the world, without dogmas, without hierarchies and without limits to the possible enjoyment of life'.

Watching the sky lighten, seeing the familiar humpbacked outline of Rome emerging from the darkness, Sin muses that the next pope will probably face more pressure than any other pontiff. There will be those who resist the slightest change, there will be others who demand dramatic and great changes. The new pope will have to be strong enough, spiritually and physically, to find ways of adjusting the Church to a rapidly changing world, without compromising the basic principles which have served as its foundation for almost two thousand years.

Perhaps, muses Sin, Aramburu is right. Only a very fit man can even begin to take up the challenge. The cardinal from Manila decides at the beginning of this momentous day that he will not be able to vote for Luciani. He has no one else in mind to support. Yet he is not worried. He feels in his bones, this deeply devout man, that the Holy Spirit will guide him when the time comes.

*

Cody is also up and about early, his ample form dominating the breakfast room at Villa Stritch. The staff wonder where he gets his energy; perhaps from the half pint of fresh orange juice he drinks every morning, or the pile of bacon and eggs and the toast and coffee he consumes. Whatever his secret, Cody shows virtually no signs of

168

fatigue from the hectic round of private luncheons, dinners and receptions he has attended and given for his brother cardinals. He has also been to all nine *Novemdiales*, listening to the sermons of Siri, Felici, Confalonieri and others, each of them praising Paul and his goals, thereby adroitly draping his mantle over their own shoulders, making it difficult for opponents to claim Paul as their own.

Cody recognizes the strategy. He is something of a buff on papal election tactics and knows these particular ploys can be doubled-edged. In 1958 and 1963 the conservative curial faction paraded its own *papabili* as the only true heirs of the previous pope – and lost out in the balloting to compromise candidates. Cody has detected that this time the traditionalists – unlike Sin, he does not mind such tags – have been smarter. They have kept a low-key public profile, saving their real politicking for the aftermath of long leisurely dinners. Cody cannot remember dining in Rome so well as he has done of late; not only has he tasted all viewpoints, he has drunk some of the choicest wines and eaten some of the best food in the city. Gradually, over a series of *digestivi*, he has realized that even unyielding conservatives like Felici are coming to recognize there is going to have to be compromise.

Indeed, Felici said as much over dinner the previous night. There had been a good sprinkling present from the traditionalist bloc of forty-four – Cody is equally precise about the number of progressives, he thinks they come to twenty-five – and they had dined late. Over coffee and liqueurs Felici told them that his search in the Secret Archives had produced nothing, adding grimly that this made the situation even more serious; Felici was certain 'dirty tricks' were operating to influence the deliberations of Conclave. Cody was not surprised; he thinks he has been the victim of its Chicago branch for years.

By the end of the evening Felici had dropped his normal technique of edging forward by polite indirection, and said he had settled on Luciani as his stalking horse in the initial round of voting. This for Felici was indeed compromise.

Cody had nodded non-committedly. But he was not going to be rushed.

He feels the same way this morning. He thinks there is still time for more 'consultations'. And he will go on taking soundings right up to the moment the talking has to stop and the voting is about to start.

*

Waiting at the German-Hungarian College for his breakfast guest – Koenig has chosen the venue because it has the best *Wurst* in the city – the Viennese is quietly certain of several things. He has prepared himself mentally for Conclave: every evening and morning he has been in Rome he has taken time to pray and to meditate, refreshing both his soul and body. It has helped him put into perspective everything that has happened these past three weeks.

There have been some difficult moments. While it is perfectly true he favours the idea of a non-Italian pope, Koenig is not asking – as some in the media have suggested – for any firm promises from his fellow cardinals. He is as aware as they that any previous commitment, however freely given, is not binding within Conclave. Each cardinal, before casting his ballot, must solemnly swear he is voting only for the person who he thinks is best qualified to be the Supreme Pontiff. Koenig is satisfied no prelate will lightly make such an oath. He is equally sure there is a misunderstanding in the secular press over what is being called papal politicking. He is certain that, in the end, the cardinals will do all they can to exclude any temptation from their minds and focus only on what is good for the Church; they will continue to pray a great deal that their judgements possess integrity. For his part, Koenig has tried to avoid the endless discussions which so many cardinals have favoured, not because he does not believe them to be useful but because he likes to take time to collect his own thoughts before he explores them with others.[1]

This approach has enabled him to evaluate the likely effect of much of the peripheral pressures for the sort of man who should be the next pope. Koenig, after reflection, does not think CREP will have any real impact beyond splashy headlines; it's a stroke of American flummery the very European Koenig does not much care for. He puts CREP in the same category as those three hundred nuns in Pittsburgh attending a convention of the National Assembly of Women Religious who have issued an open letter requesting the College of Cardinals 'incorporate into the election the voices of those whom the present Church excludes from participating'. Koenig feels there are more important issues to be faced before embroiling Conclave in tedious women's lib.

Various other *papabili* come to mind, some comparatively young, such as Sicily's Pappalardo, another good candidate who peaked briefly and has fallen back into the general mass behind the front runners. That's the way the newspapers put it – as a race. It makes Koenig sigh, this talk of favourites and odds. He really cannot understand how the media can be so crass.

He is pretty sure his breakfast companion is not on any list. And yet, as he settles Karol Wojtyla at their table and smiles happily at the Pole's delight over the selection of *Wurst* and yoghurts and warm, freshly-baked rolls, Koenig wonders again how long it will be before other cardinals recognize that here is a man with the qualities to satisfy almost all the requirements the next pope is thought to need.

Koenig has known Wojtyla for fifteen years and can well remember that day in 1963 they first met at the Polish border. Wojtyla turned up in a shabby cassock and battered hat. He continues to look like a character out of the Father Brown series: Wojtyla has either never heard of the House of Gammarelli or, more likely, is simply not prepared to spend a goodly portion of his income on expensive tailored garments. On *this*, Koenig would bet with anyone. The other memory which stands out from their first meeting is Wojtyla's friendliness and his wide range of reading. It is the same now: Koenig's guest grins broadly as he discusses some of the latest books he has read while in Rome.

The more he has come to know Wojtyla – who has taken to stopping off frequently in Vienna on his way to and from Rome – the more Koenig has come to appreciate his clear mind, the way he thinks through a problem completely before passing judgement. He gives the impression of being willing to listen and to weigh each point carefully, but in the end he makes up his own mind. And once he does, nothing will change it. His intellect is formidable, his faith unshakeable. Koenig knows how rare it is to find a man whose spiritual strength matches that of his physical power. Wojtyla is a very fit fifty-eight-year-old; he can ski down the steepest of Polish slopes and walk a man half his age into the ground.

While Wojtyla is shy about discussing himself, during previous meetings Koenig discovered by careful questioning that the very special qualities his guest has are determined to a large extent by his background. Wojtyla read Polish language and literature at Cracow University, which claims Copernicus and Lenin as luminaries. There, his already strong sense of nationalism was sharpened. Cracow is one of Poland's old provincial capitals and is steeped in the nation's often bitter and violent past. In 1939, after a year on the campus, Wojtyla saw another unhappy chapter written. Cracow, and then Poland itself, fell to the Nazis. Wojtyla abandoned his plans to become an actor in favour of the priesthood. Toiling by day as a slave labourer, he secretly studied theology at night. Late in 1944 he became a seminarian, and lived for the rest of the war hidden in the archbishop's palace in Cracow where he was spared the excesses of the retreating Germans. He was ordained in 1946 and found himself a priest in a Poland under a new and, in some way, even crueller regime. The Russians correctly saw the Church as the main stumbling block to creating a perfect Communist state; once more the Polish clergy were hounded. Wojtyla was sent by his bishop to Rome. He spent two years there. He returned home and for the last thirty years has been steadily climbing the Polish Church ladder. At the age of thirty-eight he became the youngest of Poland's eighty bishops. Six years later he was archbishop of Cracow. By then he had established his own attitude towards the Communist regime: he staged few trials of strength, working instead within the system, secure in the knowledge of the Church's special position in the minds of Polish people. Outside Poland he established a reputation for making thinking men's speeches. He drew wide support at the Second Vatican Council with a calm call for religious liberty and with a plea for a dialogue with atheism rather than rejecting it outright. He became a regular visitor to Rome, establishing a close relationship with Paul who made him a cardinal in 1967. Wojtyla was just forty-seven years old. Four years later he was appointed to the permanent council of the Synod of Bishops; it was a perfect vantage point to observe from a distance the working of the Curia. He travelled widely, including a visit to the United States where he stayed with his fellow Pole, Cardinal Krol of Philadelphia. He speaks several languages fluently, though he still finds problems with English.

This morning, as usual, he and Koenig converse in Italian and German, discussing issues dear to them both. Where should *Ostpolitik* go now? How will the Polish regime, indeed the whole of the Soviet Bloc, respond to the change in direction the Church must now take? Neither believes the *status quo* can survive or that it is desirable it should. While agreeing there seems no outstandingly obvious candidate for the papacy – though they do think it likely he will emerge from among the Italian cardinals – even if he is a pastoral pontiff he will have to look again at the whole issue of Marxism.

They are still discussing the possibilities the future holds when it is time for them to robe for the Mass for the Election of a Pope. As they part, Koenig is sure of one thing. Wojtyla is not a man to seek easy accommodations. That is what makes him so charismatic. His clear-cut beliefs are the best possible answer to that tired old question, the one Stalin is supposed to have posed about how many divisions a pope has. Wojtyla is the man, Koenig believes, who single-handedly proves that faith can be more effective than any force.

*

At ten o'clock this Friday morning four cardboard boxes are carefully loaded into a van outside 34 Santa Chiara, a small nondescript square behind the Pantheon. This is where the House of Gammarelli has its tailor's shop. Each box contains a complete set of papal vestments: extra large, large, medium and small combinations of white silk cassock, red velvet stretch slippers with a small gold cross embossed on each, a white silk sash, a rochet, a mozzetta, a red stole embroidered in gold, a white skullcap and white cotton stockings. They have all been made under the personal supervision of Anibaile Gammarelli. Working from his own highly secret in-house list – based, it seems, on information supplied by sources as mysterious as those Greeley consults – Gammarelli has prepared these papal sets. The cassocks have not been completed, their backs and hems are held together by long looping stitches. The sleeves are also deliberately unfinished. These will all be adjusted by Gammarelli moments before the pope steps for the first time as Pontiff onto the central balcony of St Peter's. Gammarelli delivers the boxes to the Vatican. From the time Conclave begins, the conscientious tailor will remain close to a telephone waiting for the summons to return and make the final adjustments. Now, driving back across Rome, he sees the limousines taking cardinals to the Vatican for their pre-Conclave Mass. He is quietly confident that the one among them who will be the next pope is a medium-sized Italian who will be elected quite quickly. So Gammarelli's sources have told him.

*

Studiously avoiding the slightest suggestion of speculation in anything he says, MacCarthy is one of a team of broadcasters setting the scene at the Mass for the Election of a Pope. He quietly describes the procession of cardinals filing into St Peter's. There are some faces missing. The Chinese cardinal who suffered a heart attack during Paul's funeral died a few days ago; America's John Wright and an Indian and Polish cardinal are still too ill to attend. As the Sistine Chapel Choir begins to sing an anthem, MacCarthy makes the point that an atmosphere of prayer is manifesting itself. He reminds his listeners that the Mass will ask the cardinals to keep before them the words of the gospel, to remember 'the Holy Spirit, whom the Father will send in my name will teach you everything and remind you of all I have said to you.'

As the service gets under way there is a brief commotion in the press pen during the singing of the antiphon; a French photographer is objecting to Britain's Peter Hebblethwaite joining in the singing: the former Jesuit is making a name for himself reporting the events in a strongly individualistic way. In the end, as Hebblethwaite puts it, they 'give each other the kiss of peace'. Decorum descends once again.

When the Mass is finished, the cardinals hear a ten-minute homily from Villot. The Camerlengo has chosen as his text John 15: 9–11: 'As the Father has loved me, so I have loved you. Remain in my love.' Villot urges them to see this as proof they are not alone in the forthcoming deliberations.

Then, led by Noé, the cardinals file out. His big moment is yet to come.

They will all assemble again in five hours to enter Conclave.

*

It must, by any yardstick, be one of the most remarkable sights in Rome this Friday afternoon. Here is Pericle Felici straddling an upright wooden chair, his two pudgy hands cupped under his double chin. Facing him is Albino Luciani, also seated on a wooden chair, cassock pulled up, bare feet in a plastic bowl filled with the amber liquid the patriarch and his housekeeper swear has helped his phlebitis.

The two men are having a serious discussion in Luciani's bedroom about the method of folding Conclave ballot papers. The subject had previously been debated for a full twenty minutes by the assembled cardinals at one of their daily morning meetings in the Sala Bologna. Felici and Luciani leisurely review the arguments which eventually swung the cardinals in favour of remaining with single folding. In reality they, and the third man present, Diego Lorenzi, know that Felici is actually here to explore whether Luciani will still allow himself to go forward as a candidate. News that Aramburu has switched camps has come as a blow to the patriarch's supporters, and Felici has been deputized to see whether the Argentinian's attitude has had any effect on the Venetian cardinal.

The 'consultation' is supposed to be secret, but in the feverish atmosphere of Rome – where, as Koenig forecast, nothing will remain confidential for long – sufficient details will eventually leak to reveal Felici in irascible form, Luciani at his smiling best and Lorenzi standing between them, not so much a referee, more a timekeeper, the secretary wondering how long both cardinals can continue this obtuse manoeuvring before it is time to go into Conclave.

Felici – and on this the conjecturalists will later agree – lobbed a casual question about Benelli's phone bill. Nine days ago the cardinal archbishop of Florence had suddenly returned to his city to preach a sermon in which he made it clear he was happy just going about his pastoral duties. Everybody in the know thought the implication clear: Benelli was saying he would leave it to others to plot in the heat of the noonday sun. That really did raise smiles. Yet another of those leaks has brought Felici the news that Benelli has pushed hard by telephone from Florence for support for Luciani from among conservative cardinals. Benelli is now back in Rome, still plugging away on the phone, stressing the patriarch's opposition to Communism, to divorce, to abortion; he almost made Luciani sound like Lefèbvre's disciple. Who is going to pay for all those calls? It's Felici's little joke, of course. No one is about to ask Benelli to account for them. It is simply Felici announcing he is aware of Benelli's role. But what he really wants to know is whether – God forbid – there has been anything promised Benelli for his tireless hustling? He doesn't put it like that – God forbid.

Luciani avoids making clear whether he approves of Benelli's support or, for that matter, the help Felici is anxious to provide; there is no way either his fellow cardinal or secretary can know at this stage what he thinks. Luciani seems to have gone into some sort of spiritual retreat.

Felici is not a man to give up as he probes for a reaction to the way the Luciani bandwagon is rolling. Naturally he does not use such crude words as 'bandwagon' and 'rolling'. That would certainly be outside the spirit of 'consultation'. Instead Felici is so circumspect even Lorenzi is unable to grasp all the subtleties. Nor, in spite of the informality of the occasion, is Felici ever less than formal. His questions are invariably prefaced by 'Your Eminence', or 'Cardinal Patriarch'.

Luciani merely says he has spoken to many cardinal electors and there are a number of very worthy *papabili* for the Holy Spirit to look upon with favour. This, too, is likely to be a simplified translation of the unusually oblique way the patriarch is speaking.

Benelli, continues Felici, as though he has not heard, has been talking to some of the Third World cardinals, who suggest the next pope should have a working-class background, if only to identify the Church more with the masses.

They both know Luciani comes from a humble family.

The next pope, muses Felici, should be genuinely concerned about the poor of the world; not, he adds quickly, that he is saying Paul wasn't. There is simply a need for a more obvious commitment.

It is another cause close to the heart of Luciani. He merely responds that so many fellow cardinals have the qualities needed. His smile denies any guile; he clearly genuinely believes this.

Luciani takes his feet from the bowl and dries them carefully. Then he puts on his socks and his shoes, old but well cared for.

Only now – it is later reported – does Felici, almost as an afterthought, ask why Luciani has been bathing his feet. And, of course, to complete the story, the patriarch's response must be suitably significant. The rumour mills will grind out that Luciani looked carefully at his guest before replying that the Holy Spirit knew the reason, and that was why it would be wrong to impose a further burden on him. That is the story. And when it begins to circulate beyond this room it will no longer matter.

*

Seated before a television monitor in Vatican Radio's Studio One, MacCarthy scribbles on a pad details of the scene unfolding on the screen. The monitor is relaying pictures from cameras strategically placed around the Conclave area. Because the scene switches from one fixed camera position to another it provides a more comprehensive view of what is happening than reporters can see from the temporary press pen inside the Sistine Chapel. Until the cardinals go into closed session, MacCarthy will rely on the monitor to act as his 'eye on Conclave'. He is nevertheless working under considerable pressure. He is due on the air shortly for his evening radio broadcast to Africa and wants to incorporate a description of the start of Conclave.

MacCarthy watches the screen as the cardinals emerge from the Ducal Hall and move into the Pauline Chapel. They are led by Noé. A pace behind him, towering over the master of ceremonies, comes Villot. He walks alone, a brooding, sad face on a frame which looks angular even under his voluminous cardinalatal robes. MacCarthy feels sorry for the aged Camerlengo: he thinks Villot has been the butt of some very spiteful gossip. He seems the man who will be most relieved when the whole business is over. Behind Villot come fifty-five pairs of cardinals, all dressed in scarlet cassocks, capes and birettas, moving slowly, their entrances widely spaced.

Pericle Felici is one of the first to appear. In his robes he more than ever looks a Roman emperor; he seems not so much holy as majestic.

Others make an appearance as MacCarthy makes notes. 'Their faces are grave, no doubt in remembrance of the charge given them this morning at the Mass. They must elect a pastor both capable and worthy and, in the words of the Mass, do so by leaving aside all worldly considerations and having God alone before their eyes.'

The screen fills with the limping presence of perhaps the most striking figure of all – Pio Taofinu'u, the cardinal who has come furthest to be here. He administers to the spiritual needs of the islanders of Samoa in the Southern Pacific. On the day Paul died, Toafinu'u was travelling by canoe to visit an outlying island when a wave capsized his craft, throwing the cardinal onto a shard of coral which badly injured his foot. On reaching his destination he had learned Paul was dead; consequently Taofinu'u, his foot swathed in bandages, was paddled back to Samoa town. There he took a plane to New Zealand and flew on to Rome – in all a thirty-hour journey with a painfully inflamed foot. In Rome his foot was operated on. Taofinu'u has been a cardinal for five years and wears his robes, notes MacCarthy, 'with the dignity of a tribal king'. He also remembers something else about the islander. Taofinu'u likes to lead his congregation in hymn-singing to the accompaniment of jungle drums and knuckle-bones.

Another picture, and there is the cardinal from Guatemala, who rides around his troubled diocese protected by armed guards. It is the only way the government can guarantee his safety in that strife-torn country. The cardinal from Boston, Humberto Medeiros, appears. MacCarthy recalls he likes to travel on long-distance Greyhound buses. He is followed by John Dearden of Detroit, who likes to walk everywhere.

MacCarthy scribbles a note. 'All are princes of the Church. But some live the life of the poor. Here are philosophers, administrators, diplomats, bureaucrats, scholars, teachers and priests. They come from all walks of life. They have tastes ranging from frugal to sybaritic, with social and theological styles embracing the extremes of conservatism and liberalism. Some live in palaces, others in modest apartments. Some have medieval cathedrals, others humble mission churches. The College of Cardinals is more diverse than at any time before. For this reason alone no one can predict with confidence what the outcome of Conclave will be.'

The shot switches. The new picture shows a group of cardinals walking slowly. Some are bent and aged: they remind MacCarthy of Paul. He wonders, briefly, whether they will elect an old man. And then this thought changes as, coming behind the procession of cardinals, he glimpses their attendants for Conclave – the confessors, a doctor, two John of God nurses, the team of nuns who will cook and clean. There, too, is the barber, who carries enough razor blades for Koenig not to worry about growing a beard. Beside him is the electrician with sufficient adapter plugs to resolve the concern of Cardinal Carberry of St Louis, who has publicly wondered whether he will be able to connect his American razor to an Italian socket. Behind the electrician is the plumber who will ensure the deliberations are not disturbed by gurgling pipes or blocked toilets. And behind him is a pair of blue-suited men. MacCarthy is not certain, but he thinks these are probably the electronic surveillance experts Ciban has ordered to sweep the Conclave area for recording or transmitting devices. Although MacCarthy doesn't know the details, there's a wild story doing the rounds that some of his colleagues are intending to bug Conclave. He refuses to believe it.

The camera shot cuts to pick up the purposeful figure of Koenig. The cardinal is unaware Greeley has already elected him; Greeley has told NBC's *Today* he thinks Koenig will be the next 'elderly interim' pope. Even if he had known what Greeley predicted, such speculation would not trouble Koenig. Besides, he is far more concerned with the very threat MacCarthy discounts. Koenig fears the Soviet Union or one of its satellites might attempt to penetrate Conclave electronically; he admits he has no firm basis for this fear, except that he knows the Russians are capable of anything. Nor does he think it necessary for them to plant a bug inside the Conclave area. Sophisticated equipment – Koenig has been told by his contacts in the world of secret intelligence – now make it possible to monitor from a distance.

In SJUDIO One the screen fills with the smiling faces of Cardinals Gordon Gray of Edinburgh and Reginald Delargey of Wellington, New Zealand. Both men exchange greetings with the crowd behind the crush barrier and Delargey replies to a call from the press pen – 'How long you going to be, Reggie?' – with the equally breezy forecast, 'See you all Monday.'

MacCarthy scribbles a reminder. 'Short Conclave? If election goes past Monday it means there will have been twelve inconclusive ballots. Deadlock. But seems unlikely.'

Wojtyla marches steadily across the monitor. He exudes vigour. There is a set to his strong square chin and a relaxed look in his eyes. MacCarthy notes: 'A charismatic Pole. Some combination!' The camera picks up Hume; the Englishman seems pensive and withdrawn, but to MacCarthy, 'He is the epitome of how a cardinal should look going into Conclave: solemn, hands clasped, head lowered as in silent prayer.' Benelli bounces in, radiating confidence. Luciani appears; everything about him suggests uncertainty: his smile, the way he keeps adjusting his biretta. MacCarthy wonders: this is the Italian some of the secular press are saying is *papabile* – how can they be so sure? It sounds to MacCarthy very much like another of those campaigns which have been expanding and bursting during the past few days.

He writes: 'Conclave can elect any baptized male Catholic, though this is unlikely to happen. This is also the largest Conclave ever, a hundred and eleven voters. The Americans, with eight, are the second biggest national group. But none of them have curial experience.'

Inside the Pauline Chapel, Cardinal Krol of Philadelphia waits patiently, a strikingly handsome figure with a strong Polish face, silver hair brushed straight back. Krol does not come to Rome very often and that is the way he prefers it. But, like Cardinal Terence Cooke of New York, he has kept up his Italian. And, if nothing else, it has helped Krol pick his way through the two weeks he's been in Rome. As the ranking US cardinal, Krol has chaired regular meetings at Villa Stritch where he and his American colleagues compared notes. He is absolutely certain none of them has indulged in any lobbying, and he is angry with Greeley for doubting the cardinals are meeting for any purpose other than 'to inform ourselves on possible *papabili* – we have to be informed electors'. Krol thinks Greeley has 'a personality problem', the way he keeps on carping about the Church and its princes.

The prime target for Greeley's vitriol remains Cody, who stands near

Krol looking a little out of breath following his walk from the Ducal Hall. He stares fixedly at Michelangelo's awesome 'Conversion of Saul' and 'Martyrdom of St Peter' which cover two walls of the Pauline Chapel. Like Marcinkus, Cody is now certain the incessant attacks on him will continue in the next pontificate. Baggio, for one, will not let go. Nor will the Chicago *Sun-Times*. Thank God, at least, he has told people, for the *Chicago Tribune*. But it is not just whether he gets a good or bad press which must be concerning Cody: there is a rumour going about — sufficiently virulent for at least one newspaperman to have tackled him on the matter — that the Inland Revenue Service is going to be taking a long hard look at the finances of the Chicago diocese. That is certainly not a nice thought to be carrying into Conclave.

On MacCarthy's monitor the camera in the Pauline Chapel continues to favour the Italian cardinals. It focuses on Poletti, leaving ample time for MacCarthy to jot down that the vicar-general of Rome has been dedicated to pastoral work; it's the sort of fact he can always slip in if for some reason there's a need for him to expand his commentary. The shrewd face of Paolo Bertoli is next lingered upon; in his robes he appears an intimidating seventy-year-old. Siri is seen, but his impassive face shows no sign that he knows he is being scrutinized. The camera settles on Villot as he leads the cardinals in brief prayers.

Now, at last, it is the turn of Virgilio Noé. Firmly clasping before him the gold papal cross, he leads the cardinals in procession to the Sistine Chapel. Watching them pass once more across the monitor, MacCarthy notes: 'It is only a journey of a hundred feet. But what lies at the end will be the start of the most important decision these men can now make.'

A new camera position — this time from inside the Sistine Chapel — and with it comes the sound of singing. MacCarthy begins to tape-record the choir of the Sistine Chapel singing the hymn *Veni, Creator Spiritus*. He will use snippets of the tape in his broadcast. He notes that the Chapel is alive with light and movement, enhanced by the camera panning slowly over art treasures unequalled in the Western world. MacCarthy reminds himself that for centuries this was the private chapel of the popes, and that only in the last hundred years has it been the setting for papal elections. As a protective measure the floor of the Chapel has been raised and covered by blockboard carpeted with cheap fawn-coloured felt. A purple-draped desk stands before the altar. The Scrutineers' tables and chairs are nearby. Behind the altar with its silver candlesticks hangs a tapestry depicting the first Pentecost. And behind this, soaring to the ceiling, Michelangelo's magnificent 'Last Judgement' broods over the assembly.

The cardinals, their places marked by name cards, begin sitting behind the two rows of long, narrow tables which face each other across the Chapel. Their chairs, finished in red velvet, are straight-backed and look very uncomfortable.

And there, in a corner of the Chapel, surrounded by tubular scaffolding to keep it away from the wall and to protect the frescoes, is the celebrated chimney in which the results of the ballots will be burnt. MacCarthy remembers he plans later to broadcast a separate item on the chimney and its history.

Suddenly, the monitor is filled with the beaky face of Noé. For a moment he looks around, aware he is the centre of attention. He wets his lips. Then, in a clear voice he speaks the only words he is allowed, to mark this unique moment.

'*Extra omnes!*'

Everybody out! His speaking part is temporarily over. But the order is enough for the choir, altar servers, invited guests, journalists and television crews, to leave.

Moments later the monitor in Studio One goes blank. MacCarthy makes one final jotting: '4.59 pm – area cleared. Conclave under way.'

17

There are still other formalities to be observed. Escorted by Noé, Jaime Sin, who has been specially chosen by his fellow cardinals for this role, walks towards the sculpted main wooden door of the Sistine Chapel. The Filipino, mindful of his responsibilities, has read up on Conclave. He now knows enough to have made even Martin nod approvingly. Sin can see the prefect standing on the other side of the open door, watching them approach, inscrutable as ever. The cardinal has sometimes wondered how Martin, given his many duties, manages to find time to search out all the information he possesses, though Sin can now well understand the fascination that delving into the unique papal election procedure holds for the prefect.

For Sin it has also been a richly rewarding journey into the past, going back to those first Conclaves when priests were literally thrown, screaming protests, into the business of producing a new pope. Indeed, it had not even been clerics who invented the process. Conclaves were created for pragmatic reasons by hard-headed secular rulers in a century – the thirteenth – when Europe was dominated by the papacy. Then, the security of every throne on the continent depended on its relationship with the Roman pope. His policies, his wishes and preferences, his likes and dislikes, his vendettas and quarrels, even the interests of his family and the particular dynasties he favoured: all these could unseat a king or queen, emperor or empress, prince or princess of the blood. Consequently, when the chair of St Peter fell vacant – and some interregnums lasted for years – the stability of Europe, its political institutions, its international trade, the very peace of the entire area was threatened. To survive, the Europe of 750 years ago needed a pope. Yet in Rome itself at this time, following the death of Innocent III in 1216, the cardinals were so at loggerheads with each other they could not find agreement on anything – except that they alone held the power to appoint the next pope. In this turbulent mood they met in Perugia to elect Innocent's successor. They were still bitterly feuding when the local authorities locked the doors on their meeting place. The result was gratifying: the cardinals, frightened by this unexpected imprisonment, quickly chose Honorius III as pope. If not exactly a proper Conclave it had prepared the way.

Honorius was followed by Gregory IX in 1227. And it was he – with his ineffectual ways, his foolish alliances and his military and political posturing – who led the Church and Europe to the collision point only a formal Conclave would eventually solve. Having antagonized England, Spain and France, Gregory next tangled with Frederick II, emperor of all Germany. It was a fatal mistake. Frederick's armies steamrolled down through Italy almost to the gates of Rome. The sight of their vast encampment stretching out over the hills undoubtedly contributed to Gregory's demise. With a strangled moan – he may have been asking for God's forgiveness – Gregory fell to the ground and died of a massive heart attack. Perhaps his age also had something to do with his dying: Gregory was almost one hundred years old.

His death on 21 August 1241 caused new and increasingly squalid divisions within the College of Cardinals. They could not agree who to elect as the man most likely to appease the wrath of Frederick. At this time Rome was governed by one of the Orsinis, the most powerful lay family behind the papacy. Orsini recognized his own future was at stake: if a pope was not quickly produced to open a dialogue with Frederick, Rome, like the rest of Italy, would fall under hated foreign domination. Orsini set about ending the friction among the cardinals in typical fashion. He had each one bound hand and foot and publicly flogged. Afterwards, the brutalized cardinals were thrown into the Septizodium, a massive three-tiered structure which had already stood on the Appian Way for nearly a thousand years. Orsini ordered its door be locked and the windows blocked in. Sentries were posted around the building and on its roof with orders to kill anybody attempting to enter or leave. The ten cardinals found themselves incarcerated in appalling conditions: bedding that was filthy and food barely edible; their lavatory buckets were not to be emptied until after they had produced a pontiff. When one cardinal looked like dying he was quickly placed by the others in a crude coffin and its lid was lowered. Inside, the suffocating cardinal could hear the chanting of the Mass for the *already* dead. The roof sentries, forbidden to leave their posts, used the gutters as latrines. Whenever the violent Roman summer thunderstorms struck, the roof drains became clogged with the sentries' refuse. Nevertheless the cardinals needed over two months to agree that a Milanese cardinal – he looked not unlike Paul – should be their new pope. He took the name Celestine IV, but died two weeks later without having been consecrated. Frederick finally stepped in. He demanded a replacement pope – fast. The cardinals hesitated. Once more Frederick set about convincing them; he began systematically to destroy their personal property, a military juggernaut which moved from one estate to another. The cardinals eventually saw the wisdom of meeting again to produce a pope. Frederick's sword, serving as Conclave key, created Innocent IV.

And so it had begun – this process of election behind locked doors and sealed windows: there would still be problems, but the pattern was set for organized Conclave coming to reasonably quick decisions. And, since 1271, there have always been a trio of men standing outside the entrance to the Conclave area just before the deliberations are due to begin – even as Prefect Martin, the governor of Vatican City and the commandant of the Swiss Guard, all now stand outside the Sistine Chapel's main door waiting for Noé and Sin to reach them.

Martin and his companions are responsible for securing the exterior approaches to the Conclave area; Noé and Sin are responsible for the security of the interior. Between them they must ensure there is no infraction of secrecy. That is what lies behind the ritual which follows. At a nod from Noé, Martin shuts the door of the Chapel. The commandant turns the key and the tumblers in the great lock drop into place. The governor then turns the handle, endeavouring to open the door. When he has failed, Noé, on the other side of the door, repeats the attempt. Satisfied he is securely locked in, he repeats his hallowed line: 'Extra omnes!'

Noé and Sin then walk to the Parrot Courtyard. There, a stout wooden wall has been temporarily erected to block off the courtyard from outside access. Fitted into the wall are two revolving drums. The larger one is to pass in extra food and supplies should they be required. The smaller is for the sole use of Cardinal Paupini, prefect of the Apostolic Penitentiary, the aged Italian who told Paul these are 'black days' for the Church in matters of conscience. Paupini's tribunal decides important cases where Catholics request guidance in problems of conscience, dispensation from Church law or forgiveness for trespasses. The presence of this smaller drum symbolizes the priority of God's mercy over all other duties of the Church, including electing a pontiff: through here may pass only sealed communications which require Paupini's urgent attention.

The master of ceremonies stands by the drum and solemnly repeats: 'Extra omnes!' There is no response from beyond the partition. He revolves each of the drums. Satisfied they are obstruction-free, Noé and Sin continue their tour of inspection, checking that every window which could give access to the Conclave area is sealed with the lead strips handed down through the centuries for this purpose.

Finally they return to the Sistine Chapel. Sin takes his seat near the end of one of the rows of cardinals and Noé reports to Villot the Conclave area is secure.

There are yet more formalities to come.

*

Outside in the courtyards adjoining the area, Swiss Guards are posted and snap to attention as Martin and his colleagues complete their tour of inspection. Abroad, some of the papal nuncios and delegates advise their host governments Conclave has started. Radio, television and newspapers carry the same message. In Vatican Radio's main studio, high up on Vatican Hill within the mock palace built by Leo XIII, the team of the prestigious *Four Voices* programme prepare to help keep the world informed of developments. The studio looks no different from any other – except that a tiny buzzer has been secretly wired into the control console. It is the receiver for at least one bug which has been secreted into Conclave.

*

The man who carries the transmitter is among the attendants in the Sistine Chapel. The bug is in the shape of a shirt button. To activate the device he merely has to squeeze the button. It simultaneously produces a low-pitched sound in the radio studio console. He will squeeze the button a prearranged number of times the moment a pope has been elected. The man has been assured there is virtually no risk involved. But listening to Villot he hears what will happen to him should he be discovered.[1]

Villot is reading aloud from Paul's *Eligendo* how his successor must be chosen. The 5,600 Latin words fill sixty-two pages. The Camerlengo sternly reminds his listeners that if one of them is found using 'any type of transmitting or receiving instrument', that person will immediately 'be expelled from the Conclave and subjected to grave penalties'. It takes Villot a sonorous thirty minutes to read the sixty separate conditions Paul has laid down.

Even then the Camerlengo is not done. Villot reads again the solemn Conclave oath binding everyone present to accept each of Paul's conditions, to reject outside interference and, above all, to keep the deliberations secret.

The Camerlengo consults a list of typewritten names. He calls out the first one. The Egyptian patriarch of Alexandria rises and walks to the purple-draped desk before the altar where Villot is standing. The patriarch places his right hand on a copy of the Gospels and swears to uphold the Conclave oath, adding 'so help me God and these Holy Gospels which I touch with my hand'.

The patriarch returns to his seat and Villot calls the next cardinal to come forward.

*

In *L'Osservatore Romano*, editorial staff check the twelve different proofs of the newspaper's front page. Each dummy contains a photograph and potted biography of one of the cardinals the editors have predicted will be the next pope. Eleven they will happily discard. But if all twelve prove to be wrong, their carefully laid plans will come to nothing and there could well ensue the nearest thing to a good, old-fashioned panic of a newspaper trying to meet a deadline.

*

It needs an hour for the cardinals and their attendants individually to swear the Conclave oath.

But Villot is not finished; some of the Italian cardinals – flagrantly breaking the very pledge they have made – will later put it about that the Frenchman now behaved as if he is stage-struck. Yet Paul's *Eligendo* requires the Camerlengo to address them further, as he does, on the importance of their deliberations and the need to keep the 'good of the Church' uppermost in their minds. It takes him ten minutes. Only then does Villot conclude.

'May the Lord bless you all. Amen.'

*

Koenig has drawn cell eleven in the pre-Conclave balloting for accommodation. It is in a small, partitioned room. On the other side of the plywood divider, he can hear Cardinal Hume walking on the parquet floor. Across the corridor Koenig listens to an American voice telling somebody it's like being back at school. It sounds like either Manning or Krol; Koenig cannot be certain because the partitioning produces a baffle-effect which muffles voices.

Walking from the Sistine Chapel to his accommodation, Koenig glimpsed a few of the other cells and knows he is lucky: some of them are really poky, the result of a small salon or office being divided into three and even four living spaces. Each cell – the term goes back to Leo XIII who was the first pope to decree cardinals must have separate rooms in Conclave so they may meditate in peace – is furnished in virtually the same discount-store manner. There is a bedside lamp, a washbowl and pitcher, a plastic bucket, a hard-backed chair and a stark wooden prie-dieu. Above it is a single wooden crucifix. Beside the pitcher is a bar of soap and two small towels. On the bedside cabinet is a single roll of toilet tissue, a dozen sheets of writing paper and a couple of ballpoint pens. Alongside each bed is a strip of floral patterned carpet. Beneath almost every bed is the result of some intensive searching by Villot's staff, who have combed Rome's monasteries and nunneries to borrow what the Americans call Uncle Joe's and the Italians refer to as *vasi da notte*. Koenig prefers the English, chamber pots. His is plain white with a sturdy handle. Villot has decided the walk to the toilets might be too far for some of the older cardinals to make during the night.

Like the other beds, Koenig's has been borrowed from a Rome seminary. It is narrow with a thin mattress over wire mesh, rather different, he muses ruefully, from his splendid interior-sprung feather-bed in Vienna. Not that Koenig minds. He sees the spartan living conditions as epitomizing the virtues of Conclave. He quickly unpacks and kneels to pray at the prie-dieu. All around him other cardinals are doing the same.

*

Watched by Noé – who is most curious to see what might happen – the two electronic surveillance technicians walk through the Conclave area. Each man holds a slim black sensor in his hand, rather like a photographer's light meter, which he moves back and forth. The sensors have a range of twenty feet and can penetrate through walls and wooden partitions. The men move unobtrusively, following the signposts at various intersections which indicate the way to the dining hall, toilets, the Sistine Chapel and the various cells.

Suddenly needles on the sensors begin to twitch. The technicians separate to get a cross-bearing; their instruments are designed to lock on to each other so as to pinpoint a target more accurately. Moving slowly, eyes on the needles, the technicians pad up the corridor. The needles become steady. There is a buzzing sound from a bedroom. Then the technicians and Noé relax. The sensors have picked up someone using a battery-operated razor. The search continues.

*

The food is as simple as the cells. It has been prepared by the nuns who operate kitchens for some of the poor of Rome, and are renowned for their gentleness as much as for their ability to make pasta seem even more unpalatable to many of the non-Italian cardinals. The sisters have set up a glorified field kitchen in a high vaulted room in the Borgia apartments. From here they dispense the first meal of Conclave – a supper of bread, spaghetti with a meat sauce, bowls of fruit and pitchers of red and white wine. There is also beer and mineral water. The dining room is the Hall of the Popes, once the armoury of the Borgia family:

thirty-five feet above the refectory tables is a fifteenth-century fresco by Pinturicchio.

Koenig sits opposite Wojtyla. Like the Canadian, Léger, the Pole enjoys the simple fare and tells his neighbours it reminds him of the trips he regularly makes into the steppes: a bottle of wine and a chunk of bread can be quite enough for a man in those circumstances, he says, grinning hugely.

Wojtyla has one of the smallest cells in the area; it is little larger than a broom cupboard. Yet Koenig has never seen the Pole happier; he is laughing and joking and listening, and doing all at the same time. One moment he is vibrantly strident, the next he speaks in the gentlest of tones. It is an actor's delivery, but there is nothing actorlike in his honesty. Wojtyla radiates sincerity, making Koenig think again that here is a man of exceptional qualities, one who combines high intelligence with a big heart.

Everywhere the conversation is relaxed and wide-ranging. The Latin Americans and the Spanish are at one table. Aramburu prefers to listen, sitting with hands on the table, straight-backed, nodding at the points his colleagues make. His composure hides inner distress. Shortly before entering Conclave the aristocratic Argentinian telephoned Buenos Aires to learn that President Videla plans to be in Rome when the next pope is crowned. Videla will be coming at a time when feelings against Italy are running high in Buenos Aires because of the way the Italian president snubbed Videla; inevitably this Argentine reaction has provoked a mood of reprisal in certain Italian quarters: Rome's newspapers have published some very unflattering stories about Videla's bloody background. It could become very nasty if Videla struts along in the wake of the next pontiff.

Preoccupied by such concerns, it is perhaps understandable that Aramburu has not told his companions why he no longer supports Luciani's candidature. It may also be that, following the strictures of Paul's *Eligendo*, Aramburu does not wish to exert any influence on their decision-making.

Luciani is flanked by Felici and Benelli, while across the table sits the striking figure of Bernardin Gantin, his ebony-black face shining with perspiration in the muggy atmosphere. Within the hall, where at best conditions are hot and stuffy in August, now, with over one hundred cardinals present and without the benefit of air conditioning, they are becoming oppressive.

Ratzinger of Munich shares one of what will become known as the 'European tables'. He too has entered Conclave in a far from ideal frame of mind. The reason is not hard to discern: Rome is plastered with newspaper placards announcing Küng's blueprint for the next papacy.

Ratzinger finds almost everything Küng advocates unacceptable. Yet among certain cardinals Ratzinger has detected a measure of cautious support for some of the theologian's ideas. Naturally he will not identify those cardinals who do not completely reject Küng's beliefs, but Conclave attendants are whispering that there seems to be a certain coolness between the Bavarian Ratzinger and Willebrands, the Dutchman from Utrecht.

Enrique y Tarancon, the cardinal from Madrid, is among the first to leave the dining hall, his tinted glasses shielding his eyes from the extra lights slung from the ceiling. Shortly afterwards the influential Spaniard is seen strolling in the San Damaso Courtyard, deep in conversation with Suenens, the charismatic Belgian.

*

This sort of detail will enable a certain person inside Conclave to produce a highly secret and totally illegal diary which he will claim actually to have written while in this forbidden area. It will largely consist of impressions, overheard conversations, trivia about the personal habits of cardinals. More importantly, it will record the results of the ballots in the powerful mystery of a papal election. The diarist is a lowly attendant. He will insist he is keeping his record because he thinks what is happening is 'the most historic decision since Pilate washed his hands'. Hyperbole apart, he also thinks the secrecy is pointless, that it has no real part to play in the process of choosing a modern man to become the Vicar of Christ, that Conclave should be seen for what it is, basically a simple act of election. Commendable though such thoughts may be to those outside Conclave, the attendant nevertheless intends to preserve his diary in the security of a Rome bank vault, with instructions that it must not be released until after his death. Since he is only in his early forties, it could be the next century before the full extent of his jottings surface. However, to substantiate his claim to have written the diary while in Conclave, he will reveal segments that, on cross-checking, seem accurate, so providing a tantalizing insight into who did and said what in the drama about to unfold.

*

The atmospheric fog thickens after dinner as cardinals light up cigarettes, cigars and pipes. While forbidden to smoke in the Sistine Chapel during the forthcoming long hours of balloting – though there is no specific ban on Krol's penchant for chewing on an unlit cigar – they are permitted to smoke in the adjoining corridors and their cells. This proviso makes the two firemen attendants nervous; their duties

188

include not only maintaining the ballot-burning stove, but also they must keep wary eyes open for any casually disposed smouldering butts.

Felici is one of several Italians who have brought bottles of *digestivi*; the liqueurs act as a welcome lubricant for the 'consultations' which begin in the cells.

Gantin prefers to keep his discussions on the move. He strides first with one cardinal, then another, and everyone who listens to this tall, handsome man cannot but be struck by his intelligence and gentleness – and courage sufficient for him to have been a threat to the Marxist government of Benin which forced him into exile. Gantin, like the other black African cardinals, is only a fourth-generation Christian, but Villot is not alone in thinking the voices of these men in Conclave will provide an important balance to all the theorizing he has heard these past weeks. In the Camerlengo's view there is no question that the problems of the Third World must be in the forefront of the next pope's mind.

Noé and Sin make a second tour of the area; until the end of Conclave they will do so four times a day. The two men reach their last port of call, the Sistine Chapel. They pause in astonishment. There is a lone figure kneeling and staring up at the majesty of Michelangelo's art, apparently riveted by the finger of God reaching out to radiate life to Adam. Michelangelo's Adam is not circumcised – and perfectly right, too, thinks Sin, for Adam preceded Abraham – but he has a navel, and Sin has always assumed this more a demonstration of the artist's understanding of anatomy than an expression of any doubt he may have had about the authenticity of the Book of Genesis. And God – a virile, white-bearded man, old yet ageless in his flimsy pink nightshirt – is this representation a satire on religion? Such questions about the *Last Judgement* and the ceiling frescoes have intrigued Sin in the past. Now, they do not matter. They seem irrelevant in the presence of this kneeling figure. In the dim light of the flickering red lamp in front of the Tabernacle, they can see he is in fact not staring at the painting, but praying. He is motionless, hands before him, head held high, his rosary passing bead by bead through his fingers. It is Albino Luciani.

*

Koenig awakens to an unaccustomed sound – that of men quietly going about their ablutions; it reminds him of the time he was hospitalized. He can hear Hume pouring water into his washbowl and from across the corridor there's the hum of an electric razor. It is just after six am on Saturday, 26 August. It is hot and airless in Koenig's cell. Siri was right last night when he said it is like living in a tomb. On the other hand the ascetic Hume expressed the thought that the primitive arrangements ensure nothing comes between the cardinals and God. Manning of Los Angeles hasn't seemed to notice the living conditions; he is finding the entire Conclave experience novel and exciting. Koenig can well understand the reaction; he still remembers the feeling of awe which had gripped him as he entered his first Conclave fifteen years ago.

While shaving and dressing he thinks back to that time in 1963 when he personally played a decisive role in persuading Paul to accept office. Koenig and seventy-nine other cardinals had filed into Conclave on 19 June. Paul – then Cardinal Montini – was the favourite of those who wanted John XXIII's open-window policies continued. On the first ballot Montini had led with about thirty votes, but he was closely followed by two other cardinals, each with some twenty votes. The first, Lercaro of Bologna, was the choice of those who thought his simplicity, even more obvious holiness and Franciscan-like poverty, seemed to mirror better John than the cool, withdrawn manner of Montini. The other main contender, backed by Giuseppe Siri, was Cardinal Antoniutti. Deadlock ensued through the second and third ballots. Koenig and Suenens of Belgium had then intervened, arguing that Montini, with his diplomatic and bureaucratic skills, coupled with his very obvious support for John's policies, was the ideal man for both sides. In the fourth and last ballot of the day, Lercaro's votes switched to Montini. It placed him well ahead of Siri's candidate but just short of the two-thirds plus one majority of fifty-four needed to win.

At this point a certain Cardinal Gustavo Testa suddenly broke the peace of Conclave by standing up in the Sistine Chapel and loudly proclaiming he would never have been a cardinal but for John. Then he turned to his immediate neighbour, Confalonieri, and asked him to stop blocking Montini's progress. Before the astonished Confalonieri could respond, Testa had launched into an impassioned appeal for the conservatives to consider 'the good of the Church' – the very phrase Villot used when opening the present Conclave – and not to wreck everything John had achieved. With this, Testa had bowled out of the Sistine Chapel leaving his peers open-mouthed.

That night Koenig came across Montini in the Galleria del Lapidario, looking anguished. Koenig had sat with him, trying to cheer him up. Montini would not be consoled, but kept on insisting he did not want to be pope. Koenig made one last effort: 'It's dark now, and you cannot see clearly. But the light will come again and you will see what you must do.' Next day Montini became Pope Paul. If Koenig and Suenens had not intervened, the Church could have been ruled by Lercaro, who might even have moved from the Vatican and gone to live in a Rome slum. He had already turned his palace into a hostel for homeless boys. There was no telling what he would have done had he become pontiff.

In the present Conclave there was another cardinal very like the saintly Lercaro, Léger of Montreal. Koenig barely knew the French-Canadian; what he did know he admired. Not every man could give up the position, power and the comfort of diocese living to work for the dying in the depths of tropical Africa. The Church clearly needed men like Léger: he was a model for everybody seeking the true meaning of service. But a pope, especially in these troubled times, could not lead the Church cut off from the outside world, however much he might wish to. The next pope must have high ideals, unshakeable beliefs certainly. That is why Koenig thinks it may take up to a week to choose him. He doubts there will be a repeat of the one-day Conclave of 1939 which swept Pius XII into office; he hopes there will not be the prolonged impasse of 1923 when it took fourteen ballots to elect Pius XI. This time, unlike 1958 when John was pre-Conclave favourite, or 1963, when Paul had such strong initial support, Koenig does not see an obvious choice. In many ways he still wishes his co-electors would look seriously at Wojtyla.

*

Shortly after eight o'clock, the cardinals troop into the Sistine Chapel. Each genuflects before the High Altar and goes to his seat. They have concelebrated Mass and eaten a quick breakfast of coffee and rolls.

Those attendants so inclined have had a busy time trying to work out what the latest contacts may mean. There has been the intriguing sight of the 'pen pal' pacing back and forth with 'the traveller', both deep in conversation. Could this mean that Sergio Pignedoli, the nearest thing to a pre-Conclave favourite, is losing ground? Is this why this cardinal who corresponds regularly with hundreds of persons he has met when abroad is trying to persuade Baggio, the globe-travelling trouble-shooter, to be supportive? They do make an unlikely pair: Baggio is jowly, tough-minded, as rigid in some of his thinking as his stiff-legged gait; Pignedoli is languid and easy-going, his voice soft and almost sepulchral. But they have found sufficient in common to remain together right up to the moment they enter the Chapel.

Felici goes in alone. Yet the watchful attendants, scurrying about the business of making beds and sweeping the corridors, have noticed him well before then. Felici has been spotted using his skills as an advocate to push Luciani's cause. He's been seen entering the cell of Michele Pellegrino, the retired archbishop of Turin. The only question really is why Felici bothered. Almost certainly Pellegrino is already a committed supporter of the patriarch of Venice. Though he has just retired at the age of seventy-five, Pellegrino reflects — perhaps next to Léger — the nearest personality to John XXIII's. He's got the same courage and tenacity, the same simplicity: he prefers to be called 'Padre' rather than 'Eminence'; he wears simple cassocks instead of regal robes; his pectoral cross is wooden rather than jewelled; he has refused a limousine and drives a car even more modest than Luciani's – a Simca 1000 – Pellegrino has little in common with Felici. Yet the very fact that Felici has called on him is seen as a sign Felici is leaving nothing to chance. He's drumming hard. Surely that is the reason he has also been with Antonio Poma and Corrado Ursi. The Italians are very different in personality and outlook. Poma is withdrawn, at times almost reclusive; Ursi is expansive and already one of the real mixers in Conclave. If Felici has persuaded both men to follow his line on Luciani – goes the whispered scuttlebutt – then he is making serious inroads into the hopes of other *papabili*.

Three of these are seated close together. Willebrands, even in his robes, looks a man with itchy feet; the Dutchman's demeanour suggests he finds the whole business an interruption to what he likes best, travelling. There had been talk just before Conclave that the primate of Holland could easily become pope if only he agreed to follow a curial fundamental: never to speak bluntly and passionately and, above all, openly on sensitive Church matters; but the betting is it is too late for Willebrands to change his frank, outgoing approach.

Nobody seems to know how, but James Knox, formerly archbishop of Melbourne and Australia's ranking cardinal, is now on some *papabili* lists. Yet his presence there should not be a surprise. Knox is currently prefect of the Congregation for the Sacraments and Divine Worship. He is the first Australian to hold such high Vatican office. He is sixty-four, superbly fit, and in the parlance of the cricket game he adores, Knox is a very good first-wicket down bet.

Leon Duval, the cardinal from Algeria who rejoices in the nickname 'Archbishop Mohammed', because of his drive to cement Catholic–Moslem ties, has managed to remain an outside possibility. This is partly due to his rigidly orthodox stand on all matters of doctrine. If there is going to be a pope from Africa, then, after Gantin, Duval could be the one.

The eight American cardinals are scattered throughout the two rows of electors. Though some US commentators – notably Greeley and CBS broadcasters – play down their influence, the notion is not shared within Conclave. The feeling here is that the Americans, because of their numerical strength and the fact they represent some of the most sophisticated Catholics in the world, could exercise considerable sway – and may already have done so. Krol, for instance, has entered into an easy alliance with Koenig, partly because they both think so highly of Wojtyla and partly because they share a common view of where the

Church should be going. Cody has also been renewing his links with the Polish cardinals. Carberry of St Louis and Cooke of New York have proved to be ideal listening posts. They have discounted much of the pre-Conclave waffle and, at their regular briefings in the Villa Stritch, have given their colleagues a very good indication of what other cardinals are thinking. Following Krol's example, the Americans are low-key yet well-informed. They are all determined to vote only according to their own dictates; no one has given them anything resembling an instruction on how they should cast their ballots.

*

Maurice Roy of Quebec and Léger of Montreal have been blessedly free of the debating and discussion which has so preoccupied many of their colleagues.

Still, nobody now seriously thinks of Roy as a candidate. In spite of sound enough liberal credentials, Roy has fallen foul of some South American cardinals who think he is one of those who continue to drag their heels over condemning torture in Latin America; the accusation is debatable and hardly new, but in the super-heated politico-religious atmosphere of that region, Roy has been tabbed at best a fence-sitter on the issue. Some cardinals have also been reminding themselves, and smarting at the memory, that at the 1967 Congress for the Lay Apostolate – a crucial early milestone in Paul's pontificate – Roy had tried to influence the resolution-making process. The memory of his failure is now almost as black a mark against him as was his attempt in the first place to manipulate matters. Both effectively combine to douse any hopes he may have of ever becoming pontiff.

But then, as the cardinals settle in their chairs, no one really knows what may happen. As Felici says, the Holy Spirit moves in a wondrous way.

*

By 8.30 the one hundred and eleven electors are seated. Villot has observed them taking their places. The Camerlengo is aware all eyes are once more on him.

In almost every sense this is 'his' Conclave. Villot has overseen all the arrangements, made the decisions – some carefully considered, others arbitrary – approved everything, from the cost of the felt floor covering to the price of the last sack of pasta, seen something of the passions involved and judged the important issues at stake. It has been a tremendous concentration of responsibility. And now, as silence descends on the gathering, he can more easily understand how that most calm of cardinals, Pacelli, Camerlengo during the 1939 Conclave and a man renowned for his icy control which nothing could panic, had broken into a sweat at this moment in the proceedings. It is also easier for Villot now to understand the words of Cardinal Antonelli, who wrote a century earlier: 'Nothing stands between us and the Lord Jesus, between what is human and what is Divine.'

Villot waits, watching the cardinals. He knows there are three possible ways for the pope to be chosen. The first is by 'acclamation'; that is, if a cardinal feels divinely inspired, he will stand up and loudly proclaim the name of the person he appoints pope. There is even a precise form of wording he must follow for this electrifying moment: 'Most Eminent Fathers, in view of the singular virtue and probity of the Most Reverend . . . , I judge him worthy to be elected Roman Pontiff and I now choose him as Pope.' Then, if all other electors feel similarly inspired, they will simultaneously shout out their assent with the word, '*Eligo*'. Should this occur Conclave will be over. The second mode of election is by 'delegation'. Under this procedure, the electors may – if they all agree – appoint a committee of up to fifteen cardinals to select the new pope. It must be given a clear time-limit to arrive at a choice. Nobody thinks this method will be adopted today. The most likely will be the third form of election, by 'scrutiny', secret ballot.

But equally nobody can say this is certain. That is why Villot waits.

*

There are perhaps fifteen thousand people already in St Peter's Square as MacCarthy skirts it on his way to work. Everyone looks frequently towards the Sistine Chapel where the temporary smoke stack juts out from the roof.

MacCarthy probably knows more, after his research, than anyone about the chimney. He has mentally locked the facts into place in a smooth-flowing sequence that will form the basis for a commentary script.

Until 1550 – the Conclave which produced Julius III – voting papers were burnt in a *focune*, the touch-hole of a gun, lit inside the Sistine Chapel. Julius was an art-loving pope and fretted the smoke could damage the frescoes. He decreed that for all future Conclaves a stove must be installed with its chimney stack extended clear of the building. From that time crowds have appeared in St Peter's Square to watch the traditional black smoke for an inconclusive vote and white smoke for a successful election. The 1963 Conclave had produced its own problems. Klieg lights were beamed at the stack to illuminate it for the television cameras. When the smoke emerged, few could immediately decide its colour. An Italian fuel manufacturer subsequently offered to install a foolproof system to eliminate such doubts during later Conclaves. Villot refused, still preferring candles of various hues being burnt with the voting papers to enhance the colour of the smoke. In many ways, thinks MacCarthy, the Camerlengo is engagingly old-fashioned.

*

Villot is also patient. He sits perfectly still, betraying no emotion, waiting to see whether any cardinal will propose election by acclamation. Ten silent minutes go by. Only then does the Camerlengo address the assembly. There has been no intervention by the Holy Spirit; no one suggests delegation. It is time to proceed to election by scrutiny.

Master of Ceremonies Noé, who has remained in the chapel with the cardinals for this sole purpose, begins to distribute to each a small pile of identical, rectangular ballot forms. Paul, perhaps during one of those lonely nights he could not sleep, designed them, deciding their size – two inches square – and the legend they carry, 'Eligo in Summum Pontificem' – 'I elect as Supreme Pontiff'. He allowed sufficient space beneath the words to write in a name. When Noé completes his task he leaves the Sistine, shutting the door on the cardinal electors behind him.

*

What will happen now, beneath the horrors of Michelangelo's version of the Apocalypse – where Jesus is shown as judge and king, shorn of enigma, ambiguity and mystery – is supposed to remain one of the most closely guarded secrets in the world. But this is 1978, when even cardinals find themselves exposed to and influenced by the intense pressures of the Age of Communications. A few cautiously concede that, just as Michelangelo's Christ in the Last Judgement fresco towering above their heads has nothing of the subtlety and compassion of the Gospel Jesus, so the ritual of which they are now part fails to take a realistic account of the real role of the papacy on the troubled international stage; there the secular powers, perhaps more than at any other time in history, are genuinely fascinated by the process which produces a new pope. These cardinals, for the best possible motives, will tell their trusted secretaries something of what occurs. The secretaries will compare notes and, in turn, inform their closest friends of what they have learned. In no time the facts will seep down to the level of that Conclave attendant who is keeping his diary. While two and two will still sometimes make five, generally speaking the secrets of Conclave, inviolate for so long, eventually will out. It is no bad thing. The door, if not exactly wide open, will no longer be shut tight.

*

Villot asks Sin to make sure the door is properly closed. The Camerlengo moves to a desk below the altar where Noé had previously placed in a silver chalice the names of every cardinal present. Then Sin, as junior cardinal appointed for the task, joins Villot.

The Camerlengo announces that the time has come to choose by lot the Scrutineers, the three cardinals who will examine and count the votes. As well as these, three *Infirmarii* must be selected. If the need arises, they will go to the cells of any electors who are taken ill and unable to come to the Sistine Chapel. The *Infirmarii* would collect their votes and bring them to the Scrutineers.

Sin shakes the chalice to mix the folded paper slips. He draws out the first one, unfolds it and reads out the name. It is Wojtyla. The second Scrutineer selected is Lorscheider of Brazil. The third is Gantin. The *Infirmarii* are then chosen. In the same manner three further appointments are made: the Revisers, the cardinals who will check the work of the Scrutineers. Once they are chosen Sin tips the remaining slips of paper from the chalice into another receptacle.

Villot calls the Scrutineers to the altar. Sin places the now empty chalice beside a silver plate on the altar. The Filipino returns to his seat. Villot puts the plate over the mouth of the chalice. Next he addresses the cardinals, reminding them again of the very precise procedure Paul laid down for voting, slowly reading out the Latin instructions.

'The completion of the cards must be carried out secretly by each cardinal elector, who will write down, as far as possible in writing that cannot be identified as his, the name of the person he chooses, taking care not to write other names as well, since this would make the votes null; the folding of the card is done down the centre of each card in such a way that the card is reduced to the width of about one inch.'

Then Villot too walks slowly to his seat.

The concentration is so intense that a number of cardinals look around nervously at a sudden buzzing. An insect is circling inside the Chapel.

Koenig notices that one or two of the men bunched almost elbow to elbow around him are staring at the *Last Judgement*. He doubts they will find much there to inspire the choice they all must now make; Koenig has always thought the fresco weighty and overbearing, intimidating rather than inspiring confidence. He wonders – and is momentarily surprised by the irrelevance of the thought – whether Islam is right when it forbids images or representations of the Divine.

The insect sound is joined by another, equally unfamiliar. It is the scratching of pen on paper.

At the altar Wojtyla is the first to write in his nominee. He folds the ballot in the prescribed form and kneels in prayer, the paper held in his tightly clasped hands. Then he arises and, facing the altar, utters the special oath Paul ordered.

'I call to witness Christ the Lord, who will be my judge, that my vote is given to the one who before God I consider should be elected.'

Wojtyla places his ballot paper on the silver plate, pauses for a moment, bows to the altar, then tilts the plate so the card drops into the chalice.

Lorscheider and Gantin repeat the identical process.

The other cardinals complete their voting forms, endeavouring to disguise their handwriting, looking neither left nor right so as to avoid any temptation to glance at what a neighbour has written. Then, one at a time, they go to the altar to cast their votes. The order of voting is almost militarily rigid: the most senior cardinals go first, with cardinal bishops preceding cardinal priests, who in turn go before cardinal deacons.

Koenig is one of the first to walk down the aisle. His shoes echo on the raised floor whose felt covering already shows signs of wear. He reaches the altar, kneels and prays for a moment, then rises and pronounces the oath. Having deposited his folded card, he walks quickly back to his seat.

Twenty-six minutes later – Felici is keeping a timetable – the last vote is tipped into the chalice.

Koenig does not think the atmosphere has perceptibly changed. Everybody is certainly very interested in what will now happen, but he does not sense any 'special tensions' or 'mounting drama'. Everyone seems to be very calm. Perhaps Aramburu is right, 'the Holy Spirit is making Itself felt'.

Wojtyla picks up the chalice and carries it to the Scrutineers' table below the altar. Before sitting at the table, he gives the receptacle a thorough shaking, holding it firmly in his strong hands. The sound of one hundred and eleven slips of paper swishing around inside the chalice carries to all parts of the Chapel.

Gantin is seated behind a second, empty chalice. Lorscheider is on the other side of Wojtyla. He sits with arms folded, eyes moving between the two vessels, as Gantin reaches a black hand into the full receptacle to withdraw the voting slips one at a time. As he transfers each to the second chalice, Lorscheider counts them off aloud. If the total number of cards does not correspond to the number of electors, all the slips will be burnt and a second vote taken at once. The numbers tally. The Scrutineers can move to the second stage.

Wojtyla switches the chalices so that the full one is once more before him. He dips his hand into the receptacle and takes out a card. He unfolds it and writes down the name on the sheet of paper. He then passes the card to Lorscheider. He, too, writes down the name before passing the card to Gantin. Gantin looks at it for a moment. Then in his captivating voice, he reads aloud the name, as Paul ordered, 'in an intelligible manner'.

The first vote is for Pignedoli.

Gantin writes down the name he has just read. All the other cardinals do the same.

Wojtyla once more dips into the chalice.[2]

*

MacCarthy is allowing himself three minutes and fifteen seconds – precisely thirty-two lines of script – to explain the custom of a pope taking a new name when elected. It will make a nice tailpiece for his broadcast this evening to Africa. He types his thoughts straight on to an old manual typewriter.

'The tradition goes back to the eleventh century. Before that popes simply kept their baptismal name – unless it was of pagan or barbarian origin. The first pope to change his name on election was John II, who governed the Church from 533 to 535. Previously he had been called Mercury, the name of a pagan god. In 955 John XII became pope – changing *his* name from Octavian, the name of a pagan emperor.'

MacCarthy reads back what he has typed, checking it against a stopwatch. Satisfied, he continues.

'Gregory V, who was pope from 996 to 999 – an easy date to remember! – was the first German pope of the Middle Ages and had "Brun" as his baptismal name. His motive for changing it to Gregory was that "Brun" was far too "barbarous" a sound for the pontiff. Sylvester II, who succeeded Gregory in 999, changed his name from Gerbert, for the same reason.'

Another check. He is well within the time he has allowed. He consults his notepad, sorting out the notes he has made, weaving them into the next cohesive thought.

'Pope John XIV, who ruled for eight months in 984, and Sergius IV, who was elected in 1009, both changed *their* names out of a sense of respect and veneration for the *first* pope, since both had originally been baptized Peter. There is a legend, still quoted in the Church today, that only the last pope to be elected will call himself Peter, and after that . . . the end of the world.'

MacCarthy pauses. Should he include this? The entire legend is surrounded by controversy. Even the simplest details about the man originally responsible for it are open to heated dispute. Had Malachy O'Morgain actually been born in 1094? Nobody now really knew. Could it really be true he had foretold the identities of ninety-eight popes, from the reign of Celestine II in 1143 to Paul? And had his predictions really looked into the future beyond this present Conclave?

But *not*, if St Malachy is to be believed, *that* far beyond. There are many – as MacCarthy well knows – who do believe the legend of this first formally canonized Irish saint. They accept that Malachy, reputedly born of a wealthy and learned family in Armagh, had been such an astonishing visionary he was able to forecast centuries ago that, after this Conclave produced a pope, there would only be three further pontiffs.

Malachy's predictions were supposedly made in 1139 while visiting Rome where he 'saw' – and committed to paper – a series of Latin phrases describing the popes down the ensuing centuries. Except for the final apocalyptic note about Petrus Romanus, the notations are very brief, no more than a few lines for each pope indicating his family name, birthplace, coat of arms or office held before election to the papacy. Some of the phrases contain certain ingenious word-plays or even puns; others are multiple prophecies. Many seem remarkably accurate. Adrian IV, the English pope, was designated by Malachy as *de Rure Albo*, which can be translated as either 'the Alban country', a medieval description of England, or 'from a white country'. Pius III, who reigned for only twenty-six days in 1503, was aptly described as *de Parvo Homine*, 'from a little man'. His family name was *Piccolomini*, Italian for 'little man'.

Many Catholic scholars maintain Malachy had nothing whatever to do with the predictions, that they are in fact a sixteenth-century forgery, written with hindsight. But MacCarthy does not think it possible to be so certain and dismissive. If they are faked then the accuracy of the forecasts should fail dramatically after the sixteenth century. This is not the case. Benedict XV was given the chilling appelation *Religio Depopulata*, 'religion laid waste'. He ruled during World War I which 'laid waste' the religious populations of several European countries. John XXIII was designated *Pastor et Nauta*, 'pastor and sailor'. He was certainly a great pastor and, until he became pope, John was patriarch of Venice, a city full of sailors; and it was he who chose the symbol for the Second Vatican Council – a cross and a ship. The prediction for John's successor was *Flors Florum*, 'flower of flowers'. Paul's coat of arms depicted three fleur-de-lis.

And now, if Malachy is to be believed, Paul's successor will be *De Medietate Lunae*. MacCarthy, fluent in Latin, wonders which of the cardinals is best suited to fit 'from the half moon'. That is the problem with Malachy, muses the broadcaster, he is just too obscure at times for full credence to be given his predictions.

MacCarthy looks again at what he has typed about the last pope being called Peter. According to Malachy: 'During his reign, the seven-hill city of Rome will be destroyed.' MacCarthy understands only too well why the Church repudiates that prophecy. Yet there remains the uncomfortable fact that at least one pope this century had a mystical vision similar to what Malachy foretells. In 1909 Pius X closed his eyes and cried out he saw a terrifying apparition: 'What is certain is that the pope will leave Rome, and in leaving the Vatican, he will have to walk over the dead bodies of his priests.' MacCarthy is sure Vatican Radio would never broadcast that. He puts aside his notes on Malachy and goes back to his script.

'From the eleventh century on, only two popes have broken the tradition of changing names, retaining their baptismal names after being elected. The first was the Dutch pope, Adrian VI, who was elected in 1522. The second was Marcellus II, who had one of the shortest pontificates in the history of the Church, just twenty days!'

MacCarthy takes another timing. He has thirty seconds left. He continues to type.

'Originally, if a pope took the same name as one of his predecessors, he was known as "junior". If there had been more than one before him with that name he was called "secundus junior", and so on. The Roman numeral placed after the pope's name was adopted for the first time by Gregory III, who was made pope in 731 and died ten years later. This custom of a Roman numeral after the name came into current use around the eleventh century. I wonder whether our next pope will use it?'

A final check: exactly three minutes, fifteen seconds.

*

Wojtyla takes out the last voting card from the chalice, unfolds it, writes down the name, passes it to Lorscheider who also makes a note before handing it to Gantin. His voice carries clearly. It is another vote for Siri.

Gantin records this and then pierces the card with a threaded needle, as he has all the others. He takes care the needle – as Paul insisted, though nobody knows why – passes through the word *Eligo*. It takes Gantin only a moment to join Siri's to the other hundred and ten ballot cards already strung on the line. Gantin removes the needle, knots together the ends of the line and places the threaded cards back in the chalice.

The Scrutineers each add up the votes they have individually recorded. Other cardinals are doing the same. Felici is the first to finish; he has used a pocket calculator.

Villot commands the Revisers to go to the Scrutineers' table. They take turns carefully to count the number of ballot papers on the thread, and to check the voting record of each Scrutineer. Paul insisted this must be done to ensure the Scrutineers have 'performed their task exactly and faithfully'.

The Revisers return to their places.

All eyes are on Wojtyla. He begins to read out the result of the first ballot. His previous acting experience gives him a natural sense of timing as he delivers each result in a strong baritone voice.

Siri tops the poll. He has twenty-five votes. There is absolutely no audible reaction from anybody. Luciani has twenty-three votes. Felici and Benelli, on opposite sides of the aisle, are seen by other cardinals to exchange quick looks. Pignedoli has eighteen votes.

Wojtyla pauses briefly. Perhaps he is waiting to see if there is any challenge from the floor. He cannot seriously expect one – not after all the checks. Yet he waits. Then his voice picks up the count which by now most other cardinals already know from their own calculations.

Baggio has nine votes. Koenig has one less. Bertoli has picked up five, the same as Pironio. Felici is limping along with a couple, and Lorscheider also has two. Fourteen other cardinals, including Hume and Pappalardo – on whom Alibrandi, the papal nuncio in Dublin, has pinned his hopes – each have a single vote. No American has one.

Sighs of relief from the tension come from several cardinals. Others look curiously at Siri and Luciani.

Villot rises and formally announces that the ballot is inconclusive. Then, before any discussion can begin he orders Sin to summon Noé. Afterwards Villot walks to the seated cardinals and asks them to hand over any notes they have made. Sin walks behind the Camerlengo with a bin which already holds the name slips used when electing the Scrutineers, *Infirmarii* and Revisers. Under Villot's watchful eye the notes are scooped by Sin into the bin. The two men go to the Scrutineers' table. Villot takes the threaded votes from the chalice and drops them in the bin. He and Sin then wait in silence for Noé to come into the Chapel. When he appears they go to the unlit stove. Villot opens its door while Sin tips in the paper. Noé closes the door. Villot then asks the master of ceremonies to leave the Chapel. Sin checks the door is secured behind him.

Somewhere in the Conclave area, the man with the button bug presses it very quickly, twice. It is the prearranged signal a second ballot is about to begin.

18

By eleven o'clock there are an estimated fifty thousand people in St Peter's Square. Some try to follow the advice of an Irish friar who makes the Rome front pages this Saturday because he has witnessed the election of every pope since Pius XI in 1922, and who suggests the best place to stand, 'for studying the papal handwriting in the sky, is just in front of the broken clock on the façade of the Basilica so you're sort of gawking over the left shoulder of Taldoni's mighty statue of St Paul – and watch out for pickpockets: sure they'd steal the freckles off your arm.'

Like the crowd, the scores of TV and radio crews and print journalists find the waiting a tedious business. The media mood is not improved by running battles with the increasingly inept Vatican Press Office. No one can remember such journalistic frustration with the Vatican. The Press Office has even received a ringing protest in Latin about the media's *Dolore et Stupore*; now all this stupefaction and pain is exacerbated by having to hump film equipment about in broiling weather.

Reporters rework earlier copy: only forty-six popes have not been Italian, the last was Adrian VI of Flanders who was booed on his election day; the last non-cardinal was elected six hundred years ago – and this time, should there be a long delay, say several hours, between the appearance of the white smoke and that of the new pope on the Basilica balcony, it will almost certainly mean that an outsider has been chosen, and that the cardinals are waiting for him to arrive, pick a name and put on one of the vestments stitched by Gammarelli.

This sort of flim-flam helps the newsmen pass their time cobbling up despatches that somehow often manage to suggest they know what is going on inside the Sistine Chapel. Yet not even the grossest piece of speculation matches the reality of the high drama developing beneath the slanted roof with its makeshift smoke stack which is the focus of attention as noon approaches.

*

Wojtyla's richly resonant voice announces the result of the second ballot.

202

sits, isolated, not responding, a man gripped by emotions which even afterwards he will not properly be able to explain.

Baggio arrives and he and Felici retreat to the Parrot Courtyard, where they pace to and fro. Even the sharp-eared attendants cannot catch the drift of the conversation. But the outcome is not in doubt. As they separate, Felici gives Baggio a friendly clap on the shoulder and then returns to Luciani.

Pignedoli and Lorscheider are seen to meet briefly in a corridor. A few words and they, too, go their own ways. Lorscheider hurries to Aramburu's cell where the two men confer privately. Pignedoli calls on Bertoli. They also have a very private discussion: the upshot is both men arrange to see Benelli in his cell.

Benelli's participation in the brief meeting must be treated scrupulously, for the friction in the past between the three men will be sufficient to produce distortion by their supporters when the details do emerge. In Conclave each is under considerable tension and pressure; each is hampered by his own bearing, those small traits of personality which do not make it easy for any of them to accept opposing points of view.

Characteristically, Benelli is intent on coming straight to the point. But, normally an experienced and eloquent orator, he is surprisingly awkward, which adds a tone of ungenerosity to his words. He tartly tells Pignedoli that he should not expect to make a further advance in the next ballot.

Everybody knows Pignedoli is an inveterate traveller, perhaps next to Baggio the most globe-trotting of the cardinals. For months now the story has persisted that he's used the trips to mobilize support for a tilt at the papacy. Pignedoli has denied it – repeatedly. Yet the rumour refuses to fade away. Now, with his clutch of nineteen votes, it seems he *has* been attracting support from various corners of the Catholic world. With a few blunt words Benelli is saying it's all over.

Pignedoli cannot hide his disappointment; his subsequent remarks clearly indicate he hoped for more. Responding with a tartness which matches Benelli's, he says his supporters are loyal and that matters should be allowed to take their natural course. To the astonishment of the others, Pignedoli's style is not his subdued self, full of the hesitancies which nowadays characterize his speech. Instead, there's a distinctly salty air about his words, a reminder of Pignedoli's days as a naval chaplain.

In the end, though, his argument amounts to this: Luciani is a mite too liberal in some areas: being progressive is one thing, verging on the radical is another. He does not specify, but quickly moves on to suggest that Aramburu is not the only one opposed to the patriarch; there are a number of other cardinals who do not like Luciani's supposedly freewheeling ways. This time he throws in one example: the patriarch's well-known relaxed attitude towards his parish priests. Then he fires his final shot. What about Luciani's health?

The question remains unanswered. Is it Benelli's way of dismissing its implications? Or does he simply not wish to get into that sort of argument at this late stage? The issue will produce endless debate. But not now. Now, the two men wait to see what Bertoli will say.

He remains silent. It may be he feels uncomfortable in the presence of Benelli after all their wrangling during those days they were both Vatican diplomats. Or it may be he just thinks Pignedoli should recognize a lost cause. But Pignedoli appears in no way dejected; he seems to have endless ways of introducing new twists to familiar arguments. And, indeed, some of what he says is beyond dispute. There are, without doubt, certain cardinals, Hoeffner of Cologne being one, who will never endorse Luciani's election. They will either return blank ballot forms, or give Pignedoli what amounts to protest votes.

Yet it is Bertoli who finally speaks the kind of simple truth which brings together all the complexities and reduces them to one telling phrase.

'We must all, for the good of the Church, let the Holy Spirit continue to guide us.'

When the discussion ends, it is seen as significant – at least by Conclave attendants – that Bertoli goes with Benelli to Luciani's cell. This is taken as symbolic peace between the two cardinals who have battled with each other for so long.

Pignedoli repairs to his cell to pray.

Koenig and Suenens of Brussels are with Wojtyla, doing some very basic arithmetic. Luciani is twenty-nine votes short of the seventy-five needed. All three – according to one source close to Suenens – will continue to vote for Luciani. But Koenig remains cautious: while Conclave will certainly not last the week he had thought, it may well go beyond a third ballot. Anything can happen; he doesn't like racing terms for such a serious business, but they are still some distance from the finishing post.

In the midst of all this intense activity – nobody can now seriously call what is happening 'consultation', it is high-powered politicking – Krol manages to squeeze in a siesta while Cody has a lengthy discussion with Cooke, one the New York cardinal will later say has 'nothing to do with the present business'.

At four o'clock, the cardinals return to the Sistine Chapel. Fifty-five minutes later – Felici's timings are useful in pinpointing the progress of events – Wojtyla announces the result of the third ballot.

Luciani has sixty-six votes. Pignedoli has managed to acquire a further two – one is said to be from Duval of Algeria and the other from Gabriel Garrone, a French cardinal. This gives Pignedoli twenty-one supporters in the Chapel. Lorscheider is still there – but fading fast. Thirteen votes have switched from him, almost certainly to Luciani. The Brazilian now only has one; it will be an open secret in Conclave that Aramburu is staying with Lorscheider to the end.

Villot calls for an immediate fourth ballot.

It is 5.25 precisely on Felici's wrist when the first vote of this count is placed on the silver paten and tipped into the chalice. At 6.20 Gantin threads the last card onto the line. A moment later Wojtyla, beaming broadly, announces Luciani has polled ninety-six votes. In the roar of applause it is virtually impossible to hear that Pignedoli has ten votes – presumably one of them being Luciani's, for cardinals cannot vote for themselves. Lorscheider has completed the course, riding home on the one faithful vote of Aramburu.

Luciani sits with his eyes closed and lips barely moving in prayer.

Villot instructs Sin to summon Noé for the last time, raising his voice above the almost continuous hand-clapping. Then, accompanied by the master of ceremonies and the three Scrutineers, the Camerlengo walks solemnly to where Luciani is seated, head bowed.

An expectant hush settles over the Chapel.

In carefully enunciated Latin, Villot poses the first of two questions.

'Do you, Most Reverend Lord Cardinal, accept your election as Supreme Pontiff which has been canonically carried out?'

Luciani's eyes remain closed. His lips continue to move in prayer. He clasps and unclasps his hands, but whereas in his cell the movement had been an unconscious gesture, now it appears deliberate, as if he is timing himself, judging his moment. His hands become still. Everyone around him strains to see his reaction. At last Luciani opens his eyes.

Noé will have a lasting memory of the 'shiny look' now in those eyes. Koenig sees 'a certainty' which has not been there before. Gantin senses 'strength and resolve'. Sin is convinced 'It's God's decision.'

Luciani's words are all the more stunning.

'May God forgive you for what you have done in my regard.'

Villot is flummoxed. He fiddles with his pectoral cross and looks around with what Felici thinks is something akin to despair; Felici believes that nowhere in the Secret Archives is there the record of a response anything like this.

Luciani suddenly smiles the broad melon-like grin that stretches his skin and exposes those dazzling white teeth over which a Venetian orthodontist has taken such care.

'Accepto . . .'

Villot's relief is so great that he gapes. He is still standing, mouth sagging, as Luciani completes the sentence.

'. . . in the name of the Lord.'

The Camerlengo closes his mouth, licks his lips.

'By what name will you be known?'

Luciani is in no hurry to respond to Villot's question. Instead he looks at Benelli and Felici. In the interval between the third and fourth ballots, both men had suggested that when this moment came – there was by then, as Felici says, no 'ifs' or 'buts' about the outcome of the election – Luciani might like to consider the influence on him of John XXIII, who ordained him a priest, and of Paul, who made him a bishop.

In a voice strong and certain, Albino Luciani announces what he will henceforth be known as.

'I will be called John Paul One.'

*

MacCarthy is seated before a microphone in view of a monitor filled with a close-up of the smoke stack. He glances at the studio clock and continues to read his script about why a cardinal changes his name when elected. MacCarthy is keyed to abandon his talk should the chimney suddenly emit smoke. But it remains lifeless. He inserts an ad-lib into his text, telling his invisible audience, stretching from the Libyan desert to the lush green of Natal, that they, like the estimated hundred thousand crowd now in St Peter's Square, must continue to wait patiently. It is 6.30 pm.

*

At that precise moment the attendant with the secret bug goes into action. He first satisfies himself on the whereabouts of the surveillance team who have been repeatedly sweeping the Conclave area. He finds them in the Sistine Chapel, standing to one side, eyes on their sensors. The man hurries to the armoury of the Borgia Apartments. The nuns in the adjoining field kitchen have either gone to the Chapel to watch the celebrations or are busily preparing dinner. No one pays him any attention.

Before coming into Conclave he memorized a simple but effective code. It differs only slightly from the one he used when indicating a new ballot had begun; this time the duration of the individual signals will be longer. Each candidate has been given a number. The first name on the man's list gets a single, lengthy buzz, the second two, and so on. He now gives the button eleven distinct squeezes.

There are eleven corresponding bleeps from the receiver wired into the engineer's console in the Vatican Radio studio high up on the western slopes of the city-state.

The employee who has been listening for the signal waits for the buzzing to stop, then writes down one word: Luciani. He holds it up to the soundproof glass panel dividing the room from the adjoining studio. The broadcasters grouped around table microphones exchange glances. One of them begins to speak.

Vatican Radio has its scoop.

Inside Conclave the attendant, as instructed, goes to a toilet and flushes away the bug.

Shortly afterwards the surveillance team report to Noé the entire area is still electronically clean.

Noé informs Villot.

*

At 6.33 – he writes down the time on a scratchpad though he does not know why – Anibaile Gammarelli receives a telephone call from one of Villot's assistants. The tailor hurries to his car and sets off at speed through the back streets of Rome. It will take him six minutes to complete the journey.

*

The tumult of shouting and honking of car horns pours from MacCarthy's monitor. He smiles ruefully. Moments after he came off the air four puffs of smoke emerged from the stack. The roar continues to rise from the crowd as more smoke is emitted. But though the camera shows the chimney in close-up, MacCarthy is not sure of the smoke's actual colour against the pearly-white sky. The crowd has no doubt. People are shouting in delight, '*È bianco, è bianco!*' – 'It is white!' MacCarthy's screen cuts from the spectators back to the stack. He sees there is a change. The smoke is darkening. It will continue to behave capriciously, causing doubt where there is no need. His critics will blame Villot – who else – for not having installed a more reliable system.

*

Three minutes later – it is now 6.37 – the same assistant who phoned the tailor calls Levi at *L'Osservatore Romano*. The editor listens and relaxes. Levi gives the order to lock on to the press the front page matrix carrying Luciani's portrait and biography.

*

Martin waits impatiently at the open door of the Sistine Chapel. He has sent Swiss Guards down to the Arch of the Bells to escort Gammarelli to him. He wishes now he had told Ciban to arrange that Rome police provide a motorcycle escort for the tailor. But there hasn't been time. It all happened so quickly even the experienced prefect is surprised: he thinks four ballots must be close to one of the shortest Conclaves in recent history, especially as the last vote seems to have been a formality.

The prefect has heard an intriguing story. Formality apart, the fourth ballot was largely 'a confirming one', intended to show how overwhelming was the support for the patriarch. So much so it would effectively silence the dissident Lefèbvre, who previously announced he would not accept the decision of Conclave because it did not include the sixteen cardinals over eighty whom Paul's rules excluded from voting.

True or not, Martin is clear the new pontiff will find Lefèbvre's brand of religious fascism just one of the many nettles he will have to grapple with. Lefèbvre shouldn't be too much of a problem; his reactionary movement is essentially a last ditch effort of pre-Vatican II nostalgists; their outlook is little different from those diehards who rejected the socio-economic, political and theological changes which followed in the wake of the great revolutions of the last century. Martin is all for preserving the tenets of Catholic faith, and there are definite lines he will not cross. Yet he has no time for extremists and self-publicists like Lefèbvre who thrive off challenging papal authority. Firmness, in the prefect's view, will see Lefèbvre off.

But it may not be so easy with the rest of the opposition. The avowed aim of many of them is the downgrading of the authority of the Curia and the Sacred College of Cardinals by increased decentralization of the Church, so that laymen, priests and bishops far removed from the ambience of the Vatican can have a greater say in its decision-making process; these revolutionaries march behind a banner which proclaims the Church and the pope are prisoners of a rigid authoritarian system and that there is an urgent need for liberalization.

The very word is anathema to the crusty old prefect. He knows the new pope will preside over a house divided, polarized between seemingly irreconcilable tendencies. Paul had indeed not wished to go down in history as the pope who oversaw the dismantling of the Church. But he had left it so weakened, in such an impasse, that it would need a very firm hand to bring it back on course. Was Paul's successor the man to do this? Did he have the talent, the skill, the insight, the wisdom, and, Martin had to admit, the essential cunning to cope with the grave challenges of the many autonomous, loosely organized groups of varying religious and political disposition, made up of clergy and laity?

The prefect continues to ponder. Luciani is another northerner; he will be almost unknown in Rome, and in turn will know little of the inner workings of the Curia. Will he be prepared to listen? Will he come south, as Paul did, with his own entourage, to stamp a distinctive Venetian influence on the Vatican? Doubtless he will bring some close and trusted aides. But will he also accept that the best interests of the papacy, in Martin's view, will only be served if the new pontiff reappoints Paul's key nominees – of which Martin is one?

He searches his mind for what he knows about the patriarch. He has seen him around the Vatican when he came to call on Paul. But Luciani always gave the impression that he really couldn't wait to go home to his palace by the water. He's written for the press and produced a book. Martin can't, for the moment, recall which newspaper, or the book's title. Then he remembers: a copy of *Illustrissimi* had been passed around the Secretariat of State, causing some head-shakes about its contents: not everybody found it to their taste that a prince of the Church was writing letters to a puppet called Pinocchio. Martin knows he must get a copy, quickly. But that name the new pope has chosen, John Paul One, doesn't it sound a bit cumbersome? Perhaps the Romans, if they like the new pontiff, will familiarize it. Gianpaolo, thinks Martin, might do very well; it has a nice affectionate ring.

The prefect is still considering the matter when Gammarelli and his Swiss Guard escort arrive. The tailor carries a small bag. In his dark suit he looks like a doctor.

'Who is he?' asks Gammarelli.

'Papa Gianpaolo.' Martin decides to try out the name.

'Gianpaolo?'

'*Sì.*'

Martin turns and walks quickly ahead, discouraging further conversation.

Gammarelli follows closely behind. 'Gianpaolo? Is he a cardinal?'

'*Sì.* What else?'

'Of course. But from where?'

'Venice.'

'Ah, Luciani.'

Gammarelli's mind is recalling the last time he measured the patriarch as Martin leads him into the sacristy.

Cardinals are milling everywhere; it is like one of those receptions the Sacred College gives in honour of a new member.

Martin cuts through the crowd, nodding and smiling but never slackening speed, Gammarelli in tow.

They finally reach the group around the pope. Martin thinks: yes, he is definitely a Gianpaolo.

Gammarelli recognizes them all except the broad-shouldered Slav with the penetrating eyes. Later, the tailor will remember Wojtyla's worn robe and shoes and wonder who his tailor is. But now he has time only for Gianpaolo.

He is forcibly struck by the contrast with that time, fifteen years ago, when he had stood on this very spot and helped Paul to robe. Even then Paul had been distant. In the ensuing years, when Gammarelli regularly measured him, Paul showed increasing impatience with the procedure. Like so much else, clothes seemed to have lost their appeal. Gianpaolo, on the other hand, has always appreciated the tailor's skills. He has been one of those clients who invariably found the time to send a handwritten note of thanks for a new garment. Already he's glanced several times at the portable rack holding the sets of papal vestments Gammarelli has made.

The tailor goes to the rack, now in command. He selects the smallest of the cassocks and turns to Gianpaolo.

'If it pleases your Eminence.' He quickly corrects his mistake. 'Pardon, *Santissimo Padre.*'

Gianpaolo smiles. 'It will take me time as well to become used to this.'

Gammarelli helps Gianpaolo remove his cardinal's robe. He hands it to Noé, who takes it away.

The robe will be dry-cleaned, placed in a cardboard box lined with tissue paper and delivered to the papal apartment. There it will be carefully stored until Gianpaolo's death; then, unless he has decreed otherwise, it will be handed over to the senior surviving member of his family.

Gianpaolo stands in his long-tailed shirt and baggy underpants, still smiling.

The tailor notices his legs. They are swollen around the ankles and the calves are distended. Gammarelli cannot remember them being like this the last time he saw Luciani. But he has too many other things on his mind to give the matter more than fleeting concern. He helps Gianpaolo to don the cassock. The tailor stands back, appraising. It is a poor fit. The hem trails the ground, the sleeves reach below Gianpaolo's fingertips, and the garment hangs loosely on his slight frame.

The pope smiles in sympathy. 'You could not have known.'

'*Grazie, Santissimo Padre.*'

This is the moment when the tailor knows he is in the presence of 'a truly wonderful man'. Gammarelli drops to his knees, opens his bag and selects an already-threaded needle. Stitching swiftly, he quickly raises the hem. He tucks and sews the sleeves, and then nips the cassock at the back. He again stands aside to run a critical eye over his handiwork.

'It feels very fine,' says Gianpaolo.

Gammarelli nods happily. Gianpaolo is not only the most wonderful, but also the humblest man he has ever met.

He asks Gianpaolo to sit. The tailor kneels once more and removes the pope's heavy brown shoes and woollen socks, replacing them with the white stockings and red velvet slippers with their small gold crosses. They are a perfect fit. Gammarelli offers the white papal skullcap. Gianpaolo puts it on, smiling broadly.[1]

*

Greeley is in St Peter's Square. The confusing smoke has been pouring from the chimney stack for forty-five minutes. But he thinks 'the show' is over. He is about to walk away when a commanding voice booms out over the piazza's powerful address system.

'*Attenzione!*'

It is Noé uttering his first public word of the new pontificate.

A door of the Basilica balcony opens.

Pericle Felici appears, smiling. Martin is behind him, Noé close by. The balcony fills with cardinals as Felici recites the traditional Latin litany.

'*Annuntio vobis gaudium magnum!*'

A roar greets the words, 'We have a pope.'

'*Eminentissimum ac Reverendissimum Dominium Cardinalem Albinum . . .*'

The crowd falls silent. Greeley wonders: 'Albinum, who in the hell is that?'

Felici booms on. '*Cardinalem Sanctae Romanae Ecclesiae . . .*'

A pause. Then: '*Luciani!*'

The crowd goes wild.

Felici roars on. '*Qui sibi imposuit nomen Joannem . . .*'

Greeley thinks: 'So, John XXIV. That's a good sign.'

'*. . . Paulum!*'

Another huge cheer.

'*Primum!*'

There is bedlam in the square.

*

Greenan is leaving his office when the telephone rings. He hesitates. It's been a long day. But he takes the call.

'Lambert Greenan?'

The accent is American, the voice that of a stranger.

'Who is that?' asks Greenan in the guarded tone he reserves for priests looking for free copies of his paper.

'This is Cody. Cardinal Cody of Chicago. Is that you, Lambert?'

'Yes, Eminence.'

'Fine. Fine. OK. I got your letter. I would have liked to have dinner. But you know, we have a new pope. A nice little Italian fellow called Luciani. A good choice . . .'

'Eminence . . . where are you calling from?'

'From Conclave.'

'You're calling from *where*?' Greenan cannot hide his incredulity.

'It's all over, Lambert. It's all over. We've got a new pope and the phones are back on in here.'

'Yes, Eminence.'

'OK. Well, listen. About your letter. I'd love to have dinner. But not this time. I've got to get back to Chicago, fast, you know how it is . . .?'

'Yes, Eminence.'

'Fine. Fine. But stay in touch, Lambert. You hear me? Stay in touch. Keep the words coming.'

Cody puts down the phone.

Dumbfounded, Greenan reflects on the call. He thinks it is one of the most astonishing he has received in his life. Months ago he had written to Cody, on behalf of his order, asking the cardinal to dine at their priory when next he was in Rome. There had been no reply. That Cody should have called from Conclave was, Greenan thinks, 'quite remarkable', but even more so was the cardinal's familiarity. Greenan has never met him, yet Cody behaved as though they were bosom pals. Greenan shakes his head. He'll never get used to these American ways.

*

Magee sees Villot emerge onto the Basilica balcony. The secretary is watching proceedings from a window overlooking the square. It is almost the first time he has been back to the Vatican these past three weeks. Since Paul's funeral Magee has retreated to the Rome residence of his order. He has spent his days there in quiet contemplation.

In some ways he feels he is at a personal crossroads. In a month he will be forty-two. He knows he has already experienced more than most men can hope to. He has sat at the elbow of a powerful pope; he has been privy to some of the most important decision-making in the contemporary world: the Vietnam war, the endless horrors of the Middle East, the continuing divisions within his beloved Ireland – all these, and many more conflicts, he has observed from a unique vantage point. He has mixed with ranking statesmen and the merely famous. Some have impressed him deeply, a few shocked him by their venality. Yet he has never shown, by as much as a flicker of an eyebrow, his feelings in public. Long ago this ninth child of a deeply committed

Ulster republican family learned from his Christian Brothers' education that outward displays of emotion are unacceptable.

Magee fears it has made him appear almost isolated, sometimes even from old friends, like Greenan and MacCarthy. And these past three years as one of Paul's closest confidants have left their mark. He knows he *is* more reserved, *is* more secretive, *is* more demanding. But there have been compensations. His time in the Vatican has provided invaluable insights into how the Church is really run. He knows most of the important leaders of the Roman Curia. To him they are not a group of faceless men sitting in marble-floored and stucco-ceilinged offices far removed from the pressures of everyday life; instead, they are civil servants who try valiantly to apply high-level Church decisions to local circumstances. And Magee knows a great deal about the workings of the Vatican diplomatic service. Though he does not always find it easy, he has come to recognize that it is sometimes preferable to support an armed regime, usually a right-wing military dictatorship, than to accede to the local bishop's understandable desire to denounce the tyranny. He has seen it actually happen in Nicaragua, Chile and Argentina. He knows, too, the unwritten law of papal diplomacy: nuncios are the conduit between a local hierarchy and a dictatorship. If it is overthrown the nuncio can be posted elsewhere, leaving the hierarchy to build its links with the new regime.

Through all of this he has come to understand the reality and the paradox of 'spiritual power'. He knows it has virtually nothing to do with the accepted view of temporal power; the Church's power is based, in the end, on the experience of the Cross. The Evangelist Luke put it so well: 'The kings of the Gentiles exercise lordship over them, and those in authority are called benefactors. But not so with you; rather let the greatest among you become as the youngest, and the leader as one who serves.' That is the bed-rock on which the Vatican's spiritual role is built, one that allows it to follow the instruction given Peter to 'confirm the faith of the brethren'. The inheritors of Peter, the popes, have, with some exceptions, tried to do that through service, not domination. This is the strong bond which joins the Church to the New Testament.

And it is this thought that is making Magee now wonder whether he should stay in Rome, or whether he might serve the Church better by returning to missionary work in Nigeria. Should he go back to that ill-defined slice of Africa which continues to hold a magnetic appeal for him? He could resume teaching in a bush school, lead the staff and pupils in prayers, learn again to cope with emergencies which have to be resolved through whatever ingenuity is available and, above all, he could remain close to the reasons which had taken him to Nigeria in the first place. It certainly is a temptation to go back.

Like Martin, Magee has been doing some serious thinking about the problems Gianpaolo is inheriting and must overcome. The crisis of authority that began in the mid-1950s still plagues the Church; perhaps now, more than ever, there exists strongly conflicting pressures within a Church looked upon for centuries as the epitome of a solidly based, united and conservative religious organization. With the passing of Paul the call for transformation is once more to be heard. From the United States, in particular, word drifted back to Rome during the interregnum that many lay Catholics were simply not prepared to accept the present order of things.

These protest movements, with their demand for dramatic and drastic change, are different from those that surfaced within the Church in previous times. Those had generally been effectively dealt with by autocratic means. Paul was the first to discover, in the wake of the brief and revolutionary pontificate of John, that such methods no longer work. He had been reluctantly forced to loosen the reins of papal power. This did nothing to halt the anti-authority protest throughout much of the Catholic world. Even members of the hierarchy were supporting the demand from the laity for more autonomy, freedom and power in all aspects of their religious lives. They were resisting what they saw as authority exercised through domination rather than service. Consequently, the challenges to Paul's authority had left the Church badly wounded.

It was not just Lefèbvre and Küng; it is a galaxy of theologians and teachers bent on creating a surge of Catholic public opinion which could sweep away much of what Magee, for one, holds to be sacrosanct: priestly celibacy, opposition to birth control and abortion and divorce, the ruling out on scriptural and theological grounds of the possibility of women being ordained as priests. Yet, Magee equally knows there can be no returning to pre-Vatican II Catholicism, as reactionaries like Lefèbvre have demanded. Instead, there must be careful progress on moral, ecclesiastical and theological questions, a balance struck between the demands of the grass-roots and the hierarchy; a delicately manoeuvred swing away from the right of centre – where the papacy had been stuck in the last years of Paul – to somewhere which would nevertheless fall short of causing accusations that the new pope was a religious radical. Like Martin, Magee wonders whether Gianpaolo is intellectually equipped to meet the challenge.

And, watching the scene on the balcony of the Basilica, Magee can guess what some of those around the new pontiff may now also be wondering. In particular, will they be reappointed? Certainly Gianpaolo will bring with him his own 'inner cabinet', one bound to be very different from Paul's. That is to be expected. And even if Magee himself is asked to be a member, how would he slot into the new regime?

He is still contemplating the question when Villot stands aside for Gianpaolo to approach the microphone.

Magee is immediately struck by his smile; it is truly magnificent.

But will it be enough?

As the crowd roars, Magee reminds himself Gianpaolo is the man people have always liked. He has an impressive pastoral record in Venice; he is popular with his priests and seems to have had no serious problems with the Curia.

Yet things are bound to be different now. Even Paul, in spite of all his curial experience and diplomatic skills, had not found it easy to cope with Vatican bureaucracy, whose exponents Pius XII had once likened to 'the Bourbons, who learned little and forgot nothing'. Magee feels the judgement unfair – perhaps even harsh. But the system does need careful handling.

He knows through hard-won experience that the successful exercise of power in the Church rests on making proper use of the Curia. Anyone, even a pope, who does not function within the formal and informal parameters of this bureaucracy will find it hard, and often impossible, to operate efficiently in the upper reaches of the Church. Paul had discovered it was much easier to work with the Curia than to try to transform it – if only because a pope and his civil service, in harmony, form a winning team. In spite of all his *Angst* with Villot, Paul had remained attached to the Secretariat of State as an instrument of government.

Would Gianpaolo feel the same? Would he realize that if he allowed the Curia to slip totally from his control, or permit a strengthened collegial control-sharing with the Synod of Bishops – as some reformers have urged – then gradually he might become little but a figurehead? He would still be publicly loved but to all intents his power would be diminished. The only way to keep the papacy potent is to develop a sensible working alliance with the Curia. That would not be easy if Gianpaolo continued, for example, to display a break with traditionalist ideology, as he had seemed to do in his pronouncements over Louise Brown, the test-tube baby. Personally, Magee could find no fault with the sensitive and sensible approach adopted; clearly raised had been the question of potential abuse, the risks involved, the possibility of science becoming like the sorcerer's apprentice – controlling instead of being controlled. And, indeed, there had been a reasoned defence of *Humanae Vitae*. Nevertheless, his widely reported views had brought many a frown to curial brows. These powerful men would be watching

217

closely and, if the need arose, would act in their own effective way against the new pope. It is a daunting prospect.

Watching Gianpaolo extend his first papal blessing to the crowd, Magee wonders, too, how the pope will cope with the pressures building up on the question of democratization of much of the structure of the Church? The present system of nomination to positions of authority – apart from the election of a pope – functioned entirely by co-optation from above; this was under severe challenge and criticism by lower clergy.

Like so much else, Paul had shunted aside the question into some backwater; in the end he pretended the problem did not exist. It didn't make it go away. It still vied for attention, demanding a solution. Just like so many issues.

There was, for instance, the vast arena of Christian–Marxist dialogue. In which direction should it go? Paul had often encouraged a moderation towards Communism far removed from the harsh condemnation of the Pius pontificates. But that very moderation paved the way for radical Catholic forces within the Church to press for reforms well beyond those envisioned by Vatican II, which, in turn, had produced the Lefèbvre backlash. And there was the equally explosive question of the Church's long-standing involvement with Italian politics. Paul, like the Pius popes, had been an astute politician, committed to the Christian Democratic Party since its birth; indeed, he had been one of the right-wing movement's most enthusiastic early backers. He saw the Christian Democrats as the means to hold back hordes of marauding Communists from extinguishing Italian democracy: the possibility had been one of the recurring themes in his nightly soliloquies over dinner. During the bitter May–June election campaign of 1976, the Christian Democrats had received his full support as they raised the spectre of Communism at the hustings; Paul had even gone so far as to threaten excommunication for any Catholic who voted Communist. The bitter residue of that promise still permeated Italy. Gianpaolo must find a way of easing the bonds which held fast the Church to the Christian Democrats; perhaps he should begin in Rome by opening up a dialogue with the city's Communist mayor?

Again, he will have to take a long, hard look at the day-to-day functioning of his financial empire, deciding for a start whether there should be a more humane and less capitalistic use of funds, whether there is any need for the Vatican to make yet more use of its economic power, working even harder to eliminate exploitation, discrimination and oppression. This overview is quite apart from the 'local' problems of Marcinkus and Cody and their entangled financial dealings – though they, too, will require serious attention early on in the new pontificate.

So will a whole range of political problems. There is the Holy See's relationship with China. Should it be improved or left in its present ambivalent state? There is the Middle East. Will Gianpaolo do what Paul would never have contemplated and bestow *de facto* recognition on Israel? Among the strongly esconced Arabic faction in the Vatican the very thought is tantamount to heresy; in some Secretariat of State minds there still lingers a Christ-was-killed-by-the-Jews mentality. There is the spiky issue of the Jesuits. It will need more than Paul's occasional dire warnings, which in the last years had given way to an anguished silence about the matter; the disaffection of the order with the Vatican's way of thinking is a veritable theological minefield. There is the equally contentious affair of the burgeoning Christians for Socialism Movement, the self-styled 'Critical Christians'; these organized reformist priests and laymen are a recent phenomenon who began in Chile and have now spread to Europe. They are pledged to end what they see as the papacy's involvement with bourgeois political parties and capitalism. Paul pretended they didn't exist. Gianpaolo might not wish to confront them head on, but there is going to be no way he can bypass them. Coupled with the 'Critical Christians' is the liberation theology movement, freely borrowing from Marxism, bent on creating a radically new Catholic doctrine for the Latin American poor. Its priest members carry guns, fight alongside guerrillas, kill in the name of God – and ask the Apostolic Penitentiary to settle any resultant questions of conscience. In the end Paul refused even to read the shattering reports from the Penitentiary about such shocking behaviour.

There are so many – so very many – problems that the tiny white figure on the balcony of St Peter's must soon begin to contend with.

And, as he watches Gianpaolo wave repeatedly to the crowd, the fiercely dedicated Magee realizes that he cannot leave Rome; that, given the chance, he must stay and use his considerable experience to try and help Gianpaolo meet all the challenges.

*

Alibrandi knows his immediate future is settled. He will be staying in Ireland; the nuncio is certain Gianpaolo will neither have the occasion nor the inclination to tamper with his ambassadors for at least a year; new popes generally like to take their time, and soundings, before moving their diplomats. Alibrandi's initial disappointment that his friend, Pappalardo, was not elected, is eased by his feeling Gianpaolo will be 'a great pope'. The nuncio had only glimpsed him on the television screen and barely knows the new pontiff, but he was instantly able to come to one of those decisions that sometimes make other diplomats in Dublin shake their heads in exasperation.

Many of them will shortly receive identical letters from the nuncio which he hammers out on his typewriter. In all he will write a hundred notes to members of the Irish government, his fellow diplomats and the country's bishops, informing them of Gianpaolo's election. Periodically he breaks off typing to make telephone calls to implement the official celebrations which will follow the election.

As the evening wears on, an idea gradually forms in the fertile mind of the nuncio. Fortified by sips of coffee, it grows from a hesitant possibility to a confident certainty.

Shortly his new nunciature will be ready. Sited close to a busy main road, it is geographically exposed for those IRA leaders wishing to slip in secretly to brief Alibrandi on their latest proposals to force Britain out of Ulster, but in every other respect the embassy is a dream come true for the house-proud nuncio.

The finest Irish woods and fabrics have been personally chosen by him for what will be one of the best appointed outposts of the Holy See's diplomatic service – a mansion certainly more splendidly furnished than the red-brick edifice of the British Embassy, some of whose occupants Alibrandi suspects will look with grave suspicion on the plan he is formulating.

The nuncio hopes to have Gianpaolo as his first official house-guest in the nunciature as part of a triumphant papal visit which would not only include the Catholic South but extend to the Protestant Northern Ireland.

The more he contemplates the idea, the more excited he feels. He gets up, walks around his cosy study, returns to his typewriter, rattles off another letter, gets up again, thinking all the time. The idea is feasible: everything is feasible in the optimistic world of the nuncio; a life-time of diplomatically getting what he wants has taught him even more wrinkles than he has on his nut-brown face. He knows this is not a matter of sending a handwritten invitation to the pope through the diplomatic pouch; that could easily get delayed or pigeon-holed in the Secretariat of State. Curial officials have a habit of doing that if they think a nuncio is going outside normal channels.

Alibrandi realizes he will have to visit Rome to put his case to the pope personally. That, too, is easier said than done. Holy See diplomats stationed abroad, as he well knows, don't suddenly breeze unexpectedly into the Vatican on some whim. There has to be good reason. Here, at least, the nuncio has an advantage over some of his colleagues in other diplomatic missions.

Since its inception as an independent state, Ireland has always been regarded as having 'a special' relationship with the Vatican. Until 1972 the Irish Constitution actually specified that 'the State recognizes the special position of the Holy Catholic Apostolic and Roman Church as the guardians of the Faith professed by the great majority of the citizens'; this was deleted by referendum, an olive twig for the Protestant North to grasp. But the Constitution still contained an article which was a pillar of Church thinking: 'No law shall be enacted providing for the grant of a dissolution of marriage.'

And yet in spite of its close ties to the Church, all is not well in the South. The old patterns of morality are being eroded. With almost half of the country's three-million-odd population under the age of twenty-five, the sober and assiduous faith of former years has given way to a distinct drift away from the fold. The proportion of young adults in the South who are not practising Catholics has reached an alarming twenty per cent of the population. And those who do attend Mass are often no more than 'lip-service Catholics', reciting their Hail Marys but otherwise paying scant attention to the teachings of the Church. More Irish Catholic girls than ever are using some form of contraceptive – freely prescribed by Catholic doctors for 'menstrual irregularities'; more women are travelling to England for abortions; more couples are demanding legal separations. At the same time the number of young people seeking a vocation as nuns, priests or monks is declining. Alibrandi thinks he knows what is behind this dismal situation. It is all to do with Ireland's new affluence as a member of the European Economic Community. EEC grants have modernized the country's farms, making them less labour-intensive; foreign investment has attracted young country people to work in the towns. Nearly two hundred years after England's industrial revolution, Ireland is going through a similar process. The result, in Alibrandi's view, is that young, inexperienced adults are being exposed to the dangers of city life: loneliness, unsupervised drinking, drugs, a loosening of sexual standards.

This, then, is the diagnosis he will place before Gianpaolo. Properly argued, supported by reports from the Irish bishops, it will produce a powerful case for a papal visit to Ireland.

The crucial question remains when he should make his presentation. Alibrandi knows nothing of the way Gianpaolo likes to do things. But he is certain the pope will need at least a month to settle into the Vatican.

He decides: he will go to Rome in early October. That will also give him sufficient time to contact the two persons who will be invaluable for the successful outcome of his mission. Pappalardo can brief him on Gianpaolo; Magee can smooth his way to the pope's private study.

The nuncio considers the pleasures ahead. It will be mild in Rome in October, a welcome break from the onset of another grey and wet Irish winter; there will be old friends to see around the Vatican, leisurely lunches and dinners, informed gossip to exchange. And at the end of it the plum of being the man to spark off national rejoicing in Ireland with the news that the pope is coming.

The papal visit will have to be carefully promoted as purely pastoral, concentrating on the moral rather than the political problems of all thirty-two counties in the divided island; yet Gianpaolo could have a decisive effect on the violence which plagues the six counties of Ulster. It is a heady prospect which is also fraught with the most delicate of diplomatic difficulties. Alibrandi correctly sees South and North as ecclesiastically one Catholic fief – his own writ extends to all Ireland – and a papal visit which included Ulster would, so far as the Church went, offer no problems. But the nuncio is painfully aware that the more rabid Protestant elements will regard any papal incursion as an attempt to establish a Catholic claim over their domain. The nuncio thinks this view is nonsense. But how to convince the extremists? Ultimately, the British government will have to be consulted to pave the way for an 'understanding' with the moderate, if not the extremist, Protestant majority.

Alibrandi suspects such a visit would have been unthinkable under Paul: he would have shied away from the idea of walking through Northern Ireland's bitterly divided factions to spread the gospel of peace. But Paul was old and exhausted. Gianpaolo, at least on television, had looked to the nuncio like 'an adventuresome schoolboy, a pope who will try anything'.

A visit to Ulster would set the style of his pontificate. It would show he is not only ready to carry on Paul's pilgrimages, but is prepared to go further. To travel from Rome to Belfast is a mere hop when compared with some of his predecessor's marathon journeys, yet it could be the most dramatic oecumenical gesture of the decade – perhaps even of the century. All these are the arguments which Alibrandi will hone and polish and place before Gianpaolo.

Then a sudden, sickening, jolting thought strikes the nuncio. Despite the most careful planning, the very necessary checks and balances, the prior agreements, the most stringent security, the constant emphasis on the purely pastoral nature of the visit: in spite of everything, supposing one – just one – Protestant extremist decides that the pope in Northern Ireland is too tempting an assassination target to miss?

19

In overcrowded Ankara Agca feels fortunate. He is sharing this fly-blown, stinking room in the Yenisheria district of the city with only four other men; they sleep on the floor while he has a narrow truckle bed. The room is one of the Grey Wolves' safe houses and Colonel Turkes, leader of the paramilitary extremists, has passed the word that Agca is to receive favoured treatment. Food has been brought to him, and once a girl had been sent up; they had copulated and she had left. The rest of the time he has spent sprawled on the bed reading the exercise book filled with details of Paul's life and travels. Below the last entry he has drawn a dagger in a circle. It is the symbol of the Grey Wolves. When he is not reading, he spends hours patiently aiming his gun. He has heard the hammer click home on the empty chamber hundreds of times. And each time he pulls the trigger he silently mouths a name on his hate list. Yet he no longer finds this rewarding. He is puzzled and dismayed by his lack of feeling but can think of no way of retrieving the loss. Although Agca does not know it, his mental state has taken a significant turn for the worse.

Agca has been told he is being kept here until the time comes for him to kill someone. He now knows enough about Turkes and his organization to realize that spending seven days in a room which bribery has guaranteed is safe from police raids can only mean the intended victim is unusually important. The thought neither excites nor worries him. If anything he now feels indifferent to the prospect of taking life – or of putting his own at risk.

It had taken him four days to hitch-hike from Yesiltepe to Ankara. By the time he reached the city, the uncontrollable rage – which had nearly made him smash the television set because it brought news he had been denied the chance to kill Paul – had subsided. He now believes it was the will of God. And Allah, he is certain, will give him another opportunity. This, too, is only briefly exciting. All that really stimulates him now for any length of time is ugly eroticism; he will speak readily to the other men in this room of his fantasies, describing superhuman sexual feats with a vivid sense of conviction. This aberration is part of the mental change which is evolving and accelerating in Agca's mind.

On Sunday afternoon, 27 August, an aide arrives from Turkes with the curt message that Agca will not be required to execute his mission; the intended victim has fled the country.

Hardly has Agca comprehended that once more he has been thwarted when the aide repeats he must leave this safe house and find his own accommodation. As they separate, the man suggests Agca might find work in the *Kara Borsa*, the flourishing Turkish blackmarket. He gives him a name and address.

Agca's absence of any recognizable response – fury, resentment, disappointment – further suggests how far his latent depressive illness has produced an emotional blunting; a *depersonalization* and *derealization*, the labels which indicate he is increasingly no longer himself, no longer an intact personality, but rather a person who believes the outside world, not he, has altered, has become alien and unreal. Not only has his capacity to experience appropriate social feelings largely disappeared but also the emotions of hate, fear and anger have withered. It is as if – he will later admit under medical probing – his feelings have become totally unrelated to his environment. He even feels, as he leaves this safe house, that his life is virtually out of his control. He wonders again, though not with any lasting curiosity, whether this is anything to do with the extraordinary secret he has managed to keep from Colonel Turkes, the Grey Wolves and even from his mother. It is so astonishing that even now, just as he has been told to guard it, the secret remains deliberately pushed into his subconscious. And when it does sometimes emerge, though never beyond the confines of his increasingly tortured mind, he thinks the secret belongs to someone else. It seems, he has said to himself, there are actually two persons living inside his puny body, linked together by a common bond of violence.

Heading on foot across Ankara, Agca passes a newstand. Several papers carry accounts of Gianpaolo's election. He studies them avidly. There is a new caliph in Rome whose smile only conceals an evil mind dedicated to destroying Islam. Agca must kill him.[1]

Any thought of working in the *Kara Borsa* is abandoned. Instead, Agca goes to the nearest bar, orders a beer and asks for a telephone directory. For months he has pondered how best to go about what he must now do. In Yesiltepe he could have written, but he had heard the secret police frequently intercept letters addressed to these places. And it was much too risky to telephone long-distance to seek an appointment; the telephone exchanges are riddled with informers who listen in to conversations. Here, in the city, it is different. A quick local call, a request for a meeting would take only moments and even the most sophisticated equipment, he believes, would be unable to trace him.

Agca begins to search for the phone number of the Libyan embassy in Ankara.

The man who has sworn Agca to secrecy told him, the last time they met, that should the need ever arise, this was the quickest way to contact him.

20

Gianpaolo knows exactly what is going to happen to him. It's there on the typed schedule Lorenzi has placed on his desk. Every minute of his official day is accounted for. The blocks of time – some fragmentary, others lengthy – now control his life. It is all so different from the easy-going days in Venice. He pushes aside the schedule and joins his secretary at the window.

They both enjoy these private moments together; they are a reminder that what Lorenzi ruefully calls 'the system' has not completely taken them over.

For both men the past week has been a learning process. Learning, for instance, to find their way around the large papal apartment: Martin had the place springcleaned before they moved in, and the prefect wondered whether Gianpaolo would like it redecorated; he's been smilingly told there's no need – such material considerations have a low priority in the pope's mind, so much so he's sleeping in Paul's old bed and using his linen. Learning to cope with a daily workload which is endless and daunting: Lorenzi has been keeping track; on an average day Gianpaolo peruses up to two hundred separate documents – more than he would see in a month in Venice. Learning to cope with the isolation: a whole system of checks which begin at the security desk by the Bronze Doors effectively ensures nobody can drop in, quite the opposite from Venice where Gianpaolo kept open house. Learning to cope with the formality: Lorenzi still finds it surprising how unbending nearly everybody is in the Vatican. He supposes it's another throwback to Paul's pontificate. Gianpaolo is trying to change this, but it's going to take time. Some of the older curialists are so stiff they almost creak when they speak.

Normally at this hour on Sunday morning – it is barely seven o'clock – St Peter's Square is deserted. Not today, 3 September. Scores of *sampietrini* are busy in the piazza making the final preparations for Gianpaolo's coronation later in the day. And beyond them, ringing the great square, are groups of armed policemen, some with sniffer dogs to check for explosives. Their presence is a reminder that in this respect, nothing has changed since the days of Paul. Gianpaolo had been stunned to learn how many threats to his life there have already been during the eight days he has held office. Almost certainly all of the telephone calls and anonymous letters are the work of cranks. Yet nobody can be sure. Consequently, Ciban has ordered a further tightening of security. When Gianpaolo queried its need, Villot sent him a file detailing terrorist outrages against the Church, showing this is not a passing phenomenon but one which grows almost daily as its bishops and priests assert the claims of the underprivileged, the impoverished and the suffering. Gianpaolo affixed to the file a handwritten note asking the Secretariat of State to research one of the initial important questions of his pontificate: did the Church have anything to answer for in shaping the minds of terrorists? He wants the answer ready for the time he will carry out his first overseas visit – to Mexico this coming October for the conference of South American bishops.

Lorenzi gently reminds Gianpaolo that, like the Vatican workmen in the square, he, too, must put the finishing touches to his coronation preparations: the secretary has managed to juggle the schedule to allow the pope a full hour for this purpose. Lorenzi turns from the window and leads Gianpaolo back to his desk. When the pontiff is seated, and Lorenzi is satisfied there is no more he can do, he leaves.

Gianpaolo resumes drafting the address he will make at his coronation.

Unlike Paul, who almost never committed himself to paper until he had thought out exactly what he would say, and then wrote without hesitation to the end, Gianpaolo writes down a thought, reads it back, amends it, reads it again. It is a slow, laborious process, one perhaps not made easier by the way he constantly consults the mass of papers on his desk. One good thing about being pope, he has told Lorenzi, is that he has unrivalled sources of information at his command. In the past week the Curia has furnished him with any number of facts and figures: from the Secret Archives have come the coronation speeches of pontiffs going back to Gregory VII who was crowned in 1073 and decreed that the pope had the right to depose emperors and kings, to be judged by no one, and that he alone was entitled to expect his feet 'to be kissed by princes'. It was Gregory who abolished simony, the sin of buying Church privileges, and ended clerical marriages.

Now, over nine hundred years later, in another briefing paper on his desk, the question of celibacy is demanding Gianpaolo's attention. The Congregation for the Sacraments and Divine Worship has sent him a strongly worded recommendation it stop handling the hundreds of applications from priests wishing to give up holy orders, generally because they wished to marry, until Gianpaolo considers the entire matter. To help him decide what should be done, the Congregation has made some specific proposals which are far more rigorous than those applied by Paul. Requests for laicization in future would be addressed directly to the Congregation headquarters in Rome and not to local bishops; they should only be granted in those cases where a 'lengthy period' has elapsed since the petitioner 'lived as a priest', or if his superiors are able to satisfy the Congregation they made an 'initial mistake' in not recognizing the person in question to be unsuited for the celibate life. But even this would do nothing to end the extraordinary situation in the Philippines where hundreds of priests have 'a lasting relationship with a woman', seemingly with no adverse effect on their pastoral duties. Should he make reference in his coronation speech, however obliquely, to the teaching that celibacy is forever – everywhere Church writ runs? To do so would surely require him to refer to related issues: the question of priests and nuns who no longer wear suitable religious garb, and those women, especially in the United States, who are demanding the right to be ordained and whose slogans are disapprovingly laid out in the Congregation document: 'God is an equal-opportunity employer', 'A woman's place is in the sanctuary', 'Equal rites for women'.

Gianpaolo, in the end, decides a coronation is not the place to begin the task of settling such vexed issues. But he will handle them – and soon.

Equally his speech must strike a response in each one of the eighteen per cent of the world's population – in total over 740 million souls – for whom he is ultimately responsible in all matters of religion.

Amid the paperwork which overflows from his desk onto the floor of his study – the one where he does his serious work, adjoining his bedroom, not the second-floor salon in the Apostolic Palace where he receives his endless flow of visitors – there is one memo which Gianpaolo repeatedly reads. He has plucked it out of the previous night's tray from the Curia. There are two typed sentences. The first states that at 3.42 pm on 9 July 1978, the world's population reached 4.4 billion. The second sentence predicts that 73 million people will be born this year, most of them in the Third World.

He finds the statistics mesmeric. He has told Lorenzi that, more than anything, they remind him of his awesome responsibility and the size of the kingdom he now spiritually rules.

On a wall of the study, near one of the speakers through which Paul used to listen to *Jesus Christ, Superstar*, Gianpaolo has had pinned a map of the world. He hardly needs look at it to know there are few places where there are no native-born Catholics: Afghanistan, Bahrain, Faroes, Greenland, Oman, the Maldives, the two Yemens. But elsewhere, numerically the Church has never been stronger. Sixty-three out of every hundred persons in teeming Latin America – from Mexico to Chile – profess the faith. In Western Europe forty per cent of the population is Catholic. The Philippines claim thirty-six million souls. In the rest of Asia and Africa the number of Catholics is growing at such a rate that by the year 2000 – when Gianpaolo could still be ruling – almost seventy per cent of all baptized Catholics will be in the Third World.

This, he knows, is the area which will in particular be looking to him for strong leadership. In the minutes he has left to complete his coronation address, Gianpaolo makes another important decision. During the past week he has received invitations to visit the old heartlands of European Catholicism – Spain, France, Portugal, and West Germany, where, as a result of a fear of Communism, the Church has in recent years gained membership sufficient that, for the first time since Luther, Catholics now outnumber Protestants. There has been a request – slipped in by Cody – to visit the United States. All these are certainly possibilities. But before he makes any such visits he must first travel extensively in the Third World. He knows, after what he has read, it will not be enough to offer promises at his coronation that the Church will become more involved in the problems of this vast area, with its estimated 400 million unemployed, even more living on the starvation line and with poverty the like of which the First World, Europe, cannot envisage. He must go himself: move amongst these people, pray with them, make them feel he is part of them.

When Lorenzi returns, he is startled to be told by Gianpaolo that he wants briefing papers on every Third World nation where there are Catholics.

'It could take months,' says the secretary hesitantly.

Gianpaolo nods. 'It could. But it mustn't.' He smiles. 'Weeks at the most.'

Lorenzi grins. There are going to be some very late nights at the Secretariat of State. No matter: it is time its officials realized that from now on things are going to be very different in the Apostolic Palace.

*

MacCarthy is conscious he has a privileged role in history in the making. He knows every detail of the coronation service: the timing, the order, the drama of the pageantry, the reason for every ritual, the symbolism behind each of the movements which will shortly unfold in St Peter's Square on this late Sunday afternoon.

He has immersed himself in the forthcoming ceremony and has no doubt about the importance of the event for the Church, for Vatican Radio and for himself. He also knows the broadcast will only fully succeed for him if those who hear it feel they are participating in a service of great religious significance. He is deeply conscious of the responsibility upon his slight shoulders: for the next two hours or so he will act as one of the many radio voices bringing the events in the piazza to an estimated worldwide audience of six hundred million. MacCarthy's commentary position is high up on top of Bernini's colonnade, with the Basilica to his immediate right and looking down on the altar set forward on the rim of the steps, where the great papal throne has been placed before the central door of St Peter's. Some of the secular broadcasters around him suggest that a papal coronation is an incongruity and an anachronism, unworthy of the 262nd successor of Peter the Fisherman and descendant of the Vicar of Christ. He is disappointed they do not grasp that the event has not only supreme spiritual importance but is also historically rooted. It was conceived and developed, like so much of the ceremonial of the papal court, in imitation of the first Christian Roman emperors; the coronation is an exaltation of the papacy, a visible proclamation of the ascendancy of the spiritual over the temporal in which the steps of the Basilica act as the sanctuary and the immense curving piazza the sweeping nave of the church. Wisely, it has been decided to begin the ceremony at six in the evening when the shimmering heat of the Roman September day is somewhat abated.

There is an even bigger crowd, MacCarthy reflects, than on the previous Sunday when, at noon, Gianpaolo made his first Angelus address from the same third-floor window of the Apostolic Palace so long used by Paul. Already, in the public's mind, the memory of the severe pain-racked face of Paul is fading, replaced by the increasingly contagious smile of Gianpaolo. MacCarthy does not know of a more auspicious Angelus address by a new pope. Almost every sentence was punctuated by thunderous applause and appreciative laughter. Even Gianpaolo's first, beautifully timed word – 'Yesterday . . .' – received an ovation. He had to pause a full ten seconds before he was allowed to continue.

The next day he took his first administrative decision, reappointing all the officials in the Curia. Martin was back as prefect of the Casa Pontificia and Magee accepted an invitation to work alongside Lorenzi as the pope's other private secretary.

Gianpaolo told a meeting of curial officials and cardinals that he didn't know much about the running of the Church and was counting on their support. His words became endlessly quoted in the Vatican corridors of power: 'The Way of the Cross is the way of the popes. I hope the brotherly cardinals will help this poor Vicar of Christ to carry the cross with their collaboration.'

MacCarthy was not the only one to note the pope had dropped the formal and aloof style of the previous incumbent, and used the simple 'I' instead of the majestic 'We'. It was a small but indicative pointer with which to judge the form the pontificate was assuming.

There were others. Gianpaolo had gently chided journalists he received in audience regarding the dangers of trivializing the papacy, and then, with a grin, added, 'The public does not want to know what Napoleon III said to William of Prussia. It wants to know whether he wore beige or red trousers or whether he smoked.' The message to the media was clear: there is a need for balance. Gianpaolo had next talked to diplomats accredited to the Holy See about the function of Vatican diplomacy. Speaking in fluent French, he said: 'Obviously we have no temporal goods to exchange, no economic interests to discuss. Our possibilities for diplomatic interventions are limited and of a special character. Our diplomatic missions, far from being a survival from the past, are a witness to our deep-seated respect for lawful temporal power and our lively interests in the human causes that the temporal power is intended to advance.' This was correctly seen as a clear statement affirming the separation of Church and state.

After only eight days, it is obvious to MacCarthy Gianpaolo is making plain what his role will be: that of supreme teacher of the Catholic world, the clarifier of its spiritual and social doctrine, the stout defender of a threatened Christendom. Gianpaolo is suggesting his will be a pontificate in the Constantine tradition, with less politicking and more praying. In some ways, thinks the broadcaster, Gianpaolo has quickly shown a clear understanding of the real world in which he must now mediate; it is a world where the common man lives in a diversity of races, beliefs, national and cultural backgrounds, where one out of every three persons survives under Communism, where one Christian out of every two is not a Catholic. It is still too early, MacCarthy realizes, to put a firm interpretation on all the ideas and aspirations which have begun to evolve. But Gianpaolo's rare gift of holy simplicity should not be seen merely as an absence of complexity; more likely his smiling spirituality is in fact a catalyst for a fusion of important thoughts. This is already clear at the end of his first week as pope. For all his grins and jokes, everything Gianpaolo says and does bears the mark of careful preparation, paving the way for consolidating the very best aspirations of the two predecessors whose names he bears. Yet there are indications that while he recognizes the need to provide continuity in this period of orientation – and knows he requires a seasoned and proven team by him to do so – he will, nevertheless, go his own way. He will do it with that smile, with warmth and friendliness. Even so, there is a steely edge discernible. MacCarthy is certain Gianpaolo will soon start surprising people.

But now, for the moment, both the pontificate and the Church must pause as, in centuries-old symbolism and pageantry, Gianpaolo's papacy is acclaimed with public pomp.

There are nearly three hundred thousand sitting or standing in the square, and MacCarthy uses their mood of expectancy to start weaving his own carefully prepared commentary. He explains how they have been arriving in the piazza from early morning, how they have waited patiently in the heat for perhaps just a glimpse of the new pontiff. He mentions, too, the presence of over twelve thousand police and *carabinieri* to protect the galaxy of distinguished guests. MacCarthy does not develop the thought: he hopes he will not have to, that all he has heard about the possibility of trouble is really no more than rumour-mongering.

He begins to describe the procession making its way into the square.

'The Holy Father comes in the procession, like everyone else, on foot. This is another of his many innovations. He has rejected the famous portable throne on which on all such occasions, for centuries past, popes have been borne aloft through their congregation with a fanfare of loud trumpets. But for this coronation there will be no trumpets, no escort of Roman nobles. Most of the gleaming uniforms belong to the distinguished guests. Papa Gianpaolo – that is what everyone in Rome now calls him – prefers to walk among his people.'

MacCarthy's words match in style and tone the endlessly unfolding scene below him.

'The cardinals, in pairs, venerate the open-air altar. And this inaugural Mass is another of the changes the pope has introduced. The liturgy is new. It's been devised by Monsignor Noé, who has been reappointed master of ceremonies, and a commission of experts who have worked all this past week to prepare it. The Holy Father made it clear he did not wish an ostentatious ceremony. Indeed, he has even refused to wear the papal crown, which popes for hundreds of years have received on this occasion. Instead, he wants his insignia, the badge of his office, to be spiritual, a reflection of his pastoral authority. That is why he wears, rather than a crown, the mitre, the tall head-dress, the emblem of pastoral authority.'

MacCarthy does not try to be coldly objective, to remain emotionally outside the event he is describing. To him this is not a procession of quaintly dressed figures: it is a vivid evocation of the true power of the Church.

'The whole world is here. The King of the Belgians. The presidents of France, Austria and Ireland. The prime ministers of Italy and Canada. There are princes and princesses, dukes and duchesses. The vice-president of the United States is here. There are also high officials of state from Communist countries. And the representatives of all the major non-Catholic churches. They are all here. But so is the ordinary world; they have come from every corner of the globe. This is truly a United Nations of men, women and children.'

He describes the Swiss Guards, the *bussolanti* in their violet cassocks and capes, the penitentiaries in solemn black, the chaplains in red, and then, row after row of white-mitred and caped patriarchs, bishops and cardinals.

'Soon it will be time to surrender ourselves to the Mass, to the music, to the singing of the Sistine Choir, to a splendour that some of us may not see repeated. Remember, the last four popes lived into their eighties. That means we can expect the present pontificate to last at least fifteen years.'

MacCarthy pauses as spontaneous applause marks the approach of Felici to where Gianpaolo is seated.

'The cardinal removes the pope's mitre. What is to happen now is the very central point of the ceremony. It is called the Imposition of the Pallium. This is the ultimate symbol of a pope's pastoral office, the sign he has entered the fullness of his pastoral ability.'

MacCarthy explains the symbolism of the circular band of white wool, with its back and front pendants, which Felici places around Gianpaolo's neck. 'It's the sign of the authority which derives from Christ through St Peter the Apostle, and at the same time it's a sign of service towards the People of God and all our neighbours. The pallium expresses the pope's special commitment to promote with all his might the unity of the Church and his fidelity to the doctrine of the Apostle.'

Singing and organ music well up from the square. Then, when the booming voice of Felici pronounces the Latin benediction that concludes the cardinal's role in the coronation, MacCarthy expertly translates into English: 'Blessed be God who has chosen you to be pastor of the Universal Church, and who has clothed you with the shining stole of your apostolate. May you reign gloriously through many years of earthly light until, called by your Lord, you will be re-clothed with the stole of immortality in the Kingdom of Heaven. Amen.'

MacCarthy prepares his listeners for the next part of the ceremony. It is the turn of the cardinals to make their way, one at a time, to the pontiff, and to kiss Gianpaolo's Fisherman's Ring. In return, he embraces them. Some he has to steady as they appear to falter in the heat. A few linger for a word, anxiously watched by Noé.

The long, solemn pontifical Mass begins; the Epistle and Gospel are sung in Latin and Greek. There are scripture readings in nine languages to mark the universality of the Church. Shadows are settling over the square as Gianpaolo begins to read his address. He starts in Latin, switches to his agreeable French and concludes in lilting Venetian Italian. It includes an engaging plea that he will continue to receive the support of those he is pledged to serve: 'Surrounded by your love we begin our apostolic service by invoking a resplendent star on our way, the mother of God, Mary . . .'

Suddenly there is a commotion in the crowd. Angry shouts are followed by leaflets being scattered in the air. Police begin to push through worshippers. From several points around the piazza balloons drift upwards. All carry the same legend: VIDELA-ASSASSINI!

In the distinguished visitors' enclosure, President Jorge Videla of Argentina, who has defied Aramburu's last-minute appeal to stay away, turns whiter than his bemedalled admiral's uniform. Close by, Aramburu has a mortified look on his face. Videla's presence has cast a pall over the ceremony.

On the fringes of the crowd armoured cars inch forward attempting to intimidate the demonstrators. Police move in and there are violent struggles.

Gianpaolo's voice, amplified by a score of loudspeakers, reminds his listeners this 'is a day of fraternal union and joy, and let us be guided by Him.'

By the time he completes his address, the police have made the first of 282 arrests. Demonstrators are hustled away to police vans while the choir intones the credo.

As the offertory procession begins – the prelude to Communion – the police fan out through the congregation trying to locate those who have released the balloons.

MacCarthy continues to ignore the interruption; his listeners will never know it has happened. He describes the timeless ceremony of the Eucharist, the liturgy of thanksgiving.

'The priests who will distribute Communion to the crowd hold the ciborium, the gold cups containing the bread which will be transformed into the body of Christ.'

The police pounce on more demonstrators. There are scuffles. As the protesters are hauled away, the Sistine Choir sing the Lord's Prayer.

'Now, as Communion begins, it will need two hundred priests to distribute it. And the assembly is singing "Lamb of God who takes away the sins of the world, have mercy upon us."'

Another fierce fight breaks out beneath Bernini's columns between police and dissenters.

The choir sings the Communion canticle as scores of people run from the square pursued by police. The 'Te Deum', an anthem of praise and acknowledgement, ends the Mass. A squad of police close in protectively on Videla. The last sight his fellow heads of state have of the Argentinian is of a frightened man being bundled away for his own safety.

Seemingly oblivious of what has happened, Gianpaolo rises and walks into St Peter's. It's another innovation, this casual, unaffected departure from his coronation. It is also a further sign he intends to break with the past. The historically minded in the square are now certain that a new era is actually dawning.

*

Shortly before eight o'clock this Sunday evening, a vigorous woman with a strong face uncorks a glass jar of boiled sweets in the kitchen of the papal apartment and begins carefully to select an assortment which she arranges in a cut-glass bowl. This is Sister Vincenza, Gianpaolo's housekeeper and confidante, whose pride in her consecrated virginity she still regards, after a lifetime of chastity, as a special grace from God.[1] In everything she says and does Vincenza embodies the only official Church document on the subject, Pius XII's Encyclical on Holy Virginity, which insists virginity is more perfect than the state of marriage because it transcends the condition where 'our bodily powers and passions darken the mind and weaken the will'.

Vincenza cannot begin to understand the movement for change among nuns in many parts of the world. For her it has always been enough to confine the body in order to free the spirit; the core and secret of the deep contentment she possesses is her certainty of the happiness to come. She has offered her life and love to the glory of God because the afterlife is forever. In Venice she had only been vaguely aware that not all nuns feel as fulfilled as she does. But this first week in the Vatican has opened her eyes, and frequently shocked her, to the fact that after fifteen centuries demands for change can be heard on all sides. Nuns want holidays, the right to dress as they please, to have male friends; she has heard staggering tales that in some American ghettos nuns are on the pill for fear of becoming pregnant if raped, that nuns wear bikinis and go to public swimming pools and some even ride motorcycles. Centuries of tradition are being heedlessly abandoned in the name of 'modernity'. The belief which has supported her from the day she assumed the cloistered existence — that the life she has chosen is a preparation and waiting for death, and though there will be purgatory, it will be followed by joyous redemption — Vincenza now realizes is no longer sufficient for her fellow sisters. Every nightly tray that comes from the Curia, the pope has sadly confided to her, contains its quota of petitions from nuns wishing to leave their orders. Ironically, it is those orders – particularly in the United States – that have become the most liberal which are losing the most members. For Vincenza the moral is plain, and when Gianpaolo had sought her opinion she had urged him to remember it: too many sudden freedoms could erode the very basis of an institution which has served the Church and human needs for fifteen hundred years. He promised to remember her warning.

Having filled the bowl, she recaps the jar and places it back on the shelf. Nobody else, Vincenza has ruled, is to touch its contents. Apart from the sweets on the shelf, there are other little delicacies the pope likes: a variety of nuts, tins of his favourite coffee, a pot holding refined brown sugar.

In her full-length black habit – Vincenza is thankful her Order of Maria Bambini has not introduced the modish calf-length habit some orders now favour – and with her head-dress, she has a timeless look, like a figure from a medieval manuscript. She is somewhere between her fiftieth and sixtieth birthday, but like so much else about her, she keeps the exact year secret. She knows some people in the Apostolic Palace find her sharply discouraging about any personal questions about herself or the man she now finds it strange, after all their years together, to call Holy Father. She still lapses back to Padre Albino. Prefect Martin, she realizes, does not like to hear such familiarity, but young Padre Magee, though he sometimes speaks so softly she has to strain to catch his words, has said it's all right, that everybody can see how devoted and loving she is towards the pope. And friendly sounding though the name Gianpaolo is, Vincenza finds the appellation hard to get used to; in a way it reminds her of those distant days when she made her final, solemn, binding vows, taking on a new identity, accepting that from then on, for the most part, she would merely be called 'Sister'. Gianpaolo has always addressed her, from the first day she came to cook and clean for him, as 'my little Vincenza'.

Then, she never dreamed of one day effectively being the mistress of the most important household in the Church. When Gianpaolo phoned her in Venice and asked whether she would move to the Vatican, she was too overwhelmed except to whisper, 'Si'. That had been a week ago.

Now, she feels fully able to cope with the papal apartment. The marvellous thing is how easy she finds it to run. She has three nuns to help her and the sort of labour-saving gadgets the patriarch's palace did not possess: here, there is a waste-disposal unit, a fully automated laundry, the very latest electric ovens and hobs and equipment to take away the ache of bread-making and food preparation. There is even a vacuum cleaner so silent she hardly knows when it is working. For someone who has been nurtured in the sternness of monastic simplicity – she well remembers those long hours on her knees as a postulant polishing floors to a fine finish by hand because her Mother Superior insisted the only way for a nun to get to heaven was on her knees, be it praying or scrubbing – the modernity of the apartment is almost overpowering.

Yet she has already stamped her own personality and authority on many of its eighteen rooms. Even if the pope doesn't want the place redecorated – she could have told Martin before he had made the suggestion that Gianpaolo just wasn't interested in such things – Vincenza has set about brightening up the uniformly neutral beige and grey tones Paul so cherished.

As she marches out of the kitchen carrying the bowl of sweets on a silver tray, she can see everywhere evidence of the changes she has so far introduced. Striding down the central corridor of the apartment which eventually leads to Gianpaolo's bedroom, she glimpses through open doors – the pope insists they remain open to give the apartment a more homely atmosphere – her handiwork: colourful cushions on chairs and settees, familiar ornaments and oil paintings from Venice and everywhere photographs of the pope's relatives. There are family snaps on the dining room sideboards, more in the drawing room and, on his study desk, a striking portrait of his favourite niece.

Passing the study, Vincenza sees it occupied by Magee and Lorenzi. Both are so intent on their paperwork they do not even look up. She admires their ability to concentrate on an immediate task to the exclusion of all else. She's also glad of the rapport between the two secretaries. She had thought at first it might be difficult for Lorenzi. He had done everything in Venice except pay the domestic bills, which she had settled. Here Prefect Martin takes care even of these, after he has carefully checked each item. Vincenza doesn't like the arrangement but Magee has soothed her. He is a born diplomat: he knows how to handle everybody. Only tonight he'd given another demonstration, this time in the wake of the violence which marred the closing stages of the coronation. From her bedroom window Vincenza had seen the demonstrators being rounded up. She felt the police were right – a papal coronation is no place to protest. Shortly after Gianpaolo arrived back in the apartment, Villot and Aramburu had come to say how upset they were. That, at least from what she'd overheard, was their intention. But Magee had quickly intervened. Following a few whispered words, the Secretary of State and the Argentinian cardinal left, apparently satisfied. Though he has only been back in the apartment for a few days, Vincenza realizes Magee is very attuned to Gianpaolo's ways. One of the things the pope dislikes is pointless inquests. To discuss the scenes in the square came into that category.

Vincenza reaches the pope's bedroom door, the only one that is closed. He is in the second-floor salon, receiving more dignitaries. The nun enters.

Here, too, her touch is discernible. There's a rug which matches the colour of the lampshade on the bedside table. Both come from Venice, but the settee she found in that Vatican warehouse filled with centuries of discarded papal artifacts. Vincenza thinks there is sufficient furniture stored there to equip all the palaces of the cardinals, and her well-developed social conscience wonders why better use is not made of it instead of simply storing the furniture from one pontificate to another.

She places the bowl of sweets beside the short stack of books on the bedside table. For as long as she can remember the man she must now call *Santissimo Padre* – at least in front of others – has liked to suck boiled sweets while he reads before going to sleep. Every evening at this hour she places a fresh bowl by his bedside.

Vincenza turns back the sheet and lays out his pyjamas. Then, her work in this room completed for the night, she goes to a window and stares out through the parted curtains. Almost miraculously, the square has virtually returned to its usual empty grandeur: carpets have been rolled up, the altar moved back into the Basilica, thousands of chairs stacked away, crash barriers removed. Only the patrolling policemen remain. She still can't believe what she has heard: that there are people somewhere out there who would kill Gianpaolo, not because of anything he personally has done, but because he is pope. She cannot comprehend how anyone can hate to that extent.

The nun starts to wonder, not about such possibilities, for there is nothing morbid about her. Nor is she normally introspective. But still she wonders how much time Gianpaolo may have left.

Twice in the past week he has called her to his bedroom, asking her to bring a bowl of hot water and the bottle of herbal elixir they both feel is so beneficial for his phlebitic condition. In Venice she regularly sat with him while he soaked his feet and ankles, and she had sometimes knelt and used a cloth to bathe the calves below his rolled-up cassock. She has done the same here in the Vatican. But whereas in Venice the swelling at least temporarily receded, here it has not done so. His ankles and calves have remained puffy.

Vincenza asked him to consult Dr Buzzonetti. The pope simply shook his head and gently told her there was nothing to worry about, that it's probably caused by no more than a change of location and when his body adjusts to the Roman climate everything will be all right. He sounded so convincing she accepted this. Only later, after looking in a medical book, has she learned that phlebitis is not affected by climatic conditions.

*

Magee and Lorenzi look up this time as Vincenza pauses by the study door on her way back to the kitchen. The men smile when she says dinner will be on time. During this settling-in period of the pontificate meals have tended to be taken by Gianpaolo and his secretaries at all hours. Frequently the pope has eaten from a tray at his desk to try to keep up with the sheer volume of paperwork. The fare is simple: soups and puddings with a nutty flavour. Gianpaolo is a poor eater, 'a nibbler' Magee calls him. But, like the Irishman, the pope cleans his plate. It's a common legacy from their childhood, when each learned the virtues of waste-not, want-not. Vincenza moves on, her habit swishing from her brisk pace as she hurries to the kitchen.

The secretaries consult their list of the pope's appointments for the remainder of the evening. In a few minutes the elevator should bring him back to the apartment after his last public engagement of the day, a ten-minute meeting with a group of American bishops. They are fortunate to have been given even this amount of time. On the pope's tight schedule some people are granted literally only a brief moment to greet Gianpaolo, exchange a few words, pose with him for an official photograph and receive his blessing before Martin escorts them out and ushers in the next visitors. If it wasn't for the photograph, Magee thinks wryly, some might later have trouble convincing themselves they had actually been in the presence of the pope. It is nobody's fault: there are just so many people demanding to see Gianpaolo – the requests for personal audiences received this first week have doubled from the five thousand Paul received weekly at the height of his popularity. Martin has worked wonders sifting the requests and squeezing in audiences between more serious papal meetings. But even so Gianpaolo's daily schedule extends far beyond that of Paul's.

Tonight, at the end of a day which has already lasted fourteen crowded hours, there are two further appointments.

Benelli is scheduled to arrive with the pope and spend thirty minutes with him. But because of his status as a close adviser to Gianpaolo, the cardinal from Florence often ignores the clock and goes beyond his allotted time; not even Martin's freezing stare has always been able to prise him away from the pontiff before Benelli was ready to go. Tonight, after seeing Benelli and following dinner, a forty-five minute item on his schedule, Gianpaolo will return to the study to confer with

239

Cardinal Felici, who, even more than Benelli, is now firmly entrenched as the pontiff's most trusted adviser. The space allotted for him is open-ended. Thankfully, at least, there are no curial trays expected tonight; the coronation has temporarily halted the flow of paper. Tomorrow it will be business as usual.

Lorenzi leaves the study to wait by the elevator for Gianpaolo and Benelli. This custom of one of the secretaries meeting the pope every time he returns to the apartment is another of the changes that Magee recognizes sets the domestic side of this pontificate apart from its predecessor's. Even excluding Vincenza's innovations, the life-style within the papal apartment is dramatically different. Gone with Paul's vials of Mogadon and those mysterious capsules of Fontana's – the old doctor has retired leaving the medical care of the pope in the hands of Buzzonetti – is the deadening silence which permeated the place during Paul's long months of dying. Now it is generally filled with the cheerful voices of the nuns; the only time they become respectfully silent is when visitors arrive. And even then the sounds of their occasional giggling from the kitchen gives a homely touch. Perhaps most important of all for Magee has been the way Vincenza and Lorenzi have integrated him into this new order. They regularly draw on his experience of the previous pontificate and, in turn, brief him on Gianpaolo.

Magee finds the pope delightfully informal around the apartment. He calls his entourage by their first names, something Paul never found easy to do, and frequently stops his staff to enquire how they are settling in. During the evenings, when his official day is done, he likes nothing better than to sit in this study listening to Magee describing the inner workings of the last pontificate.

Initially, the secretary was surprised by what Gianpaolo wanted to know: he is deeply interested not only in everything Paul did, but how he did it: what parts of his daily routine he enjoyed most, which he disliked. Magee apologized he could not be as helpful as he would like, explaining he entered papal service when Paul was already an old man, well into senescence, his eyes, sunk into his head, often looking out at the world with a look that appeared pleading or helpless. Gianpaolo had asked what made Paul like this, and Magee explained, with compassion and love, about the inner torment which had racked the old pope, eventually making Paul a man who retreated almost totally into the privacy of his own mind. Interposed were the moments when Paul whispered, 'I am alone too much', in the voice of someone both puzzled and intimidated by the world. Change was often the hardest thing for him to understand.

Gianpaolo had nodded sympathetically and continued with his

quietly probing questions, explaining it was important for him to understand so he could better see where he must introduce change, revise procedures, and make decisions which Paul, for all the reasons Magee gives, failed to implement.

Everything he has heard from Gianpaolo suggests to Magee that the papacy is about to take a dramatic change of direction.

There are small pointers. The way Gianpaolo publicly addresses people as 'brothers and sisters', instead of Paul's 'sons and daughters'. The way he canvasses the widest possible opinions on almost every matter: lowly members of the Curia who had never spoken to Paul suddenly find themselves encountering Gianpaolo during one of his prowls through the Apostolic Palace and having their views on a subject earnestly sought. There is the tremendous attention he gives to all his public speeches: it has sometimes taken him a dozen drafts to get the right tone, which is becoming very much stamped by seemingly spontaneous asides that have in fact been carefully rehearsed. Gianpaolo is very much the writer-actor.

There are larger indications. Though it is clear the main thrust of his mission will be pastoral, he is quickly coming to terms with the political-spiritual strength of the papacy. The signs are he will use it to make the Church less authoritarian and more responsive to progressive ideas.

But only so far. The purpose of this meeting with Benelli is an indication of that.

The meeting is very much part of the most significant pointer of all: how he intends to handle the Curia. Gianpaolo has made it politely clear to his civil servants that he is fully aware of their power, that he respects their rights to exercise it and does not intend to resurrect the sort of innovations John XXIII introduced which led to the crisis over ideology and organization that Paul, despite his reforms of the Curia in 1967, failed to solve. Having said that, Gianpaolo has gone on to indicate there should be a shift in emphasis, more consultation with the local bishops, more meaningful dialogue between the Curia and those whom it serves. It has all been very low-key, punctuated with the now familiar smile. Yet the curialists have been left in no doubt as to what the pope expects.

It is too early yet to see if it will work. But the signs are good.

Magee is still buoyed by such thoughts when Gianpaolo and Benelli arrive with Lorenzi. He closes the door behind him, a sign of the sensitive nature of what is to be discussed.

Benelli wants to settle the Küng question. He feels the matter has dragged on far too long. Eight years of bitter wrangling have passed since the Swiss theologian first described Paul's decisions on birth control, celibacy, and mixed marriages as 'efforts to restore a pre-conciliar theology'. Since then, in spite of the plainest of warnings, Küng has continued his assault through a series of articles and books. Even the full weight of *Mysterium Ecclesiae* – issued by the Congregation for the Doctrine of the Faith, successor to the Holy Inquisition – has not stopped Küng. The document was published specifically to counter his rejection of papal infallibility. It is the most that could be done to punish such heresy, now that burning at the stake is no longer permissible. According to some accounts of this meeting between Gianpaolo and Benelli – one thing which has not changed in the new pontificate is the number of moles willing to spill some of the beans in exchange for money, preferably American dollars[2] – Benelli genuinely regrets it's no longer possible to cast to the flames the likes of Küng.

The cardinal explains that at Paul's behest the Vatican tried to have Küng repudiated by his peers. This failed. Next, Küng had been 'invited' to Rome to explain his views before the Congregation for the Doctrine of the Faith. But he's avoided that. And, since the theologian was a diocesan priest employed by a secular university, he has also been able to shrug off any Vatican threat to his living. Paul – and Benelli produces these facts more in sorrow than anger – felt Küng's popularity, coupled with his scholarly reputation and the oecumenical importance of the views he expounded – Paul was very sensitive to anything that could cast the Church as trampling on oecumenical advance – had combined to make it difficult for the pope to intervene more forcibly. But Paul's death did not mean Küng was going to stop his challenge. Far from it: Benelli's sources have told him the theologian is winding himself up for another tilt at the papacy. What's particularly distasteful to Benelli is that Küng shows every sign of enjoying his ecclesiastical skirmishing. In the cardinal's view there is only one answer. Gianpaolo, through the Congregation for the Doctrine of the Faith, should publicly and unswervingly condemn Küng.

Gianpaolo says he will review the entire case. He agrees Küng's views are divisive, and promises Benelli his answer in a month. He makes it clear there is no more to be said for the moment.

After dinner Felici is shown into the study. Once more Lorenzi closes the door and the two secretaries start to take notes while the cardinal argues the time has come for Gianpaolo to end the defiance of Marcel Lefèbvre. Felici is well briefed; his review is masterful and authoritative. He ends by saying Gianpaolo should either pronounce a sentence of formal excommunication or hand the case over to the Congregation for the Doctrine of the Faith for trial under canon law.

The pope listens carefully until Felici finishes. Then he asks questions, each posed in a gently enquiring way. Has not the Vatican's canonical endorsement of Lefèbvre's seminary at Econe been with-drawn? Has not the archbishop already been suspended *a divinis*, forbidden to exercise his priestly and episcopal functions? Had not Paul already censured him in a way no other bishop has been condemned by a pope this century? And yet what has all this achieved? Is there not a danger further punitive action will merely endow Lefèbvre with an importance he does not deserve? Should he not be left to fade into oblivion, remembered only perhaps as *L'Incident Lefèbvre*, a tiny footnote, insignificant when measured against any proper reckoning of Paul's pontificate?

The four men in the study know that no answers are expected now. It is not because the hour is late. It is because the questions have been posed so that Felici can go away and ponder them at leisure. When he feels he can answer them, he should return.

This is part of the style of the new pontificate.

*

Noé realizes there is another, and for him, unwelcome, aspect, when he picks up the phone in his apartment very early – barely dawn – on Monday morning, 4 September. Yet it is not that Ciban is calling at this outlandish hour which upsets him; he gets on well with the security chief. One of the qualities the master of ceremonies likes in Ciban is his calmness: in the past he has always sounded and behaved as though nothing could shake him; not even his failure to track down the culprits who bugged Conclave had ruffled his composure. But now Ciban's voice is shaky as he recounts what has happened.

The master of ceremonies arranges to meet Ciban and Martin – who has already been informed – behind the papal art museum.

Hurrying from his apartment through the Vatican grounds, Noé thinks over what Ciban has said. It all fits a pattern; perhaps manifestation would be a better word to describe some of Gianpaolo's behaviour. During the past week the pope has become almost eccentric in the eyes of the protocol-steeped and staunchly traditionalist Noé.

There was his insistence on having the Coronation Mass rewritten: the Mass which had bound each pope to the Church since the Treaty of Westphalia in 1648, when the nations of Europe were allowed to go their own religious ways; the Mass that was said for Clement V, the only pope to be crowned in Lyons, France; the Mass seven other successive popes received during the long exile of the papacy in Avignon; the Mass which had remained virtually unchanged since the papal crown was placed on the head of Leo X with the words: 'Receive the tiara adorned with three crowns and you know that you are father of princes and kings, victor of the whole world under the earth, the

Vicar of Our Lord Jesus Christ to whom be glory and honour without end.'

Gianpaolo dispensed with such terminology – because he also refused to wear the crown pontiffs had worn even before the days of Charlemagne.

Noé sees the crown as a potent symbol which helped the Church rise triumphant from the pillaging of Alaric the Visigoth, Genseric the Vandal, Barbarossa of Prussia, Napoleon of France. Leo I wore it when he assumed the old Roman title, *Pontifex Maximus*, Supreme Pontiff. Boniface VIII placed it on his head the day he made his immortal declaration: 'The Church has one body and one head, Christ and Christ's Vicar, Peter and Peter's successor: in his power there are two swords, a spiritual and a temporal sword; both kinds of power are in the hands of the Roman Pontiff.'

Further, Gianpaolo had virtually dispensed with the plural majestatis, 'We'; it had been the way popes from Silvester I to Paul had spoken: it was another way for them to show they thought of themselves as kings, and of the Church as their kingdom. Even John XXIII, who introduced so many other ideas Noé found difficult to accept, had not gone so far as to speak in the singular 'I'.

But then, the master of ceremonies can reflect as he hurries to meet Ciban and Martin, most previous popes were nurtured and shaped almost exclusively by the Roman Curia, that kingdom within a kingdom which knew how to prepare potential pontiffs.

Gianpaolo is not an 'insider', someone who has spent his working life in and around the Vatican. Therefore, in Noé's view, he is not properly grounded in what is permissible – and what is not. There is no question about it: papal infallibility doesn't extend to a pontiff doing what he likes. Gianpaolo is as bound by rules and regulations as those who serve him. If only he realized that, there would be no need for Noé to come trotting up to Martin and Ciban behind the museum.

The prefect looks nonplussed. What has happened is outside his experience. He listens dolefully as Ciban explains the events to Noé.

One of the Vigilance had called the security chief with the news that shortly after daybreak the pope had walked past a dumbfounded Swiss Guard on duty at the Porta Sant'Anna, and stood for some minutes on Italian soil looking up and down a thankfully deserted street. Then he had just as casually strolled back through the gates, wishing the guard a cordial good morning before going on his way. The man had been so thunderstruck by what had occurred that when Ciban subsequently questioned him, he was barely coherent.

Ciban's immediate concern is for security. If just one member of the

Red Brigades happened to have been passing . . . He does not need to complete the thought.

As well as this nightmarish possibility, Noé and Martin are concerned with another aspect – the diplomatic gaffe the pope caused by walking onto Italian territory. As head of state, says Noé crossly, Gianpaolo should know he is simply not permitted to stroll into another country unannounced, and especially unescorted. This sort of behaviour must stop; others can decide how far the pope can go on matters of dogma, theology and doctrine. When it comes to throwing protocol out of the window, then it is very much Noé's business to halt the slide. He asks where Gianpaolo is now.

Ciban says one of his guards is trailing the pope through the Vatican gardens. He speaks into a handset, puts the receiver to his ear and listens to the crackling response. Gianpaolo is walking on one of the upper terraces.

Noé and Martin brace themselves, and with Ciban set off in pursuit.

They find Gianpaolo talking animatedly to one of the gardeners. The pope waves cheerfully as the trio bear down on him.

The gardener backs away. In all his years of Vatican service he has never encountered such a distinguished gathering at such an early hour. The man continues to stay within earshot, and later will recount how Noé takes Gianpaolo firmly by the elbow and lectures him on the personal risks he has taken and the diplomatic rumpus his action could have triggered – and might yet, if word leaked.

The Italians are very sensitive about such things, says Martin morosely. He rocks back and forth on his heels, a sure sign he is agitated. Ciban has a hurt look; it's as though he thinks the pope is personally determined to make his life a misery.

Gianpaolo nods thoughtfully. In the gentlest of voices he says he had not meant to create problems. Then he bestows a winning smile. No harm has been done. And think what has been achieved.

Achieved? Noé repeats the word, as if he thinks he must have misheard what was said.

Gianpaolo positively beams. Yes, *achieved*. He doubts any of them have been out of bed this early. They should look upon what has happened positively: it has given them the perfect start to their day.

With another cheerful wave he begins to walk back to the Apostolic Palace.[3]

*

'He's vanished!'

Ciban cannot believe what Martin is saying. He has barely got over Gianpaolo's dawn escapade. Now this.

'What do you mean "vanished"?' The security chief has difficulty in forming his words.

'He was here. Now he's gone.' Martin is impatient. 'You must find him.'

'Where are you?'

'In the apartment.'

'And the Holy Father was there?' There is something almost reproachful in Ciban's question. This really cannot be happening to him. He asks Martin to explain further.

There is little more to say. After breakfast the pope went to his study to listen to the morning radio news. Magee saw him there. A little while later, when Martin arrived to escort Gianpaolo down to the second-floor salon for the first meeting of the day, the pope was no longer there. Lorenzi has gone to stall the visitors, some African bishops. Martin has searched the apartment, without success.

Ciban pulls himself together. He tells the prefect he will telephone his guard posts around the Apostolic Palace. Within minutes he is satisfied. The pope has not slipped past his men.

In the meantime Martin is leading a search party from the apartment. The prefect says gloomily it could take days to check every room in the rambling palace. Vincenza brims with good humour: she says Gianpaolo has done this before, popping out of the palace in Venice without telling anybody. Many a time he'd slip into an old cassock and a pair of sandals to spend an evening incognito in his favourite restaurant eating seaweed pizza.

Martin is open-mouthed at the revelation.

The posse rides down in the elevator to the third floor where the Secretariat of State warren is coming to life. Its staff look curiously at the pope's personal aides peering around doors.

Vincenza finally locates Gianpaolo in the room where Macchi had fed Paul's personal papers into the shredder.

By then word had reached Villot. He lopes from his office to find the pope and his staff standing by the shredder.

Gianpaolo smiles at the Secretary and explains, almost apologetically, that none of his aides can make the machine work. Can Villot help?

Thoroughly bewildered the most senior diplomat in the Vatican begins to feed in paper.

Like Ciban he can't quite believe what is happening to him.[4]

*

It is eight o'clock on Tuesday morning, 5 September, when Gianpaolo arrives in the spacious salon on the second floor of the Apostolic Palace with its three windows overlooking St Peter's Square. Here, where Paul took such careful pains to stamp his authority, Gianpaolo has almost casually asserted his personality. There are snapshots of his relatives on the sixteenth-century desk, a series of smiling faces in simple wooden frames standing between the gold-topped roll blotter and the scissors letter-opener which Paul was never known to touch, but which Gianpaolo uses to prepare the slips of paper he utilizes as markers to insert between the pages of important files.

One of the files is a slim, buff-coloured folder containing his handwritten notes of everything Felici and Benelli have formerly told him about the financial operations of the Vatican. The pope had informed his secretaries over breakfast that for the next ninety minutes he does not wish to be disturbed while he reviews the file. Its contents have a bearing on his first meeting, scheduled for 9.30 sharp.

Gianpaolo has no real head for figures, even less for an easy understanding of the complexities of international finance. But he instinctively recognizes the smack of scandal, and the sordid saga Benelli and Felici had previously unfolded wiped away his smile and left him wrinkling his nose in disgust; once or twice, at some particularly shocking revelation, he smacked his hand on the desk and asked, 'Why?' It had been his only audible reaction during the several sessions the two cardinals needed to brief Gianpaolo.

First they detailed the tangled financial dealings which have bound the IOR – Vatican Bank – to Sindona even after the Sicilian's financial empire collapsed in 1974 in New York. The latest news from there is still alarming for the Vatican. Sindona is trying every legal move available in the American courts to avoid being extradited back to Italy; at the same time he is dropping dark hints that if he is returned, he will detail precisely how far certain others in the Vatican were aware of his own crooked dealings.

Felici and Benelli fear Marcinkus might have known far more than he has ever admitted. Equally, both cardinals are satisfied Marcinkus has not been involved personally in any financial chicanery, that he has not acted for personal gain and does not have a secret bank account somewhere. Felici's verdict is that Marcinkus is 'overambitious'; Benelli's judgement is that he is 'incompetent and inexperienced'.

Now, in the wake of *il crack Sindona*, another scandal is brewing. Potentially even more dangerous than the Sindona scandal for the Vatican – for its financial credibility and moral authority – is the astonishing way Marcinkus has blithely allowed Vatican Bank to become entangled with Roberto Calvi.

Ironically, Sindona introduced Calvi to Marcinkus. They were immediately drawn to each other, sharing a similar passion for secrecy and financial wheeling-dealing. Shortly after meeting with Marcinkus in 1971, Calvi and Sindona set up Banco Ambrosiano (Overseas) in Nassau. Three years later, as Sindona's world collapsed, so Calvi's fortunes rose. He became president of Banco Ambrosiano, with its holding company based in Luxembourg and branches throughout Italy and abroad. The Nassau bank was only a single tentacle of this vast financial octopus spreading over fifteen countries. But it was unusual in at least one respect: on its board of directors was a certain 'Mr Paul Marcinkus'.

Vatican Bank took up four per cent of the Ambrosiano Luxembourg stock and eight per cent of the Nassau stock – and began to act closely with Calvi's Italian-based banks. In its immune position, Vatican Bank could move abroad millions of lire, circumventing Italian laws designed to restrict such transfers. But now, the Bank of Italy is about to begin an extensive audit of Calvi's financial empire. Both Benelli and Felici fear it will uncover not only serious breaches of Italian law, but also show how extensive are the complex interlocking relationships between Vatican Bank and the increasingly dubious-looking Calvi empire. Even if Marcinkus is shown to have been at best naive and, at worst, rashly incompetent, the ensuing scandal will cause great harm to the Church.[5]

At the same time, apart from Sindona, there are currently two other financial time-bombs ticking away in the United States which could detonate at any moment with further devastating results for the Vatican.

The first concerns the possibility the US Justice Department might make public its so-far highly secret report on investigations in 1973 into organized crime. Justice Department agents have uncovered a plot by the Mafia to use European businessmen to borrow vast sums of money against counterfeit stocks and bonds of American corporations. The investigators had privately interviewed Marcinkus in his office in the Vatican; so secret was their visit not even Ciban knew of it. The investigators wanted to know whether Marcinkus had any suspicion the Mafia was planning to launder the best part of $900 million profit from the counterfeit securities swindle through Vatican Bank. Marcinkus's answers had so far remained a secret of the Justice Department. One suggestion is that President Nixon himself ordered that the report must not be published. But with Nixon disgraced, there is no guarantee it will remain unpublished.

The second time-bomb is Cody. It is not so much the amount of money involved: compared to the Vatican's estimated loss in *il crack Sindona* it is modest: the Chicago cardinal's caper runs to probably no more than a couple of million dollars. It's the salacious background which most worries Benelli and Felici: the whiff of moral lapses, a touch of *la dolce vita* that can only evoke unhappy memories of earlier princes of the Church who strayed. Coupled to all this is the way the Internal Revenue Service is stalking the financial doings of the Chicago diocese. Not to mention the journalistic pack sniffing in Cody's wake. It all bodes ill.

Gianpaolo continues to ponder over the notes he has made during meetings with Benelli and Felici. They had explained that the Vatican's entanglement in such unsavoury financial affairs came at a time when it was, and still is, reeling from a succession of other monetary blows. There has been a fall in the number of financial bequests to the Church; during the past five years the amount has slumped by thirty per cent. The annual contribution of Peter's Pence has declined steadily since the days of John. Allowing for inflation, in true worth the amount collected is now only sixty per cent of what it was a decade ago. Against this, salary increases for curial employees – whose numbers have tripled these past fifteen years – had to be given just as Italy's inflation peaked.

And only now, three years later, is the full extent of the financial disaster of the Holy Year of 1975 clear. The Church had invested huge sums trying to attract pilgrims to Rome. They did not come. As a result the Vatican was forced to dip heavily into emergency contingency funds to meet a deficit equal to some six million dollars. This position has worsened despite the most stringent cuts. The projected deficit for 1978 – quite apart from the expense of Paul's funeral and the ensuing Conclave and coronation – is expected to be eleven million dollars.

Now, eight years after Paul launched his angry attack on critics who spoke disturbingly of the Vatican's 'fabulous wealth', it is the Church's deteriorating investment position which most worries Gianpaolo. Holdings in real estate, art, rare books and all the other treasures the Vatican possesses still make it in a sense one of the richest organizations in the world. But the capital it has available to invest is dropping all the time – because of bad management. It began when Paul signed that secret deal with Sindona taking the Church's portfolio outside traditional Italian markets, where the Vatican could exercise rigid control over its investments, into the financial markets of Europe and the United States.

Gianpaolo learned that plunging, often as a major shareholder, into multinational conglomerates had resulted in a diminishing of the Vatican's influence in the financial world. No longer could the Church wield the power it previously possessed when it held sway over companies and could ensure they did not engage in dubious practices; there had been mistakes made then, too, but nothing on the scale that has happened in the last five years.

Close to 9.30, Gianpaolo finishes reading. His thoughts at this moment remain his alone, shared with no one.

Yet already Felici and Benelli have told several people of that earlier moment when the pope looked at them and, in a voice they had not heard before, said this must stop; that an end must be put to policies which left the Vatican financially defenceless and at the mercy of profiteers, speculators and high-flying con men like Sindona and Calvi.

For the moment, he decides, Marcinkus will remain at the helm but, like Küng and Lefèbvre, the future of the banker is under review. In the meantime the Church must urgently seek new ways to make use of its funds.

Exactly at 9.30 Martin ushers in Bernardin Gantin. Gianpaolo leads the tall black African cardinal to a sofa and sits beside him. Gianpaolo comes quickly to the point. He outlines what he has learned and what he wants to do.

Gantin is frank – and will later make no secret of it. Paul, possibly partly because of his own financial experience, had, in the closing years of his pontificate, developed an entrenched fear of the Italian Left. This, coupled with his increasing conservatism, had decided him to move the Vatican's money beyond the reach of those in Italy he felt might one day grab it. He had acted from the highest motives and no one, least of all Gantin, wanted to see the Church's money put at risk in unstable Italian stock. Equally, if the Church is to continue to be seen as the church of the poor, especially in the Third World, it must ensure it does not appear blatantly materialistic and must divert some of its still considerable financial resources to more humane causes. Gantin urges that the Vatican use its investment, wherever possible, to help stop socio-economic injustices and exploitation. Vatican finances should be used to support worthwhile redevelopment schemes in Africa, Asia and South America. There could still be acceptable profits – and such a policy might also virtually put an end to the growing criticism from Catholics and non-Catholics about how the pope's financial empire functions.

For the first time Gianpaolo smiles. There *are* going to be changes. For a start he wants Gantin to take charge of Cor Unum, the Church's powerful organization for international aid. Until now this important and delicate position belonged to Villot.

Gantin accepts.

*

When Gantin emerges from the pope's salon, Martin, waiting in its crowded ante-room, sighs. His carefully prepared schedule is already overrunning. It really is so irritating, the prefect has complained to Magee and Lorenzi, the way the pope simply refuses to keep to time. Martin has tried everything. He has come in and stood pointedly inside the door. Gianpaolo either ignores him or cheerfully waves him away. He has tried to devise a 'fifty-minute hour', allowing a ten-minute interlude between appointments. That hasn't worked either. The pope simply runs on.

Martin finds all this upsetting enough. But matters are exacerbated because there often seems no good reason why the pope uses his valuable time talking to people who, really, in the end, are relatively unimportant. For instance, Gianpaolo has had in some of his former archdiocese priests for a chat which had run on well beyond the allotted span. Again, between meetings that are important, Gianpaolo sometimes wanders off and talks with anybody he comes across in the corridors of the Apostolic Palace or the San Damaso Courtyard.

The prefect had needed his considerable tact and experience to smooth the ruffled feelings of several cardinals making their farewells before leaving Rome, who found themselves kept waiting beyond their appointed time. Cody, for one, was not pleased. Nor was Aramburu. Others, like Koenig and Sin, had been more philosophical: they felt running late was just part of the papacy shaking down.

Martin feels relieved that the imposing figure he has been engaging in polite conversation while waiting for Gantin to finish, seems in no hurry.

Everything about the Metropolitan Nikodim, Archbishop of Leningrad and Novgorod, reminds Martin of a bear. The man has a huge, bear-like head, thick bear-shaped neck and shoulders, a bear-like belly and hams of arms which he uses to fan himself like a bear swatting flies. And even in the voluminous regalia of the Russian Orthodox Church the Metropolitan is clearly a hairy man. He has a full, flowing beard which extends from just below his eyes to the start of his ample stomach; there are tufts of hair in his ears and on the back of his broad fingers and hands; when Nikodim strips off for his regular swim in a Rome hotel pool, the thickly matted hair on his body causes heads to turn; he stands close to six feet and weighs about three hundred pounds.

Born in a small town a hundred miles outside Moscow, he has clung to his native peasant patois. Nobody is really fooled. Nikodim's mind is sharp enough to make more than one member of the Soviet Politburo — as Casaroli has informed Gianpaolo — ponder anxiously the strength of Christianity under Communism. In the Vatican, Nikodim is also seen as a powerful bridge-maker between the Church and non-Catholic Christian churches. The Metropolitan has been allotted a full fifteen minutes in which to speak privately to Gianpaolo about the problems of religious worship in Russia.

Martin finally leads him into the salon. While introductions are made Vincenza enters with a tray bearing a coffee set. The prefect leaves with her.

Gianpaolo will now be the only witness for what happens. He will recall precisely the sequence of events and, natural reporter that he is, pare them to the essentials for the subsequent benefit of Magee, Lorenzi and others. It won't change anything.

For a moment he talks to his visitor. Then he pours two cups of coffee. He offers the Metropolitan cream and sugar: Nikodim accepts a little of each. They are standing by the pope's desk. Nikodim takes a sip from his cup. Gianpaolo is about to do the same when he pauses, startled.

A stricken look crosses Nikodim's face. Cup and saucer drop from his hand. The saucer shatters on the desk top; the cup spills coffee on the carpet which the thick pile quickly absorbs. Nikodim clutches his chest, makes a choking sound, and then topples backwards, crashing to the floor. His mouth and eyes remain open. But Gianpaolo knows instinctively his guest is dead.

The pope picks up the white telephone and dials Lorenzi, telling him to get a doctor.

Almost immediately Martin and Magee rush into the room. Buzzonetti quickly arrives.

The doctor kneels beside the body, listens for a heartbeat, checks for a pulse. He stands up, shaking his head.

Martin suggests Gianpaolo cancel the rest of the morning's appointments.

'No!'

Magee is startled by the sharpness of the pope's response.

'No. These people have come to see me. They will.' Gianpaolo looks down at the body. 'That is what this good man would have wished.'

The corpse is still warm when the rumour starts. Nikodim is the victim of a confusion with poison; he had sipped lethally contaminated coffee which was actually meant for the pope.

It is both vicious and untrue. The Metropolitan died from a massive coronary. But the story continues to spread.

*

Behind Gianpaolo is the towering figure of the Risen Christ in a mass of jagged bronze, the dominant feature of the Nervi Audience Hall. Facing him, only held in check by steel crush barriers patrolled by anxious security men, are some twelve thousand men, women and children, all gripped in high emotional fervour. There may be more. Shortly before the doors closed, there was a final surge of people into the Nervi, and now there may be so many crammed into this vast indoor arena that public safety laws are being broken. Nobody seems to care. The fifty or so television and still-cameramen encroaching on the huge stage where Gianpaolo sits on his throne; the two hundred reporters in their gallery set into one wall; the radio broadcasters in the adjoining booths; the forty cardinals and almost a hundred bishops seated with them on the stage; and, above all, the public who stretch row after jam-packed row so far back that from the throne the faces meld and blur: all are totally absorbed by the extraordinary performance Gianpaolo is giving during his first Nervi audience, on Wednesday, 6 September.

People who have been coming here for fifteen years cannot remember Paul, at his most relaxed, behaving like this. Indeed, there may have been nothing quite like it in the entire history of the papacy. Two months ago Paul had spoken to them in terms often obscure, his dogma impeccable but frequently so hedged with caveats many could not follow his meaning.

The journalists came then expecting – perhaps even half hoping – there would be trouble: that the supporters of Lefèbvre might disrupt Paul's words; that somewhere in the crowd would be followers of Küng. But now the journalists are almost all here for a very different reason. They simply want to see what Gianpaolo will say and do after their own close encounter with him at their special audience a few days ago. He had offered the evocative thought that the Church is 'like a clock', its 'hands give certain rules to the world', and 'the Church itself needs winding up, which is the Curia's job.' He'd asked and answered the question as to what distinguished him from every other pope since the year 914: he was the first for over a thousand years entitled to add a 'One' after his name. The journalists decided he was going to be a most quotable pope. This is why they are here: to witness the captivating performance Gianpaolo has put on since coming into the Nervi, skullcap askew, face lit up with irrepressible humour.

It had taken him thirty minutes to walk from the rear of the hall to the throne beneath the Risen Christ. Along the way he shook hundreds of hands, exchanged even more greetings and behaved, one reporter noted, 'like a humble, godly man, his skew-whiff skullcap suggesting a degree of lovable incompetence which is in no way threatening.'

From the moment Gianpaolo speaks the entire gathering is in his hands. He begins by saying he intends to 'imitate Paul, in the hope that I, too, will be able, somehow, to help people become better.' It is straight to the point, not stuffy theology, more like crisply spoken journalism.

'We must feel small before God. When I say, "Lord, I believe", I am not ashamed to feel like a child before his mother. One believes in one's mother. I believe in the Lord, in what He has revealed to me. The commandments are a little more difficult to observe, but God gave them to us not to satisfy a whim, not in His own interest, but solely in our own interest.'

He pauses and looks at them all in turn: his cardinals and bishops, some smiling uncertainly, for they, too, have witnessed nothing like this; at the film crews and the reporters high up in their gallery. They respond by recording his smile, the way he gives his cap an even jauntier angle. Then he looks out over the great mass of people and, with an aplomb a stand-up comic would envy, says he is going to tell them a story.

'A man went to buy a motor car from the agent. The latter talked to him plainly. "Look here, it's a good car. Mind that you treat it well. Premium petrol in the tank and oil for the joints. The good stuff."'

He pauses; his timing perfect.

'The man replied, "Oh no, for your information I can't stand the smell of petrol or of oil. I'll put champagne, which I like so much, in the tank, and I'll oil the joints with jam."'

Appreciative laughter sweeps the Nervi. A quick wave of Gianpaolo's hand and there is silence for the punch-line. 'The agent said, "Do what you like. But don't come and complain if you end up in a ditch with your car!"'

Another burst of laughter. Then the point of the story, delivered with a surge of feeling.

'The Lord did something similar with us. He gave us this body, animated by an intelligent soul, a good will. And he said, "This machine is a good one. But treat it well."'

Thunderous applause. He silences it by beckoning a choirboy to join him on the platform. His name is James and he is just ten years old, an angelic-faced child. With him Gianpaolo reveals another gift: his sure way with children.

'James, have you ever been ill?'

'No.'

'Ah, never?'

'No.'

'Never been ill?'

'No.'

Chuckles come from all over the hall.

'Not even a temperature?'

'No.'

'Oh how lucky you are!'

Another burst of delighted laughter. Gianpaolo pats James on the head. The child has paved the way for the moral he wants to convey.

'When a child is ill, who brings him a little broth, some medicine? Isn't it his mother? That's it. Afterwards you grow up, and your mother gets old. You become a fine gentleman, and your mother, poor thing, will be in bed, ill. That's it. Well, who will bring the mother a little milk and medicine. Who will?' He waits for James to digest the scenario.

'My brothers and I.'

Gianpaolo beams. 'Well said!' He addresses the audience. '"His brothers and he", he said. I like that. Did you understand?'

A mighty roar of agreement.

'But it does not always happen. As Bishop of Venice I sometimes went to homes. Once I found an elderly woman, sick.'

Gianpaolo pauses, looks at James, smiles, prepares himself to play both the part of the visiting clergyman and the ailing woman.

'"How are you?"'

The pope subtly changes his voice. He sounds like a frail old woman. '"Well, the food is all right!"'

'"Are you warm? Is there heating?"' He's the caring cleric.

'"It's good."'

'"So you are content?"'

'"No."' He adds adds another voice to his repertoire, that of a neutral observer. 'She almost began to cry.'

He switches again, back to the concerned priest. '"But why are you crying?"'

'"My daughter-in-law, my son, never come to see me. I would like to see my grandchildren."'

In the hall people are actually crying.

Gianpaolo raises his voice. 'Heat and food are not enough. There is the heart. We must think of the hearts of our old people. The Lord said that parents must be respected and loved, even when they are old. And besides the parents, there is the State, there are superiors. May the pope recommend obedience? Bossuet, who was a great bishop, wrote: "Where no one commands, everyone commands; where everyone commands, no one commands any longer but chaos." Sometimes something similar is seen in this world too. So let us respect those who are our superiors.'

He smiles at James, gives him a final pat on the head and sends the boy back to his place.

He is not finished. Gianpaolo tells them charity is the soul of justice, but that he has always recommended not only great acts of charity, also little ones.

He says he wants to repeat a story he read in Dale Carnegie's *How to Win Friends and Influence People*.

'A lady had four men in the house: her husband, a brother, two grown-up sons. She alone had to do the shopping, the washing, the ironing and the cooking. Everything, all alone. One Sunday they came. The table is laid for dinner, but on each plate is only a handful of hay.'

Another perfectly-timed pause. As the laughter erupts, he quells it.

Gianpaolo spreads his hands expressively. '"Oh!", the others protest and say, "What? Hay?" And she says, "No, everything is ready. Let me tell you. I prepare your food. I keep you clean. I do everything. Never once have you said, 'That was a good dinner you made for us'. Say something! I'm not made of stone!"'

Now he lets the applause come. He bides his time. Then he quickly delivers the message. 'People work more willingly when their work is recognized. These are little acts of charity. In our homes, we all have someone who is waiting for a compliment.'

As the applause eventually dies, Magee thinks Gianpaolo has done more in ten minutes than some Church leaders achieve in a lifetime. He has created a means by which he can funnel his teachings, knowing they will be warmly received. It has been a tremendous performance – perhaps one powerful enough to make his opponents pause.

21

The opposition grew.

Within his city-state – with its thirty squares and streets, parish church, grocery store, post office, car pool, garage and bookstore – the voices of dissent became more vocal, more malicious and more bold in their rejection of what the pope said and did.

When he smiled and laughed, they smirked. When he quoted not only Dale Carnegie, but also Jules Verne, Mark Twain, Napoleon and St Bernard, they said he culled his philosophy from the Reader's Digest. The more his audiences were attracted by his direct, common-sense approach, the fiercer grew the opposition; the more the crowds cheered, the more the Curia growled. They picked over Gianpaolo's words, looking not so much for hidden meaning – there was almost none – as for a chance to ridicule and repudiate with that special kind of subtle viciousness curialists can use when they feel most threatened; these were the jibes of single-minded men whose outlook had been shaped in part by grappling with such travails as birth control, pre-marital sex and the increasing threat of women being ordained as priests.

These were men who had come to believe in the closing years of Paul's pontificate that, unless the slide was halted, by the end of the century there would no longer be a religious institution which they, in any event, recognized as the Roman Catholic Church. All around them they perceived opponents tearing at the very fabric they held sacred in order to achieve that change even sooner. There were priests in open rebellion against their bishops; bishops in revolt against the authority of the Vatican; black, yellow and all shades of brown, Catholics all, insisting their will be done in the name of their brand of racism and under threat of separation from the parent Church; nuns who refused to wear habits or even work alongside priests because it offended their new-found religious women's liberation. There were Catholic Gay Churches, Catholic Yogis, Catholic Pentecostalists, Catholic Processeans; they are to these men in the Curia what the Dancing Dervishes were to mainstream Islam.

For years – say the curialists – the deviates have had sympathizers in high places in the hierarchy; any number of cardinals who should know better continue to pay at least lip service to the demands of those determined to bring about change and the havoc their opponents fear.

They had almost welcomed the passing of Paul. For them, he had become simply too feeble to handle the crisis of Communism, contraception and theological revolt. Not only had he finally failed to walk alone on the peaks of decision, but he had lurked in the foothills, pleading and scolding, and trying to please all sides. Under him papal authority had reached a new nadir. The Church had been eviscerated by his weakness, his indecision, the lack of real authority that greatness demanded. Paul, in their eyes, became a pygmy pope leading the pygmy masses to the abyss.

They had expected, they said, so much from his successor: that he would refute moral support for terrorists in Latin America and elsewhere; that he would temper sympathy for Third World causes; that he would voice his objection to Marxism in all its many guises; that he would stamp – hard – on the concept of a 'people' church where everyone was allowed to go their own way; that he would tell Catholic homosexuals and divorcees they could never be allowed full religious rights; that he would denounce all those priests and nuns hell-bent on the destruction of the social order which the Church must have to survive. This, at the very least, they had hoped for.

Instead, Gianpaolo gave them parables about Pinocchio and, perhaps even harder for these arch-conservatives to accept, photographs of himself shaking hands with the Communist mayor of Rome.

In the embattled world of the diehards, this was tantamount to a declaration of war between them and the pope. He was, they shuddered to one another, almost certainly going to realize their worst fantasies: there would be more homosexual marriages; would be more denials of the Virgin Birth and the Resurrection; would be an increase in tactile prayer, Satan–Jesus cults, masses celebrated by women in living rooms, nude altarboys, rock masses, black revolutionary Christs, female Holy Spirits; there would be a burgeoning of clerical posturing and theological absurdities.

They all had hoped for a successor in the mould of Pius XII, a true Prince of Power, imbued with a real feeling for traditional values, a model – they added – all popes should aspire to follow. Instead they had acquired a pope who insisted he was more of a mere man than even John had proclaimed, who had, within a few days of being elected, indicated change was inexorable, and that the Church had already passed through a momentous trap-door – the Second Vatican Council – from which there could be no turning back. In all Gianpaolo said and did – for his opponents – he seemed to be suggesting the Church was out of date and the only way it could contribute to the immense problems and possibilities it faced was to 'adapt'. The very word was anathema.

When he told the College of Cardinals in the first week of his pontificate that he had no real idea how the corporate structure of the Church worked, they had not objected. There had been popes in the past content to leave everything to the Curia and virtually rubber-stamp what it ordered. It had worked very well. But Gianpaolo was different: he poked his smiling face around every door – so much so that Villot, for one, always so exasperatingly courteous in the French way, and so tolerant of human failings, was tearing at his full head of hair. So they said. And the husky, balding Benelli – whom entrenched curialists unfailingly called 'the Gauleiter' – was being allowed to flex his muscles. That may not, in the end, have mattered: after all they had seen Benelli off once already. What really distressed the diehards was that, in spite of all his happy wanderings up and down the corridors of power, Gianpaolo still did not seem really to understand what his priorities should be.

He spent long hours preparing his apparently spontaneous homilies and Sunday Angelus asides. It got him a great deal of publicity. But the curialists fretted that even in his third week as pontiff, he appeared uncertain how many sacred congregations there were and seemed to have little grasp of the subtleties of interrelationship between those which he knew. While the maze of congregations, tribunals, secretariats, commissions and offices of the Curia might indeed appear cumbersome to a newcomer and in need of streamlining, they insisted this complicated labyrinth was well integrated and worked because everyone recognized the demarcation lines. No pope – said the men who manned the lines – could possibly ignore the recommendations of his civil service and hope efficiently to rule the Church. But that was what Gianpaolo was doing: he was falling behind with his paper work.

They said he appeared to have only a hazy notion of the many splits in the Church: the rift between the bishops of Latin America and the United States over the need to co-exist with, or continue to reject totally, Communism; the division within the intellectual life of the Church over what was acceptable and what was not; the argument over what could be done to halt the steady drift away from the priesthood. In so many ways Gianpaolo had taken over a house divided.

Even his most implacable enemies conceded he could not simply sit back and do nothing; that would assuredly have allowed the dam which Paul's policies had cracked to be totally breached. So: something had to be done.

What Gianpaolo did – they insisted – was something worse than doing nothing. He increasingly showed he had little patience with the daily grind, the decision-making and the politicking, while at the same time he liked to be involved in everything. He was, in the words of one Irish curialist, 'a messer'.

The criticism was both unfair and untrue.

Even before 6 September, when Il Mondo, Italy's leading financial journal, published a detailed exposé of the Vatican's financial morass, almost confirming what Gianpaolo learned from Benelli and Felici, he had already begun to untangle the machinations of Marcinkus, who had been firmly asked for an accounting. And Baggio had been put back on the Cody trail.

Casaroli, for one, was quickly impressed by Gianpaolo's grasp of the Church's relationship with the regimes of Eastern Europe. Casaroli placed seven crucial questions before the pope; Gianpaolo answered five of them *promptly and asked for time to ponder the other two. Paul had never been so positive.*

The inescapable truth was that Gianpaolo had deliberately decided to take a long view. He did not feel it mattered he was not grasping such trifles as who did what, where and why; what concerned him was that he could be the pope who led the Church into the third millennium. In the year 2000 he would be eighty-seven, not an unknown age for a ruling pontiff. To guide the Church into the next century successfully he must function less as a monarch and more as a colleague and pastor. He must bring the full promise of Vatican II to fruition, making it an instrument of genuine reform and reunion. This called for a new kind of papal leadership, less rigid, more open. That was why, when speaking to a group of visiting American bishops, he had not only warned of the dangers of divorce, but also admitted there were many questions on the issue yet to be discussed. In other words, the door was not firmly closed. He used his Angelus talks on Sundays and his Wednesday audiences – both with their frequent references to Pinocchio – as a genuine attempt to foster a rekindling of faith. He was going unashamedly for mass appeal: this was the basis of his remarkably effective catechetical style, his polished microphone manner, his powerful attraction for the ordinary people of the world. He was a magnificent communicator and the papacy gave him a platform which had never before been available to him.

He used it shrewdly from the outset. He identified one crucial issue as collegiality; it was essential for power and decision-making to be more widely diffused, and there must be a genuine increase in the sharing of responsibility between himself and his bishops. He said – and meant it – that he needed the collective wisdom of the episcopate to resolve the pressing questions facing the Church. He was more than willing to decentralize authority and at the same time give greater autonomy to episcopal conferences and diocesan councils. And he wanted this sort of co-operation to permeate all levels of the Church. In no way, he said with his usual winning grin, was he ceasing to be head of the Church, the ultimate arbiter. Far from abrogating his responsibilities, he was showing a new understanding of them by emphasizing his role as someone who ruled within, rather than over, the Church. Enforced imperialism had no place in his pontificate.

He quickly demonstrated too – which may explain much of the opposition – that the Curia held no fear for him. He would build from where Paul had left off, internationalizing the Curia still more. He planned to introduce foreigners in increasing numbers into middle-management posts; eventually there might even be non-Italian nuncios. And he wanted younger people in the Curia – the average age of his civil servants was currently 60.2 years. He also saw a need to increase the number of religious and lay women from the present paltry few; while it would require a great deal of 'understanding' – another of his words which drove opponents to reach into their office cupboards for drink – the day could soon come when women held important executive positions in the Curia. It would all fit in with his overall concept that the Curia must be more pastoral, service-oriented and much more in keeping with the requirements of the Church he wanted to lead.

Gianpaolo revealed an immediate ease with his prime responsibility of preserving the unity of faith and communion. And he was always willing to try and capture the popular imagination to do so. He studiedly remarked that God was 'even more our mother than our father'. When he was challenged – as he full well knew he must be – he gave the perfectly correct response that the idea was not his but Isaiah's. More important, it was yet another way for him to stimulate debate on such issues as Christology, Mariology, the sacraments and communal absolution. It became quickly clear he would pay the most careful attention to the responses to such serious theological issues. He warmly embraced the concept that, 'free from anxiety', he would give positive guidance in all decisive questions affecting life and death, good and evil, including matters where human sexuality was involved. Nor would he be a doctrinaire defender of the ancient bastions. Rather – and always paying proper attention to consistency with the Church's teaching – he would be a pastoral pioneer, encouraging responsible religious debate and ready to guide and correct when necessary.

In his inaugural address he set another measure of his pontificate: 'The danger for modern man is that he would reduce the earth to a desert, the person to an automat, brotherly love to a planned collectivism, often introducing death where God wishes life.' He made it clear he would use his greatest asset – the morality and the inspirational authority of the papacy – to correct this situation. He would do everything he could to move the minds and hearts of people through exhortation and example. The wounds society inflicted on its members – and he was thinking in these first weeks of his pontificate of the Middle East and Iran – could be healed by love, hope and truth: all offer the only way to create a new sense of spiritual brotherhood. He intended to foster this feeling by travelling; he hoped his journeys would further demonstrate his visible solidarity with other faiths and creeds.

Gianpaolo made it plain in his first speeches that he was painfully aware that of the four billion-plus people on this planet, sixty per cent of them lived below the level of subsistence. He would, in all humility, like to be their spokesman, the pope who would plead for this voiceless majority; he would say and show, wherever possible, that the dispossessed, the oppressed, the disadvantaged and the poverty-stricken should regard him as their advocate. He was determined to sensitize the consciences of the wealthy and powerful and encourage them to develop a worldwide economic and political system based on justice and not on exploitation. In saying this he had not forgotten the words of Bernardin Gantin.

Nor indeed had he overlooked that, as leader of the largest Church in the world, he could exercise unique moral suasion to further oecumenism. Close to a quarter of a million people in St Peter's Square and an estimated hundred million around the world heard his clear-cut credo: 'We intend to dedicate our prayerful attention to everything that would favour union. We will do so without diluting doctrine, but at the same time without hesitation.' Here was clear notice Gianpaolo meant to foster evangelical spirit, reject authoritarianism, unite Christians and to improve existing ties between Jews, Moslems and the peoples of other religions.

In all he said and did he struck a universal chord. He received more attention and coverage than even John managed at the outset of his reign. It continued like this through the sunny weeks of September. In the process it seemed as though his opponents, like so much else, were being swept away; their angry voices were lost in the roar of the crowd.

People began to say this could be the beginning of perhaps the most triumphant pontificate this century.

At his Wednesday audience, on 27 September, sixteen thousand people somehow manage to squeeze into the Nervi Hall. He stuns them by speaking in excellent English on a subject he knows a great deal about: love.

Even his opponents admit that he is expert at dispensing it.

22

As during Paul's pontificate, Romans measure Gianpaolo's reign by small things. Now, the fountains in St Peter's Square play all night, their splashing drowned by the rumble of traffic constantly passing below his bedroom. The pope sleeps with the shutters open, the way he did in Venice, when he lay in bed listening to the shouts of the gondoliers. He's coming to tolerate the distinctive *tufo* sound of the city just as he is becoming used to the rolling syllables of the Roman accent. What he finds hard to fathom are some of the minds of his Curia. They are not only as devious as he has been told to expect but also often petty and unpredictable. Senior civil servants leak their squabbles with each other, and with him, to outsiders. All sorts of tales have begun to appear in the Italian press. It is mostly unimportant tittle-tattle, nevertheless it is not what he likes or expects. But at least nothing has appeared about the crucial meeting he is going to have later this Thursday morning, 28 September.[1]

Gianpaolo has tried to ensure only six other people know of it: Villot, Felici, Benelli, Baggio, Magee and Lorenzi. He has involved each of them after the most careful thought. Villot because, as Secretary of State, his presence is mandatory for the matter under discussion; Felici and Benelli will attend as his two most trusted advisers; Baggio because he has been principally responsible for gathering the latest evidence; Magee and Lorenzi are included since eventually they will have to prepare the final all-important document on what Gianpaolo recognizes is the most critical test so far of his authority.

For the past ten days the four cardinals have been preparing in their own handwriting a series of position papers; Gianpaolo had ruled the topic to be so delicate and serious that not even their private secretaries should be informed. Each cardinal placed his papers in envelopes which he secured with his personal seal. The envelopes were then collected by either Magee or Lorenzi and brought to Gianpaolo. He personally opened each envelope and read the contents several times. What he has learned deeply disturbs and frightens him. The matter is far more serious than the financial bungling he is trying to untangle. It is immeasurably graver for the Church than any of the secular disputes the Holy See is involved in under his aegis: Lebanon, Rhodesia, Poland.

In all the 'consultations' before and during Conclave, no one had mentioned a word about this crisis to him. Yet, when he studies the evidence – the meticulous paperwork the four cardinals have prepared – it is clear Paul had begun to grapple with it. Then, perhaps from exhaustion, or fear, or because he could not face such a confrontation, Paul had not pursued the problem.

Gianpaolo knows he cannot do this. He sees the crisis – this is the word he has repeatedly used after reading the position papers – as one which threatens the very stability of the Church. Unless he deals with it properly and quickly, his own pontificate will lose the credibility he has worked so hard to achieve these past thirty-two days. That is why he has called this ultra-secret meeting in the seclusion and security of his own study.

The meeting is still over five hours away when, at exactly 5.15 am, the pope appears at first one, then the other of his bedroom windows. Unlike Paul he does not lurk behind the curtains, afraid someone might see him staring out over a troubled Rome. Instead, Gianpaolo stands boldly at the windows, visible from anywhere in the square and, through a telescopic gunsight, from further beyond. Villot has asked him not to be so conspicuous, pointing out, perfectly correctly, that the pope makes an easy and distinctive early-morning target for a terrorist bullet. Gianpaolo responded, very firmly, that he was not going to change a lifelong habit: from his youth he has stood at his bedroom window every morning to greet the new day. He will continue to do so – however great the danger. Besides, he had grinned, softening his sharpness, his policemen friends in the square will protect him.

They wave at him – something they would never have dared do in Paul's days – and Gianpaolo waves back. It's hard to realize, the policemen tell each other, that Gianpaolo is really a head of state and the world's most powerful religious leader. He behaves like a country priest. They also think 'the system' – the same term Lorenzi uses to describe the way many in the Vatican apply rigid precedent to everything – is beginning to stifle the pope.

It is a week now since Gianpaolo was last seen walking in the Vatican gardens; Ciban deployed a posse of men to keep people at bay. It looked more like an American president on a carefully managed walkabout than the universal pastor taking a stroll around his back garden.

At his Wednesday audience, Gianpaolo is now so hemmed in by curial monsignors and security men that people can barely see him as he is hurried along the central aisle to his throne in the Nervi Hall. And his speeches are being edited; all those enchanting 'I's' are being changed in *L'Osservatore Romano* to the deadening 'We'. The editors are also rationing the number of papal jokes and asides they will publish, and often ignore Gianpaolo's carefully rehearsed departures from his script.

There had surfaced what amounts to a Curia within the Curia. Its presence is not new; it tried to make its influence felt in Paul's closing days. But then the papacy was barely ticking over and there was very little they needed to do about the few decisions being taken. Yet this inner elite is determined to shackle Gianpaolo. Individually tied to the Vatican since their seminarist days, tempered by heated political battles amongst themselves, weaned on conspiracies and secretiveness disguised as piety and protocol, they want to assert their authority over the new pope. The struggle provides another game for the bored policemen in the piazza. They like to bet with each other on the outcome.

When Gianpaolo turns away from the window he is into the second hour of the nineteen-hour day he regularly works. It is an astonishing feat of physical stamina and mental discipline, a punishing routine which begins at 4.30 every morning when Vincenza leaves a flask of coffee outside his bedroom door, and which the pope drinks after his first devotions.

Gianpaolo is no insomniac as Paul was; he is more like a veteran combat soldier who can awaken, fully refreshed, after the shortest of sleeps. It is this ability which enables him to do what he finds so fulfilling (and here he is like Paul), namely to read and ponder quietly in these first hours before Martin's schedule claims almost every other minute he is awake.

Again, like Paul, Gianpaolo has made it clear he must not be disturbed during this period except for the gravest of emergencies. There is a designated chain of command who can intrude. Vincenza is top of this very short list. Then comes Magee. His precedence over Lorenzi is seen in the gossipy Apostolic Palace as significant, it being interpreted that the pope has 'promoted' Magee to senior secretary. This is not so: the men have equal status. But in the divide-and-rule mentality of the curial cubby-holes it's a useful item to juggle with.

But it is not nearly so intriguing as having Vincenza head that list. Her relationship with Gianpaolo is the subject of the most intense speculation. Nobody is suggesting any impropriety – God forbid. It is rather that curial officials remain uncertain about her. And that, to them, is in itself worse than any impropriety.

They had understood, if not liked, the first woman to have a decided impact on their relationship wth a pope. She was the haughty Pasqualina, Pius XII's housekeeper. The sturdy Bavarian peasant had begun to take care of Pius when he was nuncio in Nazi Germany. She was barely twenty, a pretty rosy-cheeked girl, when she came to keep house for him. Pasqualina – in spite of the Church rule which forbids young women to live in the households of priests – stayed with Pius to the day he died. Throughout this period she used her position shrewdly. So had Giacomina who handled Paul and the Curia with a skill even Casaroli ruefully admired. Once, she had interrupted a briefing to say that Paul was tired, and would Casaroli please come back in the morning to talk about the possibility of nuclear war?

No one in the Curia quite knows how to handle Vincenza – or how she manages Gianpaolo. Like her predecessors she is certainly more than a housekeeper. Visitors to the apartment are surprised to find how wide-ranging is her grasp of events. It is clear she has the pope's ear. At meal times he often includes her in matters under discussion; her opinions are short and sensible. Occasionally, with Gianpaolo's agreement and to Martin's *Angst*, she has slipped in a visitor or two – usually from Venice – to see the pope between his scheduled meetings.

All this has helped the more perceptive curialists to look upon her with grudging respect. Yet the question remains: how far does her power extend? Has she, for instance, played any part in shaping Gianpaolo's speeches? He likes to read them to her, and she is certainly an appreciative audience, laughing in all the right places and often clapping her hands with delight. Is she the one who encourages him to use children during his Wednesday audiences as conduits for the points he wants to put across? She herself comes from a large family and is said to have been good with the children of Venice who regularly visited Gianpaolo's palace when he was patriarch. Is it Vincenza who tells Gianpaolo to continue to poke around in the most unlikely places? Perhaps. After all, she does just that, once even walking into Villot's office by mistake. The Secretary had been too startled to say anything before she retreated with a cheerful 'Scusi'.

Whatever her status, there is no need for Vincenza to disturb the pope this morning. He continues to ponder the meeting he has scheduled.

It centres on a frail old man who controls an extraordinarily powerful organization from a cluttered complex of buildings on the Borgo Santo Spirito near the Tiber embankment, a few hundred yards from the Apostolic Palace. Even now Gianpaolo cannot fully grasp why this ailing man, probably still asleep on the far side of St Peter's Square, should have condoned, if not actively encouraged, a determined, carefully prepared and totally unacceptable campaign which mocks the special vow of fealty he and some of his priests have solemnly sworn to the pope.

Yet there is no denying the evidence against the largest, most prestigious, and often the most controversial men's order in the Roman Catholic Church, the black-cassocked battalions known as 'the pope's light cavalry', or his 'spiritual Marine Corps', news-magazine labels that are a reminder the Society of Jesus was founded in 1540 to check the advance of Protestantism during the Counter-Reformation; since then the Jesuits have served as front-line educators and missionaries. For centuries they have set an example to all Catholic institutions by their loyalty to the pope and their dedication to spreading the approved doctrine of the Church. Then, and Gianpaolo cannot pinpoint the precise moment, the Jesuits set off on a new and radical direction, placing its twenty-seven thousand members on a direct collision course with orthodox Church dogma.

After four hundred and fifty years of history – during which it was never without the enemies its founder, St Ignatius Loyola, a Basque nobleman, said were so essential – the Society has now gathered more opponents within the Vatican than all other Catholic organizations combined. The order that had trained Molière, Voltaire, Descartes and James Joyce, and which risked the lives of its missionaries to bring the Word to princes and peasants on five continents, was allowing its members to wage its latest campaign against much that the Vatican held inviolable. Jesuit theologians continued to challenge the validity of *Humunae Vitae*, the need for priestly celibacy, the banning of women from the priesthood; Jesuits supported left-wing, and even openly Communist, guerrilla movements. In Nicaragua they helped socialist revolutionaries seize power and are deeply committed to similar movements in Guatemala and El Salvador. They opposed the Vietnam War and urged the impeachment of President Nixon over Watergate. In every liberal cause are to be found Jesuits. Some have openly engaged in acts of civil disobedience and become stormy figures in the tensions between liberals and conservatives.

The position papers Gianpaolo received from his task force of four cardinals list hundreds of infractions; it is a dismaying catalogue of how determinedly out of step the Society is with the Church. The cardinals have laid much of the blame at the door of the sickly but still iron-willed Superior-General of the Society, the gaunt-faced Pedro Arrupe, like the order's founder, a Basque. He is a man whose living quarters Gianpaolo can clearly see from his own bedroom window.

Every morning, after waving to the policemen in the square, the pope has looked across the piazza, willing himself – he told his secretaries – to try and understand what has made Arrupe behave as he has.

Gianpaolo has read everything the cardinals provided on Arrupe. He knows he spent twenty-seven years in Japan where he was known as the 'Shinto Jesuit', that he was in Hiroshima in 1945 when the first atomic bomb fell on the city and that Arrupe helped to save many lives. Gianpaolo also knows Arrupe was elected to lead the order in 1965 and immediately set about implementing liberal policies. He sent his priests out to work even more actively with the poor and underprivileged. He deployed Jesuits in Asian and African ghettos. In India, the order's institutions were moved from cool hill stations to the steaming back streets of New Delhi and Madras.

If this had been all, Gianpaolo told his task force at their last secret meeting to review the situation, then, of course, there could be no cause for complaint. But, as they all now recognized, Arrupe has gone much further. He is, they think, allowing the Society to be aligned with the forces of Communism; he is seemingly advocating what amounts to spiritual sedition, challenging the very tenets the Church holds most sacred.

The previous meeting agreed the matter must be resolved – swiftly. This morning the task force will assemble again to recommend how it can be done.

In the end Gianpaolo alone must decide. There is no way he can, or wants to, shirk his responsibility. That does not make it any easier to bear as he leaves his bedroom to begin what he believes may be the most difficult day so far of his pontificate.

*

At seven o'clock, having prayed together, Gianpaolo, Magee and Lorenzi meet for a buffet-style breakfast. Vincenza has laid out baskets of freshly-baked breads, dishes of fruit, platters of yoghurts, jams and cheese. There is a special bowl of peeled nuts at the pope's elbow. And this morning there is also a small bottle of tablets. Gianpaolo calls them his 'age aids', implying they are one of those marginally beneficial substances which are claimed to ward off the inevitable effects of advancing years.

The secretaries know the truth. Four days ago Gianpaolo's Venetian physician visited Buzzonetti in the Vatican. Afterwards both doctors called on the pope and, in spite of his mild protest that he never felt better, they examined him. Subsequently they insisted Gianpaolo take these tablets. The pills are to help his weakened heart. The doctors stressed to the pope and his secretaries there was no cause for immediate alarm. The tablets are merely a precaution to combat the relentless pace Gianpaolo insists on maintaining.

Today will be another gruelling day. Apart from the secret meeting with regard to the Jesuits, there are to be thirteen official audiences as well as the regular twice-daily briefings by Villot and the routine three hours of curial paperwork Gianpaolo must attend to before dinner.

He takes his tablet with coffee, nibbles at the nuts and keeps up a lively commentary about the contents of the morning newspapers on the table. Like Paul, Gianpaolo reads them quickly. He does not dwell on personal attacks or criticism of his pontificate. There is in fact very little of either and what there is does not trouble him: he sees any admonishing as well-intentioned and a reminder there is always room for improvement. He circles a number of articles for his secretaries to cut out; the reports contain points he thinks could be useful to slip into his next public speech. Gianpaolo likes to be topical: it's a good way to enhance his rapport with his audience.

There's another story this morning concerning one of the currently contentious issues facing the Church: the theology of liberation, the campaign to liberate the poor through Church-bound social action. When he goes to Mexico in October to address the conference of South American bishops, Gianpaolo will be expected to pronounce on the subject, yet another of the problems Paul carefully skirted.

In 1968, when the question first surfaced, Paul approached it with nervous even-handedness. At times his reaction suggested he saw the concept as little more than an interesting academic exercise, this idea that Christian doctrine may acquire new meaning and purpose for the impoverished tens of millions of Catholics in South America if their salvation can be expressed through freeing themselves from oppression and injustice. Catholic liberation theologians postulate that, using this approach, the Bible takes on a new meaning: Moses becomes a political leader, the Magnificat a manifesto, and God is on the side of the poor and no longer the protector of an unjust social system which must be destroyed – and that the Church must participate in this destruction.

Before they left Rome after the coronation, Gianpaolo carefully questioned the nineteen cardinals from Latin America who, between them, are responsible for the souls of almost half the world's Catholics, the vast majority of whom *do* live in abject misery. He learned that liberation theology is far from academic.

During the past five years, over one hundred thousand *comunidades eclesiales de base*, basic Church communities, had been formed throughout the continent. Cardinal Arns of São Paulo, Brazil, told the pope that the groups 'work in the gospel spirit' but take many of their ideas 'directly from Marxism'. Indeed, many liberation theologians identify the Gospel poor with Marx's proletariat: their speeches are filled with references to achieving victory in the class war; they approve the classic Marxist defence of violence whereby it *is* acceptable when used to redress the inbuilt violence of oppressive regimes; they endorse

Marxist criticism of capitalism, and believe only revolution can purge them of an unjust society. Afterwards, there will be reconciliation – on their terms. The only apparent difference between this brand of thinking and the doctrine of Communism is that the liberation theologians do actually reject atheism.

Inevitably the communities have come under attack from right-wing regimes. Gianpaolo listened, horrified, as the cardinals related a long litany of torturings, assassinations, kidnappings, arrests, intimidations and trials of community leaders; all told seven hundred priests and nuns and lay workers have been murdered in the past five years. This violence produced still more extremism: priests were openly fighting alongside guerrillas in Colombia and Argentina. The Church's well-established tradition of political quietism was wrecked by the theology of liberation. The more oppressive the juntas, the more radical the priests.

Gianpaolo sought the advice of Baggio, who was president of the Pontifical Commission for Latin America. Baggio was emphatic. The pope must condemn the communities and their Marxist attitudes. It is the only way to preserve the integrity of the Church and avoid its universal persecution throughout South America.

The pope knows there is no way he can remain neutral. He must come down on one side or the other, making a judgement which literally will decide the future relationship between Church and State in South America. It will also inevitably affect the Church's position elsewhere, in countries where conflict between the government and the priesthood is also on the increase.

But, he confides to Magee and Lorenzi on this Thursday morning, he still has not made up his mind about what to say at the forthcoming Mexican conference. In part it will depend on the outcome of the secret meeting to settle the crisis with the Jesuits.

*

At 8.30 Martin appears in the dining room with a copy of Gianpaolo's appointments schedule. For the next fifteen minutes he sits at the table and goes over the list. Gianpaolo nods approvingly.

At 8.55, the two men descend to the second-floor salon. Gianpaolo settles behind the desk which bears the scratch marks left by Metropolitan Nikodim's shattered saucer, and waits for Martin to show in his first visitor.

Precisely at nine o'clock the prefect leads in Patriarch Hakim, whose Melchite-rite flock is scattered across Lebanon and Syria. The patriarch's aide has an armful of gifts. After Hakim and Gianpaolo embrace each other, the patriarch hands them to the pope. Both manage to remain oblivious of the circling papal photographer, Luigi Felici.

Gianpaolo is genuinely delighted with the gifts of icons of Christ and the Virgin Mary, and a Damascene tablecloth. He tells the gratified patriarch the icon of the Virgin is a worthy companion to one he has brought from Venice. Fingering the tablecloth he grins. 'Too good for me.'

'No, no,' insists Hakim. 'You must use it.'

'Then I will, I will,' says Gianpaolo. 'It will be a fitting reminder of you.'

Martin takes this as his cue to motion the photographer and patriarch's aide to leave the room with him. For the next ten minutes Hakim and Gianpaolo discuss without interruption the worsening situation in the Middle East.

At 9.15 Martin is back, standing meaningfully inside the door.

Instantly Hakim rises. And, notes the prefect appreciatively, Gianpaolo does the same. The pope is learning to be pope, thinks Martin: he's keeping to time, taking his cues; it really is getting so much easier. The prefect judges this pontificate could turn out to be far more congenial than he had ever dared hope.

*

In the next hour Gianpaolo receives three further visitors. None of them overruns Martin's schedule by as much as a minute. But even Martin remains ignorant of the true purpose of the block of time between 10.30 and noon which is marked: Discussion.

*

At 10.30 exactly, Villot is the last to enter the salon. Felici, Benelli and Baggio are on the sofa facing Gianpaolo. Magee and Lorenzi sit behind him. Villot's arrival is a signal for the pope to call the meeting to order.

For the next ninety minutes they debate. Unlike Conclave, there will be no leaks from this most secret discussion. Nobody outside this salon will know who said what in which order. It is a perfect example of the way the papacy has handled such ultra-sensitive matters down through the centuries.

But by the end of the morning a decision *has* been taken. This much will later become evident: Arrupe and, through him, the Jesuits, are to be firmly told their attitudes must change. No longer will they be allowed so openly and defiantly to involve themselves in secular politics; instead they must revert to their traditional role as teachers and advisers on Church dogma. Gianpaolo has also decided what he should say in Mexico next month: he will condemn out of hand liberation theology.

Magee and Lorenzi will prepare and type up the momentous document the pope plans to read to Arrupe in this very salon tomorrow morning. The Superior-General will be brought here to be solemnly reminded of his personal oath of fealty and sternly sent away to convey to all his men the very real displeasure of the pontiff.

*

At five o'clock another running problem surfaces – again – in the course of Gianpaolo's second formal discussion of the day with Villot. Magee shows the Secretary into the salon and remains nearby, awaiting the outcome of a matter in which he has a close interest.

Villot asks Gianpaolo – in the unbending voice that makes him seem so frosty – whether the pope has yet made up his mind about two key appointments? The first is who should fill the empty seat of Patriarch of Venice. The second is whether the present Primate of All Ireland should be elevated to cardinal.

Gianpaolo has been considering the matter for a couple of weeks. Villot thinks this is long enough, and has made as much clear. The stumbling block is not Venice; after a certain amount of discussion, Villot accepts that Gianpaolo will probably appoint Marco Cé as his successor.

The difficulty is Ireland. Gianpaolo is hesitating over promoting Archbishop Tomás O'Fiaich to the Sacred College of Cardinals. In spite of O'Fiaich's image among Ulster Protestants as being sympathetic to the IRA, he is nevertheless considered by many – including Villot and Magee – worthy of promotion. But Gianpaolo's papal delegate in London, the perceptive Archbishop Bruno Heim, has made it clear that the British government will not exactly welcome the elevation of O'Fiaich.

Heim indicated that O'Fiaich is an Irish nationalist who, like Magee, was born and raised in the virulent atmosphere of that area of Northern Ireland which borders the Republic; alleged sympathies for the IRA apart, O'Fiaich is thought to be far more openly anti-British than the Catholic majority in the South. To make him a cardinal would not only upset Ulster Protestants but might not necessarily be welcome among many of those same southern Irish politicians who are already uneasy about the Dublin nuncio Alibrandi's close connections with the IRA – maintained in the guise of what he sees as acceptable diplomatic conduct, of course.

Gianpaolo readily agrees to a suggestion from Magee that it could be helpful to get the latest soundings from Ireland when the nuncio arrives in Rome in early October. He does not mention to the pope Alibrandi's desire to return to Dublin bringing news of a forthcoming papal visit to Ireland. But whether that becomes a reality or not, Magee hopes that at the end of Alibrandi's interview with Gianpaolo, in face of the nuncio's renowned skill as a persuader, there could still be cause for an Irish celebration – O'Fiaich's promotion.

Yet Gianpaolo realizes the situation is not simple. Basil Hume, whom Gianpaolo instinctively trusts, has quietly conveyed the profound mood of anguish in Britain over the running sore of Ulster. In a short private audience with the pope, Hume deftly sketched in the parameters of the problem, and made it tactfully clear that the question of appointing a new cardinal for Ireland is a most delicate decision.

It is even more remarkable, then, that Villot chooses to misunderstand Gianpaolo's hesitation. The Secretary has been pushing hard for O'Fiaich's promotion. He sees the pontiff's continuing uncertainty almost as a challenge to his own position.

But Gianpaolo will not budge. It is much too soon, he says, for him to decide which cardinals to create, and in particular to pass judgement on the controversial O'Fiaich.

Villot strides out of the salon, his irritation perfectly plain.

*

Later – there will be questions.

Have the trays from the Curia on this Thursday evening been unusually full? How did the pope cope with the paperwork: from the Secretariat of State, the nine Sacred Congregations, the three Tribunals, the Secretariats for Christian Unity, Non-Christians, and Non-Believers, the Pontifical Commissions, Councils and Committees, the Apostolic Camera, the Prefecture of the Economic Affairs of the Holy See, the Welfare Service of the Holy Father, the Office for Personnel Relations of the Holy See, the Reverend Fabric of St Peter's, the Apostolic Vatican Library, the Secret Archives, Vatican Press and Vatican Publishing House? Were there more documents than normal from these, and even more curial departments, causing him concern and worry?

Had he seemed tired afterwards? His secretaries will insist not, remembering that when the pope went to change for dinner, he was cheerful and made a joke about wanting a machine to do his paperwork for him.

When he emerges – Vincenza will recall – he stopped by the kitchen, just as he used to do in Venice, and wrinkled his nose with pleasure over the meal she was about to serve. Felici, Baggio and Casaroli are dining with the pope and his secretaries, and she has taken special care to cater for their liking for good food.

His guests will remember how he greeted them warmly, and how, over *aperitivi*, he had listened attentively while Casaroli expounded on internal American politics and changing American attitudes towards Western Europe. Casaroli felt the United States was becoming more insular as a result of the deep wounds of Vietnam and Cambodia. He and Baggio both doubt that President Carter will win another term. Even with a change of leadership, Felici thinks the United States would still not allow full ambassadorial-level diplomatic ties with the Holy See. He suggests that part of the problem might be the poor American press the Church has received over *Humanae Vitae*. The encyclical's true purpose, he claims, is misunderstood and under-appreciated; this had undermined respect for the papacy in the minds of some Americans and created a shift in its importance in the eyes of others.

Felici states there is only one way to resolve the situation. Those around the table will remember how he looked at Gianpaolo, then, nodding his great Roman emperor of a head, the cardinal had thundered: 'You should go to America, soon.'

Over coffee, Felici returns to the idea. America's fifty million baptized Catholics, he declares emphatically — even in normal conversation Felici has this disconcerting habit of speaking loudly and aggressively — are in need of a firm reminder of what their faith should mean. They have been led astray. Though he does not say so directly, it is clear Felici is thinking of the Jesuits.

Casaroli remarks he's had several conversations with Henry Kissinger who thinks a papal visit to the United States could be beneficial. Baggio adds that his visits to Chicago and New York in recent months suggest such a visit would have tremendous pastoral benefits. Gianpaolo listens carefully. It is obvious he finds the idea attractive.

At 9.30, the guests leave the apartment and Gianpaolo goes to his study.

On the desk, in a space which has been cleared of the clutter of paper, is a memo and a red-coloured folder. The memo is a typed aide-mémoire from Lorenzi which he prepares every night to remind the pope of forthcoming matters: tomorrow the first of the curial reports on the Third World is due to be delivered; a decision must be made about Küng this coming Monday morning when Benelli is scheduled to discuss the theologian; there is a need to read the latest file on Cody before a meeting Monday afternoon.

The pope turns to the folder. It contains the draft of the document he intends to read aloud to Arrupe in the morning.

He takes it with him to his bedroom, pausing on the way to thank Vincenza for dinner. They speak together for a few minutes.

A little after 10.15, she watches him close the door of his bedroom. She cannot remember when he last retired so early.

*

The policemen in St Peter's Square see that by 11.30 all the lights except one are extinguished in the papal apartment. This is normal. Gianpaolo's bedroom windows stand out as small squares of brightness. The betting in the piazza is that they, too, will go black within the hour. At one am the windows remain lit. The policemen wonder what can be keeping the pope awake so late. An hour later the light is still on. The policemen confer among themselves. Even the insomniac Paul had not worked this late. At three am the windows continue to glow in the darkness. The policemen no longer bet: they believe they know why. Gianpaolo must have fallen asleep before switching off his bedside lamp. It's just the sort of thing which makes him so lovable to these hardened men. At four o'clock the light comes on in Vincenza's bedroom. It's the time she gets up every morning.

*

Shortly before 4.30, dressed in her habit and lace-up black shoes, carrying a tray holding a flask of coffee, a cup and saucer, a bowl of sugar and a jug of cream, Vincenza walks to the pope's bedroom door and leaves the tray on a small table beside it.[2] She returns to the kitchen where some of the other nuns are beginning to prepare breakfast.

A little before five o'clock, Vincenza goes to collect the tray. She is surprised to find it has not been touched.

She hesitates. Should she remove the tray? Or leave it here? This has never happened in all the years she has brought him his first coffee of the day.

Vincenza leans towards the door, listening for a sound. She thinks perhaps the pope has overslept and is now too busy to take coffee. But then she reminds herself she cannot recall him ever once oversleeping.

There is no sound from the bedroom.

The nun glances over her shoulder. There is nobody in sight to tell her what to do now. She looks back at the door. Once more she listens, finally pressing her ear to the door. There is still no sound from beyond.

Vincenza gently knocks. There is no response.

She does so again, harder. She feels certain someone, *somewhere*, will have heard her and must appear shortly. She hopes it may be Magee or Lorenzi; they will know what to do.

Nobody comes.

A new thought enters her head. If the pope doesn't want to open the door, he could at least call out. Maybe he hasn't heard. She knocks more insistently.

There is no reply.

She hesitates, increasingly confused.

Vincenza looks at the door handle and the keyhole beside it. Suddenly, her mind made up, she kneels, putting her eye to the keyhole, squinting to see better into the bedroom. The light is on. She feels relieved. He must be awake. She moves her head. All she can make out is the foot of the bed and part of the carpet. She rises as another thought strikes her. What if somebody had seen her peeking through the keyhole? How could she explain her unease? And what would they think about what she intends to do now?

Quickly, before her resolve weakens, Vincenza reaches for the handle and turns it slowly, opening the door a few inches so she can peer into the room.

The nun stops, frozen.

Gianpaolo is sitting up in bed and appears to be staring strangely at her. She can see he's been reading, and his glasses are way down his nose. His knees are drawn up and his hand is holding a file.

Vincenza begins to ease shut the door. There is something terribly wrong. The pope's right hand is dangling oddly, the fingers half-clenched. And the file he's holding is empty, the papers scattered across the bed sheet and onto the floor. But it is the look on his face which most frightens Vincenza. His lips are drawn back, exposing gums, giving his mouth an alarming, savage look. His eyes are bulging in their sockets, and the veins in his neck stand out.

'*Santissimo Padre*?' she asks fearfully.

There is no response.

'Albino?' She uses the name she has sometimes used when they are alone.

He continues to stare.

Vincenza fully opens the door.

His contorted face does not change. The tilt of his glasses magnifies one eye.

She screams.

The pope continues to stare sightlessly back at her.

Vincenza turns and runs still screaming down the corridor.

*

Magee shoots up in bed, blinking furiously.

Vincenza backs away. She has run into the secretary's bedroom, switched on the light and shaken him awake.

'What do you want?' Surprise gives his soft voice an edge. 'What's the matter?'

'*Santissimo Padre* . . . something's happened . . . '

Magee leaps out of bed. '*What's* happened?'

She is trembling. He thinks the nun is on the verge of hysteria. He repeats his question, more firmly. 'What's happened?'

'Padre Albino . . . He looks strange.'

Magee completes buttoning a soutane over his pyjamas. He runs from the room.

The pope's bedroom door is ajar. Magee looks at Vincenza. 'Didn't you close it?'

'I came straight to you, padre.'

'Please wait here. Nobody is to come in until I say so. Understand?'

'Yes, padre.'

Magee enters the pope's bedroom, closing the door behind him. He stands for a moment, taking stock.

There is no doubt at all what has happened. But he must be absolutely certain.

He walks to the bed, noting the copy of Thomas à Kempis's *Imitation of Christ* on the bedside cabinet, on top of a pile of other books. He glances at the scattered papers. They are what Gianpaolo planned to read to Arrupe this morning. Magee sees the bowl of sweets beside the telephone. They appear untouched.

Magee places his hand against the pope's right cheek. It is icy cold.

He picks up the telephone and dials Villot.

'*Oui?*'

'It's Magee. The Holy Father is dead.'

There is a pause. 'Are you certain?'

'I'm in his room.'

'*Mon Dieu*. This is not possible.'

Magee can sense Villot struggling to shake off sleep and comprehend what he has been told.

'He is dead, Eminence.'

'How long?' Villot's voice is barely a whisper.

'Probably several hours. There's rigor mortis.'

'*Mon Dieu*.'

Magee waits, giving Villot time to collect his thoughts.

'Have you told anybody else?'

'No. But his nun found him, Eminence.'

'Keep her there, outside his room. Nobody is to talk to her until I arrive.'

'Yes, Eminence.'

Villot again pauses. Then he issues orders. 'Stay in the bedroom.

Lock the door. Phone Buzzonetti. Wake up Lorenzi. Get him to call Confalonieri and the others. There's a list, isn't there, from last time?'

'There's a list, Eminence.'

'Good. Get Lorenzi to do that. I'm coming straight over.'

Villot breaks the connection. Magee recognizes that already the Secretary has once more donned the mantle of Camerlengo.

*

At 5.20 Magee unlocks the bedroom door and Villot strides in. He has managed to shave and comb his hair. He looks immaculate. He is carrying the same small bag he had brought with him to Paul's death bed.

The Camerlengo is faced with a ticklish problem. His question to Magee about when the pope died is linked to Absolution, the granting of the forgiveness of sins. The much-debated theological point is how long after death may total Absolution be granted. It revolves around the vexing question of how durable a soul can be. There are some Catholics who argue that if a Catholic succumbs following a long wasting illness, cancer for example, the soul might leave the body relatively quickly, possibly within thirty minutes of death. But if a person has been healthy before being fatally struck down, his soul could remain in the body three or four hours, perhaps even longer. To non-Catholics the proposition may appear fanciful, but it can afford great comfort to Catholics.

In Villot's judgement, the soul of Albino Luciani, Pope John Paul I, the 262nd successor to the Throne of St Peter, has not yet departed.

He reaches into his bag and removes a vial of holy water. Villot opens it and presses it to his thumb. He places the vial on the side table and then turns to the bed. In a hoarse whisper, Villot begins to chant.

'*Si capax, ego te absolvo a peccatis tuis, in nomine Patris, et Filii, et Spiritus Sancti. Amen.*'

'If it is possible, I absolve you from your sins in the name of the Father, and of the Son, and of the Holy Ghost. Amen.'

He makes the sign of the cross on Gianpaolo's forehead. Then he rapidly moves his thumb up and down, back and forth, touching the pope at each station of the Cross.

'*Per istam sanctam Unctionem, indulgeat tibi Dominus quid-quid deliquisti. Amen.*'

'Through this holy anointing, may God forgive you whatever sins you have committed. Amen.'

Villot then administers the Apostolic Blessing.

'*Ego facultate mihi ab Apostolica Sede tributa, indulgentiam plenariam et*

278

remissionem omnium peccatorum tibi concedo, et benedico te. In nomine Patris, et Filii, et Spiritus Sancti. Amen.'

'I, by the faculty given to me by the Apostolic See, grant to you a plenary indulgence and remission of all sins, and I bless you. In the name of the Father, and of the Son, and of the Holy Ghost. Amen.'

Villot steps back from the bed, recorks the vial and places it back in his bag.

Buzzonetti arrives. The doctor is ashen-faced and tieless. As he closes the bedroom door, Magee hears Lorenzi making another telephone call from Gianpaolo's study. He has placed Vincenza in there.

Confalonieri arrives with Martin and Noé as Buzzonetti completes his medical examination. He turns from the bed and addresses the others. 'A coronary occlusion. He felt nothing.'

'When?' Villot's question is flat and expressionless.

Buzzonetti clears his throat, thinking. 'I estimate the time of death between 10.30 and eleven o'clock last night.'

Villot bends down and opens his bag. When he straightens, he is holding the tiny silver hammer Magee had last seen him produce in Paul's bedroom at Castel Gandolfo.

Villot stands by the body and carefully removes Gianpaolo's spectacles. He folds them and places them on the side table.

Then, just as he had with Paul, Villot taps the pope on his forehead with the hammer and solemnly enquires whether he is truly dead. When he has asked the question three times and received no reply, he informs those present that Albino Luciani is dead according to the rites of the Holy Roman Catholic and Apostolic Church.

He places the hammer in the bag, closes it and addresses Magee. 'Bring in the nun.'

Magee fetches Vincenza.

She is dry-eyed and totally composed as she stands before Villot and recounts what she had seen and done. Villot thanks her and asks her to return to Lorenzi.

When Magee has once more closed the bedroom door, the Camerlengo stands with his back to the group and makes decisions that are going to have a devastating effect.

Villot decrees the world must be told a story which departs from the truth in several places.

Vincenza's involvement is to remain secret. She and the other household nuns are to be returned as soon as possible to the mother house of their order where they are to remain, away from any public contact, for the rest of their lives.

The official Vatican version will be that Magee, waiting to escort the pope to early morning Mass, discovered him dead in bed. And, says

Villot, indicating the document chastising Arrupe, no mention must be made of it. The world will be told that Gianpaolo died reading *Imitation of Christ*. Villot explains that the astonishing camouflage is to avoid 'unfortunate misunderstandings.'

Buzzonetti next makes his contribution. He says he cannot straighten the body. Villot orders that Zega and Co. should be contacted. Martin uses his bedside telephone to call the firm of morticians.

At 6.10 the Zega employee known as the Technician arrives with an assistant. The Technician carries a small suitcase. He opens it and the others are amazed to see it contains several lengths of rope.

The Technician explains what he and his colleague must do.

'Then do it,' orders Villot.

The morticians take up positions on either side of the bed. The Technician knots a rope around Gianpaolo's ankles and another across his knees. He and his assistant grasp the ends of the ropes. The Technician nods and they pull steadily. Gianpaolo's knees unbend. The men tie the ropes to the bed frame. They place a different rope around the pope's chest and pull it taut to straighten the trunk. Each man then takes an arm, straightening it by physical force so it rests at the side of the body. Each limb is now held in place by rope. The restraining cords will stay until rigor mortis has passed and the body is pliable once more. The men move to the head, one firmly grasping it while the other slowly manipulates the jaw to a normal position. They cover the body with a bed-sheet, tucking it neatly into the side of the mattress, leaving only the head exposed. They close its eyes and mouth. Gianpaolo appears to be sleeping peacefully.

Magee escorts the men from the room and arranges for their return next morning to embalm the body.

The secretary will not be here to meet them. He is about to find himself caught up in a staggering twist to the drama of the death of a pope who has ruled for only thirty-three days. It will involve the KGB, the Soviet intelligence agency, and the chilling charge that Gianpaolo was murdered by poison.

23

It's Saturday morning, 30 September, and Franz Koenig's mood matches the Roman weather: heavy. He's reeling from what he has just learned. That is why he's closely watching each of his fellow cardinals as they drift into the Sala Bologna. He keeps wondering which of them might have swallowed the carefully prepared and cunningly dangled bait. Even now, as he sits here in his purple silk mourning robe, well inside the Vatican, Koenig is sure the sophistry is still working its deadly effect far beyond the Leonine Walls. Reporters are clearly devouring it: Koenig thinks grimly that this is to be expected. The material is so temptingly prepared it's a gift-horse for sensation seekers.

But members of the press are not the only ones deceived. Some of the radical voices in the Vatican can be heard in the corridors and courtyards saying that for the first time in history, there should be an autopsy performed on a pope: that Gianpaolo's body should be opened and his organs removed for laboratory analysis to see if he has been poisoned. The very idea makes Koenig shiver.

If it was only members of the Curia who were suggesting the post-mortem, that would be quite bad enough. But a meeting of the Sacred College of Cardinals, the first of this interregnum, is about to begin in this salon to consider whether there should be an autopsy to try and quell all the rumours. This is what Koenig finds especially disturbing. This is why he continues to watch the other cardinals for signs any of them has swallowed the simulacrum and will be pushing for an autopsy – so falling into the trap which has been prepared by the Soviet organization above all others that Koenig hates and despises, *Komitet Gosùdarstvennoy Bezopasnosti*, the KGB.

Koenig is one of the few cardinals in the room who has seen at first-hand the machinations of the KGB, and everything he has learned confirms this is one of their operations. He is certain he recognizes the agency's *modus operandi;* the footprints, invisible though they may be to others, in his mind lead all the way from Rome to Moscow, to the building in Dzerzhinsky Square where the KGB shares its headquarters with the infamous Lubianka. Very possibly the importance of the operation means it was cleared, perhaps is even being directed by, the agency's chairman, General Yuri Andropov. Koenig knows how efficient the general can be: over the years Andropov has done his share of besmirching the Church. And just forty-eight hours ago, when Koenig was in Helsinki on 'Church business', he had heard of yet another KGB drive being prepared against the Church behind the Iron Curtain.

But even that pales against this – a full-scale plot to destabilize the entire Church through the smear that the pope was murdered by his trusted aides. The very concept of the plot is so staggering that even now, with the evidence of its success so far only too clear, Koenig cannot quite believe the KGB hope to get away with it. But they have – and they are. If they hadn't, there would not be this meeting. So many of the things that have occurred since Koenig heard Gianpaolo was dead would not have happened.

His secretary had awoken him in his Helsinki hotel with the news. Even a strong mind like Koenig's can absorb only so much. He simply refused to believe, hoping against hope, refusing to think the unthinkable, clinging to the thought there had been a mistake. Then it hit with a force which made him physically gasp: a promising pontificate was cruelly over and the Church was again vulnerable until a new pope was installed. He had sat on his bed and prayed. By the time he was being driven to the airport, Koenig was again his composed self. As the taxi pulled into the terminal, he heard Finnish radio announce that there were reports the pope had been poisoned by 'persons unknown'. That was the beginning. By the time he reached Vienna – staying only long enough to pack for Conclave – Koenig's staff were fending off newsmen following up wire service reports from Rome on the same theme. That was when his suspicions hardened. But only when Koenig reached Rome and discovered people inside the Vatican were suggesting an autopsy would 'prove' the pope died of natural causes, did he become certain what was happening bore the hallmark of the KGB.

That was yesterday. Today he knows the plot has a firmer grip than he could ever have thought possible. The very credibility of the Church, the Vatican and the papacy is being eroded. It is truly frightening.

Looking around the Sala Bologna, Koenig wonders what support he can expect for his plan to stop the KGB's machinations.

He has been one of the first to arrive and occupies the same seat he had during the last interregnum, when the Sacred College met here every morning to settle important Church matters. The salon is just as grandly impersonal as he remembers it: the frescoes and the fine art collection almost casually hanging on the walls of this high-ceilinged room do nothing to hide the fact that the Sala Bologna is hardly ever used except on such momentous occasions as interregnums.

The long table at which Koenig sits is standard multinational boardroom length; the chairs might have come from any conference supplier. Koenig wonders whether the drinking water in the glass jugs placed at regular intervals on the table has been changed since last he was here.

Most of the cardinals are in shock so severe that they sit in numbed silence waiting for the meeting to start. Koenig is positive none of them anticipated Gianpaolo's death. That is what makes the evil campaign so horrific.

Koenig is even sure he knows which section of the KGB spawned it: it bears the malevolent mark of Department D – for *dezinformatsiya* – of the First Chief Directorate. Only Department D could have moved so swiftly, been so well organized, calling upon its vast experience in the area of grand deceptions designed to mislead, confuse or influence world opinion against the Church. What has occurred reeks of the opportunism which in the past saw other Department D provocations grow to monstrous proportions. The Vatican has been thrown into panic.

The KGB success and the attendant repercussions both largely stem from decisions taken by Villot. Koenig and the other cardinals who see the spectre of Department D – they include Joseph Ratzinger of Munich, Joseph Hoeffner of Cologne, Giuseppe Siri of Genoa and the Poles, Stefan Wyszynski of Warsaw and Karol Wojtyla of Cracow – find it virtually impossible to make sense of the Camerlengo's behaviour. They feel that from the moment Villot invented the nonsense about Magee finding Gianpaolo in bed reading *Imitation of Christ*, the Camerlengo has played into the hands of Department D. This criticism is both carefully restrained and further muted by compassion. The years had taken their toll on Villot even before he assumed the intense pressures of the last interregnum and Conclave. And, if only because of his close contact with the pope, the shock of Gianpaolo's sudden death has been all that much more traumatic for him. It has left his decision-making capacity fatally flawed.

This may account for the strained, almost haunted look about the Camerlengo. Seated at one end of the table, Villot appears a very old man who realizes he has lost his grip on events, but cannot quite understand how. And even Koenig, despite his certainty that the KGB is behind the plot, finds it hard to provide satisfactory answers to all aspects of the calumny.

*

For whatever reason – whether he is in fact recoiling from shock, whether there is something close to hysteria behind the tightly controlled mask of a face – Villot has not been his normally careful and far-seeing self since he made the first extraordinary decisions in the pope's bedroom.

To attempt to hide that Gianpaolo was reading the indictment of the Jesuits is understandable; the pope's death effectively puts into limbo the crisis with the Society of Jesus.

But to try and excise the presence of Vincenza from the timetable of Gianpaolo's death, and place discovery on Magee, borders on the irrational.

In any event, shortly after Villot made these decisions, a sequence of happenings occurred which, within a matter of hours, torpedoed whatever thinking might have induced him to attempt such fabrications in the first place.

*

This much is known:

Around seven am on Friday – when word was officially given by Vatican Radio that Gianpaolo was dead – Franco Antico receives the first of many calls he will accept and make during the rest of that day.

Antico is the secretary-general of Civiltà Cristiana, the aggressively right-wing organization which plastered Rome during August with posters demanding: ELECT A CATHOLIC POPE. It supports Lefèbvre, opposes many of the changes introduced by Vatican II. More important for what is to follow, Civiltà Cristiana believed Gianpaolo 'a good man' bent on a project dear to its heart – reforming the Curia, which the organization identifies as the enemy of Lefèbvre-like traditionalism. The international media had briefly spotlighted Civiltà Cristiana during the last interregnum. But since then it has virtually dropped out of sight. Membership is beginning to fall from a claimed peak of 50,000 in forty-one countries. Civiltà Cristiana badly needs something to get it back to those heady days when *Time* and other news-magazines gave it space and the contributions came rolling in.

To the journalists who interviewed him in August, Antico seemed someone who would have been a success with the Medici popes. He is a romantic and trustingly naive. He also sees conspiracies where most people don't. Antico is very responsive to what the press likes to hear: he's the sort of man some journalists simply can't do without. These qualities are about to have a disastrous effect when he takes that first early-morning call.

With the stubbornness which is another of his traits, Antico will go to his grave refusing to name his caller. He will merely contend he is 'a person with good Vatican connections'. In the scenario which now develops, all the cardinals who insist this is a KGB plot determinedly cast Antico's caller in the role of *agent-provocateur* for Department D, Later Casaroli, Martin, Magee and Noé, people not usually given to wild words, will also insist the man is a KGB agent.

Antico is shocked by what his caller tells him.

By the end of their conversation – Antico thinks it may have lasted twenty minutes – he has a very clear picture of what must be done. With his penchant for conspiracies, the secretary-general has not needed much convincing that, in the name of Civiltà Cristiana, he should immediately call for an autopsy, and that the reason for doing so is to establish whether the pope was murdered 'by persons unknown'.

Since 1959, when Department D was formed, it has achieved its most conspicuous successes by distributing its fabrications through a gullible medium most unlikely to be thought associated with Soviet duplicity. The devoutly Catholic Antico perfectly fits the Department's requirement.

Who his caller is must remain a matter for speculation. KGB disinformation operations have always differed from conventional Soviet propaganda insofar as extraordinary care is taken to conceal the originating source. In this case, as Koenig accurately perceives, the plan has been well-laid, suggesting that careful fieldwork established the pipeline to Antico. Almost certainly there are several cut-out points between Department D officers and the person who actually telephoned Antico. In the event of a subterfuge going wrong at any stage, tracing it back to the KGB would be a near impossibility. Perhaps it is as Koenig says, a matter of recognizing the footprints.

In this case the fuse had been laid, but remains to be lit. It is the Vatican Press Office which applies the match. About the time Antico is having his momentous conversation, Fr Romeo Panciroli clears with Villot the official announcement of Gianpaolo's death: 'This morning at about 5.30 am, the private secretary of the pope, Father John Magee, entered the bedroom of Pope John Paul I. Not having found him in his chapel as usual, he was looking for him in his room and found him dead in bed with the lights on as if he were reading.'

At 7.30 on the Friday morning, Panciroli telephones this statement to major foreign and Italian news agencies in Rome.

About thirty minutes later, Ansa, an Italian wire service, receives a call from Antico. He reads out a statement which states categorically that Vincenza found the pope and that she 'dashed down the corridor' to awaken Magee. Gianpaolo had 'a few sheets of paper in his hand', which Antico identifies as 'highly secret documents'.

The Ansa reporter's excitement is understandable. In almost every respect Antico's version contradicts the Vatican's.

Shortly after eight o'clock Ansa begins to transmit Antico's staggering demand for an autopsy to ascertain whether the pope has been poisoned.

By then other correspondents in Rome are being phoned by Antico with the same astounding tale.

Few, if any, stop to ask basic questions. What is the nature of the evidence? Has it been handed over to the Italian police? Are there sworn statements and witnesses? No such challenges are offered. It is simply enough that Antico is an official of an organization which had been taken seriously in August. His utterances are now accepted at face value again.

The reporters begin to call Panciroli. He is still bruised from his abrasive encounters with the media during the previous interregnum and Conclave, and reacts badly: he is cooler than usual. It makes him no new media friends; the reporters accuse him of covering up. Panciroli calls Villot. The Camerlengo orders the Press Secretary to put up the shutters. The suspicion of conspiracy gains strength.

Nobody will know if Villot stops to think how it is that the perfectly accurate account of Vincenza's involvement has emerged so quickly.

By mid-morning on the Friday, Antico and Civiltà Cristiana are firmly back in the spotlight. He is taking media calls from all over Europe. If the reporters suspect the real status of his imposing-sounding organization – a small, fading institution that clings to the hem of Lefèbvre's cassock – it does not trouble them. As the press had built up the archbishop, so it now endows Civiltà Cristiana with a significance it does not deserve. Perhaps, then, it is inevitable that Antico, with his heady blend of romance and suspicion, should soon be claiming, 'We have concrete evidence to back our demands for an investigation. But we can't release it at this time. We want to preserve the legal niceties and work through channels.'

He helpfully suggests the reporters call Vincenza and Magee.

Faced with Panciroli's freezing refusal to comment, journalists try to reach the nun and the secretary. They are too late. On Villot's orders, three hours after she found Gianpaolo, Vincenza and her nuns were bundled out of the Vatican and driven away into the Church's equivalent of purdah. When the Vatican switchboard contacts Magee and says reporters wish to speak to him, the secretary prudently calls Villot first. Magee is stunned by the Camerlengo's reaction. Villot instructs him to pack at once, leave the Vatican for a seminary well outside Rome, and to stay there until further notice. The bewildered Magee follows the nuns into exile.

It does not take long before Antico is calling the press with this latest news. The reporters check. The Vatican Press Office says Magee has 'left the country', and that the nuns are 'inaccessible'.

So the conspiracy theory has grown to the point where the Sacred College is having this Saturday morning meeting.

*

Of all the many questions which deeply trouble Koenig as he sits in the Sala Bologna one in particular predominates: how had Antico's caller been so well informed so quickly? Accepting he was a Soviet *agent-provocateur*, an even more shattering question remains to be answered: is there somewhere within the Vatican a KGB mole?

It is unthinkable. But as Koenig knows too well this is the era of the unthinkable.

*

Felici is the last to enter the Sala Bologna. For the past month he has been virtually at Gianpaolo's elbow, every kilo of his bulky frame fostering his appearance of being the confident confidant. Now Felici seems to have physically crumbled: his huge head and neck look too large for his body.

Benelli also appears to have shrunk. His eyes are hollow, his cheeks caved in: he seems a man who has recently done a great deal of crying.

Nobody doubts both Felici and Benelli will recover; it's not in their nature to do otherwise. But for the moment their world has collapsed.

It is difficult to gauge the mood of Siri of Genoa. Behind his horn-rimmed spectacles he is more inscrutable than ever. Perhaps he is mulling over what his sources in the Italian intelligence service have told him about the KGB's operation. Or maybe he feels like someone who has been given a second chance at the papacy – which, at the age of seventy-two, Siri must surely expect to be his last tilt. It may also be that his twenty-five years as a cardinal have taught him to maintain an expressionless face on such uncertain occasions as this.

Beside Siri sits Salvatore Pappalardo. He seems to be concentrating solely on his writing block; one has been set before each cardinal for any notes they care to make. Pappalardo arrived on an early-morning flight from Palermo and is still mildly perplexed over having been buttonholed by Baggio about the need to resist any move to conduct an autopsy. This was the first Pappalardo had heard of the proposal. He finds the suggestion repugnant. Not only does it fly in the face of precedent, a post-mortem will cause further offence to all those Italians who disliked the idea of Paul being embalmed.

There are thirty-four cardinals in the salon when Villot, at precisely eleven o'clock, starts the meeting. The remainder of the Sacred College have yet to reach Rome.

Carefully eyeing Felici, Villot first asks those present if they have each received their letter, signed by him, requesting they take part in Conclave. Villot is not going to allow Felici the chance to attack him again for his lapse at the outset of the last Conclave. Only after he gets an affirmative nod from each cardinal does Villot continue.

He repeats, almost word for word, the bald nonsense of the press statement he had approved, adding that at the pope's bedside was a copy of *Imitation of Christ* and that Buzzonetti concluded death was from a massive heart attack which probably occurred around eleven o'clock the previous Thursday night.

There are no questions.

Villot proposes the funeral should be in five days time, Wednesday, 4 October, the feast day of St Francis, the patron saint of Italy.

There are no objections.

Everybody is waiting. The lengthening silence is broken from an unexpected quarter. Few can have expected the Dean of the Sacred College to be the one to raise the subject. But Confalonieri says there is a need to act decisively to end the malicious campaign that is now well underway. Distasteful as it may seem, it is nevertheless now necessary to have an autopsy. Oblivious of the reaction to this – there are a number of surprised gasps – he goes on to say the world must accept what everyone in this room most assuredly knows: that Gianpaolo has been peacefully called home; brief though it had been, his pontificate was not uneventful. Secure in that knowledge, it would be both sensible and desirable to take the only possible course to end this dastardly campaign of vilification. He will support any vote for a post-mortem.

Koenig waits while the others consider what they have heard. He is himself as astonished as any at the line Confalonieri has taken. The Dean's view will, undoubtedly, have a powerful effect on those who are still undecided. It will be all that much harder for Koenig to win them over – let alone change the minds of those already committed to Confalonieri's point of view. Not for a moment does Koenig think the Dean has been influenced by anything other than the highest of motives. Certainly there is no question of anybody in this room – let alone a KGB mole – being able to nobble Confalonieri. He has clearly come to his decision after the most careful consideration. The fact that Koenig thinks Confalonieri is wrong in no way alters his respect for the cardinal.

Koenig begins to speak, slowly measuring his words. There is the matter of a lack of precedent. So far as he knows, there has never been an autopsy on a pope. Therefore, would it not be best to wait for a vote of the full College to make the decision? Will not a post-mortem fan the fires they all want to douse? Though the time left before the funeral is short, is it not better to reflect further and consult quietly among themselves over the weekend? Surely this is too grave a decision to rush?

It is the familiar Koenig technique, this posing of carefully enunciated questions. He moves on, calm and deliberate, confident of his argument.

There is the matter of secrecy. How could an autopsy be concealed? Outsiders would have to be involved. However trusted they were, there is no certainty there would not be a leak. And if there was an attempt at secrecy, and it was discovered, wouldn't the damage be all the greater?

Further, assuming that prior notice is given, think how it could be exploited. Would it not be easy for the KGB to say it was no more than a cosmetic operation? Look at the outlandish lies they were already successfully spreading without any basis. Imagine, then, how much more effective their propaganda would be if they actually had something tangible to hang it on? And when the result is known, and the outcome is as irrefutable as they all know it must be, what then? Will the attacks cease? Assuredly not. More lies will follow. He finishes as he began, suggesting again that at the very minimum they should wait until the full College is assembled.

There is another silence. Villot waits to see whether anyone else will speak.

It is Felici who causes the second surprise. He argues that the presence of all the cardinals will not resolve the issue. There are likely to be just as firmly held opposing views then as there are now. Besides, it is possible some of the cardinals will not reach Rome until the day of the funeral. In view of the lying in state which is mandatory, it is impossible to wait until then. Nor, indeed, can the matter be delayed beyond Monday at the latest for 'practical reasons'.

Felici has been speaking to the Technician, and he now knows a great deal about the bodily chemical changes which occur after death.

He proposes that three doctors externally examine the pope's body. Afterwards they should prepare separate reports on the 'medical advisability' of an autopsy. These ought to be available for the next meeting of the cardinals on Monday.

He suggests the names of a Rome pathologist and two physicians.

Villot pauses a moment and then asks for a vote.

Twenty-nine of the cardinals support Felici.

*

Under the polite but watchful eyes of two Swiss Guards, Lorenzi leads a team of Vatican workmen on a tour of the papal apartment. It is early Saturday afternoon and they are making a final check that no personal effects have been left.

Before going, the nuns removed all evidence of their presence. Vincenza has taken her stoup of holy water, the black wooden cross over her bed, her small collection of well-read books, a picture of the Virgin, the vacuum flask she kept by her bedside during the night in case she was thirsty.

In the past twenty-four hours the workers have also emptied the apartment of any sign that Gianpaolo lived here. Rubber-wheeled trolleys moved from room to room, gathering up boxes and chests which Lorenzi, often close to tears, had packed. One holds Gianpaolo's wardrobe of Gammarelli cassocks and other clothes, some so new they have not been taken out of their tissue paper. Another box contains his modest collection of shoes, well worn uppers, heels that need repairing, and among them a pair of felt carpet slippers, the sort an old-fashioned gentlemen's haberdashery sells. Two chests hold his personal papers, the letters from his family and friends, old birthday and Christmas cards, notes from world leaders congratulating him on his appointment, letters from bishops and priests wishing him the long pontificate that was not to be, laboriously written requests from children in his old diocese asking whether they might visit him in the Vatican. There are his books, among them a surprising number of contemporary novels, a popular history of the world, several volumes of nature study, and of course the classics of philosophy and theology which helped him write *Illustrissimi*. There are magazines and the files of clippings from newspapers which he collected as part of his research material for those speeches which so captivated the world. There is a cassette-recorder and the tapes he sometimes used to try out a phrase or a whole section of a particularly important speech: he would play them back, listen, and continue to record until he was completely satisfied he had his delivery and timing word-perfect. There are his family photographs, each individually wrapped by Lorenzi in old newspapers that Gianpaolo liked to keep. There are the paintings and etchings, the ornaments and colourful cushions Vincenza so carefully displayed, a small chest which holds the tins and jars from that special shelf in the kitchen where she kept his nuts, coffee and sugar. Everything had been methodically packed and labelled, and taken down to a store-room in the basement of the Apostolic Palace. In all it comes to some thirty containers. They will eventually be handed over to the pope's family.

Lorenzi leads the workmen into the pope's private study. Here, more than anywhere so far, he has learned the hard facts of papal death. The secretary still remembers that particularly painful moment when, shortly after formally pronouncing Gianpaolo dead, Villot walked into this study holding the Fisherman's Ring which he had removed from the pontiff's finger. He asked Lorenzi for an envelope into which he casually dropped the ring. Later it would be ceremoniously broken before the cardinals. The Camerlengo brusquely informed Lorenzi that Secretariat of State officials would soon arrive to remove all official documentation of the pontificate. They had taken away three large chests.

The desk at which Gianpaolo worked in such a clutter is now bare-topped; the overflow of paper has been removed from the floor, the wall-map taken down. The study is as dead as a show-room.

To make doubly sure nothing remains, the men open and close drawers and cupboards. They work, as they have done since starting their task, in almost total silence. At first Lorenzi thought this was out of respect, or perhaps awe at being able to handle the intimate objects of a pontiff. But gradually he has concluded the workmen are merely indifferent: they have been in Vatican service much of their working lives and the routine of fetching and carrying for popes and powerful prelates has long lost its fascination. The men are mostly bored. There is nothing to say, so they say nothing.

Satisfied the study is cleared out, Lorenzi conducts the men to the pope's bedroom.

The secretary still finds it difficult to enter the room, the very hub of activity in the immediate aftermath of Gianpaolo's death. Here throughout Friday morning, had come an endless procession: the Vicar for Vatican City who blessed the mortal remains; the President of the Council of State who stared at the corpse and left as silently as he entered; the Prelates of the Ante-chamber; the Almoner of His Holiness; cardinals and bishops. Lorenzi finds it astonishing how many persons had a need, if not a right, to come and stand at the bedside and look and whisper to each other. Noé, Martin and Villot have been in and out, conferring, planning, deciding, not so much reverential, more quietly businesslike.

Contrary to the arrangement made with Magee, the Technician and his assistant had returned to the apartment around mid-morning Friday; by then Magee had gone. Their arrival was the signal for Villot to order everyone from the bedroom. Lorenzi already knew there would be no autopsy until the Sacred College ruled on the matter. He also knew it would be impossible to conduct a post-mortem once the body was drained and filled with the Epic Corporation's embalming fluids. An hour after they entered the bedroom the Technician and his aide leave.

The secretary was one of the first to return to the room. He found Gianpaolo lying on the bed, fully dressed in papal vestments, a mitre on his head, arms neatly folded, wrists lightly dusted with power to hide the chafe marks where the restraining ropes held them until rigor mortis passed. The face has also been carefully made up. But without his spectacles and with lips tightly pursed, Lorenzi thinks the pope bears little resemblance to the smiling, twinkle-eyed man he had served and loved.

Shortly afterwards the body was carried on a stretcher by Swiss Guards through the apartment to the high-ceilinged Sala Clementina. Here, in the vaulted vestibule to the papal apartment, beneath the priceless art work of Giovanni and Cherubino Alberti and Paul Bril, Gianpaolo was placed on a bier and the vigil of the Swiss Guards began.

That was twenty-six hours ago.

Now, the bedroom has a desolate air. The horse-hair mattress on its ancient frame is covered by a single sheet. The bedside lamp and rug have gone. The prie-dieu stands forlornly in a corner. The bowl of sweets has been removed. From the bathroom Gianpaolo's toiletries have been packed and taken away.

But there remains one item, to Lorenzi the most symbolic of all, that he has yet to remove. He goes to the wardrobe and opens its door. Reaching to the top shelf he takes down the cardboard box which contains the dry-cleaned cardinal's robe Gianpaolo had changed out of in the Sistine Chapel. Lorenzi cradles the box under his arm and walks sorrowfully from the bedroom.

Behind him one of the men closes the wardrobe door. A Swiss Guard waits until all have left the bedroom, then closes its door and follows the group down the corridor.

Villot and Martin are waiting at the entrance door to the apartment. They stand aside, saying nothing, as Lorenzi and the workmen pass. The guards take up position on either side of the door. Villot removes a key from his robe and locks the door. Then Martin affixes the lead seals across the door and its jamb. They will not be removed and no one will enter the apartment until a new pope is chosen.

*

All day Vatican radio messengers have brought slips of paper, copies of official communications, to MacCarthy's desk. Royalty, statesmen, religious and secular leaders in almost every country have been telexing, telegraphing and telephoning their condolences. The Secretariat of State has been overwhelmed by the sheer volume of the expressions of sorrow. Its communication system is further choked by reports from nuncios describing the profound sadness around them:

Alibrandi, for instance, has painted an evocative portrait of a mourning Ireland. Thousands of Catholics, important ones like Edward and Ethel Kennedy, and unknowns like a family in Berlin, have communicated their sense of loss: the German family's telegram spoke of 'our grief at the departure of a dear friend'.

MacCarthy doubts whether anyone in the Vatican had fully realized the extent to which ordinary people had either read the pope's speeches, listened to him on the radio or seen him on television and become attached to him. And it is not only Catholics who have felt a rapport: Anwar Sadat of Egypt cabled a dignified tribute, Indiri Gandhi of India sent a touching message. Rapid communication undoubtedly heightened the international sense of sympathy: film of the pope lying in state was flashed simultaneously to New Zealand and the Soviet Union.

The universal mourning is very different from that expressed for Paul. Then the tributes were stiff and formal, as if even in death Paul should not be treated with familiarity. But now they are often movingly informal: a group of Italian children he had greeted at his last Wednesday audience sent a collective telegram: WE WILL MISS YOU. It is a common sentiment, seldom expressed so succinctly. UN Secretary-General Kurt Waldheim personally telephoned the Vatican to sum up what so many feel. 'He radiated hope and warmth. His directness, his simplicity and his candour gave evidence of an obvious determination to use his great office for the vital purpose of all humanity.'

MacCarthy types up the judgement. It will make a fitting penultimate paragraph for the script he is preparing on the world's reaction. But he still needs a closing thought, one which will encapsulate the great sense of loss felt by ordinary people.

He rifles through the pile of messages. Poignant though many of them are, none contain exactly what he wants.

Then he remembers his own first reaction to the news: 'It is as if a parish has lost its priest.'

MacCarthy begins to type.

*

Greeley is busy as usual making all sorts of judgements: he is upset by the ghoulishness of the reporters and photographers in the Sala Clementina; he's sure Gianpaolo shook the papacy to its core; he thinks: 'The big question now is whether they will simply pull out the notes from the last time and do the same thing all over – that is, pick the next one down on the list'; he believes that the short gap between the funeral and the beginning of Conclave, a mere ten days, perhaps gives Benelli 'less time to concoct a plot'.

It's vintage Greeley.

Now, on Saturday night, he's one of the hundred thousand gathered in St Peter's Square to see Gianpaolo's bier born shoulder-high by the papal throne-bearers from the Apostolic Palace across the piazza to the Basilica.

In spite of the pleasantly warm evening and the reverent mood of the crowd, Greeley is feeling somewhat miffed. What upsets him this time is that he'd swallowed the Vatican Press Office announcement stating the pope died reading *Imitation of Christ*. Lorenzi has now said he was reading 'personal papers'. And further, the secretary 'blames the pope's death on a great sorrow; he had been deeply moved by the outburst of terrorist assassinations, the news of which he had heard just before he retired.' It really must be rather confusing for Greeley, and he is coming around to the idea that maybe he's a naive American.

Of course he's picked up Antico's allegations. But Greeley is not that naive. He does not take seriously the conspiracy to murder theory. Besides, he has a more important matter to worry about – deciding who is going to be the new pope. The fact he has been wrong before is no bar to trying again.

Nor is he alone.

*

Felici and the three experts he has requested assist him continue their search of the Archives. Outside, the rectangle of sky, walled in by massive stone buildings, fades into inky-black night, and the cool wind which often swirls around the flagged courtyard adjoining the room where the men work shakes the old orange trees and threatens to dislodge the roosting pigeons.

This Saturday night it is the extraordinary life of a pope, Pius VII, whom Napoleon had the audacity to arrest and deport to France as if he were a common felon, which continues to keep Felici and his companions seated at study tables so ancient their original wood is blackened. Each desk has a slotted lectern to support the heavy volumes brought by the archive attendants, often from the most restricted areas of this most secret of buildings in the Vatican.

Felici has come here straight from the meeting of the cardinals. He is certain his memory has not failed him; somewhere in this labyrinth among the millions of rare books and documents he believes is one which will prove Koenig is wrong; that there *is* a precedent for a papal autopsy.

Stored away in Felici's prodigious recall is the memory of coming across the hint that a post-mortem was performed on Pius VII.

It is not much of a clue, and Antonio Samore, the cardinal archivist, has said so. But it has been enough to spur on Felici; his sheer energy and enthusiasm persuaded Samore and his staff to join the thrill of an intellectual hunt over a course which is a hundred and fifty years old.

Nobody is better at finding their way round the obstacles to this plunge into the past than the two monsignori Samore has called upon to assist: the prefect of the archives, the gentle and erudite Martino Giusti, and the senior archivist, Charles Lamb, who, after twenty years in Rome, still retains his Scottish burr.

Between them they have combed for clues the most likely of the 684 indexes, many handwritten and barely decipherable; these offer the only guide to the contents of this cloistered store-house of astonishing secrets.

The hunt has been made that much more difficult because, like other popes, the life and times of Pius VII is not contained in one section but is scattered under various headings: parts are secreted in the *armadi*, the closets of the *Miscellanea* whose index uses the coded letters of the Greek alphabet; parts are in the *fondi*, various collections of documents which possess only *onomastic*, by name, indexes.

But Felici, with a gambler's instinct, has brushed aside the difficulties. He *knows*, he repeats, that somewhere in this building is what he wants.

It is Lamb who suggests a search is made of the Chigi family library. The Vatican had acquired it early in World War II when many of the great private archives of Europe were handed over for safekeeping because, in common with the cities of refuge in ancient Hawaii, the Vatican is inviolate from war. The Chigi family, like that of the Borghese, have for centuries been part of the papal court, collectors and discreet chroniclers of the secrets of successive popes.

Unlike many of the others, the library is well catalogued and sensibly arranged.

In no time the four men are once more immersed in that period onwards from 6 July 1809, when Pius walked out of the papal apartment and down the great staircase into the Court of Honour which the soldiers Napoleon had sent to arrest him had already desecrated. The Chigi papers detail the forty-two days of forced travel which took the prisoner-pope from Italy over the Alps to Grenoble, Avignon, and then back to Nice to the tiny fortress-town of Savona on the Gulf of Genoa. For two years Pius VII languished there.

Then, continues the Chigi diary, in June 1811, Napoleon discovers the English fleet plan to rescue the pope. In frail health – Pius VII has a mysterious stomach malady Felici reads with quickening interest – the pope is unceremoniously carted off in the dead of night northwards to Fontainebleau. Here he languished a further three years.

It is not until Napoleon is exiled to St Helena that Pius VII can recuperate in the peace of the Vatican.

Felici is certain he remembers: it's not enough, but it's coming back. He has been here before – to these well-ordered papers of the Chigi's. He still can't quite recall the reason, nor does it matter. Not now. He tells the others the search could soon be over.

They too begin to concentrate on the area Felici is trawling through, the closing stages of the life of Pius VII.

It remains a laborious process. There are cross-references to follow up which send Lamb and Giusti hurrying to collect yet more folders. Nobody minds. Caught up with Felici's relentless pursuit, they enjoy the spirit of the chase.

Felici reads on, his excitement contagious as he comes to the long account of the death agony of a pope who has already suffered so much. His pontificate of twenty-three troubled years closed with an ever-present Chigi to record his last words. Pius VII died mumbling: Savona and Fontainebleau.

And at the end of the report is the probable cause of his death: a weakened heart.

Felici is nonplussed. It is simply not possible: his memory, he is sure, has not played tricks. He turns the file over. There, on the back, is yet another maddening cross-reference, pointing him towards a new *fondo*.

Lamb returns with files from it, silently placing them by Felici's lectern.

The cardinal is more perplexed than before. These *buste* cover part of the brief papacy of Pius VIII, who reigned for less than a year.

Then Felici *really* remembers. He had been wrong. His memory has played a trick. But his instinct has finally given him the answer. All those years ago, when he had first stumbled upon the clue which has kept him and his helpers poring over papers for the last six hours, he had come here to read the history of papal medals. Paul had wanted the information and for some reason insisted Felici personally obtained it for him. Felici discovered that Pius VIII had created the *benemerenti*, the medals popes award to those they decide have given outstanding service to the Church. And there, in this file which contains much about the life of a pope who had been largely dull and blameless, is that elusive clue. It is another cross-reference on the inside cover of the *busta*.

Now, Felici has no doubts. It takes only minutes for Lamb to return with the file. He is smiling. Felici suspects the archivist has looked inside and knows. No matter: Lamb is also entitled to feel triumphant.

They gather around Felici as he opens the *busta*. It contains the original diary of Prince Agostini Chigi, who had been marshal of Conclave after Pius VIII's death.

Felici begins to read out Chigi's graphic account of the pope's 'frequent convulsions' before he died. He turns another yellowing page, his finger moving over the lines which Chigi's quill-pen scratched onto the parchment paper.

And at last he finds what he seeks. It is Chigi's detailed account of how an autopsy had been secretly carried out on the pope the day following his death to establish whether he had been poisoned. The doctors who opened up Pius VIII found: 'the organs healthy; the only thing noticed was some weakness in the lungs and some said his heart was weak'.

Felici smiles triumphantly. He has his precedent.

*

It may be that Benelli is unaware or perhaps he no longer cares. But he is being overheard and his words will be touted to some of the journalists arriving in Rome to cover Gianpaolo's funeral and the ensuing Conclave.

Cardinal-watching is back in vogue. There isn't a member of the Sacred College who can safely expect, between now and the moment he enters the Sistine Chapel, to escape surveillance by tipsters.

Media interest in the Holy See started relatively recently. Fifty years ago few newspapers outside the strictly Catholic press carried regular Vatican news; it was not until 1927 that even *L'Osservatore Romano* reported directly a pope's remarks. The Press Office opened in 1945 and remains a place where a reporter cannot ask real questions and expect answers. Nor does it as a rule arrange interviews with Vatican staff. Consequently a system of informers has sprung up.

Some informers are on retainers. Some, like Paolo Rossi, make a decent living. Rossi is the man who once got hold of an advance copy of *Annuario Pontificio*, the red-covered yearbook which lists the current Church hierarchy throughout the world and is an invaluable Who's Who to those in the Curia. *Annuario* has been published since 1716 and the pope receives the first copy of the new edition printed every January. Rossi beat him one year because he had inside information that the latest directory showed that the head of the Orsinis – who have served the papacy longer than any other Roman family – had no longer retained his traditional post as Assistant to the Throne. It was the pope's way of showing his displeasure that Prince Filippo Orsini, one of Rome's more attractive married playboys, was too close a friend of a famous actress. Rossi spilled the beans in advance of publication. He has been twenty years in the business of gathering such titbits. He boasts all sorts of Church connections. Certainly he is a grafter. And clearly one reason for his success is intelligent anticipation.

This Saturday night he has booked a table for himself and a companion in the one restaurant in Rome where he can reasonably expect to uncover at least one cardinal. It's L'Eau Vive in the Via Monterone, a nondescript back street near the Pantheon which tourists tend to ignore. For more years than anybody can be certain, this is the place senior members of the Vatican dine; ninety per cent of the clientele come from the Church. The prices are much too steep for a mere parish priest; even monsignori have to save before paying a visit to one of the culinary showplaces of Rome. It is not only the delectable food and vintage wines which attracts *bons vivants*. It is the service provided. L'Eau Vive is run by a female missionary order. The sister who acts as hostess has chosen with care the staff who wait at table. Each girl is young, often tall and usually strikingly beautiful: all have been given special leave to exchange their usual attire for filmy and elegant dresses – some split to expose dusky thighs – which cling demurely to their bodies. Only the gold crosses on neck chains signify the vocation of the waitresses. Their soothing voices and soft smiles are often long remembered even after the agreeable food fades from memory. For the appreciative prelates this is pleasure without temptation.

Rossi has obtained a table in the coveted back room of the restaurant – where cardinals always dine – by a ruse he has used before. He wears a clerical-black suit with a gold cross in his lapel. If challenged he will say he is a religious editor. He looks the part and has never been stopped in the years he has been coming here to listen and afterwards peddle what he has heard.

Tonight he had not expected such a windfall.

A corner table is occupied not only by Benelli, but by two other cardinals, Suenens and Willebrands. They are members of that loose coalition people like Greeley say set Luciani's bandwagon rolling.

They have dined well, but have confined themselves to generalities during the meal. Only when coffee, laced with fragrant anise, is served does the conversation become more serious and worthwhile for Rossi.

Suenens begins by suggesting that the problems of the Church are once more where they were at the time of Paul's death: there is still a need to settle the role of the Synod of Bishops, to overcome the confrontation between the Church's moral principles and the modern ethics of lay society, to resolve the special problems of the Third World, to stabilize relations with the governments of Eastern Europe – and, perhaps most important of all, to find a means to end the falling-off of religious fervour within and without the Church itself. It is barely a month since Gianpaolo began to face these problems. He had shown signs he would tackle them; yet no one could seriously argue he had left a heritage which was much more than a promise of things to come. Gianpaolo had indeed given every indication of being different. But there is now no way of knowing just how different. Equally the Church must not slip back to the era of Paul. The dialogue Gianpaolo began must continue.

Benelli nods periodically. Rossi decides this is only out of politeness, that it's Suenens 'clearing the ground'.

The amplified voice of the restaurant hostess stops further discussion. She orders the waitresses to take up their position before the large statue of the Virgin which stands in its grotto in a corner of the restaurant. Hands clasped in reverence, the girls stare shiny-eyed at the plaster Mary. Then the voice of the hostess, coming from hidden loudspeakers, invites the diners to join the girls in the speciality of L'Eau Vive, singing a hymn over coffee.

The rich voices of the three cardinals lend authority to the timeless words of *Ave di Lourdes*.

Afterwards Willebrands picks up the thread of the discussion. There must surely be an expanded role for the Synod of Bishops in the next papacy; it is the one most effective way for the pope to handle the problems Suenens had indicated. Given greater authority, the bishops could effectively end the rebellion of Lefèbvre and Küng, hopefully without a need for further theological bloodletting. It could not be done at once and there would have to be give and take. But none of this could be achieved before a strengthened working relationship is established between the Synod and the next pope.

Benelli's balding head continues to nod in agreement. Then, in the aggressive voice that people often resent or are intimidated by, he intervenes: what about the Jesuits? Look how Arrupe has responded to Gianpaolo's death; the briefest of statements, not so much tinged with sadness, more with stoicism. Wasn't this an indication the Society of Jesus would continue as before? Shouldn't the next pope come down once and for all on them and, if needs be, frog-march Arrupe back into line – and be seen to be doing it?

Rossi is all ears: this really is news – Benelli laying down rules on how the Jesuits should be tamed.

The cardinal from Florence is in full flow now. The next pope must be 'vigorous', appeal to the progressives, 'but not offend the conservatives'. He must move Vatican II appreciably on, and do it early in his pontificate. But he 'must not disinherit the Curia'. They, too, have their part to play in bringing 'the malcontents' to heel.

Rossi has no doubts: this is not only very saleable material, it is

Benelli signalling he's most ready and willing to go forward as a candidate for the papacy. Rossi's basis for his conclusions may be too obtuse for many people, but he has spent sufficient time eavesdropping on prelates to recognize the often-obscure language of cardinal-speak. Rossi is satisfied he has heard enough to peddle the story that once more the archbishop of Florence, the mercurial Giovanni Benelli, is back on the ramparts and ready to defend his right to go for pope.

*

Shortly before eleven o'clock on Monday morning, 2 October, eighty-five cardinals assemble in the Sala Bologna. Their mood is tense and expectant. They know about the widespread calls for an autopsy and the campaign of calumny which many readily accept is KGB-inspired. What else, they have asked each other en route to this meeting, can explain the way suspicions have been fanned until one of Italy's most responsible newspapers, *Corriere della Sera*, has just stated that Gianpaolo's death raised such grave doubts that 'We cannot understand why an autopsy was not performed, especially since the Vatican constitution does not explicitly forbid this.'

Felici has been busy throughout Sunday calling his media friends to campaign for a post-mortem. He really believes it is the only way to end the terrible smears. More and more newspapers and radio commentators are lending their authority to this view. Many point out that the world has lost confidence in official versions of events – citing Watergate, the assassination of President Kennedy, the Aldo Moro murder investigation, the Lockheed scandal: *ipso facto* the Vatican version Villot approved should not be believed. Indeed, the original scenario for the death is in tatters, and the Camerlengo's prestige has suffered a severe blow both in and outside the city-state.

Villot has before him a file filled with evidence of how the campaign is escalating. Antico's *Civiltà Cristiana* continues to rampage through the media. But Villot has decided that to censure him publicly would only attract even more odium to the Vatican, and to approach Antico privately is too unthinkable for the Camerlengo to consider. Consequently the secretary-general of this recently obscure organization is continuing to receive the sort of attention usually reserved for ranking statesmen. Antico appears to be relishing every moment. And the more his views are reported, the more support he acquires.

One of Lefèbvre's aides reportedly rants, presumably in jest, 'It's difficult to believe that the death was natural considering all the creatures of the Devil who inhabit the Vatican.'

A Spanish organization, Fuerza Nueva, semi-religious, pro-Franco and hitherto almost unknown, attracts wide media attention with its ridicule of the Vatican's press statement.

An obscure philosophy professor in Madrid gets huge coverage by postulating how the pope could have been murdered.

Edition by newspaper edition, bulletin by radio bulletin, newscast by television newscast, the dreadful story spreads: anything and anybody is dragged in: the Borgias, the medieval popes with their penchant for hemlocking opponents – it's all grisly grist for the rumour mills. No wonder even the most level-headed of the cardinals in the Sala Bologna come to accept that the KGB is masterminding it all.

At eleven o'clock the doors of the salon are closed and Villot starts the meeting. He announces that the three doctors have submitted their reports. In a toneless voice he reads out the first.

It is signed by the two physicians. Their conclusions are largely based, they admit, on the original medical findings of Buzzonetti, who examined the body 'within seven hours of death'. He had found there was no discoloration of the face, no suffusion to suggest a stroke; rather the skin was 'white as chalk', indicating blood/oxygen starvation. In their considered opinion Buzzonetti had been correct in his diagnosis of a myocardiac infarct, probably preceded by fibrillation, an a-rhythmic heart action and swift death. In their view there is no need for an autopsy.

Their pathologist colleague disagrees. Speaking 'purely medically', there is no way, almost forty-eight hours after death, the lapsed time before he examined the body, for him to be positive death resulted only from a massive heart attack. He is quite willing to accept this as the most likely cause. But to be clinically positive there should be an autopsy.

Villot says the majority medical vote is 'negative et amplius', a clear rejection. Unless he hears to the contrary he proposes to call for a vote on this expert opinion. He pauses and looks meaningfully down the table at Felici.

For the second time in two days Felici surprises his colleagues. He sits arms folded, saying nothing. He has decided – he will say later – there is no point flying in the face of expert testimony. It will be the only comment, brief though it is, he will permit on the matter; it will become another enigma in the Felici legend.

Villot continues to wait.

Some cardinals, like Krol, Cooke, Cody and Carberry, have just arrived in Rome. They and the rest of the North American bloc are firmly with Koenig: there is no need for an autopsy. Krol is confident, 'If there had been any reason to suspect foul play, the Vatican would have investigated it fully. There wasn't. Hence there isn't any need for formal denials. They wouldn't satisfy the people clamouring loudest for an autopsy – nothing would.'

Enrique y Tarancon and the other Spanish cardinals are equally emphatic: a post-mortem will only pander to the public appetite for sensation. There is murmured agreement around the long table.

Sensing it, eager to catch this favourable wind, to steer himself and the Vatican free of the unholy mess his original mishandling of the situation is responsible for, Villot quickly calls for a vote.

It is virtually unanimous. There will be no post-mortem; there is quiet confidence that the rumours will fade and wither as nothing fresh emerges to feed them. But Koenig has a new fear.

Now that the KGB has scored such a success it will surely want to try again.

24

To the end it maintained its simplicity – the wake and funeral for Gianpaolo. Over six hundred thousand ordinary people – the same kind as those who attended his Wednesday audiences – filed past his body before the coffin lid was closed prior to the funeral on Wednesday afternoon, 4 October.

The words of the Mass were essentially the same as the ones expressed over Paul's coffin. The setting was identical: the piazza of St Peter's. But the pomp and the glory, the presence of the high and mighty, were markedly absent this time. Jimmy Carter sent his mother to represent the United States. Mayor Edward Koch represented New York. Everybody was relieved President Videla of Argentina stayed home to watch the outdoor service on television. Thirty-one countries took the pictures from the square. But the major networks weren't inclined to send their star commentators to Rome. As a CBS executive said, 'We did this show last month.'

The funeral was a damp affair. It rained on and off for most of the ninety-minute ritual. Several times the tall paschal candle seemed about to flicker out in the wind. But the water-soaked pages of the Bible stayed open at the Gospel of St John.

At precisely 5.50 Rome time, twelve frock-coated pall-bearers bore the coffin into the Basilica and afterwards on down to the grotto. There it was placed in the sarcophagus which already carried his name. The tomb was covered by a heavy stone slab. Above it two fifteenth-century marble bas-reliefs of flying angels watch over the pope. They have smiles on their lips.

PART THREE

CONSPIRACY

*Cursed be the heart
    that thought the thought,
And Cursed be the hand
    that fired the shot*

— Ballad (undated)

25

Even if he begins to suspect and wants to unravel the carefully conceived manipulation, the nurtured exploitation of his strengths and weaknesses and the deadly way his condition was recognized and seized upon: even if he grasps any of this, the road along which Agca is travelling on this Thursday morning, 5 October, is not the place to try to begin to understand.

For a start the truck he is driving demands all his attention. The 1960 Dodge is well beyond its normal lifespan and has been sorely neglected. Its tyres are balding, its gears crash and grind; there is a disconcerting knocking sound in an engine which should have been replaced a hundred thousand miles earlier. Apart from the speedometer/milometer, the dashboard instruments no longer function. The brake linings are worn and the lights out of alignment. In most Western countries the vehicle would not even interest a rapacious scrap dealer. But in Turkey the truck is unexceptional. Its one functioning gauge confirms what Agca has carefully noted on a piece of paper he taped beside the indicator at the outset of his journey; that since then he has driven this decrepit truck over one thousand kilometres. The instrument cannot reveal that covering this distance has meant a numbing, jolting lonely week in the cab, continually fighting a stiff steering wheel to avoid the worst of the pitted road surface. His route has brought him across the Cappadocia, that eerie volcanic area which extends for hundreds of miles south-east of Ankara; a surrealist landscape of towering stone cones and plunging ravines. He has passed the rock chapels of Göreme, the troglodyte village of Aveilar and the ancient underground cities of Kaymakli and Derinkuyu. Later he turned east into that part of Turkey which was once Upper Mesopotamia where, two thousand turbulent years before Christ, man had struggled to survive in this hostile landscape.[1]

Like the truck, Agca blends easily into his surroundings. He wears heavy, army-style lace-up boots which he uses constantly on brake and accelerator. He is dressed in rough serge trousers and a faded flannel shirt, old-fashioned enough to have a hole for a collar stud. A cloth cap is on his head, its greasy peak pulled well down on his forehead so no one can easily see his eyes. He does not like people to stare into them; this is another of his recent peculiarities. His beard and moustache form a thick stubble. Agca looks what he wants to be taken for – a countryman about his business.

At the start of his long journey considerable care was taken by others to enhance this impression. The Dodge's licence plates were rubbed with mud, obscuring the numbers, giving an appearance common enough in the empty hinterland beyond Ankara. On the run down to Harran, the truck had been filled with rickety furniture: if he was stopped Agca would have said he was delivering it to a family in Harran whose relatives had died in Ankara. At Harran the chattels were off-loaded and replaced by a consignment of maize and chickens. Many will die before Agca reaches his next destination. He does not care. In a way this is symptomatic of what is happening to him.

During the five weeks since he left the safe house of the Grey Wolves in Ankara, the changes in Agca have been so insidious he himself barely recognizes them. But they are there, changing and shaping him, subtly altering his personality, making him more malleable and receptive. All Agca is aware of, apart from his eroticism, is that he feels increasingly dead; he is in fact no longer locked into his environment by the repertoire of emotional responses that have sustained him for years.

The reason which has brought him on this bone-jarring journey across Turkey to the Syrian border initially excited him – this possibility of getting help to kill the new pope in Rome. But long befo4e he reached his first destination, Harran, he heard that this pope, too, was dead. News which once drove him nearly to smash the family television and to retreat howling to his bedroom to chant the mantra of his hate list, this time had been received with indifference. It was the will of God at work, and if God willed it, he would be given another opportunity. That possibility, at least, has not lost its appeal.

In this frame of mind Agca is continuing his journey. Now and then he recites his hate list. Yet for the most part the old rewards – the feelings of elation, domination and intense physical pleasure – have largely gone; he only really feels the familiar excitement, a rekindling of anger and hate, when he reminds himself of all the evils his imagination places at the door of the pope and the Roman Catholic Church.

And another part of Agca's mind also functions as clearly as ever; it is his well-developed sense of secrecy and cunning. He has wrapped his treasured Mauser and bullets in oilskin; then, along with the exercise book filled with details about Paul, the first pope Agca wanted to kill, he concealed the items in a flap he cut under the truck seat. It is one of the tricks he remembers from that period which he still manages to keep hidden even from his mother. And now he is certain that she – and also Turkes and the other Grey Wolves – have no idea he is actually here, on the road from Harran.

Yet, despite the precautions he has taken, Agca knows he will need all his wits and prayers to avoid arousing the suspicions of the Turkish Army which patrols this border area with Syria. The last of the summer tourists have long gone; for another year there will be no sightseers gawking at the sacred carp in the pool beside the Mosque of Abraham at Urfa, four hours away in the Dodge bouncing noisily through one mountain pass after another. Anybody who moves along this ancient trail – two thousand years earlier King Antiochus I had travelled this very route to conquer the local tribes – is automatically frowned upon by the patrols during the long months of autumn and winter.

For here, above the gorges, well concealed from any tourist cameras, between where the Euphrates and the Tigris have their sources, the US Central Intelligence Agency has its listening posts; radar dishes beam north-east and south, sufficiently sensitive for their attendant computers to isolate and identify individual telephone calls in Damascus, Tehran and even further afield, deep inside Russia. And beyond the gorges are the massive black basalt walls of Diyarbakir, the provincial capital of this desolate area, with its modern air base from which black-painted American spy planes take off to photograph military movements in Syria, Iraq, Iran and the Soviet Union. The American presence confirms the strategic importance of Turkey in the overall NATO defence plans for southern Europe and the eastern Mediterranean. It is this entire system which Agca and the countless members of the Anarchy wish to overthrow.

With his blinkered vision, Agca has no difficulty believing implicitly what he was told in Harran: that the Americans, for whom, like the Church, he has not lost his hatred, are powerful enough in this area to have persuaded their Turkish allies – Europe's largest land army – to deal swiftly and harshly with anyone acting even remotely sus- piciously. The dreaded military prison at Diyarbakir is full of men being detained only for this reason.

Agca has also been told if ever he comes under suspicion, both his Turkish and American enemies will use all available means to extract from him everything he learned from the man at the meeting which brought them together briefly in Harran, the Biblical village of strangely domed dwellings where Abraham lived for several years and which is mentioned in the Book of Genesis. As a result of that meeting, Agca is now driving a further eight hundred kilometres north-east to another Old Testament shrine, Mount Ararat, where Noah's Ark rested until the Flood subsided. There, close to that part of Turkey which borders Iran and Russia, Agca hopes for more news from the one other man who has had such a complete influence on his life for the past eighteen months.

Both the man he met in Harran and the one he will meet at Ararat form the crucial human elements in the secret Agca has kept for all of this time.

But even without the hazardous driving conditions – several times he has barely avoided minor landslides caused by the sound of the truck's protesting engine echoing around one of the narrower ravines, bringing shale skeetering down onto the road – and the constant threat of encountering army patrols, it is still hard, because of the psychological changes he is experiencing, for Agca to have a sustained and clear recall of how it all began.

*

The events, it will later emerge, are deeply rooted in his subconscious. When Agca does think of them he has the feeling they involve another person, one he has permitted to inhabit his body for reasons he cannot explain, even to himself. This inner world is not equipped with the normal guidance system which would allow him to differentiate clearly for himself between what really happened and what was delusion.

His condition will subsequently make it that much more difficult for the psychiatrists and interrogators to understand and accept his motives. They will note his predominating mood, the long periods of morose and unproductive silence, and they will wonder how long he has lived in this half-way house between normality and psychosis. They will realize that, as part of his condition, he has no real insight into it, and that he does not see himself as disturbed.

They will also discover that driving along this Turkish road, Agca is content. His future is being decided by others. This is how it must always be from now onwards, said the man he has just secretly met in Harran before he faded back across the border into Syria. He is Sedat Siri Kadem. They have been friends for a long time.

*

This much will become known:

For five years Kadem sat at the adjoining desk to Agca in Yesiltepe School. He is older than his classmate by almost three years, a short, muscular figure with crinkly black hair and coal-black eyes. Kadem is one of the few boys who does not tease or beat up Agca because of his scholastic abilities. In return Agca helps Kadem with his lessons. Both graduate the same year with equal marks. It's Kadem who paves the way for Agca to get a job driving for the local Mafia. They remain friends, but after Agca enrolls in the Grey Wolves, Kadem suddenly drops out of Malatya's small but thriving underworld. Nobody is very interested why or where he has gone; already the Anarchy is seeding itself through the land and it is assumed Kadem joined one of the roaming bands of killers, intent, for whatever reason, on disestablishing Turkish democracy. In January 1977, Kadem reappears in Yesiltepe, calls on Agca and resumes their friendship as casually as he interrupted it. One night in Kadem's room in Malatya they become lovers. Agca finds the experience exciting. The eroticism has already taken root; sexuality accompanied afterwards by unpleasant accusatory thoughts, will torment him. Pledging Agca to secrecy Kadem tells him where he has been during the past year – a training camp in the Lebanon. There he learnt the latest techniques for 'liberating' Turkey, ending the hateful system of corrupt Western democracy, removing the country from its position as NATO's farthest outpost in the Middle East and returning it to a closed Islamic society. Kadem expresses perfectly the driving force which has sustained Agca for some time. He offers to take Agca back with him to the school for terrorism near the road to Damascus.

*

The Dodge safely passes through Diyarbakir. There are soldiers everywhere. But they give no more than cursory glances at the battered truck, its driver and the bags of maize and crates of clucking chickens. Beyond the city the threat from army patrols recedes with every mile the protesting truck covers on the windswept barren road to Bitlis. There are no CIA bases out here amid the snow-capped mountain vastness.

The Romans and the Parthians, the Byzantines and the Sassanids grappled to occupy this place of howling gales. None of them succeeded: they were driven from their freezing forts by sweeping sheets of rain and snow.

Even now the weather is seasonal: a blistering wind buffets the truck, chilling to death the weaker chickens, forcing the others to huddle together.

Agca grips the wheel harder, hunches himself against the dark, glowering skies on all sides. Soon the peaks are lost beneath a canopy of cloud and mist which swirls so low it often reduces visibility to feet. Even in the cab, with a padded jacket buttoned to the neck and the heating full on, Agca feels iced to the bone. He shouts the names on his hate list and, whether from the cold or because his hatred is once more burning brightly, tears trickle down his cheeks.

He will remember this journey well. Just as he will never forget the last time he entered this impregnable area.

*

This, too, is known:

On 10 March 1977, a Thursday, Agca and Kadem board a bus in Malatya, the first of several they travel on to bring them, two days later, to Mardin, a southern Turkish city as dazzling white as the surrounding snow peaks. From there they walk for an entire frozen night further south, crossing the border into Syria during the small hours when the Turkish guards huddle in their pill-boxes. They walk another half-day to the Arab shanty town of Senyurt. A waiting truck takes them to the training camp. After reaching its perimeter Agca seldom sees Kadem. He has no time to think about this. There are hundreds of recruits in the camp who are drilled from dawn until far into the night. After a month Agca is transferred to an inner compound within the main complex. He receives intensive training with a variety of weapons, Russian and American. He is coached in sniper tactics, and learns how to carry out assassinations under various conditions.

*

Psychiatrists will wonder whether with total confidence they can know anything more. They will note Agca's memory gaps, his compression of events, his constant lack of emotional response, and they will ponder whether, in their lingua franca, this is all associated with 'a loss of the ego boundary', whether in fact the essential and the non-essential, the relevant and the irrelevant have become equal in Agca's mind.

His interrogators will ask the psychiatrists to get names and descriptions which can be checked against those in computers of a dozen intelligence agencies. The doctors will return with more questions. What names did the instructors have? What did they look like? What accents did they use? Arabic? Turkish? Maybe – Russian? They will pose hundreds of questions, taking him back and forth through his time in the camp. And so by this careful process they will come to the name of the man Agca is now driving to meet.

*

Again, known:

It is Saturday morning, 30 April 1977. Agca's last day in the camp. His bag is packed; he is returning to Turkey with no mora than he came. He is thinner and fitter than he has ever felt. He is called to the camp office. Kadem is there. They briefly embrace, then Kadem leaves the room. Moments later Teslin Tore enters. He has one of those faces easy to label. Jaw, eyes and nose all convey the same enveloping hardness. It extends to his neck, shoulders and barrel of a chest, and to his biceps and thighs. He wears the same battle fatigues as the last time they met, in the Sinan Hotel on Malatya's Kisla Cad. Then, Tore was distant and dismissive as he paid Agca for a successful drug run. Now he is cordial and effusive. Tore drives Agca westwards, across Syria, towards the Mediterranean. At dusk they reach the frontier post of Ciivegozu. The Syrian soldiers wave them through. Two hundred yards up the road, at the Turkish checkpoint, the barrier is raised without the car having to stop. Tore drives them into Turkey. Two hours later the car reaches the regional capital, Iskenderun. They spend the night in separate rooms at the Guney Palas, a second-class hotel on Temmus Cad. Next day Tore drives them to the airport, fifteen minutes from the hotel. He buys a one-way ticket to Istanbul on THY, Turkish Airlines. He gives the ticket to Agca, embraces him, but more formally than Kadem had done, and leaves. Four hours later Agca is back in Istanbul.

*

The psychiatrists and the interrogators will pounce. How can he remember this sort of detail? When, precisely, did he go to the Sinan Hotel? Had he seen anyone else there? How long had he worked for Tore in Malatya? Had he not wondered what Tore was doing in the camp? Was he an instructor? A recruit? Why had he driven Agca hundreds of miles? What time exactly did they cross the border? Could he identify the faces of the guards if they showed him pictures? Where did they buy petrol? What time did they reach the Guney Palas Hotel? Could he recognize any of the staff from photographs? Did he register in his own name? And Tore – did he use an alias? How did Tore pay the bill? How did he pay for the ticket?

The questions will come: flat, doubting questions; clever, pliant questions; harsh, threatening questions.

They will all be to no avail.

*

It is dark when the Dodge drives along the sweeping curve of the highway to Bitlis, its worn tyres humming on the highway, suddenly asphalt. Agca can relax his concentration, think once more about the little book, no thicker than a passport which, as part of his secret world, he has kept tucked inside his underpants. This book is as precious as the exercise book and the gun and bullets hidden under his seat. He realizes his mother knows about them: she had not been as clever as she thought; he knew every time she had disturbed the books on the shelf in his bedroom. But she will never know of the little book.

313

No one must. Kadem made him promise this before he handed it to him.

*

Desperate for a breakthrough, the psychiatrists and interrogators will reveal to Agca that they know about the little book; that it is a passbook for the main Istanbul branch of *Turkeye Is Bakasi*, a bank; that on 13 December 1977, an initial forty thousand lire – about three thousand American dollars – was put on deposit in the name of Mehmet Ali Agca.

But who had forged his signature? Why? What was the money for? Where had it come from?

Why? Why? Why?

*

The truck passes through Bitlis around midnight. Agca has driven almost two thousand kilometres since leaving Ankara. Beyond the sleeping town he pulls off the road, and, as on previous nights, he sleeps in the cab. Behind him the few surviving chickens cluck feebly. By morning they will almost all be dead either from thirst or the biting cold.

Two hours later he awakes. He is not refreshed. But he cannot sleep longer. He has this strange compulsion to go on and on. He can't explain it – and certainly didn't to that official from the Libyan Embassy when he had met him in Ankara.

As he had been instructed, he had used Tore's name when his call to the embassy was answered. After a brief hesitation he was asked to wait. Then another voice came on the line, suggesting a meeting at the bus terminal on busy Hippodrome Cad. It had been a brief meeting, merely long enough for Agca to explain he wanted to see Kadem or Tore as soon as possible. The Libyan suggested they should meet again at the terminal in two days. When they did, he handed Agca a wad of lire and told him to collect a vehicle from a garage on Ataturk Boulevard.

It is the Dodge that now, well before dawn, Agca guides around the icy shore of Lake Van near the Turkish eastern border with Iran.

He is ahead of schedule. Kadem estimated he would not reach here until sunrise. Steering with one hand he chews *yufka*, unleavened bread, and swigs from a bottle of *raki*, aniseed spirit potent enough to make his eyes smart. It has been his only nourishment for days.

Agca can still recall the burning intensity of Kadem's promise. It was after he had explained – again – about all the names on his hate list and why he had felt impelled to come on this long and dangerous journey, to seek help to kill a pope who is no more. It was then that Kadem made his vow. He had held Agca's hands in his and said that soon those other enemies will be dealt with, that the demanding hatred he carries in his head will be quenched.

This prospect still sustains Agca as he continues his lonely journey.

In two days' time, at the location Kadem gave him, Agca will meet Tore on Mount Ararat.

Like Kadem, Tore is under the direct control of the KGB.

26

Villot sighs irritably. One of the African cardinals wants to be able to see the moon. Noé sympathizes with the Camerlengo's exasperation: this really is too much.

It is Monday morning, 9 October, and they are in Villot's office trying to finalize the arrangements for Conclave, due to start this coming Saturday. The open windows do little to reduce the fug of Gauloises around Villot. He is already well into his first packet of cigarettes, though it is only just nine o'clock, and by the end of the day he'll be close to emptying three. His normal forty-a-day limit has consistently been broken this past week. The usually fastidious Villot now resembles an even sadder and seedier version of the xenophobic Frenchman journalists portray: he is more pinch-nosed and purse-lipped; when he does smile, rare enough in itself nowadays, it clearly comes nowhere near reaching behind his spectacles. And ash sprinkles his wool soutane – it's autumn now and the old Camerlengo has given up his fine silk cassock of summer.

Villot is still badly rattled – there is no other word for it – by some of the excesses of the Italian press. They are not letting up with their innuendoes about Gianpaolo's death. The autopsy issue lives on, abetted by a call for all cardinals eligible to vote to have a medical before Conclave – and that the results should be circulated before any balloting. There is even the rumour that Karol Wojtyla had an electrocardiogram before coming to Rome.

The point which concerns Villot about the health issue is not so much that it flies in 'the face of tradition and papal dignity', but the expense. To give one hundred and eleven mainly elderly men a thorough check-over would mean sending them all to the Gemelli Hospital; it would cost a great deal. Villot knows only too well that the forthcoming Conclave and its attendant coronation are financial burdens which the Vatican can ill afford at a time when its expenditure is going up while income declines. There has, naturally enough, been no contingency made for a second Conclave coming so quickly. Consequently, Villot has had to do his share of barrel-scraping to distribute the cost of

Gianpaolo's funeral and find the cash to meet the considerable expense of electing his successor.

It has not been easy, the Camerlengo querulously tells Noé, trying to balance everything, satisfy everybody, and still stay within budget. The same amount of money as before has been allocated for this Conclave. But since August prices have risen, to be sure only a few lire for this item, a few for that. But on the scale Villot operates – accommodating and feeding some three hundred persons for an indeterminate period – the increase is bound to be substantial; he has calculated that overall this Conclave may in the end prove a whopping fifteen per cent more expensive. To juggle successfully with it all needs the combined skills of a quartermaster, accountant and hotelier. (The thought of Villot's equal in a secular government, a Foreign Minister, being personally involved in such petty-fogging detail is clearly preposterous, but it is an indication of the endearing Ruritanian-like atmosphere which pervades the upper echelons of the Holy See. Senior Vatican staff frequently settle very minor matters which in other administrations are dealt with by junior members of a department.)

Noé clucks sympathetically and helpfully suggests that this time the African cardinal should be allowed to have his moon: it would save both labour and materials if Conclave windows were not painted over.

Villot agrees. They move on to another request, one of a small pile before him which have come from cardinals who, two months ago, filed into Conclave willing to accept what they were given. Now they are seasoned campaigners, and ready to display their princely power. Carberry of St Louis has been telling the Rome press corps that in August, 'We felt as though we were going into a dark tunnel; now it is as though we are entering a bright room.'

But clearly not bright enough for Cody. He has sent a handwritten request on Chicago diocese bonded notepaper for the whole lighting system in Conclave to be improved.

Villot rejects the idea. That would cost even more than full medical examinations. The Camerlengo turns to another suggestion. It is from Felici. He thinks each cardinal should have a proper bedroom, not the thinly partitioned salons of August when, Felici writes, he was unable to sleep because of the snoring from the cubicles on either side.

The Camerlengo and master of ceremonies consult the floor-plan of Conclave. The usable area around the Chapel has been considerably extended. Sleeping accommodation will be on three floors. Felici can have a corner room on the upper floor; it has a bathroom attached. That should keep him satisfied.

Noé picks out another request. One of the Americans wants a bedside ashtray; last time, he complains, he had to use his chamber pot. Villot checks one of the many lists which his staff have prepared. In August twenty-five ashtrays were allowed for. He sees no need for this number to be increased. The Camerlengo dictates a brief note to a hovering priest-secretary suggesting the cardinal brings his own ashtray.

He moves on. A European cardinal has complained about the mattress and bed he had last time. There will be the same narrow beds and slim mattresses this time, along with the same well-laundered sheets and the same thin blanket for each cardinal. There is a request for more writing paper. This is also refused. Each cardinal will still only get five sheets on which to scribble his thoughts – or, as Wojtyla and Koenig did in August, to use for playing tic-tac-toe between their 'consultations'.

Noé checks a memo. It is from one of the French cardinals. Can he have Vichy water, preferably two bottles a day? Villot refers to a price list. Vichy costs more than Italian mineral water. But he approves the request. The Camerlengo is partial to Vichy himself.

Ratzinger of Munich wonders whether it's possible to have a shaving mirror? Noé remembers that one of the Conclave staff, chasing up chamber pots, came across hundreds of tiny plastic-framed mirrors in a Rome convent. They would do. Each cardinal will have one for shaving.

Manning of Los Angeles wants to know if there will be a bar-kitchen where the cardinals can make themselves coffee and tea, or perhaps collect a snack from a well-stocked refrigerator?

Noé checks another list. A fridge from the pope's kitchen had been temporarily moved down to the Conclave area before the papal apartment was sealed.

Aramburu asks whether there can be more South American dishes on the menu; he is one of those who became bored with the common diet of pasta last time.

Villot consults the produce list. This is where he has made a substantial saving. In August supplies had been bought for a week. But with that Conclave lasting little more than a day, there had been a huge surplus which the Vatican distributed free to the poor of Rome. Villot this time has allowed food for only four days, nearly a fifty per cent cut in costs; if the need should arise, more can be sent in through those revolving drums. And the Camerlengo has gone further, substantially reducing the amount of rations for each person. Their beer and wine allocation has been cut by half.

Regretfully, he dictates to Aramburu, there is no way to include regional dishes on the Conclave menu.

A German cardinal has a query about the infirmary. The room set aside last time had electric lights but no proper wall socket, let alone modern monitoring equipment. Could not adequate power be laid on and a basic resuscitation trolley provided? Ideally there should be oxygen and ECG facilities. Surely these could be rented?

Villot shrugs. They could, but the cost is beyond his budget. He dictates an explanation to the German. It will be hand-delivered, like all the other notes, before the day is over to cardinals scattered throughout Rome. Some things will not be curtailed – among them the courier service of priests Villot uses on these occasions.

He and Noé begin to check shopping lists. Two hundred toilet rolls have still to be bought. A similar number of table place settings – a single knife, fork and spoon for each cardinal and Conclave attendant – must be rented. Richard Ginori, one of Italy's leading crockery manufacturers, has offered to provide the china. A sample plate is enclosed with the offer. It is a tasteful beige. Villot dictates grateful acceptance.

More lists. To be rented: dustbins, clip-on reading lamps. To be borrowed from convents and monasteries: tablecloths and napkins, prayer stools and night tables.

Villot picks out yet another letter. It's from one of the Italian cardinals, Corrado Ursi of Naples. He politely wonders – his diffidence can be sensed in his prose style – whether there can be a little extra elbow room in the Sistine Chapel this time to help preserve the secrecy Paul's *Eligendo* requires.

The Camerlengo gives another weary sigh. He sympathizes with Ursi. But there is no way of making more space in the Sistine.

And once again it will be possible for leaks. Whatever else has changed since August, Villot is sufficiently realistic to accept that the human frailties of some of those directly involved in the forthcoming proceedings will not have altered.

*

Nor will the role of the Vaticanologists change. They blissfully continue to interpret the uninterpretable, judge the unjudgeable, put flesh and blood on the Holy Spirit, and perhaps even give It shoes to see where the Spirit goes in order to postulate why. The experts are legion: the priests in the pay of newspapers; the religio-sociologists under contract to those television networks that thought Gianpaolo's funeral wasn't worth sending a team to Rome for but have decided Conclave is good for their ratings; the religious editors with mysterious pipelines which need a lot of expense-account maintenance; the specialist writers who handle the event as though it's just another routine assignment; the hard-news reporters who hold court in the bars of the Rome Hilton and decide among themselves which rumour is floatable and which should be sunk with large gins and tonic. Nearly a thousand of them have registered with the Vatican Press Office; this entitles them to pick up the cardinals' biographies left over from last time.

Like all other 'ologists', Vaticanologists are really no more than outsiders peering in, attempting to penetrate the impenetrable. In between they squirrel around Rome, listening to anybody with a rumour to peddle, a fact to sell.

Paolo Rossi, the doyen of the tipsters, has made more money these last ten days than in the previous two months. A score of journalists have bought his account of what happened at L'Eau Vive. Now he has another Benelli story for sale. This past Sunday, Rossi has learned, the cardinal's secretary lunched at the Polish Church of St Stanislaus near the Piazza Venezia. Also present were Wojtyla and two Polish bishops, Andre Deskur and Ladislaw Rubin. It may not sound much of a titbit, but in Rossi's experienced hands it is transformed into high-value intrigue. Benelli's secretary, claims Rossi, had been sent along to enlist Wojtyla's vote in return for the assurance that in a Benelli pontificate the Synod of Bishops would be given increased importance; Rubin is the Synod's secretary-general and Wojtyla has been a member of its permanent council since 1971. The item is fleshed out Rossi-style; who sat next to whom, what they ate, who drank what, even how much. It *sounds* authentic. But it has to be taken on trust – and Rossi's reputation for worming out such details.

Most of the cardinals are now back in Rome after a long weekend outside the city when all kinds of pacts, deals, schemes, agreements, bargains and plots were hatched. So runs the scuttlebutt.

Not even the indefatigable Greeley can check them all out. The last time round he and CREP had their moment with the job-definition for the papacy. Now Greeley – of whom Cody has increasingly been heard to ask plaintively whether no one will rid him of this meddlesome priest – has come up with another gee-whizz wheeze. He and his associates are going to pre-empt Conclave by telling the cardinals, and the world, who, according to their complicated calculations, the next pope should be. For, as well as CREP, Greeley is associated with another acronym, NORC, the National Opinion Research Center in Chicago. NORC has used computer models to simulate Conclave. Data on the 'attitudes and behaviour' of each cardinal elector, gathered from 'people in a position to know' – none of whom in the Greeley way of doing things are named – have been acquired. Further, 'a number of experts on the College of Cardinals rated each of the cardinals on a scale of relative influence from one to five, five indicating a highly influential cardinal and one a cardinal with relatively little influence on others'.

Felici, Benelli and Lorscheider scored five, suggesting they held the greatest sway over their fellows. Siri, Baggio, Arns of São Paulo and Madrid's Enrique y Tarancon received four. Among those rating three were Koenig, Gantin, Sin, Suenens and Willebrands.

In addition: 'Using a complex decision-making model', the creation of NORC, 'a weighted profile which calculated the attitudes and behaviours which would be most typical of the College was constructed from the data. Each of the cardinals was then assigned a score based on his deviation from that profile, a score on a scale running from zero to two hundred.'

And this was how it was done. With hey-presto verve Greeley has his order of 'profile deviation'.

It's bad news for Benelli. Greeley and NORC have him at number twelve. Bertoli can do no better than come in at eleven. Felici is at ten. Poletti sticks at nine. Koenig, who last time Greeley elected beforehand as an 'interim pope', is now well out of the running, at eight. Pironio, a curial favourite, is one place above. Pellegrino, another Italian, makes it to the number six spot. And at five – certain to be a real headline-grabber for all the English journalists in Rome – is Hume. Immediately above him is Baggio. Willebrands is third from the top of this astonishing list. If only he knew, there's little doubt nuncio Alibrandi would be close to clapping his hands in delight because his close friend, Pappalardo, has such a small 'profile deviation' that he's come second. And at the number one spot, the first pope in history to be chosen by a NORC computer, is the cardinal who wrote so politely to Villot asking for more elbow room when the votes which really matter, those cast in the Sistine, are made. It is Corrado Ursi.

Greeley means to release this list on Thursday. It's not only perfect timing to get him more useful publicity, but he has an idea the cardinals will look seriously upon what at best seems about as tasteful an exercise as the betting book Ladbrgkes ran on the first Conclave.

*

Greenan has no patience with gimmicks like computer forecasts; he sees them as part of the journalistic tomfoolery which this Conclave is attracting. Equally, the sharp-minded, and sharp-tongued, editor has to prepare his own in-house list of *papabili* so that *L'Osservatore Romano* can pre-set another batch of front pages which hopefully will include the cardinal to be selected at the forthcoming eighty-third Conclave, dated from 1241 when accurate voting tallies started.

This Tuesday afternoon, 10 October, he is at his desk, itself covered by the jumble of papers he finds both reassuring and rewarding. They form, he can reflect, the proof that old-fashioned methods still pay off best.

Greenan has acquired copies of everything all the cardinals have said publicly since assembling in Rome: their sermons, the occasional press conference the Americans and some of the Europeans give, newspaper accounts, transcripts of their radio and television statements. He has coupled reports from these with the genuine network of contacts he has within the Sacred College and the Curia. For Greenan – trained in that most skilful of Vatican techniques, how to differentiate between an event and its interpretation – the result has been some important discoveries.

The sermons preached at the *Novemdiales* Masses are especially revealing. Basil Hume, in his own careful English way, suggests – Hume is not one to make dogmatic assertions at any time, let alone on such a sensitive issue as this – that there should be no temptation, having buried Gianpaolo, to forgo all the hopes and expectations which his pontificate had indicated. The move towards a collegial style of Church government must continue. And yet the astute Greenan detects that many cardinals want to redraw the one outstanding memory of Gianpaolo's reign – its pastorality.

It is now no longer enough, as it was in August, to define pastoral merely as 'from a diocese'. That had created its own problems for the Curia on how divisive issues could be settled. It might well be illusory, but the image had been forged, and stuck, that Gianpaolo was little more than a happy-go-lucky pope who adored children, cared about the poor and vaguely saw his mission to be in the Third World; he was the world's favourite small man, battling against strong opposition. Like his beloved Pinocchio he was always getting into trouble – in his case with the Curia.

In their subtle and wily way which Greenan, an old trouper in this baroque circus, long ago learned to spot, some cardinals are saying there is nothing wrong, as such, with the next pope being 'pastoral' – given one important proviso. The meaning of 'pastoral' should not be taken to suggest their choice of pontiff be restricted to again plucking somebody from a diocese, especially someone who might not grasp, or may not care to learn, how an organzation as complex as any multinational works.

Krol offers the intriguing thought that a cardinal who works in the Curia and is involved in settling divorce questions, can be 'profoundly pastoral'; Dearden of Detroit goes further: *all* curial cardinals are men of compassion, which is Dearden's way of saying 'pastoral'. Gantin reinforces this with the attractive idea that 'all the cardinals are in some sense pastoral men – and many of them have been in a diocese, including myself'.

Is Gantin declaring, by way of cardinal-speak, that he's ready to become the firt black pope? Greenan thinks surely not. Gantin is not that naive.

The editor senses what lies behind this determination to make 'pastoral' a broken-backed word. Redefined, it can now be applied to every one of the cardinal electors. Nobody this time will be able to get a bandwagon rolling by promoting the 'pastorality' of a *papabile*, as had happened with Luciani.

Greenan continues to work his way through the sermons. He has read them several times already, underscoring passages which offer him important clues as to how the campaigns – all naturally called 'consultations', all cleverly within the limit of what Paul's *Eligendo* states is permissible – are developing.

Confalonieri, though himself well past the voting age limit, is determined his fellow cardinals will know what sort of a pope he hopes they will choose. The Dean of the Sacred College has spelled it all out. In an oblique tribute to the cosmetic skills of the Technician and his embalming aids, Confalonieri has spoken about Gianpaolo's smile, 'hovering on his lips even in death', a reminder that he had been 'a meteor which unexpectedly lights up the heavens and then disappears'.

Greenan has already underlined the words. He sees them as a clear indication – indeed remarkably so, in the otherwise often obscure prose of the sermon – that the Dean wants a second, similar shining star to emerge smiling from Conclave. But, and here there is another clue for the prescient editor to ponder, the next pontiff must not only have faith and the perfection of Christian life, he must also understand and know how to come to terms with 'the great discipline of the Church'.

There it is again: what amounts to a call for a curial cardinal, one who will smilingly put a stop to liturgical abuses and get back to good old doctrine.

But who?

Siri, with his clutch of votes which Greenan thinks are probably as committed to him now as they were back in August, is very much in the running. He has paid his public tribute to Gianpaolo – nicely formed phrases delivered to full effect. But the overall impression of Siri's real judgement – carefully buried beneath the layers of politeness – is that Gianpaolo might not have proven such a good pope when judged against the themes the conservative archbishop of Genoa holds sacred: 'primacy of the spiritual', 'ecclesiastical discipline', 'separated spirituality'. Greenan interprets the code-phrases as Siri suggesting the next pontiff would do well to remember these totems.

And, in spite of his obligatory denial, Siri is *papabile*. Everybody knows this. He goes onto Greenan's list.

So does Felici — if only because he virtually declared his own candidature during a remarkable sermon largely devoted to reminding everyone how close he was to Gianpaolo; who better, then, than the man who has been a pope-maker to become pope? That's the message wrapped up in all the references from Corinthians and the other Gospels which Felici used as essential ballast to give a weighting for something very basic. Felici would love to be pope.

But where does this leave Gianpaolo's other great advocate, Benelli? Not to mention the possible non-Italian *papabili*?

Greenan realizes he has a lot more reading to do before he can type his final list. To help him along with his task he goes to an office cupboard. When he opens it, his eyes take on an anticipatory gleam. Facing him, neatly arranged so their labels can be read instantly, is a selection of bottles. Each one contains a vintage Irish whiskey. Greenan selects a bottle and pours himself a generous measure. Then he continues reading. It is going to be a long day and he knows he will need to make several visits to this place which the few who are aware of it have dubbed Greenan's Cupboard of the Holy Spirit.

*

One after another, spaced throughout Wednesday, 11 October, arriving and departing between their other engagements, a large number of cardinals come to the Collegio Pio Latino on the Via Aurelia. Here, where Albino Luciani presented copies of *Illustrissimi* and spoke movingly about his reasons for writing it, these cardinals now discuss the very different style of another author. The well-stocked Latin American College library is one of the few places in Rome which still has ample copies available of *Segno di Contraddizione*. This is the Lateran Retreat which was preached in 1976; each year, and at the request of the pope, a version of the Retreat is presented before him and the Curia. Traditionally the discourse is given by an Italian Franciscan, or another Rome-based bishop. Two years before, Paul invited Karol Wojtyla to write and deliver the Retreat.

All the cardinals coming to the Collegio Pio Latino are non-Italian. They include Enrique y Tarancon who is already familiar with, and approves of, this particular Retreat. But he goes to the College late in the afternoon because here is a chance for him to hear how other visitors are reacting. The senior Spanish cardinal is gratified. Aramburu and Arns, São Paulo's archbishop, both of whom are carefully monitoring reactions, say the response has been unanimous. The Dutch cardinals are particularly impressed by what they have read. The German cardinals — all five of them — have been equally complimentary. The Asians and the Africans, especially the Polynesian, Pio

Taofinu'u, who still hobbles after his boating accident off Samoa just before Paul's funeral, appear undivided in their enthusiasm. The seven French cardinals have been led in praise by no less than the Chancellor of the Gregorian University. Gabriel-Marie Garrone, who used to send Paul intellectual teasers, and says that what he's read in the College library is as theologically impeccable as anything he has studied during thirty years of Church service. Garrone is conservatively minded. What interests Enrique y Tarancon is the reaction of François Marty, archbishop of Paris. He's a liberal, far across the religious spectrum from Garrone. Yet Marty, too, seems completely satisfied and, like Aramburu and Arns, the other seventeen Latin American cardinals have also found much to appreciate in Wojtyla's words.

The visits to the Collegio Pio Latino library have come about through Koenig. He had been studiously casual over the whole matter, murmuring the idea to one cardinal as they strolled into a meeting of the Sacred College in the Sala Bologna, dropping the thought into a conversation with another while they walked through the Vatican gardens. Koenig is adamant he is not running any sort of campaign. Indeed, the very idea, he will patiently insist, is quite absurd; such politicking is fine for the Morris West novels Wojtyla likes to read, but things are rather different in reality. Koenig maintains he is merely being 'helpful'; no cardinal, he argues reasonably, can know all there is to know about his peers. All he is doing in Wojtyla's case is offering some useful pointers they may care to think about. Just that, and no more.

No doubt responding to such a courteous approach, the cardinals have been equally receptive to Koenig's suggestion that, having read Wojtyla's Retreat, they might find the time to dip into his other writings. These have been neatly flagged in the Collegio library, all in the cause of being helpful, naturally.

There is the speech on the liturgy Wojtyla made in a Vatican II aula on 7 November 1962; it is an erudite call for a more Biblical and less clerical approach to the Church. The address is as carefully balanced as another, this one on the sources of revelation which he delivered at another Vatican Council session, on 21 November 1962. Even a quick perusal of his writing shows Wojtyla is no peasant pietist clinging to outmoded ideas. Nor is Garrone the only cardinal to believe that here is impeccable theology, very much in tune with current curial thinking, delivered with a realism in keeping with the ethical philosopher which Wojtyla is by training. (Cardinal Wojtyla was one of the most prolific writers in the Sacred College. Polish history and culture provided him with an endless stock of references and symbols which he consistently drew upon. In the past two years his work had become increasingly known to his fellow cardinals.)

And there is still more to make these busy cardinals pause and ponder and, in some cases, cancel appointments so they can continue to read. Here is Wojtyla on Communism and atheism; Wojtyla's rejection of theologians who sow seeds of doubt by questioning such fundamentals as the Trinity, the evidence of Christ, the real presence of Jesus in the Eucharist, the indissolubility of marriage; Wojtyla on the importance of Mariology; Wojtyla on the need for a strong Catholic identity, a call for a ringing proclamation of faith in a world which is increasingly losing its religious way.

It is all here in the library of the Latin College, clearly referenced, so cardinals can easily discover where this Polish bishop stands on issues they hold dear: ingenuous statements which reveal both a fidelity to traditional commitments and yet leave sufficient room for the more liberal cardinals to feel a warm glow of approval.

For instance, there is Wojtyla's grappling with atheism. He shows a refreshing openness which appeals to the likes of Suenens, Sin and Willebrands. Wojtyla is not in favour of an outright condemnation of atheism because this would end any hope of dialogue on the matter. Instead he leans towards the 'heuristic approach', aimed at finding common ground with unbelievers. It is an attitude which extends throughout Wojtyla's thinking; he begins and ends with the idea that everything stems from the thick of human experience, that the Church itself is involved in a continuous process of search, that there is no room for pointless moralizing, 'or the suggestion that we have a monopoly of the truth', and that, above all, the Church must never appear as an authoritarian institution. He first said this on 21 October 1963, and he has been restating the view regularly ever since.

It is indeed, as Koenig indicates, all very interesting. Something to keep at the back of a cardinal's mind. But not too far back. Not with the growing indications by this Wednesday night that the Italian cardinals are hopelessly divided on who they should support. For the first time in 455 years there is a feeling – small and subdued though it is – that this time a non-Italian has at least a chance of being chosen pope.

*

Kite-flying, MacCarthy tells a Vatican Radio colleague dismissively, 'it is all pure kite-flying'. They are on the station's second floor beside the bank of wire-service teletypes churning out stories on Greeley and NORC's forecast of who will be pope.

MacCarthy is hard put to recall the former Chicago priest among the scores of other observers who for the past two weeks have been constantly drifting in and out of the building, seeking the help of Vatican Radio staff in understanding the many mysteries surrounding the election of a pontiff. MacCarthy is almost certain not one of his colleagues would have any part in this caper. But there it is, the Associated Press, cheekily catch-lining its story 'Vatican City' – perhaps to give it more credibility when the actual office of the agency is in the centre of Rome – boldly stating: COMPUTER PICKS URSI AS NEXT POPE.

A messenger tears off the message and adds it to a pile of others in a tray marked: CONCLAVE.

Though it is only mid-morning of this Thursday, 12 October, the basket is filled with the outpourings of the wire services. It has been like this all week, evidence of continuing, and increasing, media interest in the forthcoming Conclave.

MacCarthy tells his colleague, 'The whole thing is being over-played – there's this idea something quite extraordinary can happen. I don't buy it.'[1]

Much of what rests in the basket is assuredly pure speculation, often reflecting the attitude of reporters who, unlike MacCarthy, cannot accept that the Holy Spirit has an incalculable role to play.

Yet, Greeley's computer caper aside, the basket also contains proof there is no let-up in the concerted effort by the Italian press to get Siri elected. It has been forging ahead for three days, printing flattering profiles and glowing assessments of the archbishop of Genoa. To suggest this has any connection with 'consultation' is nonsense; what is happening is nothing less than a well-organized offensive, a determined bid to concentrate wonderfully the minds of the cardinal electors. This very Thursday morning, RAI, Italian state radio, broadcast a ten-minute eulogy about Siri, displaying the sort of unctuousness RAI in the past has reserved only for an elected pope.

MacCarthy's colleague, in fact one of the radio team which last time scooped the world with the help of the Conclave bug – he himself will insist he had no prior knowledge of the affair – sees the entire Siri operation as permissible psychological warfare; if successful, it could rule out any desire to penetrate this Conclave electronically and illegally. The man points to yet another wire service report clattering off the teletype. It claims Siri has a 'packet' of fifty committed votes.

He thinks, as do many others, that behind this sustained press campaign is the Curia once more intervening in the choice of a pope. The curial cardinals are trying to stampede those still uncommitted electors to throw in their lot with Siri, who has been given an editorial facelift in the media, so much so he is barely recognizable. The theory is plausible, given the 'soft centre' of the present Sacred College, evinced by how quickly these 'centrists' jumped on the bandwagon which swiftly put Gianpaolo into office.

MacCarthy remains sceptical. Assuming any of this is true, could it not be, he ponders, a cunning ruse by Siri's opponents? Perhaps they have arranged to focus all this attention on Siri on the basis of 'setting him up to knock him down', a phenomenon not uncommon in the politics of MacCarthy's birthplace. His enemies will have realized that Siri's record of arch-conservatism cannot stand up to the intense publicity he is getting; the more the lily is gilded, the more inevitable it is that an abreaction will set in. Indeed, continues the shrewd Irishman, indicating a UPA story, there is more than a hint this has already started. 'Informed sources' – MacCarthy smiles wryly at the words, wondering whether once more they indicate flummery rather than facts – are starting to remind people who Siri really is: the cardinal who detested John XXIII and Paul, the bishop who traduced the Second Vatican Council as 'the greatest disaster in recent ecclesiastical history', the prelate who drags his feet in the face of anything remotely 'liberalizing'. Is this the man, then, the agency story quotes those 'informed sources' as asking, who should be the next pope – no matter that Siri now calls himself a 'centrist', a 'moderate' and, even more whimsically, an 'independent'?

Reminded of this, McCarthy's suddenly crestfallen companion thinks not. He rifles through the basket, pausing at an Agence France Presse story. The agency claims the French cardinals believe it will be a short Conclave, 'no more than three days' is the reported confident prediction of Marty of Paris. AFP suggest the 'collective French view', drawing another wry smile from MacCarthy, is that, should Siri's bid fail, Felici will be the 'acceptable' compromise Italian candidate. No named source is given for this. Nor can MacCarthy divine who are the 'high sources' in another agency story which states that if the split in the Italian ranks continues, Hume, Willebrands and Gantin could all become candidates.

'So could everybody else in the Sacred College,' he growls.

MacCarthy, moulded by the inviolate rule of Vatican Radio, that nothing can be broadcast unless it is properly sourced, repeats it is all kite-flying. He and his colleague walk away from the teletypes.

*

Martin is entertaining Noé to lunch on Friday, 13 October, in the prefect's handsomely furnished apartment near the San Damaso Courtyard. The actual *cortile* has been boarded off in preparation for Conclave: this time the deliberating cardinals will have the benefit of striding over flagstones which the Renaissance popes first trod.

The elderly prefect asks again – indicating the newspaper open between them across the dining table – what will the cardinals make of *this*? It is a prominently displayed article in L'Osservatore della Domenica, a popular weekly illustrated companion of *L'Osservatore Romano*.

The article carries the staid headline, PROPHECY AND REALITY. But the clue to its potential impact, the reason for Martin's question about how the cardinals will react, is its author. Monsignor Corrado Balducci is a senior official in the Congregation for the Evangelization of Peoples, the old De Propaganda Fide. Around the Vatican, Balducci is known, not altogether facetiously, as the Resident Demonologist, the prelate who has made a study of the supernatural and in particular predictions of disaster. This time Balducci has been doing research which closely resembles that which MacCarthy did on the eve of the last Conclave. But whereas MacCarthy had then been certain Vatican Radio would never broadcast some of the direst predictions of the Irish saint, Malachy, Balducci has had no problem publishing Malachy's apocalyptic portrait of the next pontificate: 'There will be a great disaster, which could very likely be World War III.' In support of Malachy he cites the mysterious Third Secret of Fatima, the one only a new pope can see. Balducci ends his article with the warning: 'God cannot prevent such a scourge if mankind does not deserve it.'

Dire though the warning is, it is the relevancy to the papacy of what Balducci is saying which fascinates Noé and Martin. Coming as it does on the eve of Conclave, published in a most impeccable outlet, the article is bound to be seen as a timely reminder that in a threatened world only a strong-minded pope can lead the faithful from such a disaster. This is no time for mere 'pastorality', for trading jokes with children, for making analogies with Pinocchio. This is very much the time to go back to the hellfire-and-brimstone days, to remind the faithful what sort of faith is needed to ward off the evil eye. Unwritten though it is, the message is very clear to Noé and Martin: the cardinals must elect a man sufficiently resolute to take the Church through the stormy days ahead.

Balducci's position in the Curia, and the timing of the article, indicate the Siri faction has far from given up hope of having him elected. It is as clear as the sunlight streaming into Martin's dining room that Balducci's piece is meant to suggest that apocalypse soon can only be averted by electing Siri now.

But he is about to commit an astonishing act of *felo de se*.

*

Koenig cannot believe it. Yet there is the evidence — a couple of thousand words which must effectively put paid to Siri's chances of *ever* becoming pope.

It is breakfast time in the German-Hungarian College on Saturday, 14 October. This is normally the quietest period of the day when the cardinals and their entourages munch cold sausages and cheese and say little to each other.

Now, the room is awash with incredulous voices trying to make sense of what Siri has done. By any yardstick it is incredible – this most astonishing interview the archbishop of Genoa has given to *Gazzetta del Popolo*. He has trampled all over the memory of Gianpaolo by ridiculing the late pope's inaugural address. He has hit out at Villot by criticizing the way his Secretariat of State is run. Then, hardly pausing for breath, Siri swept aside any idea of serious collegiality among bishops during the next pontificate. The hapless reporter who sat through the tirade describes how he himself suffered Siri's wrath. Politely asked a question, the cardinal reportedly bristled, 'It is one I would only take from my confessor.' Asked another, Siri thundered, 'I don't know how you could ask such a stupid question. If you really want an answer, you will have to sit there and shut up for three hours.'

Koenig reads the story a second time. It appears even more incredible.

What can Siri have been thinking? The intemperate tone, the shocking personal abuse shown towards the reporter, this surely cannot be typical of a man who throughout the week has been running sure-footedly, so sweetly-reasonable through the media? Above all, why permit the interview to be published now – only hours before the cardinals go into Conclave, allowing no time for any of the heat to cool, when every damning word is at its most lethal?

Koenig does not know the answer.

But, just as Siri's outburst is so extraordinary, so are the reasons for its publication. Siri gave the interview the previous day on the strict understanding it would be embargoed for at least forty-eight hours, by which time all his fellow cardinals would be safely locked with him in Conclave and therefore unable to read what he'd said. The reporter agreed to Siri's proviso. Then, later on Friday, Siri gave a Genoa radio station an interview which was a watery version of what he had told *Gazzetta del Popolo*. It was broadcast within the hour, as, curiously, Siri made no embargo request of the station. Ansa, the Italian news agency, carried a brief account of the broadcast. Their wire-service teletype was seen in the newsroom of *Gazzetta del Popolo*. The editors concluded Siri had himself broken the embargo and decided to run their far more explosive interview this Saturday morning.

Even before Koenig reads it, Siri puts out a denial he gave the interview. The newspaper reporter immediately offers to make public his tape-recording of their meeting. Siri backs off. He has done himself even more damage.

As Koenig prepares to participate in the Mass for the Election of a

Pope, he delivers a final prediction on Siri. In his most velvety of tones, the Viennese murmurs to other cardinals waiting for the Mass to begin that if Siri is elected pope, he would 'have a simple, humble ceremony in St Peter's Square, but then afterwards, in private, he would have a marvellous coronation with all his friends present and incense billowing all over the place'.

They are *mots* which spell the *coup de grâce* for Siri. His chances are dead.

But Benelli's live on. Is this why, wonders Felici, the archbishop of Florence is taking in a typewriter to Conclave – so that he can type out his acceptance speech?

*

Dining alone on Saturday night does nothing for Greeley's spirits. For a start there is the attitude of the American cardinals – 'absolute pushovers for curial propaganda'. He is especially aggrieved with Carberry, not just because he's taken into Conclave ten chocolate bars, or because he has apparently told the American press now isn't the time for a non-Italian pope. That's fine by Greeley: he's still clinging to the hope Ursi will win. What irks him about Carberry is that 'the good cardinal of St Louis does not seem to comprehend that people are not expecting a Xerox copy' of Gianpaolo as the next pontiff.

And, nothing new in this, he's angry too: 'All right, we lost John Paul' – Greeley tells himself after dinner – '*why* is God's problem. If John Paul is replaced by business as usual, the people will be profoundly disillusioned. That's where lots of Catholics are today. They went through an interlude of being proud of Catholicism and had it snatched away from them; they want it back. Yet many of these clowns who are doing the voting don't perceive that.'

Some of these 'clowns' might also be hard put to it to understand why Greeley appears unable to refer to the last pope as everybody else does, with affectionate sadness, as Papa Gianpaolo.

Perhaps his attitude might stem from a confession he has put on tape about his sources.[2] There just don't seem enough of those unidentified yet wonderfully described figures he gives such colourful pseudonyms to. In fact there might be only one, 'Deep Purple', alias the Cincinnati Kid, the prelate whom some Vaticanologists think is Greeley's main informant, the archbishop of that city, Joseph Bernardin.

Right now the archbishop is back home. Which also might explain why, when Greeley returns to St Peter's Square and stares up at the moonlit outline of the Sistine Chapel in the sealed-off Conclave area, he asks himself plaintively one question. What's going on up there?

27

Over dinner in the Borgia Apartments – altogether too grand a setting for the modest fare of fettuccini *and* gelato di frutta *washed down with pitchers of wine – several cardinals venture Conclave might go into Monday. The observation is solemnly noted by the minor attendant who is once more keeping a secret diary.[1] Late into Saturday night he watches the 'factions' forming. The Italians, all twenty-seven of them, loosely divide their allegiance between four candidates: Benelli, Ursi, Felici and, in spite of his gaffe, Siri. Some of the Africans and Asians, if the free exchange of views in the corridors is any guide, are drawn either to Ursi or Benelli. Aramburu and some of the other South Americans also lean towards the archbishop of Florence. No other trend is discernible.*

Koenig, who until entering Conclave worked so assiduously promoting Wojtyla, retired early without appearing to have 'consulted' with anybody. The last cardinal is asleep by midnight.

Before breakfast next morning, Sunday, 15 October, Wojtyla in cell ninety-six was already engrossed in the latest statement from the government minister responsible for Church matters in Poland; under Communism, religion has a special political department in that country to watch over it.

Suenens of Belgium had an early meeting with Enrique y Tarancon of Spain; they spent the time talking about the state of the Spanish Church after Franco, and the crucial duty that the Spanish cardinals have to ensure their country's new-found democracia *does not lead to undesirable excesses.*

Both men must have been well aware of the role the quiet and thoughtful Enrique y Tarancon has created for himself. In previous Conclaves the influence of Spain's cardinals was, at best, minimal. Almost invariably they were firmly placed with one of the Italian 'factions'. But Enrique y Tarancon, during the nine years he has been cardinal, had been preparing his country for the momentous events which followed the death of Franco. To make the transition from dictatorship to democracy more bearable, he encouraged his bishops and priests to look beyond Rome. By doing so, he told them, they would be able to find what is good and could be adapted to the new mood of freedom in the Spanish Church. It had been a genuine voyage of discovery which was not always fully appreciated by Spanish traditionalists, inured and set in the religious mortar Franco used to bind the Church to him. Along that journey,

Enrique y Tarancon had discovered Wojtyla. He found that the Pole's vision of how the Church should develop was close to his own. When Koenig, an old friend, suggested the time had come for a non-Italian pope, Wojtyla came naturally to mind. During the past week, with all the instinctive good manners which make him such an engaging figure, Enrique y Tarancon had been pushing the Polish cardinal. It had been a discreet and dignified campaign.

Lorscheider of Brazil, following doctor's orders and as part of his recovery from recent heart surgery, walked steadily through the corridors, pausing to speak to everybody he met.

Two Africans, Gantin and Joseph Malula, archbishop of Kinshasa, strolled back and forth across the San Damaso Courtyard. Malula told Gantin what he had already told Time *magazine: 'All the imperial paraphernalia, all that isolation of the pope, all that medieval remoteness and inheritance that makes Europeans think that the Church is only Western – all that tightness makes them fail to understand that young countries like mine want something different. They want simplicity. They want Jesus Christ. They want change.'*

'That's why we're here,' said Gantin cheerfully. 'To make change happen.'

Breakfast was quickly over. The coffee was as dreadful as Sin remembered from last time. Along with the other hundred and ten cardinals he hurried to the Sistine Chapel, eager to start. There, the formalities – the election of Scrutineers, Infirmarii and Revisers – were swiftly completed. Noé departed and voting began.

The expected Italian challenge was obvious well before the last card was pierced by the threaded needle through the word 'Eligo'.

As in August, Siri topped the poll, this time with twenty-three votes. When news of this reached the general Conclave area, it caused considerable speculation. Siri's brutally frank interview, coupled to Balducci's call for an iron-fisted pope to ward off Armageddon – or something very close – was interpreted as indicating that the conservatives, far from running scared, were going all out for a quick victory. The twenty-three votes provided a respectable platform from which the Siri campaign could grow, attracting those 'soft centrists' willing to overlook some of his wilder pronouncements in the hope Siri would be the salve for the doom-laden future Balducci had indicated was waiting around the corner. Difficult though it may be to accept in a secular sense, Balducci's article had a marked effect on the minds of some cardinals. Many brought copies with them into Conclave where Balducci's warnings were a source of lengthy debate. The outcome had been this remarkable support for Siri.

Benelli received twenty-two votes. Nobody was very surprised; a good Benelli showing early on was a foregone conclusion. The question was whether his supporters would stay with him for the next ballot, when a more definite pattern might begin to emerge, or desert him for all the old reasons: the unease, suspicion and even distrust the archbishop of Florence could still evoke among his peers.

Ursi had eighteen votes. The general consensus among Conclave staff was that he was well placed, although not exceptionally so. Depending on continuing 'consultations', support could drift to him from Benelli, or vice-versa.

With seventeen votes, Felici surprised a number of people. Their interpretation – even allowing for Conclave's glasshouse atmosphere where so many opinions were forced to the surface before they could properly mature – had a certain fascination. Felici is almost as conservative as Siri. Perhaps Felici was making a showing as an alternative in case it should emerge that, after all, Siri would remain unacceptable even on the Day of Judgement for some cardinals.

A genuine surprise was the fifteen votes recorded for Pappalardo. What indeed could this mean? Nobody was quite sure, but the feeling was that he was a genuine compromise candidate, somebody to rally behind if the four Italian front-runners locked horns.

Wojtyla had five votes. The word was that his only visible response was to crease his broad Slav forehead with a frown. Such a modest return for all the hard work Koenig had put in may account for what some attendants insisted was barely disguised disappointment on the face of the archbishop of Vienna.

Among the remaining contenders receiving votes in this ballot were Poletti, who got four, and Gantin who had three. (One source insisted both Hume and Sin each received a vote.)

Everybody agreed that by mid-morning on Sunday it looked like a straight fight between the Italians.

The second ballot shortened the field. The results produced the first murmurs of real astonishment. Siri had suddenly fallen away. Only eleven cardinals, the very core of the curialist diehards, stayed with him. But it was all over; there was no way Siri could come back. The speculation on why he had failed would come later. There would be talk of deals and promises, of, as the secret diarist would write, 'the Holy Spirit and reality intervening'. It would all be irrelevant. The salient point was that shortly before noon, Siri was out of the running.

Ursi clung doggedly to his eighteen votes. His bolt was also shot. He had made no progress. In the next ballot his supporters would assuredly transfer their loyalties. Pappalardo's had already done so. He was no longer a contender.

Felici had climbed strongly with thirty votes. Almost all of them, it was assumed, came from Siri supporters. Felici was the cardinal the majority of the conservatives were indicating could be the man not only to ward off Balducci's predicted almost-end of the world, he might also achieve the equivalent of a miracle: bringing enough of the liberals over to him to get a quick victory.

There was only one flaw in this attractive scenario. Benelli had leapt ahead with forty votes. There will be talk that all his travelling, all his careful preparations, all those dinners at L'Eau Vive – all were beginning to pay off.

But he was still thirty-five crucial votes short of the seventy-five needed to win. There was a long way to go.

Wojtyla trailed with nine votes. This time he did not frown. He looked astonished. So they said. Many Conclavists found his modest advance puzzling. Who were those nine cardinals who felt compelled to support him?

Koenig was certainly one. In half a dozen separate conversations this Sunday morning he made it very plain where his loyalty lay.

Enrique y Tarancon was another. Yet only a few people found his support for Wojtyla significant. They were the ones who became aware of a brief meeting after breakfast between the Spaniard and Koenig. The alliance between the Viennese and Enrique y Tarancon was a bridge to the all-powerful voting bloc of South America, Africa and Asia. Enrique y Tarancon was not only the undisputed leader of the Spanish Church, he had tremendous influence in the Third World. Even the autocratic Aramburu was prepared to listen to him. With the Spaniard committed from the outset to Wojtyla, the way was open to garner in the forty-four other votes available from Spain, Latin America, Asia and Africa. It would also be reasonable to assume that Australia, New Zealand and Western Samoa could be persuaded. But the evidence of common attitude between Koenig and Enrique y Tarancon largely escaped notice.

So, too, did the equally crucial support of Krol. Almost certainly he had been one of the initial five who supported Wojtyla. The archbishop of Philadelphia knew his fellow Pole well, had entertained him in America, and had begun quietly to tell others that here indeed was a person of impeccable credentials. On this second ballot, Cody and Cooke came in to support the candidature of Karol Wojtyla.

But it did not look very serious. How could it? In spite of the fact that Koenig, Enrique y Tarancon and Krol had the closest possible connections and between them considerable influence over more than half of the cardinal electors, they had apparently so far been able only to marshal six others in the Sistine Chapel to vote for Wojtyla.

During lunch – a heavy meal of macaroni and similar pasta dishes accompanied by rather fruity red wine – there was some speculation about whether the Austrian–Spanish–American triumvirate had tried and failed to influence their colleagues, or were actually waiting to see how and where the Italian challenge would develop in the next ballot before they again took the initiative.

After lunch, Cody, Krol, Koenig and Enrique y Tarancon were repeatedly seen walking back and forth across the San Damaso Courtyard, deep in conversation. Later they were joined by Suenens and Marty. They subsequently returned to the Sistine Chapel for the third ballot.

Its result showed a further narrowing of the field.

Felici had been stopped. His total tally had slipped to twenty seven. He sat in his seat, drumming his fingers, a set, determined look on his face. So they said. Felici felt 'total acceptance'. So he said.

Eighteen voters remained loyal to Ursi. The question was not only why, but for how long?

Siri somehow still had five supporters. Nobody could understand this senseless squandering of votes.

Wojtyla's nine maintained what looked like a lost cause. The feeling was that they must soon leave this Pole alone with his charisma. There seemed no way he could improve his position.

Poletti and Gantin had dropped from view.

It was Benelli's round. He had forty-five votes.

Villot suggested there should be a thirty-minute pause before the fourth and final ballot for the day was cast.

Several significant meetings occurred during the break.

Enrique y Tarancon, Willebrands and Koenig met. Then the Spaniard had a meeting with Aramburu. At the same time Koenig was talking to both Sin and Gantin, key members of the Asia–African bloc. These meetings attracted interest, and there was speculation Koenig was going to throw in the towel and accept the fact that Wojtyla was now an also-ran. But for once there were no leaks; nobody really knew what was afoot.

Villot and Baggio met with Pignedoli in the bar-kitchen. Sipping coffee, they were overheard expressing their determination to stop the unthinkable happening: having to swallow the bitter past and, in the colourful words of that secret diarist, 'kiss the Florentine's Fisherman's Ring'. They would, of course, do precisely that if Benelli was elected. But, equally, they were determined to do everything possible to see it did not happen. Villot was deputized to call on Felici. While the Camerlengo shambled off, inevitable cigarette in mouth, yet another 'consultation' was under way.

Pappalardo, Poletti and Ursi met Benelli. The only sure thing about this encounter was that it was short. The four Italians separated with Benelli apparently having failed to get his companions' agreement to come over to his side.

It did not seem to matter much. In the next ballot, Benelli acquired a further twenty votes, giving him a total of sixty-five – a mere ten short of victory.

And Ursi's supporters had finally done what was expected of them hours earlier. All but four had left the agreeable archbishop of Naples.

It was where Ursi's erstwhile supporters went which surprised so many.

Wojtyla suddenly had twenty-four votes. The significance of the quiet 'consultations' Koenig, Enrique y Tarancon and Krol had initiated became clear. Yet their real sway had only just started. Whether it could gain momentum at this late stage – with Benelli in sight of the Throne of St Peter – was anybody's guess.

The speculation this caused was only matched by the buzz of astonishment which followed the announcement that a new contender had entered the list. He was Cardinal Giovanni Colombo, the seventy-six-year-old archbishop of Milan. He had not been thought papabile *when he came into the Conclave. But with some firm persuasion from Villot and Felici – the outcome of their meeting had evidently been a strengthening of the stop-Benelli movement – Colombo had agreed to be cast in the role of the Curia's compromise candidate. He would take up the mantle originally meant for Felici. Colombo was, in the convoluted language of one curialist, 'a conservative moderate'. He was somewhat to the left of Felici but nowhere near Benelli, who was characterized as a captive of the non-Italian cardinals, as the Italian who would destroy the Italian papacy, and as the old foe of the Curia who had already caused havoc by imposing an inexperienced Gianpaolo on the Church's civil service.*

Colombo was there to stop Benelli. That he was old, frail, and not too bright, did not matter. He was Italian and quite possibly the only candidate able to halt Benelli. Colombo would keep the papacy well and truly in the family.

Fourteen cardinals had voted for him.

It was a fitting end to a remarkable day in the Sistine Chapel.

*

After supper – pasta in brodo, insalata *and beer or wine – Koenig, enrique y Tarancon and Krol were busy stressing to various cardinals there really was no basis for the somewhat desperate case against Wojtyla which had emerged from the Benelli camp: namely, that to elect a pope from behind the Iron Curtain would have extraordinary political consequences for the Church. The risks, Koenig patiently and quietly insisted, could be far outweighed by the benefits.*

Each of Wojtyla's three advocates had their own very different manner of promoting his cause.

Koenig correctly gauged that, in Europe, the support of the five German cardinals was crucial; any wavering among the French and Dutch would almost certainly cease once the Germans were fully committed. And the German Church was heavily involved in supporting the Third World: Ratzinger and Hoeffner in particular could be expected to lend their considerable authority to round up any remaining Third World candidates. Koenig intuitively pitched his arguments on a level his listeners could hardly resist. He reminded them Wojtyla was a resilient enemy of Communism, itself a perpetual bogey in a country which borders Eastern Europe and whose populace firmly believes the day may come when the Russians will roar up the Autobahn, overrunning West Germany on their way to conquering all of Free Europe. As pope, Wojtyla would be able to call upon his already vast experience of the Communist menace, as well as making the best use of his formidable strength to face the challenge of religious persecution behind the Iron Curtain. Finally, Koenig shrewdly reminded the Germans Wojtyla had publicly asked the German

Church to forgive the Polish Church for 'whatever offences' it had committed. It was the clincher – and placed all five Germans in the Wojtyla camp.

Krol stressed the qualities of the man he knew well: Wojtyla's fearlessness, his physical prowess, the way he could ski, fish and run with the best of them; his poetry, his modesty, his 'sensible attitudes' to Church dogma as a firm middle-of-the-roader; in short, the sort of person who, but for an accident of birth, could have been a typical, and ideal, American: Krol's fellow Americans were impressed.

Enrique y Tarancon looked into the future. Wojtyla's background, he told colleagues from Latin America, would make him the perfect type to deal with the problems of the Third World. They listened attentively.

The lobbying was low-keyed and relaxed; so much so that some of the Americans – Manning, Carberry and Dearden – would later insist there had been no electioneering. Several cardinals retired early on Sunday night to read copies of Wojtyla's Segno di Contraddizione, *the Lateran Retreat which Koenig had thoughtfully brought into the Conclave. It was all part of the careful light-touch strategy.*

*

Conclave was barely stirring on Monday morning, 16 October, when news swept the enclave that Colombo, after a night of prayer and reflection, no longer wished to be considered. (One source insists Colombo made his decision on Sunday evening after he was visited by Benelli. Benelli denied any such meeting took place.) It was sensational enough for Felici to hurry to Colombo's room. The two men spent a short time together, perhaps no more than five minutes. Felici emerged, according to one eyewitness – not a cardinal – even more set-faced than he was when his own candidature had collapsed in the Sistine Chapel. Felici then went to Villot. They were still together when breakfast was announced. By then most people knew Colombo was out. He was himself one of the first to sit at table; an observer said the old man looked ten years younger.

Wojtyla appeared with the senior Polish cardinal, Stefan Wyszynski. They took their places opposite Koenig and Krol. Koenig raised his coffee cup in silent salute. Krol smiled warmly at Wojtyla and said, in Polish, 'It's okay.'

There was no response. Wojtyla sat, head down, eyes fixed on his plate. Nobody could really tell what he thought.

The Benelli camp occupied the long centre table in the dining room. The predominantly Italian faction was accompanied by some of those outsiders whom the curialists accused the archbishop of Florence of selling out to: there was Owen McCann, the archbishop of Cape Town; Lawrence Picachy, a Jesuit, archbishop of Calcutta and president of the Indian Bishops' Conference; Antonio Ribeiro, patriarch of Lisbon; Franjo Seper of Yugoslavia; Stephanos Siderouss of Egypt. It was a mixed bag but one capable of exerting itself vigorously.

With Colombo departing as swiftly as he had been pressganged into entering, his fourteen votes would have to be redeployed.

The possibilities for even more drama was clear to everybody. It was likely the four votes for Ursi would now switch to Benelli. There was a mood among the increasingly gloomy Italians that even Benelli, in the last resort, was better than losing the papacy to a non-Italian. If the switch did occur, then it would need just six of those fourteen Colombo votes to see Benelli elected. The feeling was that even among the diehards six might be persuaded to endorse their old enemy, if only for the sake of Italian continuity in the papacy.

Amid considerable expectancy and some tension, the cardinals filed to the altar to cast their first votes of the day.

Benelli moved up to seventy votes, just five short of victory. Wojtyla had forty.[2]

Villot ordered a break of fifteen minutes for those who wished to take coffee or other light refreshments.

Wojtyla promptly went to his room and pointedly closed the door, a clear sign he did not wish to be disturbed.

Wyszynski huddled with Koenig and Enrique y Tarancon outside the Sistine Chapel. The Pole and the Austrian spoke German, which Koenig translated into Spanish for Enrique y Tarancon.

There was no need for Koenig to translate Wyszynski's vigorous assertion, 'Es wird passieren.'

Enrique y Tarancon agreed, 'Sí, esto ocurrirá.'

Certainly it could happen. But Benelli was very, very close. The next ballot might well see him elected.

It was not to be. In the course of fifty-five momentous minutes, no fewer than eleven votes switched from Benelli to Wojtyla. The tally was now fifty-nine to Benelli and fifty-two for Wojtyla. It was all over for the archbishop of Florence. But this did not guarantee that Wojtyla would win. He still needed at least twenty-three more votes.

The cardinals broke for lunch. Hemmed in by supporters determined he should not now retire to his room, Wojtyla was led into the dining hall.

Wyszynski took him by the arm and whispered in Polish, 'The Holy Spirit demands you accept what is happening.'

Koenig quickly translated the words into German and Spanish. Encouraging responses were directed at Wojtyla. He seemed to Koenig 'a good example of pale and pensive'. The Viennese poured himself some wine from one of the pitchers on the table and raised his glass towards Wojtyla. This impromptu toast led to others. Soon cardinals as far up the table as Basil Hume of England, ten places from Wojtyla, were turning and toasting the Pole. For a while he remained silent. Then, in a low and intense voice, he said, 'No, no, no.'

Enrique y Tarancon, fearful of any disruption to the new-found momentum, *quickly intervened, 'Sí, sí, sí.' Pointing at the food, cannelloni, the Spaniard said, 'Buen* provecho!'

Wojtyla grunted, 'Smacznego.' He began slowly to stuff forkfuls of the rolled pasta into his mouth.

The Benelli table – not a strictly accurate description, for his supporters were scattered all around the room – was downcast.[3]

Lunch was an unusually lengthy one: nobody seemed anxious to leave in case they missed a new development. When dessert was served, a straight choice between ice cream and fruit, Willebrands and Baggio came over to Wojtyla. They simply stood close to him, saying nothing, lending him their silent approval.

Finally, when the nuns began rather pointedly to clear the tables, the cardinals drifted out, many heading for the sunny confines of the San Damaso Courtyard.

There Ratzinger and Hoeffner quietly concentrated on any Third World cardinals they thought might still be hesitating. During the course of the next hour the archbishops of the Dominican Republic, Guatemala, Sri Lanka and Indonesia were all gently spoken to.

In the meantime Koenig and Wyszynski were closeted with Wojtyla in his room. Wojtyla sat on his bed, hands clasped between his knees, head bowed. Wyszynski perched on the edge of the only chair in the room. Koenig leant against the closed door, effectively barring entry to anyone who might wish to come in.[4]

Wyszynski spoke first. Gripping the arms of the chair he said to Wojtyla, 'You will have to accept.' He turned to Koenig. 'You tell him.'

Koenig shrugged. 'I have.' He looked at Wojtyla. 'You simply must face the truth. This is what the Holy Spirit wishes.'

'It is a mistake.' Wojtyla's response was barely audible.

'There is no mistake. Look at the figures. There is the proof.' Koenig's deeply felt compassion for Wojtyla softened the words.

Wyszynski rose from his chair and stood over Wojtyla. The old cardinal reached out and gently touched the younger man's bowed head. 'Please, Karol. This is right. For the Church. For Poland. For you.'

There was no response.

'Please, Karol. Do not resist what is right.'

This time there was the tiniest of head movement, so slight Koenig could not be certain what it meant.

'You will accept?' Koenig's voice was uncertain.

'If that . . .' Wojtyla did not complete the sentence.

'It is. It is right,' insisted Wyszynski.

This time Wojtyla's nod was more discernible. 'Let us see what happens this afternoon.'

Koenig moved away from the door, lowering his voice. 'That is right. But you must prepare yourself now for the outcome.'

When it became clear that Wojtyla was not going to respond, Koenig continued. 'You must be called John Paul the Second.'

Wojtyla raised his head and looked at Koenig.

Koenig smiled. 'Do not look so worried. You have been chosen for this. That is clear. You are *going to be elected pope. And you* must *be called like that because that is a mark of the continuity we all want.'*

Wojtyla asked that they now leave him so he could pray alone.

'We shall all pray,' promised Koenig.

*

The first ballot of the afternoon was decisive.

Wojtyla had seventy-three votes. Benelli's support had dropped to thirty-eight.

At 5.20 in the afternoon, the result of the eighth and final ballot was read out.

Wojtyla had ninety-seven votes.

Thunderous and sustained applause swept through the Sistine Chapel. Then Villot rose and began to walk towards the slumped figure of the archbishop of Cracow. Wojtyla sat, head in his hands, tears running between his broad fingers, a suddenly lonely and isolated figure beneath Michelangelo's apocalyptic 'Last Judgement'.

28

The door of the Sistine Chapel opens and Noé stands there, looking inside. He is transfixed by what he sees.

Behind him, craning their necks, is a group of open-mouthed attendants who have been drawn here by the thunderous noise. Within minutes the corridor is completely filled by supporting players in the drama which has occurred. Nuns come rushing from the kitchen; the barber and the electrician, the bed-makers and the floor-sweepers, even the counter-electronic surveillance men with their sensors are pushing and shoving to see what is happening.

Noé remains in the doorway, overwhelmed. He is certain there have never before been scenes quite like this in the Sistine. Here, where Philibert of Orange once casually stabled his horses while his army pillaged and raped its way through the Vatican, bringing a fear not since equalled, there is on this sunny Monday evening four hundred years later a joy also unequalled.

Most cardinals are on their feet, still clapping wildly. Others, the Africans and South Americans, are using their clenched fists to hammer the table tops. Polynesia's Pio Taofinu'u is swaying gently to his own rhythm. Several of the Italians are shouting 'Viva! Viva!'

Koenig, architect of the victory, alternately takes off his spectacles, polishes them, and puts them on again – only to have to remove them once more when they mist up. If he is not crying, it is something remarkably close.

Enrique y Tarancon also displays a repetitive reaction. He stands up, sits down, and stands up again, applauding and smiling non-stop; no one has ever seen this serious-faced Spaniard so happy in public.

Krol is talking animatedly to some of the other Americans, communicating to them his 'elation and exhilaration'. In all the hubbub his listeners can hardly hear him.

Felici has balled one fist and is pounding it into the other; he looks more than ever like an emperor bestowing his accolade.

Siri manages a wintry smile. Yet his applause is as sustained as any of the cardinals'.

The Germans are ecstatic. Not only are they congratulating each other with formal handshakes, but Ratzinger, in a totally unexpected demonstration of emotion, cries out that the Holy Spirit has prevailed.

Basil Hume shows more restraint. His smile is reserved, but his approbation is genuine.

Benelli is gracious in defeat, grinning and nodding towards where Villot now towers over Wojtyla.

He remains a bowed and isolated figure, hands locked tightly together, apparently oblivious of the noise.

The Camerlengo extends his arms, slowly dipping them in an ungainly movement, like a tired old bird flapping its wings. It is his way of asking for silence.

Noé turns and motions the crowd in the corridor to stand back. They reluctantly retreat a few feet. There are excited whispers of, 'Who is it?'

Ignoring them, Noé moves inside to Villot.

The ovation continues. Villot's movements become more agitated; his arms have a formication all of their own. He looks around, beseechingly.

Gradually the clamour dies. The cardinals resume their seats, staring at the isolated figure of Wojtyla.

Noé nudges Villot. The Camerlengo coughs.

Wojtyla's head remains bowed.

Villot taps him lightly on the shoulder.

At last Wojtyla raises his head.

Koenig, seated a few feet away, is relieved. Whereas in Albino Luciani's countenance there had been 'a certainty', there is in Karol Wojtyla's 'a firm resolution, the face of a man who has come to terms with what God wants of him.'

Krol thinks he is witnessing 'not the loneliness of the long-distance pope but a strong man taking up a great task.'

Hume's reaction is equally interesting. He feels 'desperately sad for the man. Yet somebody has to carry the tremendous burden.'

Clasping his hands before him, Villot peers down at Wojtyla.

Cody is not the only person present to realize the significance of the moment: 'This is no eyeball-to-eyeball; this is the abnegation of the old order, the end of the Italian domination of the papacy, the start of the new order from Poland.'

For a long moment – Felici thinks it may have been a full thirty seconds – the two men continue to stare wordlessly at each other.

Then, in Latin, Villot poses his first question.

'Do you, Most Reverend Lord Cardinal, accept your election as Supreme Pontiff, which has been canonically carried out?'

The tears which Wojtyla had wiped away before raising his head well up once more.

Felici is deeply moved. He thinks it takes an unusually balanced personality to display emotion so freely: 'This is not a neurotic response, it is a man responding from the heart about what he feels.'

Wojtyla quickly blinks his eyes. Then in a steady and resonant voice, carefully pitched to reach all corners of the Chapel, he makes his response, also in Latin.

'With obedience in faith to Christ, my Lord, and with trust in the Mother of Christ and the Church, in spite of great difficulties, I accept.'

Tumultuous applause sweeps the Sistine. It is taken up by the Conclave staff bunched in the Chapel doorway.

Villot flaps his arms. But it is now just a meaningless gesture. The old Camerlengo is smiling as hugely as everybody else.

Finally, undoubtedly eager to hear the answer to Villot's next question, the cardinals subside. Noé glances towards the doorway. It is enough to stop the excited whispering there.

Villot asks: 'By what name will you be known?'

Koenig glances at Wyszynski. He is staring intently at Wojtyla. Wyszynski's lips are trembling, whether in prayer or excitement, Koenig cannot tell.

In a voice even more declamatory, Karol Wojtyla announces his decision.

He will be known as John Paul the Second.

Villot smiles, turns to face the altar and then, departing from protocol, he impulsively swings back to embrace the new pope.

Noé, mindful of the need to adhere to precedent, goes to the door and gives his first instructions of the pontificate. He orders an assistant to have the Conclave area opened, to give Martin the news, to have the prefect summon Gammarelli, to remove the seals on the papal apartment and to request a team of nuns dust off and air the place. Then Noé hurries back to Villot. John Paul is receiving one joyful cardinal after another. Villot respectfully intervenes and, accompanied by Koenig, Krol and Enrique y Tarancon, he takes the pope to the sacristy to await the arrival of the tailor.

John Paul walks directly to the rack holding the vestments the House of Gammarelli delivered just before Conclave. He inspects them briefly and then makes his choice.

'I don't need anyone to dress me,' he says jovially to Koenig, in German. (John Paul converses in a mixture of Polish, German, Italian and a little French. Many present in the sacristy well remember how even there he switched from one language to another with ease.)

The pope dons the white linen cassock and secures its white sash. The robe is a reasonably good fit. When moments later Gammarelli is ushered into the sacristy by Martin; the tailor can immediately see that it will take him only minutes to make the minimal adjustments required.

*

'*Un polacco?*'

Greeley fancies he hears the word repeated endlessly across crowded St Peter's Square. The disbelieving whisper rustles through the throng, passing on the news that the first non-Italian pope since Adrian VI died on 14 September 1532, is a Pole. Greeley, putting behind him the computer prediction that Ursi would be the man shortly to step past the glass doors opening onto the central balcony of the Basilica, senses the 'angry, confused and sullen' mood of the crowd. They continue to stare incredulously up at Felici who has just made the historic announcement: '*Habemus Papam. Carolum Sanctae Romanae Ecclesiae Cardinalem Wojtyla.*'

Felici is joined by Noé and together they drape a red-bordered white papal tapestry over the balustrade. It still bears the coat of arms of Gianpaolo.

Someone asks Greeley whether the pope is a black.

'*No.*'

'*Asiatico?*'

'*No. Un polacco.*'

'*Un polacco?*'

Felici and Noé leave the floodlit balcony briefly, then they are back, standing either side of the door, looking expectantly into the Basilica. There is movement there. But nobody in the square can actually see what is happening.

*

Gammarelli makes a final adjustment to John Paul's cassock. Satisfied, the tailor steps back. There is no doubt about it, he murmurs to Martin, no pope has looked finer in his vestments.

John Paul's red velvet mozzetta is a perfect fit, resting comfortably on his broad shoulders, its golden-trimmed front falling cleanly over his chest. The white silk skullcap is firmly in place, enhancing his strong, broad face.

In the past few minutes, between the walk from the sacristy to where John Paul now waits to step onto the balcony, his tailor has detected a definite change in the pope's demeanour.

There is a look in the deep-set eyes which was not there before; it was present when Gammarelli made that final adjustment: almost a warning that this is not a man who wants to be bothered with the trifles of life. There is now also an impatient thrust to John Paul's strong chin.

345

He really wants to get on with it, thinks the tailor; he is clearly anxious to get down to the real business of being a pope.

John Paul stands a few feet from the doors to the balcony. Straight ahead is the towering obelisk of Caligula, where Nero had burned the Christian martyrs, where St Peter was crucified and St Paul beheaded. Beyond runs the Via della Conciliazione, lined with the buses which have brought the faithful and the merely curious to the great piazza.

Close behind John Paul is Villot and other cardinals. But most have retired to their rooms to rest before dinner.

The pope begins to move onto the balcony when Noé motions him back. John Paul hesitates for the merest fraction. Then, picking up stride, he brushes aside the master of ceremonies with one impatient flick of his hand.

At 7.21 pm precisely he steps into the spotlight.

*

MacCarthy feels a sudden tension. He is in Vatican Radio's mobile studio atop Bernini's colonnade. It offers a near-perfect vantage point from which to view the scene on the balcony. But for once there is almost nothing for the broadcaster to do. A Vatican Radio microphone is on the balcony to pick up the first public words of the pope for transmission live around the world.

Waiting for him to appear, MacCarthy has tried to place the election in some sort of perspective. He sees the pope's choice of name as significant, a clear-cut statement that the papacy will continue a line which did not have time to be consolidated during the short pontificate of Gianpaolo. The relative youth of the new pope, fifty-eight, removes any thought he was elected only as a transition pontiff; instead he could be reigning at the start of the next century. Yet now, in the first minutes of his reign, John Paul might stumble.

Looking down on the piazza, MacCarthy senses this is predominantly a Roman crowd, one used to Italian popes. A slip now, and this newcomer will be lost, perhaps forever. The word would spread. Everything John Paul would subsequently do or say could have appended to it the pejorative: 'un polacco'. The Romans can be very cruel to their own, as Paul had learned. With an outsider they could be vicious. This is why MacCarthy continues to feel tense as John Paul steps forward to the microphone.

The pope stands directly under the name of the Borghese Paul V, emblazoned across the façade above the balcony. He lifts his arms in a gesture of greeting and acknowledgement, a shy smile on his lips. Then in a strong voice he gives his first blessing to the city and to the world.

'All honour to Jesus Christ,' he chants.

'Now and forever,' responds the crowd.

He lowers his hands and grips the top of the tapestry. For a moment he waits. There is nothing nervous about the pause. It is the action of a man who knows the effect he wants to create. When he speaks there is a surprised and delighted roar from the piazza. He looks *un polacco*, but his Italian is almost perfect.

'May Jesus Christ be praised.'

'Now and forever,' roars the crowd.

'Dearest brothers and sisters . . . '

There is wild cheering. The throng does not need reminding this was how Gianpaolo used to address them.

'We are still all grieved after the death of that most beloved pope . . . '

John Paul waits, content to let the applause roll on.

MacCarthy relaxes. It's going to be all right, he tells himself, it really is going to be all right.

The pope's voice booms out and the crowd obediently falls silent.

'Behold, the most eminent cardinals have called forth a new Bishop of Rome, called him from a far-off country, far, but still so near, because of the unity of faith and Christian tradition.'

Huzzahs of encouragement rise from the square.

'I was afraid to receive this nomination . . . '

Another pause. Sections of the crowd shout out he has nothing to fear.

John Paul's voice changes. It becomes deeper and more vibrant.

'But I . . . but I accepted out of love and veneration for Jesus Christ and the Holy Mother . . . '

He stares down at them. They stare back.

'I don't know if I speak your . . . ' A suspicion of a chuckle. '*Our* Italian . . . '

A delighted burst of laughter.

'*Our* Italian well enough. If I make a mistake you will correct me.'

The ecstatic cheering of the crowd continues unchecked for a full half-minute.

John Paul's arms are extended again.

'Thus I present myself to you in our mutual faith and confidence in the Mother of Christ and our Church. And, also, to start on that road, the road of history and the Church, beginning with the help of God and the help of men.'

Now there is no stopping the crowd. The joyous tumult nearly drowns the sound of the six great bells of St Peter's ringing out their jubilation.

The pope stands perfectly still. He spreads his arms wide in embrace. Almost magically the noise stops.

'Blessed be the name of the Lord,' he chants.

'Now and forever,' responds the crowd.

'Our help in the name of the Lord,' intones the pope.

'Who has made Heaven and earth.'

With a majestic sweep of his arms, John Paul traces his first papal blessing in the Roman night air.

'May the blessing of Almighty God, Father, Son and Holy Spirit, descend upon you and remain forever. Amen.'

He turns and leaves the balcony as the huge ovation continues.

*

Lambert Greenan is relieved he is not involved in the production of the special edition of *L'Osservatore Romano* to commemorate the election. The possibility of a Polish pope was never seriously considered by any of the editors asked to submit short-lists. The result is confusion.

Thankfully, thinks Greenan, the panic is happening well away from his quiet enclave. There are still two days to go before the press date for his weekly English-language edition. The timing of the new pope's election suits him perfectly: there is time to think, time to shape those elegant phrases Greenan is famed for, time to make a more mature assessment.

Sipping a whiskey – he has chosen a twelve-year-old Irish to mark the occasion – Greenan sits at his desk, Roman collar unbuttoned, sleeves rolled up, glasses perched on the end of his nose, alternately reading and pondering before occasionally making a brief, cryptic note.

He is convinced that not only is the election of a Polish pontiff in itself an event of extreme importance, but in choosing the first non-Italian for almost five centuries the normally cautious College of Cardinals displayed an imaginative rashness which has moved the papacy from the conventional certitude of the old Roman order to somewhere potentially far more exciting – yet possibly fraught with dangers.

Greenan expects that John Paul, simply because of his background, must possess a very particular experience of some of the greatest problems confronting the Church.

He's a Pole, the editor reminds himself, and Poles have their own special national attitudes stemming from that country's historic and geographical situation.

'The Irish of Middle Europe?' he scribbles. Greenan sips whiskey and adds, 'Perhaps not. But close.'

The editor ruminates. Above all John Paul will undoubtedly have been raised in the tradition that the Polish Church remains, in spite of Communism, the true custodian of Polish nationhood. Greenan knows that during the long, dark period of foreign occupation, first under the

Germans and then the Russians, the Polish Church had been directly responsible for preserving the identity of the country. It continues to do so. Despite brutal pressure from Poland's Communist Party, the Church has managed to keep itself an intact institution without whose consent the nation cannot properly be governed.

In recent years – Greenan makes another note that coincidentally this is the period during which John Paul's own career in the hierarchy developed – the Polish Church has reached a more stable understanding with the Polish government; there is cautious recognition on both sides of the need for coexistence. The pressures are still there, but the Church in Poland flourishes. Either despite persecution or because of it, the churches are full; in terms of faith, the Holy Roman Catholic and Apostolic Church of Poland is stronger than in any Western country.

Once more Greenan reaches into his own background for a comparison. He makes another jotting: 'Stronger even than Ireland where religion and nationalism go hand in hand.'

Greenan wonders whether this could be one of the underlying reasons John Paul was elected. Is this the Sacred College's means of coping with the undeniable problems of Euro-Communism, the way its creed has eaten even into the Catholic strongholds of Western Europe? Is not John Paul's own success in battling with Communism a shining example showing that the Communist doctrine is not invincible, that in the competition for the confidence and support of his people, the Church not the Party has emerged victorious?

It is very possible John Paul's experience of living under Communism has not only tested his faith and his courage and given him the inner strength which comes only to those who have learned to resist, but it may also have convinced him that a godless authoritarian structure can only successfully be resisted by a God-fearing one. It would be good if this were so, Greenan decides; firmness is a valuable quality in these times when Christian values are being eroded on all sides.

Yet the real issue, the editor thinks, may be a more subtle one: can a pope who has been schooled in the direct confrontation between an embattled Polish Church and an atheist government possibly possess the subtlety and flexibility of thinking needed to cope with the many more challenges – far more varied than any Poland can throw up – which the Church faces throughout the world?

Greenan slowly sips his whiskey, lost in contemplation. Overnight the entire Church has been set on a journey the end of which cannot be known. The Polish regime, and behind them the Russians, will undoubtedly not like the idea of a Polish pope, one whose election is bound to have the effect of strengthening still further religious faith under Communism. Equally, oppressed Catholics throughout Communist Europe will see John Paul's election as confirmation of the Church's continued concern for them; it will be a beacon which will point them forward. But where could all this ultimately lead? Bold and brave though the decision to elect a Polish pope was, Greenan is suddenly aware it has also created a situation where dangerous human, political and religious forces alien to the Church could be unleashed.

The phone interrupts Greenan's meditations. (Greenan will remember this call just as vividly as his earlier one from Cody; he thinks it 'may be because it isn't every day I get called by an exalted cardinal.')

'Lambert?'

'Cardinal Cody?'

'Who else? How you been?'

'Fine, Eminence.'

'Well, I got bad news for you.'

'Not again, Eminence?'

Cody had previously provisionally accepted Greenan's second invitation to dine with him this evening at his priory.

'The pope wants us to eat and pray with him. Very Polish.'

'Also very Irish, Eminence.'

'Polish. Irish. Same thing where I come from,' growls Cody. 'OK. You ask me again. Understand?'

'Perfectly, Eminence.'

A sudden thought strikes Greenan. The Chicago cardinal has a large number of Poles in his diocese. It's worth a try.

'Eminence, what's the new pope like?'

'Huh?'

'You've met him, of course?'

'Sure. Lots of times. A great man. Let me tell you a few things . . . '

For the next twenty minutes Greenan listens to one cardinal's very personal view of the new pontiff. The editor will decide that what he hears is too privileged ever to be revealed.

The riveting call ends on a high note.

'Lambert, you listen to me. This is going to be the greatest pope, ever. You got that? Ever.'

Without waiting to say goodbye Cody rings off.

*

During dinner in the Hall of the Popes, John Paul moves among his cardinals.

He has a friendly word for each, physically embracing many. When Wyszynski struggles to rise from his place, the pope gently eases him down and bends to whisper in his ear. The old warrior nods. Both are close to tears.

John Paul moves on. As he reaches Villot he quietly enquires whether any champagne is available.

Villot grins. *'Oui, Santissimo Padre. Mais oui!'*

Tight though his budget has been, the Camerlengo presciently purchased three crates of champagne to be brought into Conclave. He somehow had a feeling the wine might be needed.

He passes the request on to Noé.

The master of ceremonies is dumbfounded. 'Champagne? Here?'

'Oui! Et tout de suite!' replies the delighted Frenchman.

Soon afterwards nuns arrive with bottles and trays full of fluted glasses. They hover, uncertain.

The pope beckons them to him. He takes a magnum and expertly uncorks it. He tells Noé to begin opening the others.

Then, tray-bearing nuns in tow, John Paul moves around the Hall, pouring each cardinal a glass. When a bottle is emptied he hands it to a nun and takes another from Noé. Caught up in the spirit of the occasion the master of ceremonies is soon drawing corks with the aplomb of a wine steward.

As John Paul gives Krol his champagne, he says, 'I must return to Philadelphia soon so you and I can sing together again.'

Krol replies, 'Any time, any day.'

Perhaps it was overhearing this which gave Terence Cooke, archbishop of New York, the idea. He turns to Krol.

'Why don't you sing now?'

Krol hesitates. 'Sing here? What?'

'Anything. Something appropriate.'

Krol sips champagne. 'Perhaps something they like in Poland?'

'Good. That would be very good.'

Krol rises, Gradually his rich voice can be heard round the room, quelling all conversation. He is singing the Latin lament, *Plurimos annos plurimos*, a wish for a long life.

Other cardinals begin to join in. They stand.

John Paul grins and continues pouring champagne with, if anything, more verve.

Krol comes to the end. There is applause. The pope beams approvingly, clearly enjoying the impromptu celebration.

'Sing "The Mountaineer",' suggests Cody, expansively waving his glass. 'Sing "The Mountaineer". It's a great favourite of His Holiness.'

'In Polish,' adds Wyszynski. The old cardinal has a look of triumph and anticipation in his eyes. Possibly more than anyone in the Hall, he recognizes the deeper implications for both the Church and the secular world of having a Polish pope. In fractured German he tells Koenig, 'Everything is going to be different, very different.'

Koenig nods in agreement.

Wyszynski repeats that Krol should sing the words in Polish.

Clearing his throat, the archbishop of Philadelphia launches into the traditional *Goralu, czy ci nie za.*

There is silence as people begin to lower their glasses and listen to Krol's powerful voice. Few of them understand the words: 'Mountaineer, why are you leaving your beautiful hills and silvery brooks? – For bread, Lord, for bread.' But the words do not matter; the feeling conveyed by Krol transcends any need for translation.

He comes to the end of his rendition.

There is quiet applause as people look towards the pope.

In the gentlest of voices John Paul speaks. 'That was beautiful. Would you please sing it again?'

Wyszynski has a suggestion. 'Instead of singing "For bread, Lord, for bread", sing "For You, Lord, for You".'

Krol nods. Again his voice fills the chamber.

While he is singing, John Paul quietly continues pouring champagne. When Krol finishes his second version, the pope has another request.

'Sing it once more.' It is not a command, more a plea.

'And I will join in,' says John Paul.

Krol launches himself for the third time into the evocative ballad.

Martin shakes his head disbelievingly at Noé. The prefect probably knows as much as anyone present about papal elections but he has never seen, or heard of, anything remotely like this. As Martin watches, the pope, still singing in accompaniment with Krol and having finished dispensing champagne to the cardinals, now begins to serve the nuns.

For Noé, steeped in the stifling tradition of the Italian papacy, this is simply incredible. The pope is casually pouring champagne for nuns and singing as though he's been doing both all his adult life.

'It must be the Polish way of doing things,' says Martin in wonderment.

When the song ends, amid the applause Krol and the pope embrace. They converse happily in Polish. Some of the Italian cardinals, whose language has so often dominated such occasions, are seen to exchange wan smiles with each other. They have no idea what is being said.

Jaime Sin is not the only one in the Hall to be overheard wondering whether this is the Italian way of putting on a brave face – or whether it may possibly signify something else.

*

Agca has been back in Istanbul a week – back in this stinking rented room off Orou Cad, behind the great Mosque of Sultan Süleyman the Magnificent.

Before they parted on the freezing slopes of Mount Ararat, Teslin Tore told him that a further thirty thousand lire would be credited on this Monday to his account at an Istanbul branch of the *Turkye Is Bankasi*.

A few hours ago, as Tore had instructed, Agca went to the bank with his passbook. A teller took it from him and he was asked to wait. When the teller returned he handed back the passbook to Agca. It contained the new lodgement.

Agca had returned to this room, to flop on its rickety bed and endlessly study the passbook. On paper, by Turkish standards, he was now a wealthy man. He has the equal of almost five thousand American dollars to his name, more money, he is sure, than anyone in Yesiltepe can ever dream of possessing.

But Tore was adamant. Agca must not withdraw any of the money until told. Tore had explained this was 'a test'.

Agca understands. In the Grey Wolves there are constant tests, designed to measure a member's loyalty, his strengths and weaknesses.

It is the instructions Tore has given him about the Grey Wolves which Agca finds puzzling. Tore ordered that no one in the organization must become aware of their secret meeting on Mount Ararat. Yet he also insisted he has the same goal as Colonel Turkes – to drive out of Turkey all hated Western influence and return the country to the 'old ways'.

Turkes, Tore claims, is personally ambitious and extremely dangerous to anybody who recognizes him for what he is: someone simply not powerful enough to carry out such a cleansing operation. That, Tore adds, is yet another reason for Agca to keep from Turkes and his Grey Wolves any hint of their secret meeting. Agca agrees.

Nor does his disoriented and disassociated mind find any difficulty accepting what Tore has said his new role must be within the Grey Wolves. To the organization Agca must appear as enthusiastic and fearless a member as ever. At the same time he must take the greatest care not to attract the interest of Turkey's authorities; he must stay away from his old criminal haunts and lead an exemplary life.

Agca agrees to it all.

*

Chaotic though his attitude may seem, psychiatrists will subsequently conclude these are recognizable clinical responses. They go with Agca's vague feeling that his will-power has been weakened, that his thoughts

353

and sometimes even his words are all being imposed from 'outside' – and are largely beyond his control. The psychiatrists will speak of *personality ambivalence*. But only later.

*

This Monday night it is enough for Mehmet Ali Agca to recall, as he lies in this foetid room contemplating his bank passbook, trusted Mauser beneath his pillow, that Tore has promised the time will soon come when he can begin to kill some of those enemies whose names he carries in his head.

After listening to the news on a radio in the café below his room, a new name has been automatically added to his hate list. It is that of John Paul II.

29

In the aftermath of John Paul's election all sorts of attempts were made to get into his mind: to define and explain, elucidate and exemplify the reasons for his election and the direction of his mission.

The very fact he is Polish was seized upon. The choice of a pope from that crucible, and the cautious acceptance of his election by the Polish state and the wider Soviet orbit, was taken as an admission that even within the Communist empire there were things which were Caesar's and others that were God's.

By choosing him, the Church was entering with new vigour the gavotte between Christianity and Communism. His election was interpreted as a decisive advance not only in Rome's claim to the leadership of Christendom, but in the more important quest for an understanding with all sorts and conditions of men.

Here was a pope who, having lived through decades of confrontation between his own Church and a Communist regime, could create a real impact on relations with Marxism throughout the world; who could lead from the front the Holy See's search for a modus vivendi with the governments of Eastern Europe; who, coming from one of the historic frontiers of the Church's encounter with the modern world, could provide a new image of Catholic universality, a revitalized sense of the Church's involvement in the actual passions of ordinary people; whose message need not be the comfortable one of bourgeois Catholicism, but an appeal for all Catholics to find their human dignity through fidelity to the crucified and risen Lord.

When John Paul announced, as one of his early administrative decisions, that the Latin American bishops' conference – twice postponed because of the death of his predecessors – would take place in the coming January, immediate debate began on how a pope who recognized certain praiseworthy elements in the Marxist ideology of social transformation would regard the theology of liberation so strongly supported in parts of South America. His intellectual consistency, speculated Vaticanologists of all persuasions, should at least ensure he did not indulge in Paul's fire-and-brimstone threats to excommunicate Catholics who aided the liberation movement. They pointed to lessons of John Paul's past, to Cracow, for instance, where he had won important concessions from the government for the building of more churches and the improved religious education of children; his promise in return that Cracow Catholics

355

would stop killing policemen had not meant he had sold his congregation short or compromised himself. Equally, he had been one of the leading supporters of the strikes in 1976 which led to the Student Solidarity Committee in Cracow; when one of its members died in suspicious circumstances he had vigorously pursued the authorities. He had encouraged the now-famous 'flying university' of historians and scientists who taught aspects of subjects banned from the official curriculum.

Nor had he been afraid to condemn those most unsavoury skeletons in the Polish Church's own cupboard: racism and, in particular, anti-semitism. His denunciation was discerned to have been markedly stronger than the Polish Church's official position required. His own life of suffering, endurance and hardship was undeniably imprinted on his face. That he had, in contrast to most Catholic prelates, attended a secular university, that he was an accomplished author, linguist, philosopher and traveller – he had made repeated trips to North and South America and even voyaged as far as New Zealand – all these suggested to Vaticanologists he was likely to move the emphasis of papal activity away from theological debate and concentrate more on the social responsibilities of the Church. So ran the speculation.

John Paul had once said: 'We cannot be Christian and materialist.' Where, then, did this leave the growing number of people committed to the theology of liberation? Surely with the hope that here, at last, was a pope whose own background had demonstrated – impeccable though his anti-Communist credentials were – that he had come to terms and could coexist with Marxism; here also was a pope who, by one of those elisions of opinion, was not only instantly seen as the spiritual leader of Eastern Europe, but also as the pontiff for Africa, for Asia, and for Latin America. There Marxism and Catholicism had been forged to prepare for revolution. If he would not actually lead it, would John Paul at least condone it?

He would not.

In the plainest of language he warned those who were attempting to 'mould Christ, to adapt Him to their own dimensions', that they would find naught for their comfort in his pontificate. Commentators began to book their plane tickets for Puebla, the site in Mexico for the bishops' conference. The whiff of a coming confrontation was in the air.

In the meantime there was much else of more immediacy to consider and ponder upon. In his first message to the world, again delivered directly and succinctly, blessedly devoid of ecclesiastical obscuration, John Paul made it clear his being Polish was 'of little importance'; no one should be distracted from the universal character of his office and the message he had to proclaim. With an actor's delivery, judged to win unstinted enthusiasm from the quarter of a million people in St Peter's Square, he promised to be 'the witness of the divine tool, reserving to all the same benevolence, especially to those being put to the test'.

That, said the Vaticanologists, was most definitely political, was assuredly directed at the continuing destruction in the Lebanon and Cambodia and every place on earth where there was strife. He would use the full influence and authority of his office to end it.

Yet in the same homily he also spoke of his intention to avoid interference in temporal politics. The fact that the Holy See had diplomatic relations with many countries should not be taken as implying approval for a given regime. In turn, Holy See diplomacy must have 'an appreciation of possible temporal values; an interest in, and help for, human issues. These must be prompted, sometimes by direct intervention, but above all through formation of consciences, bringing a specific contribution to justice and peace on the international plane.'

The words were examined endlessly. Clearly they did not suggest a political quietness in this pontificate; they were also anything but a supine respect for temporal power: John Paul's goals in this area were plain. He was determined to make any wayward regime with whom the Holy See had diplomatic ties recognize the true worth of 'liberty, respect for life and for the dignity of persons – who are never instruments – fairness in dealings, professional conscience in work, and the loyal search for the common good, the spirit of reconciliation and an openness towards spiritual values.'

Some said that Paul's Ostpolitik had just been updated. And that, in spite of John Paul's wish to minimize the importance of his background, only a Pole could have expressed it so feelingly.

But while his utterances were being dissected, for many in the Vatican this first momentous week of his pontificate was virtually a holiday as staff made good use of the $200 equivalent granted each of them by the pope to celebrate his election. The bonus to mark a new reign was an old custom. So was John Paul's reappointment of all heads of departments, with the exception of the ailing American cardinal, John Wright. Yet there was one important difference: the reappointments would not necessarily run for the normal five years. Curialists could expect changes after the pope had time properly to assess his civil service. There was immediate uncertainty and even alarm around the Curia. No other Pope had ever treated them like this before.

Questions were added to all the suppositions. In particular, could such a powerfully dominating personality satisfy another early promise: to bring the world's Catholic bishops into the sharing of responsibility for governing the Church, the collegiality which was so much discussed during the Second Vatican Council? John Paul had spoken of shared responsibility, but he had yet to reveal how he saw it actually working. Did he envisage more power for the Synod of Bishops? Or more decision-making on a local level, with a consequent general reduction in the need to refer to Rome? Nobody was certain. They comforted each other this was all part of the exciting style of the new pontificate. Camelot had come to the Vatican. Most questions were lost amid the admiration for John Paul's sheer drive, most marked in his frequent reiteration of the

357

fundamental relationship between Christ and Peter, and the unbroken line that had made him the 263rd successor to the throne of the Apostle. And yet, of course, his inheritance was more than the tradition of nearly two thousand years. It was also the lessons of the past six weeks, when the catalytic effects of Gianpaolo's pontificate had created a new kind of papacy. It was Gianpaolo's short reign which prompted a new self-awakening in the Church; it was Gianpaolo whose thirty-three days had purged the pessimism, the admonitions and laments of Paul's pontificate; it was Gianpaolo who had tilled and sown the ground with new compassion and hope.

But, swept up in John Paul's great charisma, this was largely forgotten. The new pope was endowed with magic. He became the object of fan-magazine hero-worship. A typical reaction was that of Archbishop Derek Worlock of Liverpool who reportedly described John Paul as 'the greatest intellect I have ever met . . . he has a wry, wrinkled smile and is a man of wonderfully exuberant good spirits. He possesses a fantastic ability to analyse and weigh up everything.'

No doubt that was all true – but no clear picture emerged of how different in everyday, human terms John Paul was from the predecessors whose names he now bore.

*

At exactly five o'clock in the morning of Sunday, 19 November 1978, the lights on the top floor of the Apostolic Palace come on. The policemen in St Peter's Square stamp their feet and move around, trying to look busy. It is still dark and the great piazza is deserted. But the patrolmen can never be sure when Monsignor 'Gee-Whiz' – they latched onto the name when they overheard Marcinkus use it on the very first day of the pontificate – might come stalking past the Bronze Doors to see whether they are keeping a proper watch.

This is Day Thirty-Four of the new reign – the policemen keep count though they half joke that after Gianpaolo there will be no betting between them on the length of John Paul's pontificate – and Gee-Whiz goes on giving people a hard time. He is everywhere and at all hours, a glint-eyed, black-soutaned figure with an imperious nose and a sharp tongue which can lash out equally well in Polish, Italian, French and German. The men think it uncanny the way he is able to sniff out anything not in keeping with the new order. Twice already this past month they have seen Gee-Whiz lope along in the darkness behind the chipped supports of Bernini's colonnade. What did he expect to find, grumble the policemen? Despite the Red Brigades and talk of Rome being now one of Europe's breeding grounds for urban terrorism, this is still Vatican City to these hardened patrolmen; in their view there is no need for Gee-Whiz to behave like this. It makes everybody nervous.

The patrolmen have been told by their commander to be particularly vigilant. His orders came from the Italian Minister of the Interior. The minister had been asked by Villot to tighten up security in the piazza. Gee-Whiz made the demand to the Secretary of State. The question which intrigues the policemen in the square is: did Gee-Whiz first consult the pope, or was it another of his unilateral actions?

This, the policemen grumble, is very possible. Nothing they have heard, either from inside the Vatican or at police headquarters, suggests the pope is in any more danger than his predecessors. Nevertheless, now that the lights burn brightly in the papal apartment, they move purposefully around, their automatic weapons and flak jackets making their movements ungainly, their hands cupped around their cigarettes; Gee-Whiz doesn't like people smoking on duty.

The policemen have made it their business to learn all they can about Gee-Whiz. They know his real name is Stanislaw Dziwisz. He is barely thirty-four years old, is now the pope's senior private secretary and has been with him for the past thirteen years. They have seen that the relationship between the two men is the close one of a father and son. The patrolmen believe John Paul indulges Dziwisz; that the pope is letting his secretary run loose through the Vatican to roust out the lethargy and dead wood. The policemen don't mind that: after all, they chuckle, wasn't it John XXIII who, when asked how many people work in the Vatican, had said, 'About half.' It is the way Dziwisz goes about his duties which annoys the patrolmen. He expects to be instantly obeyed and can be brutally frank and dismissive, in a way not even Macchi was. Whenever he gets the chance, he lapses into Polish, much to the consternation of the Italians in the Vatican. In manner and style, the policemen have recently heard Villot whisper, Dziwisz appears like a reincarnation of one of Richard Nixon's aides; Villot is believed to be again seriously wondering whether it isn't time to step down and avoid all the *Angst* Dziwisz seems to thrive on.

And just look at the way he's tamed Martin, the policemen tell each other as they circle the square, regularly glancing up at the brightly lit papal apartment. Although the prefect has been reappointed, it's said things are different. While he still has the privilege of walking in unannounced and uninvited on the pope, now he almost never does. Not after Dziwisz sharply told him John Paul doesn't like this sort of interruption. And the daily list of appointments have first to be approved by Dziwisz; it is he, not Martin, who goes over them with the pope. Again, when the prefect is present, Dziwisz has the disconcerting habit of speaking Polish – leaving Martin frozen-faced and effectively frozen out of the conversation.

Yet this is nothing, the policemen remind each other, to the way Noé is treated. He has again been appointed master of ceremonies. But several of the patrolmen have bets among themselves for how long. Some wager Noé will be gone within a year, fast by Vatican standards. Others think he might last a little longer; that removing Noé too soon would be seen as an anti-Italian bias in the new pontificate. Most certainly Noé's days are numbered – perhaps were from the moment he tried to shoo back the pope from the balcony of St Peter's. Since then they have repeatedly clashed. When the pope appears in public, Noé positions the microphone one way and John Paul invariably changes it; during a procession, the master of ceremonies will attempt to stride almost beside the pope who will curtly motion him away; at a reception, Noé hovers at the pontiff's elbow and is studiously ignored. Only the previous Wednesday, as the pope was about to enter the Nervi Hall for his weekly audience, Noé had fussed over the position of John Paul's skullcap. The pope angrily upbraided him. The policemen, from their own experience, know Noé cannot and will not change; it is in his nature to fuss and be a stickler for perfection. Frail old Paul and easy-going Gianpaolo tolerated his attentions. But John Paul clearly will not. Behind his smile there is an explosive temperament. One day, think the policemen, Noé will go too far. That's what makes the betting so interesting – knowing the moment may not be all that far off. In the meantime they can still tell their families and friends how different things are now in the papal apartment.

*

Thirty minutes after the policemen saw the lights come on in the apartment, the pope had shaved with an old-fashioned open razor and showered, running the water icy-cold for the last rinse; he has recommended this to his personal staff as a way to maintain good blood circulation. Then he dressed himself in a white linen cassock, a white skullcap on his head, his feet shod in sturdy size ten shoes. He is ready to start another of his eighteen-hour days.

As he does every morning after his ablutions, he returns to his bedroom and prays before a striking portrait of the Madonna, hanging on the wall above the prie-dieu. The picture has come from John Paul's bedroom in Cracow. It is the only visible link with his past throughout the entire apartment. There are no discernible mementoes, souvenirs or keepsakes; some visitors wonder if this is an extension of the pope's desire to play down his background.

Yet his devotion to Mary is very much a part of his Polish heritage. During the few weeks he has been pontiff, John Paul has constantly reminded the world that the Marian shrines of Poland loom large in his own life and piety. He plans to return to the theme later today, at his noon Angelus: it is so natural for him to do so he would assuredly be surprised if anyone should remark on it.

At 5.45 he rises to his feet and strides from the bedroom.

*

Dziwisz and Magee are waiting for the pope inside the apartment's private chapel. It is now three weeks since Magee was summoned back from his enforced exile. John Paul personally sent for him, appointing the Irishman as his English-speaking private secretary. The pope knows Magee is ideally suited for the delicate task of building bridges between the new papal family and the Curia. But in a conversation with Dziwisz Magee made it plain – insists the Vatican's still thriving 'Irish Mafia' – that he wouldn't tolerate any interference. Dziwisz had promptly responded in Polish. Magee coolly interrupted him, and apologized for not being fluent in the language; he suggested in future Dziwisz and the other Poles on the pope's personal staff should try and use the common language of the Vatican, Italian. Or, with Magee, they could try English or French. But Polish was pointless. The Irish Mafia relished the story.

This morning both secretaries greet John Paul with the traditional *Santissimo Padre*. Then they follow him to the altar to celebrate the first Mass of the day.

*

At 7.30, the pope leads his secretaries into breakfast. Already present is the pope's Polish doctor, Mielyslaw Wyslocki. He is a member of the entourage John Paul has imported from Cracow, Warsaw and other Polish dioceses; in all some forty Polish priests and nuns are scattered throughout the Vatican. They report directly to Dziwisz.

Wyslocki's presence reminds Magee of the unhappy position of Buzzonetti, who attended two previous popes and, though he is the Vatican Health Commissioner, has yet to be reappointed physician to the papal household. This is upsetting enough for Buzzonetti but what concerns him more is that his efforts to give the pope a thorough physical examination have been thwarted. Dziwisz has repeatedly said John Paul has no time and, besides, he is in robust health. Buzzonetti accepts this is probably the case, but he understandably wants to check for himself. And, try as he might, Buzzonetti has not been able to see John Paul's medical history.

Magee realizes he is going to have to tackle Wyslocki about all this. But now is not the time. The doctor is tucking into a plate of Polish ham and sausages. Every week the Polish airline LOT, on flight 303 from Warsaw, flies in quantities of provisions including Polish beer, *chleb*,

Polish bread, and the buckwheat to make *blinis*, the pancakes served with sour cream which the pope relishes.

The kitchen invariably serves traditional Polish peasant food. Magee finds it palatable enough, though after the frugal tables of Paul and Gianpaolo the portions are often too substantial for him to complete.

John Paul, however, has a healthy appetite; he frequently takes second helpings. Over breakfast this Sunday, as usual, he confines himself to domestic talk.

He wants to know the reaction to his latest edict: that all the papal staff should give up their afternoon siesta and work 'a normal day'. Dziwisz reports there have been no problems.

What about the tennis court? The pope has requested one be renovated for his use. Dziwisz looks at Magee. He says the matter is in hand. John Paul has another question. Could a swimming pool replace the cleverly concealed roof garden Paul had installed? He would like nothing better than to get in a dozen lengths first thing in the morning. Magee explains a previous survey had shown it was impracticable to install a pool atop the Apostolic Palace. The pope persists: in that case, couldn't one be built at Castel Gandolfo? Then at least he could swim throughout the summer.

Dziwisz intervenes. He speaks rapidly in Polish to the pope. Magee waits patiently until the exchange is finished and then asks Dziwisz for a translation. It is all very relaxed. But no one can deny there are undercurrents at work.

*

At 8.30 John Paul takes the private elevator – the one nobody else can use unless invited to do so – to the third floor. The Swiss Guards on duty drop to one knee. The blue-uniformed Vigilance outside the pope's official study noticeably stiffen. When they do so the outline of shoulder holsters becomes more visible under their jackets.

For the next three hours the pope works at his desk on the final draft of his Angelus address. He writes slowly, thinking deeply about everything he pens; it is part of his intellectual make-up, part of his scholastic discipline. He writes on a large blockboard; the penmanship is bold and distinctive.

*

At 11.30 Dziwisz enters the study with Noé. The master of ceremonies carries a red velvet cloth etched with gold.

They move quietly past the pope to the central of the study's three windows. Dziwisz opens the window. From the square below comes cheers and applause. Dziwisz thinks there must be close to two hundred thousand people down there. It has been like this for each of John Paul's Angelus addresses. The secretary helps Noé neatly drape the velvet over the window ledge. Next they clip into place on the ledge a heavy glass lectern. Finally Noé positions the microphone. The two men stare for a moment longer down at the piazza, at the rows of television cameras, at the enclosure filled with still photographers, at another packed with reporters.

Behind them John Paul is reading aloud, rehearsing his speech. Key words have been underlined. The delivery is measured, the place for pauses noted. On one level this is the natural actor determined to give a good performance; on another level the words are a further indication that in this pontificate papal theology and policy seem to be swiftly intermixing while the range of pastoral solicitude is ever expanding.

At one minute to noon the pope rises from his desk and walks to the window. Noé and Dziwisz stand well clear.

John Paul begins to speak.

*

His words, like everything else he said publicly in the following weeks, were examined, given their place in the chronology of pronouncements and directives which flowed from the pope. They were related to the personal predilections, attitudes and convictions which were rooted in his youth. When John Paul stressed human dignity, Vaticanologists who had travelled to Poland to probe further into his past reminded themselves that as a young man he had heard the cries of those randomly rounded up by the Gestapo; he came of age with the terror on his own doorstep in Cracow's Debniki Square, the entrance to a specially built Jewish ghetto. Auschwitz, symbol of modern technological genocide, is in a corner of his old archdiocese. Was this, then, why he felt compelled to remind everybody that he still believed, regardless of the horrors he had been privy to, there was an inherent dignity in human beings; that just as the Nazis failed to extinguish it, so, too, would their successors, in spite of their more sophisticated modalities of dehumanization? Was he putting Russia and its satellites on notice? Was he warning them in particular that though he had placed behind him his Polish background – a valiant effort which proved impossible – he could not, would not, stand idly by if Communist oppression passed a certain stage in Poland? It sounded very much like it, and Vaticanologists were not the only people who sensed the shivers in the Vatican. Several ambassadors attached to the Holy See informed their governments that this was showing signs of being the most politically explosive papacy since the days of Pius XII.[1]

And certainly John Paul was more direct than his predecessors. Not even Gianpaolo, for all his Pinocchioisms, had been so assertive. John Paul was determined there could be no doubt about the emerging motifs of his pontificate.

Nor was there any indication of corporate thinking in what he said, no suggestion of many hands labouring over various drafts. Instead there was a personal resonance and style, quintessential idioms and syntax, an individual selection of terms and scriptural loci: all combined to identify the pope as sole author. Even his inaugural homily and his first encyclical, Redemptor Hominis *– the latter written first in Polish and then translated by himself into Latin – were pre-eminently personal testimonies.*

It became quickly apparent that his assertions were meant to underpin a deep conviction about the irreplaceable worth of life from 'within the womb to natural death'. In this world abortion was too unthinkable even to be mentioned as something always to be rejected. It was a clear warning he would have no time to hear any pleas for change. The same would apply to divorce and birth control: they were not matters for debate.

John Paul was making vivid the timeless and awkward truths about the Church; that it had survived because of its core of strong convictions; that its continued existence required him to nurture, defend and transmit those truths. A diluted faith could not compete with the distractions of the modern world: a reluctance to accept authority rooted in tradition should be seen as the sin of pride, the foolish assumption that there is nothing to learn from previous experience.

Three months after his election, it was clear that a cardinal who, in Poland, was a tenacious adversary of an overbearing state, had become, in Rome, a vigorous enforcer of orthodoxy. No one should have been surprised.

Behind the smile, the warmth of his personal contact, the way he found the time to return to his original role as a parish priest and solemnize a marriage, his ability to don an unadorned black cassock and sit in one of the confessionals of St Peter's giving penance, his sudden and unexpected visits to the sick in Rome hospitals, the way he lifted up a child and looked lovingly into its face, his easy communion and fraternal relationship with his fellow bishops, his inborn sense of dignity which came from being energized by his own experiences, his overall image as a Supreme Pastor who was determined to resist the usual deadening institutionalization of the papacy: behind all this was an implacable traditionalism. His doctrinal attitudes, his views on worship and pastoral care, on every contentious issue his pontificate faced he was rigidly orthodox. He would not move from well-prepared ground. He was not going to be an innovator; he was going to be a constant reminder of the old Catholic truths. There were some who wondered whether he drew too much comfort from the cheers which greeted him in the Nervi Hall on Wednesdays and from his balcony overlooking St Peter's Square on Sundays; whether he realized that beyond his immediate horizons there were Catholics who were beginning to stir uneasily.

Yet he could still surprise.

*

Shortly before 2.30 on the sunny afternoon of 21 November 1978, a Mercedes saloon drives down the Via della Conciliazione, cruising slowly between the stone benches and imitation obelisks which border the road, bunching together the constant stream of traffic honking and crawling towards St Peter's. The car's silver paintwork is coated with the mud and dust of some seven hundred kilometres of travel.

Almost two days have passed since the driver – a member of an elite corps known as Chauffeurs de Monseigneur, specially established for the sole purpose of transporting one person around Europe, the man in the back of the Mercedes – set out on the tiring journey. When they had started from the remote Swiss village of Riddes, the old man had sat bolt upright. Now, thirty-six hours later, with brief stopovers for food and rest, having been driven out of Switzerland over the Alps, into Italy down through the wine valleys of Lombardy and finally along the helter-skelter *autostrada* to Rome, seventy-two-year-old Archbishop Marcel Lefèbvre still sits proudly and defiantly erect. He has barely spoken to his chauffeur during the drive. The man does not mind; for him it is a privilege just to be in the presence of a prelate he venerates even more than the pope. He is one of twenty drivers ready, willing and able, at any time and at their own expense, to carry Lefèbvre anywhere in Europe he wishes to go in order to voice his objections, celebrate his illegal Masses and to continue to challenge the authority of the man he will shortly face, John Paul. It is a confrontation which makes the chauffeur tingle with apprehension. He is both bewildered and overawed that his passenger can remain so stoically calm. Not even since joining up with their two-car escort on the outskirts of Rome for the last stage of this historic journey has the archbishop shown a flicker of emotion. His face, for all his frailty, is set and resolute. No one, thinks the chauffeur, not even the Polish pope, will shake the determination of Marcel Lefèbvre.

As the Mercedes turns left into the Via del San Uffizio, the escort cars follow closely behind. Seated in the first, in full regalia, is Cardinal Giuseppe Siri. This is his first time back in the Vatican since he left Conclave, the sound of champagne corks popping and Polish songs still ringing in his ears. His face, too, is a mask. The passenger in the second car is Silvio Oddi. He is a curial cardinal; some say he is even more of a Catholic extremist than Siri. Between them they have exerted considerable pressure for this meeting to take place. Yet the two cardinals remain surprised the pope has agreed to it. They can see no way there can be compromises, no possibility of Lefèbvre retreating. Indeed, when they had met just now on the other side of Rome, the archbishop made it icily clear that he had not come here to listen; for him this was not a peace mission.

At the Arch of the Bells newsfilm cameramen, photographers and reporters await their arrival. Informed of the meeting, they have assembled, as they have so often in the past thirteen years of Lefèbvre's rebellion, in the confident expectation that when he emerges from the Vatican he will tell them how he trounced this pope – just as he had so many times defeated Paul and would undoubtedly have triumphed over Gianpaolo.

Lefèbvre motions the driver to stop. The archbishop rolls down the back window, ignores the reporters' questions and stares bleakly into the cameras. Satisfied the moment has been recorded, he closes the window and orders the chauffeur to drive on. As the car bounces over the cobblestones, Lefèbvre disregards the salutes of the Swiss Guards.

The cortège drives around the back of the Basilica, crossing Parrot Courtyard and on into the larger San Damaso Courtyard. The cars park on the far side, near the elevator to the Secretariat of State and the papal apartment.

Dziwisz and Magee greet the visitors. Then, preceded by the two secretaries and flanked by Siri and Oddi, Lefèbvre is escorted to the salon where John Paul conducts most of his audiences.

The pope is standing in the centre of the salon, hands entwined, when his visitors arrive. He moves forward quickly and embraces first Lefèbvre and then the two cardinals before leading them to a side table where coffee and biscuits await. The secretaries act as waiters. The talk is small and stilted.

Siri and Oddi have not only sponsored this meeting but they have advised the archbishop what he should say, and how and when he should say it. They are his champions in every sense. But they will not be allowed to take part. That was made clear to them before the pope agreed to the meeting. Gradually and discreetly, Dziwisz and Magee move them from the salon. Magee closes the door behind him.

For fifteen minutes it remains shut. Then it suddenly opens. John Paul stands there. He is holding Lefèbvre by the elbow. The archbishop looks dazed. As they stand in the doorway the pope once more embraces the archbishop warmly. He says, in excellent French, 'It will be all right, it will be all right.' Lefèbvre nods. He does not speak.

Escorted by the secretaries and cardinals, the archbishop returns to his car. The convoy drives from the Vatican. At the Arch of the Bells, it accelerates past the media gaggle.

The rebellion Marcel Lefèbvre first proclaimed on 8 December 1965, and which he subsequently cleverly subsidized with well-publicized conflicts, is over.

But how did it end? Who won?

*

Greeley believes he knows what happened: the dynamic pope simply charmed the crusty old archbishop. It is another of Greeley's cryptic conclusions to slip into the book he is rushing out about this past summer in Rome. Other theorists thought that, during their fifteen minutes alone, Lefèbvre somehow came to realize that tradition is not bound only in a row of books on a shelf, but can be altered and added to by the ongoing experience of life. This is also too attractively neat. Again, harking back to his past, some said the pope was 'kind and understanding' during the meeting, that he had said it was 'right' for Lefèbvre to express his fears and bring them to a man who understood the old values.

The truth is far different.[2]

John Paul, with a forcefulness which stunned Lefèbvre, stated he could excommunicate the archbishop – and might yet do so before Lefèbvre left the Vatican. In his tone and his choice of words, the pope was cold to the point of brutality. When Lefèbvre tried to speak, he was angrily told to remain silent. For ten uninterrupted minutes, the pontiff lectured his visitor, pointing out that the Tridentine Mass was not the only issue; that so much Lefèbvre said and did was misguided and even illegal in the eyes of the Church; that by attempting to turn back a clock that could not be turned back he was being disobedient to papal authority. Much else was said in this vein. Then, abruptly switching direction – which may account for the ensuing dazed look on Lefèbvre's face – John Paul stated that if the archbishop persisted in remaining outside the mainstream of Catholic thinking, he might be allowed to stay in his Swiss mountain fastness; but his well-known penchant for publicity, the way he had over the past thirteen years used the media to attack previous popes – this must stop, now and forever. There must be no more reporters invited to Lefèbvre's seminary; there must be no more articles filled with the desperate rhetoric of archaism revivified; no more promoting of Lefèbvre's book, *I Accuse*; no more well-staged television appearances; no more public speeches such as the one Lefèbvre delivered at Lille in 1976 in which he had repeatedly used the word *bâtard* to describe the new Mass – 'a bastard rite, bastard sacraments and bastard priests'. All this must stop. Further, Lefèbvre must ensure his followers also desist from their public promotion of doctrine which is against the Church's present teachings. Otherwise they too will face excommunication.

The pope had fallen silent. The minutes dragged on. Then, in little more than a whisper, Marcel Lefèbvre capitulated. He would remain secluded and silent in his lonely Swiss seminary.

John Paul took him by the arm and gently ushered him to the door.

*

Throughout the remainder of November and into December, the door of the pope's salon opened and closed at least thirty, and often forty, times a day, marking the coming and going of a continuous procession of people, ushered in and out by Martin. Some spent less than five minutes with John Paul; others were closeted with him for an hour or longer. The pope generally kept his comments to a minimum, but he showed no hesitation in interrupting those cardinals and civil servants, no matter how important they were, who strayed from the topic or repeated the obvious. More often than not he anticipated a point, and with a well-aimed question got a quick conclusion. Yet his impatience was mitigated by the way he gave his full attention to every speaker, focusing on each person those penetrating deep-set blue eyes, absorbing a prodigious amount of detail but never losing sight of the broader picture. He could also be disconcerting, as Villot had discovered early on. The Secretary was ruminating about the possibility of a fresh Vatican approach in the Lebanon when the pope suddenly said now was not the time, abruptly rose to his feet and escorted Villot to the door.

Despite Martin's scheduling and the careful vetting by Dziwisz and Magee of everything which came before the pope, and their constant reminder that John Paul put great store on brevity and punctuality, he was sometimes an hour behind schedule by the end of an invariably demanding and long day. It was not unusual for the last visitor to depart just before the Vatican exits were closed at midnight.

Saturdays and Sundays were no exception. Rest periods were confined to the fifteen minutes the pope would occasionally catnap after a late lunch. Even when he exercised – he nearly always managed to find an hour in his day to walk around the roof garden – John Paul was usually accompanied by a visitor, with either Magee or Dziwisz hovering in the background to record any decisions taken. The relationship between the secretaries was cordial but lacked the warmth of Magee's associations with Lorenzi and Macchi. Neither Dziwisz nor John Paul had shown much interest in how things had been done in the previous pontificates. They wanted everything done their way – a thoroughly Polish system whose hallmark was careful preparatory work.

As well as the official calendar of audiences published in L'Osservatore Romano, the pope also had a number of other meetings, each strictly off the record, many categorized as secret. The latter included early in his pontificate briefings by the Italian government on the Red Brigades. He received senior officers of the American Central Intelligence Agency who outlined likely Soviet global strategy in the coming months. Members of the Egyptian Intelligence Directorate briefed him on the Middle East. He matched all this against what he had been informed by Casaroli, whom he had told on their first meeting after becoming pope: 'I want you to be my eyes and my ears.' It was a role for which Casaroli was ideally suited. John Paul also received a number of Poles who appraised for him what was happening in the growing movements against the Polish regime.

Developments during a particular day often meant new meetings had to be squeezed in. Minutes were literally trimmed to make them possible. During the first weeks John Paul managed to see a surprising number of people whom certain of his staff ruefully called 'non-essentials' – Polish reporters, clerics and friends from Cracow, others from his days in Rome as a student; now there was no time to receive them. The sheer daily grind of meetings and discussions excluded such pleasures. But he did everything possible to avoid what had happened to his predecessors. He strongly resisted attempts by the Curia to make him rely totally on official channels to know what was going on. He asked to read the newspapers, not curial digests of the press. He demanded time to listen to the radio and television bulletins. He made it clear that, on a day-to-day basis, the more his mind was exposed to what was happening beyond the Vatican walls, the more effective he would be as a pope. He told his secretaries he did not want any screening out of criticisms. He showed a compulsive curiosity about what people thought of his pontificate. It was all very laudable.

In some ways it was also unrealistic. The papacy was simply not designed to work the way John Paul wanted. But still he tried.

Curialists were ordered, wherever feasible, to keep briefing papers to no more than a page. And the pope showed that despite his episcopality – epitomized by his regular visits to the parishes of Rome – he had a good administrative grasp. The nine Sacred Congregations were expected to keep him briefed on all the options open on every current issue under review. He did not want predigested and fully formed verdicts: he wanted the facts fairly presented; then, when it was his responsibility to do so, he would make up his own mind. A number of curialists did not like the approach. There was a resurgence of defensive bureaucratic reaction to what was happening.

These misgivings began to deepen into a distrust which became mutual. During his years with the Synod of Bishops, on his regular visits to Rome and in his contacts with other cardinals, John Paul had seen what the Curia could do. He was determined they would not do it to him. Conflict was made more inevitable by the pope's refusal to leave the legislating solely to his civil service. He repeatedly told them – in detail – what he wished done. And, like any chief executive in a hurry, John Paul sometimes did so with a minimum of courtesy.

Such lapses were largely overlooked – except by the diehards – because the pope was obviously pushing himself hard and thrived under pressure. Disappointments only made him more determined. When he heard from Pericle Felici that Hans Küng was bestirring in his redoubt in Tübingen, the pope wearily asked, 'Why does he do this?' As Felici began to explain, John Paul interrupted. 'No, no. Not now. Later. There is so much else to concern us. Besides, Küng may realize there is a different pope now – one he shouldn't play with!'[3]

The self-discipline John Paul showed, and expected in others, became a byword. There was both a rhythm and single-mindedness about this pontificate which stemmed from the top. Yet what could have been dour dullness was relieved by the pope's humour. It flowed from him spontaneously; the wit was neither feigned nor forced and was sometimes earthily Polish. In public, especially at the Wednesday audiences, John Paul did not pause to signal an impending witticism or even wait to see how it was received; a joke or two was included as a natural element of what he was saying. The same wit often punctuated the opening and closing of his office door. It was his way of trying to remove the sting from some unusual decisions.

Baggio came to brief him on Cody. He was listened to for twenty minutes. Then Dziwisz was summoned. The three men conferred for a further thirty minutes. The final decision must have astonished Baggio. Those months of travel, the careful gathering of evidence, the confidential reports to first Paul and then Gianpaolo; all were seemingly to no avail. John Paul decided Cody should not be pursued further. If Baggio was given a reason, it has remained part of the secret deliberations in the pope's salon on that winter's morning. It would not stop the speculation. But then, John Paul had made it plain he was largely unconcerned by what was said outside the Church; his preoccupation was with what happened within his immediate orbit of authority. He did not seem to be aware that the Cody scandal was now of equal interest inside the Church and out.

Marcinkus was summoned on Friday, 1 December 1978. He spent an hour alone with the pope. No mention was made of the bulky dossier which Benelli and Felici had collated about the financial activities of the Vatican bank. The file lay on the pope's desk, apparently unopened. But both Marcinkus and Felici would subsequently agree on one thing: the pope had undoubtedly read it. Yet on this Friday afternoon he preferred to discuss the first major foreign trip of his pontificate – to Mexico, a spiritual cauldron every bit as dangerous for the Church as anything the Communists had stirred in Poland.

The pope wanted Marcinkus back in a familiar role, acting as his papal bodyguard for the Mexican trip. The fifty-six-year-old banker could be forgiven for believing the months of financial unhappiness he had experienced were behind him; that he was completely returned to favour, riding shotgun for a pope who might well have posed some very pertinent questions after reading that file on his desk.

That they were not asked would later cause yet other questions to be raised.

*

Though he has not been here for almost a year, Alibrandi knows his way instinctively. He knows every flight of stairs, every bend in the corridors. The paintings on the walls are the same and the Swiss Guards do not look any older. Nothing has changed. Yet everything is different.

There is an 'air' about the Apostolic Palace which was not there before. There is a feeling of real purpose, much more than the nuncio can recall from his visits during the last years of Paul.

Magee is waiting for him outside the pope's salon. The secretary looks as relaxed as when Alibrandi last met him. They speak for a few minutes about mutual friends in Ireland, the parlous state of that country's economy, about the nuncio's flight from Dublin; it is inconsequential chit-chat to bridge the moments before the nuncio's appointment.

Alibrandi has been allotted ten minutes. It is all Magee has been able to get on this particularly busy December day.

'Good luck,' murmurs the secretary, glancing at his watch, then knocking and opening the door.

The pope is completely absorbed reading a paper; he continues to concentrate on the document, seemingly unbothered or unaware of the approaching men. When they are close to his desk he puts down the paper and rises to his feet, smiling broadly, coming from behind the desk to embrace the nuncio and lead him over to a sofa.

Magee leaves.

Alibrandi, knowing the pope will have already read the brief he sent on the Irish Church, does not waste time repeating the details. He comes straight to the point.

'Your Holiness, will you honour Ireland with a visit?'

The pope smiles. 'We shall see . . .'

'Next year is Knock's centenary . . .'

In 1879 the Virgin Mary is believed to have appeared as one of three illuminated figures before some twenty-two people in the Irish village; the other two, they attested, were Joseph and John the Evangelist. Since then Knock has taken on a significance similar to Lourdes for many Irish Catholics.

'21 August 1979 is a hundred years. It would be a most appropriate time to come,' concludes Alibrandi.

'We shall see . . .'

Alibrandi beams. 'Sì, Santissimo Padre. Sì.'

He is certain his journey has not been wasted. He translates 'we shall see' into positive acceptance. Knock, after all, is a Marian shrine. And the nuncio knows enough about the pope to believe he would look favourably upon visiting any shrine to the Madonna.

The nuncio moves to the second item on his list.

'Santissimo Padre, it would be wonderful if your visit could be preceded by the appointment of a new cardinal for Ireland.'

Another smile. 'We shall see . . .'

Alibrandi beams his thanks. He has recognized the subtleties of this

371

world of underplay and the unspoken. The nuncio is now sure that whatever the opposition – and no matter that John Paul has appointed London's Basil Hume as his own successor on the Council of the Synod of Bishops – soon Tomás O'Fiaich, Archbishop of Armagh and Primate of All Ireland, will be elevated to cardinal. The promotion will have an important bearing, the nuncio believes, on everything he wants to happen in Ulster.

*

The appointment of Hume – a cardinal increasingly regarded as the essence of progressive-minded intellectualism – was seen as a definite sign for the direction the pontificate was travelling. On his return to London, Hume had obligingly helped matters along by explaining to his priests his own hopes for the Church under John Paul: there would be more 'dialogue', more stress on 'serving God and our neighbours in a pluralist and secular world'. Hume spoke about a brave new era where the pope would heal divisions both inside the Roman Church and between it and other Christian churches. Though Hume did not mention non-Christian religions, the objectives he outlined sounded most promising.

But closer to hand an unhappy relationship developed between John Paul and the liberal-minded Argentinian, Eduardo Pironio. Like John Paul, Pironio had personally experienced oppression and violence. In 1976 the cardinal had been hurriedly removed from his diocese of Mar del Plata in Argentina where his name was found on a death list prepared by right-wing terrorists. Paul had made Pironio prefect of the Congregation for Religious and Secular Institutes. He had been a compassionate administrator, one who was more ready than most to treat sympathetically any priest who wanted to relinquish holy orders. During a sharp, short meeting in December 1978, John Paul told Pironio he wished his Congregation to discipline 'difficult' members of religious orders. Pironio objected. Angry words were exchanged. There would be some dispute later about whether Pironio stormed out or was ordered to leave the pope's salon.

Afterwards John Paul sang Christmas carols with children in St Peter's Square.

It steadily became clear that his concept of the papacy, when applied to governing the Church, was very much keyed in the tradition of the Pius popes. The power John Paul possessed he felt was there to be used, without guilt, as the quickest way to get what he wanted done. That was the long and short of it. There was no question of being overawed by the authority he possessed.

There was also an innocence which was both revealing and thought-provoking. Early in December he had asked Casaroli to make arrangements for the pope's first Christmas Pontifical Mass to be celebrated in Bethlehem, 'without any Israeli–Vatican City protocol to be observed or precedent to be established.'⁴

Casaroli was astonished. He began to explain the problems: the lack of time, the fact that there was no diplomatic relationship with Israel, the potential personal risk for the pope. John Paul cut him short. As a cardinal he had travelled to Bethlehem incognito when it was under Jordanian jurisdiction. There had been no problems then. Why should there be now? Casaroli went off to make a tentative approach to the Tel Aviv government. The Israelis vetoed the idea on grounds of security. Given the news, John Paul merely shook his head. Casaroli felt he clearly did not understand that in such matters a pope was very different from a cardinal.

John Paul preached his Christmas sermon in the Basilica: Urbi et Orbi: He is Our Peace. It was a fitting conclusion to a momentous year for a most complex man.

But the storm was gathering.

*

At 12.35 on the afternoon of 6 January 1979, the Aeromexico DC-10 – irreverently code-named *Aeropapa* by Mexico City air traffic controllers – makes another course change. Six miles below are the jungles of Central America, a dense green carpet stretching from the shores of the Pacific on the aircraft's port side to the slopes of the Yucatán Mountains rising to starboard. Beyond the peaks is the hazy outline of Cuba. The rain forest, the highlands and the island are all very much on the pope's mind as he sits in his day cabin aboard the jet with Marcinkus and Dziwisz.

Sombrely, John Paul tells his listeners that what has already occurred in Cuba has undoubtedly helped to create the disturbing situation now prevalent not only in Central America but extending thousands of miles down through South America.

For centuries Cuba was regarded as a model outpost of the Church. Ninety-five per cent of its population was Catholic. When Fidel Castro swept to power in 1958 he wisely decided to leave religious behaviour alone. Then came the Bay of Pigs fiasco in 1961. Instigated by America's first Catholic president, John Kennedy, this disastrous attempt to overthrow the Communist dictator was not only quickly repelled but also led to a violent upheaval between the Castro regime and the Cuban Church. Castro suspected, not without grounds, that many of the Church's hierarchy were ready to welcome the invaders from Miami. He promptly set about 'regulating' the Church, expelling some 600 priests and more than 2,000 nuns. Catholic schools were nationalized, the number of priests limited to 200, and serious obstacles placed in the way of Catholics wishing to enter public life. During the past fifteen years, coupled to a population explosion, the number of Cuban Catholics had fallen to less than forty per cent among a population of nine million.

Most of those expelled by Castro made their way initially to the long strip of land passing below the papal jet. Here, in the swamps of Central America, many of them gravitated into the theology of liberation movement. They immersed themselves in the fight against the authoritarian regimes which started in San Salvador, continued on down into Paraguay and spread even further, to Brazil and Argentina. They spoke out against the multinationals which ruthlessly stripped local economies of basic raw materials. They continued to challenge every kind of repression. Many of the priests and nuns still face, as a matter of daily routine, torture, imprisonment and death. They believe the risk is worthwhile, that anything is acceptable providing it helps bring about change.

To sustain them these priests and nuns have found Marxism a comfort. The Jesus of Central America – a dead god, tortured and scourged, a figure invariably portrayed clad in either black or dark red, the colour of congealed blood – has been given new emphasis: he is the Saviour predominantly of the poor; the revolutionary Christ who was himself poor, behind whom the new poor of Latin America, all millions of them, can rally and stage revolution in the security of the Lord. This has drawn the Church directly into the political turbulence of the entire region – and to the point, insists the pope, where it is no longer acceptable.

Marcinkus and Dziwisz are content to listen uninterruptedly to John Paul speaking. They recognize not only the importance of what he is saying, but hope it may also take his mind off the unpleasant scenes he had been caught up in a little earlier aboard the DC-10.

The aircraft was chartered by Marcinkus on behalf of the Vatican. Considerable modifications have been made. Behind the flight deck a small bedroom has been installed for the pope. It has a crucifix attached to a bulkhead, a special pile carpet on the floor and bedding brought from the Apostolic Palace. Next to the bedroom is the pope's day cabin, equipped with a dining table and armchairs. Behind that is the special papal galley, its refrigerator filled with frozen Polish food. Adjacent to the galley is the First Class area. Here Marcinkus, Dziwisz, Noé and other dignitaries have their seats. Ciban and his security men occupy the last two rows. Their orders for the flight are specific: keep 'them' from entering.

'Them' are the throng of reporters, photographers and television and radio crews occupying the Tourist Class. To help defray costs, seats on the flight have been sold to the media. In return for paying rather more than the ordinary full fare, each news person receives a pre-packed meal and unlimited cocktails. There has been a good deal of drinking and ribaldry during the flight from Rome. After a brief stopover in San Domingo, the journey had continued on across the Caribbean towards Mexico. The boozing and joshing continued.

As Central America came into sight the pope decided to visit the press compartment.

It was not a casual decision. John Paul had repeatedly made clear his desire for good relations between his pontificate and the media. He sees this as a necessary extension of what he is about: educating, persuading, reminding and mobilizing opinion within the Church. These can best be achieved, he has told aides, by making proper use of the media.

This does not mean he always appreciates the way Church affairs are reported; three months into his reign he has been seen to frown and even occasionally to narrow his eyes in anger over some of the stories he reads. What especially annoys him are those reports which are clearly based on curial 'leaks'. He has let it be known that anyone discovered 'leaking' can expect a severe reprimand. Nevertheless, he is anxious on this, his first trip abroad as pope, to have a good press. That is why he decided to visit the press section.

At first all went well. Confronted by tape recorders and film cameras, accosted by reporters, John Paul accepted questions and provided answers of substance as he moved down the aisle.

Suddenly, half way down, certain journalists began to climb onto seats and over the backs of colleagues, pressing in on Ciban and his men, elbowing aside Press Secretary Panciroli and Noé in order to get nearer the pope. Cursing broke out, language so unsavoury even some of the correspondents on board were embarrassed. A reporter who may have taken excessive measures to fortify himself for the flight, tangled with a television cameraman. Their exchanges were too much for the pope. He turned on his heel and walked back to his day cabin.

But, as the plane begins its descent into Mexico City, John Paul knows the misbehaviour of a handful of journalists is inconsequential when measured against what lies ahead. For a start, Mexico is the one Latin American country which constitutionally forbids 'religious propaganda'. It acknowledges no Church – and refuses to recognize the sovereignty of the Vatican or consider forming the loosest of diplomatic ties with the Holy See. Yet there are three times more baptized Catholics in teeming Mexico City than among Rome's population of three million. By the year 2000 it is estimated thirty-one million people will be living in the city.

The dichotomy of a secular regime controlling a predominantly

Catholic nation is only too evident as the DC-10 rolls to a stop outside the terminal complex at Benito Juarez Airport, eight miles east of the city where the papal tour is due to begin.

*

At one o'clock exactly, John Paul appears at the front exit of the plane.

Behind him, Noé murmurs, '*Santissimo Padre*, remember the air is very thin – you must not exert yourself.'

Dziwisz immediately mouths something at the master of ceremonies; one of the ground crew atop the mobile steps thinks the secretary told Noé to keep quiet.

The pope ignores those behind him and walks down the steps.

A cheer comes from three thousand hand-picked Mexicans perched on two custom-built platforms. A *mariachi* band, its musicians decked out in traditional dress complete with sombreros, swings into a popular Mexican ditty, *Cielito Lindo*, a tune about a 'pretty little heaven' and a comely young woman.

John Paul reaches the foot of the gangway. He looks around briefly, then hoists his silk papal cassock a few inches, displaying a pair of brown shoes and white linen socks, before dropping on his hands and knees to kiss Mexican soil.

This seemingly spontaneous gesture is the result of careful research by Dziwisz and Magee. They have studied all the trips abroad Paul had taken. The most successful gesture of Paul's was his kissing of the ground the moment he reached a country. John Paul has included it in his repertoire.

Just as he rises to his feet a gust of wind catches his yoke-cap, blowing it over his head. Helping hands rush forward to smooth it away. The pope stands there beaming. His staff, led by Marcinkus, rush down the landing steps, grouping themselves protectively around John Paul.

Mexico's president and his wife step forward. She gives the pope a bunch of red roses, which John Paul passes to Noé. The president, mindful of his government's ferocious anti-clerical posture, keeps his welcome speech short. It is remarkable for its banality and the fact that John Paul is never once referred to as pope. He is merely a 'distinguished visitor'. The president and his lady leave the airport which has been closed since dawn to all other air traffic because, in the words of an official spokesman, somebody might 'wish to bomb the pope'.

Only after the presidential cavalcade is clear of the tarmac can the local bishops extend their welcome. They come forward hesitantly, wary of the heavily armed policemen forming a perimeter around the aircraft. The clerics wear black trousers. There is virtually no way of telling they are priests: none of them displays a cross or other religious emblems. Mexican law forbids priests and nuns to wear their habits outside consecrated ground. Villot has personally negotiated with the Mexican government permission for the pope to travel about the country in his pontifical garb.

John Paul has hardly begun to greet his bishops when the press disgorge from the plane. They swoop on the papal party and the welcoming committee.

Marcinkus does not hesitate. Using his fists, elbows and the sheer bulk of his body, he begins furiously to push aside the press. The violence of his response causes the media momentarily to draw back. Marcinkus grabs the pope and hustles him towards a single-decker bus whose roof has been cut off. The strange-looking vehicle is draped in the Vatican colours, yellow and white. Marcinkus plumps the pope on a platform just behind the driver. The rest of the papal retinue scramble for seats. With Marcinkus standing towering, glowering at the reassembling press corps, and John Paul hanging onto a metal bar, the machine – quickly christened a popemobile by a reporter – sets off for Mexico City.

Behind, the police start to fire tear-gas grenades into the media mêlée. Then they move in on the reeling reporters and photographers with heavy boots and swinging truncheons. It is a foretaste of what is to come.

*

Preceded by a police motorcade and flanked by policemen dressed in tight-fitting black tracksuits who trot alongside, the popemobile travels towards a city guarded for the occasion by another hundred thousand policemen and soldiers – including a thousand marksmen placed on roofs from which the vehicle is visible. Twenty helicopter gunships constantly fly back and forth above the route. Two thousand doctors and six thousand nurses stand by at first-aid posts.

Judging by the crowds, all of Mexico City's twelve million inhabitants plus an estimated two million visitors who have come for the occasion appear to be lining the route. There is one thing about them the pope cannot fail to notice: they are mostly young; half the population of Mexico is under fifteen.

As the cavalcade moves on, the millions of voices are raised in a continuous scream of *Viva El Papa!* Confetti and fresh flowers shower onto the papal vehicle. Soon its occupants are ankle deep in blooms.

One of the reporters who has managed to escape from the police bashing at the airport and has caught up with the popemobile, thinks that 'the white, open-armed figure seems to be repeating a mythical return – the return of Quetzalcoatl, the legendary Aztec god who sailed back from the east and came into his own here in this upland capital. The white pope brings his own *mysterium* with him. He seems astonished, moved and delighted.'

But Noé is worried. No matter what Dziwisz says, the high altitude can cause giddiness and heart palpitations which may make even strong men keel over, unconscious.

It is mid-afternoon when the popemobile reaches Mexico City's magnificent sixteenth-century cathedral in Zocalo Square. Two hundred thousand people are crammed around the towering edifice. Here there are more clashes between police and press: thirty reporters are injured.

As the popemobile judders to a stop, Noé darts forward and speaks to Marcinkus.

'*La turista*,' insists the master of ceremonies. 'It can be very bad.'

Marcinkus looks bewildered. 'Which tourist is bad?' He glares around him. The police are driving back the press.

'No, no, no,' snaps Noé. 'The altitude.'

Marcinkus shrugs. He has no idea what the master of ceremonies is worrying about now. The giant bodyguard is suffering no ill effects from the change in atmospheric pressure.

Noé falls in behind the pope for the ceremonial procession into the cathedral. He has no doubt: John Paul shows increasing signs of fatigue. His gait has slowed and he appears to have trouble keeping his head from sagging; he barely acknowledges the four thousand guests packing the cathedral, including women in black lace mantillas who attempt to kiss his hands as he passes. When he reaches his throne, Noé bends down and murmurs in his ear.

'It's the altitude. Breathe slowly. Then it will be all right.'

The pope nods.

When he speaks his strength returns. His voice has its usual vibrant timbre as he delivers his homily word perfect in Spanish. First he pays tribute to Mexico's patron, the Virgin of Guadelupe, and to the importance of Mary's religious example.

He pauses before saying '*Mexico siempre fiel*', an adaptation of the Polish motto, *Polonia semper fidelis*. Thunderous applause sweeps the cathedral.

John Paul waits, beaming. He looks down at his script. His lips are seen to move silently. When he lifts his head his smile has gone. There is a sternness about his mouth which gives the languid Spanish phrases a clipped finality.

He says he deplores 'theological deviations'. That there is no such thing as 'a new Church'. Nor is there a Church 'born from the people'.

There are no 'new arguments'. In a dozen different ways he warns that liberation theology is anathema. Not only is it to be rejected, but he demands that all the Catholics of Mexico, and beyond – he waves vaguely in the direction of South America – must declare their fealty to the papacy and also subscribe to his version of what is the Church. Raising his voice, staring about him, now ignoring a script he clearly knows by heart, John Paul says only the established Church can nourish and create a people able to grow in faith, hope and fraternal love. Liberation theology – the words themselves do not actually cross his lips, not that it matters – must never be spoken of in the same breath as the Risen Christ and the Universal Church.

He delivers a papal blessing. It is over. But nobody thinks it is the end.

*

Two days later, John Paul, dubbed *Su Santidad* by the adoring masses, visits the sanctuary of the Madonna of Guadelupe. The sermon he will deliver here will formally inaugurate the Latin American bishops' conference at nearby Puebla.

There are a million people around the Guadelupe shrine. Forty thousand riot police wall them in. Helicopters clatter overhead. Half-tracks lurk on the fringes. It looks more like a military exercise than the peaceful assembly of those who wish to pay homage to their spiritual leader.

Apart from waving at the vast throng, the pope almost ignores their presence. He intends to concentrate largely on the nuns and priests standing before him. The nuns have not stopped applauding since he arrived. This visibly annoys the pope; Noé finally shushes them by placing his fingers to his lips. John Paul's anger is still evident as he delivers his biting words.

He jabs a finger towards the nuns. 'Remember who you are. You are the mystical brides of Christ.'

He reproaches them for thinking action is a substitute for prayer. 'You must give up the pursuit of socio-political matters and radical ideologies.'

The nuns stir uneasily. 'You must stop seeking new horizons and experiences.'

John Paul warns them to be careful in their choice of companions. Those they mix with must always be selected 'according to evangelical criteria'. It is a blunt reminder they must not consort with liberation theologians. He gives them one final piece of advice. They should all pray more.

The nuns who have come to cheer, to show their pleasure at his presence, sit there dismayed. Several seem to be on the verge of tears.

John Paul turns and faces the ranks of Mexican clergy.

His voice even harder – 'a judge not a pastor', scribbles one journalist – the pope reminds them of their duties.

'You are priests and members of religious orders, not social or political leaders.' A pause, then: 'Let us have no illusions that we will serve the Gospel if we dilute our charisma by showing an exaggerated interest in temporal problems.'

The priests are stunned. Many wonder what the morrow will bring when John Paul delivers his keynote speech to the cardinals and bishops at Puebla. Everybody realizes his address will set the tone for the most important conference in the modern history of the South American Church; it may also even more clearly reveal the future direction of this pontificate of constant surprises.

*

Visibly tired, and thinner – he has already lost three pounds through an attack of 'Mexican tummy' – John Paul, his face wan in the harsh tropical light, leans for support on the rail of the popemobile as it travels slowly through the streets of Puebla. There are an estimated two million persons lining the route. It is Sunday morning, 28 January, the one free day in the week-in week-out existence of these pitifully poor people. They stand in their best clothes over which they have draped strips of yellow and white paper or fabric in honour of the pope. When the papal vehicle approaches they extend their rosary beads and crucifixes towards John Paul, shouting for him to bless them. It is both moving and not a little frightening. Marcinkus looks more vigilant than ever. Ciban and his security detail trot alongside the popemobile as do some of the ten thousand policemen drafted into Puebla for the occasion.

By late morning the convoy reaches the Palafoxian Seminary on the outskirts of Puebla where the bishops' conference is being held.

An altar has been set up on the seminary's football field. Nearly four hundred thousand people stand on the pitch and the open ground beyond.

Once more, as he reaches his throne, the pope's attention focuses on those immediately below him. In the first row are the nineteen cardinals from Latin America. Aramburu looks stern – but satisfied; the autocratic Argentinian has let it be known he endorses the tough line the pope is taking. Lorscheider and Arns, both Franciscans and renowned liberals, seem pensive. They have tried, and failed, to get sight of the much awaited speech John Paul will deliver to the bishops after lunch. Baggio, who is Lorscheider's co-president at the conference, claims the pope insisted on the embargo. It is not a good omen for the liberals. As well as the cardinals, there are some hundred bishops and *monsignores* seated in the front rows.

When he speaks, John Paul makes it plain that the small, privileged group sitting in comfort before him are his messengers – the prelates charged with going forth from here and persuading the three hundred million other Catholics in Latin America to accept the uncompromising message he now delivers.

John Paul first restates the Church's position on divorce, which is a 'threat to the solidarity of the family'. Therefore all good Catholics must ignore the dangerous new divorce laws recently passed in several Latin American countries. It is short and sharp.

Next he turns to birth control. He is as vigorously opposed to it as were previous popes, perhaps more so. There must be no 'indiscriminate effort to reduce the birth rate at any cost – what my predecessor, Paul VI, called "reducing the number of guests at the banquet of life".'

The liberals listen in dismayed silence to a stricture delivered in Mexico, a country which doubles its population every ten years, and to a continent, South America, where almost half the babies born are illegitimate.

On this sobering note, followed by a smile and papal blessing for the crowd, John Paul departs for lunch. He eats very little, talks even less. He is a man clearly preoccupied with what he must do next.

Early in the afternoon he goes to the seminary hall and takes his place in the middle of a long table. He is surrounded by the hierarchy of all Latin America. He sits, his head bowed over the script he has written first in Polish, revised, and then translated into Spanish. No other hand has touched the text. It is entirely his own work. Now, as he begins to speak, free of cameramen and the watchful reporters, John Paul makes no effort to be the smiling and relaxed pastor.

He starts with the reminder that ten years have passed since their last conference. Then Paul had addressed them. Now, he has come to remind them of some important truths. A great deal that was positive had stemmed from the 1968 conference. But there is also no way to 'ignore the incorrect interpretations which have at times been made'.

Lorscheider begins to take notes. Arns is openly unhappy, nervously drumming his fingers on the table. Baggio looks at him. When Arns stops his tapping, the Vatican trouble-shooter resumes staring impassively ahead.

The pope's words roll inexorably on; the delivery is flat, brooking no contradiction. He says he is deeply dissatisfied with certain 're-readings' of the Gospels. This has caused 'confusion'. People must not be confused over what 'true liberation' really is. 'True liberation' is 'liberation from sin', nothing more nor less.

He pauses to turn a page. Up and down the table comes the sound of scratching pens.

The pope resumes speaking. The main mission of pastors, he states, 'is to be teachers of the truth – not a human rational truth, but the truth which comes from God.'

It is a devastating body blow to one of the cherished beliefs of the theology of liberation. This holds that 'the truth which comes from God' can only be discovered within the present-day political and social world. For them, spiritual truth cannot be separated from worldly reality, nor is it enough to proclaim the Gospel faithfully; it must be lived through identifying with the oppressed.

Displaying a remarkable insight into the new doctrine he clearly opposes, John Paul continues to dissect and reject liberation theology in favour of the traditional interpretation of the scriptures. To 're-read' the Gospels is simply 'theoretical speculation rather than an authentic meditation on the word of God'. The 're-read' view of Jesus does not 'tally with the Church's catechesis'.

Another pause for a sip of water. He turns and looks at the cardinals seated on either side and immediately across from him. His next words are for them. He reminds them of what he had said in Rome the night he was elected and just before they had all prayed together in the Sistine Chapel: concern for social ecclesiology would be paramount in his pontificate.

A number of cardinals nod, remembering.

John Paul smiles briefly before turning back to his script. It is because, he continues, he is anxious to develop his pontificate along these lines that he is now so vigorously opposed to any suggestion there can be two Churches.

He looks up, watching the surprised reactions. 'Two Churches,' he repeats. 'How can this be?' He tells them the institutional and official Church is now under attack by those who have erroneously judged and found it to be wanting; they have chosen therefore to follow 'a new church', a church which 'springs from the people and takes concrete form in the poor'.

John Paul stops once more. He spreads his hands. He seems to be saying he cannot believe it needs stating, but that he will, nevertheless, state it. There is only one Church, the one they all belong to, the one of which he is the head.

'Preaching the Gospel is not an individualistic activity. It is not subject to the discretionary power of individualistic criteria and perspectives, but to that of communion with the Church and her pastors.'

Anything else is the result of 'familiar forms of ideological conditioning'. In other words, Marxism.

Another pause. The pope is in no hurry. This is a watershed. He has delivered his judgement in all its severity. He wants time for it to be fully absorbed.

Now he begins to build. He tells the conference they must never forget that the essential Christian message is primarily about God and his action in the world. He goes on to examine a paradox which contemporary philosophers have also pondered: this is an age when ever more is being written and spoken about liberty, yet in reality it is an era of unsurpassed enslavement and torture.

He begins to suggest a solution. Whereas Christian humanism consists of more than that which humanity alone can provide against oppression, atheistic humanism leads directly to man 'being deprived of an essential dimension of his being, namely his search for the infinite, and thus having his being reduced in the worst way'.

The words symbolize John Paul's mastery of religious intellectualism. He has meditated on philosophy and on action. Not only is his mind creative, it is also analytical. What he is saying is that, in a secular sense, a search for 'liberation' may in fact lead to enslavement.

He tells them how this can be overcome – through proper use of the 'Catholic social doctrine' which lays such store on human dignity. The pope is back on familiar ground. He goes on to remind the bishops that 'this complete truth about the human being constitutes the foundation of the Church's social teaching and the basis also of true liberation'.

It is balm. But can it soothe the earlier stings?

*

The reaction was expectedly swift. Baggio and other curialists were blamed for 'badly advising' John Paul to make such statements; his critics would not – or could not – believe the pope was sole author of the judgements at Puebla. A bitterness entered into the statements they issued to the thousand news people covering the tour. A leading liberation theologist said a commitment to 'liberation according to the Gospel' was what counted; that 'theology is what you do in the evenings, when you're tired'. Another insisted the pope was 'talking in a realm of ideals. The reality is too dramatic, too tragic to be ignored. The pope has an idealist spiritual reading of the scriptures.'

It was the beginning – the end of the honeymoon of John Paul's pontificate. Few recognized what had happened. Least of all perhaps the pope. He remained caught up in the uncritical enthusiasm of the enormous crowds he drew everywhere he went.

Before boarding the plane to return to Rome, he offered a final thought. 'I came with a message of love. The love of God, the Virgin Mary, the Church and the pope. I leave you the greetings of a friend. To all of you, to your children and families, a brother's embrace.'

Then Juan Pablo Segundo *was airborne. None of the thousands who saw his departure were aware of what he had told the bishops' conference. But for them it was enough that there had been six days of religious fervour which provided a temporary respite from the reality of the daily struggle to stay alive.*

Nobody really thought anything would change. How could it? The question was too ridiculous, said a liberationist, to warrant thinking of an answer.

In its way that was an answer. The pope had spoken. The hierarchy had listened. Yet in the final analysis those who probably mattered the most: the priests in the shanty towns, the Catholic doctors and nuns who routinely prescribed contraceptives up and down this vast continent, and above all the millions who had found the militancy of the new Christianity worth grasping: they would continue as before.

It would not matter that the Puebla conference reiterated the pope's conservatism, largely because of the magisterial grip Baggio held all the way through. It would not change anything when, as a rider to the book-length final document, it was admitted that not all the leaders of the Latin American Church had distanced themselves far enough from the rich and politically powerful, or 'identified themselves sufficiently with the poor'.

Nothing would matter for the poor. Nothing would change for them. This they knew. So did everyone who had been involved in a visit which had produced so much in theory and would result in so little in practice.

*

Practice and the techniques he learned in the Syrian training camp have brought Agca undetected to where he now stands at five o'clock on the freezing afternoon of Thursday, 1 February 1979. He is on a corner of Nuruosmaniye Caddesi, the Istanbul street which houses the headquarters of Turkey's most important newspaper, the independent daily, *Milliyet.* There are three hours to go before Agca intends to commit murder.

Even here, as he stands shivering – partly in excitement, partly from cold – Agca cannot believe how quickly it has all happened.

The previous Monday he returned to his room near the Süleyman Mosque to find a piece of paper under his door. It asked him to telephone an Ankara number he knew: 27 48 92. It is the Libyan Embassy. When he called he was directed to collect a letter left in his name at the Istanbul Hilton. That evening Agca picked up the letter and, as instructed on the telephone, did not open it until he was safely back in his room.

The letter was unsigned. But Agca recognized the writing. To make doubly sure, however, he compared it with a piece of paper he carried in his bank passbook. Its writing matched that of the letter. Each had been written by Teslin Tore.

Tore's instructions in the letter were specific. Agca must persuade the Grey Wolves that the time had come to kill Abdi Ipekci. Ipekci is not only the editor of *Milliyet* and one of the most respected of Turkish journalists, he is also vice-president of the International Press Institute. There were other instructions, all of which Agca carefully memorized. Included with the letter were twenty thousand Turkish lire in notes. They came with a final instruction. Having read the letter Agca should burn it. This he did.

Next day he placed the money in his savings account.

After visiting the bank he called on the Istanbul leaders of the Grey Wolves, Mehmet Sener and Yavus Caylan. Both agreed Ipekci should die. There was little discussion over why the editor had been chosen. It was perhaps sufficient that Sener categorized Ipekci as a 'moderate'; there was no place for such a person in the fanatical world of Agca and his companions.

The assassination details were quickly settled. The three men would shadow Ipekci during the day before Agca actually killed him at night. They had picked up the editor this morning as he left home in his car. Caylan, the son of a cab owner, had borrowed his father's ageing taxi for the purpose. They had trailed Ipekci to the *Milliyet* office. Later, when he emerged for lunch, they staked out the restaurant. Then they had walked behind the editor as he went back to the newspaper. Once Agca had casually overtaken him and turned and looked quickly at Ipekci, remembering his face. It was a trick he had learned in Syria.

Now, as Agca waits on the windy street corner, his Mauser concealed under his sweater, he knows Sener and Caylan are somewhere nearby in the taxi. They will reappear moments before eight o'clock – the planned hour of Ipekci's execution.

Agca works his way quietly through his hate list. Then, as the time approaches, he runs through the details of the approaching murder with the same fixation as he has repeated the list.

At 7.50, Agca walks slowly down Nuruosmaniye Caddesi until he reaches number 65, the *Milliyet* headquarters. There are few people about and the traffic is light. Agca takes up position across the street, standing against a wall, watching the newspaper's works entrance, the one he now knows Ipekci uses when he comes and goes from his office. Agca hopes he is not too conspicuous.

He removes the Mauser and holds it behind his back.

Shortly before eight o'clock Ipekci emerges, as he does every night he is on duty, to drive home for dinner. He begins to walk towards his parked car.

Agca follows.

At the top end of the street Caylan appears with the taxi. Sener is in the back, holding the passenger door slightly ajar. The cab cruises slowly down the street.

Agca is a few feet behind Ipekci. He has the automatic in his right hand. He glances quickly over his shoulder. The taxi is twenty yards away – exactly where they planned it would be.

Suddenly Ipekci turns. He looks uncomprehendingly at Agca. As the gun comes up level with the editor's eyes, he shouts one word: 'No.'

Agca shoots Ipekci in the head. He slumps to the ground, blood running from his nose, ears and mouth. Agca stands over him and empties the Mauser's magazine into the already-dead body.

The taxi draws alongside. Sener throws open wide the passenger door.

Agca looks again at Ipekci and, as instructed in Tore's letter, shouts, 'The Grey Wolves take vengeance!'

He utters the traditional howl of the organization. Then, gun in hand, he jumps into the taxi. Caylan races the cab down the street.

The first screams over what has just happened are drowned by the noise from the taxi's faulty exhaust pipe.

*

The murder shocks Turkey. It is widely reported internationally. The killing is seen as a further deterioration in law and order; there is speculation that Turkey is now more ungovernable than ever. *Milliyet* and the Turkish Journalists' Union offer a reward of six million lire – over a hundred thousand American dollars, a fabulous sum in such an impoverished country – for the capture of Ipekci's killers. Eyewitnesses have seen them escape. Agca's defiant words about vengeance and his chilling howl almost automatically mean the crime is laid at the door of the Grey Wolves.

This is what Teslin Tore had planned.[5] The KGB-controlled terrorist who has been running Agca for months, who arranged his grooming in that school for terror in the Syrian desert, who has been supplying him with substantial sums of money which have almost certainly come from his own Soviet paymasters – Tore can now feel completely satisfied it has all been a good investment. His protégé, despite his mental disturbances, and perhaps even because of them, has performed his first, and very professional, assassination.

*

The crime attracts the special interest of two foreign embassies in Ankara.

The first is the Holy See's Nunciature in the quiet suburb of the capital's Cankaya district. The nuncio has just received a most confidential report from Villot requesting he begin exploratory talks with the Turkish regime for a visit John Paul desires to make to Istanbul to celebrate the Feast of St Andrew, the patron of the Church of Constantinople. The pope wishes to use the occasion as a means of reconciliation between the Roman Catholic and Orthodox Churches. The feast is in late November, ten months hence.

The Ankara nuncio is already nervous about the political instability and the relentless wave of violence sweeping Turkey. He decides that the murder of Abdi Ipekci will make an ideal case-study to illustrate his fear that it is simply too dangerous for the pope to come to this troubled country. He starts to collect data on the Ipekci murder to support his contention that the same fanatical mentality which struck down the editor would not hesitate to attack John Paul.

A few streets away from the Holy See Nunciature is the heavily guarded Israeli Legation, at 43 Farabi Sokak. Apart from the Russian Embassy, no other building in Ankara is better protected than this redoubt where a dozen Jewish diplomats and their families live.

As a matter of course, details of Ipekci's murder, together with the surprisingly accurate descriptions of his killers — the one of Agca is particularly good and has been provided for the Israelis from sources in MIT, Turkish intelligence — are sent by short-wave radio to the Foreign Ministry in Tel Aviv. There, on a highly secure teletype, they are relayed to the nearby headquarters of the Central Institute for Intelligence and Special Missions, MOSSAD. The description of Ipekci's killers are fed into the agency's sophisticated computers to see whether they match any of the thousands of terrorist profiles already on tape. They do not. But because the Ankara Legation has tagged Agca as the leader of the three killers — though his name is still unknown — his physical description is transferred to a second computer bank. It is the one in which MOSSAD stores the names of those terrorists it believes are most likely to strike again.

30

Why should he wear a bullet-proof vest under his cassock? John Paul angrily throws the question across the breakfast table in the papal apartment on Monday morning, 28 May 1979.

Four of his listeners — Dziwisz, Magee, Martin and Marcinkus, sitting in front of the debris of food, as Polish and substantial as ever, wait for the fifth man to respond. Agostino Casaroli steeples his fingers together and says the suggestion should be seen for what it is — a ploy by the Polish Communist Party leader, Edward Gierek. In five days' time the pope is due to begin a full-scale visit to Poland. This is Gierek trying to sabotage it. Casaroli argues that in spite of the Polish leader's assurances to the contrary, almost certainly if the pope wore a flak jacket, the news would be leaked to the media to bolster the insidious campaign the Polish authorities have been waging that the pope is a security risk even in his own homeland.

'Very crude,' concludes Casaroli. 'And also very typical.'[1]

The pope agrees.

Equally, cautions Casaroli, to disregard what on the surface seems to be Gierek's concern no harm should come to the pope could leave the Vatican open to accusations of irresponsibility. Accompanying the request for John Paul to wear protection is Gierek's reminder that the Polish government knows of the numerous threats the Vatican has received against the pope's life. Consequently, continues Casaroli, it would be wise to pack a flak jacket in John Paul's luggage.

'I will never wear it,' pronounces the pope.

'Of course not,' concedes Casaroli.

What he does not add is that when Gierek's request arrived in the Secretariat of State, Casaroli had sent word to Gammarelli to tailor a number of papal cassocks cleverly designed to conceal a bullet-proof vest underneath. The cassocks would be delivered to the Vatican before the pope left for Poland. They would be in his baggage, placed there at Casaroli's specific instruction. If, by any chance, the situation in Poland warranted it, Casaroli intends to persuade John Paul to wear a protective vest. Until then there is no need to discuss the matter further.

This foresight is typical of the man who is now Secretary of State following the unexpected death of Villot in March. John Paul had waited six full weeks before appointing Casaroli to this most senior position in the Curia. What made him hesitate is Casaroli's strong views on *Ostpolitik*, the building of bridges between the Church and the godless regimes of Eastern Europe. The pope does not always share Casaroli's enthusiasm for *Ostpolitik*. He has let it be known he wants to 'reflect' further on the best way to have a 'dialogue' with Communism. Finally, though, recognizing the extraordinary diplomatic gifts Casaroli possesses, John Paul made him Secretary. In the two weeks he has been in the job, Casaroli has displayed considerable flair balancing what John Paul wants against the demands of the secular world, a world which the pope's globe-trotting is bringing ever nearer – and sometimes, as in the case of the forthcoming Polish visit, close to the point of conflict.

The talk turns to how the approaching visit has made Poland the very epicentre of Eastern Europe's Catholic revival.

Dziwisz says that almost every day he receives reports of peasant revolts against Communism across the country. The secretary is spending hours on the telephone to Poland, double-checking arrangements for the visit. At Zbrosza Duza, a sooty hamlet with a history of religious militancy, the villagers have paraded a slogan through the streets – *The Church is our government* – and formed a Believers' Self-Defence Committee. Potential meddlers from the secular government are greeted by Believers armed with pitchforks. At another village, Opole Stare, a church has been built: overnight two steeples rose from the roof of a cottage. Thousands of Catholics came to dedicate this modest, and illegal, Church of the Blessed Maximilian. Warsaw's central government ordered the structure torn down, just as Opole Stare's previous church was demolished twenty years earlier. But now, with the impending papal visit, the villagers are resisting. They have organized guard patrols and an alarm system of bells which will ring in six neighbouring communities if government forces dare to attack their church.

It is not just Poland, explains Casaroli, but the entire Eastern Bloc which has been put on notice that its relationship with the Church is in a challenging new phase. In Lithuania and the Ukraine, in Hungary and Czechoslovakia – where the Church has suffered the severest of brutal oppression – there are signs of a new boldness among the faithful.

The pope listens carefully. Over the past months he has made plain how much store he places on this sort of informal briefing. The breakfast session typifies the rapport between the pope and his personal staff. With them – these insiders inevitably dubbed around the

Vatican as the 'Polish Mafia' – he is informal without being over-friendly, demanding yet generally relaxed; his occasional explosive outbursts of anger are therefore the more surprising. Afterwards John Paul generally makes clear no one must forget that he alone bears the responsibility of the papacy, yet at the same time he expects those close to him to give advice as well as to take orders.

Casaroli, for all his recently acquired authority, is still a relative newcomer to this kitchen cabinet. After listening to him for a few minutes, the pope begins to nod impatiently; every bit as well as the Secretary, John Paul knows the overall developments in Eastern Europe. The pope turns to Dziwisz.

'Tell me more about our Poland,' he says. It is a request he never tires of making these days.

Dziwisz reveals that one Polish diocese has collected seventy thousand signatures for a petition demanding that Mass be broadcast on radio and television. For the first time there has been open criticism of religious persecution from the pulpit of St John's Cathedral in Warsaw – at a time when its congregation was sprinkled with Party functionaries.

Everything Dziwisz says makes it obvious that Poland, earnestly Catholic for longer than a thousand years – once Rome's eastern bulwark against Mongols, Turks and Russians – is showing that its Church, shorn of its extensive landholdings, persistently harassed and poor, is now respected all the more for leading resistance against Communism. The harder Party cadres try to consolidate their power, the more the Polish Church becomes the fount of national pride and lost freedoms.

Dziwisz's words draw murmurs of approval from the pope. More than anybody around the table, the secretary thinks the pope's thoughts and speaks the pope's language. By temperament he is very like the side of John Paul which only these insiders are privileged to see. On these occasions Dziwisz is far removed from the Gee-Whiz character the policemen in St Peter's Square resent and fear; here, in the pope's dining room, he has the same articulate and soft-spoken delivery, the same low-keyed restraint that characterizes John Paul in private.

The visit to Poland, insists the secretary, will be an unqualified success.

Magee, Marcinkus and Martin each assuredly know what lies behind this resounding declaration. It is Stanislaw Dziwisz trying to soothe away some of the criticism John Paul's pontificate is openly attracting.

*

Nobody can be certain when it began. Was it that morning the first mocking newspaper cartoon appeared? It depicted John Paul walking across the water of his newly built swimming pool at Castel Gandolfo. As he walked, looking suspiciously like Jesus Christ, Superstar, the cartoonist had the pope declaiming, 'A few years of this and I'll set up on my own.' Other, even less amusing, allusions followed, sniping at his Polishness, his conservatism, his travel plans. In the wake of the cartoons came the poor-taste jokes. A nadir was reached with the tale of Jesus approaching as an apparition in that most secluded part of the Vatican gardens where the pope liked to jog. The punch-line of the jibe was Jesus saying there would be no more Polish popes – 'at least not in my lifetime'.

The jogging part was true. Whenever he could, the pope donned a tracksuit and trotted around the grounds of the Apostolic Palace. One of Ciban's Vigilance discreetly followed. Sometimes Marcinkus joined him for a run. An easy and close relationship developed between them. This did nothing to stifle criticism. The drip of gossip hinted Marcinkus had bamboozled the pope into ignoring the precarious financial situation of the Vatican Bank – the Italian authorities were urgently investigating its links with Sindona and Calvi – and that the banker had somehow persuaded John Paul to concentrate on his pastoral work and let the business side of the Church remain largely in the hands of Marcinkus. There was no real evidence to support this. But, like the cartoons and the jokes, the idea persisted.

So did the fable that 'apparently' Cody 'has successfully played the Polish ethnic card to frustrate attempts by responsible Church officers to remove him'. The charge, hardly surprisingly, comes from the self-appointed bête-noire of the papacy, Andrew Greeley. He claimed Cody 'parlayed his past financial contributions to Poland – and some new contributions, according to Chicago sources – the size of the Polish population in Chicago, and his alleged friendship with the pope into a successful counter-offensive against his enemies'. Greeley alleged the pope offered Cody a job in Rome – not specified, but presumably to keep a closer eye on the cardinal – and that Cody declined. Greeley's flim-flam continued with his judgement that John Paul was 'reluctant to act against a cardinal who helped elect him.' But Greeley couldn't let the matter rest there. He felt compelled to deliver a final jab at the pontiff. John Paul's alleged behaviour over Cody 'must raise serious questions about personal weakness'. Cardinal Krol was not the only prelate to believe it also raised serious questions of personal spleen in Greeley.

Those who actually know John Paul are genuinely baffled by any suggestion he could be capable of the slightest personal weakness. Magee, in particular, had come to appreciate the pope's constant strength. It stemmed from a disciplined and analytical mind; even John Paul's instincts emerged from cool reasoning rather than intuitive hunches. Yet behind his careful pragmatic approach there was a compassion that permeated everything he did. There were also other qualities which had shaped his mind, and further discounted the idea of personal weakness. His confrontation with Communism hardened his will to resist anything he saw as a threat to the Church.

It also heightened his political awareness; in this arena he could more than hold his own with Casaroli. The two men spent many a long night reviewing the state of the secular world. Of all the documents the pope perused, the intelligence digests from the Secretariat of State were read the most avidly. These were sometimes accompanied by reports from the Central Intelligence Agency on Soviet intentions. (Approval for the pope to be briefed by the agency was apparently given by President Carter and reiterated in a personal letter Mrs Rosalynn Carter delivered during a private audience with him early in his pontificate.) All this enhanced his natural capacity for growth. He brought to the papacy an already well-developed curiosity about almost everything. He was prepared to listen to anybody with something to say; conversely, those with nothing to contribute made him impatient.

Impatience was one of the hallmarks of his pontificate, undoubtedly helping to create an environment where criticism could thrive. His impatience was most noticeable when he sensed others did not recognize his total commitment to internal discipline in the Church – epitomized for him by the question of celibacy. He had a heroic concept of the priesthood, coupled by a sweeping and compelling vision of 'the grandeur of priestly celibacy'. He was determined to underwrite the old piety that a priest was married for life to his vocation. Consequently, he had so far refused all petitions from priests wishing to be released from their vows.

John Paul enshrined his views about the priesthood – who was eligible to belong and on what terms – in a lengthy document: Letter to All the Priests of the Church. *Each cleric had been sent a copy in April. The reverberations were still crashing against the Leonine walls; the thunder of controversy and obloquy permeated even the Apostolic Palace.*

The pope simply could not understand this reaction to an appeal which began with the personal touch that characterized his discourses. He wrote to his priests in the hope 'I may be permitted to speak here of my own experience.'

The letter had continued in this vein, a moving soliloquy of the pope as priest, writing to equals, speaking at every turn of his eloquent text of 'our priesthood'.

But behind the mellifluent words was an iron resolve. John Paul offered his own reasons why the issue of celibacy had ever arisen: 'Perhaps in these recent years – at least in certain quarters – there has been too much discussion about the priesthood, the priest's "identity", the virtue of his presence in the modern world and so on, and too little praying.'

His Letter *was not intended, he made clear, as a theological treatise on the ministry; instead it should be seen as encouragement, as one priest offering support to another in a difficult moment, as a reminder of old principles: 'It is a matter here of keeping one's word to Christ and the Church. Keeping one's word is at one and the same time a duty and the proof of the priest's inner* maturity.' Therefore, he continued, there should not, 'especially at moments of crisis' be 'recourse to a dispensation'.

Requests for dispensation continued to stockpile in the Vatican. After these first seven months of John Paul's pontificate, there were close to five hundred priests seeking release from their vows. Those who sought to do so in order to marry were told they would not be released. There need be no further discussion on the matter; they would simply have to abide by their oath if they wished to remain Catholics in good standing. Only a few old priests, close to death, would be seriously considered for dispensation.

The battle lines were drawn. Any priest wishing to marry would have to choose between a personal relationship and his relationship with the Church – a choice he was presumed to have made before taking holy orders in the first place. A priest who 'attempted marriage' would be instantly excommunicated.

The response to the Letter was predictable. The pope was accused of being too simplistic, too closely linked with a theology which had not assimilated the orientations of the Second Vatican Council. He was charged with failing to recognize that it was not fidelity to a state of life that had priority but rather fidelity to the ministry which had been entrusted to priests in the service of the community. Opponents bitterly rejected John Paul's comparison between the sacrament of marriage and the promise of celibacy a priest made at his ordination; certainly, they conceded, marriage was the sacrament of love, but ordination was not the sacrament of celibacy.

Hans Küng entered the fray. He condemned the pope for 'violating the human right to marriage within the Church while posing as the defender of human rights outside'. The judgement seemed harsh on a pope who had actively fought in Poland to stop his priests being jailed, tortured and murdered, who had opposed every attempt to deny religious and civic rights, who had done as much as anyone to uphold the Church in his homeland.

The row roared on. Koenig tried to cool matters by telling priests in Vienna that the pope was attempting to elevate the question of celibacy above the level of 'mere administrative acts and to show that sacred promises and deep convictions of conscience are involved'.

Koenig's attempt at balance was lost in the rush to other judgements. The not altogether invidious comparison was made that, like Paul's Humanae Vitae, John Paul's Letter had fuelled the very controversy it was meant to quench. Throughout the Church liberal theologians – few of whom could match Küng's intellectual fire-power – continued to take pot-shots at the pontificate. Mexico, they said, had clearly not been a one-off: it was not just the theology of liberation that was being chopped; felled with it were all the other expectations they had held for the new reign. They feared this was the onset of an era of toughness, one which would make Paul and even Pius XII look like milksops when it came to administering the magisterium. Nobody doubted John Paul's appeal for the masses, his magnetic personality, his charisma. But his *opponents feared he would use these qualities to batten down the ecclesiastical hatches. That he was, in short, going to be Polish. Nobody really explained what that nasty little ethnic smear meant.*

But in the first week of June 1979, the critics fell silent. Not one of them could but be enthralled by the image of a devout man who had last seen Poland as a cardinal now returning home as the pope. There had been nothing quite like it in the entire history of the papacy.

*

During the day some three hundred thousand Poles assemble in the square in the centre of Warsaw where Tsar Alexander I had reviewed his troops, where the Germans had erected a V-shaped monument to their occupation, where the Red Army had conducted executions. It is the place the Polish Communist Party has called Victory Square.

This Saturday evening, 2 June, the start of the pope's visit, the presence of a vast peaceful throng in the square is a vivid indication of the crushing defeat the Party has suffered. All its attempts to impede, frustrate, play down and nitpick over the visit have been a glorious failure. Many of those in Victory Square were present the previous Thursday night when a low-loader lorry had driven across the cobblestones to a large wooden platform, covered with hessian and painted to look like granite. On the truck was a cross, thirty-five feet long, carved from solid oak and attached to tubular steel. A crane had hoisted the cross into place on the platform. Since then it has become a symbol for Poland and the outside world, an object of wonder and hope. Below the towering cross is the altar, its front draped with the Polish crown and eagle. It offers a magnificent provocation to the nearby grey edifice of Communist Party headquarters.

Earlier this Saturday Noé had added a third symbol. From a window behind the platform – a position reluctantly agreed upon by the authorities – the master of ceremonies had unfurled the pontifical coat of arms. This, for the crowd, is the final stirring proof that 'Jan Pawel' has actually come home.

For hour upon patient hour, waiting for the Mass to begin, they have stood here, in a heatwave temperature, staring at the emblem, noting with quiet satisfaction the prominence given to the two figures central to the pope's life since boyhood: Christ and Mary. There is a simplicity and personal theological affirmation about the banner which appeals to the crowd. They note that the emblem's cross is sufficiently off-centre to allow room for the red silk-embroidered initial M – for Mary – to be symbolically placed by the foot of the Cross of her Son. He has not forgotten, they are glad to see, his heritage. How could he?

While they wait they endlessly repeat their jokes. 'Why isn't there any yellow paint left in the shops?' 'Because it's all been bought by the police to paint their truncheons to look like candles.' 'Why can't you buy black and white cloth?' 'The militia have taken it all so they can dress up as nuns and priests for security purposes.'

Security had been used in a last desperate effort to downgrade the actual start of the visit. Only five hundred people were allowed into Okecie Airport to greet the pope on arrival. As he reached Polish soil he kissed it. The official Party welcome was coolly cordial, though the greetings were peppered with the term 'Your Holiness' and there was a measure of national satisfaction over the fact the pope was Polish. John Paul responded that he had come for strictly religious reasons. Edward Gierek next received him at the city's old Belvedere Palace. Some observers suggested that when he playfully tapped the pope on the chest Gierek was really checking to see whether John Paul was wearing a flak-jacket under his cassock.

This was all skirmishing before the first big celebration of the tour – the Mass in Victory Square.

Suddenly, in the late afternoon sun, here he is – a sturdy, slightly stooping figure appearing before the altar. Prolonged clapping greets him. He raises his arms in greeting. He waits for a minute. Then he lowers his arms. The clapping stops. It is a poignant demonstration of the control he has over this congregation.

John Paul begins to speak. His voice is richly powerful, echoing and re-echoing around the square, bouncing off the stone buildings, a cacophony of sound that sometimes, because of a fault in some of the loudspeakers, gives his message a hiss and crackle which makes it difficult to follow. It does not matter. The gist is clear.

First he reminds them that Paul had wanted to come to Poland. He pauses. There is no need to say more. Everyone present knows the regime had refused to grant him a visa. Then he says the desire of Paul to come to Poland was so strong that he himself had been unable to resist the pressure.

'The pope could no longer remain a prisoner . . .'

The pause is brief. But the allusion is not missed. There is a renewed outbreak of clapping.

'. . . of the Vatican . . .'

Laughter. This is the pope showing he has not forgotten the rules for getting around things: that he still knows how to outsmart the opposition.

He comes to his first declaration. 'The Church brought Christ to Poland, and this points the way to an understanding of the great and fundamental reality which is man. For man cannot finally be understood without Christ, or rather man cannot ultimately understand himself without Christ. He can understand neither who he is nor what his proper dignity is, nor his vocations or final destiny; he cannot understand any of this without Christ. That is why Christ cannot be excluded from man's history anywhere in the world.'

It is out – a crystal-clear statement that Communism cannot ultimately triumph. The applause is unrestrained. It rolls on minute after minute. Here is Jan Pawel spelling out the Christological foundation for human rights. Here is a Polish pope telling the entire world that after thirty years of Communist oppression and indoctrination the Church in Poland will never abdicate its responsibilities.

*

For the next seven days John Paul proclaimed his vision, that through faith human rights would be restored to all those presently denied them. It would take time, but it would assuredly happen. His veiled attacks on first Polish then the wider Soviet repression drew roars of approval. Pointedly looking eastwards, to where Europe stretches to the Urals, he repeatedly said he had come to gather all the oppressed – the Slavs and the Croats, the Moravians and the Slovaks, the Serbs and the Ruthenians, the Latvians and the Estonians – to the heart of the Church. He was certain they would hear him in spite of all the obstructions to a free exchange of views. To everyone he offered an uncompromising proclamation of the Christian view of man. He told them he was well aware mankind was divided in many ways; he was also aware – perhaps above all – of the ideological divisions inherent in different systems. And he promised that 'the search for solutions which would enable human societies to cope with the task confronting them and live in justice is perhaps the main sign of our times'. It was enough. John Paul had achieved what he had set out to do: increase the self-respect and confidence of all those Catholics living under Communism. He had won an astonishing confrontation between spiritual force and material power. He brilliantly exploited the prerogative of the papacy – had he been a mere priest uttering these things he would surely have been imprisoned – to give real hope not only to his fellow countrymen but to everyone, everywhere, living under tyranny.

*

Sunday, 10 June, is another fine day. The sun beats down on the Russian-built TU–134A airliner of LOT, the Polish airline. It has been freshly painted a gleaming white for the flight to Rome. The plane's interior has been totally renovated. There is a salon up front with armchairs and a bed for the pope. There is champagne on ice in the galley, plus vodka and caviar and all kinds of other fish morsels. The cabin crew have been instructed that any food not used on the flight must be brought back to this tiny airport in the suburbs of Cracow.

Early in the afternoon John Paul arrives. He looks very tired. During the past week he has delivered thirty-two sermons and speeches, every one written solely by himself. He has been to Auschwitz, 'this Golgotha of our time', he called it; to his beloved mountains and the major Marian shrines of Poland. Everywhere he has drawn adoring crowds. Now he is about to leave Cracow aboard the LOT airliner.

There are, perhaps, a hundred thousand people lining the approaches to the airport. Many are crying.

Party officials bustle around the tarmac as the pope appears. One of them makes a politically orientated speech, claiming the State shares the concerns John Paul had mentioned during his stay. The pope sits quietly.

Then it is the turn of Cardinal Wyszynski. The Primate of Poland has hardly left John Paul's side during the trip; his every gesture has been an embodiment of Polish patriotism, his shrewd slate-grey eyes have narrowed and darted constantly, still protective towards the younger man.

The faith and Poland are what matters to them both. They have said so, in different ways, a hundred times on this trip. Now the Primate says so again. Staring into John Paul's face, in a voice broken with emotion, Wyszynski pleads, 'Before Polish wings carry you to Rome, look once again at your children and your countrymen, and bless the dear homeland.'

Visibly moved, close to tears, John Paul makes his farewell.

'Back there, beyond the Alps, I shall hear in my soul the sound of bells calling to prayer the heartbeat of my compatriots.'

It is a final reminder that it is the Church, not the state, which matters.

He kneels quickly and brushes his lips against the tarmac. When he stands tears are running down his cheeks. In a heartbroken voice he declares, 'On my departure I kiss this soil from which my heart can never be separated.'

He turns and walks slowly towards the plane.

Wyszynski follows a pace behind, his face flushed with emotion.

The pope and the cardinal look at each other for the last time at the foot of the ramp. They gaze into each other's eyes for a brief moment. Neither can trust himself to speak.

Wyszynski is the first to step back. It is only a pace. But it is enough. John Paul turns and slowly climbs the steps into the aircraft.

At the door of the plane he turns and smiles through his tears. Those at the front of the ramp think he says, 'Courage, Christ be with you all.'

Nobody can be certain because at the same moment the jet's engines are boosted.

The pope disappears into the cabin. Moments later he is seen at a window. He is still crying as the airliner taxis away towards the runway and Rome.

*

Analysts on the Polish Desks in Western intelligence agencies – particularly the CIA – interpreted the visit as a serious setback for the Polish Communist Party. The pope had only too closely shown the full extent of the power of the Church in his homeland. Nor indeed, assessed the analysts, could the Kremlin be anything but uneasy over John Paul's great personal triumph. Despite tight reporting restrictions – only heavily censored media coverage of the visit was allowed in Communist countries – the analysts believed word of mouth, that most effective of all grapevines within the Soviet satellite system, would ensure the pope's message did get through. Consequently, they reasoned, the Russian Politburo would have to take note of the impact of this very Polish pope on their overall strategy. No Western analyst, however, was in a position to predict what course a Soviet response would take. All they knew, based on past form, was that the Russians would undoubtedly make one.

*

Late in the afternoon of Sunday, 24 June, 1979, a lottery ticket salesman enters Istanbul police headquarters. He is known here as an informer on the *Kara Borsa*, the thriving black market. For a reward equal to the profit on a handful of his tickets the salesman regularly tips off the police about the petty criminals he spots in the cafés and clubs where he does his selling.

Today he believes he has information so important he will never again have to work. The reward this time, he thinks, will make him a Turkish lire millionaire.

When he tells his story to the desk sergeant, the salesman is gratified by the response. A squad of heavily armed police are swiftly assembled. They climb into two trucks. The salesman is squeezed into the cab of the first. Twenty minutes later the vehicles are in the city's Beyoglu District, a raffish area of night clubs and brothels. The trucks pass the massive six-hundred-year-old Galata Tower and stop outside the nearby Maramara coffee house, open only a few months but already an established haunt of the Grey Wolves.

The trucks block the road either side of the coffee house, sealing off escape. By then the policemen are pouring inside, fanning out among the startled customers.

Agca stands to greet them. He begins to shout defiantly that he hates all policemen. He is hit, hard, across the mouth, by one of them. Another snaps handcuffs on Agca's wrists. A third policeman pushes him towards the door. The snatch squad ignores Agca's companions and moves out of the café.

Waiting on the sidewalk is the lottery salesman. Agca looks at him carefully. Then he smiles.

The informer smiles back, uncertain. Perhaps he is thinking of the six million Turkish lire reward for turning in Agca. He is still smiling when Agca lashes out with his foot, kicking the informer viciously in the groin. The pedlar crumples to the ground in pain. The policemen ignore him as they bundle the most wanted man in Turkey into the back of the nearest truck.

*

Kartal-Maltepe. It is an area feared by all those brought to that complex of squat buildings set well inside the high security fence which encloses the entire area. Istanbul is twenty miles, and light years, away. This is a place of torture, sometimes refined, more usually primitive. Kartal-Maltepe is where the tottering left-wing government of Turkey holds the most dangerous members of the Anarchy. Many never leave here. After being tried and condemned to death by one of the military courts that sits from dawn to dusk inside the compound, they are either hanged or shot and then buried within the keep of this most frightening of all Turkish military prisons. The soldiers patrolling its perimeters have a standing order to shoot to kill anybody attempting to scale the perimeter fence.

The layout of the prison is so designed that the most violent prisoners are held in a building at the very centre. To reach it requires passing through eight separate security checkpoints. Each is constantly manned by two men. They have orders to kill any unauthorized person who tries to pass them.

The building itself is a concrete and steel bunker made to withstand all but the heaviest of weapons. Eighty soldiers per shift guard its forty cells. Each is small, with a door of reinforced steel. There are no lights. The only furniture is a drop-down steel flap bolted to the wall and suspended on chains. This doubles as a bunk and a table on which to eat the two meals a day prisoners receive. There is no bedding. An opening in a corner of the floor of each cell is the toilet. All prisoners have their belts, braces and shoe-laces removed to minimize their frequent attempts at suicide. Death is infinitely preferable to existing in these conditions.

It is to this maximum security wing that Agca is brought following his arrest.

Twenty-four hours after he is incarcerated, on the evening of Monday, 25 June, Agca receives his first visitor. Minister of the Interior

Hasan Günes has been flown from Ankara in a military aircraft which touches down on the dusty airstrip inside the prison perimeter.

Even among his Socialist government colleagues, Günes is known as a radical left-winger, ardently pledged, by his own admission, to use every means available to convict those right-wing terrorists guilty of the worst crimes committed in Turkey. Politically, Günes is very close to the extremism Teslin Tore expounds – though he in no way endorses Tore's violent methods of achieving what they both want: a purging of the country's right-wing and the creation of a Socialist state which will look with particular favour on the Soviet Union.

Günes meets Agca in the prison governor's office. The minister and Agca are alone for forty minutes. Günes then returns to Ankara.

Nearly five months must pass before Agca gives his version of what happened.

But now, to the astonishment of his guards and fellow prisoners, Agca returns to his cell whistling and smiling.

*

The normally effervescent high spirits of Alibrandi are bolstered by the satisfaction of knowing that everything which can be done has been accomplished. The nuncio's excitement is evident in his bouncy step, in his voice, in the smile he bestows on everybody around him. Tomorrow, Saturday, 29 September 1979, will see the climax of months of hectic preparations. Alibrandi has lost count of how many telephone calls he has made to Ireland's new cardinal, the prelate the nuncio had pushed for so hard, Tomás O'Fiaich, created by John Paul in July at the same time Casaroli received his red hat; calls to government ministers responsible for the secular side of the event, to the bishops of Ireland and, above all, telephone calls to the Vatican. Alibrandi thinks there must have been dozens of calls to and from Rome since the moment he heard officially that the pope would be coming to Ireland. Tomorrow morning, John Paul will land at Dublin airport.

This Friday night Alibrandi sits in his nunciature on the city's Navan Road quietly contemplating the likely effects of the historic three-day visit. Though it is being called purely pastoral, everyone, particularly the politically aware nuncio, hopes it will have a positive influence on the deteriorating situation in the North. The whisper from Rome is that the pope will speak frankly about the need to end the mindless violence. What John Paul intends to say exactly is still a closely kept secret. Not even Magee, who is Alibrandi's direct conduit into the papal apartment, has been able to tell the nuncio just how far the pope will go, or how hard a line he will take.

The need for mediation is more urgent now than ever. Only a month earlier, at the end of August, the IRA had claimed twenty-two further victims in a single day: England's much beloved Lord Mountbatten and three others on board his holiday boat cruising off County Sligo were murdered; eighteen British soldiers died in an ambush in County Down. Protestant outrage in Ulster and universal revulsion in Britain was so great Casaroli had actually told the pope it might be sensible to postpone the visit.

O'Fiaich and Alibrandi in Ireland and Magee, at the pope's elbow, mounted a successful counter-campaign. Casaroli, they intimated, was, for once, wrong. Now, more than ever, the pope's presence in Ireland was needed.

John Paul agreed. He would not only come and indulge his passion for visiting spots associated with the Virgin Mary – in this case Knock in County Mayo – but he would say something about the North.

To help 'the Holy Father have a full perspective', Alibrandi has fed him a series of position papers on the province. Some of Casaroli's advisers in the Secretariat of State claim that, in spite of the diplomatic suavity of the language, Alibrandi's arguments display his Sicilian vindictiveness towards Ulster Protestantism. It is an accusation the nuncio hotly disputes. He maintains he is even-handed in his condemnation of all violence, whether it originates with the IRA or its opponents; he argues, with truth, that few other foreign diplomats have taken such interest in the crisis – and that his commitment, made on behalf of the Church, is for a just and lasting peace.

Alibrandi lays equally great stress on the view that, historically speaking, Britain is an occupying power which, in the case of Ulster, is holding a Protestant enclave in an island that is traditionally Catholic. Alibrandi believes that the pope's own background makes him a committed foe of all occupations – especially those who do it in the name of religion.

In the nuncio's opinion – welcome though the gestures are – it does not ultimately change anything that the British Army in Ulster has sent down tents so that 2,500 Southern Irish school children may camp out before the pope says Mass at Drogheda, or that most Protestant churchmen in the North support the pope's visit. The nuncio wonders how much of this is lip-service, a mere papering over of the cracks; whether this is only a temporary respite in the relentless war of bigotry some Ulster Protestant clergy feel compelled to wage in the belief they are saving Northern Ireland from falling into the clutches of Rome. So many of them, Alibrandi has mused in the past, seem to thrive on the propagation of anti-Catholic myths. He also now believes that if anybody can overcome their antipathy to Catholicism, it is John Paul.

Alibrandi is convinced that the pope, making 'full use of his pastoral powers', will repeat what he did in Poland and speak out plainly in Ireland to achieve an end to the violence. In turn this will pave the way for the old ogres – Alibrandi's 'Brits' – to leave. It is a massively exciting thought for the little nuncio to contemplate.

Alibrandi cannot later be certain, but the prospect may still have been on his mind when the telephone rings yet again this Friday evening.

It is Casaroli calling from the Vatican. The Secretary does not waste time.

'Please listen carefully. We have just had information that if the Holy Father sets foot in Ireland he will be executed.'

Alibrandi is stunned. He manages to utter one word: 'Executed?'

'Yes. Murdered. Executed. That is what we have been told.'

The nuncio is trembling. 'Is the report reliable?'

Casaroli ignores the question. For whatever reason he will not inform Alibrandi he has received this devastating report from the British Minister to the Holy See who, in turn, has been given it from Britain's Secret Intelligence Service in London.[2]

The nuncio tries again. 'Ever since Mountbatten, I have feared this possibility. There is a link.'

'That could well be. What is important is this. The threat is serious. We are viewing it as such . . .'

'It could most likely happen in Drogheda. It's close to the border . . .'

'It could happen *anywhere*.'

'Please God, not.'

Casaroli continues. The trip cannot be called off at this very late stage.

'Thank God,' breathes the nuncio.

'The Irish police must be alerted. The Holy Father must be given the best possible protection.'

Alibrandi promises he will ensure this. When the shattering call is over he stands drained of all emotion. He wonders how the police can achieve this. How can anybody be fully protected in this island of inflamed passions?

Slowly the nuncio gathers himself together. He consults his address book and picks up the phone.

*

Alibrandi's telephone call, to the head of the Special Branch at Garda Headquarters in Dublin, produced an effect which began the moment the pope made his now obligatory stoop, this time to kiss the tarmac at Dublin Airport on his arrival on Saturday morning. There were armed detectives within feet of him and a hurriedly arranged security cordon which extended far beyond the papal presence. The Irish police were reasonably confident they could spot an assassin. But nobody minimized the risks. The pope's appearances around the country made it relatively easy for a gunman to attack. It happened often enough in the crowded, heavily defended streets of Belfast and Derry. Ultimately security rested in the hands of the Irish Special Branch team whose defence of the pope would depend very much on their ability to spot potential trouble before it surfaced and to respond swiftly to any emergency.

Marcinkus and Ciban and his Vigilance were on hand. Ciban, in particular, knew how vulnerable the pope was in this divided island; he had been specially briefed on the problem by a senior Irish police officer; he was also aware of the report Casaroli had received. Ciban had reminded his men of what the King of Italy said in 1897 after dodging the knife thrust of a would-be assassin: 'Sono gli incerti del mestiere' – 'These are the risks of the job.' On the flight from Rome he warned his men that they must absorb the risks, even to the point of being ready to give their own lives for the pope.

Against this background the visit began. It was meant, in its broadest sense, to be an act of recognition by the Holy See of Ireland's fidelity for a thousand years, and more, to the Church. From the outset it was a highly charged affair. Some one and a half million people filled Phoenix Park on the outskirts of Dublin for the first Papal Mass. There were also huge crowds in Galway and at the Knock shrine to the Virgin. To his rapturous audiences, John Paul brought a familiar and welcome message. He reminded them of the historical links between Ireland and Rome; he praised their commitment to their faith: he extolled the virtues of the family. And he constantly told them the facts of Catholic life.

'Marriage must include openness to the gift of children. Generous openness to accept children from God as the gift of their love is the mark of the Christian couple. Respect the God-given cycle of life, for this respect is part of our respect for God himself, who created male and female, who created them in his own image, reflecting his own life-giving love in the patterns of their sexual being. And so I say to all, have an absolute and holy respect for the sacredness of human life from the first moment of its conception. Abortion, as the Vatican Council stated, is one of the "abominable crimes". To attack unborn life at any moment from its conception is to undermine the whole moral order which is the true guardian of the well-being of man. The defence of the absolute inviolability of unborn life is part of the defence of human life and human dignity. May Ireland never weaken in her witness before Europe and the world to the dignity and sacredness of all human life from conception until death.'

Alibrandi could relax. The pope was doing all he had hoped he would do in restating the old patterns of morality; the lapsed and the careless were being asked to think again.

And so he came to Drogheda in County Louth. Over a quarter of a million people, many from Ulster's Catholic ghettos, had crossed the nearby border to participate in a moment of high drama. For it was here that the pope chose to deliver what would be the keynote speech of the trip. Here, in the damp Irish climate, with the wind tugging at his cassock, he made a passionate and moving plea for an end to violence. While there must be a Christian solution to social or international injustice, 'Christianity does forbid solutions to these situations by the ways of hatred, by the murdering of defenceless people, by the methods of terrorism. Let me say more: Christianity understands and recognizes the noble and just struggle for justice, but Christianity is decisively opposed to fomenting hatred and to promoting and provoking violence or struggle for the sake of struggle. The commandment, ''Thou shalt not kill'', must be binding on the conscience of humanity if the terrible tragedy of Cain is not to be repeated.'

He reminded them violence destroys what it claims to defend, the dignity and freedom of human beings. Instead it shatters the very fabric of society; it is always a crime against humanity.

Then, his voice booming over the crowd, he made a direct appeal: 'Now I wish to speak to all men and women engaged in violence. I appeal to you, in language of passionate pleading. On my knees, I beg you to turn away from the paths of violence and to return to the ways of peace. You may claim to seek justice. I, too, believe in justice and seek justice. But violence only delays the day of justice. Violence destroys the work of justice. Further violence in Ireland will only drag down to ruin the land you claim to love and the values you claim to cherish. In the name of God I beg you: return to Christ who died so that men might live in forgiveness and peace. He is waiting for you, longing for each one of you to come to Him so that He may say to each of you: your sins are forgiven; go in peace.'

Soon afterwards an IRA spokesman pointed out that the pope had not actually been on his knees when he made his appeal. It was a cynical reminder that the killing would continue.

Like Mexico and Poland, nothing would really change in Ireland. But at least nobody had killed John Paul.

*

All this morning, Thursday, 11 October 1979, Mehmet Ali Agca lolls in the dock, alternately yawning or picking his nose. He is wearing the clothes he was arrested in. They have been washed and pressed for the occasion – his trial for the murder of Abdi Ipekci. Agca has been shaved and given a haircut. He has a court-appointed lawyer but has insisted he will conduct his own defence.

When he entered the dock the prosecutor asked him two questions. Had he been physically abused while in custody; had he been subjected to psychological pressure? They are routine questions to try and combat the invariable defence accusations that prisoners are automatically tortured. Everybody expects Agca to deliver a diatribe against his captors. Instead he answered each question with a monosyllabic: 'No.'

Then he had smiled vaguely around the packed courtroom. Since then he has shown no further interest in the trial.

His attitude goes unremarked upon. Bravado and dumb insolence are common among the terrorists who pass in and out of the dock on the way to life imprisonment or execution. No one will ponder over the physical awkwardness and curious posture Agca displays, the way he constantly twists one leg around the other, curls his hands into his armpits or clenches his fists as though expressing his inner feelings in mime. There is about him something the psychiatrists will decide is a 'misuse of symbolization'. But that will come later, when they try to piece together what makes Agca behave as he does in this airless courtroom.

The prosecutor is in no hurry to outline his case. He knows the outcome because Agca has already pleaded guilty.

Yet this is an important trial for the state. A decision has been taken at government level that the evidence must be fully presented so as to offer convincing proof that not only does justice prevail in Turkey but nobody can escape proper retribution.

The judge sits, barely able to conceal his impatience, as the minutiae of the police investigation are paraded: seventy officers have worked on the case; 245 suspects have been questioned, eighty of whom are still being held in connection with other crimes; 456 bullets similar to the one which killed Ipekci underwent ballistic tests. Then had come the breakthrough. The court hears how Agca had been caught on 'information received'.

Before his guards can restrain him Agca is on his feet addressing the judge.

He is rambling and incoherent but his attitude is domineering and irritated.

Psychiatrists will later think this manifestation could be part of Agca's general thought disorder. It is a symptom common to the condition known as *talking-past-the-point syndrome*, a clumsy translation from the German word, *vorbeireden*. The clinical picture is of a patient who talks a great deal, but not completely relevantly; he does so not because he misunderstands his situation, but as a tactic to avoid contact with his immediate surroundings. Yet when they suggest this is a possible explanation, the psychiatrists cannot be certain because so much time will have elapsed after the outburst Agca now delivers to the court.

He speaks of a deal.

The prosecutor rises to his feet, objecting.

Agca ignores him, racing on, his words tumbling out. The court stenographer can barely keep track of his outpourings.[3]

'After I was captured, Minister of the Interior Günes came to prison and talked to me. His proposal was a deal.'

Agca's lawyer is on his feet, urging his client to be silent.

He is ignored. Agca continues. 'There was a deal. A deal! A deal! A deal! It was offered to me. I would say it was a high official of the Grey Wolves who ordered me to kill Ipekci.'

The prosecutor jumps in. He tells the judge Agca has yet again admitted to committing murder.

Agca goes on. 'If I confessed I was promised . . .'

The prosecutor says this is irrelevant.

The judge agrees.

The guards pull Agca back down to his seat. He again smiles vaguely around the courtroom.

Soon afterwards the judge adjourns the hearing for two weeks.

*

This much will become known:

Shortly after Agca was returned to the maximum security wing at Kartal-Maltepe, he received a letter. This alone contravened prison regulations. The note was unsigned, but Agca recognized the writing. Once more Teslin Tore had made contact. Agca memorized the contents and, as instructed, ripped the letter into pieces and dropped them down the toilet hole.

As well as being permitted to receive a letter there were additional indications Agca had been singled out as a favourite prisoner. He was shown no violence and allowed to exercise regularly. He was permitted to buy his own food rather than having to eat the vile slop served to other inmates. He paid for his meals with some of the money he had been allowed to retain on his person; that too was a breach of regulations. The money was part of the funds he had withdrawn from his bank account; permission to do so was given him by Tore in a previous unsigned note, delivered to Agca shortly after he murdered Ipekci. Following Agca's arrest, the balance left in his account was withdrawn. In this latest letter, Tore informed Agca that the money had been converted into suitable currency as part of the next stage of a carefully concocted plan.

It began to unfold when Agca next appeared in court. He calmly told the judge he wished to change his plea to not guilty. Agca now insisted he had not killed Ipekci but that he knew who had. The judge put one question. Would Agca name the persons or person concerned? The response was surprising: 'Not today. When we meet again.' The judge once more adjourned the hearing, this time without saying when the trial would be resumed.

*

Magee can, if asked, date it from the first dismaying report which arrived on his desk in the Apostolic Palace seven days after John Paul

406

returned from the United States. The paper was marked for the personal attention of the pope, a request reinforced by Casaroli's spidery initials. The document was a lengthy analysis of the papal visit by the apostolic delegate to North America and the Holy See's Permanent Observer to the Organization of American States, Archbishop Jean Jadot. The carefully chosen words epitomize the old-fashioned diplomacy which made Jadot so successful as the pope's representative for more than fifty million baptized members of the Church in the United States. Jadot has spelled out the often emotional and sometimes disruptive repercussions of John Paul's visit.

Since then there have been reports from the American cardinals. They have put on as brave a face as they can. Krol mentions the electrifying effect the visit had on Catholics and non-Catholics alike. Cody, almost wistfully, remembers the unprecedented television coverage which he feels helped ordinary Americans become aware of the pope's spiritual presence. Manning in Los Angeles and Cooke in New York are both optimistic the visit has left a clear impression that Catholic life has a strong spiritual foundation, and that the pope's embodiment of the power of the Holy Spirit must have a good effect.

It is the precise nature of this effect which, no matter how Jadot and the cardinals cushion it, has brought back to the papal apartment some of the anguish Magee thought had perished with Paul.

The disappointing news from America – one of the largest of the Churches within the Holy Roman fief – has produced a pronounced physical and mental strain on John Paul. This past month he has begun to look much older, greyer, more bowed than the person who for an entire week had helped fill the television screens and newspapers of America. He no longer sings as he strides through the Apostolic Palace. He seems a person badly hurt, bewildered as to why it should have happened.

All he had done, he told Magee, was to restate established doctrinal orthodoxy.

Indeed he had.

From the moment he arrived in Boston from Ireland he enumerated only too clearly a long list of breaches among American Catholics which had been brought to his notice. These must stop. He had not come to argue but to state; he was not here to listen to excuses but to expect obedience.

If John Paul was not actually ordering, he was certainly not making an appeal – nor would he listen to any appeal against what he held to be true. He said it all with natural charm and a deal of good humour. But the message was unequivocal: the emphasis on materialism and permissiveness must stop; 'escape in sexual pleasures, escape in drugs, escape in violence, escape in indifference' must stop; the suggestion that the priesthood is for anything less than a lifetime must stop; the thought that women can ever be ordained must stop; the idea that homosexuality is not always 'morally wrong' must stop; the attitude that priests and nuns may dress as they like must stop; the argument that in certain special conditions abortion is permissible must stop; the claim that the marriage bond can be broken must stop. He repeated it all after Boston in New York, Philadelphia, Chicago and Washington. Then, after addressing the United Nations – stressing to a rather sceptical audience that war and the arms race must stop – the pope returned to Rome.

Now, on Tuesday, 20 November, when John Paul has been back for six weeks, the Vatican is still receiving reports from the United States on the adverse reaction to the visit.

It is clear that, as with Mexico, Poland and Ireland, a pattern has been maintained. Throughout Latin America the liberation theology has, if anything, gained ground; in Poland the regime is tightening its grip; in Ulster the killing goes on. And in North America, despite John Paul's specific request for change, there has not been one. Catholics continue to seek divorce, continue to use contraceptives, continue to enter into homosexual liaisons, continue to undergo abortions, continue to support euthanasia. Priests and nuns continue to wear non-clerical garb, continue to petition to leave holy orders. Women continue to seek permission to be ordained. Virtually throughout the American Church there is somewhere exhibited the same stubborn desire to reject, the same scorn for traditional dogma, the same willingness to experiment dangerously in theological areas which the pope holds sacrosanct. Magee, studying all the reactions to the American trip, becomes convinced that what has happened is not of the pope's making – but that of certain radical elements within the American Church who can produce the smallest quiddity to support their call for change. It is they, not the pope, who have unleashed the forces which are tearing and pulling at what has been unquestioned for centuries.

The secretary also knows that John Paul's visit to America has confirmed for him the view that the United States is the world's most advanced example of the 'consumerism' he abhors: he fears 'consumerism' can be as big a threat to human dignity and survival as godless Marxism.

During the past month, in the aftermath of the trip, there has been talk in the papal apartment that John Paul should make his displeasure known. Some curialists argue he ought to go further and use the sanctions of his office to obtain obedience and submission. Casaroli firmly opposes such a move. The Secretary has argued it could be disastrous: faced with sanctions many American priests and nuns might well defect. And were that to happen the domino effect would be incalculable; an upheaval in the United States would certainly have religious repercussions throughout Latin America, Africa and Asia. It is best, advises Casaroli, to act cautiously.

Better than most, Magee knows how difficult it is for John Paul to comply with any suggestion which involves putting off action. The secretary has never known a pope who so consistently pushes himself to the limits of physical tolerance. There is a rumour which just will not die that John Paul's hectic pace stems from a prediction made by the late Padre Pio, the Franciscan whose hands bore the wounds of Christ and who was credited with second sight. John Paul reportedly visited the monk and was told his pontificate would be short and end in bloodshed. Magee knows the story to be apocryphal. But in part – however unintentionally – the pope helps keep it alive by his own remarks. Only two Sundays ago, on the feast day of his patron saint, St Charles Borromeo, the pope told a crowd of almost a quarter of a million in St Peter's Square that the saint was an example of pastoral love and episcopal service, linked to a dedication which 'ignored fatigue and even mortal danger'.

The words, Magee knows, are not without special significance. They are John Paul's way of publicly saying he will not be deterred from what he must do.

That includes visiting Turkey at the end of this month. Magee is not alone in thinking the dangers facing John Paul in Istanbul are the greatest any pope has encountered in living memory.

*

Evening roll-call at Kartal-Maltepe is later than the customary six o'clock on Friday, 23 November. The military court has sat late in order to catch up with a backlog of cases. It is almost seven o'clock before the count can begin. It takes an hour to check the 629 prisoners. For eight of them this is to be their last night on earth. They have been condemned by the court to die at dawn. The doomed men are in cells all around Agca. He can hear some of them praying. He begins to recite his hate list.

He is still doing so when a squad arrives in the maximum security wing. It is led by no fewer than six officers, the most senior of whom wears the uniform of a *yarbay*, a lieutenant-colonel in the Turkish Army; there are two *yuzbasis*, captains, and three *tegmen*, lieutenants. The dozen soldiers are led by a *bascavus*, a sergeant-major. All the troops except one carry a single carbine; this soldier has two. The officers wear side-arms.

The presence of the squad in the wing is not unusual; in the past it has collected those scheduled for execution before their appointed hour so as to avoid getting up before dawn to escort prisoners to the execution yard.

The sound of boots trampling down the corridor silences those in the cells. The squad has its own routine for the occasion. It suddenly stops outside a cell door. The *yarbay* consults loudly with his officers about whether the prisoner inside is to be shot or hanged. When the squad hear sounds of fear from beyond the door – which never fail to materialize – it moves on to pause outside another randomly selected door. It is the squad's idea of a joke.

This is how they come to stop outside Agca's cell.

But here there is no discussion. The bolts of the door are slid open. The *yarbay* and the two *yuzbasis* enter. The other officers and men take up positions in the corridor. One of the captains begins to strip off his baggy battle fatigues. Beneath, he is wearing a second uniform. He hands the fatigues to Agca who puts them on over his clothes. The entire switch takes only moments.

Preceded by the *yarbay* Agca walks from the cell. He is handed one of the two rifles the soldier has bought for this purpose. The squad forms a protective screen around Agca. A *tegmen* closes the cell door, securing the bolts. The squad tramps back down the corridor and out of the building.

During the next ten minutes it passes through the eight separate checkpoints which must be navigated before the perimeter of the prison is reached. Beside the final guard-house is a truck pool. The *yarbay* leads the squad to a three-tonner. Agca climbs into the back with the soldiers and all but one of the junior officers. The lieutenant gets in the cab with the lieutenant-colonel and drives the truck past the guard-house, out of the prison camp and onto the road to Istanbul.

In the back of the truck Agca strips off the fatigues. On the outskirts of the city the truck stops long enough for him to clamber over the tailboard onto the road. Tucked in his waist band under his shirt is a pistol one of the captains gave him. In his trouser pocket are several thousand Turkish lire. In his head are all the instructions the *yarbay* had whispered to him in the cell.

These orders completely contradict the earlier instructions Teslin Tore gave Agca in that letter smuggled into the prison.

For the moment Agca puts from his mind both sets of orders.

He strolls down the road, in the opposite direction to the truck, disappearing into the maze of backstreets he knows so well. Now he is keyed up, full of anticipation. He reaches a narrower, darker street, slips into a recess and waits. He knows the person's habits. Some time later he sees him approaching, going home after another day of peddling. Agca lets him go past. Then he steps from the recess and walks after the man. He taps him on the shoulder. The man turns. Before he can open his mouth to speak, Agca shoots in the head the lottery ticket seller who had betrayed him.

Agca turns and walks swiftly away. Nobody pursues him. Such murders are almost commonplace in Istanbul.

*

The escape from prison was organized by the Grey Wolves. Some of the military officers and men who spirited Agca out are members of the organization. The *yarbay* gave Agca instructions to go to a Grey Wolves safe house in Istanbul; it would have drawn unnecessary attention for the truck to have driven him there. Instead Agca wreaked the revenge he had promised himself.

Now, ignoring his instructions to go to the hideaway, Agca follows the very different orders Teslin Tore had secretly given him. He goes to a café, orders *cay* and pays for writing paper and an envelope. With a pencil he borrows from the waiter, Agca writes a letter and addresses it to the editor of *Milliyet*. He posts the letter.

It galvanizes the editor immediately he receives it. He scraps all other plans for the front page and designs a layout which will prominently display Agca's words. Next he calls the prime minister's office. He promptly orders steps to be taken to concentrate the search for Agca in Istanbul. Hundreds more soldiers and police are drafted onto the streets. Whole districts will be combed in what is to be the biggest manhunt in Turkish history. The prime minister telephones the Holy See's nuncio in Ankara. He places a priority call to Agostino Casaroli in the Vatican. By then the duty officer at the Israeli Embassy has picked up what is happening from his own source in *Milliyet*. The information is teletyped to Tel Aviv. There it is assessed in the light of what is happening elsewhere: in Madrid three bombs have exploded outside an airline office; in Beirut MOSSAD agents warn that there could be similar attacks planned for other European cities. MOSSAD interprets the threats as part of a well-organized protest against the pope's visit to Turkey – in part a reminder that for all its importance to NATO, not everybody thinks John Paul should visit a country where basic human rights are so abused.

But MOSSAD in Tel Aviv, Casaroli in the Vatican, the prime minister and nuncio in Ankara, and the editor in Istanbul will all be unable to answer one basic question. Is Agca working alone or is there a wider conspiracy at work which has made him write to the newspaper that he intends to kill John Paul during his two-day visit to Turkey?

That question takes on new urgency the morning of Wednesday, 28 November, when the papal jet enters Turkish air space.

*

Before leaving Rome Ciban had checked on the latest developments in the hunt for Agca.

Now, at Esenboga, Ankara's shabby international airport – a place of peeling wallpaint partially concealed by hundreds of police posters of men and women wanted for political crimes against the state – the Vatican security chief makes further urgent enquiries. His Turkish counterpart, a full blown *orgeneral* with four stars on his broad red epaulettes, shrugs. In Turkey it is not easy to trace anyone on the run. But the pope will be well protected. The *orgeneral* turns and indicates the line of tanks, half-tracks and troop carriers filled with soldiers in full combat dress. This military might cordons off the papal party from the handful of sightseers standing well beyond. And, says the *orgeneral* proudly, it is only a small part of the total security precautions. Forty helicopter gunships – some borrowed from American airbases in Turkey – will hover over the pope. There will never be less than ten thousand troops guarding the routes he will travel. Ciban thinks gloomily this is Mexico all over again. But this time the threat is far more direct.

Agca is out there somewhere. Nobody knows when or how he will strike. The *orgeneral* thinks a man who can escape from Kartal-Maltepe is capable of anything. His remark does nothing to reassure Ciban. He fervently wishes to God the pope had listened to those, led by Casaroli, who had urged that the trip should be cancelled. Instead John Paul had said nothing he had heard gave sufficient reason for him to change his mind. During the flight Ciban had briefed John Paul on the situation. The pope's response moved the tough security man deeply. He looked Ciban in the eyes and said, quietly, 'I trust in God.'

Stepping onto Turkish soil the pope manages to kiss the ground before impassive officials from the Turkish Foreign Ministry. He rises to his feet and glances towards the soldiers.

Noé, standing at his elbow, murmurs: 'There will be no speeches.'

John Paul nods and looks away. He has spent a precious hour memorizing the correct pronunciation for Turkish phrases of greeting.

He walks slowly towards the bus which will convey him and his party, including Cardinals Hume of Westminster and Baum of Washington, into Ankara. It is wedged between two tanks, whose turrets constantly revolve menacingly during the forty-minute drive into the city. In Ankara there are only a scattering of Catholics among

412

the few thousand Orthodox Christians, themselves largely the last survivors of the Greek Empire. This is one of the reasons the Turks have decided that the pope should be treated only as the head of state of a small country with diplomatic links to Turkey; in area the Vatican is hardly bigger than some of the villages the pope passes through on the twenty-two-mile drive to Ankara.

John Paul is not here as a religious leader. That point was made very clear before the trip was agreed upon. Now he has arrived, the regime does all it can to play down the visit. It is, frankly, an embarrassment. Conditions throughout the country are more unstable than ever. On average there is a politically motivated murder every eight hours. And there is the delicate matter of Turkey's relations with adjoining Iran, where the murderous regime of Ayotallah Khomeini is in full Islamic fury. Khomeini is holding fifty Americans hostage in the US Embassy in Tehran. Having just visited the United States, the pope, in the Ayotallah's mind, is another of those 'tools of Western Imperialism' who can be consigned to what Khomeini chillingly calls 'the dustbin of death'. And the Turkish regime, reasonably enough, suspects Khomeini thinks the same goes for a country which seems so friendly to someone looked upon with such disfavour by the Ayotallah. All in all, the presence of John Paul in this Moslem country of forty-five million Turks is not the most timely.

Then there is the menace of Agca. The prime minister has said that heads will literally roll should Agca manage to carry out his threat. In the past twenty-four hours there have been close to two hundred arrests. Anybody suspected of knowing Agca, however slightly, is being questioned. But as yet there is no sign of him.

The pope is bundled into the chapel of the Italian Embassy in Ankara where he pays a fine tribute to the strength of Islam. He points out that Moslems venerate Jesus as a prophet and honour the Virgin Mary, even invoking her in their devotions. He quotes approvingly from the Koran.

The papal entourage flies on to Istanbul for the high spot of the visit. The city has been the Constantinople of the early Church. It is filled with Christian relics. Paul came here a decade before. Then there had been no threats. But now, on Thursday, 29 November, as John Paul greets Dimitrios the First, who still bears the ancient title of Oecumenical Patriarch of Constantinople, Noé thinks the menace is 'thick enough to cut'. The pope and patriarch take part in a joint liturgical celebration of the eucharist in Dimitrios's Cathedral of St George. While they pray together two Turkish soldiers sit a few feet away with sub-machineguns on their knees; they are almost certainly unaware of the significance of the occasion. John Paul is the first pope

413

to be present at an Orthodox Mass since the schism of 1054. He is careful, though, note the handful of Vaticanologists making the trip, only to be a witness, not a participant.

There are brave words from the two brother patriarchs about their 'sister churches'. They exchange gifts, and John Paul expresses the hope he will soon have Dimitrios kneeling beside him in prayer at the tomb of St Peter as proof of their 'impatient desire for unity'.

Nobody is unkind enough to enquire when this might happen. No one in the papal entourage wants to start such a discussion in the super-tense atmosphere of Istanbul. Their main desire, as Ciban is overheard telling Noé, is to 'get the Holy Father back home unharmed'.

On Friday, St Andrew's Day – after celebrating with Dimitrios the feast which provided the reason for John Paul to come on this bizarre pilgrimage – he leaves Turkey the way he arrived: behind a cordon of bristling guns.

Although Agca has not made his attack, he is still free.

*

Officers of MIT, Turkish military intelligence, have picked up his trail. As the pope's jet climbs into the Turkish sky, two cars filled with MIT agents are driving through some of the most spectacular terrain in Asia: the great mass of Eastern Anatolia, the part of Turkey which borders Iran and Russia. It is an endlessly stretching landscape of ash-grey, rust-red and tawny-yellow, a turbulent frontline between Eastern and Western cultures.

The MIT team finally reaches the mountain city of Erzurum. They have come to question a guide named Timar Selcuk. He makes a meagre living showing the few summer tourists around Erzurum's magnificent Byzantine fortress. The officers suspect he makes far more money acting as a guide through the mountain passes in and out of Iran.

Selcuk is surprisingly forthcoming.[4] Shown a photograph of Agca he readily admits he met him two days earlier in the town's modest Hotel Efes. Selcuk insists he had no idea who Agca was. But he does agree that he had taken Agca part of the way along a smuggling route through the mountains.

The MIT men press. Why only part of the way? Why not into Iran itself?

Selcuk has a plausible answer. With Khomeini's bands running amok, it is too dangerous. Besides, he adds, there was a man waiting on the trail for Agca.

The MIT men ask Selcuk to describe him. They become impatient with his vague description. One of them produces a photograph. Selcuk studies it. He says it is the man he saw on the trail.

The photograph is of Teslin Tore.

31

The more openly John Paul pursued his rugged activism, with its attendant helicoptering to Italy's working-class districts and the seemingly endless pleasure he obtained lifting children high over his head; the more he filled the media with pronouncements, addresses, homilies and messages; the more he revealed a natural facility for tailoring his Sunday Angelus blessings for the evening television bulletins; the more he wrote; the more problems he tackled; the more he appeared to be commanding totally not only the immediate Vatican stage but the vastly greater one beyond; the more he used every possible occasion – whether announcing another curial appointment, lamenting the death of someone close or important in the Church, even commenting on a new Vatican postage stamp – to speak to a larger audience; the more he did all this and far more, the more enigmatic and worrying he became to his critics.

They attacked him on all levels. Conceding he was undoubtedly a pope for his time, if only because he recognized the revolutionary changes sweeping the Church and the world, they went on to assail him for allowing the mantle of papal tradition to rest so visibly upon his shoulders. It was true that he displayed a deep awareness of the role of all public sacramentalia. Processions and extra liturgical devotions never failed to suggest they formed part of the forces of natural worship that were his well-spring. Religious panoply, with its accompanying adoring throngs, seemed to stimulate him. His critics argued that these very visual reminders of how unique the Catholic Church was only emphasized its differences from other modes of Christian worship. They were especially censorious of the way the pope enjoyed the public paraphernalia of his Wednesday audiences in the Nervi Hall, or, in fine weather, in St Peter's Square: the obvious satisfaction he got from the presence of cardinals in red silk capes trimmed with ermine; the Swiss Guards in helmets and cuirasses carrying the pikes which symbolized the cantons of their homeland; the archbishops and bishops, the abbots and generals of the religious orders all in their finery; this, they said, did nothing for oecumenism, and was not the best way to win the hearts and minds of millions of other Christians who anyway did not necessarily accept John Paul's interpretation of the mystery and revealed truth about man.

Such criticisms were borne stoically. Occasionally, usually over a meal with his staff, John Paul discussed some of the attacks. He accepted that many of *them were the work of critics with a long record of misjudging papal motives. The censures were seen as part of a wider problem, the one which faced any new pontiff: introducing a proper sense of reality after the initial euphoria. The criticisms were rejected on the ground that they failed to appreciate that the renewed emphasis on the timeless power and magisterial authority of the papacy was deliberate. It was yet another reminder that however variegated, contrary and contradictory they might seem to non-Catholics, the triad of the pope, the papacy and the Vatican, for Catholics, remained a complex and comforting authority which condemned, forbade, judged, punished, allowed and ruled with a certainty no other faith could surpass. Within this framework John Paul had decided to play the classic role for which the papacy was designed. From the very beginning he felt it important to assume all the mystique of a leader; he wanted to make clear in everything he said or did that he epitomized the charisma of power. That was what lay behind the increased emphasis on visual traditionalism; the rolling Latin phrases of all official pronouncements, a style Gianpaolo had mused might not always be appropriate; the pomp and the glory which in the final years of Paul had declined. These trappings were all part of John Paul's policy to revitalize the papacy, to remind Catholics they must accept the pope as the Vicar of Jesus, that in obeying the pope they were actually obeying Jesus; that to disobey or reject what the pope said was to disobey or reject Jesus.*

This did not pacify his detractors. They claimed he showed signs of functioning as more of a monarch than Paul had ever done; that while it was right and proper he should rebuke – though not necessarily publicly – any affront to his office, he need not have gone so far as he had in maintaining the status quo.

They instanced his first crucial curial appointment. In September 1979, on the death of Cardinal Wright, he filled the vacancy of Prefect at the Sacred Congregation for the Clergy with Oddi, one of the most influential of curial reactionaries and the person who had helped arrange Lefèbvre's meeting with the pope. The news astonished and then delighted most curialists; in their wildest dreams they could not have expected the pope to show his hand so clearly. They saw Oddi's appointment as a plain signal of how the pope intended to settle the still contentious question of celibacy. Oddi, with his well-entrenched devotion to the traditional caste-system, had been put in charge to ensure that everybody finally understood that the priesthood really was for a lifetime, would remain celibate and totally masculine. All this talk of married priests and women being ordained was a dead issue. Oddi was there to preside over the burial.

There was shock and dismay in various quarters. In the United States, particularly, there was a wave of resentment among many priests and nuns over Oddi's appointment. But most of those far-off criticisms were blocked off long before they could reach the papal presence. In a way that was worse: the

417

resentment festered, breeding a rebellion which could only grow in face of what they viewed as stony indifference to heart-felt protest.

To them it appeared that the great initial sunburst which had dazzled everyone had faded; that so many of their expectations and hopes had been dimmed in the process; that this Polish pope was really from an Italian mould; that in spite of its high efflorescence, this pontificate was firmly bedded in old soil; that the wisdom on offer, for all its glittering presentation, was a disappointment.

The pontificate's defenders – and they were still in the majority – pointed to the situation John Paul had inherited: falling attendance at Mass, emptying seminaries, a Church drifting out of control, threatened both from within and without. John Paul had set about stopping the decline with a directness of language no one could fail to understand. If it seemed to some people he was not being democratic, where was it ordered that the Church must be a democracy? John Paul was doing what popes had always done: shoring up the faith against the slings and arrows of a world which, in his view, was becoming increasingly evil. This was not a time for snickering and bickering inside the spiritual barricades he was erecting; this was a time to remember the old realities. Otherwise the Church would be lost. Matters had, he made plain, gone too far down the road of conformity which must eventually lead to subjection to secular values. That is why he opposed all the tumult for an easing of what was traditionally sacred.

They still queried what they saw as his near obsession with Mary which only antagonized non-Catholics. And some within the Church wondered whether John Paul had gone too far when he extolled the Marian shrines in Paraguay and Uruguay as being responsible for the well-being of the Church in those countries, without uttering a single word of condemnation of two regimes which persecuted all Catholics – priests, nuns and laity alike – who dared challenge their repressive policies. When Bolivia staged its 212th military coup, John Paul merely hoped the fratricidal fighting would end after he had prayed for the intercession of the Virgin of Copacabana, a local Marian shrine few in the Vatican had previously heard of.

Those critics failed to appreciate that Marian Devotion was ingrained in his Slavonic past. Indeed since 1658, Mary has been Queen of Poland and has remained a distinctive feature of Polish spirituality, the transcendental authority which shaped the pope's own religious outlook in so many ways. It was, said his aides, unrealistic to expect him to reject her. Mary was an essential support in his responsibility for preserving faith and morals; her presence was a reminder of the historical consciousness and doctrine of the Church, helping to maintain what the pope had himself called 'the objective importance of the magisterium'.

They wondered what exactly he meant by his repeated commitment to Vatican II. In the second year of his pontificate everybody recognized that the full promise of the Council had yet to be realized; that there was indeed a long way to go to reach John Paul's desired 'maturity of movement and life'. But pessimism had replaced hope. When he had said that the first main task of his reign would be to promote 'with prudent but encouraging actions the most exact execution of the norms and direction of the Council', it turned out – said his critics – that what he really meant was that Vatican II was an end, not a beginning; it resolved issues rather than rekindled them. Liberation and reform sounded fine, but they were poles apart from ideas of liberty and reform – and this Pole was going to keep them very separate.

The concept did not recognize a fundamental truth. Vatican II had brought the Church to a crossroads. There were hard choices to be made, and only the pope could make them. There was no way – none at all – that John Paul would give free rein to all the spin-offs being demanded. Equally he could not ignore the facts of secular life. John Paul was caught, in the words of one defender, 'in a no-win situation'. In the end he decided to mark time on certain Vatican II recommendations. He wanted to settle other issues first. The alarm bells, he told his staff, would have to go on ringing.

His opponents argued about his attitude towards collegiality: that there was no real evidence to show that power and decision-making were more widely diffused, that there had been an increase in the sharing of responsibility between John Paul and his fellow bishops. Further: there was nothing to suggest that he recognized the collective wisdom of his episcopate as being a way to solve the serious issues facing the Church or that he seriously subscribed to decentralizing his authority; that in short he would fulfil the promise of Gianpaolo. Instead the Synod of Bishops, though it met more often, seemed to function too often as an echo-chamber for what the pope decided. To this extent collegiality withered. So ran the criticism.

As with so many of the accusations, there was a modicum of truth in this one. He had written his controversial Letter to his dioceses. He did tend to expound his own position – as at Puebla – and then leave the bishops to settle the details among themselves. He did expect them to follow his broad policy lines. He was not interested in a 'loyal opposition' within the Church to correct him. Equally, he did listen. His office door – if not always actually wide open like Gianpaolo's – was far from shut. During his first year in office, John Paul received more people than Paul had in the last three years of his life. Everybody was entitled to their say. But he would not be swayed. Collegiality had to stop at some point, otherwise certain functions of the papacy would cease. So argued his defenders.

Many in the Curia thrived on the controversy; divide and rule was manna in their idea of heaven. John Paul – faced by all the other issues, caught up in a very real desire to take the papacy to the people, increasingly preoccupied with the international arena – after his first hint of change by refusing to reappoint his departmental heads for five years, did almost nothing to alarm his civil service for over a year.

The Curia continued on its well-ordered way. The appointment of Oddi was a constant reminder no matter what this vigorous, unHamlet-like pontiff meant to the world – and that was a great deal – inside the Leonine Walls, in all those corridors and offices of the Apostolic Palace, John Paul had shown the good sense to play the game the curial way. There would, for instance, be no dramatic increase in the number of women civil servants. And there were few surprising promotions. The Poles he imported, to sit in L'Osservatore Romano, *in Vatican Radio, in the congregations, commissions, tribunals and secretariats, all were comfortingly conservative. Even the surprises did not alter the Curia's traditional* figura di bronzo, *its poker face. For the first time Casaroli's deputy, his* sostituto, *was a non-Italian, and a Lithuanian was brought into the senior echelons of the Holy See's diplomatic service. The appointments were interesting but hardly earth-shattering.*

Nevertheless, John Paul's critics in the Curia told each other that, for all his style, his warmth, the way he had popularized the papacy like no other pope in living memory, despite this they still hankered for the days of Paul; they also admitted that in his day they had yearned for Pius, proving, if nothing else, that every generation remembers its youth. Yet they did find grounds for complaint. They moaned that while it was true he had visited their offices – though not with the same frequency, or in the way Gianpaolo popped in and out like a jack-in-a-box – John Paul did not appear to know what he wanted from them. He asked a lot of questions, but he almost never seemed to act on the answers. Less important documents and papers had begun to pile up on the desks of Magee and Dziwisz. When they fed them into the pope, he often placed them to one side. He was not a tidy administrator: his desk was usually disordered, though he seldom had difficulty locating any paper of importance. Some curialists began to fear they were being cleverly moved into a limbo; one disgruntled monsignor said: 'We do our thing, and the pope does his, and rarely do the twain meet.'

In November 1979 came the rude awakening. In their clerical cubicles, well out of sight of the Apostolic Palace's magnificent corridors, staircases and salons, in tiny, uncarpeted rooms with worn furniture and dull walls, amidst a clutter of filing cabinets and waste-baskets – unkindly said to be receptacles for so many of the suggestions submitted by priests and bishops beyond Rome – in this closed, suspicious world, curialists put aside their book-keeping, cataloguing and filing to ask one question: what was the reason behind the staggering news that, at extraordinarily short notice, every living cardinal was being ordered to fly to Rome. Only serious illness would be accepted as an excuse for absence. The cardinals were told to cancel or change their schedules and come to the Vatican. This had last occurred during a pontificate four hundred years earlier. Nobody could easily recall which of the seven popes between Pius III in 1503 and Paul IV in 1555 had sent out the last call. Or why.

This time the disturbing reason surfaced quickly. Among the subjects to be discussed between the pope and his cardinals was curial reform. After four days of intermittent debate, the civil servants could breathe easy. In spite of all the whispered leaks from inside the Sala Bologna about restructuring and economising, it turned out there was nothing for them immediately to worry about. There was going to be some rationalization, a mild cut here, an amalgamation of two small departments there. But really nothing to give any curialist palpitations. Indeed, the curial cardinals had even managed to get John Paul to pay due tribute to 'the substantial validity of the present structure'. Still, the pope had tried to slip one past them, said a few curialists. In some of the cubby-holes in the Apostolic Palace where paranoia thrives, that was seen as a precursor of worse to come. Perhaps not tomorrow. But come it would. Mark their words. The pope was unpredictable. After all, just look at the way, the quite extraordinary way, he had openly discussed that most secret of all matters – Vatican wealth.

*

John Paul had told the one hundred and thirty cardinals participating in the event in the Sala Bologna that the time had come to dispense with, at least as far as they were concerned, the 'fables and myths' about the wealth of Vatican State and the Holy See. He reminded them of the need to keep such matters secret; the fact that he felt compelled to issue such a warning indicated how aware he was of the leaks which continued to seep from his pontificate.[1]

The balance sheet had been initially prepared by Marcinkus. Then it was worked further upon by two other financial experts in the Vatican: Cardinal Egidio Vagnozzi, head of the Prefecture for Economic Affairs; Cardinal Giuseppe Caprio, President of the Administration of the Patrimony of the Holy See (APSA). Finally, Casaroli had reviewed the figures. The only other cardinal to see a copy beforehand was Sergio Guerri, administrator of the governatorato which ran Vatican City. They flanked the pope as he came straight to the point.

The 1979 deficit was the equivalent of $20.2 million. The projected deficit for 1980 was over $28 million. The current loss was equal to one-third of the entire annual budget. On present trends, the Vatican – 'in a book-keeping sense' – would be bankrupt by 1984. Therefore, continued John Paul, there was an urgent need to 'consider the matter objectively'.

There was not a sound in the elegant salon. The atmosphere was more electrifying, Felici recalled, than when they had sat here and heard how the KGB tried to exploit the death of Gianpaolo. John Paul had revealed an even greater threat to the Church.

He spoke for an hour. He explained that the Vatican had been in 'serious economic difficulties' since 1975. Paul had rejected the proposed budget for that year and demanded immediate and substantial cuts.

John Paul stated this had not proved possible as the Vatican had doubled its *staff during Paul's pontificate. The wage bill now stood at $22 million a year. Salaries were index-linked to the Italian economy, a costly device in a country where inflation was now running at over twenty per cent.*

There were other equally heavy expenses. Vatican Radio presently cost $11 million a year to run. L'Osservatore Romano was losing $2.7 million a year. The overall cost of maintaining the Vatican's printing outlets was almost $15 million a year.

Next the pope dealt with the ten Vatican museums. Not one of them was in profit in spite of an increase in the number of visitors and in admission charges. Between them the museums were losing $2 million a year. There was the cost of the upkeep of the Sistine and other chapels, the Raphael loggia and apartment, the dozen galleries and the magnificent staircases, all open to the public, all showing losses which, when measured against maintenance costs, showed a debit of $1.5 million a year.

There were the increased expenses of the diocese of Rome. It now cost $1.3 million to administer.

And finally there was the massive charge for maintaining the Church's present pre-eminent position as missionary. It now cost $50 million a year to keep all its priests, nuns, doctors and nurses in the field.

John Paul turned to income.

He revealed that the 1979 Peter's Pence collection amounted to $4 million. Traditionally popes used this money, collected from churches throughout the world, either for major charitable work, such as aiding disaster relief, or paying for papal trips, or for financing major Church meetings: under John XXIII, the costly Vatican II was largely paid for by Peter's Pence. Paul had regularly used the money to help offset the budget deficit.

Collections organized by Propaganda Fide produced $44 million. The figure had not significantly changed during the past three years. In true value, measured against inflation, it was now worth considerably less than in 1975.

Profits from the Vatican's duty-free concessions came to $8 million. This showed a drop from the previous year.

Commemorative stamps had brought in $3 million. It was an improvement on 1977, but this was probably due to what the pope referred to as 'special circumstances', the results of two Conclaves. There was no expectation that this figure would be maintained in future years.

Profits from rents from properties owned worldwide by the Vatican had raised no more than $9 million.

He came to the last item on the balance sheet. John Paul revealed that revenue from Vatican investments had produced $28 million.

Everybody realized how carefully he had chosen his words – and their implication.

For the first time a pope had declared openly – even if only within the supposed security of the Sala Bologna – figures which hitherto had never been mentioned outside a small circle of the most trusted of senior Vatican staff.

Some of those present felt it significant that John Paul had broken this strict tradition. They looked curiously at Marcinkus. He remained impassively tight-lipped.

Not even Benelli or Felici, despite their exhaustive investigations for Gianpaolo, could now be sure what the true position was at the Institute for Religious Works (IOR). The closer he had become to John Paul, the more unforthcoming Marcinkus appeared about the affairs at Vatican Bank. He was still reportedly furious that the latest annual report of the Bank for International Settlements in Basle – which regularly analyses the foreign currency positions of banks in the ten largest industrial nations, plus Switzerland and offshore banking centres – showed that in 1977 the IOR had foreign deposits of $100 million. Benelli and Felici had calculated that the IOR held between $600 and $700 million of the Vatican's money on deposit; the bank's total deposits at home and abroad, might come close to $1.5 billion.[2] On top, the saleable value of all Vatican-owned properties could amount to an estimated $2 billion.

None of these figures was mentioned by the pope.

Bernardin Gantin, for one, was dismayed. He did not need to be told that John Paul's assessment had just put paid for the foreseeable future to most, if not all, of those plans Gianpaolo had outlined to Gantin: the schemes to divert further Church money into the Third World, to try and achieve a more humane and less capitalistic use of Church funds, to create jobs which would alleviate hunger and suffering in the poorer countries. On the facts John Paul has presented there was little if any real money available for such dreams. The Vatican's finances, suspected Gantin, would have to continue working in traditional areas. Nevertheless, Benelli and Felici were only two cardinals who still wondered how badly the IOR had been damaged by the Sindona–Calvi affair. Was the position made to appear worse than it really was?[3] Had John Paul been advised that the only way he could expect the cardinals to support his closing plea for urgent help – presumably through additional fund-raising and contributions from their dioceses – was to paint a picture of unremitting financial gloom?

No cardinal knew. And the Sala Bologna, they decided, was not the right forum in which to raise such matters. For the same reason that they did not question John Paul, so they chose not to examine Marcinkus about the astonishing series of banking disasters he and the IOR had survived. Yet standing at the pope's elbow as they trooped out, more than one cardinal subsequently remarked, Marcinkus seemed without a care. Could there, after all, be some solid business excuse for his attitude? Or were there perhaps other reasons?

*

Everyone knew what made John Paul deal with Hans Küng. The aftershock of the American visit had rumbled on. The pope was bluntly accused of being out of step with contemporary American Catholicism, especially in matters of sexuality.

Into this argument stepped Küng. He had set about the pope in a review of John Paul's first year in office. He doubted the pope's claim to be a genuine spiritual leader, a pastor, a supporter of collegiality, an oecumenist and someone with a mind open to the world. Küng even wondered aloud whether the pope was a Christian in the accepted sense of the word. No one could remember such a venomous, vituperative and maledictory denunciation against a living pope; not even Paul had drawn such fury. Küng particularly denounced John Paul's position over such rights as that of priests to marry – which Küng claimed was guaranteed 'in the Gospel itself and in the old Catholic truths'; the right to leave the priesthood with official dispensation, 'after a thorough examination of conscience, rather than the inhuman practice introduced by this pope of forbidding bureaucratically this dispensation'; the right for theologians like Küng to express their opinions; the right of nuns to dress as they pleased; the right of women to be ordained, 'as can certainly be justified by the Gospel of our contemporary situation'; the right of married couples to control conception and the number of their children.

The review became the most widely read challenge yet to the pontificate. Some thought there had been nothing like it since Luther stormed out of the Church. Others said Küng's outburst was far worse than any of the disobediences of the Jesuits. There, John Paul carried through what his predecessor intended: he had summoned the dying General, Pedro Arrupe, and spelled out what he expected: an immediate end to the crisis between the Church and the Society of Jesus. Arrupe had promised this would be done. That appeared to end the matter. But Küng was something else. By going public, by personally attacking the pope's principles and, worst of all, by continuing to question the validity of the doctrine of papal infallibility, the theologian was obviously not going to be silenced by stern words. John Paul sent for the bulky dossier kept under lock and key in the Sacred Congregation for the Doctrine of the Faith. What he read deeply angered him. He did not hide his feelings from those he consulted on the case. They were Benelli, Felici, and Ratzinger of Munich whom the pontiff had already earmarked as a replacement for the ailing Franjo Seper as head of the Doctrine of the Faith. Theologically Ratzinger shared the outlook of the pope. He was also in the same tough mould; behind his mild-mannered appearance was a steel-trap of a mind as many a diocese priest had learned. John Paul and Ratzinger had several lengthy telephone conversations on the matter of Küng.[4]

With a speed which astonished everyone – not least Küng – he was ordered to Rome, escorted to the third floor of the forbidding Doctrine of the Faith building and paraded before its officials. They listened and swiftly pronounced. Unusually, the verdict was released through the Vatican Press Office, a certain sign John Paul wished the world to know the fate of Hans Küng. He was 'no longer a Catholic theologian, nor able to function as such in a teaching role'.

The oecumenical fallout continued into 1980. The entire episcopate of Brazil refused to support Küng's suspension. The German Church murmured its collective Mein Gott. *Like so many others this storm would not blow over.*

Suddenly – in a move some Vaticanologists suggested made the pope seem like a religious Red Adair, the legendary fire-fighter who takes calculated risks to douse the flames – John Paul moved again. He had just returned from a triumphant African tour – six countries, seventy sermons, each personally written, as many Masses celebrated, all done in enervating tropical heat – and was preparing to celebrate his sixtieth birthday, 22 May, before setting off for France. That was the moment he chose to 'finally settle' – the words he used to Ratzinger when he briefed him by telephone what was about to happen – 'once and for all this Küng business'. In faultless German the pope strongly defended his suspension of Küng to the West German bishops. He associated infallibility with 'the prophetic vision of Christ and the Church', and with the 'office of Christ' which was conveyed by Him to the Apostle Peter and consequently to the pope. But John Paul went further, identifying inerrancy not only with the pope, but also with the Church's bishops when they met in council.

Küng's silence, noted Lambert Greenan, was 'deafening; he had got his final come-uppance'. The editor shared a common and satisfying view in the Vatican that here was a pope who could deal forcibly with his critics, and was not afraid to be seen doing so.

But there was a secret side to the pontificate which only a very select few knew about. Its genesis came from an even greater, and increasingly public, confrontation – the one between John Paul and those forces which he felt threatened both the Polish Church and what little freedom remained in his beloved homeland.

*

From the beginning John Paul had involved the Holy See in world affairs – despite an avowed intention not to do so expressed in his inauguration address. He denounced the neutron bomb and racism; he oversaw the mediation between Argentina and Chile in their war-threatening dispute over the Beagle Channel, an important sea passage at the tip of South America. He spoke out, frequently, on the turmoil in the Middle East. No one in the Secretariat of State could remember anything like this diplomatic drive in the past. But it was only the very visible side of what in another instance was an ultra-secret initiative.

This arose directly from the pope's increasingly pointed references to Communism. He attacked it intellectually and on moral grounds. Nobody was surprised. It was, after all, to be expected of a pontiff who had made a hard-line policy against all oppression a major element in his pontificate. In part, too, John Paul was responding to criticism from Catholics within the Soviet bloc, and strongly anti-Communist elements in the West, who argued that the only way to get concessions was to end the policy John XXIII had started; one in which he had deliberately switched from confrontation to détente, from denunciation to discussion. Dialogue would continue, but from the Vatican's point of view under John Paul it would be conducted from a far more realistic position where he could use his formidable strengths to promote religious and other freedoms. Yet, secretly, telling only those who had to know, the pope went far beyond his public posture. He had symbolically taken the papacy in his capable hands and was using it as a weapon to help protect a vision which was maturing in Poland. The risks were monumental – to him and to the man he was clandestinely advising in Poland; at times the pope must have wondered whether the fragile stability of their homeland would not be torn asunder in the outcome. And yet John Paul felt he had no option from that day, a month after his return from Cracow at the end of his Polish visit, when he had received a confidential report on what the trip had achieved. There was a growing mood among the congregation of Poland's eighteen thousand churches which was directly linked to the challenge of a young man who, next to the pope, was becoming the most exciting figure in recent Polish history. His name was Lech Walesa. He had yet to become an international figure. But within Poland, Walesa symbolized a dream. He had promised that the lick-spittle government trade unions would be replaced by an organization which would have real bite and power – and would not be afraid to use it. It was called the Solidarity Movement. Walesa was its most vocal and articulate leader. The union's name had been chosen by Walesa after he read the pope's encyclical, Redemptor Hominis, *with its direct appeal for 'acting together'.*

John Paul had sent a secret message to Walesa in July 1979, expressing his approval of the choice of name.[5]

So began a relationship only few knew of – in the Vatican they numbered Casaroli, Marcinkus, Dziwisz and Magee. At all hours of the day or night John Paul telephoned Walesa at his home in Gdansk to discuss what was happening. The conversations were brief and usually innocuous. Both men were only too aware that almost certainly the Polish authorities were tapping Walesa's telephone. But the pope's calls were not primarily intended for receiving information; he had other ways of checking that: the Polish Church provided him with excellent intelligence. John Paul chiefly wanted Walesa to know he had a powerful friend, one who was decidedly in favour of the birth of Solidarity.

The pope told those privy to what was happening that Walesa was going to provide perhaps the most important challenge the Polish Communist Party had ever faced; if Solidarity became a reality, the first truly independent trade union in the Soviet bloc, it would also revolutionize the situation in other East European countries. Some of those around John Paul at times had the impression the pope believed Walesa might achieve even more than he had.

During his French tour – where he chided the French faithful over falling baptismal figures, a decline in Church attendances, Church marriages and those entering Church vocations, coupled with a slackening off in the traditional prohibitions of divorce, birth control and priestly celibacy – John Paul still managed to stay in touch with Walesa.

The pope urged the trade unionist to be cautious. Casaroli had been taking soundings in Eastern Europe. The indications suggested the Russians were becoming restive about Solidarity.

Back in the Vatican, the French firmly put in their religious place, John Paul and Casaroli drafted a note to Walesa. It made clear that although the pope firmly intended to remain available in the background offering support and counsel, the trade unionist should now follow a policy of moderation; this was not the time for precipitate action. It was a period for calm and careful advances. The report was couriered to Poland. On Wednesday, 11 June 1980, the courier returned on LOT flight 303, landing at Leonardo da Vinci airport. A Vatican car drove him to the Apostolic Palace. From his Secretariat of State briefcase the man produced Walesa's response. Walesa said he would be careful. But there was now no way he could, or would, stop the momentum of events.

The pope called an immediate meeting in his study in the papal apartment.[6] *Casaroli, Marcinkus and Dziwisz were among those present. One important question was discussed: what was the likely response to Solidarity from the Soviet Union? The Polish Communist Party would take its cue from Moscow. A number of possibilities were examined. The Russians would do nothing. The Russians, through the Polish regime, would exert political pressure. The Russians would initiate indirect military action against the Polish workers. The Russians would intervene directly – invade Poland.*

The first option was quickly discounted. Everyone agreed there would be some response by the Soviet Union. Casaroli felt strong political pressure was a real possibility, at least initially. Threats would be issued through the Polish regime to cow Solidarity; every effort would be made to separate the workers from the leadership, to sow doubt and dissension. There would be concurrent offers of better conditions, an improvement in the food ration, an easing of restrictions. It would all be a standard ploy to remind the Poles that the status quo was better than the unknown.

The argument was plausible. But in the end, insisted Marcinkus, there would be a show of physical strength. There always was. It was part of the Soviet tradition in settling any threat to its existence.

John Paul agreed. The question then was: would the force be Russian-backed – or direct?

Based on the evidence available, mostly reports funnelled to the Secretariat of State from Eastern Europe, no one could be certain.

It was decided to include Koenig in future deliberations. Better than anybody, with his unique experience of Soviet intentions, his unsurpassed connections behind the Iron Curtain, the cardinal in Vienna was ideally placed to know what the Russians might be intending to do.

Casaroli undertook to continue tapping the CIA connections he had nursed along since coming into office.[7]

There remained one other issue to be discussed. Everyone quickly agreed John Paul must go ahead with his most taxing journey so far, the forthcoming twelve-day, eighteen-thousand-mile tour of Brazil. During it he would deliver forty-seven addresses, each of which he was writing in the Portuguese language he learned for the occasion. Using language-laboratory discs and a tutor, for the past few weeks the pope had studied a couple of hours daily, between midnight and two am, so that he could communicate directly with Brazil's one hundred million Catholics, the largest single Catholic population in the world.

At the end of June he set off. Special arrangements were made to keep him informed of developments in Poland.

Arns and Lorscheider were on hand to conduct the pope through a seemingly endless land filled with nightmarish social problems. The contrasts visibly disturbed John Paul: slums and skyscrapers side by side; incredible wealth and unimaginable poverty; above all a smiling military government ruling a country in which, during the past decade, the pope knew nine bishops had been arrested, thirty-four priests tortured and at least eight killed.

As usual John Paul tailored his words for the occasion. After dealing with what a member of his entourage called 'the old faithfuls' – divorce, abortion and birth control – the pope spoke brave words about the need for land reform, the rights of minorities and, significantly, at Manáus on 10 July, on the rights of workers, including their right to strike.

The day before, he had received word from the Apostolic Palace that Solidarity was mobilizing itself for confrontation. Walesa had said he would call a national strike unless he got what he wanted.

The pope's tour continued, during which he stressed the primacy of the spiritual and the need for priests to stay out of politics. There was nothing in his voice to show how poignant and ironic were his words.

The tour closed on a down note. John Paul sharply rejected any thought of the Brazilian bishops being allowed to ordain married men from the favelas, *the shanty towns, despite a belief that this was the only means to strengthen the Church's influence in these places. The pope was not even swayed by the thought that it would ease the hold of the theology of liberation movement in the slums.*

During the long flight back to Rome, John Paul barely discussed the Brazilian trip. His mind was on events in Poland. There was nothing he could do publicly. Casaroli had warned that such a course might well delay, if not defeat, the very thing the pope wanted achieved – the peaceful creation of Solidarity. This John Paul accepted. Equally, he refused to consider any suggestion that Walesa should be told to put an end to his plans. After a year of covert papal support, that would be too severe a blow for the young trade unionist to bear; Walesa was already under considerable pressure in Poland.

John Paul moved for the summer to Castel Gandolfo. The secret meetings continued in the summer palace in the Alban hills. Increasingly the question narrowed down to: how best could the pope intervene?

On Monday, 4 August, came the news he most feared. Koenig's finely attuned ears in Vienna had picked up alarming signals the Russians were seriously considering ordering the Polish regime to conduct a purge of Solidarity's leadership while at the same time warning the population that if there was any further rebellion, martial law would be imposed. If that provoked resistance, the Red Army would roll into Poland. It was a dire situation.[8]

Only John Paul knows precisely when he finally decided that he, and he alone, had to act – and act urgently. It may have been during one of those early-morning walks around the gardens of Castel Gandolfo; it may have been over a meal with his secretaries; it may have been during one of those times he was swimming his daily dozen lengths of the pool. It may even have been when he knelt in prayer in the small private chapel attached to his bedroom where Paul had died two years before to the very week. Somewhere, sometime, in the first week of August 1980, John Paul decided he must write the most extraordinary letter any pontiff had ever penned.

John Paul wrote, in Russian, a single handwritten page on his personal stationery with the papal coat-of-arms in one corner, to President Leonid Brezhnev of the Soviet Union.[9]

The pope told the president he believed Poland faced a Soviet invasion. John Paul warned Brezhnev that if this did happen, he would relinquish the throne of St Peter and return to stand at the barricades beside his fellow Poles.

The pope concluded the letter, 'Yours in Christ.'

He addressed the envelope in his own handwriting to Brezhnev in the Kremlin.

There remained the decision as to who should courier the letter to Moscow.

There was no question of using one of the Secretariat of State priest-couriers. The matter was far too delicate, far too politically explosive for such a course.

Koenig would be a good choice. But his absence from Vienna could cause comment. It would have to be someone from the Vatican.

Dziwisz was excluded because of his comparative lowly rank. The aim was for the letter to be delivered personally to Brezhnev. A monsignor, even if he was the pope's secretary, was of insufficient importance to impress the president of the most powerful Communist nation on earth of John Paul's earnest intention to resign his office and help lead his people's resistance against the Red Army.

Casaroli was a possible choice. He spoke Russian and knew the Soviet mind. The Secretary would be a powerful emissary, one who could without doubt make those in the Kremlin sit up and take notice. But the absence from the

Vatican of the Holy See's equivalent of Foreign Minister might also lead to what John Paul so badly wished to avoid – any hint of what he was doing surfacing.

There was another possible person: Marcinkus. (The use of Markincus would go some considerable way towards explaining why, after all the financial disasters the IOR experienced under him, Marcinkus would, at least for some considerable time, remain in office. The pope is not one who easily forgets great personal favours, and this may have helped Marcinkus when there were demands in 1982 for John Paul to rid himself of the banker.) The IOR governor had impressive qualifications. He was a close confidant of the pope; his advice during the whole affair, like Casaroli's, had been a great help; he also spoke Russian; he was not a man to be awed by Brezhnev; and, as the Vatican's banker, it would not be unusual for him to travel anywhere in the world at short notice on the pope's business. But was he reliable?

The letter was reportedly hand-delivered to Moscow in the second week of August 1980. There followed two months of intense, highly secret shuttle diplomacy between Warsaw, Moscow and Rome, paving the way for the historic agreement signed early in November 1980, between Solidarity and the Polish regime.

On 12 November, the pope told a crowded Wednesday audience in the Nervi Hall of his 'joy at this wise and mature agreement'. He went on, in the only public reference to everything that had happened, to state that the 'maturity which in the last few months has characterized our fellow countrymen's way of acting will continue to be typical of us.'

The Russians had not invaded. But nor could Brezhnev forgive or forget John Paul's position on Solidarity; the defiant Polish pope was indeed a man of immense influence and real power. He might prove even more troublesome to the Soviet authorities in the future.

32

Agca has taken to wearing a *kaffiyeh*, the flowing Arab headdress held in place by a single knotted cord. It provides protection both against the cold of the Libyan night and scorching daytime sun. He also wears a pair of desert boots which Teslin Tore bought for him in Beirut. They go well with Agca's faded US Army fatigues, part of a surplus consignment for the Vietnamese War that, after years, found its way to this training camp forty-five miles south of Tripoli City. It is on the road to Al-Qyaddahiyal where Colonel Muammar al Qathafi,[1] ruler of this desert nation, was born in a goatskin tent not unlike the one Agca has shared these past two months.

Once, he had seen Qathafi's helicopter hovering over the camp. His instructor, the short burly American everybody simply calls 'Major Frank', told Agca that Qathafi regularly likes to be flown out and look down on this place. It's here, Major Frank likes to boast, 'the cream' — the most promising terrorists — are put through their paces. This, the major never tires of saying, is 'the graduation class.'

Frank is the first American Agca has ever met. The experience initially confused him. For years Americans and the United States have had a position high on his hate list. That remains so. But Agca nevertheless finds Major Frank likeable. He decides it is mainly because of the very factual way the American talks of killing. Major Frank has told Agca he has killed over twenty men, and in the past month he has been demonstrating just how to do so with a variety of weapons. Agca has been deeply impressed. He would like to know more about Major Frank. But the rules of the camp forbid him asking. It is a necessary precaution in the event any of the students here are afterwards captured. Major Frank has told Agca chilling stories of what the Israelis do to the terrorists they catch.

Major Frank should know. For a spell he trained Israeli officers in counter-terrorist methods. That was when Frank Terpil was a CIA field officer, one of the agency's experts on sabotage. Now he is a fugitive from American justice. A grand jury in Washington indicted him for supplying explosives to Libya, conspiring to assassinate one of Qathafi's opponents in Cairo, recruiting former American military pilots to fly Libyan aircraft and recruiting Green Berets to help him run the training camp Agca is now in. Terpil is far more dangerous and deadly than any of the hundred men he and his team are instructing. That also makes Terpil attractive to Agca.[2]

The camp is very different from the one Agca went to in Syria more than two years ago. Here he is not subjected to political lectures on the history of the PLO and its long struggle for a Palestinian homeland, or on the evils of Zionism or the threat of Western Imperialism. Here such discussions are taboo. Agca soon discovered why. In this camp there appear to be terrorists of all political persuasions. They come to receive training and then they depart. Nobody asks where they have come from or where they are going. It is another firm rule of this place that such questions are never put.

Now, Agca himself prepares to move on. He removes his headdress, desert boots and fatigues and changes into a three-piece suit manufactured in East Germany, as were his cheap suitcase and other clothes. He is given a one-way tourist-class ticket for the Lufthansa flight which will take him to Sofia in Bulgaria. He has been told that Tore will meet him there.

*

Agca's mind can no longer recall in any logical manner everything that had happened to him since Tore took them through the mountain pass east of Erzurum out of Turkey and into Iran, at the end of 1979. Some incidents remain vividly clear, others contain gaps. The psychiatrists will later wonder whether, in a clinical sense, this is one of those periods when he was 'lost' in a catatonic stupor. That could explain both the memory gaps and the astonishing detail which Agca will remember about certain of his experiences: whole conversations, who had been unkind to him, who was helpful.

The initial trip south from Iran into Syria was a blur; it may have taken a month or more. But by February 1980, Agca and Tore were in Damascus. There they had met Kadem. He and Agca resumed their homosexual relationship until Kadem left the city, telling Agca he was going to Libya. At the end of April, Tore showed up in the room he had rented for Agca with a two-day-old copy of *Milliyet*. It contained news that Agca had been sentenced to death *in absentia* by an Istanbul court. Agca remembers how he shrugged and giggled for hours over the report. This, too, was in keeping with his mental state.

The next memory he has is of Tore arriving in June with an Indian passport which he gave to Agca. Tore had said, 'From now on you are Yoginder Singh.' Just as he had spent hours in Turkey staring at the bank passbook, so Agca took endless pleasure studying this imperfectly forged document.

On 3 July, Tore arrived once more in Agca's room with a travel bag and $500. He spoke carefully to Agca, making sure his instructions were clearly understood. He made Agca repeat them back. Then they took a taxi to Damascus International Airport. There Tore gave Agca a ticket to Sofia. Agca can remember Tore complaining about having to pay the airport tax of ten Syrian pounds.

From Vrajdebna airport Agca took a taxi for the six-mile journey to the Vitosha Hotel in Sofia's downtown area. He checked into Room 911 which had been pre-paid. A note from the management on the bedside table informed Agca that he had been given credit facilities to dine in the Vitosha's restaurant and use the hotel's room service.

On the evening of 5 July 1980, he received two visitors. The first said his name was Omer Mersan. The other merely identified himself as 'Maurizi'. They quickly convinced Agca they knew Tore and Kadem. The three of them then spent, Agca will recall, several hours together.

Maurizi asked Agca about his life after leaving Yesiltepe. He made him repeat his hate list, in full. He carefully questioned Agca about his religious attitudes and asked to see his scrapbook on Paul. Maurizi leafed through it, asking Agca to explain some of the entries. He asked him why he felt compelled to kill a pope. Agca had given his reasons and then ordered dinner to be sent to his room. During the meal Maurizi had continued probing. He went back over Agca's religious attitudes. But he gave no sign whether he approved or disapproved of them. Finally he had sat back. Mersan then asked Agca to produce his Indian passport. He flipped through it, shaking his head, saying how lucky Agca had been to cross any frontier with such a clumsy forgery. He handed the passport to Maurizi who pocketed it. Mersan then produced another passport. It was Turkish, number 136635, made out in the name of Faruk Ozgun and already bore immigration stamps for London (Heathrow), Paris (Charles de Gaulle) and Munich (Rheims). The passport contained a photograph of Agca and details which aged him five years, giving his year of birth as 1953. Mersan handed Agca the passport. He told him to use it for all future travel until otherwise instructed.

The two men had left. For Mersan, a Turkish smuggler based in Munich, his part of the operation was over.[3]

But 'Maurizi' is known to Western intelligence services as Maurizi Folini, a senior KGB agent in the Balkans with good connections to extreme left-wing elements in Italy's Red Brigades.

In the next four months, Agca met Folini on two further occasions. The first time Folini gave him $500 spending money. The second time

he informed Agca he would be going to the training camp in Libya.
Kadem was there when Agca arrived but left shortly afterwards. It was
the last time they would see each other.

At the camp Agca met four other men who are to play an important
role in his life, Ali Chafic, Omer Ay, a Turkish-born terrorist and
member of the Grey Wolves, Ahmed Jooma and Ibrahim El Haya. (In
December 1981, Chafic, Jooma and El Haya were named by the US
government as members of a Libyan hit-squad on its way to the United
States to assassinate President Reagan. There was a world-wide alert for
the men. In January 1982, Omer Ay was arrested by West German
police in Hamburg. Turkey demanded his extradition. The German
authorities refused to hand him over until he had been dealt with for
crimes in their country.)

Like Agca they have been coached in the art of assassination, car
bombings and urban mayhem of every kind. Special training has been
given to them all in the skills needed to carry out a successful
'operation', Terpil's generic word for murder in crowded public places.
They have been taught the importance of ground work, positioning
and anticipation, and how to create a diversion. They have studied film
of the assassination of President Kennedy in Dallas and successful
attacks on politicians in Spain and other countries. Finally they have
worked together as a team under the watchful eyes of their instructor.

*

Now, while the others are to remain at the camp, it is time for Agca to
travel. Physically he is even fitter than he had been in the Syrian camp.
And during his stay in Libya he has regularly seen a doctor who asked
many of the questions Folini had posed: about Agca's hate list, his
religious obsessions, his compulsion to kill a pope. The doctor
prescribed anti-depressant drugs: largactil and phenelzine. The latter
has produced side-effects from which Agca continues to suffer: a
dryness of the mouth, constipation, sudden waves of dizziness, a
lowering of sexual feelings, difficulty in urinating. Worst of all to bear
are the sudden pounding headaches that come and go without
warning. The doctor has told Agca these pains are also common
side-effects from phenelzine, but that he must continue to take both
medicines. Agca accepted this and a six-month supply of the drugs is
packed in his suitcase as he leaves the camp. It is the only indication he
has he will not be returning here until well into 1981. But even of that
he cannot be certain. Nor can Agca possibly know as the Libyan
Airways 737 climbs away from Tripoli airport that he has finally begun
his journey into the history books.

*

Cardinal Sin can barely contain himself. For weeks he has been assailed on all sides. From their fortified palace President and Mrs Marcos – the famous 'conjugal dictatorship' – have used every ploy to exploit the pope's presence in the Philippines. The formidable pair have asked to fly aboard the pope's jet; they have wanted to say Mass privately with him; in a dozen different ways they have tried to turn the visit into a papal endorsement of their authoritarian regime. Sin has successfully resisted them. At the same time he has faced a running battle with his own clergy. Many oppose the visit not only because it could comfort the regime but also because they fear John Paul's views do not fit the local scene. The Church in the Philippines is trying to divest itself of its image of being the acquiescent supporter of the wealthy and powerful. Even more than in Latin America, Filipino priests and nuns are openly militant.

It is against this background that the papal party jets into Manila on 17 February 1981. From the moment John Paul rises from kissing the ground at the airport, he finds himself in a tense situation. Remembering the attempt on Paul's life when he had visited Manila, the regime has hemmed in John Paul behind a security cordon reminiscent of the way he was guarded in Turkey. Sin remains his moon-faced impassive self. The cardinal is waiting for the moment when the pope will say what he thinks.

That moment comes later in the afternoon of the first day of the visit when John Paul pays an official call on the Marcoses and members of the government. The world's press is on hand, sensing confrontation. It is swift in coming. His voice steady and measured – signalling to veteran Vaticanologists there is trouble on the way – John Paul reminds everyone this is a pastoral visit, that he is here 'in the name of Jesus Christ'. The pope turns and looks squarely at the president and his wife. He fixes them for a long moment with his eyes. There is a steely look in them. Noé, standing almost at the pope's elbow, knows the look well. He has seen it in John Paul's eyes when he is angry. This time, the pope's passion is the more formidable because of the cold way he delivers his attack. He reminds everyone – and as he does so he glances quickly at the suddenly uneasy president, his wife and their government – that nothing can justify violation of human rights. He then delivers a drubbing of all the regime represents. He ends with a direct appeal to the ministers present 'to see enacted those reforms and policies that aim at bringing about a truly humane society, where all men and women and children receive what is due to them, to live in dignity, where especially the poor and underprivileged are made the priority concern of all'.

Sin is content. He has advised the pope the only way to make the visit work is to speak out, to take sides, to let the Marcos regime know exactly where he stands.

The pope and the cardinal leave the crestfallen administration behind. There are further home truths to be uttered. John Paul intends to make the clergy understand their position. He tells hundreds of them in Manila's cathedral: 'You are priests and religious, you are not social or political leaders or officials of a temporal power.'

He goes further in his next address. He warns another great assembly of priests and nuns about resorting to violence: 'The road towards your total liberation is not the way of violence, class struggle or hate. It is the way of love, peaceful solidarity.'

Marcinkus and Casaroli can recognize that the words are also a warning signal to the other side of the world. It is John Paul's way of telling Lech Walesa and his Solidarity Movement not to push too hard. Not now, when they have achieved so much.

Here, in the Philippines, the pope feels he has delivered two telling blows. He has put both the regime and the episcopate on notice they had better mend their ways if they are to remain Catholics in good standing.

On 23 February, it is time for John Paul to fly north to make his contribution to a wider issue. He goes to Japan, to speak first in Hiroshima and then Nagasaki about the perils of nuclear war. His words are among the finest of his pontificate. Realizing the pope knows the contents of the third secret of Fatima, and remembering the article by Balducci published on the eve of the Conclave that elected John Paul, some of those in his entourage wonder whether the pope believes a nuclear holocaust is closer than many realize. It is a sombre note on which to end the Asian sortie.

*

On Good Friday, 17 April 1981, the first day of the Easter Holiday, Istahäk Cahani, the recently appointed defence attaché at the Israeli Embassy in Ankara, receives a telephone call from a contact in MIT.[4] Cahani learns that, using the name of his false passport, Agca has enrolled for a language course at the University for Foreigners in Perugia, Italy. A Turkish 'casual' – MIT parlance for a member of the network of informers it maintains throughout Europe's Turkish community – has recognized Agca. It is the description of his two companions which at first excited Cahani's MIT contact and now produces the same response in him: Agca was seen in Perugia with one man who looked like Tore: the other's description fitted Folini.

Cahani is a resourceful professional intelligence officer. One of the functions of his profession, he has been known to quote, is 'hearing voices through the noises'. As the senior member of the Israeli intelligence team in Turkey, Cahani has problems extracting those 'voices' from some very distorted 'noises'. The various factions of the Anarchy tend to lie as a matter of course; so do the regime's security forces, including MIT. But, in spite of his caution, Cahani has come to believe, based on everything he now knows, that Agca is not just another run-of-the-mill Turkish terrorist.

His own growing file on Agca confirms this. There is the fact that Agca was sprung from his Istanbul prison in an operation which bore all the marks of a professionalism MOSSAD itself could not fault. Though the escape had been carried out by Turks, they almost certainly were advised either by the KGB or another Eastern Bloc intelligence agency. That suspicion alone had been enough for Cahani to be aroused. But there was more. Despite being the subject of an Interpol Red Alert – the most serious arrest-on-sight order the international agency distributes to its member police forces – Agca remains free. Yet in the past three months he has flitted in and out of West Germany and Switzerland. Each time he disappeared through that most famous of bolt-holes, Checkpoint Charlie in East Berlin. Cahani had listened sympathetically as his MIT source explained the chagrin of other MIT officers who tailed Agca on these trips. On the German leg the Turks were accompanied by a team from BND, the German secret service. The BND had apparently told their Turkish counterparts they would not allow Agca to be arrested on German soil for his two murders; they feared it might provoke a revenge reaction from one of the many Turkish terrorist groups which have based themselves in West Germany.[5] Besides, the BND might well find it more interesting to let Agca come and go virtually as he pleased in order to see where eventually he might take them. This situation has caused friction between the two intelligence services, contributing to the reasons Agca remains free. Yet Cahani suspects there are other reasons. On his trips through Europe Agca has stayed in good hotels, appears to be well-funded. Only a very generous paymaster provides such cash. Cahani knows this also points towards a KGB involvement.

But the final 'voice' had come to Cahani from a MOSSAD agent stationed in Sofia. Alerted by Tel Aviv, the Israeli agent had quickly picked up Agca's trail when he arrived back in the Bulgarian capital from Libya. A few days after again settling into the Hotel Vitosha, Agca received Abuzer Ugurlu, known throughout the Balkans as 'the Godfather' of the area's thriving underworld. Ugurlu's smuggling activities into Turkey produce an annual turnover of millions of dollars. His total Euro-wide connections have made him a multi-millionaire. He has an imposing home in the most select quarter of Sofia; his neighbours are senior members of the Bulgarian Communist Party.

The reasons for Ugurlu's power and position is known to Western intelligence agencies. Their files on him all indicate the same story: he has been allowed to build up his personal fortune and acquire his privileges in return for the invaluable service he provides. For years Ugurlu's smuggling network has been the most effective way to distribute huge quantities of weapons to Turkish terrorists, of all persuasions, as part of a deliberate attempt to dismantle Turkey, NATO's vital outpost. The computers of CIA, MIT and Britain's SIS confirm what the MOSSAD agent in Sofia has told Tel Aviv: Ugurlu has the most direct and closest of links to the Bulgarian secret service. In turn, no other Eastern Bloc intelligence agency is more closely tied to the KGB.

The fact Ugurlu called on Agca not only strengthened, at least in the view of MOSSAD analysts, the conclusion that Agca had connections with Soviet intelligence, but was also a clear indication of his growing importance to the KGB.

Still interpreting those 'voices', Cahani had made a number of deductions. Ugurlu's network is the one Agca has used to travel so successfully around Europe. The purpose of the journeys, Cahani decided, is so that Agca can become familiar with the area in which he will sooner or later carry out some mission. At first the defence attaché thought Agca would be used for an attack against a Jewish installation either in West Germany or Switzerland: an embassy, legation, El Al office, a Jewish bank – anything with an Israeli connection. Warnings were sent out from Tel Aviv, security tightened on all Jewish property in both countries. MOSSAD passed on their fears to the BND and Germany's other counter-terrorist force, the BKA. The response was cool.

Then Agca disappeared once more through Checkpoint Charlie. For weeks Cahani has waited patiently for news.

This latest sighting in Perugia is important. With Tore and Folini seemingly in tow, Agca could be going to strike at one of the many Jewish targets in Italy.

Cahani goes to the embassy's cipher room and begins to encode a telex to MOSSAD in Tel Aviv.

*

On Saturday, 18 April, the DIGOS office on the third floor of Rome police headquarters receives news that a possible terrorist squad is in Perugia. MOSSAD is given as the source. The squad is identified as 'Mehmet Ali Agca alias Faruk Ozgun, Teslin Tore and Maurizi Folini'. After Agca's name comes a copy of the Interpol Red Alert. Tore and

Folini are identified imprecisely as 'Soviet intelligence'. DIGOS is Italy's justifiably famed anti-terrorist squad, set up to fight the Red Brigades. It is overworked and understaffed. It does not have a good working relationship with MOSSAD; like the German BKA, harassed DIGOS feels the Israeli agency has a penchant for sending out too many fliers.

The duty officer in Rome calls the local police in Perugia. Their enquiries meet with a blank response. This is the middle of the Easter holiday weekend. The University for Foreigners is closed. There is no way the Perugia police can easily run checks on something which anyway sounds rather unlikely: the idea a terrorist squad would find anything suitable to attack in Perugia seems rather far-fetched. There is little more to be done until Tuesday.

Then, when checks are completed, the Perugian police are not surprised to have found no trace of Agca and his companions. Although a Faruk Ozgun had indeed registered at the University, he had not turned up for classes. No one has even heard of the other names. It is not an uncommon situation; a great deal of police work is foot-slogging investigation. The Perugia police inform DIGOS in Rome. The message goes back up the line to Interpol in Paris – the clearing house for all such traffic – and on to Tel Aviv: if the terrorist squad has been in Perugia, it is not there now.

DIGOS in Rome thinks none of the team may even have entered Italy.

Tel Aviv again telexes Cahani in Ankara to continue listening to his 'voices'. He does not have much hope. But he goes on listening. Something tells him Agca is set to strike soon. And while he cannot know where, Cahani is confident who the target is going to be: either a Jewish person or a building. The attaché is not a betting man, but he would bet a month's pay on that.[6]

*

On Wednesday, 6 May, John Paul allots two full hours – ten am to noon – to discuss an issue his staff think is beginning to vie with Poland for his attention. It is the delicate question of the Holy See's relationship to the Republic of China.

Casaroli heads a group half a dozen strong at the Secretariat of State who have been working on the problems for months. Some of them travelled with the pope to the Philippines and Japan so they could renew informal contact with the Chinese Church; a year earlier, in March 1980, John Paul had sent Koenig to Peking to report on the situation. Koenig returned after ten days pessimistic: Catholics in China, to survive in a religious sense in a basically hostile climate, had to keep a distance from Rome. They were only allowed to practise their

439

faith under the auspices of a government-sponsored organization called the National Association of Patriotic Catholics. The Association has since 1949 elected its own bishops without the approval of the Vatican.

The elections are illicit but not invalid. Though they do not have the seal of Holy See approval, they do represent the all-important continuity of ordination. And the Chinese bishops have the support of Marcel Lefèbvre in his mountain redoubt in Switzerland because they say the Latin Tridentine Mass for China's three million Catholics.

They are the product of three centuries of relationship between China and the Church. It began when the Jesuits walked into Peking in the sixteenth century. They were warmly received. Then, in a momentous blunder, Rome rejected the Jesuits' idea of integrating Chinese and Catholic culture. Had this been allowed China might very well have become a Catholic country. But when the proposal was turned down, Catholic influence faded; the Chinese Catholics remained a small minority, sometimes tolerated, more often persecuted, but always tenacious of their faith. Since coming to office, John Paul had uttered several conciliatory statements towards the Chinese Church.

But he longed to do more.

This morning's meeting in his salon is to discuss the possibility of a full-scale pastoral visit to China, in which he would be the first pontiff to celebrate Mass in Peking's nineteenth-century French Gothic-style cathedral, and to say other Masses in Canton and Shanghai. It would not only be a splendid act of bridge-building between two of the oldest powers in the world, but also an open declaration of the Holy See's recognition of the vast importance of China. And if that was seen in Moscow as an indication of what the pope felt about the Soviet brand of Communism, so be it.

Casaroli reports that one seemingly insurmountable problem remains: Taiwan.

The Peking government will not consider allowing a papal visit until the Holy See ends its diplomatic ties with the Chinese Nationalist government of Taiwan.

Everybody in the room knows the dilemma: the Church flourishes on Taiwan. It has two hundred thousand Chinese Nationalist Catholics. They have a laudable education system which includes the world's only Chinese Catholic University. Just as the United States in the secular world had been pledged not to turn its back on Taiwan, so the Holy See is committed to maintaining its spiritual support.

This, John Paul insists, cannot change. And yet, he adds, a way must be found to reach Peking.

Casaroli says there are a number of possibilities to consider.

There should be a follow-up to the meeting John Paul had in Manila with a hundred Chinese Christians who had flown from Peking specially for the occasion. The pope had told them the past was over: mistakes had been made; this was freely acknowledged. But what mattered was the future. The thoughts had been guardedly received in Peking. Now, suggests Casaroli, was the time to capitalize on this reaction and make another approach to the government-approved Bishop of Peking. An appropriate letter could be sent from the Secretary enquiring about the possibility of a personal meeting. Casaroli was himself prepared to fly to Peking for talks.

John Paul gives his approval.

Next there is the more delicate matter of the Chinese Jesuit who had been released after twenty-two years in prison the previous September. This was clearly, in Chinese eyes, an olive branch. Why not then, suggests the Secretary, reciprocate? Would it not be appropriate, he asks the pope, to elevate the Jesuit to be Archbishop of Canton? This could only be seen in Peking as a genuine desire on the part of the Holy See to be allowed once more to become involved directly with the Chinese Church.

The pope agrees. (In June 1981, the Holy See announced the appointment. The National Association of Patriotic Catholics attacked it. Next came a strong denunciation by the Chinese government for the Holy See illegally interfering in the internal affairs of the Chinese Church. The door was once more closed. But only for a time. By 1982, the dialogue between Rome and Peking was again in full flow, part of potentially the most important contemporary advance in Church–State relations. Nobody doubts that what is happening is of immense significance. The Soviet Union views the Church's Chinese Connection with the deepest of misgivings. It has aroused barely dormant fears in the Soviet Communist psyche, the idea that the combination of Chinese and Holy See cunning is too strong a match for any secular power. It is yet another reason for Moscow to regret the appointment of John Paul.)

That Wednesday afternoon John Paul drives from the Vatican in his now familiar white-painted jeep-like *campagnola*, the popemobile. There are some fifty thousand people in St Peter's Square to greet him. Smaller than the crowds were in the early stages of his pontificate, they are nevertheless numerically far larger than his predecessors generally attracted. It continues to be a constant headache for security chief Ciban. Today, for the first time, his Vigilance have some real support. As well as the Rome police there is a squad of DIGOS agents spaced apart and moving watchfully near the popemobile as it crawls around the piazza with the pope smiling and tending his blessing.

John Paul's outstretched arms embrace those widely separated points of the crowd where five men watch the popemobile's progress. They leave the piazza without showing the slightest sign of recognition of each other. They have been particularly warned against this by Maurizi Folini and Teslin Tore, their KGB controllers. The five men are Ibrahim El Haya, Ahmed Jooma, Omer Ay, Ali Chafic and Mehmet Ali Agca.

THE POPE AND THE JACKAL

*If it were done when 'tis done, then 'twere well
It were done quickly: if the assassination
Could trammel up the consequence, and catch
With his surcease success; that but this blow
Might be the be-all and the end-all here,
But here, upon this bank and shoal of time,
We'd jump the life to come.*

— Macbeth (I vii 1)

Absolutism moderated by assassination.

— Definition of the Russian
  Constitution by an unnamed Russian
  recorded in Count Münster's
  *Political Sketches of the State of
  Europe, 1814–67*

33

The solitary night duty operator in the Vatican telephone exchange, an elderly nun, puts down her book and looks at the rows of buttons and lights on the switchboard which runs the length of this beige-coloured room. From dawn to midnight the exchange is manned by shifts of half a dozen sisters who daily handle thousands of calls. But this is almost three o'clock in the morning of Wednesday, 13 May 1981, and outwardly the Vatican sleeps. The nun knows better. That is why she has put down her book. Her head-set is clipped over her coif and a cross on a gold chain hangs from her neck. Her face is composed. But her eyes remain watchful. The nun is waiting for a signal.

Before her, on a typed card, is a list of emergency telephone numbers. They begin with Ciban's bedside extension. Next on the list is the night extension of Buzzonetti, now reinstated as papal physician. Then comes the number of Casaroli's bedroom telephone and the bedside extensions of Dziwisz and Magee. They are followed by the numbers for Martin and Noé. At the bottom of the list are two numbers written in longhand. The first is the general number of Rome police headquarters. The next is the main number of the Gemelli Hospital. They have both been on the list since the end of April.

The nun suspects, but cannot be certain, that their presence is connected with a noticeable increase in security in and around the Vatican. She has seen how the Swiss Guards now ask for identification from even long-serving Vatican employees, how the Vigilance have increased their patrols of the grounds, how there are more policemen on duty in St Peter's Square. The precautions have puzzled her. And everybody else she has spoken to – her fellow operators, clerical workers in the Apostolic Palace, the staff in the duty-free store – seem equally mystified by the sudden increase in security.

There is nothing prescient about it. Casaroli has designated the Gemelli as the hospital which will handle any serious medical emergency involving John Paul. The Secretary had told the others privy to this decision – Marcinkus, Buzzonetti, Dziwisz and Magee – that in the event of the pope becoming ill, he wished to avoid the criticism which arose from the way Paul's final illness was handled and the extraordinary aftermath of Gianpaolo's death. This time, Casaroli has ordered, at the first sign of any medical complication, the pope is to be sent to the Gemelli. The listing of city police headquarters is also innocent enough: the presence of its number in the Vatican exchange is merely part of Ciban's regular review of standard security procedures. He has received no sudden tip that trouble is in the offing; indeed, the latest information from his contacts at headquarters suggests that the relentless, but unpublicized, combined efforts of the police, Carabinieri and DIGOS are at last making Rome too hot for the Red Brigades.

The nun, of course knows nothing of this. All she knows is that at three o'clock – the appointed time – the signal she expects every hour comes. One by one the Vigilance night patrols call in from various posts inside the Vatican. The nun switches each call through to the guard-house behind the Arch of the Bells. When all the calls are in, she picks up her book. Hopefully, she can get in another hour's reading before the process is repeated.

*

Shortly after four o'clock a shadow detaches itself from the darker mass of Bernini's colonnade. It is a Rome policeman, one of twenty-four now stationed around the silent piazza. The patrolman walks towards the obelisk. A colleague waits there. They light cigarettes and stare, bored, at the darkened Vatican buildings. They hate night duty; nothing ever happens.

An hour later, the first light appears in the papal apartment. Thirty minutes later there are lights everywhere on the top floor of the Apostolic Palace. The policemen extinguish their cigarettes. One of them, a lapsed Catholic, asks his companion a familiar question: whether it is a life of celibacy which makes everybody in the pope's entourage get up so early. Just as he had hoped, the question stimulates his companion to begin another discussion about the private habits and foibles of the pope. Does he bathe or does he shower? Sing Polish hymns or pop songs as he goes about his ablutions? Does he still eat all that Polish stodge for breakfast or has he gone Roman and settled for coffee and a bread roll? They continue in this vein to the end of their shift. As they go off duty they promise each other they will tap their contacts around the Apostolic Palace for the answers.

*

At eight o'clock John Paul returns to the private study down the corridor from the dining room. His eating habits have not changed: a substantial breakfast, a light lunch and then a good dinner. More than anywhere in the apartment, the study reflects his tastes and personality. There are photographs of his parents in wooden frames on his desk. The titles in the bookshelves are predominantly Polish. Where Paul's copy of Mailer's *The Naked and the Dead* had stood, there is now the latest Morris West confection, *The Clowns of God*. It is all about a pope who claims he has received a private revelation of the end of the world and the second coming of Christ; he resigns his office to save mankind. Curialists who have read the book think it's clever nonsense. They, of course, have no knowledge of how closely it parallels John Paul's letter to Brezhnev.

*

A maid pauses outside the door of Room 31 on the third floor of the Pensione Isa. It is a small hotel near Rome's main railway station. Most of its clients are students or tourists of limited means. The hotel provides reasonably priced, comfortable accommodation for those who wish to make the fifteen-minute walk to St Peter's Square. Most guests leave early, breakfast in one of the nearby coffee shops, and return in the early evening to freshen up before going out again for dinner. It is a routine which allows the hotel to get by with a small cleaning staff: since all the rooms are generally vocated for the day by around nine o'clock, the handful of maids employed at the Pensione Isa can go about their work uninterrupted.

For the past two days the maid who services Room 31 finds its occupant has spoiled her routine. He comes and goes at all times, then returns to spend hours in the room. Sometimes she has heard him muttering away in a foreign language. She wonders whether it is anything to do with the bottles of tablets she has noticed he keeps on his bedside table. The maid thinks he must be quite ill to be taking so many medicaments. He arrived on Monday, carrying a briefcase and flight bag. He paid in advance for three nights. That means, thinks the relieved maid, he will be gone by the morning and she can return to her well-ordered ways.

She listens outside the door, her basket of cleaning cloths and sprays in her hand. There is no sound from within. Perhaps he slipped out when she was servicing one of the other bedrooms. The maid knocks lightly and enters the room. She is wise in the ways of hotel guests; nothing surprises her any more. Nevertheless, she is still astonished by the reaction she gets. The man in the narrow single bed leaps to the floor and stands facing her in his vest and pants. He is crouching as if expecting to be attacked, elbows tucked into his waist, fists clenched in front of his face. He is shouting at her in a language she cannot understand. But his meaning is clear. He wants her out of the room.

Uttering excuses, the maid backs towards the door and closes it behind her.

Agca turns and climbs back into bed.

*

At noon John Paul and Casaroli meet in the pope's private study to discuss the latest crisis in Northern Ireland – one that placed the Holy See on a collision course with the British government of Prime Minister Margaret Thatcher.[1] Both the pontiff and the Secretary had been told there was at least some circumstantial evidence that the British government may have allowed to be undermined a highly secret Holy See initiative to try and save the life of IRA prisoner Bobby Sands.

His hunger strike in the notorious Maze Prison in Belfast had focused world attention on the entire matter of Britain's involvement in Ulster. While imprisoned, Sands had been elected a member of the British House of Commons. He had vowed to die for the cause he espoused all his adult life – an Ulster free from what he saw as British domination. From the day he went on hunger strike there were widely expressed fears that his death would spark more such actions and create a serious general escalation of violence in the province.

The pope had asked Magee to act as his co-ordinator over what was happening in Northern Ireland. Magee remained in close contact with Alibrandi and O'Fiaich. All three had the uneasy feeling their telephone calls may have been monitored – perhaps by one of the agents of Britain's Secret Intelligence Service who were widely thought to have been operating on both sides of the Irish border for some time. In the Republic they were suspected of working directly out of the British Embassy in Dublin. In the North, O'Fiaich's palace – his friends say – may be under electronic surveillance if only because, like Alibrandi, the cardinal felt it essential to talk to all those involved in the sectarian conflict – and that naturally included those with affiliations to proscribed organizations whose every activity is of interest to the security forces. Consequently, the conversations between Magee's office, Alibrandi's study and O'Fiaich's palace had been necessarily cryptic.

But towards the middle of April, with Sands weakening daily, Magee was in no doubt the messages he was getting from Ireland came down to one matter: it was time for the Holy See to intervene.

On Thursday, 23 April, Magee had raised the idea with John Paul. The pope listened carefully but gave no decision. Next day, Friday, he discussed the question with Casaroli in Magee's presence. The Secretary had steepled his fingers in that familiar gesture and made a suggestion: the Holy See should not only intervene but Magee himself should travel to Belfast to make a direct appeal to Sands to call off his hunger strike. At the same time Casaroli would try and persuade the British government to make some concessions to the IRA prisoners in the Maze H-Block.

Throughout the weekend, 25–26 April, Magee remained in close contact with Alibrandi and O'Fiaich while Casaroli had several meetings with the British Minister to the Holy See. The Secretary also called Cardinal Hume in London and the pope's apostolic delegate to Great Britain, Archbishop Heim. Between them they kept Downing Street informed of developments; there was a desire in the Vatican that there should be no misunderstanding of what it was trying to do. In particular Hume and Heim both stressed that this initiative should not be seen as in any way offering comfort to those who committed violence; the Holy See was intervening solely on humanitarian grounds. Hume and Heim reported back to Casaroli they were satisfied this message had got across.[2] That the response in Whitehall appeared cool was, they counselled, understandable. What was being proposed required a great deal of thought. To make it work would need much give and take on both sides. But if the will was there it might just succeed – providing a spectacular triumph for what the Holy See had always been good at: patient and secret negotiation.

By Monday, 27 April, the situation had hardened to the promising point where the Sands family, through O'Fiaich, had indicated they would welcome Magee and that Bobby Sands would see him in his prison cot, seriously weak though he was. A ticket was booked for Magee to fly to London and then on to Belfast. The British Minister to the Holy See informed the Foreign Office in London. This was normal procedure. Magee would travel on a red-covered Holy See diplomatic passport and would expect to receive all the courtesies normally shown to an important papal envoy. But there was one specification about the trip that the Secretariat of State felt worth restating to the British Minister: secrecy was of paramount importance; there must be no leaks at any stage. The Sands family had pledged their co-operation and O'Fiaich was satisfied that for once the IRA would not try and capitalize on the visit. So concerned was Casaroli with letting as few people as possible know exactly when Magee would be travelling that Hume and Heim were not given his flight times. There was really no need for them to know. London was merely a short stopover to Belfast. But the British Minister was given full details: Magee would fly on Tuesday morning, 29 April, on Alitalia to London and would then take the British Airways shuttle to Belfast. The details were passed to the Foreign Office in London.

What happened next continues to infuriate John Paul and Casaroli because, despite the insistence on secrecy, there is no doubt that a leak did occur. Magee was still on his way to London when the British media knew he was coming. Numerous reporters had called Northern Ireland's Protestant leader, Ian Paisley, to ask his views. They were predictably outraged. He saw Magee's visit as 'the unacceptable involvement of the Roman Papacy' in the affairs of 'Protestant Ulster'.

Magee's carefully conceived secret mission was in shreds even before he touched down at London Heathrow. There he was met by Peter Blaker, Foreign Secretary Lord Carrington's deputy, and Michael Alison, Minister of State at the Northern Ireland Office. They made it clear the British government was not prepared to make concessions to IRA inmates – they wanted to be allowed to run their own affairs in prison in much the same way as prisoners of war do – while under duress. Magee found both men icily formal. He found the headlines dismaying: there was no way, ran the reports, that Ulster Protestants would help save Sands if it meant the British government having to give ground to 'terrorists'.

For two days Magee shuttled to and from Sands's prison bedside. In the end Magee had been unable to extract a single concession from the Thatcher government. He left Belfast convinced the Holy See had been 'double-crossed' by London. If there had not been what he perceived as a carefully managed publicity storm it might have been possible to have avoided the impasse. But in the super-heated glare of the media there had been little chance of Magee successfully carrying out John Paul's wishes – finding the compromise solution the pope had sincerely hoped existed.

Immeasurably sadder – and, he told his friends in the Irish Mafia, 'wiser to the wiles of the Brits' – Magee had continued to do all he could from the Vatican to diffuse the hunger-strike crisis. He was still trying when Bobby Sands died.

Now there has been a second hunger-strike death. More were expected.

After reviewing the situation John Paul and Casaroli call in Magee and tell him that the Holy See cannot involve itself further in such a public way. It will continue, however, to work behind the scenes.

Magee leaves to inform O'Fiaich and Alibrandi.

*

This much will become known:

Agca spends most of the morning in Room 31. He re-reads notes he has made. They detail the final instructions he received from Teslin Tore when they last met, this time in Milan. Tore does not know Agca had made these jottings which, if discovered, could compromise all the months of training and planning that have gone into the forthcoming operation: Agca, in his wilful way, which all the medicaments he has been taking cannot change, nevertheless went ahead and wrote down his instructions.

Folini had given Agca two million Italian lire to cover his expenses in Rome. Folini also repeated what he had almost certainly been instructed to say by the

KGB: when Agca had completed his mission he would receive three million Deutschmarks, yet another identity plus sanctuary in Bulgaria. Agca did not doubt any of this. Ever since that first deposit of forty thousand Turkish lire in his name on 13 December 1977, in the Turkye Is Bankasi, he had received ample proof that those who now controlled him had the finances and resources to back up Folini's words.

In Milan Agca had also received further proof of how careful Tore and Folini always are to avoid anything which would directly implicate them. Tore's final instruction to Agca was that he should go to Milan railway station and collect a packet left there in the name of Faruk Ozgun, the alias Agca was still using. Then, after quick handshakes, Tore and Folini had left him. They were due to meet Agca in the Vitosha Hotel in Sofia this coming weekend.

He had gone to the left luggage office, produced his passport and collected his packet. It was surprisingly heavy for its size. He had gone to the station toilet, locked himself in a cubicle and opened the packet. It contained a Belgian-made Browning 9-mm semi-automatic pistol and bullets. The gun had been bought in Austria, with money almost certainly provided by Folini, by yet another sinister figure in the conspiracy. This man's name is Horst Grillmeir, an old associate of smuggler Omer Mersan and the Bulgarian Mafia Godfather, Ugurlu.[3]

The instructions Agca received tell him what he must do with the gun at this stage. He now places it in his flight bag.

Some instructions he had disregarded. He will not dye his hair. Nor will he wear a cross to pretend he is a Catholic pilgrim. Even the idea of placing around his neck the symbol of a person he hates passionately is enough to make him feel physically ill.

Just before two o'clock, Agca takes his anti-depressant drugs: in Milan Tore had given him a further supply, sufficient to last until he reaches Sofia. Agca plans to begin the journey this very evening, taking a train to Florence and flying from there to Geneva where there were connections onward to Sofia. His co-terrorists will go their separate ways to their pre-determined destinations.

Agca is not concerned about them. He knows they are merely supports for what he will do. He only wishes his headache would go away.

He strips and shaves and washes. Then he settles back on the bed and quietly begins to recite his hate list, glancing frequently at his watch.

*

By three o'clock there are about eighty thousand people in St Peter's Square. They include an elderly American woman, Anne Odre, from Buffalo, New York, and a pert Jamaican girl, twenty-one-year-old Rose Hall. They have chosen their positions with care. They are right at the front of the fenced-off route the popemobile will travel and both are also quite close to the platform from which John Paul will deliver his weekly address. The women stand a few feet apart, with their backs to the right-hand curve of Bernini's colonnade as they look towards the Basilica. Behind them, and just in front of the colonnade, are two trucks. One is a mobile first-aid post, the second is selling Vatican stamps. An ambulance edges its way through the crowd and parks beside the post-office trailer. The women notice there are plenty of policemen around, but security seems very lax. The checks seem casual on those with passes to enter the special pens immediately below the dais.

The crowd is even larger than the women had expected. Though they do not know each other, there had been a common thought in their minds when they chose their positions: they are ideally placed to leave the square quickly when the ceremonies are over.

Standing on an upper edge of one of the square's fountains, another American, Lowell Newton, also thinks he is well positioned. He can see over the heads of the crowd and the light is right for what he wants to do.

Like everybody else in the ever-filling piazza, the three Americans wait patiently.

*

At four o'clock John Paul goes to his bedroom and changes into a freshly pressed pristine-white silk cassock. It has a tailored cape that Gammarelli has cleverly modified to enable the pope to wear a flak jacket beneath the cassock. The tailor's skills have been wasted. The pope continues not only to refuse wearing any protection but has ordered the flak jacket to be removed from the apartment. The very thought of it, he has angrily told his secretaries, goes against all his office stands for.

John Paul leaves the bedroom and joins Dziwisz in the nearby study. The secretary will accompany him in the *campagnola* during its customary two-circuit drive around the square. Then Dziwisz plans to hurry back to this study to prepare yet another brief on what is happening in Poland. Just as Magee is determined to keep before John Paul what is occurring in Ulster, so Dziwisz makes every effort to keep the pope informed on the latest manoeuvrings between the Polish Church and the regime in their homeland. And Dziwisz can take satisfaction in that he has even managed to persuade the pope to slip in some references about Poland in his homily this afternoon. Both he and the pope agree the words will be a further welcome boost for Solidarity.

*

Dressed in a sports jacket, white shirt open at the neck and a pair of black trousers and shoes, Agca edges his way past where Lowell Newton is standing to a position almost facing Ann Odre and Rose Hall. He carries his flight bag on his right shoulder. Its zipper is closed.

Minutes later Omer Ay makes his way through the crowd to stand at Agca's right elbow. His body masks the flight bag.

Neither man gives any sign of recognition.

Some distance away, quite close to Newton, waits Ali Chafic.

On the other side of the piazza, near the Arch of the Bells, Agca knows that Jooma and El Haya should now be in position.

*

At 4.50, John Paul and Dziwisz arrive in San Damaso Courtyard where the popemobile waits. Casaroli is there. So is Martin and Noé. The pope takes the Secretary aside for a brief conversation no one can overhear. Then John Paul turns to Martin and reminds the old prefect he wants time set aside in the morning to review 'papers'. Martin promises to rearrange the schedule.

Dziwisz climbs into the *campagnola* and sits in the white leather padded seat immediately behind the pope.

John Paul takes up his accustomed position. He stands and grips the steel white-painted handrail. Luigi Felici, the papal photographer, sits in a seat opposite Dziwisz; Felici is there to get some action shots the pope wants to send to close friends at Christmas.

At five o'clock precisely, the popemobile drives out of the courtyard.

Ahead, from the square, though nobody there can yet see anything, the cheering begins. The crowd knows he is coming. On these occasions his timetable and route never vary.

As the *campagnola* approaches the Arch of the Bells, Vigilance, DIGOS agents and uniformed Rome City policemen begin to walk ahead and immediately behind the vehicle. Their presence, if anything, makes the small popemobile appear more vulnerable. As it emerges into the piazza the noise rises to a roar. There are now well over a hundred thousand people in the square and they are cheering wildly.

John Paul waves and smiles. The *campagnola* moves past Jooma and El Haya.

With a couple of hundred yards to go before the *campagnola* reaches him, Newton raises his camera and readies himself.

Ann Odre finds the sun is reflecting off her glasses. It is difficult for her to see. She thinks: 'It's crazy; I've come all this way and now the sun's going to blot out things.'

Rose Hall has never heard so much noise. She tries to tell a neighbour it is not even like this at carnival time in Jamaica. Her companion shakes her head. Rose cannot be heard above the tumult.

Agca and Ay smile and wave towards the pope, as they have been told to do. They can glimpse the white figure in the popemobile greeting those standing at the bottom of the square.

The vehicle moves at two miles an hour. John Paul is now facing inwards, waving and smiling at the tens of thousands surrounding the obelisk in the centre of the piazza.

As the *campagnola* approaches, Newton lowers his camera. The pope has his back to him. Then he remembers: on the vehicle's next circuit around the square the pope will be facing outwards, towards him.

Following orders, detective Vito Ceccarelli continues to work his way through the crowd. He is following his nose, heading for those parts of the square where experience has taught him he might make an arrest. Ceccarelli is a member of a plain-clothes detail of Rome City policemen on the look-out for pickpockets. He dislikes the work because of the way he has to shove and elbow his way through the throng; he gets a lot of hassle and very little thanks when he makes an arrest. As the *campagnola* passes, Ceccarelli is facing the Basilica, near one of the square's fountains. He begins to shoulder his way up towards the right-hand side of the colonnade. The area is a favourite spot for pickpockets as it offers an easy escape route into the surrounding maze of streets.

Like Newton, Ann Odre and Rose Hall can only see John Paul's broad back as the popemobile passes. They know next time around he will be facing them.

It is exactly 5.15 when the *campagnola* begins its second circuit.

John Paul moves to the other side of the vehicle and faces outward, partially blocking Dziwisz's view. Photographer Felici, having taken several rolls of film over the pope's shoulder, has dropped off the popemobile and is now among the security men walking ahead of the vehicle. Felici is taking pictures of the crowd's rapturous reception and the pope's obvious happiness.

At 5.18, the popemobile passes Newton. John Paul appears to be waving directly into his camera. It's a better photograph than Newton ever imagined he would get.

The popemobile continues along to where Ann Odre and Rose Hall wait. They are both cheering and laughing as is virtually everybody around them.

Nobody notices the flight bag being unzipped and a hand reaching inside. It emerges holding the Browning Agca has brought to the square.

Detective Ceccarelli is still doggedly working his way through the crowd as John Paul passes. Ceccarelli notes, almost automatically, that the pope gives a particularly broad smile to a group of people waving a Polish flag.

After the popemobile passes, the detective continues on up the square. He is heading towards the post office trailer. That's where, with a bit of luck he'll nab a pickpocket, so giving himself some satisfaction for his tiring afternoon in the piazza.

Dziwisz sees there are about sixty feet to go before the *campagnola* completes its second circuit.

Impetuously, John Paul does something which always makes the secretary nervous. The pope reaches into the crowd and plucks up a child being held at arm's length. It is a little girl, with tousled blonde hair. He hugs and kisses her and then hands her back to her ecstatic mother. Dziwisz is always worried that a child will somehow wriggle clear of the pope's grasp and fall, creating a nasty accident. But whenever he mentions to John Paul the possibility, the pope only grins. Now, as Dziwisz continues to watch nervously, the pope bends down and leans out of the *campagnola* to give his hand to another little girl, dressed in Communion white. He straightens and looks about, wondering who else he might personally embrace or greet. It's his way of bringing the papacy to the masses in even the largest of crowds.

John Paul is now no more than twenty feet from Ann Odre and Rose Hall.

The first shot rings out.

*

Various individuals hear it differently. Ann Odre believes it is a car back-firing. She looks towards the two parked trailers and ambulance.

Rose Hall thinks someone has let off a fire-cracker. She thought they only did such things at Kingston carnivals.

Ceccarelli instinctively identifies the sound as gunfire. But even then he is confused. His experience is limited to the Rome City police range with its excellent acoustics. Here, in the crowded square, the direction the sound came from is not easy to locate. The detective begins to cast around, ruthlessly elbowing people out of his way. Other policemen stationed in the crowd are doing the same.

*

Even before the first echo fades, Dziwisz knows what has happened. There has been a shot. For a fleeting second – too short for the secretary subsequently to measure – he does not know who, or if anyone, has been hit.

John Paul remains upright, gripping the handrail.

Dziwisz is about to yell, 'Sit down!', when the pope starts to sway.

Agca's first bullet has penetrated John Paul's stomach. It has produced multiple wounds in the small intestine, in the lower part of the colon, in the large intestine and in the mesentery, the tissue which holds the intestine to the abdominal wall.

Instinctively, John Paul places his hand over the entry wound to try to stop the spurting blood.

Luigi Felici sees the shocked and bewildered look in the pope's eyes and lowers his camera.

John Paul starts to falter and crumple, desperate though he is to remain upright. He uses his left bloodstained hand to grip the handrail for support. His right hand is bunching the cassock in a futile attempt to quench the flow of blood. His face grows increasingly creased with agonizing pain. He begins slowly to collapse onto Dziwisz.

*

Extending his right arm, Agca draws a new bead with the Browning. His feet are placed firmly on the ground, a foot apart, the best position, he has been drilled, to keep him rock steady in a crowd. He remembers what his instructors in Libya had drilled into him: Take your time. Line up the target. Remember you have surprise on your side.

Agca fires again.

A second 9-mm shell hits the pope, in his right hand. It falls uselessly to his side.

Agca can see bright red blood spurting onto the white cassock.

He pulls the trigger once more.

The third shot hits John Paul in the right arm.

*

The *campagnola* driver twists in his seat. His mouth is open. But no word comes.

Dziwisz cradles the pope in his lap. John Paul is saying, 'Thank you. Thank you.'

The secretary starts to scream at the driver in Italian. 'Move! Back and forth! Move! Get us out of here!'

All around there is madness.

Dziwisz is shielding the pope with his body and screaming at the driver to go faster.

The phalanx of security men are whirling, guns drawn, shouting orders and counter orders.

The crowd itself is beginning to sway as if being buffeted by a great wind. One shocking sentence is repeated from mouth to mouth, rippling ever outwards from the scene of carnage. In a dozen different languages the same thing is said: 'The pope has been shot!'

Luigi Felici crosses himself. As he does so, a policeman bundles him aside.

The popemobile continues at an agonizingly slow speed through the throng. Its interior is a place of deepening horror. Blood continues to fountain up through John Paul's cassock, staining his cross, spattering all those around him; blood is soaking into the white leatherwork and dripping onto the floor.

The pope is barely conscious. His eyes open and close. He is whispering in Polish. Dziwisz holds him tight, murmuring words nobody can clearly understand. The secretary is saying a Polish prayer for the dying.

*

Ann Odre turns in the direction of the shooting. Another shot rings out. She is hit squarely in the chest. She collapses, seriously hurt.

Another shot.

The bullet hits Rose Hall in the left arm. She falls to the ground.

Two innocent bystanders have now been badly wounded.

Agca glances to his right. Ay has gone.

Agca, gun in hand, sets off after him. He is heading in the direction of the trailers and ambulance parked in front of the colonnade.

*

The third shot gave Ceccarelli a bearing. He is moving, bulldozer-like, even before the sounds of the other shots. Head down, arms flailing, he beats a path through the crowd. He, too, is heading for the trailers and ambulance.

*

Newton has left the fountain and is moving in the direction of the gunfire. As he does so, he sees a young man burst from the crowd, running very fast and holding a black revolver in his right hand.

Fearing he himself might be shot, Newton quickly turns away from the terrorist, hoping to give the impression he hadn't noticed him. The man passes within ten feet of Newton. The intrepid cameraman swings around and photographs him fleeing.

It is Ali Chafic.

On the far side of the square, Jooma and El Haya – placed there for the very purpose of providing an effective back-up – have run from their post well before the *campagnola* approaches.

Like Chafic and Ay, these other members of a hit-squad trained in part by a renegade CIA officer in a Libyan school for terrorism and financed by the KGB, believe Agca has totally succeeded in a mission that has been conceived as a suitable response to a pope who has dared to challenge Communist Russia.

*

Agca is almost there. The crowd continues to open before his waving gun. As he reaches the post office trailer he tosses the Browning away, sending it skidding under the trailer.

At the same moment his legs are cut from underneath him.

Detective Ceccarelli has made his arrest.

*

The popemobile lurches through the Arch of the Bells. An ambulance is parked there, engine running. Its crew swiftly transfers John Paul to a stretcher and lifts him into the ambulance.

Dziwisz goes with him.

Lights flashing and siren wailing, the ambulance heads off at speed for the Gemelli Hospital.

Inside, John Paul repeatedly whispers one word that both the Italian ambulance crew and the Polish secretary can understand.

'Madonna. Madonna. Madonna.'

During the desperate twenty-minute drive to the hospital through three kilometres of twisting city streets crowded with rush-hour traffic, behaviour patterns emerge in the ambulance which will be endlessly repeated as news of the shooting spreads.

The two attendants riding in the back reflect an attitude which becomes common. As they bend over the pope, making him as comfortable as they can, the men are filled with incredulity and outrage that this has happened to one of the most revered figures in the world. They are also themselves so shocked they partially forget to follow their training. Instead of keeping the pope quiet, they allow John Paul to go on repeating his beseeching, 'Madonna'. Every time he gasps the word his face contorts in pain and another spurt of blood comes from his stomach wound.

Dziwisz crouches on the floor of the wildly swaying ambulance as it careers over sidewalks and through traffic lights at speed. The secretary holds the pope's shattered right hand. Blood continues to flow from John Paul's wounded right arm, dripping onto his Fisherman's Ring. Dziwisz is tough. He has seen his share of violence in Poland and he knows that in such situations coolness is imperative. But while he remains outwardly calm he is gripped with an inertia which has stopped him asking a basic question: has anyone radioed ahead to alert the Gemelli?

No one has. Hands gripping the wheel, the ambulance driver is preoccupied using every trick he knows to get to the hospital. For all his skilful manoeuvring and the precious seconds he is saving, the fact no one thinks to warn the Gemelli to stand by is a serious mistake.

One of the attendants glances up from the pope long enough to look out of the window. He turns back to John Paul and smiles reassurance.

'We shall soon be there.'

The pope whispers, 'Thank you. Thank you.' The effort produces another surge of blood.

The ambulance skids to a halt by the Gemelli emergency entrance.

The driver leaps out and dashes past the doors, shouting at a startled nurse.

'It's the pope! It's the pope!'

She turns and runs into a room, and almost immediately returns with two doctors and three other nurses. In a group they run to the ambulance, pushing a trolley ahead of them.

The doctors jump into the ambulance. One of them almost collides with Dziwisz. They ignore him and look at the pope.

One of them turns and, too shocked to speak, motions for the nurses to help lift the stretcher from the ambulance onto the trolley.

As they do so, John Paul murmurs, '*Perchè l'hanno fatto?*' – 'Why did they do it?'

Now professionalism begins to take over. There is no time to answer questions. Half running, the medical team wheel John Paul into the Gemelli.

Dziwisz follows. He feels lost in these unfamiliar surroundings. His sense of shock and grief deepen.

He will not remember travelling up in the elevator that brings the pope to the ninth floor of the hospital, to a self-contained suite: an induction room, an operating room, a recovery room equipped with all the latest intensive-care facilities. This is where Giancarlo Castiglione, chief of surgery at the hospital, operates on his private patients. But Castiglione is in Milan. His associate, Francesco Crucitti, has already ordered a call placed for Castiglione to return urgently; he is about to fly by private plane to Rome as Crucitti enters the induction room.

The surgeon joins the team of doctors and nurses around the trolley. Here, at the eye of the drama, there is no panic, no wasted movement or word. Here, all is quiet urgency and tightly controlled discipline. Here, for the first time since John Paul had collapsed into his arms, Stanislaw Dziwisz can feel the beginning of hope.

Even before Crucitti arrives, a great deal has been done. John Paul's bloodstained cassock, vest and underpants have been expertly cut away from his body. The bloodstained cross on its solid gold chain has been removed from around his neck and placed on top of the ruined clothes in a corner of the induction room. Green surgical towels have been draped over the pope's nakedness. A saline drip has been set up. His Fisherman's Ring has been taped over, a necessary precaution to avoid the slightest possibility of it acting as a conduit for any of the steadily increasing pieces of electronic equipment being wheeled into position, EEC and ECG monitors among them. Gloved hands reach for, fetch and carry in silent rhythm the first of the instruments needed in a struggle the team are only too familiar with.

John Paul has been rapidly examined physically by a junior doctor. He has made a note of his pulse rate and heart beat. His eyes and chest have been examined. A sample of his blood has been taken. The lab report is there for Crucitti to see. John Paul is Type A Rh-negative, a not too common type.

Crucitti orders up five pints of blood from the hospital blood bank.

The surgeon then makes his own examination. The arm and hand wounds are relatively unimportant. It is the hole in the pope's abdomen which most concerns Crucitti.

Straightening from his inspection, he quickly gives the order to prepare John Paul for immediate surgery.

The words end Dziwisz's silence. He bends his head close to John Paul, noting the pope's slow shallow breathing and his deathly white pallor. The secretary whispers in the pope's left ear the last rites of the Church and bends even closer to hear the pope's confession.

Dziwisz steps back. His priestly duties are done. Now it is up to other skills to save the life of a man he looks upon as a second father.

The pope's last word before he is anaesthetized is a final agonized, 'Madonna.'

THE STORY
THEREAFTER

34

The pope was on the operating table for five and a half hours. In all he received six pints of transfused blood, three-fifths of the body's normal circulating volume. A temporary colostomy was performed. He was given the first of massive doses of antibiotics. He was taken to the recovery room and regained full consciousness close to midnight. In his first recorded words, whispered to Magee and Dziwisz through a post-operative blur, he forgave his assailant.[1]

*

Throughout the night police continued to question Agca in a bare-walled room in central police headquarters in down-town Rome. He was not beaten or threatened; his interrogators realized such methods would not work. He made little sense to them as he frequently responded to their questions by reciting part of his hate list. When they strip-searched him they found a note he admitted writing: 'I am killing the pope as a protest against the imperialism of the Soviet Union and the United States and against the genocide that is being carried out in El Salvador and Afghanistan.'

That was almost certainly the moment the Rome police knew Agca was no ordinary terrorist.

In the early hours of 14 May – after Room 31 in the Pensione Isa had been searched by police and the meagre evidence there gathered up – the first of the psychiatrists who work closely with the Italian Secret Service and the psychiatrists of other intelligence agencies, arrived. He questioned Agca for an hour, read his note, and made his initial assessment. He decided Agca was not clinically mad, but might well be suffering from hebephrenic schizophrenia. It was much too early to be certain, but the signs were there: *depersonalization, derealization.* He warned that Agca was a suicide risk. Other psychiatrists followed, to probe and check for themselves what they learned from the Turkish authorities about Agca's medical history. They would get to know him well in the coming weeks as they continued in their patient process of building up a psychological identikit portrait of Agca. Ultimately the doctors would disagree as to the exact nature of his illness. By then it would only be of academic interest. Other and perhaps more important truths would have been settled.

They began to emerge when three senior officers from West Germany's *Bundeskriminalamt* (BKA) flew to Rome to interrogate Agca secretly. According to the stenographic records they brought back to their headquarters in Wiesbaden, 192 questions were put to Agca on the afternoon of 15 May. The interrogation procedure was cumbersome; the Germans had put their questions through an Italian State Prosecutor. Nevertheless, what the BKA team discovered was so sensitive in parts only portions of their findings were passed to Interpol in Paris for circulation on a 'need to know' basis to police forces around the world. The full BKA report was sent to the office of the then West German Chancellor, Helmut Schmidt. Its contents have yet to be published.

On the day the BKA officers returned to Germany, two senior MOSSAD officers flew from Tel Aviv to Rome on El Al flight 385. In their briefcases were detailed dossiers on Agca's life and times which had been prepared by the defence attaché at the Israeli Legation in Ankara, Istahäk Cahani. In part the BKA team had been hampered because none of them spoke Turkish. The men from MOSSAD suffered no such handicap; both were fluent in Agca's native tongue, and the Italian police allowed the Israelis to question Agca directly. For three days, over five separate sessions, the MOSSAD officers pieced together the story of Agca.

During the weeks which followed, files of evidence accumulated in the offices of DIGOS, in the offices of the Italian Secret Service, in BKA headquarters in Wiesbaden, in West Germany's BND secret service complex at Pullach near Munich, at CIA headquarters in Langley, Virginia, at SIS headquarters in Century House, Westminster, London, at Austrian Security Headquarters in Vienna, at MIT headquarters on Atatürk Boulevard in Ankara, at MOSSAD headquarters in Tel Aviv. Like Topsy, the evidence would grow and grow, stored on computers and microfilm; millions of words of reports, statements and assessments.

Not one scrap of information from these agencies was presented before the Rome Assize Courts in the last week of July 1981 when Agca came to trial. The brisk three-day hearing shed no light on his motives; it appeared to most observers that every care was being taken it should not. Agca was sentenced to life imprisonment; with good behaviour he would be eligible for parole in the year 2009. He spent the first year of his sentence in solitary confinement, visited only by Western intelligence officers. Their interest faded as Agca's mental aberrations grew more pronounced. He began to fantasize to men who knew the reality of fantasy. They stopped coming. Agca had no more to tell them.

*

John Paul made a remarkable recovery. Typically, his first thoughts were for others. He ordered flowers sent to the two women who had been shot with him in that appalling moment in St Peter's Square. When children gathered beneath his hospital window to serenade him with folk songs, he sent Dziwisz bustling down with a joyful message: 'I bless you and I would like to kiss you all, one by one.'

In the late summer and autumn of 1981 he convalesced at Castel Gandolfo and began to plan other trips; to Britain and Spain. He still dreamed of going to China.

Slowly and steadily, under the watchful eyes of his doctors and the adoring looks of his staff, he gathered his strength and returned to his familiar position – at the very centre of the Church stage.

He continued to tread the delicate path between his role as spiritual leader and that of undoubted political force. Increasingly, the two melded over Poland. He would not be dissuaded from speaking out in defence of the principles of Solidarity; his third encyclical, *Laborem Exercens, On Human Work*, appeared at the time of the first wave of Solidarity strikes; the more the Polish regime threatened reprisals, the more the words of this encyclical – regarded by many as his best yet – were seen as John Paul linking human dignity with the right to do meaningful work under just conditions: to have the privilege to organize into unions and strive for equitable labour standards and to improve the general welfare of working people. Just as an early encyclical provided inspiration for the name Solidarity, so this one became part of its rule-book.

When Solidarity was banned and Lech Walesa arrested, John Paul began yet another extraordinary secret initiative. Working through Archbishop Glemp – who replaced Wyszynski after his death as Primate of Poland – the pope began to deal with the Polish regime, and therefore in effect with the Kremlin. With President Brezhnev dying, throughout much of 1982 John Paul found himself to all intents and purposes negotiating with Yuri Andropov, who had been head of the KGB at the time of the Agca assassination attempt. It was an ironic situation.

Guided by the same small group who initially advised him on Solidarity – Casaroli, Marcinkus and Dziwisz – the pope began the delicate task of trying to have Walesa freed and martial law lifted in Poland.

For ten months, although repeatedly rebuffed, John Paul inched towards what he wanted. Whenever he felt despairing, Marcinkus proved a tower of strength. Vilified in the media and himself under the most intense pressure – the Italian authorities continued to hint they very much wanted to question him – Marcinkus devotedly supported the pope. Perhaps more than anybody, the Vatican banker played the most supportive role.

Encouraged by him John Paul persisted. Then, in November 1982, Brezhnev died, and Andropov took his place. That very day, from Warsaw, came the news Walesa would be released.

The announcement was received with quiet satisfaction in the Vatican.

Beyond Poland, the pope presented himself as a spiritual leader who transcended racial, regional and theological boundaries and disputes. He continued to pray for a better world where mankind would be enchanced through the transforming power of prayer and faith. He remained implicitly wedded to the 'old faithfuls' – opposing birth control, divorce, abortion and premarital sex – with a vehemence not always understood.

He brushed aside anything which threatened the stability of the Church, such as the continuing financial scandals involving, for instance, the revelations in 1982 of how deeply implicated the Vatican Bank was with the discredited Banco Ambrosiano. Marcinkus, sheltering in the lee of a still powerful and robust pontiff, continued to survive. The more he was attacked, the more serene and secure he appeared. But he, better than anybody, knew there was no telling what the morrow might bring.

Those closest to John Paul – from March 1982 they no longer included Noé who had been abruptly replaced then as master of ceremonies by Magee – became convinced that, in the wake of the shooting, the pope was motivated, perhaps even obsessed, by the thought something dramatically decisive will happen to the world by the year 2000. He has said so on more than one occasion as he sat with his trusted and beloved Polish Mafia in the papal apartment. They have noticed his growing commitment to eschatology, which incorporates the view based on Biblical teachings that God will inaugurate his kingdom through a series of 'happenings' to close the second Christian millennium, 31 December 1999.

This sense of premonition, suggest his confidants, accounts for John Paul's mysticism and the increasing feeling he displays that he sees himself leading a Church – purified and revitalized by his teachings – into the third millennium. Everything he says and does reaffirms his theology that the birth, death and resurrection of Jesus Christ is the pivotal event in all human history; that accepting the spiritual certainty of the second coming of Christ is the only way to ensure redemption for each man, woman and child, be they Christian or non-Christian.

Inside this loose and necessarily controversial framework, one in which he sees theological principles not as didactic arguments but as working tools to solve the social and ethical problems of the age, John Paul continues to promote the teachings of the magisterium – the authority he shares with the Church's hierarchy – as encouraging secular responsibility, a heroic view of the priesthood and in particular a positive attitude towards mankind.

He remains what he was the moment he gave his firm response to Conclave in October 1978: a pope who will make all major decisions alone, a pope who knows what path he wishes to follow. Some feel he is more of a prophet than a ruler, more a preacher than an administrator, more of a charismatic mystic than a confirmed pragmatist.

John Paul is a mixture of each. Above all he is true to his passion. Knowing as he does why he was shot, the attempt on his life has in no way diminished his role of leading the voices for human justice and dignity. He continues to oppose Marxism with a force and urgency which suggests he believes time could be against him. John Paul, even better than those pledged to protect him, knows that the further he is from the last assassination attempt the closer he could be to the next. There is always another jackal awaiting.

Only a very special kind of person can live with such knowledge – while at the same time showing such a reassuring smiling face to the world.

Note on Sources

This book is the result of twenty-two months of research in Italy, Turkey, the United States, Spain, Syria, Lebanon, Bulgaria, West Germany, France, Austria, England, Ireland, Canada, Africa, Asia: in all 200,000 miles of travel, over a hundred interviews which transcribed into some six million words; a further eight million words of documentation: a rich haul that included Agca's school books, Paul VI's will, an invaluable Austrian intelligence service file, and much, much else. When we began our investigation we knew it could never be easy; we never realized how difficult it could be. We would have failed totally but for the extraordinary patience and understanding of our sources. They guided us through the intricacies of Church government, ecclesiastical history and Vatican tradition. They taught us how to interpret the subtlety of Vatican moves, how to read correctly a minor change in the liturgy, a word deleted from an old prayer, a papal audience that lasts a little beyond the allotted time, a brief sentence inserted in an otherwise routine speech, an encyclical presumably on one subject but actually designed to emphasize another matter. These are the ways of the Vatican. Secrecy prevails there on a scale almost unimaginable.

Yet there are ways to penetrate it. Risking automatic excommunication, with absolution possible only from the pope, Vatican employees and cardinals spoke to us with astonishing and moving frankness. Some have died in the course of our research. They said their deaths would free us from our pledge to keep secret their help. In some cases, where it is pertinent, we have named these sources. But for the most part our sources are alive and well and will consequently remain protected. That is the only bargain we struck with them in return for assistance.

Other sources are professional intelligence officers. They opened doors to their twilight world which could never otherwise have been opened. They did so for any number of reasons. None of them are relevant here. It is enough that they helped.

Textual Notes

CHAPTER 2

1 A personal visit to Yesiltepe during the winter of 1981–2 provided the authors with invaluable insights. They were accompanied by armed officers of MIT, Turkish military intelligence. These insisted on remaining alongside at all times in order to afford what the most senior of them, Ahmed Tok, called 'necessary protection'. On that level their presence was welcome. Yesiltepe remained as untamed as it was at the height of the Anarchy: during this on-site research one murder and three attempted killings took place in the tiny community. MIT sources in Ankara provided copies of medical reports on Agca, the result of investigation into his mental state after he left Yesiltepe. Inevitably part of the reports delved into his formative years; these helped the authors reconstruct his psychological development from an early age. In Yesiltepe Agca's school-teachers and some of his classmates were interviewed. This served as useful preliminary work for lengthy interviews with the family. Working through an interpreter provided by the Turkish regime – never the best way, but there was no choice in the matter – and aware that Tok was recording every question and answer, it was nevertheless possible to compare the external recollection and clinical evidence with the intensely personal account of the Agca family. Suspicious at first, openly resentful at the presence of police in their home once again, the family gradually thawed over a period and for the first time began to talk openly about Mehmet Ali. Adnan Agca was especially forthcoming. He clearly recalled conversations and incidents involving his brother, and pointed out Mehmet Ali's shelf of books, the place he had kept his exercise book and the box where he stored his Mauser. Adnan recalled how his brother had, in his late teens, increasingly expressed his hatred of all non-Moslem religions and especially the Roman Catholic faith. Had he heard Mehmet Ali actually say he wanted to kill a pontiff? Adnan paused. Then in a low, intense voice, very reminiscent of his elder brother's, he said: 'Many times, many times.' And so the family portrait of

Mehmet Ali Agca came very close to matching, in a broad sense, the more official picture of a disturbed personality. It became clear why one doctor had observed that in Agca's case, 'the primitive angry impulses and fantasies of his inner world became greater than the living ones. From early on he had believed only bad could be expected of him.'

CHAPTER 3

1 Villot's account of life with Paul was recorded in various forms: internal Secretariat of State memos, less official letters to other prelates, the stories he sometimes recounted over dinner to friends; these sources provide a rich trawl of contemporary life in the papal apartments.

2 A senior curialist, one of half a dozen who discreetly guided the authors through the papacy, insisted that the Secretariat of State files for the period contain ample evidence to support this view. To corroborate his claim he produced, in February 1982, several memos he had written on comparatively minor matters of state in 1978. None of them had been answered; indeed Villot had scrawled across the bottom of one, 'for later'. The curialist insisted that at this time 'nobody was doing a thing. Everybody was just keeping their seats warm. I wrote a lot of personal letters to friends. It was the one way to let off steam.' Some of the letters he kindly retrieved for the authors; they contained fascinating glimpses of life in the Apostolic Palace while waiting for a pontiff to die.

CHAPTER 4

1 The authors learned there are at least two unpublished studies in the Vatican on the question of why so many contemporary terrorists have Catholic backgrounds. One study was commissioned in the aftermath of the Moro murder; the other was produced a year later. Both are believed to contain considerable testimony about the theology of liberation movement in South America in which a great number of Catholic priests are actively involved; the movement claims, among other things, that it can be permissible to commit acts of violence in certain circumstances. Hardly surprisingly, this view finds no favour in the Vatican. Like so much else, Paul had put off dealing with the movement, preferring to leave it an issue for the next pontificate.

CHAPTER 5

1 As terrorists become bolder there is a growing fear that an attempt
will be made to land inside the Vatican and hold its occupants to
ransom. Special security precautions have been introduced to thwart
this.

CHAPTER 7

1 The Vatican officially provided such details. It is the framework for
the more unofficial recollections of those present at Castel Gandolfo
which the authors obtained between December 1981 and June 1982
in Rome.

2 He remained so until his death in 1982. Right to the end Cody
insisted he was a victim of an unparalleled smear campaign. There is
some truth in that. Nevertheless the evidence against him remains
formidable.

CHAPTER 9

1 Two senior Irish politicians separately confirmed that the nuncio's
position was 'informally' discussed at cabinet level in 1976 during
the government of Liam Cosgrave.

2 Archbishop Alibrandi's account is part of a lengthy taped interview
he gave the authors on 23 April 1982. On several occasions he
requested that the taping cease so that he could speak even more
frankly; subsequently he asked that some portions of his interview
remain confidential. That was agreed.

3 Cardinal Aramburu's views were revealed to the authors in May
1982. Aramburu was in Rome to advise Pope John Paul II on the
Argentinian Church's position in the Falklands crisis. The pope was
about to make a pastoral visit to Britain. Many Vatican advisers felt
he should not go. Aramburu argued 'forcefully', he told the authors,
that the pope should visit both Britain and Argentina in the hope of
producing a peaceful settlement. This the pontiff did in June 1982.
But there was still war. In the end Britain recaptured the islands
which had been occupied earlier in the year by Argentine forces.

4 The matter of speculation was one Cardinal Koenig dwelt upon in his
discussions with the authors. He accepted that part of the problem
arose from traditional Vatican obsession with secrecy, and cautiously
agreed that a responsible use of information might dispel some of the
outlandish reporting. On that basis he spoke as freely as he felt able
to.

CHAPTER 11

1 Villot's views are on record in the Secretariat of State files for the Archdiocese of Chicago. They became known to the authors in June 1982. Cody was dead and there was no way to check directly the veracity of Villot's judgement.
2 MacCarthy made available to the authors his script and programme notes for the entire period.

CHAPTER 12

1 Recalling for the authors the incident, Mrs Agca's own religious fanaticism surfaced. One of the few times during the interviews that she displayed emotion was when she admitted Agca had broken Moslem tenets – drinking alcohol and going to brothels. She wondered if somehow he had become contaminated through handling the newspaper cuttings on the pope he had accumulated. Gradually she began to seek answers for her son's behaviour in the Koran. Time and again she would say it was the will of God which motivated him. Given this outlook, it seemed perfectly obvious to Mrs Agca that her son could only have fallen by the wayside because he had somehow become contaminated by what she saw as 'dangerous forces' bent on destroying the all-important will of God. Her ideas doubtlessly played their part in forming the personality of her son.

CHAPTER 13

1 Luciani's medical condition was an open secret in Venice. Several diocesan priests recounted to the authors examples of Lorenzi's devotion. These recollections helped shape the portrait of a hardworking secretary whose own modest assessment of his role was that he was merely doing the job God had chosen for him.

CHAPTER 15

1 The CIA reportedly told Casaroli later it would have been relatively easy to bug Conclave. A Secretariat of State memo dated 25/9/81 reveals Villot's anxiety; he writes of conducting a 'proper study' to see whether future Conclaves can be made more electronically secure.
2 The authors were greatly assisted in unravelling the workings of the IOR under Marcinkus by Tana de Zulueta, Rome correspondent of

the London *Sunday Times*, and two cardinals, Felici and Benelli, who died a few months apart in 1982 when they were still collating evidence of IOR's tangled finances and relationships.

CHAPTER 16

1 Koenig insisted most cardinals feel as he does, and that the secular media has vastly overstated the wheeler-dealing.

CHAPTER 17

1 His identity was revealed in June 1982 to the authors, who agreed to keep it secret.
2 We have two sources for our Conclave voting details and have no reason to doubt their reliability.

CHAPTER 18

1 Recalling the moment, Gammarelli told the authors Gianpaolo subsequently wrote to thank him in one of the first letters of his pontificate.

CHAPTER 19

1 Independent of Agca's own subsequent account of his movements at this time, which the authors have studied in police files in Ankara and Rome, there is other evidence to support this portrait of his mental state. It is in the files of the psychiatrists employed by intelligence agencies who have had cause to study Agca's behaviour. In October 1981 MIT, Turkish military intelligence, established Agca's contact with the Libyan embassy in Ankara through sources MIT understandably do not wish to reveal. An MIT report on the matter was submitted to the ruling junta in Ankara in late November 1981. It remains pigeon-holed. One MIT source stated over dinner in the Grand Hotel, Ankara, on 19/1/82 that the likeliest reason was that the ailing Turkish economy cannot afford to endanger its trade links with Libya. Publicly involving Libya with Agca could well do that. Nevertheless, the MIT man urged the authors to make the connection public. Further checks revealed that almost certainly MOSSAD and West Germany's BND, the country's secret service, were aware of Agca's approaches to the Libyans.

Chapter 20

1 The details of Vincenza's life in papal service were made available to the authors under the pledge they would not reveal the source. The person remains active in Church service.

2 The authors obtained details of this meeting without payment.

3 The incident is part of Vatican folklore. There are various versions: the authors have chosen the least sensational.

4 Villot's subsequent account of the episode shows the Secretary to be rather more endearing than his public image suggests.

5 In June 1982, Calvi fled Italy en route for England in a cloak-and-dagger operation well-matched to his financial machinations: the banker was huddled in the back of a motor launch normally used for running contraband to Yugoslavia. When he reached London he immediately went into hiding, in Chelsea Cloisters, an apartment block off the King's Road. Had he stayed in Italy he faced, among other things, four years in prison and fines of at least £7 million for exchange control violations.

Investigations for a detailed special report published in the *Sunday Times*, 13 February 1983, suggest, 'The Vatican has so far been less than totally frank' when describing the role of the IOR in Calvi's manipulations. While it is unthinkable that the Vatican was knowingly involved or took part in a deliberate fraud, it is nevertheless hard to understand how Marcinkus could have remained totally unaware of Calvi's dubious manoeuvrings.

In any case, Calvi's former international good name had gradually become publicly to be called into question through a smear campaign said to have been directed by his former mentor, Sindona. Calvi was blackmailed and arranged for over half a million dollars be paid to Sindona. Worse, a Bank of Italy enquiry into Calvi's affairs resulted in him being arrested in May 1981, tried and found guilty, and then released on bail pending an appeal trial.

Afterwards Calvi became increasingly withdrawn and, untypically, began to mix with some distinctly unsavoury underworld characters. A few days before his appeal trial was due to begin, on 11 June 1982, he had left Italy on the launch and reached London on 15 June; in great secrecy he moved into the Chelsea Cloisters flat.

Then, at 7.30 am on 18 June 1982, Calvi was found dead – hanging from scaffolding under Blackfriars Bridge, suspended by the neck on a three-foot length of rope, his pockets filled with heavy stones plus his passport, spectacles and £7,000 in cash.

CHAPTER 22

1 The authors learned of this meeting in December 1981. A senior curialist reminiscing about Gianpaolo's style let slip some of the details. Six further months were needed to piece together further particulars, most of them surfacing in intentional leaks usually aimed at promoting a certain position. The authors believe they have avoided special pleading in their account.

2 Vincenza's movements and reactions were subsequently obtained and published by Civiltà Cristiana, the right-wing organization which sprang to prominence in the August Conclave. Independently of this the authors obtained their own account of the nun's behaviour from a curialist who can only be described as a person in a position to know.

CHAPTER 25

1 In January 1982 Agca's route was retraced by the authors in a taxi almost as ramshackle as the Dodge, and with an MIT escort.

CHAPTER 26

1 The patently honest broadcaster will later ruefully recall this conversation and suggest it as 'perhaps worthy of inclusion in any how-wrong-can-you-be anthology'.

2 The existence of the tape would only be revealed in *Chicago Lawyer* in 1981. While affording a sobering glimpse into Greeley's methodology, it is nevertheless possible to sympathize with him. Like anyone attempting to penetrate the Vatican, Greeley clearly found it necessary to rely on information provided on a strictly non-attributable basis. There is a well-established reluctance among Holy See employees to go on the record. They point to the fate of those in the past who have risked identification: banishment to some remote Church outpost or even dismissal, in the case of lay staff, from Vatican service. This does not mean their evidence is less credible. It simply indicates the difficulties any researcher faces in obtaining it.

CHAPTER 27

1 He will be one of three sources for this Conclave who, in return for guarantees of anonymity, will provide a worthwhile account of the proceedings. Morally dubious though they may appear to some for their willingness to tell the secrets of Conclave, their accounts,

furnished quite independently, do show a remarkable conformity. And their testimony in part was reluctantly confirmed by certain of the cardinals. They, too, mindful no doubt of the severe warning about security Villot delivered at the outset of Conclave, asked for and received guarantees they would not be quoted directly. There is no evidence to suggest Vatican Radio staff or anybody else attempted this time to bug Conclave.

2 One source disputes this tally and insists there was an even bigger sensation: that Jan Willebrands of Holland received a number of votes. These were presumed to be from those cardinals who felt electing Wojtyla was too fraught with political dangers for the Church. The same source claims that when Willebrands saw this he immediately became a strong supporter of Wojtyla. This may also be what prompted Cardinal John Carberry to tell a press conference on 17 October 1978, 'I would like to tell you everything. It would thrill you. But I can't.' A pity – because Carberry might well have provided corroboration of Willebrands's candidacy.

3 One source subsequently claimed, with enough conviction for Greeley to publish it, that Benelli was 'bitter because Wojtyla was a year younger than Benelli and age had been used against him in his candidacy.' There is no other evidence to support such an unlikely reaction: Benelli was far too shrewd a tactician to display such emotion openly.

4 The details of this historic meeting were made available by Koenig to the authors for the first time in 1982. He recalled not only word by vivid word what was said, but also the physical actions of the three cardinals present.

CHAPTER 29

1 Reports from the Holy See missions of the United Kingdom, Australia and the Republic of Ireland offer striking proof of this.

2 Two well-placed Vatican staffers provided virtually identical accounts to the authors.

3 Felici relished telling the story up to his death in 1982.

4 The words are from a confidential Secretariat of State file on the matter shown to the authors in 1982.

5 Tore's role was made clear for the first time when the authors met with officers of MIT, Turkish intelligence, in Ankara and Vienna in December 1981 and January 1982. Those officers provided substantial evidence to support their contention that since 1977 Tore had been used by the KGB to foment unrest in Turkey. Corroboration for their claim came from Major Otto Kormek of the Austrian Security

Service in a series of interviews with the authors in his Vienna office from 9 to 13 December 1981.

CHAPTER 30

1 Casaroli's words are included in a subsequent minute of this meeting. Details leaked from the Secretariat of State in November 1981 when relations between the Holy See and the Polish state worsened markedly as a result of the pope's support for Solidarity.

2 On 23 April 1982 Archbishop Alibrandi revealed this extraordinary conversation to the authors. Though more than two years had passed he was vividly clear about everything, except where Casaroli's information came from. It is not the first time that friendly intelligence services have tipped off the Holy See. Both West Germany's *Bundesnachrichtendienst*, BND, and Israel's MOSSAD informed Secretary of State Villot of a terrorist plot to kidnap Pope Paul VI and take him to Libya early in 1978. Britain's SIS had been monitoring any threats against the pope on his Irish visit for weeks. Apart from this one, the others were discounted as utterances of cranks. It is reasonable to assume that – mistaken or not – with London knowing Alibrandi's sympathies for an end to British rule in Ulster, the SIS would not wish him to know they were in any way involved in actually protecting the pope. One SIS source suggested this could 'lead to all sorts of future complications.' This would then explain why Casaroli did not inform the nuncio of his source.

3 The stenographic record of his trial subsequently disappeared from the Istanbul Security Department. But several accounts of the trial exist in Turkish-language newspapers. However, the most authoritative account is that by Claire Sterling in the *Reader's Digest*, September 1982. She reveals it was Günes himself who told her about Agca's mention of a deal. Mrs Sterling adds that Günes insisted 'if all the charges made against me were true, I'd have been hanged long ago.' It is a good answer – but is it a completely satisfactory one? Günes refused to elaborate any further, thus leaving open one of the tantalizing gaps in Agca's story.

4 In meetings with MIT officers in Ankara in February 1982 the authors were shown the interrogation reports of Selcuk. Subsequently they also visited Erzurum where Selcuk substantially confirmed the account.

CHAPTER 31

1 The authors were able to piece together a detailed reconstruction of

the meeting from some of those who were present. They were also considerably helped by Tana de Zulueta, the distinguished Rome contributor to the London *Sunday Times* whose own reporting on the tangled state of Vatican finances is a benchmark in investigative financial journalism.

2 Benelli indicated before his death in October 1982 that between $5 million and $10 million a year of IOR profits go directly to the pope.

3 Two Vatican sources in a position to know insisted to the authors that the final Vatican losses were far smaller than had been expected. One curialist put it like this: 'Marcinkus saw at the last moment what was happening and by some very adroit financial footwork was able to claw back a great deal of the money which would otherwise have been lost; he may have got back as much as forty per cent, a remarkable achievement.' The second source spoke of an 'unofficial official policy' to play down this idea: 'It does not fit into the impoverished image now being promoted.'

4 Fr Bruno Fink, personal secretary to the cardinal, told the authors in May 1982, after Ratzinger had been appointed prefect of the Sacred Congregation for the Doctrine of the Faith, the old Holy Office, that undoubtedly the advice Ratzinger gave the pope over Küng had been 'of great importance'. Fink denied there had been any witch-hunt against Küng. The secretary claimed 'Küng brought the matter onto his own head. He can have no cause for complaint. The whole matter was handled on evidence. And that went against him.'

5 The authors first learned of the message on 9 December 1981 in Vienna from Austrian intelligence officer Major Otto Kormek. He indicated that the information had come to him from 'Church sources'. He would not elaborate. Subsequent checks with another Austrian intelligence informant whom the authors are pledged to keep secret strongly suggested the information came from Cardinal Koenig's palace. On this subject the normally helpful Koenig would not be drawn, on the grounds such matters 'are best not put on the record'. Perhaps the words should be seen as an example of cardinal-speak: they can be interpreted at face value or have a deeper meaning attached to them. In Wiesbaden, West Germany, head-quarters of the country's equivalent to the FBI, the *Bundeskriminalamt*, two senior police officers, Kommissar Helmut Bruckman and Kriminalhauptkommissar Hans-Georg Fuchs, conceded that the pope's covert support for Solidarity at this stage had a crucial bearing on what was to happen to the trade union – and subsequently to John Paul.

6 Details of this meeting are necessarily incomplete. Only two copies of the minutes exist. One is apparently held in Casaroli's office; the

other remains in the pope's private papers. Almost two years elapsed before the authors learned in May 1982 what had happened. Two Vatican staffers each independently revealed what appear to be the essential elements. In Vienna, that trusted intelligence source, tapping his own well-established contacts in Poland, was able substantially to confirm what had occurred in the Vatican in the summer of 1980. Nevertheless, this account may only afford a partial recounting of the event. Until any of those directly involved in the drama decide to furnish further details, the account, imperfect though it may be, must remain as a broad statement about the meeting and subsequent developments.

7 Like so much else, the precise role of the CIA in this affair has yet to be clarified. The agency, despite efforts by the authors to prise out even a clue with the help of the Freedom of Information Act and other means, has managed to keep the hatches battened down. But Fuchs and Bruckman in Wiesbaden and Kormek in Vienna told the authors their agencies believe the CIA played an important role briefing Casaroli on the Polish situation.

8 It remains unclear whether independent confirmation of this scenario was provided by the CIA. Certainly nothing surfaced publicly in Washington, DC. Not that CIA confirmation would have made any real difference. Koenig's information was undoubtedly trusted. And there is every possibility his own sources could have included the CIA office in the American Embassy in Vienna. On such matters Koenig maintains silence. But others were prepared to point the authors in the direction of the CIA.

9 Details of the letter were first made public by the US network NBC on 21 September 1982. It claimed it had received the information from a source inside the Vatican. Officially, perhaps not surprisingly, the Vatican subsequently denied the NBC story. Nevertheless, other sources in the Vatican suggested the leak was approved by the pope in view of what had happened in Poland.

CHAPTER 32

1 The name has several English spellings. Gaddafi, Qaddafi and Khadafy are the most common variations. All are correct. Since the name is transliterated phonetically from the Arabic there is no single agreed English spelling. But on the advice of his Viennese lawyer, the authors have used the English translation the colonel himself prefers: Muammar al Qathafi.

2 Later in 1981 Frank Terpil gave a remarkable television interview which formed the basis of a programme about his terrorist activities,

entitled *The Most Dangerous Man in the World*. In the film he described how he had trained Agca. The interview was filmed in Beirut. Shortly after it was completed, in December 1981, three men called at Terpil's apartment and took him away. He has not been seen since. He is still a wanted man in the United States. His former employer, the CIA, refused to confirm or deny persistent reports in the Middle East that Terpil had been a deep-penetration CIA agent who worked his way into Qathafi's confidence and provided invaluable intelligence on the colonel's plans. Subsequently, goes the story, Terpil's role was discovered; he had fled to Beirut and given his interview in the hope the publicity would save him from the vengeance of the Libyan leader. The story raises more questions than it answers. If he was a CIA undercover agent, why did the agency not quietly withdraw him instead of allowing Terpil to go public? His revelations could do nothing to enhance the name of the CIA. Who were the men who took him away? One suggestion is that they were CIA operatives come to return Terpil to the fold. Another, and perhaps more likely, explanation is that they were Libyans. Whatever the truth, it is ironic that Terpil disappeared before the film was shown around the world. In 1982 two witnesses who would have given evidence against Terpil, should he be found, died in mysterious incidents. One disappeared after his boat exploded off the Bahamas. The other, a former CIA employee, Kevin Mulcahy, who single-handedly had persuaded the US government to prosecute Terpil, was discovered dead in Virginia in November that year in equally puzzling circumstances.

3 In 1981, after being questioned by West German police, Mersan disappeared from his Munich haunts into Eastern Europe. He was seen in Warsaw, East Berlin and Sofia before he dropped out of sight. Police and intelligence agencies in half a dozen Western countries still want to question him about his relationship with Agca and 'Maurizi'.

4 Details of the call and Cahani's role were made available in February 1982 in Ankara. This new information goes a long way towards explaining how intelligence data on Agca accumulated.

5 The allegation that the BND acted this way was repeated to the authors by Major Otto Kormek of Austrian Security. The charge has also been made at a diplomatic level by the Turkish government to the West German authorities. A government spokesman in Ankara, Varol Akcin, told the authors the 'German response is totally unsatisfactory. They just wriggle and wriggle.' The BND also vetoed a suggestion that the MIT agents should kidnap Agca and spirit him back to Turkey from West Germany.

6 In February 1982 the authors spoke by telephone to Cahani in Ankara and told them what they had learned. His comment was, 'Now you know, why call me?' He then terminated the call.

CHAPTER 33

1 It must be self-evident why the authors cannot directly reveal their sources for this situation, revealing, as it does, one of the most important initiatives attempted by the Holy See in Northern Ireland. Those persons are still actively involved in Church affairs in Ulster, the Republic of Ireland and the Vatican. In two cases they specifically asked not to be named for the good reason that, given the killings, to do so could, very easily, physically endanger themselves or their families, and at best seriously jeopardize their professional lives. It should also be sufficient to state that the minutes of this important meeting are on record and extracts from that record were made available to the authors in May 1981 in Dublin, and subsequently in more detail in December of that year in Dublin, and finally, in still more detail in April–May 1982 in Rome.

2 The London reaction is in the files of the Secretariat of State. There is no reason to doubt that the minuted responses of Hume and Heim are anything less than totally accurate. One Irish source, however, did try to convince the authors that Hume was opposed to the idea of sending Magee because of the secretary's republican background. There appears to be nothing to support this contention. Indeed all the evidence points to Hume's enthusiasm for anything which would ease the tension in Ulster.

3 On 13 December 1981 the authors were handed, in the Intercontinental Hotel, Vienna, a complete copy of the Austrian Security Service file which details how the gun came into Agca's possession. The file gives a graphic account of how painstaking the Austrians were in pursuing a trail that leads back to Otto Tintner, a seventy-year-old gun dealer with the twinkling eyes of a cartoon patriarch. Tintner runs his deadly business from a tiny shop in the remote village of Muhldorf, a three-hour drive from Vienna. Normally his paperwork for transacting his business is impeccable. Strict Austrian legal requirements do not allow otherwise. But, as the file shows, records involving the Browning were destroyed. Nevertheless, the Austrian Security Service were able to implicate Grillmeir as having purchased the weapon. Like so many of the others involved with Agca, Grillmeir subsequently disappeared, almost certainly to Bulgaria, where, notes the file, he was already 'a frequent visitor'. The file also throws light on the way intelligence

organizations view each other. One of its documents suggests that MOSSAD may have somehow been involved in Agca's mission. In a far from convincing analysis the writer, a member of the Austrian Security Service, traces a convoluted argument which finally withers away in some rather unpleasant anti-Semitic smears. But this comment, it is fair to say, is rather the exception to some excellent Austrian investigative work which does offer a stark picture of not only the extent of terrorism in Europe but also how involved the KGB are in encouraging it. There is perhaps one last thing worth mentioning: the reason this file was handed to the authors. The person who made it available said he hoped by doing so to bring out the truth of what he saw as bitter rivalry inside his security service: 'We are far too politically controlled; we are often not able to do our jobs if it involves embarrassing somebody with a "good connection". There is no doubt at all that in the case of Agca there was some very bad mishandling. The file shows that.' Indeed it does.

In February, 1983, Austrian police arrested Grillmeir for attempting to smuggle a large quantity of 'war materials' into the country. A pick-up truck with Vienna licence plates had been stopped at an Austrian border checkpoint with Czechoslovakia. It was discovered to contain seven Soviet Dragunov sharpshooter rifles, the first of their kind to reach the West; the Dragunov has a telescopic sight and a bayonet that folds into clippers capable of cutting barbed wire. The truck also contained a huge quantity of other arms. Grillmeir, who had just returned from Bulgaria, insisted he was importing the guns for a West German in Munich named Paul Saalbach. When the Vienna police appealed to their colleagues in West Germany to detain Saalbach, they were told that he worked for the BND, the Federal secret service which had been involved in the Agca case. The BND refused to comment. The notion that the BND was using Grillmeir as a gun-runner – in all, the truck contained over 700 weapons and 15,000 rounds of ammunition – infuriated the Austrians, who speculated whether Grillmeir had been able to avoid them for so long with the help of the BND. Inevitably, the question arose: how involved was the BND in the case of Agca? Had the agency, as one Austrian put it to the authors in February, 'looked the other way while Agca travelled through Germany on his way to Rome'?

CHAPTER 34

1 In the aftermath of the assassination attempt there was vigorous disagreement within the Vatican over whether the wider question of

a conspiracy should be pursued. There were those, led by Cardinal Casaroli, who argued that to pursue the matter could create further problems with the Soviet Bloc; Casaroli argued there was nothing to gain by branding the KGB as being involved. On a more personal level he argued that to allow publicity to be continually focused on the papal shooting could only encourage further attempts on the life of the pope by cranks not connected with intelligence agencies. Casaroli's fears were reinforced when the pope visited Portugal in early 1982 and a mentally disturbed priest tried to attack John Paul with a knife, claiming the pope was 'selling out the Church'. The priest had belonged to Archbishop Marcel Lefèbvre's organization but had been asked to leave because he was too extremist. The attitude of the Vatican partially explains the somewhat lethargic posture adopted by the Italian Minister of Justice with regard to the shooting. Initially insisting that Agca was no more than an unbalanced religious fanatic acting alone, he seemed as anxious as Casaroli to have the shooting swept out of sight. For almost a year the position remained like this, in spite of some strong prodding by the press. Then, coinciding with the deepening chill between the Holy See and the Polish regime, a decision was taken within the Vatican, one which the authors were told the pope approved, that the attempts on his life must be pursued , if need be, to Moscow's door. The Italian investigation was revitalized, placed in the hands of one of the country's most experienced investigative magistrates, Ilario Martella. Working in the utmost secrecy – actively assisted by MOSSAD, DIGOS, West Germany's BND and Turkey's MIT – Martella assembled a case which enabled him, in December 1982, to announce publicly that he had issued arrest warrants against seven persons. Five were Turks, two Bulgarians. One was named as 'Oral Celik', the alias Timar Seluk, the contact man in Erzurum, assumed in 1982. MIT sources told the authors that Seluk is 'now almost certainly' in Bulgaria. Martella also conceded that the men named in his warrants are only 'messenger boys' working for Folini and Tore.

Suddenly the Bulgarian Connection assumed a momentum of its own. Italy's Defence Minister, Lelio Lagorio, produced the most substantial public evidence so far – outside that which the authors have documented in this book – of Bulgarian complicity not only in the assassination attempt on the pope's life but in the kidnapping of NATO General James Lee Dozier by the Red Brigades in December 1981. Mr Lagorio revealed in the Italian parliament that Italian counter-intelligence had long been monitoring radio transmissions by the Bulgarian Secret Service. There had been 'unusual traffic around the time of the shooting of the pope, especially in the days prior'. The coded signals, according to the minister, were for agents already in Italy, including almost certainly Folini and Tore. Mr Lagorio further revealed that the Italian government was satisfied that three diplomats attached to the Bulgarian embassy in Rome 'were accomplices in the attack on the pope'. All had left Italy some months before this disclosure; covered by diplomatic immunity they had returned safely to Sofia.

Within hours of these disclosures, the Vatican discreetly leaked the news that it was considering breaking 'all ties' with Bulgaria; this leak coincided with Italy's Foreign Minister, Mr Emilio Colombo, stating that the Italian ambassador in Sofia had been recalled to Rome, that Bulgaria was removing its own ambassador from Rome and that there was a very real possibility of a total diplomatic rupture between the two countries.

In Sofia, the Bulgarian government, facing unprecedented diplomatic pressure from the West, panicked. It staged a press conference in Sofia to rebut all the accusations. Journalists from all over the world were invited to attend. The conference was a shambles. Few journalists were convinced by Bulgaria's claim of being a victim of an 'evil-minded campaign'. Many felt that the evidence for Bulgarian involvement in the papal plot had been strengthened by the ill-supported denials.

These developments were closely followed by the pope personally. Over the 1982–3 Christmas period, traditionally a time for quiet reflection and prayer in the papacy, John Paul II held several meetings with Casaroli and other senior advisers to discuss the situation. Sources close to the pope told the authors early in January 1983 that John Paul II 'now has no doubts that the Russians were behind Agca's attempts to kill him'.

The pope was all for letting the world know that the Cross was in the Soviet cross-hairs. Drawing on his previous briefings from the CIA and other intelligence agencies, the pope argued that the entire assassination operation bore the classic stamp of the KGB. He pointed out that great care had been taken to establish a direct link to Moscow; that was the reason why the Bulgarian Secret Service, a virtual subsidiary of the KGB, with well-established 'rat lines' for running spies and arms into Italy, had been used to front the operation. Again, standard KGB procedure had been used in the choice of Agca. He was publicly associated with the Right – in this case the neo-Nazi Grey Wolves – and was a man with nothing to lose. To muddy the waters further, the pope now believed Agca had been deliberately trained in Libya at the behest of the KGB.

Though he had survived, John Paul II had come to believe that the assassination attempt had been successful in many ways. In Poland Solidarity had been crushed. The Catholic Church had been shown that not even the pope was inviolate. The Russians, he concluded grimly, had only made one mistake: the KGB had neither managed to arrange for Agca's escape from prison – or have him killed. Now, by 1983, it was too late. Agca had disclosed KGB complicity.

Conceding all this to be very possibly the case, Casaroli – again according to Vatican sources trusted by the authors – argued that there could be a very real possibility that the KGB was content to let the world know it was implicated – that it deliberately wanted the attack on the pope to be seen as a stark message that Russia had the capability to eliminate opposition anywhere. On that assumption, argued Casaroli, to further spotlight the KGB involvement was only 'playing' into Soviet hands. At the most, argued the canny Secretary of State, events should be allowed to unravel without any undue prodding from the Vatican.

And so 1983 began with a split within the papal ranks as to how public the papacy should go, one as deep as in the immediate aftermath of the shooting. Observers began to wonder how far the Vatican had been intimidated. They pointed out that suddenly discreet Vatican support for anti-Communist forces in Latin America had been curtailed; that in the United States bishops opposed to the Reagan administration's hard-line on nuclear deterrents received no rebuke from the Holy See; that the pope had received Yasir Arafat, in one of whose Syrian camps Agca had received basic terrorist training. And so on. The astute American writer, William Safire, asked in the *New York Times* a question many were pondering: 'What is behind this pattern of retreat from the Vatican's staunchly anti-Communist and anti-terrorist posture of only two years ago?' Safire felt that 'as no pope since Peter', John Paul had realized 'his Church must get along with Caesar'.

But for how long? Everything the authors know, and have been told about John Paul II, strongly suggests that he is merely biding his time, that he is determined the full and total truth about why he was nearly assassinated should surface, and that he, for one, believes a book like this one can only further his determination to see that truth becomes public.

Abbreviated Bibliography

AMBROSINI, MARIA LUISA. *The Secret Archives of the Vatican*. London: Eyre and Spottiswoode, 1970.

BULL, GEORGE. *Inside the Vatican*. London: Hutchinson, 1982.

CASTLE, TONY. *Through the Year with Pope John Paul II*. London: Hodder and Stoughton, 1981.

CLANCY, JOHN G. *Apostle for Our Time*. London: William Collins, 1964.

CRAIG, MARY. *Man from a Far Country*. London: Hodder and Stoughton, 1979.

GRANFIELD, PATRICK. *The Papacy in Transition*. Dublin: Gill and Macmillan, 1981.

GREELEY, ANDREW M. *The Making of the Popes*. London: Futura Publications, 1979.

HASLER, AUGUST B. *How the Pope Became Infallible*. New York: Doubleday & Company, 1981.

HEBBLETHWAITE, PETER. *The Year of Three Popes*. London: William Collins, 1978.

LUCIANI, ALBINO. *Illustrissimi*. London: William Collins, 1978.

MARTIN, MALACHI. *The Decline and Fall of the Roman Church*. London: Martin Secker and Warburg, 1982.

NICHOLS, PETER. *The Politics of the Vatican*. London: Pall Mall Press, 1968.
— *The Pope's Divisions*. London: Faber & Faber, 1981.

ST JOHN-STEVAS, NORMAN. *Pope John Paul II*. London: Faber & Faber, 1982.

WHALE, JOHN (Ed.) *The Pope from Poland*. London: William Collins, 1980.

Index

abortion 59, 167, 216, 364, 403, 408, 428, 466
Absolution 278–9
Administration of the Patrimony of the Holy See 98, 421
Adrian IV, Pope 199
Adrian VI, Pope 200, 202, 345
Africa 425
Agca, Mehmet Ali 7–15, hate list 9–11, 354, 433; his mental state 13, 223–4, 310, 353–4, 405, 432, 434, 463–4; family background 123–5; in Ankara 223–5; in Syrian training camp 307–12; Teslin Tore and 312–15, 351, 431; kills Ipekci 384–7; description filed by intelligence services 387; arrested in Istanbul 398–400; in Kartel-Maltepe prison 399–400, 406, 409–11, 437; on trial 404–6; shoots lottery ticket seller 410–11; threatens John Paul II 411–12; hunted by MIT 414–15; in Libyan training camp 431–4; in Perugia 436–7; in Rome 442, 447; assassination plan 451; shoots John Paul II 453–8; arrested 458; questioned by police 463–5; his trial 464
Alexander III, Pope 164
Alexander VI, Pope 3
Alexander VII, Pope 66
Alexandria, Patriarch of 118, 184
Alfrink, Cardinal Bernard 130
Alibrandi, Archbishop Gaetane 90, 97, 102–3, 219–22, 272–3, 293, 370–72, 400–404, 448–50
Alison, Michael 450
Almoner 64
Andropov, Yuri 282, 465, 466
Angelus addresses 230, 362–3, 416
annulments, marriage 57
Ansa 285–6, 330
Antico, Franco 284–7, 294, 300
Antonelli, Cardinal 194
Antoniutti, Cardinal 190
Apostolic Camera 84, 273
Apostolic Palace 35
Apostolic Penitentiary 57–8, 183
Apostolic Signatura 118

Aramburu, Cardinal Juan Carlos 92–5, 118, 168, 234, 237, 251, 324, 325, 380; in Conclave (August) 187, 197, 204, 205; in Conclave (October) 318, 332, 335, 336; Luciani and 132–3, 166
Arch of Bells 32
Argan, Giulio Carlo 77
Argentina 93–5, 187, 215, 425
Arnau, Cardinal Jubany 129–30
Arns, Cardinal Evaristo 37, 269, 324, 325, 380, 381, 428; influence of 321
Arrupe, Pedro 267–8, 271–72, 274, 299, 424
atheism 326
Attachés of the Ante-chamber 64
audiences, papal 43
authority, church's 364
Ay, Omer 434, 442, 453, 454, 457

BKA (Germany) 438, 464
BND (German secret service) 437, 438, 464
baciamano 43
Baader-Meinhof gang 26
Baggio, Cardinal Sebastiano 40, 72, 100, 118, 134, 380, 381, 383; ambitions 40; Cody and 73–4, 76, 115–16, 179, 259, 370; in Conclave (August) 191, 201, 203, 205; in Conclave (October) 321, 336, 340; influence of 321; John Paul I and 263, 270, 271, 273–4; *papabile* 139, 140, 321; troubleshooter role 29
Balducci, Monsignor Corrado 329, 436
Banco Ambrosiano (Overseas) 248, 466
Banco di Messina 156
Banco di Roma per la Svizzera 156
Banco Privata Finanziaria 156
Bank of Italy 248
Baran, Archbishop 142
Baum, Cardinal 412
Bea, Cardinal 130,
Benedict XV, Pope 61, 199
Benelli, Cardinal Giovanni 39–40, 97, 99, 134, 287, 293, 297, 424; in Conclave (August) 178, 187, 201, 203, 204, 205, 206; in Conclave (October) 332, 333–5, 336, 338, 339, 343; influence of

Benelli, Cardinal Giovanni—*contd.*
320–21; John Paul I and 239–40,
248–50, 259, 263, 271; *papabile* 104–5,
139, 160–61, 298–300, 320, 321, 324,
331; support for Luciani 174; Vatican
finance and 423
benemerenti 296
Bengsch, Cardinal Alfred 128
Bernardin, Archbishop Joseph 74, 331
Bertoli, Cardinal Paolo 97–8, 118, 134; in
Conclave (August) 179, 201, 203, 205,
206; *papabile* 161, 321
birth control 51, 167, 216, 241–2; John
Paul II and 364, 381, 424, 427, 428,
466; practised by Catholics 19
bishops: Latin American conference
379–83; consultation with 241, 260;
gifts from 28–9; *see also* Synod of Bishops
Blaker, Peter 450
Bolivia 418
Boniface VIII, Pope 244
Brazil 425; John Paul II's visit to 428
Brezhnev, President Leonid 429–30, 466
Britain 448–50; death of Paul VI and 85
Bulgaria, Agca and 438, 451
Buzzonetti, Dr Renato 106, 238–9, 240,
252, 268, 278–80, 361, 445

CIA (Central Intelligence Agency) 368,
392, 438, 464
CREP (Committee for Responsible Election
of the Pope) 68, 170; *see also* Greeley,
Andrew
Cahani, Istahak 436–7, 439
Calvi, Roberto 247–8, 391, 423
Cambodia 357
Camerlengo 36–7, 82, 101, 165; *see also*
Villot, Cardinal Jean
campagnola, papal 441, 452
canon law revision 99
Canterbury, Archbishop of 99, 117
Caprio, Cardinal Giuseppe 65, 77, 79, 84,
421
Carberry, Cardinal John 118, 177, 193,
301, 317, 331, 338
Cardinals: called to Rome 85; called to
Rome (November 1979) 420–23;
College of 57, 133; created by Paul VI
37; creation of 133–4; eligible to vote in
Conclave 133; European 128–30;
European progressive 113; German 338;
growth in number of 42; influential
134, 320–21; Italian 166; Latin
American 131–2, 166, 193; North
American 192–93, 301, 331, 338;
pre-Conclave meeting 101–2; privileges
134; proposed autopsy and 281, 287–9,
300–302; Third World 175, 189, 338;
see also Conclaves

Carter, Lilian 68
Carter, President Jimmy 303, 392
Carter, Rosalynn 108, 114, 117
Casaroli, Cardinal Agostino 266, 285, 445;
bugging of the Vatican and 142–3; Cody
and 73–5; Communism and 87, 128;
John Paul I and 259–60, 273; John Paul
II and 368, 388, 392, 401–3; as
Secretary of State 389, 390, 421,
426–30 *passim*, 439, 441, 453, 465;
warned of danger in Turkey 411–12
Castel Gandolfo 26–7, 62, 64–7, 391
Castiglione, Giancarlo 459
Catholic Action 126
Catholic Church, the: democratization of
218; division within 45–9, 257–8, 257;
Italian politics and 218; numerical
strength of 228–9; Paul VI's view of 33;
problems facing 59, 167–8, 216–19,
298, 418; separate from state 231; social
responsibilities of 356; *see also* Papacy,
the
Caylan, Yavus 385
Cé, Cardinal Marco 272
Ceccarelli, Vito 454–8
Celestine II, Pope 198–9
Celestine IV, Pope 42, 182
Celestine V, Pope 38
celibacy, priestly 19, 59, 216, 242, 267;
John Paul I and 227–8; John Paul II
and 392–3, 417, 424, 427, 428
Central America 373–84
Chafic, Ali 434, 442, 453, 457
Chagall, Marc 44
Chauffeurs de Monseigneur 365
Chicago 74–5
Chigi, Prince Agostini 297
Chile 215, 425
China, Communist 52–3, 439–41
Christian Democratic Party 218
Christians for Socialism Movement 219
Church *see* Catholic Church, the
church attendance 168
church unity *see* oecumenism
Ciban, Camilio 49, 51, 441, 445; bugging
of Conclave and 141–44; John Paul I
and 243–6, 264; John Paul II and 374,
403, 412, 414
Civil Guards 29, 34
Civiltà Cristiana 138–9, 284–5, 286
Clement V, Pope 243
Clement XIII, Pope 66
Cody, Cardinal John 131, 151, 229, 251,
301, 350; accused of racism and
financial maladministration 74–6, 116;
in Conclave (August) 111–13, 168–9,
193, 206; in Conclave (October) 335;
Greeley and 127, 178–9, 320; Greenan
and 213–14, 350; John Paul II and 391,

407; problem of 28–9, 38, 218, 248–9, 274, 370; Vatican finances and 159
Collegiality 217, 260, 322, 330; John Paul II and 357–8, 419
Colombo, Cardinal Giovanni 337, 338
commemorative stamps 422
Commission for Justice and Peace 135
Communism 58, 218, 355; attacked by John Paul II 425–6; in Eastern Europe 87–9, 171–2; Jesuits and 267, 268; in Poland 348–50, 363–4, 396, 398; in Western Europe 229
concelebration, rite of 99
Concesio 31
Conclave (August) 101–2, 175–209; first ballot 195–201; second ballot 202–4; third ballot 206–7; fourth ballot 207–8, 210; betting on 138, 161; bugging of 184, 186, 208–9; food for 186; Mass 173; media coverage of 175–80; Paul VI's guidelines for 36, 101, 184, 185, 196; secret diary kept 188; speculation about 104–5, 112–13, 127–30, 137–40, 159–63; theologians' letter to 137
Conclave (October) 316–45; first ballot 331–3; second ballot 334–5; third ballot 335–6; fourth ballot 336–7; fifth ballot 339; sixth ballot 339; seventh ballot 341; eighth ballot 341; accommodation 317–18; factions 332; media coverage of 319–21, 326–8; NORC prediction 320–21, 326; secret diary of 332; speculation before 319–31
Conclaves 36–7; the Camerlengo's role in 36–7, 184–5; Cardinals' rooms 185–6; history of 133, 164–5, 181–3; *Infirmarii* 196; Paul VI's guidelines for 36, 101, 133, 166; Revisers 196, 200–201; Scrutineers 196, 200–201; secrecy of 166, 183, 195; smoke 202, 204, 209, 213; types of election 194
Confalonieri, Cardinal Carlo 77, 79, 84, 101, 139, 169, 190, 278, 323; at Paul VI's funeral 118–19; proposes autopsy 288
Congress for the Lay Apostolate (1967) 193
conscience 357
Consistory 133, 145
consumerism 408
Cooke, Cardinal Terence 118, 178, 192, 206, 301, 407; in Conclave (October) 335
Cor Unum 250
Coronation, Pope's 229–33, 243–4; inaugural mass 232, 233–4, 243
Corriere della Sera 300
Council for the Public Affairs of the Church 73

crack Sindona, il 150–59
Crucitti, Francesco 459–60
Cuba 373–4
Curia, the 37, 85, 215, 299; John Paul I and 230, 241, 257–66; John Paul II and 357, 369–70, 419–20; opposition to 210–11; Papacy's problems with 217; Paul VI and 45, 217; power of 37; reform of 421; support for Siri 327; as a training ground for Popes 244

DIGOS (Italian anti-terrorist squad) 438–9, 441–2, 453, 464
Dar-es-Salaam, Archbishop of 118
Day of the Jackal, The 8
Dearden, Cardinal John 177, 322, 338
debate, religious 261
Delargey, Cardinal Reginald 178
Deskur, Bishop Andre 320
dictatorships 215
Dimitrios, Patriarch 413–14
diocesan councils 260
Diocese of Rome 422
diplomatic relations 35, 52–3, 56, 215; archival records 146; John Paul I on 231; John Paul II and 357
divorce 51, 167, 216, 408; John Paul II and 364, 381, 427, 428, 466
doctrinal policy 35; traditional, rejected 408
Drogheda 403
duty free concessions 65
Duval, Cardinal Leon 139, 192, 207
Dziwisz, Stanislaw 358–60, 361, 362, 366, 368, 370, 373, 374, 388, 389, 420, 426, 427, 429, 445, 465; assassination attempt and 452–60 *passim*

Eastern Europe 53, 396; bugging of the Vatican and 142–3; church's relations with 87–9, 259–60, 355, 389; *see also* Communism
Egyptian Intelligence Directorate 368
El Haya, Ibrahim 434, 442, 453, 457
El Salvador 267
eschatology 466

Fatima, Our Lady of 148, 436
Fazzini, Pericle 44
Felici, Luigi 128, 239, 271, 453, 456, 457
Felici, Cardinal Pericle 100, 118, 131, 169, 213, 273–4, 331, 370, 424 archive search for papal autopsy 294–7; in Conclave (August) 187–9, 191, 200, 201, 203, 204, 205; in Conclave (October) 332, 334, 337, 342; coronation role 233; conservative views of 139; influence of 319, 320; John Paul I and 240, 242, 248–50, 263, 271;

Felici, Cardinal Pericle—*contd.*
papabile 324, 328; pre-Conclave activity
169, 174–5, 176; proposed autopsy and
287–9, 300, 301; secret archives and
145–8, 169; Vatican finances and 423
Finabank 156
finance, Vatican 61, 148–59, 218, 259;
analysis of (November 1979) 421–3; fall
in bequests to the Church 249; John
Paul I and 246–50; John Paul II and
370, 391, 420–23
Fisherman's Ring 25, 82, 83, 109, 233,
291, 460
Folini, Maurizio 433, 438–9, 442, 450–51
Fontana Dr Mario 19, 21, 33–4, 68, 70–71,
77–81, 106
Formosus, Pope 3
Frank, Major 431
Franklin National Bank 159
Furstenberg, Cardinal Maximilian de 130

Gammarelli, House of 24, 84, 172–3,
209–13, 344–5, 388, 452
Gantin, Cardinal Bernardin 37, 135, 322,
328; in Conclave (August) 187, 189,
196, 197–8, 200, 204; in Conclave
(October) 333, 334, 336; influence of
321; investment in Third World and
423; John Paul I and 250, 261
Garrone, Cardinal Gabriel-Marie 57, 207,
324–5
Gazetta del Popolo 330
Gemelli Hospital 445–6, 458–60, 463
Gentlemen of the Pope 64
Ghezzi, Franco 22, 24, 52, 59, 60, 64
Giacomina, Sister 22–3, 27, 30, 53, 54, 59,
61, 64, 68, 70, 77, 79–80, 102, 266
Gianpaolo *see* John Paul I, Pope
Gierek, Edward 388, 395
Ginori, Richard 319
Giusti, Martino 295–6
Glemp, Archbishop 465
Governatorato building 65
Gray, Cardinal Gordon 178
Greeley, Andrew 68, 74, 83, 108, 111,
178, 192, 213, 320–21, 326, 331, 345,
391; attacks Macchi 72–3; John Paul I's
death and 293–4; Lefèbvre and 367;
requirements for the next Pope 126–7
Greenan, Father Lambert 96–100, 117,
425; Cody and 213–14; list of *papabili*
127–30, 159–63, 321–4; view of John
Paul II's election 348–50
Gregorian University 57
Gregory III, Pope 200
Gregory V, Pope 198
Gregory VII, Pope 227
Gregory IX, Pope 182
Gregory X, Pope 164

Grey Wolves 7, 12, 13, 124, 223, 224, 353,
385–6, 406, 411
Grillmeir, Horst 451
Guatemala 267
Guerri, Cardinal Sergio 421
Guitton, Jean 70
Günes, Hassan 400, 406

Hajnal, Giovanni 44
Hakim, Patriarch 270–1
Hall, Rose 451–7 *passim*
Hall of the Popes 186, 350
Hebblethwaite, Peter 108
Heim, Archbishop Bruno 272, 449
heroin 9–10
Hoeffner, Cardinal Joseph 128–9, 206,
283; in Conclave (October) 337, 340
Holy Office 57
Holy See, the: administration of 55–8;
politics and 55; role of 35; *see also*
diplomatic relations
Holy Year of 1975, 249
homosexuality 408
Honorius III, Pope 164, 182
human dignity 363, 383, 408
Humanae Vitae – On Human Life 45, 59, 99,
137, 168, 217; opposition to 19, 50,
127, 267, 274
humanism 383
Hume, Cardinal Basil 112, 113, 131,
139–40, 322, 328, 372, 412; in
Conclave (August) 178, 189, 201, 203,
204; in Conclave (October) 334, 343;
Ireland and 273, 449; John Paul II and
372
Hungary 53

IOR (Instituto per le Opere Religiose)
149–59, 247–50, 423, 466
IRA *see* Ireland
infallibility, Papal 168, 242, 244, 424
Innocent III, Pope 181
Interpol 437; red alert on Agca 438–9
Ipekci, Abdi 385–6
Iran, 261, 413
Ireland 89–92, 272–3; Bobby Sands
448–50; papal visit to 220–21, 273,
370–72, 400–404
Islam 14–15, 413
Israel 372–3, 432–3; Ankara legation 386;
Vatican recognition of 219; *see also*
MOSSAD

Jadot, Archbishop Jean 407
Japan 436
Jesuits 66–7, 267, 271–2, 274, 299, 424;
in China 440
Jesus Christ 358, 466–7
John XII, Pope 3, 198

John XIV, Pope 3, 198
John XXIII, Pope 31, 45, 88, 140, 148, 199, 208, 359; his reforms 241, 244
John Paul I, Pope (Albino Luciani) 240–41; absolved 278–9; announcement of 213; audiences 239, 252–6; autopsy on, proposed 281, 285–9, 316; coronation 226–35; daily routine 265, 268–9; death of 275–80; fitting of robe 212–13; funeral of 301; illness 238–9, 266; leadership style 259–60; life threatened 226–7; opposition to 257–61; popular appeal of 260; reactions to his death 292–3; security and 243–6, 264; view of his role 230–1; walks out of Vatican 244–5; *see also* Luciani, Cardinal Albino
John Paul II, Pope (Karol Wojtyla) 344–6; administration 369, 420; assessment of 467; attempted assassination of 452–9; audiences 368–9, 419; bullet proof vest for 388, 452; changes made 360–61; his concept of the papacy 372; criticism of 390–91, 416–19; daily routine 360–61, 368–9; doctrinal attitudes 364, 392–4, 403–4, 406–8; first appearance 346–8; his humour 370; influences upon 362–3; kissing of foreign soil by 376; letter to Brezhnev 429–30, 447; mass appeal of 393–4, 416; mysticism and 466; pastoral work 364; his personal staff 389–90; his political awareness 392; recovery from shooting 465; secret meetings 368; sources of information 368; his strength 391–2; swimming pool for, 362, 391; visits USA 406–9; visits Africa 425; visits France 426–7; visits Japan 436; visits the Philippines 435–6; *see also* Poland *and* Wojtyla, Cardinal Karol
Jooma, Ahmed 434, 442, 453, 457
Julius III, Pope 194
justice, violence and 404

KGB: death of John Paul I and 281–3, 289, 300, 301, 302; involvement with Agca 433, 437–8, 451, 457
Kadem, Sedat Siri 310–11, 312, 432
Kempis, Thomas à, *Imitation of Christ* 277, 280, 294
Kennedy, David 156
Kennedy, Edward 108, 114, 117, 293
Khomeini, Ayotallah 413
Kissinger, Henry 274
Knock 371, 401
Knox, Cardinal James 192
Koenig, Cardinal Franz 58, 86, 113, 118, 119, 134, 139, 189–90, 251, 329–31, 352; his assessment of Paul VI 103–4;

on celibacy 393; Cody and 74; in Conclave (August) 177, 185–6, 189–91, 192, 196, 197, 201, 206; in Conclave (October) 332, 335, 336, 339, 340–41, 342, 344; influence of 321; his knowledge of Communism 87–9, 427–8; *papabile* 100–101, 321; pre-Conclave activity (August) 104–5, 166–7, 169–72; proposed autopsy and 281, 288–9, 301; report on China 439–40; support for Wojtyla 325–6, 332, 335, 337
Krol, Cardinal John 118, 172, 301, 322, 351, 391; in Conclave (August) 178, 188, 192, 206; in Conclave (October) 335, 337, 338, 342, 343, 344
Küng, Hans 85, 129, 137, 187–8, 299; John Paul I and 241–2, 274; John Paul II and 369, 393, 423–4; Luciani and 162

Laborem Exercens – On Human Work 465
Lagorio, Lelio 485
Lamb, Charles 295–6
Last Judgement 189, 195, 196, 341
Lateran Palace 84
Lateran retreat 324
Latin America 229; bishops' conference 355, 379–83; Marxism in 45, 269–70, 354; Pontifical Commission for 270; problems of 93–5, 193; *see also* theology of liberation movement
Lebanon 357, 368
Lefèbvre, Archbishop Marcel 45–8, 57, 59, 85, 138–9, 210, 216, 218, 286, 299, 440; John Paul I and 242–3; John Paul II and 365–7
Léger, Cardinal 187, 191, 193
Leo I, Pope 244
Leo X, Pope 243
Leo XI, Pope 42
Leo XIII, Pope 185
Lercaro, Cardinal 191
Libya 15, 225, 431–2, 434
Lorenzi, Diego 130–33, 174; after John Paul I's death 290–92; private secretary to John Paul I 226–7, 229, 230, 237, 239, 263, 265, 271, 274, 278
Lorscheider, Cardinal Aloisio 37, 113, 380, 381, 428; Cody and 74; in Conclave (August) 196, 197–8, 200, 201, 203, 205, 207; in Conclave (October) 333; influence of 134–5, 320
love, John Paul I on 262
Luciani, Cardinal Albino (Pope John Paul I) 118, 130–33; in Conclave (August) 178, 187, 189, 201, 203, 204–8; elected Pope 207–8; health 131, 166, 168; *Illustrissimi* 131–2, 162, 211; *papabile*

INDEX

Luciani, Cardinal Albino—*contd.*
161, 162–3, 166, 169, 174–5; *see also*
John Paul I, Pope

MIT (Turkish intelligence) 387, 414–15,
437, 438, 464
MOSSAD (Israeli intelligence) 26, 387,
411, 437, 438, 439, 464
McCann, Cardinal Owen 338
MacCarthy, Father Sean 95–6, 117,
118–19, 133–4, 194, 198–200, 208, 209,
293; reporting John Paul I's coronation
229–35; reporting the August Conclave
163–5, 173, 175–80; reporting the
October Conclave 326–8, 346–8
Macchi, Don Pasquale 21, 22, 26–7, 28–9,
30, 38, 40, 44, 49, 51, 59–61, 64–5,
70–73, 76, 78–81, 82, 135, 359; after
Paul VI's death 109–11; press campaign
against 72–3; Vatican finances and 156,
159
Magee, Father John 285, 286, 445; after
Paul VI's death 114–15; becomes Master
of Ceremonies 466; Bobby Sands and
448–50; at John Paul's election 214–19;
importance of 27–9; Ireland and 221,
272–3, 371, 400, 401, 452; private
secretary to John Paul I 230, 236–40
passim, 252, 256, 263, 265, 271–2,
276–80, 284; private secretary to John
Paul II 361, 366, 368, 388, 390, 401,
408, 409, 420, 426; private secretary to
Paul VI 30, 38, 44, 49, 51, 59–61, 64–5,
70, 72, 78–81, 84
magisterium 467
Malula, Cardinal Joseph 333
Malvinas, the 94–5
Manning, Cardinal Timothy 118, 407; in
Conclave (August) 166, 189; in
Conclave (October) 318, 338
Marcellus II, Pope 200
Marcinkus, Bishop Paul 40, 72, 358;
Brezhnev letter delivered by 430; John
Paul II and 370, 388, 390, 391, 403,
426, 427, 430, 466; Mexican visit 373,
374–5, 377; unpopularity of 150;
Vatican finances and 148–59, 218,
247–50, 259, 421–3, 423
Marcos, Imelda 117
Marcos, President 435–6
Marian shrines 418
Maritain, Jacques 32–3
Martin, Cardinal Gonzales 129
Martin, Monsignor Jacques 64, 78–81,
113, 134, 352, 445; Conclave (August)
and 181, 183, 209, 210, 211; John Paul
I and 226, 236, 237, 239, 245–6, 250–2,
266, 270–71; after John Paul I's death
285, 291, 292; John Paul II and 359–60,

388, 390, 453; pre-Conclave speculation
135, 328–9; role of 41–3
Martin, Malachi 153
Marty, Cardinal François 113, 325, 328; in
Conclave (October) 335
Marxism: Catholicism and 45, 172; in
Central America 374
Mass Ordinal 46–7
meat on Fridays 104
Medeiros, Cardinal Humerto 177
media, papacy and 231, 297–300, 319–21,
375
Melitone, Metropolitan 99
Mersan, Omer 433, 451
Mexico 227, 269, 370, 373–84
Michelangelo 189, 195, 341
Middle East 219, 261, 368, 425
Milan 154
Milliyet 411–12
missionary work 422
mixed marriages 99, 242
'moles', Vatican 242
Monreal, Cardinal Bueno y 129
Montini, Giovanni *see* Paul VI, Pope
Montini, Ludovico 77, 79, 80
Montini, Marco 77, 79, 80
Montreal, Archbishop of 118
Moro, Aldo 25–6, 39, 53–4
Moscow, Patriarch of 117
Mysterium Ecclesiae 242

Nervi Hall audiences 29, 32, 43–4, 49–52,
251–2, 416
neutron bomb 425
Newton, Lowell 452–7 *passim*
Nicaragua 215, 267
Nikodim, Metropolitan 251–2
Nixon, President Richard 10, 248, 267
Noble Guard 34
Noé, Monsignor Virgilio 84, 106–7, 173,
176, 291, 328–9, 351, 445; in Conclave
(August) 179, 181, 186, 195, 201, 204,
208; in Conclave (October) 316, 342,
344; John Paul I and 232, 243–5; John
Paul II and 359–60, 363, 376, 378, 394,
412, 435, 453, 466
Novemdiales 101, 169, 322
nuclear warfare 88
Nueva, Fuerza 300
nuncios 56, 90–92, 291
nuns 235–6, 409, 424

Oddi, Cardinal Silvio 365, 417, 420
Odre, Ann 451, 453–5, *passim*
oecumenism 3, 85, 99, 168, 242, 416;
under John Paul I 262
O'Fiaich, Cardinal Tomas 272–3, 372, 400,
401, 448–50
Opus Dei 100

Orsini, Prince Filippo 297
Orsinis, the 182
Orthodox Church 387
L'Osservatore della Domenica 328–9
L'Osservatore Romano 63, 72, 96–9, 127, 138, 185, 209, 297, 321, 348, 422; *see also* Greenan, Father Lambert
Ostpolitik *see* Eastern Europe
Ozgun, Faruk 451

Pacelli, Cardinal 193–4
Pacem in Terris 88
Paisley, Ian 449
Palatine Guard 34
Pallium, Imposition of 233
Panciroli, Father Romeo 40, 72, 80–81, 83, 140; death of John Paul I and 285–6,
papabile 127–8, 160–62, 321–4; *see also under names of cardinals*
Papacy, the: authority of 216, 417; foreign travel 168; Italians in 202; new name taken by popes 198–200; origin of 3; Paul VI's view of 33; requirements for 137–8; spiritual and temporal power 244, 465; violence and 3; *see also names of popes*
Papal apartments 20–21, 236–8, 446–7; sealed after Pope's death 84, 289–92
Papal Briefs 56
Pappalardo, Cardinal Salvatore 102–3, 201, 219, 287; in Conclave (October) 334, 336; *papabile* 170, 321
Parrot Courtyard 183
Pasqualina, Sister 23, 265–6
pastoral, definitions of 322–3
Paul VI, Pope 3, 168, 208, 240; administration 55–8; Agca and 14–15; alarm clock 21, 80, 81; assessments of 50–51, 60, 99, 100, 103–4, 258; books read by 32–3; clothes 24; his conservatism 44–5; his correspondence 60–61; criticism of 31; his daily routine 21–37, 41–4, 53–5, 59–61; death of 79–84, 92; his early life 31; election of 190; embalmed 105–7; foreign travel 50–51, 55–6; his funeral 101–2, 117–19; guidelines for choosing a successor 36, 101, 184, 185, 196; his illness 21–2, 33–4, 42, 68–72, 76–81; Lefèbvre and 45–8; his life threatened 25–6, 34–5; his linguistic ability 42–3; lying in state of 106–10, 114; music and 61; newspapers ready by 30–31, 32; his papal apartment 20–21; his private secretaries 28–9, 30; his private chapel 29; his racial equality work 74; Sindona and 153–6; theological influences on 70; tributes to 84–5; Vatican finances and 153–4

Pauline Chapel 176
Paupini, Cardinal Giuseppe 58, 183
Pellegrino, Cardinal Michele 321; in Conclave (August) 191–2
Pertini, Sandoro 93
Peter's Pence 422
Philippines, the 26, 35; priestly celibacy in 228
Picachy, Cardinal Lawrence 338
Pignedoli, Cardinal Sergio 58; *papabile* 161; in Conclave (August) 191, 198, 203, 204, 205–6, 207; in Conclave (October) 336
Pio, Padre 409
Pironio, Cardinal Eduardo 37, 201, 321, 372
Pius III, Pope 199
Pius VII, Pope 294–6
Pius VIII, Pope 296–7
Pius X, Pope 200
Pius XI, Pope 66, 191
Pius XII, Pope 20, 55, 101, 128, 130, 146, 163, 191, 217, 258, 265–6; Cardinals selected by 133; Communism and 87–8; IOR started by 149; on virginity 235;
Poland 53, 171–2, 348–9, 398, 452; Catholic Church in 398; Communism in 348–50, 363–4, 390; John Paul I's visit to 390, 394–8, 426–7; Soviet Union and 171, 427, 429–30, 465
Poles in the Vatican 420
Poletti, Cardinal Ugo 77, 79, 84; in Conclave (August) 179; in Conclave (October) 334, 336; *papabile* 161–2, 321
Poma, Cardinal Antonio 192
Pontifical Commissions 273
Pope *see* Papacy, the
population growth 228
Populorum Progessio 156
Porta Sant'Anna 61, 62
Prefecture for Economic Affairs 159, 421
Priesthood, the: dress 408; leaving holy orders 57, 228, 372, 392; in the Philippines 435; *see also* celibacy, priestly
Prohibited Books, Index of 104
Propaganda Fide 422
protocol for papal audiences 43

racism 74–5, 425
Ratzinger, Cardinal Joseph 129, 160, 283, 424; in Conclave (August) 187; in Conclave (October) 318, 337, 340, 343
Red Army Fraction 26
Red Brigades 25–6, 39, 54, 368, 446
Romano Pontifici Eligendo 101
Redemptor Hominis 364, 426
Ribeiro, Cardinal Antonio 128, 203, 338
Roncalli, Cardinal 140
Rosmini, Antonio 162

Rossi, Paolo 297–8, 320
Roy, Cardinal Maurice 139, 193
Rubin, Ladislaw 320
Russia *see* Soviet Union

SIS (British intelligence) 438, 464
St Malachy 198–200, 329
St Peter 3, 64, 198, 358
St Peter's Basilica 24–5, 64
St Peter's Square 23, 58–9, 114, 202
Sacred Congregations 273, 369; for
    Bishops 57; for Catholic Education 57,
    129; for Clergy 57, for Oriental
    Churches 130; for Religion and Secular
    Institutes 57, 372; for the Causes of
    Saints 57, 97; for the Doctrine of the
    Faith 242, 424–5; for the Sacraments
    and Divine Worship 57, 192; of the
    Inquisition 57
Sala Bologna 282–3
Salesian Congregation of John Bosco
    98
Samore, Cardinal Antonio 147–8, 294–5
sampietrini 63–4, 226
San Damaso, Courtyard of 34
Santa Anna dei Palafrenieri church 62
Schmidt, Helmut 464
Schroffer, Cardinal Joseph 129
Secretariat for Christian Unity 58
Secretariat for Non-Believers 58
Secretariat for Non-Christians 58
Secretariat of State 35, 420; departments
    of 56, 273; Office of Information and
    Documentation 98
sedia gestatoria 49
sediari 49
Segno di Contraddizione 324, 338
Selcuk, Timar 414–15
Sener, Mehmet 385–6
Seper, Cardinal Franjo 56–7, 338, 424
Sergius IV, Pope 196
sexuality 261, 407, 424, 466
Siderouss, Cardinal Stephanos 338
simony 227
Sin, Cardinal Jaime 37, 113, 118, 135,
    251, 326, 352, 435; in Conclave
    (August) 181, 183, 196, 201, 203, 204;
    in Conclave (October) 334, 336;
    influence of 321; thoughts on the next
    Pope 166–8
Sindona, Michele 152–9, 247, 249, 391,
    423
Siri, Cardinal Giuseppe 118, 169, 190, 283,
    287, 365–6; in Conclave (August) 200,
    201; in Conclave (October) 332, 333,
    334, 336, 342; influence of 321; *papabile*
    139, 160, 323; pre-Conclave interview
    329–31; supported by Italian press
    327–8

Sistine Chapel 25, 179, 191; balloting in
    144, 319; chimney 180, 194
Società Generale Immobiliare 157
Solidarity (Poland) 426–7, 428, 430, 436,
    465
sorcery 58
South America *see* Latin America
Soviet Union 15, 68; bugging and 177–8;
    Catholicism in China and 441; John
    Paul II and 349–50, 398, 458; Poland
    and 171–2, 427, 429–30; religious
    worship in 251–2; *see also* KGB
Spada, Prince Massimo 155
spiritual power 215
Suenens, Cardinal Leo 113, 190, 206,
    298–9, 324; in Conclave (August) 188;
    in Conclave (October) 332–3, 335
    influence of 321
Supreme Tribunal of the Apostolic
    Signature 58, 100
Swiss Guards 34, 49, 61–3, 67, 88, 184,
    209–11, 362, 445; attendance at the
    catafalque 106–7, 292; commandant of
    183
Sylvester II, Pope 198
Synod of Bishops 85, 99, 135, 160–61,
    172, 217, 298–9, 320, 372; John Paul II
    and 357, 419

Taiwan 440–41
Taofinu'u, Cardinal Pio 176, 324–5, 342
Tarancon, Cardinal Enrique y 134, 302,
    324; in Conclave (August) 188; in
    Conclave (October) 321, 331–3, 335, 336
    337, 339, 342, 344; influence of 321;
    papabile 129; support for Wojtyla 335
Terpil, Frank 431–2
terrorism 68, 70; in Italy 25–6, 54, 358;
    training for 307–12, 431–4
test-tube babies 68, 162–3, 217
Testa, Cardinal Gustavo 190
Thatcher, Margaret 448,
theologians 19; *see also* Küng, Hans
theology of liberation movement 219;
    John Paul I and 269–70, 272, 383;
    John Paul II and 355–6, 374, 379, 408,
    428
Thiandoum, Cardinal Hyacinthe 37, 47
Third World, the 166; Catholics in
    229; John Paul I and 261, 274; Papacy
    and 229; Vatican investments and
    250
Tomasek, Cardinal Frantisek 128, 134
Tore, Teslin 312–15, 353, 384–5, 386, 400,
    406, 411, 415, 438–9, 442, 450–51
Tridentine Mass 56–7, 367, 440
Trinh Van Can, Cardinal 134
Tucci, Father Roberto 84, 163
Turkes, Col. Arpaslan 7, 12, 223, 224

Turkey: anarchy in 7–8, 13; John Paul II's visit to 387, 409, 411–14; strategic importance of 309; terrorism in 413, 437

USA 25, 274, 417; *Humanae Vitae* and 127; John Paul II's visit to 407–9, 424; Justice Department investigations 248; nuns in 236

Ugurlu, Abuzer 437–8, 451

Ulster 90–91, 222, 401–2, 408, 448–50

underdeveloped countries *see* Third World, the

Urban VIII, Pope 66

Ursi, Cardinal Corrado 192, 319, 331; in Conclave (October) 332, 334, 336, 339; *papabile* 321

Vagnozzi, Cardinal Egidio 421

Vatican, the: Casa Pontificia 41; chapels, upkeep of 422; duty free concessions 422; gardens 63; gates of, closed 42, 61; museum 422; printing outlets 422; 'private library' 34, 38; property income 422; railway station 65; secrecy in 469; secret archives 145–8, 227, 294–7; security 29, 34, 59, 358–9, 445; telephone exchange 445 *see also* finance, Vatican

Vatican City, governor of 183

Vatican Council, Second 59, 129, 172, 218, 258, 284, 299, 328; cost of 422; implementation of 38; John Paul II and 418–19

Vatican Palace 84

Vatican Press Office 202

Vatican Radio 63, 95–6, 127, 422; Conclave bugged by 143–4, 208–9; reporting the Conclave 163–4; *see also* MacCarthy, Father Sean

Vatican State 35

Videla, Jorge Rafael 93–4, 118, 187, 303; at John Paul I's coronation 234–5

Vietnam 39, 267

Vigilance, Central Office of 61–3, 244, 362, 445, 453

Villot, Cardinal Jean 29, 43, 47, 65, 214, 351, 359, 377, 389; attacked by Siri 330; as Camerlengo after John Paul I 277–80, 283, 287–9, 291, 300–302; as Camerlengo after Paul VI 82–4, 101–2, 109, 115, 138, 141–4, 184, 193–4; in Conclave (August) 173, 176, 184–5, 189, 196, 201, 207–8, 209; in Conclave (October) 316–19, 341, 343–4; John Paul I and 237, 246, 259, 263, 268, 271, 272–73; John Paul II and 368; Paul VI and 19, 76–7, 79–80; Secretary of State 36–7, 39, 41, 55

Vincenza, Sister 131, 238, 246, 265–6, 273; John Paul I's death and 275–9, 284, 286

violence, resorting to 436

virginity 235

Volk, Cardinal Hermann 129

Waldeheim, Kurt 291

Walesa, Lech 426, 436, 465–6

West, Morris 447

Willebrands, Cardinal Jan 58, 113, 298, 326; in Conclave (August) 188, 192, 203, 204; in Conclave (October) 336, 340; influence of 321; *papabile* 130, 167, 321, 328

Wojtyla, Cardinal Karol (Pope John Paul II) 118, 140, 167, 283, 316, 320; his career 170–72; Communism and 170–71; in Conclave (August) 178, 187, 192, 196–7, 200, 202–4, 206, 212; in Conclave (October) 332, 334, 335, 336–7, 337–8, 339–41, 343–4; elected Pope 341; supported by Koenig 171–2; writings 324–6; *see also* John Paul II, Pope

women 260–61; in the Curia 420; ordination of 19, 216, 228, 267, 408, 417, 424

Worlock, Archbishop Derek 358

Wright, Cardinal John 173, 357

Wyslocki, Dr Mielyslaw 361

Wyszynski, Cardinal Stefan 118, 140, 283, 350–52, 397; in Conclave (October) 338, 339–40, 344

Yesiltepe 11–13

Yugoslavia 88

Zega and Co. 105–7, 280